D1367016

Marketing Research

A Practical Approach for the New Millennium

The Irwin/McGraw-Hill Series in Marketing

Marketing Research

A Practical Approach for the New Millennium

JOSEPH F. HAIR, JR.
Louisiana State University

ROBERT P. BUSH
The University of Memphis

DAVID J. ORTINAU
University of South Florida

Boston   Burr Ridge, IL   Dubuque, IA   Madison, WI   New York
San Francisco   St. Louis   Bangkok   Bogotá   Caracas   Lisbon
London   Madrid   Mexico City   Milan   New Delhi   Seoul
Singapore   Sydney   Taipei   Toronto

McGraw-Hill Higher Education 🖋

*A Division of The **McGraw-Hill** Companies*

MARKETING RESEARCH: A PRACTICAL APPROACH FOR THE NEW MILLENNIUM

Copyright © 2000 by The McGraw-Hill Companies, Inc. All rights reserved. Printed in the United States of America. Except as permitted under the United States Copyright Act of 1976, no part of this publication may be reproduced or distributed in any form or by any means, or stored in a database or retrieval system, without the prior written permission of the publisher.

This book is printed on acid-free paper.

1 2 3 4 5 6 7 8 9 0 DOW/DOW 9 0 9 8 7 6 5 4 3 2 1 0

ISBN 0-256-19555-2

Vice president/Editor-in-chief: *Michael W. Junior*
Publisher: *David Kendric Brake*
Sponsoring editor: *Rick Adams*
Senior developmental editor: *Tom Thompson*
Editorial coordinator: *Sasha Eakle*
Senior marketing manager: *Colleen J. Suljic*
Senior project manager: *Susan Trentacosti*
Senior production supervisor: *Lori Koetters*
Senior photo research coordinator: *Keri Johnson*
Senior designer: *Kiera Cunningham*
Interior and cover design: *Z Graphics*
Cover photos: *©Photodisc*
Supplement coordinator: *Carol A. Bielski*
Compositor: *Precision Graphics Services, Inc.*
Typeface: *10/12 Times Roman*
Printer: *R.R. Donnelley & Sons Company*

Library of Congress Cataloging-in-Publication Data

Hair, Joseph F.
    Marketing research : a practical approach for the new Millennium /
Joseph F. Hair, Jr., Robert P. Bush, David J. Ortinau.
      p.   cm. -- (Irwin/McGraw-Hill series in marketing)
    Includes index.
    ISBN 0-256-19555-2
    1. Marketing research.   I. Bush, Robert P.   II. Ortinau, David J.
III. Title.   IV. Series.
HF5415.2.H258   2000
658.8'3--dc21   99-27710

http://www.mhhe.com

This book is dedicated to my wife, Dale, and my son, Joe III.

J.F.H., Jr.
Baton Rouge, LA

This book is dedicated to my wife, Donny, and my two boys, Robert, Jr., and Michael.

R.P.B., Sr.
Memphis, TN

This book is dedicated to my family for their love and continuous support. To my mom, Lois Ortinau, and dad, Harold Ortinau, long deceased, for instilling great values and the work ethic necessary to complete this project. In memory of my brother, Don, and my grandmother, Mabel, whose untimely deaths gave me better insights and appreciation for life. To my brothers, Dean and Dennis, and my sister, Nancy, and their families for all their encouragement during the writing of this textbook. To all, my deepest love and thanks.

D.J.O.
Tampa, FL

Joseph F. Hair, Jr., earned a B.A. in Economics and an M.A. and Ph.D. in Marketing at the University of Florida. He began his teaching career at the University of Mississippi and then moved to Louisiana State University in 1977. He continues to teach at LSU, where he is the Director of the Institute for Entrepreneurial Education and Family Business Studies, and where he holds the Alvin C. Copeland Endowed Chair of Franchising. He has acted as a management consultant and/or expert witness for a variety of industries and has served on the board of directors of numerous organizations. He has been an officer for a long list of academic organizations and he is a past President and Chairman of the Board of Governors of the Academy of Marketing Science. He has been a regular contributor and reviewer, and occasionally a member of the editorial board, for such publications as *The Journal of Marketing Research, The Journal of Business Research,* and *Marketing Education Review.* The list of his scholarly publications runs to a dozen pages.

Robert P. Bush earned a B.A. in Psychology and Economic History from St. Mary's University and an M.A. and Ph.D. in Marketing at Louisiana State University. He began his teaching career at the University of South Florida, moved first to the University of Mississippi, and then to The University of Memphis, where he has taught since 1993. He was chairman of the committee on Grants and Research for the Fogelman College of Business from 1991–1997 and Director of the Ph.D. program at Memphis from 1995–1997. He has been a consultant for a wide range of corporations and institutes, as well as for the U.S. Department of Defense. He is the coauthor of *Retailing for the 21st Century* (Houghton-Mifflin, 1993) and a coeditor of *Advances in Marketing* (LSU Press, 1994). He is a regular contributor to such academic publications as *Journal of Advertising, Journal of Consumer Marketing, Journal of Marketing Education, Journal of Direct Marketing, Journal of Health Care Marketing,* and *Marketing Education Review.*

David J. Ortinau earned a B.S. in Management from Southern Illinois University–Carbondale, an M.A. in Business Administration from Illinois State University, and a Ph.D. in Marketing from Louisiana State University. He began his teaching career at the University of South Florida, where he continues to win awards both for outstanding research and for outstanding teaching. He has a wide range of research interests—from attitude formation and perceptual differences in services marketing to interactive electronic marketing technologies and their impact on information research problems. He consults for a variety of corporations and small businesses, with specialties in customer satisfaction, customer service quality, customer service value, retail loyalty, and image. He continues to serve as a member of the editorial review board for *Journal of Academy of Marketing Science* and was coeditor of *Marketing: Moving Toward the 21st Century* (SMA Press, 1996). He was co-chair of the 1998 Southern Marketing Association's Doctoral Consortium in New Orleans, and he is a past President of the Southern Marketing Association. He also served as co-chair of the 1999 Society for Marketing Advances' Doctoral Consortium in Atlanta. He has presented numerous papers at academic meetings, and he has been a regular contributor to and referee for such publications as *The Journal of Business Research, The Journal of Retailing,* and *Journal of Marketing Education.*

All marketing research books are designed to introduce students to the concepts and practices that make up the field of marketing research. *Marketing Research: A Practical Approach for the New Millennium* goes beyond that basic idea to show how marketing research tools, skills, and understanding can be applied to solving marketing problems and creating marketing opportunities within a rapidly changing information environment. With the growing availability of advanced technologies and communication systems, with the changing of internal organizational structures to improve the sharing of information, and with the movement of both large and small businesses toward the globalization of marketing practices, tomorrow's information requirements will be much more challenging than those of yesterday. We believe that we have identified several critical learning needs that other marketing research textbooks were not addressing well or were not addressing at all.

Objectives and Approach

Our objectives in writing *Marketing Research* were basically threefold. First, we wanted to provide students with a body of knowledge and a set of facts that are easy to read and understand, and that would facilitate *practical self-learning* of the basics of information research. Second, we wanted to provide students with the tools and skills necessary to solve business problems and exploit business opportunities. And finally, we wanted to provide a solid educational learning resource for instructors who strive to bring understanding to often-complex subject matter. As students develop information acquisition skills and an understanding of available research tools, they will quickly see how they can be applied to a changing marketing environment, to other academic coursework, and to their personal lives.

Changes in the business world are creating new decision situations that demand creative solutions and better skills for the acquisition and use of information. As a result of many recent advances in computer technologies (both hardware and software), high-speed communication systems, and other electronic technologies, business decision makers and the marketing research industry have been forced to rethink their notions of information and of the practices used to acquire and generate data and information. One unique feature of this book is the detailed treatment of and significantly greater emphasis placed on identifying, searching, gathering, analyzing, and interpreting secondary data and information. It offers students expanded coverage of online research techniques, database development and maintenance, and data mining.

Marketing Research offers insights into alternative ways of dealing with new information needs and demands brought about by environmental changes. These changes have had a direct impact both on marketing research practices and on the operating environments of business practitioners. In addition, there have been many changes in the educational environment that have implications for how people acquire knowledge and master the skills and tools customarily associated with the practice of marketing research. The information research process that is described here covers traditional marketing research concepts but goes on to offer insights for meeting the information challenges of the 21st century. It has been written for people at a fairly basic level, who do not need a strong background in statistics nor any prior knowledge of marketing research. It is not intended for people who wish to teach advanced multivariate data analysis procedures.

We believe that self-learning is a critical and necessary component of a student's overall educational experience. To that end we have incorporated the following characteristics into our text in an attempt to enhance the learning process:

• Easy-to-understand writing style and manners.

• Clearly presented exhibits, tables, and boxes that provide real business applications.

- Integrated examples that illustrate the links between various research concepts.
- Detailed treatment of critical information skills and tools.
- In-depth treatment of secondary data/information.

Content and Organization

Part I of this book covers marketing research and technology and contains five chapters. Chapter 1 provides an overview of the role of marketing research in the strategic marketing planning process. It offers discussions and illustrations for the various research requirements, tasks, and functions within today's complex business environments. Chapter 2 takes an information approach to explaining the marketing research process and sets the tone for the remaining chapters. It presents an overview of the four stages of the process and discusses the major steps that researchers and decision makers must take to ensure successful results. There is an important discussion of the critical role marketing research information plays in decision making.

Chapter 3 provides in-depth treatment of the most critical step in the process—determining the "right" information research problem and deciding upon appropriate research objectives. It also offers a discussion of the important ethical issues faced by both researchers and decision makers. Chapter 4 isolates strategic management issues involved in conducting secondary data gathering research. It places heavy emphasis on the search strategies needed to acquire, analyze, and use both traditional and online approaches. Chapter 5 provides detailed coverage of the use of the Internet and explores various research strategies for database acquisition and for the intraorganizational sharing of data and information.

Part II covers the various research designs used to collect accurate data and information and contains five chapters. Chapter 6 provides detailed information on the application of secondary data sources to solving business problems. It places heavy emphasis on the importance of secondary data and on knowing how to maintain databases and how to undertake data mining. Chapter 7 focuses uniquely on how research-driven decision support systems (RDSS) are created and used to support researchers and decision makers.

Chapter 8 moves from research designs that are strictly for secondary data to those aimed at the collecting of primary (i.e., first-hand) data and its conversion to useful managerial information. Heavy emphasis is placed on two widely practiced designs—in-depth interviews and focus groups. Chapter 9 presents an overview of survey research design, along with other quantitative data collection methods. It also provides an introduction to various types of errors associated with survey research designs, including their impact on the quality of the data collected. Chapter 10 provides discussion of experimental and quasi-experimental designs, along with in-depth treatment of test marketing and field simulation practices. It also explores the issues of validity and reliability.

Part III covers the process of gathering accurate data and contains four chapters. Chapter 11 introduces readers to sampling and defined target populations. It provides in-depth discussions of sampling distributions, sampling frames, sample size determination, and types of probability and nonprobability sampling procedures. An appendix shows how to develop a sampling plan and discusses each component of the process. Chapter 12 introduces the procedures used in construct development and provides an overview of measurement. It provides detailed discussions of critical issues underlying the development of basic scale measurements and information properties, and it revisits earlier discussions of validity and reliability.

Chapter 13 advances the concept of scale measurement and more complex attitude, emotional, and behavioral scales, and goes on to provide a basic overview of other types of specialty scales used in marketing research. Chapter 14 offers a detailed discussion of how the so-called flowerpot framework integrates, and has an impact upon, the various procedural steps of the design process.

Part IV covers data preparation, data analysis, and the communication of research findings and contains five chapters. Chapter 15 begins this section by offering an overview of the fundamental principles of coding requirements, the editing of data, and the preparing of raw data for statistical analysis. An appendix provides detailed discussions of several complicated issues associated with conducting field work. Chapter 16 builds on earlier discussions of basic sampling statistics and begins to illustrate how fundamental descriptive statistical analyses are used to transform raw data into more complex data structures. It provides the *how, when,* and *whys* for performing both *t*-tests and Z-tests, and explains the importance of means, standard deviations, and standard error values. Chapter 17 expands the discussion of data analysis to include testing for associations using correlation, covariance, regression, and analysis of variance (ANOVA) statistical procedures.

Chapter 18 presents a somewhat simplified overview of multivariate statistics. It provides *how, when,* and *why* discussions of discriminate analysis, cluster analysis, and conjoint analysis procedures. Chapter 19 discusses the important issues that underlie the preparation of research reports and presentations. It shows students how to develop computerized presentations (i.e., PowerPoint slides) of data structure results and research findings. Each chapter in Part IV offers SPSS data analysis exercises developed for a fictional fast-food restaurant (Back Yard Burgers). The disk with this material can be found inside the back cover of the textbook.

Pedagogy

Most marketing research books are readable, but a more important question might be "Can students comprehend what they are reading?" This book offers a wealth of pedagogical features, all aimed at answering that question in the affirmative. Here is a list of the major elements.

- **Learning Objectives.** Each chapter begins with clear learning objectives that students can use to gauge their expectations and the importance of the chapter material.

- **Vignettes.** Each chapter begins with an interesting story that describes a real-world business example that illustrates the focus and importance of the chapter's material.

- **Basic Concepts and Terms.** These are boldface in the text and are also defined again in the page margins to make reviewing easier. They are also listed at the ends of chapters and included in a glossary at the back of the book.

- **A Closer Look at Research.** These boxes, which are found in each chapter, come in three varieties—Using Technology, Small Business Implications, and In the Field. They are intended to expose students to real-world issues.

- **Ethics.** This text provides extensive treatment of ethical issues early in the book (Chapter 3) and revisits ethical issues throughout the remainder of the book. There are six carefully designed "ethics boxes" selectively placed in other chapters that provide excellent real-life examples of unethical research practices, and there are ethics-oriented discussion questions at the ends of other chapters.

- **Global Insights.** These boxes, scattered throughout the book, are intended to encourage students to see the international implications of and opportunities for marketing research.

- **Chapter Summaries.** These detailed summations, organized by learning objectives, will help students remember key facts, concepts, and issues, and will serve as an excellent study guide when preparing for in-class discussions and exams.

- **Questions for Review and Discussion.** These questions were carefully designed to enhance the self-learning process and to encourage the application of the concepts to real business situations. There are one or two questions in each chapter (**Experience the Internet**) that directly relate to the World Wide Web to provide students with opportunities for sharpening their electronic data gathering and interpretive skills.

- **Marketing Research Illustration.** This illustration, found at the end of each chapter, provides students with additional insights as to how key concepts from that chapter can be applied to a real business situation.

- **Marketing Research Case Exercise.** At the end of each chapter there is a short case with questions that are relevant to the chapter material. These cases provide an excellent opportunity for creating interactive classroom learning. A number of the cases are based on the material provided in the videos that accompany the book.

Supplements

This book offers a rich ancillary package. Here is a brief description of each element in that package.

- **Instructor's Manual.** This contains for each chapter a list of learning objectives; an overview; an outline showing where to use key terms, boxes, exhibits, and discussion questions; and a list of student projects.

- **Test Bank.** This contains for each chapter 60 multiple-choice questions, 15 true/false questions, and 4 essay questions.

- **Computerized Test Bank.** This contains the questions from the printed test bank in Diploma, the most sophisticated, but easiest to use, test generator on the market today. Diploma can create a wide array of paper tests or network-based tests, which can be automatically graded and the results pulled directly into a grade book program.

- **PowerPoint.** This program provides 15–20 slides for each chapter, which contain such elements as key terms and concepts, definitions, and exhibits.

- **Videos.** The video program contains two hours of material on marketing research from the Irwin/McGraw-Hill video library.

- **Web Site.** Students can use their Internet skills to log on to this book's dedicated Web site (www.mhhe.com/hair) to view additional useful information about marketing research and evaluate their understanding of chapter material by taking the example quizzes which are offered.

- **Back Yard Burgers Data Set.** Standard copies of the book contain a CD-ROM that provides a nationwide data set in SPSS file format. It can be used for a research project or with exercises in Chapter 15 that focus on preparing primary data for analysis and actual data analysis procedures (Chapters 16, 17, 18). The database is rich with data and covers a topic that all students can easily identify with.

- **SPSS Student Version.** Through an arrangement with SPSS, we offer the option of purchasing the textbook packaged with a CD-ROM containing an SPSS Student Version 9.0 for Windows. This powerful software tool allows for the analysis of up to 50 variables and 1,500 cases. It contains the complete Back Yard Burgers data set and can be used in conjunction with the data analysis procedures covered in the text.

Acknowledgments

While we took the lead in creating this book, many other people must be given credit for their significant contributions in bringing our vision to reality. Our Deans, Tom Clark at Louisiana State University and Robert Anderson at the University of South Florida, have given us support as has William Locander, Chairman of the Marketing Department at USF. We thank them for providing us with a workable environment that was supportive for undertaking this textbook writing endeavor.

We thank our many colleagues in academia and industry for their helpful insights over many years on many different research topics. We are grateful to several former students, Michael Powell, Julie Bjorklund, and Craig Martin, for their input and research efforts on initial materials in the early writing stage of several chapters. We are also grateful to John R. "Rusty" Brooks, Jr., and Kellye Brooks at Houston Baptist University for their outstanding efforts in the development of the exceptional learning/teaching package that supplements the book, and to David Andrus at Kansas State University for the excellent test bank program.

In any textbook project, the peer reviewers play a very significant role in helping shape content and pedagogy during the preparation of the various drafts. We wish to acknowledge our thanks and appreciation to the following colleagues for their useful suggestions for improving the quality of the book:

David Andrus
Kansas State University
Barry Babin
University of Southern Mississippi
Joseph K. Ballanger
Stephen F. Austin State University
Kevin Bittle
Johnson and Wales University
John R. Brooks, Jr.
Houston Baptist University
Mary L. Carsky
University of Hartford
Frank Franzak
Virginia Commonwealth University
Timothy Graeff
Middle Tennessee State University
Harry Harmon
Central Missouri State University
Karen Kolzow-Bowman
Morgan State University
Martin Meyers
University of Wisconsin at Stevens Point

Arthur Money
Henley Management College, U.K.
Molly Rapert
University of Arkansas
John Rigney
Golden State University
Jean Romeo
Boston College
Lawrence E. Ross
Florida Southern University
Carl Saxby
University of Southern Indiana
Bruce Stern
Portland State University
Gail Tom
California State University at Sacramento
John Tsalikis
Florida International University
Steve Vitucci
University of Central Texas

And finally, we'd like to thank the editors and advisors at our publishing house. We begin by thanking John Weimiester, our original editor at Austin Press, for his capacity to see the value of this project and Steve Patterson, our executive editor at Richard D. Irwin, for his encouragement during the always daunting reviewing process. We are grateful to Rick Adams, our new senior sponsoring editor at Irwin/McGraw Hill, for his commitment to the project and his support in getting the book into production. A very "special thanks" goes to Thomas Thompson, our developmental editor, for all his guidance through the review process and production. We are also grateful to the very professional production team—Susan Trentacosti, project manager; Kiera Cunningham, designer; Lori Koetters, production supervisor; Keri Johnson, photo research coordinator; and Carol Bielski, supplements coordinator—and last, but no means least, to Colleen Suljic, our marketing manager.

Joseph F. Hair, Jr.
Robert P. Bush
David J. Ortinau

Marketing Research Information and Technology

CHAPTER 1

Learning Objectives

After reading this chapter, you will be able to

1. Describe and explain the impact marketing research has on marketing decisions.

2. Demonstrate how marketing research fits into the strategic planning process.

3. Provide examples of marketing research studies.

4. Understand the scope and focus of the marketing research industry.

5. Understand emerging trends and new skills associated with marketing research.

The Role of Marketing Research in Strategic Planning

❝ I don't know how you're supposed to make intelligent decisions without facts. ❞

WILLIAM DILLARD SR.
Founder and Chairman
Dillard's Department Stores[1]

Marketing Research and Decision Making

Outback Steakhouse

Six years after opening its first restaurant in Tampa, Florida, Outback Steakhouse had 210 units in operation. Revenues in 1994 hit $544 million, with sales projections for 1997 at $956 million. Despite bad publicity concerning red meat, top-end steak houses like Morton's in Chicago and Ruth's Chris Steak House were flourishing. Budget eateries like Ponderosa and Ryan's Family Steak Houses were expanding even more rapidly. Yet a mid-range, casual-oriented eatery was nowhere to be found. Using carefully generated information, Outback went to work. Decision number one was to locate in suburban areas and open only for dinner. This was where the families (Outback's target market) were, and when they ate.

Decision number two was to locate in shopping centers in close proximity to residential subdivisions. Again, this was where Outback's target market resided. Decision number three was to build on the Australian theme. "Outback is a lifestyle-driven restaurant catering to the needs of the budget-minded suburban family. This whole Australian attitude is to emphasize a fun, friendly, and active environment, while offering quality food, large portions and reasonable prices."[2] Owners of Outback Steakhouse cite timely information about the market and its dining preferences as a major source of the company's success.

Natural Ovens and Pete's Brewing

Natural Ovens of Manitowoc, Wisconsin, packs a one-page newsletter with every loaf of bread it sells. Pete's Brewing Company, a microbrewery in Palo Alto, California, tucks a minicatalog into each six-pack of its beer. Thus, both companies reach customers when they are most receptive to information about their products. They also save on postage and production. The weekly Natural Ovens newsletters, printed on the flip side of the bread labels, include health tips, recipes, and letters from customers. "Thousands of people have responded about the newsletter," says co-owner Barbara Stitt. "We increased the label size to fit the newsletter, which raised the cost only one-half cent per loaf, but overall printing of the newsletter saved us $1,000 per issue."[3]

In its bookmark-size catalog, which unfolds to 13 inches, Pete's Brewing tells beer lovers about its side products of T-shirts and beer mugs. Pete's Brewing also passes out the catalog at beer-tasting festivals. Talk about reaching customers when they're feeling good!

Both Natural Ovens and Pete's Brewing contend that if it were not for direct customer input and feedback, they may have never developed such profitable marketing devices.

Value of Marketing Research Information

Outback Steakhouse, Natural Ovens, and Pete's Brewing offer just three examples of what marketing research can do for a business. Implementing a sound marketing research process based on customer inquiry and feedback allows any size business to make confident, cost-effective decisions, whether in identifying opportunities in a market or designing packaging and promotional literature.

Marketing research
The function that links an organization to its market through the gathering of information.

The American Marketing Association formally defines **marketing research** as follows:

Marketing research is the function that links an organization to its market through the gathering of information. This information allows for the identification and definition of market-driven opportunities and problems. The information allows for the generation, refinement and evaluation of marketing actions. It allows for the monitoring of marketing performance and improved understanding of marketing as a business process.[4]

Applying this definition to Outback Steakhouse's marketing research process, we can see that Outback used marketing research information to identify an opportunity in the midrange, casual-oriented restaurant market. Natural Ovens and Pete's Brewing used marketing research information to refine their promotional activities and improve marketing performance by introducing value-added products and cost-saving measures.

Included in the American Marketing Association's definition is that marketing research is a process. Specifically, the collection of information as it applies to marketing research is a systematic process. The specific tasks in this process include designing methods for collecting information, managing the information collection process, analyzing and interpreting results, and communicating findings to decision makers.

The purposes of this chapter are to elaborate on marketing research and to provide a fundamental understanding of its relationship to marketing practices. We first explain why firms use marketing research and give some examples of how marketing research can help companies make sound marketing decisions. Next we discuss who should use marketing research, and when.

Another task of this chapter is to provide a general description of the activities companies use to collect marketing research information. We present an overview of the marketing research industry in order to clarify the relationship between the providers and the users of marketing information. The chapter closes with a description of how this text is organized.

The Marketing Concept and Marketing Culture

Marketing The process of planning and executing the pricing, promotion, and distribution of products, services, and ideas in order to create exchanges that satisfy both the firm and its customers.

The fundamental purpose of **marketing** is to allow a firm to plan and execute the pricing, promotion, and distribution of products, services, and ideas in order to create exchanges that satisfy both the firm and its customers. The process of creating this exchange is normally the responsibility of the firm's marketing manager. Marketing managers attempt to stimulate the marketing process by following various decision criteria. More specifically, they focus on getting the right goods and services (1) to the right people, (2) at the right place and time, (3) with the right price, (4) through the use of the right blend of promotional techniques. Adhering to these criteria ultimately leads to the success of the marketing effort. However, the common denominator associated with each criterion is *uncertainty*. Uncertainty lies in the fact that consumer behavior is unpredictable. In order to reduce this uncertainty, marketing managers must have accurate, relevant, and timely information. Marketing research is the mechanism for generating that information.

Marketing concept A business philosophy that says a business must be consumer oriented, goal directed, and system driven.

Today, successful businesses, no matter how small or large, follow a simple business philosophy known as the **marketing concept.** According to this philosophy, a business must be (1) consumer oriented, (2) goal directed, and (3) system driven. Successful businesses produce the goods and services that consumers want, not necessarily the ones they think consumers need. They offer these goods and services to targeted groups of consumers based on the specific desires those consumers express. In addition, marketing-oriented businesses establish goals as benchmarks of success. They realize that they cannot be all things to all people; therefore, they set only those goals that accomplish corporate objectives. While most goals are in fact profit directed (e.g., 10 percent return on investment), true marketing-oriented businesses express goals in terms of their market (e.g., a 20 percent increase in core customer base, or a 10 percent increase in repeat customer purchases).

Finally, successful businesses are system driven; in other words, all of their functional units, no matter how diverse, operate as a team with a common purpose: consumer satisfaction. Being system driven allows businesses to find out what consumers want, to identify profitable market segments, and to uncover significant market opportunities. The prerequisite of any system is a rich understanding of the market dynamics, which can be developed only through marketing research.

Marketing culture   A set of corporate values and norms a business develops in order to establish a long-term relationship with its customers.

Adopting the marketing concept is the first step in generating a **marketing culture.** A marketing culture is a set of values and norms a business develops in order to establish a long-term relationship with its customers. More specifically, a marketing-oriented firm uses the following set of corporate guidelines:

1. The business is a creature of its environment and must monitor that environment, which includes both its competition and its customers. The purposes of any business are to react to its environment and to create customers.

2. If a business isn't growing it's dying. Innovation is the key to growth. Successful innovation is based on understanding both customers and the benefits those customers will receive from the innovation.

3. Success for any business comes from the careful monitoring of and long-term planning for changes in the firm's environment and its relationship with its markets.

4. Long-range planning can be successful only if it is developed with a true information system that is continuous and integrated throughout the firm.

While these guidelines are only general, they do exhibit the four major elements of successful marketing: (1) a focus on the environment and the customer; (2) customer-driven innovation; (3) long-term planning and relationship building; and (4) an integrated, continuous information system.

Marketing research plays a dominant role in the operations and decision making of any business. It is the critical link between the consumer, the environment, and the growth of the business. Marketing research provides the information managers need to identify and define opportunities; generate, define, and refine marketing actions; monitor market performance; and develop strategic marketing plans. In the next section we will explain how marketing research operates to provide information for strategic marketing decisions.

Strategic Marketing Planning

Within a strategic-planning framework, managers must make many critical marketing decisions. These decisions vary dramatically in both focus and complexity. For example, managers must decide which new markets to penetrate, which products to introduce, and which new business opportunities to pursue. Such broad decisions usually require decision makers to consider a variety of alternative approaches. Conversely, decisions regarding advertising effectiveness, product positioning, or sales tracking, while still very complex, are somewhat more narrow in focus. Such decisions usually concentrate on a specific advertising campaign, a particular brand, or a specific market segment. Such decisions often center on monitoring performance or anticipating and initiating changes in a company's marketing practices.

Regardless of the complexity or focus of the decision-making process, managers must have accurate information in order to make the right decisions. The entire strategic marketing process is a series of decisions that must be made with high levels of confidence about the outcome. It is therefore not surprising to realize that a sound marketing research process is the nucleus for strategic market planning.[5]

Exhibit 1.1 lists some of the research-related tasks necessary for confident strategic decision making. While this list is by no means exhaustive, it does provide a general illustration of the relatedness between strategic planning and marketing research. The following sections describe these relationships in more detail.

EXHIBIT 1.1	Strategic Planning Process and Related Marketing Research Tasks

Strategic Planning Process	Marketing Research Task
Marketing Situation Analysis	**Situation Research Efforts**
Market analysis	Opportunity assessment
Market segmentation	Benefit and lifestyle studies Descriptive studies
Competition analysis	Importance-performance analysis
Marketing Strategy Design	**Strategy-Driven Research Efforts**
Target marketing	Target market analysis
Positioning	Positioning (perceptual mapping)
New-product planning	Concept and product testing Test marketing
Marketing Program Development	**Program Development Research**
Product portfolio strategy	Customer satisfaction studies Service quality studies
Distribution strategy	Cycle time research Retailing research Logistic assessment
Pricing strategy	Demand analysis Sales forecasting
Integrated marketing communications	Advertising effectiveness studies Attitudinal research Sales tracking
Strategy Implementation and Control	**Performance Analysis**
Strategy control	Product analysis Environmental forecasting
Strategic information analysis	Marketing decision support systems

Marketing Situation Analysis

Situation Analysis To monitor the appropriateness of a firm's marketing strategy and to determine whether changes to the strategy are necessary.

The purpose of a **situation analysis** is to monitor the appropriateness of a firm's marketing strategy and to determine whether changes to the strategy are necessary. A situation analysis includes three decision areas: market analysis, market segmentation, and competition analysis. Within the context of a situation analysis, the purposes of marketing research are to:

1. Locate and identify new market opportunities for a company (opportunity assessment).

2. Identify groups of customers within a product-market who possess similar needs, characteristics, and preferences (benefit and lifestyle studies, descriptive studies).

3. Identify existing and potential competitors' strengths and weaknesses (importance-performance analysis).

Market Analysis

Opportunity assessment
Involves collecting information on product markets for the purpose of forecasting how they will change.

The research task related to market analysis is **opportunity assessment,** which involves collecting information on product markets for the purpose of forecasting how they will change. Companies gather information relevant to macroenvironmental trends (political and regulatory, economic and social, and cultural and technological) and assess how those trends will affect the product market.

The role of marketing research is to gather and categorize information pertaining to various macroenvironmental variables, then interpret the information in the context of strategic consequences to the firm. Marketing researchers use three common approaches in the collection of macroenvironmental information:

1. Content analysis, in which researchers analyze various trade publications, newspaper articles, academic literature, or computer databases for information on trends in a given industry.

2. In-depth interviews, in which researchers conduct formal, structured interviews with experts in a given field.

3. Formal rating procedures, in which researchers use structured questionnaires to gather information on environmental occurrences.

These procedures will be discussed further in Chapters 12, 13, and 14.

Market Segmentation

Benefit and lifestyle studies   Examine similarities and differences in consumers' needs. Researchers use these studies to identify two or more segments within the market for a particular company's products.

A research task related to market segmentation consists of **benefit and lifestyle studies,** which examine similarities and differences in consumers' needs. Researchers use these studies to identify two or more segments within the market for a particular company's products. The marketing research objective is to collect information about customer characteristics, product benefits, and brand preferences. Such data, along with information on age, family size, income, and lifestyle, are then related to purchase patterns of particular products (cars, food, electronics, financial services) for the purpose of developing market segmentation profiles.

Creating customer profiles and understanding certain behavioral characteristics are major focuses of any marketing research project. Determining why consumers behave as they do becomes the critical interaction between marketing research and marketing strategy development. Chapter 9 will focus on this issue and examine, in detail, customer-driven marketing research approaches.

Competition Analysis

Importance-performance analysis
A research approach for evaluating competitors' strategies, strengths, limitations, and future plans.

A research task related to competition analysis is **importance-performance analysis,** which is a commonly used research approach for evaluating competitors' strategies, strengths, limitations, and future plans. Within marketing research, importance-performance analysis asks consumers to identify key attributes that drive their purchase behavior within a given industry. These attributes might include price, product performance, quality, accuracy of shipping and delivery, or convenience of store location. Consumers are then asked to rank such attributes in order of importance. Following the importance ranking, researchers identify and evaluate competing firms.

Attributes on which companies are ranked high can be viewed as strengths, and those on which they are ranked low can be viewed as limitations or weaknesses. When the competing firms are analyzed in aggregate, a company can see where its competitors are concentrating their marketing efforts and where they are falling below customer expectations.

Importance-performance analysis is just one technique for analyzing competition. This and other techniques for analyzing competition are discussed further in Chapter 8.

Marketing Strategy Design

Information collected during a situation analysis is subsequently used to design a marketing strategy. At this stage of the planning process, companies design target market approaches, seek methods of positioning products and brands within target markets, develop new products, and test different markets.[6]

Target Marketing

Target market analysis
Information for identifying those people (or companies) that an organization wishes to serve.

Target market analysis provides useful information for identifying those people (or companies) that an organization wishes to serve. In addition, it helps management determine the most efficient way of serving the targeted group. Target market analysis attempts to provide information on the following issues:

- New-product opportunities.

- Demographics, including attitudinal or behavioral characteristics.

- User profiles, usage patterns, and attitudes.

- The effectiveness of a firm's current marketing strategy.

In order to provide such information, the marketing researcher must measure the key variables outlined in Exhibit 1.2.

Positioning

Positioning A process in which a company seeks to establish a meaning or general definition of its product offering that is consistent with customers' needs and preferences.

Positioning, or **perceptual mapping,** is a process in which a company seeks to establish a general meaning or definition of its product offering that is consistent with customers' needs and preferences. Companies accomplish this task by combining elements of the marketing mix in a manner that meets or exceeds the expectations of targeted customers.

The task of the marketing researcher is to provide a photograph of the relationship between competitive product offerings based on judgments of a sample of respondents who are familiar with the product category being investigated. Consumers are asked to indicate

EXHIBIT 1.2 **Target Market Characteristics and Associated Variables Measured in Target Market Analysis**

Target Market Characteristics	Key Variables to Measure
Demographics	Age, gender, race, income, religion, occupation, family size, geographic location, and zip code
Psychographics	Consumer activities, interests, and opinions
Product usage	Occasion (special use, gift); situation (climate, time of day, place); and usage context (heavy, medium, or light)
Brand preferences	Level of brand loyalty, salient product attributes, and product/brand awareness
Decision process	Size and frequency of purchase; propensity to purchase; risk of purchase (high, medium, low); and product involvement

Kellogg's Pop-Tarts is an example of new-product positioning.

how they view the similarities and dissimilarities among relevant product attributes for a set of competing brands. For example, positioning among beers may indicate that customers decide between "popular versus premium" and "regional versus national" brands.

This information is then used to construct perceptual maps, which transform the positioning data into "perceptual space." Perceptual mapping reflects the dimensions on which brands are evaluated, typically representing product features or attributes judged as important in a customer's selection process. Positioning and perceptual mapping will be discussed more fully in Chapters 13 and 18.

New-Product Planning

Concept and product testing and **Test marketing** Information for decisions on product improvements and new-product introductions.

The research tasks related to new-product planning are **concept and product testing** and **test marketing,** which give management the necessary information for decisions on product improvements and new-product introductions. Product testing attempts to answer two fundamental questions: "How does a product perform for the customer?" and "How can a product be improved to exceed customer expectations?" Product testers reshape, redefine, and coalesce ideas to arrive at a vital product that not only meets but exceeds market expectations. Specifically, product testers

1. Provide necessary information for designing and developing new products.

2. Determine whether new or improved products should replace current products.

3. Assess the appeal of alternative products for new target segments.

4. Seek to identify products that are most preferred or actively sought relative to existing competitive offerings.

Marketing Program Development

The information requirements for marketing program development concentrate on all the components of the marketing mix: product, distribution, price, and promotion. Managers combine these components to form the total marketing effort for each market targeted.

While at first this may appear to be an easy task, decision makers must remember that the success of the total marketing effort or program relies heavily on synergy. It is critical that the marketing mix not only contain the right elements but do so in the right amount, at the right time, and in the proper sequence. Ensuring that this synergy occurs is the responsibility of market researchers.

Product Portfolio Strategy

Within product portfolio strategies, the total product line is typically the focal point of investigation. Market researchers design specific studies that help product managers make decisions about reducing costs, altering marketing mixes, and changing or deleting product lines. Two varieties are customer satisfaction studies and service quality studies.

Customer satisfaction studies are designed to assess the strengths and weaknesses customers perceive in a firm's marketing mix. While these studies are usually designed to analyze the marketing mix collectively, many firms elect to focus on customer responses to one mix element at a time (e.g., satisfaction with pricing policy).

Regardless of their scope, customer satisfaction studies concentrate on measuring customer attitudes. Research indicates that customers' attitudes are strongly linked to purchase intentions, brand switching, perceptions of company image, and brand loyalty.[7] Attitude information allows management to make intelligent decisions regarding product or brand repositioning, new-product introductions, new market segments, and the deletion of ineffective products. Chapters 12 and 13 discuss the design and development of attitudinal research studies.

Service quality studies are designed to measure the degree to which an organization conforms to the quality level customers expect.[8] Service quality studies concentrate on physical facilities and equipment, appearance and behavior of company personnel, and dependability of products and programs. Specifically, employees are rated on their general willingness to help customers and provide them with prompt, friendly, courteous treatment.

A popular service quality study is the mystery shopper study, in which trained professional shoppers visit stores, financial institutions, or even manufacturers and "shop" for various goods and services. Atmosphere, friendliness, and customer appreciation are just a few of the dimensions evaluated by mystery shoppers. Some firms also patronize their competitors to see how their own performance compares. Data from service quality studies have proved to be invaluable for decision making related primarily to products or services. They allow the firm to anticipate any problems in its product or service offering before they become out of hand. Also, such data allow firms to assess themselves relative to competitors on key strengths and weaknesses.

Distribution Strategy

Distribution strategies take into account the distributors and retailers that link producers with end users. The distribution channel used by a producer can create a strong influence on a buyer's perception of the brand. For example, Rolex watches are distributed through a limited number of retailers that project a prestigious image consistent with the Rolex brand name. Three common types of distribution-related research methods are cycle time research, retailing research, and logistic assessment.[9]

With many businesses moving to control inventory costs, automatic replenishment systems and electronic data interchange are becoming widely used. Closely associated with such inventory systems is **cycle time research,** which centers on reducing the time between the initial contact with a customer and the final delivery (or installation) of the product. This research is most often concerned with large distribution networks (manufacturers, wholesalers, retailers, end users). This is not to say cycle time research ignores

Customer satisfaction studies These studies assess the strengths and weaknesses customers perceive in a firm's marketing mix.

Service quality studies Are designed to measure the degree to which an organization conforms to the quality level customers expect.

Cycle time research A research method that centers on reducing the time between the initial contact and final delivery (or installation) of the product.

shorter channels of distribution (retailer, end user), for in many cases, such as direct marketing approaches, it becomes critical in exploring ways to increase customer satisfaction and fulfillment. Marketing research becomes responsible for collecting information that will help reduce costs in the total cycle time, as well as exploring alternative methods of distribution to reduce the time frame in the shipping and installation of goods.

Two common research practices in this area are delivery expense studies and alternative delivery systems studies.[10] Both seek to obtain information related to expense analysis for alternative forms of delivery (e.g., post office, FedEx, UPS), in connection with providing a high degree of customer satisfaction. Such studies are unique in that they rely heavily on internal company records or databases. Usually referred to as secondary research, studies such as these are becoming more common than ever before. Chapters 4 and 5 are devoted to information-gathering procedures at a secondary level. Chapter 6 explores the relationship between marketing research and database development.

Retailing research

Studies on topics such as trade area analysis, store image/perception, in-store traffic patterns, and location analysis.

Retailing research includes studies on a variety of topics. Because retailers are viewed as independent businesses, all of the studies we have discussed up to this point are applicable to the retail environment. Yet, at the same time, the information needs of retailers are unique. Market research studies peculiar to retailers include trade area analysis, store image/perception studies, in-store traffic pattern studies, and location analysis.

Because retailing is a high-customer-contact activity, a majority of retailing research focuses on database development through optical scanning procedures. As illustrated in Exhibit 1.3, every time a salesperson records a transaction using an optical scanner, the scanner notes the type of product, its manufacturer and vendor, and its size and price. Marketing research then categorizes the data and combines them with other relevant information to form a database. As a result, retailers can find out what television programs their customers watch, what kinds of neighborhoods they live in, and what types of stores they prefer to patronize. Such information helps retailers determine what kind of merchandise to stock and what factors may influence purchase decisions.

EXHIBIT 1.3   **Information Collection Process through Retail Optical Scanning Techniques**

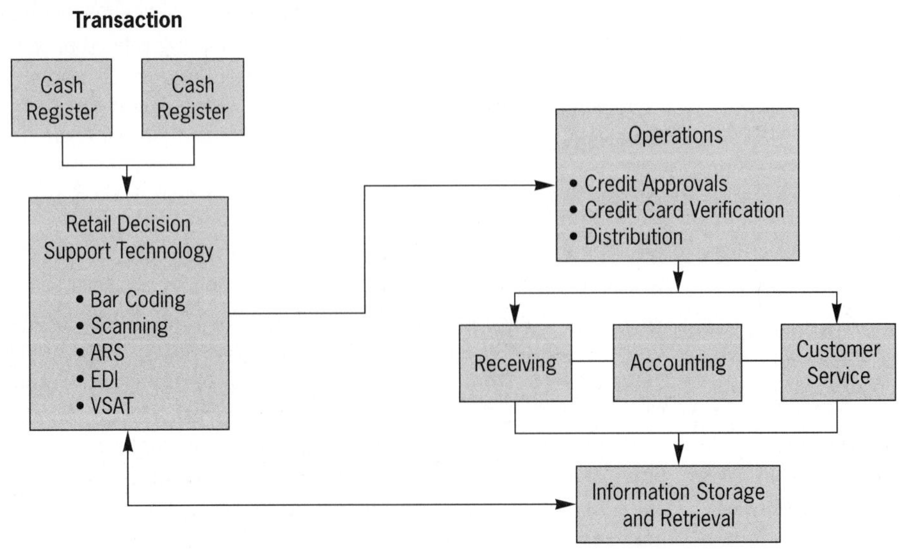

Logistic assessment
Information in logistics allows market researchers to conduct total cost analysis and service sensitivity analysis.

Marketing research related to **logistic assessment** is an often overlooked area in distribution decisions. One reason for this is that it has been traditionally driven by secondary data, that is, information not gathered for the study at hand but for some other purpose.[11] This type of information in logistics allows market researchers to conduct total cost analysis and service sensitivity analysis.[12]

Total cost analysis explores the alternative logistic system designs a firm can use to achieve its performance objective at the lowest total cost. The role of marketing research is to develop an activity-based cost information system by identifying key factors that affect transportation, inventory, and warehousing costs.

Service sensitivity analysis helps organizations design basic customer service programs by evaluating cost-to-service trade-offs. In conducting this type of analysis, market researchers look for ways to increase various basic services by making adjustments in transportation activities, inventory levels, or location planning. Each adjustment is analyzed relative to its impact on corresponding total costs.

Pricing Strategy

Pricing strategy involves pricing new products, establishing price levels in test-market situations, and modifying prices for existing products. Marketing research must provide answers to such fundamental questions as the following:

1. How large is the demand potential within the target market?

2. How sensitive is demand to changes in price levels?

3. What nonprice factors are important to customers?

4. What are the sales forecasts at various price levels?

Pricing research can take a variety of forms. Two common approaches are demand analysis and sales forecasting.

Demand analysis A research method that seeks to estimate the level of customer demand for a given product and the underlying reasons for that demand.

When a company evaluates a new-product idea, develops a test market, or plans changes for existing products, a critical research challenge is estimating how customers will respond to alternate prices. **Demand analysis** seeks to estimate the level of customer demand for a given product and the underlying reasons for that demand. For example, research indicates that customers will buy more of certain products at higher prices, which suggests that price may be an indication of quality.[13] This seems to occur most often when customers are unable to evaluate the product themselves. Conversely, the chemical firm Du Pont, using demand analysis, obtained a specific measure of nonprice factors for its products. Among those factors were delivery, service, innovation, brand name, and quality.

Demand analysis many times incorporates a test-marketing procedure. This involves the actual marketing of a product in one of several cities with the intent of measuring customer sensitivity to changes in a firm's marketing mix. Test marketing is discussed in detail in Chapter 10. Demand analysis can also incorporate end-user research studies and analysis of historical price and quality data for specific products.

Sales forecasting Uses variables that affect customer demand to provide estimates of financial outcomes for different price strategies.

Closely associated with demand analysis is **sales forecasting.** After demand analysis identifies the variables that affect customer demand, sales forecasting uses those variables to provide estimates of financial outcomes for different price strategies.

Although a variety of sales forecasting techniques exist, most can be placed in one of two categories: qualitative or quantitative. Qualitative techniques include user expectation studies, sales-force composites, juries of executive opinion, and delphi techniques. Quantitative forecasting techniques include market testing, time series analysis, and statistical demand analysis.[14]

Integrated Marketing Communications

Promotional strategies are important influences on any company's sales. Companies spend billions of dollars yearly on various promotional activities. Given the heavy level of expenditures devoted to promotional activities, it is essential that companies design studies that will generate optimum returns from the promotional investment.

Marketing research methods used to acquire information about the performance of a promotional program must consider the entire program. Employing the appropriate methodology, estimating adequate sample sizes, and developing the proper scaling techniques are just three key areas of promotional research. Each of these areas is used when considering the three most common research tasks of integrated marketing communications: advertising effectiveness studies, attitudinal research, and sales tracking.

Because advertising serves so many purposes and covers so many objectives, actual *advertising effectiveness studies* vary across situations.[15] Advertising effectiveness studies may be qualitative, quantitative, or both. They may take place in laboratory-type settings or in real-life settings. Measures of an ad's effectiveness may be taken before or at various times after media placement. Regardless, the key elements of advertising effectiveness studies are what is being measured, when the measurement is made, and which medium is being used.

Most advertising effectiveness studies focus on measuring a particular ad's ability to generate awareness, communicate product benefits, or create a favorable predisposition about a product. In attempting to accomplish such measurement objectives, market researchers usually include attitudinal research within the advertising effectiveness study.

Attitudinal research, which will be discussed in Chapter 13, can be categorized into three types. First is the cognitive approach, which attempts to measure consumers' knowledge and opinions about a given product or brand. Second, affect approaches measure consumers' overall impressions of a product or brand. These impressions are usually associated with dimensions like good/bad, pleasant/unpleasant, or positive/negative. Third, behavioral approaches seek to measure consumers' specific behaviors (brand loyalty, brand switching, etc.) with regard to a given product or brand. Because many promotional strategies are designed to affect consumers' attitudes, the results of attitudinal research play an important role in the design and implementation of promotional programs.

Personal selling also plays a major role in a firm's promotional mix. The objectives assigned to salespeople frequently involve expected sales results such as sales quotas. Nonsales objectives are also important and may include increasing new accounts, evaluating middlemen, or achieving set levels of customer service.

Both forms of objectives are commonly tied to the evaluation of a salesperson's overall performance. Several variables must be considered in this evaluation process, which uses a technique commonly called *sales tracking*. From the standpoint of marketing research, key information must be gathered on salespeople and placed into the proper units of analysis in order to provide adjustments for factors beyond the control of individual salespeople. Sales-tracking procedures allow for this adjustment by assessing a combination of objective and subjective performance dimensions. Exhibit 1.4 contains some actual data collected on a sales-tracking form. Some of the key variables are standard industrial classification (SIC) codes, annual sales, and number of employees. The form also illustrates the effectiveness of the selling function by documenting who sold the product, the number of sales calls required to close the sale, and the profit generated. A well-designed sales-tracking system such as this helps managers diagnose performance-related problems and determine corrective actions that may be necessary.

| EXHIBIT 1.4 | **Computerized Sales Tracking Form Illustrating Key Sales Tracking Variables** |

Company Id: 5012   Job No: 7012

Name: HERSHEY CHOCOLATE USA

Address: 27 WEST CHOCOLATE AVE

City ST Zip: HERSHEY   PA   17033-0819

Phone: 717-534-6488   DIV:

SIC Code: 2066   **Employees:** 5

Annual Sales: 4   **Region:** 1

Primary Bus: 4

No. of Plants: 8

Projected Growth: 7

Primary Market: 2

No. of Product Line: 4

End Product: 4

Facility Address: HERSHEY

Key Contact Person: GARY HOMMEL

Division No.:   **Location:** 1

System Price: 1   **System Profit:**

Sales Call/Close Ratio: **Sales Rep:** 52

Strategy Implementation and Control

The key to strategy implementation and control for any organization is the marketing plan. This plan indicates what the strategic goals are and how they will be accomplished. Marketing research provides managers with the information they need to analyze product markets, competition, and product performance with regard to the marketing plan.[16] Specifically, marketing research provides information for strategy implementation and long-term planning.

Strategy Control

Two key areas of focus are product analysis and environmental forecasting. **Product analysis** attempts to identify the relative importance of product selection criteria to buyers

Product analysis Identifies the relative importance of product selection criteria to buyers and rates brands against these criteria.

and rate brands against these criteria. Such analysis is conducted throughout the life cycle of the product or brand. It is particularly useful when developing the strengths-and-weaknesses section of a marketing plan. Many of the standardized information services provided by marketing research firms, such as Information Resources and ACNielsen, monitor the performance of competing brands across a wide variety of products.

Environmental forecasting A research method used to predict external occurrences that can affect the long-term strategy of a firm.

Environmental forecasting is used to predict external occurrences that can affect the long-term strategy of a firm. This technique usually involves a three-phase process that begins with a survey of customers and industry experts. This is followed with a market test to measure customer response to a particular marketing program and, finally, an analysis of internal company records to determine past buying behaviors. The net result is an accumulation of data pertaining to industry trends, customer profiles, and environmental changes that allow a company to adapt its strategy to anticipated future events.

Strategic Information Analysis

Information is vital to the strategic planning process. Just as strategic planning is the key to the long-term survival of the firm, information is key to the accuracy of the marketing plan. Strategic information allows firms to develop a competitive advantage. The role of marketing research is not only to collect and analyze data, but to categorize and process the data for maximum usage. This task is achieved through the development of a sophisticated system referred to as a **marketing decision support system (MDSS).**

Marketing decision support system (MDSS) A company-developed database used to analyze company performance and control marketing activities.

An MDSS is a company-developed database used to analyze company performance and control marketing activities. It includes standardized marketing research reports, sales and cost data, product-line sales, advertising data, and price information. This information is then organized to correspond to specific units of analysis (market segments, geographic locations, particular vendors), to be used for various decisions from reordering inventory to launching new products. The value of the MDSS becomes most apparent when the system focuses on strategic decision making. An example of this relationship between strategic planning and marketing research is Northwest Airlines' ability to use an MDSS when focusing on the needs of specific market segments. The Northwest system, which determines mileage awards for frequent flyers and provides a reservation support database organized according to market segments, reveals that the top 3 percent of the company's customers account for almost 50 percent of its sales. These key customers are highlighted on all service screens and reports. Ticket agents are alerted when one of these customers phones in or arrives, so that they can offer a variety of special services, such as first-class upgrades.[17]

New technologies for collecting, processing, and analyzing market research data are rapidly changing organizations in a variety of ways. Many experts in the field speculate that technologies associated with the MDSS will diminish the need for primary data collection methods in the near future.[18] The full impact of the MDSS on marketing research will be discussed in Chapter 7.

The Marketing Research Industry

As an industry, marketing research has experienced unparalleled growth in the past five years. According to a recent *Advertising Age* study, the revenues of U.S. research companies grew 10 percent in 1997, compared to 6.8 percent in 1990.[19] Even more dramatic were the revenues reported by international research firms, claiming a 14 percent increase in 1997. Marketing research firms have attributed these revenue increases to postsales customer satisfaction studies (claiming one-third of research company revenues), retail-driven

EXHIBIT 1.5	Research Activities of 435 Companies in 1988 and 1997

Research Activity	Percentage of Companies That Perform This Activity		Research Activity	Percentage of Companies That Perform This Activity	
	1988	1997		1988	1997
Business/Economic and Corporate Research			**Distribution**		
Industry/market characteristics and trends	83%	92%	Location studies	23	25
Acquisition/diversification	50	50	Performance studies	29	—
Market share analysis	79	85	Coverage studies	26	—
Internal employee studies	54	72	International studies	19	—
Pricing			**Promotion**		
Cost analysis	60	57	Motivation research	37	56
Profit analysis	59	55	Media research	57	70
Price elasticity	45	56	Copy research	50	68
Demand analysis			Advertising effectiveness	65	67
Market potential	74	78	Competitive advertising studies	47	43
Sales potential	69	75	Public image studies	60	65
Sales forecasts	67	71	**Sales Force Research**		
Product			Compensation	30	34
Concept development and testing	63	78	Quotas	26	28
Brand-name testing	38	55	Territory structure	31	32
Test markets	45	55	Sales promotion	36	47
Existing product tests	47	63	**Buyer Behavior**		
Packaging studies	31	48	Brand preference	54	78
Competitive product studies	58	54	Brand attitudes	53	76
			Satisfaction	68	87
			Purchase behavior	61	80
			Purchase intentions	60	79
			Brand awareness	59	80
			Segmentation	60	84

Source: Thomas C. Kinnear and Ann R. Rott, *1988 Survey of Marketing Research,* p. 43; and *1997 Survey of Marketing Research* (Chicago: American Marketing Association, 1997), p. 49.

product scanning systems (claiming an additional one-third of all revenues), database development for long-term brand management, and international research studies. Exhibit 1.5 lists various market research activities and the percentage of companies (out of a sample of 435 firms) that performed them in 1988 and 1997. In virtually all areas, the percentages have increased since 1988. Satisfaction, corporate strategy, and buyer behavior studies were high priorities for most businesses in 1997.

Types of Marketing Research Firms

Marketing research providers can be classified as either internal or external, custom or standardized, or brokers or facilitators. Internal research providers are normally organizational units that reside within a company. For example, General Motors, Procter & Gamble, and Kodak all have internal marketing research departments. Kraft Foods realizes many benefits by keeping the marketing research function internal; these benefits include research method consistency, shared information across the company, minimized spending on research, and ability to produce actionable research results.

Other firms elect to seek external sources for marketing research. These sources, usually referred to as marketing research suppliers, perform all aspects of the research, including study design, questionnaire production, interviewing, data analysis, and report preparation. These firms operate on a fee basis and commonly submit a research proposal to be used by a client for evaluation and decision purposes. An actual example of a proposal is provided in the Marketing Research Illustration at the end of Chapter 2.

Many companies use external research suppliers because, first, the suppliers can be more objective and less subject to company politics and regulations than internal suppliers. Second, many external suppliers provide specialized talents that, for the same cost, internal suppliers could not provide. And finally, companies can choose external suppliers on a study-by-study basis and thus gain greater flexibility in scheduling studies as well as match specific project requirements to the talents of specific research firms.

Marketing research firms can also be considered customized or standardized. Customized research firms provide specialized, highly tailored services to the client. Many firms in this line of business concentrate their research activities in one specific area such as brand-name testing, test marketing, or new-product development. For example, Namestormers assists companies in brand-name selection and recognition, Survey Sampling Inc. concentrates solely on sampling development for the restaurant industry, and Uniscore only conducts studies designed around retail scanning data. In contrast, standardized research firms provide more general services. These firms also follow a more common approach in research design so that the results of a study conducted for one client can be compared to norms established by studies done for other clients. Examples of these firms are Burke Market Research, which conducts day-after advertising recall; ACNielsen (separate from Nielsen Media Research), which conducts store audits for a variety of retail firms; and Arbitron Ratings, which provides primary data collection regarding commercial television.

Many standardized research firms also provide syndicated business services, which include purchase diary panels, audits, and advertising recall data made or developed from a common data pool or database. A prime example of a syndicated business service is a database established through retail optical scanner methods. This database, available from ACNielsen, tracks the retail sales of thousands of brand-name products. These data can be customized for a variety of industries (snack foods, over-the-counter drugs, etc.) to indicate purchase profiles and volume sales in a given industry.

Finally, marketing research firms can be distinguished as either brokers or facilitators. Broker services provide the ancillary tasks that complement many marketing research studies. For example, marketing research suppliers and clients who do not have the resources for data entry, tabulation, or analysis will typically use a broker service to facilitate the data management process. Brokers usually offer specialized programming, canned statistical packages, and other data management tools at low cost. P-Shat, Inc., for example, is a marketing research broker service that performs only three functions: data entry, data tabulation, and statistical analysis.

Facilitating agencies

Businesses that perform marketing research functions as a supplement to a broader marketing research project.

Facilitating agencies are companies or businesses that perform marketing research functions as a supplement to a broader marketing research project. Advertising agencies, field services, and independent consultants are usually classified as facilitators because they help companies complete broader marketing projects. Advertising agencies, for example, are in the business of designing, implementing, and evaluating advertising campaigns for individual clients. Many agencies use their own research services to guide the development of the campaign and test for effectiveness. In this instance, the ad agency provides marketing research to facilitate the ad campaign process.

Marketing research suppliers frequently employ field services, whose primary responsibilities are to schedule, supervise, and complete interviews. As a facilitating agency, a field service contributes data collection services toward the completion of the marketing research project. In addition, many independent consultants are hired ad hoc to complement strategic planning activities for clients. Many consultants, offering unique and specialized research skills, are hired by firms to facilitate a total quality management program, develop a marketing information system, or train employees in the procedures of marketing research.

As this discussion shows, marketing research is an undoubtedly diverse industry. Diversity, coupled with increased revenue growth in the industry, has created job opportunities for people with a variety of skills. Furthermore, as more and more marketing research projects take on international flavor, these opportunities will continue to expand. The following section addresses exactly what skills will be needed in the industry.

Changing Skills for a Changing Industry

Marketing research employees represent a vast diversity of cultures, technology, and personalities. As marketing research firms expand their geographic scope to Europe, Asia, and the Pacific Rim, the requirements for successfully executing marketing research projects will change dramatically. Many fundamental skill requirements will remain in place, but new and innovative practices will require a totally unique skill base that is more comprehensive than ever before.

In a recent national survey of 100 marketing research executives, basic fundamental business skills were still rated high for potential employees. Communication skills (verbal and written), interpersonal skills (ability to work with others), and statistical skills were the leading attributes in basic job aptitude.[20] More specifically, the top five skills executives hope to find in candidates for marketing research positions are (1) the ability to understand and interpret secondary data, (2) presentation skills, (3) foreign-language competency, (4) negotiation skills, and (5) computer proficiency.[21] Results of this survey thus suggest that there has been a shift from analytical to executional skill requirements in the marketing research industry. Emphasis on existing databases, multicultural interaction, and negotiation promise to be important characteristics of marketing research in the future. Marketing research jobs are further discussed in the Marketing Research Illustration at the end of this chapter.

Emerging Trends

The general consensus in the marketing research industry is that five major trends are becoming evident: (1) an increased emphasis on secondary data collection methods; (2) movement toward technology-related data management (optical scanning data, database technology); (3) an increased use of computers for information acquisition and retrieval; (4) a broader international client base; and (5) a movement away from pure data analysis and toward a data interpretation/information management environment.

The organization of this book is consistent with these trends. Part I (Chapters 1–5) explores marketing research information and technology from the client's perspective, with a primary emphasis on how to evaluate marketing research projects. Part I also provides an innovative outlook on secondary data sources, with emphasis on technology-driven approaches for collecting secondary data, design and development of databases, and the management of secondary data.

Part II (Chapters 6–10) discusses traditional marketing research project design issues (survey methods, experimental designs, and database procedures). While these methods are fundamental to the marketing research process, technological developments have changed the focus of these issues. Part II will also emphasize collection and interpretation of qualitative data, along with a practical discussion on decision support systems.

Part III (Chapters 11–14) is devoted to sampling, measurement, scaling, and questionnaire design. While the approach to these topics is traditional, practical examples illustrating how they are used today in industry facilitate the discussion. Part IV (Chapters 15–19) will prepare the reader for management, categorization, and analysis of marketing research data. Computer applications of various statistical packages provide readers with a hands-on guide to a somewhat intimidating area. The text concludes with a presentation of marketing research findings. Key elements in preparing a written marketing research report and planning an oral presentation of results are treated succinctly. Word-processing packages and graphic aids highlight the discussion of these topics.

Each chapter concludes with an actual marketing research illustration. The goals of these illustrations are to facilitate the understanding of chapter topics and to provide the reader with a how-to approach for marketing research methods.

SUMMARY OF LEARNING OBJECTIVES

Describe and explain the impact marketing research has on marketing decisions.

Marketing research is the set of activities central to all marketing-related decisions regardless of the complexity or focus of the decision. Marketing research is responsible for providing managers with accurate, relevant, and timely information so that they can make marketing decisions with a high degree of confidence. Within the context of strategic planning, marketing research is responsible for the tasks, methods, and procedures a firm will use to implement and direct its strategic plan.

Demonstrate how marketing research fits into the strategic planning process.

The key to successful strategic planning is accurate information. Information related to product performance, distribution efficiency, pricing policies, and promotional efforts is crucial for developing the strategic plan. The primary responsibility of any marketing research endeavor is to design a project that yields the most accurate information possible in aiding the development of a strategic plan.

Provide examples of marketing research studies.

The scope of marketing research activities extends far beyond examination of customer characteristics. The major categories of marketing research tasks include, but are not limited to, (1) situation research efforts (which include opportunity assessment, benefit and lifestyle studies, descriptive studies, and importance-performance analysis); (2) strategy-driven research efforts (which include target market analysis, positioning or perceptual mapping, concept and product testing, and test marketing); (3) program development research (which includes customer satisfaction studies, service quality studies, cycle time research, retailing research, logistic assessment, demand analysis, sales forecasting, advertising effectiveness studies, attitudinal research, and sales tracking); and (4) performance analysis (which includes product analysis, environmental forecasting, and marketing decision support systems).

Understand the scope and focus of the marketing research industry.

Generally, marketing research projects can be conducted either internally by an in-house marketing research staff or externally by independent or facilitating marketing research firms. External research suppliers are normally classified as custom or standardized, or as brokers or facilitators.

Understand emerging trends and new skills associated with marketing research.

Just as the dynamic business environment causes firms to modify and change practices, so does this environment dictate change to the marketing research industry. Specifically, technological changes will affect how marketing research will be conducted in the future. Necessary skills required to adapt to these changes include (1) the ability to understand and interpret secondary data, (2) presentation skills, (3) foreign-language competency, (4) negotiation skills, and (5) computer proficiency.

KEY TERMS AND CONCEPTS

Benefit and lifestyle studies 8

Concept and product testing 10

Customer satisfaction studies 11

Cycle time research 11

Demand analysis 13

Environmental forecasting 16

Facilitating agencies 18

Importance-performance analysis 8

Logistic assessment 13

Marketing 5

Marketing concept 5

Marketing culture 6

Marketing decision support system (MDSS) 16

Marketing research 4

Opportunity assessment 8

Perceptual mapping 9

Positioning 9

Product analysis 15

Retailing research 12

Sales forecasting 13

Service quality studies 11

Situation analysis 7

Target market analysis 9

Test marketing 10

REVIEW QUESTIONS

1. Provide three examples of how marketing research helps marketing personnel make sound strategic decisions.

2. What improvements in strategic planning can be attributed to the results obtained from customer satisfaction studies?

3. List the three basic approaches used in the collection of marketing research information. Briefly describe each method and comment on its application.

4. Discuss the importance of target market analysis. How does it affect the development of strategy for a particular company?

5. What are the advantages and disadvantages for companies maintaining an internal marketing research department? What advantages and disadvantages can be attributed to the hiring of an external marketing research supplier?

6. As the marketing research industry expands into the next century, what skills will future executives need to possess? How do these skills differ from those currently needed to function successfully in the marketing research field?

DISCUSSION QUESTIONS

1. **EXPERIENCE THE INTERNET.** Go online to one of your favorite search engines (Yahoo, Lycos, etc.) and enter the following search term: *marketing research*. From the results, access a directory of marketing research firms. Select a particular firm and comment on the types of marketing research studies it performs.

2. **EXPERIENCE THE INTERNET.** Using the Yahoo search engine, specifically the Get Local section, select the closest major city in your area and search for the number of marketing research firms there. Select a firm, e-mail that company, and ask to have any job descriptions for positions in that company e-mailed back to you. Once you obtain the descriptions, discuss the particular qualities needed to perform each job.

3. You have been hired by McDonald's to lead a mystery shopper team. The goal of your research is to improve the service quality at the McDonald's restaurant in your area. What attributes of service quality will you attempt to measure? What customer or employee behaviors will you closely monitor?

4. Contact a local business and interview the owner/manager about the types of marketing research performed for that business. Determine whether the business has its own marketing research department, or if it hires an outside agency. Also, determine whether the company takes a one-shot approach to particular problems or is systematic over a long period of time.

ENDNOTES

1. Annual report, Dillard's Department Stores, Little Rock, Arkansas, 1997.

2. "The Aussie Invasion, Trend or Fad," *Business Week,* March 16, 1997.

3. "New Trends in Retailing at the Superspecialty Level," *Chain Store Age Executive,* June 1997.

4. American Marketing Association, *Official Definition of Marketing Research,* 1987.

5. David W. Cravens, *Strategic Marketing,* 4th ed. (Burr Ridge, IL: Irwin, 1993).

6. "The Aging of America," *American Demographics,* April 1997.

7. Cravens, *Strategic Marketing.*

8. Ibid.

9. William Pride and O. C. Ferrell, *Marketing,* 10th ed. (Boston: Houghton-Mifflin, 1997).

10. Ibid.

11. *Research Topics in Cycle Time Research* (Memphis, TN: Center for Cycle Time Research, University of Memphis, 1997).

12. American Marketing Association, *Official Definition of Secondary Data.*

13. Ferrell and Pride, *Marketing.*

14. Ibid.

15. Tom Ingram and Raymond LaForge, *Sales Management,* 2nd ed. (Fort Worth: Dryden, 1992).

16. Ibid.

17. Cravens, *Strategic Marketing.*

18. "Value Added Research," *Marketing Research,* Fall 1997.

19. Ibid.

20. "Survey of Top Marketing Research Firms," *Advertising Age,* June 27, 1997.

21. "Fostering Professionalism," *Marketing Research,* Spring 1997.

MARKETING RESEARCH ILLUSTRATION

CAREERS IN MARKETING RESEARCH WITH A LOOK AT FEDERAL EXPRESS

Career opportunities in marketing research vary by industry, company, and size of company. Different positions exist in consumer products companies, industrial goods companies, internal marketing research departments, and professional marketing research firms. Marketing research tasks range from the very simple, such as tabulation of questionnaires, to the very complex, such as sophisticated data analysis. Exhibit 1 lists some common job titles and the functions as well as compensation ranges for marketing research positions.

Most successful marketing research people are intelligent and creative; they also possess problem-solving, critical thinking, communication, and negotiation skills. Marketing researchers must be able to function under strict time constraints and feel comfortable with

EXHIBIT 1	Marketing Research Career Outline

Position*	Duties	Compensation Range (Annual, in Thousands)
Account executive research director	Responsible for entire research program of the company. Works as go-between for the company and client. Employs personnel and supervises research department. Presents research findings to company and/or clients.	$60 to $90+
Information technician statistician	Acts as expert consultant on application of statistical techniques for specific research problems. Many times responsible for research design and data analysis.	$40 to $70+
Research analyst	Plans research project and executes project assignments. Works with analyst in preparing questionnaire. Makes analysis, prepares report, schedules project events, and sets budget.	$35 to $65+
Assistant research analyst	Works under research analyst supervision. Assists in development of questionnaire, pretest, preliminary analysis.	$30 to $45+
Project coordinator Project director Field manager Fieldwork director	Hires, trains, and supervises field interviewers. Provides work schedules and is responsible for data accuracy.	$25 to $35+
Librarian	Builds and maintains a library of primary and secondary data sources to meet the requirements of the research department.	$35 to $45+
Clerical and tabulation assistant	Handles and processes statistical data. Supervises day-to-day office work.	$18 to $32+

*Positions are generalized, and not all companies have all of the positions.

working with large volumes of data. Federal Express, for example, normally seeks individuals with strong analytical and computer skills to fill its research positions. Candidates should have an undergraduate degree in business, marketing, or information systems. Having an MBA will usually give an applicant a competitive advantage.

As is the case with many companies, the normal entry-level position in the marketing research area at Federal Express is the assistant research analyst. While learning details of the company and the industry, these individuals receive on-the-job training from a research analyst. The normal career path includes advancement to information technician and then research director and/or account executive.

Marketing research at Federal Express is somewhat unusual in that it is housed in the information technology division. This is evidence that, while the research function is integrated throughout the company, it has taken on a high-tech orientation. Marketing research at FedEx operates in three general areas:

1. *Database development and enhancement.* This function is to establish relationships with current FedEx customers and use this information for the planning of new products.

2. *Cycle time research.* Providing more information for the efficient shipping of packages, tracking of shipments, automatic replenishment of customers' inventories, and enhanced electronic data interchange.

3. *Market intelligence system.* Primarily a logistical database and research effort to provide increased customer service to catalog retailers, direct marketing firms, and electronic commerce organizations.

The entire research function is led by a vice president of research and information technology, to whom four functional units report directly. These four units are responsible for the marketing decision support system operation, sales tracking, new business development, and special project administration.

If you are interested in pursuing a career in marketing research, a good way to start is to obtain the following career guide published by the Marketing Research Association:

Career Guide: Your Future in Marketing Research
Marketing Research Association
2189 Silas Deana Highway, Suite 5
Rocky Hill, CT 06067
MRAH@aol.com

It is also a wise idea to obtain the *Marketing and Sales Career Directory,* available at your university library or by writing:

Marketing and Sales Career Directory
Gale Research Inc.
835 Penobscot Building
Detroit, MI 48226-4094

MARKETING RESEARCH CASE EXERCISE

VALUJET OR AIRTRAN, WILL IT STILL FLY WITH AIRLINE TRAVELERS?

ValuJet Airlines, Inc., was a large regional airline that offered affordable, no-frills, limited-frequency, short-haul flights primarily in the eastern United States. Its no-frills philosophy allowed the airline to offer low fares and to attract travelers who would have otherwise used ground transportation. ValuJet Airlines was incorporated in July 1992 and became a wholly owned subsidiary of ValuJet Inc. in October 1995.

In May 1996, an accident involving a flight from Miami to Atlanta, in which there were no survivors, dramatically changed the operations of ValuJet. Before the accident, ValuJet offered service to 31 markets from its hub cities of Atlanta; Washington, D.C.; and Boston. On June 17, 1996, an FAA consent order resulting from the fatal crash required the company to suspend operations. On September 26, 1996, ValuJet resumed service from Atlanta, operating with only 60 percent of its original personnel. The airline had been battling an overwhelmingly negative public perception due to negative media coverage following the crash. The company never regained its preaccident flight numbers or profitability.

In an effort to escape negative perceptions, ValuJet changed its name to AirTran Airlines on September 24, 1997. ValuJet completed a merger with AirTran in November 1997. Although AirTran Airlines will remain under strict scrutiny by the Federal Aviation Administration, the public still remains apprehensive. Or do they?

1. Research the history of ValuJet immediately before and after the fatal crash in May 1996. Look specifically at profit, market share, and number of passengers. Prepare a brief summary of your findings.

2. Based on your research, prepare a marketing research plan for AirTran. In this plan, discuss the type of research study or studies that AirTran should consider in order to measure consumer perceptions of the company and the new name.

CHAPTER 2

Learning Objectives

After reading this chapter, you will be able to

1. Describe the major environmental factors that are directly influencing marketing research, and explain some of their impact on the research process.

2. Describe and discuss the four phases and the 10 integrative task steps involved with the research process, and explain some of the key activities within each step.

3. Explain the differences between raw data, data structures, and information, and explain the process by which raw data are transformed into information that managers can use.

4. Identify the most critical task step in the research process, and explain why it is so important.

5. Distinguish between exploratory, descriptive, and causal research designs.

6. List the critical issues in the development of a sampling plan, and explain the basic differences between a probability and nonprobability sampling plan.

7. Identify and explain the major components of a solid research proposal.

The Research Process

" How do I determine whether Rosetta Technologies, Inc., is meeting the printing needs and requirements of our customers? **"**

ROB HULLAR
Co-founder and President
Rosetta Technologies

Using the Research Process to Address Marketing Problems, Questions, and Opportunities

Trish G. Byrnes is a service quality consultant from Denver, Colorado. Recently she was working with the owners of a medium-size printer manufacturing company located in New York on improving some specific internal quality processes. Toward the end of their meeting, one of the owners asked her about external customer satisfaction and customers' perceptions of the company's image as they related to quality. During the discussion, the owner stated that he was not sure how the company's printer products and services were being viewed by its actual and potential customers. He said, "Just last week, I received phone calls from three different customers complaining that either the printer they bought two weeks ago still had not arrived like we promised or that our service technician did not fix the problem they were having with their printers. None of them were happy campers." Then he asked Byrnes, "What do I need to do to find out how satisfied our customers are with the quality and services we sell?"

Byrnes suggested that the owner's situation might call for gathering and analyzing some specific types of information using a research process. The owner responded by stating, "I am *clueless* as to what you are talking about."

After Byrnes explained the basic phases of a research process and the various task steps that were involved within each phase, the owner asked, "How much would it cost me to get this new information?" Byrnes responded by asking her client if he would like her to submit a research proposal. She explained that the research proposal would serve as a framework for gathering, analyzing, and creating information needed to address his questions. The proposal would include the following elements: (1) a purpose statement; (2) a discussion identifying the type of study and specific information needs; (3) a definition of the target population and sample size; (4) a sample plan, sampling technique, and data collection method; (5) a discussion of the questionnaire needed to gather the raw data; (6) the potential managerial benefits of the study; and (7) a proposed cost structure for the total project.

Byrnes went on to explain the importance of some of the activities used to generate information. As she left the owner's office, she mentioned she would have the research proposal ready in a week but might need to ask the owner a few more questions before it was completed.

Value of the Research Process

As the chapter opener illustrates, business practitioners often identify potential problems which they need help to solve. In such situations, when some type of additional information is required, one approach is to employ the *marketing research process.* This chapter uses an information perspective to explain the marketing research process. It begins with a discussion of the critical environmental factors that directly influence the scope of the research process. The bulk of the chapter provides an overview of the four basic phases that make up the research process and the specific task steps involved in each phase, as well as activities and questions a researcher must address within each step. The final section of the chapter explains how to develop an information research proposal.

This chapter, the textbook's designated overview chapter, serves as a preview of some of the central topics in the text. You will find that much of the discussion is descriptive. Overall, this chapter provides the general blueprint for understanding the information research process. The topics introduced in this chapter will be discussed in much more detail in subsequent chapters.

Changing View of the Marketing Research Process

Over the past decade, many cultural, technological, and competitive factors have created a variety of new challenges, problems, and opportunities for today's decision makers in business. Exhibit 2.1 lists the three environmental factors that have been most influential in changing the nature of marketing research.

First, the rapid advances in interactive marketing communication technologies (e.g., online databases, interactive multimedia systems, PC networks) have increased the need for database management skills, while shortening the relative time of data acquisition and retrieval. Moreover, advancements associated with the so-called information superhighway have created greater emphasis on secondary (versus primary) data collection, analysis, and interpretation. (The terms *primary* and *secondary data* will be defined more fully in Chapter 3.) The movement is away from pure data analysis and toward information management.

Second, there is a growing movement that emphasizes internal quality improvements. This movement has placed more importance on cross-functional information than ever before. For example, traditional organization structures and functional areas (e.g., accounting, finance, management, marketing, production, engineering) are being replaced with cross-functional decision-making teams, with heavy emphasis on relationship building and information sharing. This factor will have greatest impact on how business and marketing problems and questions are defined as well as the determination of appropriate information needs. It also suggests that marketing researchers will need to better understand and interpret cross-functional secondary data as well as increase their microcomputer proficiency and database management skills.

The third factor is expansion into global markets. International expansion introduces management decision makers to new sets of multicultural interaction problems and questions. Cultural differences in these new markets alone will force marketing researchers to direct their focus away from pure market data analysis tasks and toward data interpretation and information management activities.

While there are many other environmental factors that influence the marketing research process, these three in particular are challenging decision makers to view the traditional marketing research process and its task steps from a new information management perspective.

EXHIBIT 2.1	**Critical Environmental Factors That Affect Marketing Research Practices**
Environmental Factors	**Impact on Marketing Research and Examples**
Advances in interactive marketing communication technologies	Increases the need for technology-driven databases and database management skills; shorter acquisition and retrieval time requirements. *Examples:* online computer databases, interactive multimedia systems.
Growing emphasis on internal quality improvements	Places importance on cross-functional sharing of both internal and external generated information; development of decision-making teams. *Examples:* just-in-time inventory controls, cross-functional decision team networks.
Expansion into global markets	Creates multicultural interaction problems and questions as well as opportunities; customized delivery systems and information. *Examples:* different market needs and wants, production requirements, pricing strategies.

Management Decision Makers . . .

Tend to be decision-oriented, intuitive thinkers who want information to confirm their decisions. They want additional information now or "yesterday," as well as results about future market component behavior ("What will sales be next year?"), while maintaining a frugal stance with regard to the cost of additional information. Decision makers tend to be results oriented, do not like surprises, and tend to reject the information when they are surprised. Their dominant concern is market performance ("Aren't we number one yet?"); they want information that allows certainty ("Is it or isn't it?") and advocate being proactive but often allow problems to force them into reactive decision-making modes.

Marketing Researchers . . .

Tend to be scientific, technical, analytical thinkers who love to explore new phenomena; accept prolongment of investigations to ensure completeness; focus on information about past behaviors ("Our trend has been . . ."); and are not cost conscious with additional information ("You get what you pay for"). Researchers are results oriented but love surprises; they tend to enjoy abstractions ("Our exponential gain . . ."), the probability of occurrences ("May be," "Tends to suggest that . . ."); and they advocate the proactive need for continuous inquiries of market component changes, but feel most of the time that they are restricted to doing reactive ("quick and dirty") investigations due to management's lack of vision and planning.

Information research process Refers to the 10 systematic task steps involved with the gathering, analyzing, interpreting, and transforming data structures and results into decision making information.

Consequently, we feel that a more appropriate name for the marketing research process would be the **information research process.** The term *information research* is used to reflect the evolving changes occurring within the marketing research industry and the rapid changes facing many decision makers regarding how their firms conduct both internal and external marketing and operating activities. While many of the specific task steps and activities involved in marketing research remain unaffected, understanding the process of transforming raw data into usable information from a broader information processing framework expands the applicability of the research process in solving business problems and creating opportunities.

Determining the Need for Information Research

Before we discuss the phases and specific task steps of the information research process, we want to emphasize how important it is that you understand when the research process is needed and when it is not. In addition, we want to point out how necessary it has become for researchers to interact closely with managers in recognizing business problems, questions, and opportunities.

While many marketing research texts suggest that the first step in the marketing research process is for the researcher to establish the need for marketing research,[1] this tends to place a lot of responsibility and control in the hands of a person who might not understand the management decision-making process. Until decision makers and information researchers become closer in their thinking, the initial recognition of the existence of a problem should be the primary responsibility of the decision maker, not the researcher. Decision makers and researchers have often differed in their approach to solving problems, as illustrated in the narrative profiles in the accompanying In the Field box.

To help prevent the differences between decision makers and researchers from complicating the problem definition process, the decision makers should be given the responsibility of initiating the activities involved in defining the problem. A good rule of thumb is that the information research process (or a specific task step) needs to be activated when "Yes" is the logical response to the question, "Does the decision maker require either secondary or primary data (or both)?" Moreover, if a problem cannot be solved using subjective information, then the decision maker should consider employing the research process. In most cases when some type of additional information is needed to address a problem, decision makers will need assistance in determining, collecting, analyzing, and interpreting that information.

Questions arise from the recognition that a decision is needed. In turn, decision situations are created by the awareness of either decision problems, decision opportunities, or market performance symptoms. A **decision problem** is a situation in which a manager is not certain which course of action will help him or her accomplish a specific objective. In a more general context, the word *problem* refers to an independent variable (e.g., marketing mix element, environmental condition, or situational factor) that causes the organization not to meet the specified objective. For example, problems can result from an ineffective marketing mix (i.e., the combination of product, price, promotion, and distribution); uncontrollable environmental changes (e.g., new product safety laws, increases in direct competition); changes in situational factors (e.g., increased consumer demand for quality and satisfaction); or a combination of these.

A **decision opportunity** is a situation in which a company's market performance can be significantly improved by undertaking new activities or revising existing practices. For example, a firm that understands that its customers are demanding higher levels of service quality might establish new standards of performance not only to ensure better quality but also to improve its overall image in the eyes of customers. The result of this action might be an increase in the number of quality-oriented customers. In the process of exploiting decision opportunities, decision makers will frequently require secondary and/or primary data.

Market performance symptoms are conditions that signal the presence of a decision problem or opportunity. Quite often, market performance symptoms act as signals for marketing decision makers. Remember that symptoms are not the same as problems and opportunities; rather, they are the observable, measurable results of problems and opportunities. Rarely can a decision maker adequately identify and define the decision problem or opportunity solely because he or she knows that a symptom (or set of symptoms) exists. For example, a decline in sales volume that follows a 10 percent decrease in the unit price of a certain product is not a problem, but rather a symptom of a problem yet to be identified.

As more firms employ cross-functional decision-making teams and stress information sharing, there will be a greater dependence on the information research process, and especially those task steps that focus on collecting, analyzing, and presenting secondary data. For example, information systems that are designed to accurately monitor traditional market performance measures, key marketing mix elements, or environmental or situational factors will need to incorporate the scientific principles that guide the research process.

Decision problem A situation in which a manager is not certain which course of action will help him or her accomplish a specific objective.

Decision opportunity A situation in which a company's market performance can be significantly improved by undertaking new activities or revising existing practices.

Market performance symptoms Conditions that signal the presence of a decision problem or opportunity.

An Overview of the Information Research Process

The marketing research process has been described as a set of anywhere from 6 to 11 standardized stages.[2] In this text, we will define it as an information research process that consists of four distinct yet interrelated phases that have a logical, hierarchical ordering: (1) determination of the research problem, (2) development of the appropriate research design, (3) execution of the research design, and (4) communication of the results (see Exhibit

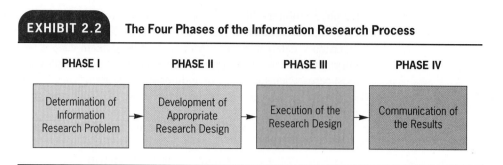

EXHIBIT 2.2   **The Four Phases of the Information Research Process**

PHASE I	PHASE II	PHASE III	PHASE IV
Determination of Information Research Problem	Development of Appropriate Research Design	Execution of the Research Design	Communication of the Results

2.2). Researchers must ensure that each phase is executed in order to achieve the overall goal of providing the necessary information to management decision makers. However, each phase can and should be viewed as a separate process that consists of a combination of integrated task steps and specific procedures. The four phases and their corresponding task steps are guided by the principles of the **scientific method,** which involves formalized research procedures that can be characterized as logical, objective, systematic, reliable, valid, impersonal, and ongoing. Somewhat different from the traditional marketing research process that emphasizes collecting and analyzing "firsthand" raw data, the information research process places equal emphasis on the interpretation of secondary data.

Transforming Raw Data into Information

As you read this chapter, keep in mind that the major goal of the information research process is to provide management decision makers with information that will assist them in either resolving an identifiable problem, addressing an existing question, or exploiting a business opportunity. Regardless of the type of information, it is important to remember that a decision maker receives it only after someone analyzes and interprets data structures and transforms those structures into narrative information that did not really exist prior to the interpretive transformation process. To clearly understand what we mean here, it is critical to realize that there are distinct differences between the terms *raw data, data structures,* and *information.*

First, **raw data** represent the actual firsthand responses that are obtained about the subject of investigation by either asking questions or observing the subject's actions. These responses have not been analyzed or given any type of interpretive meaning. Some examples of raw data are: (1) the actual responses on a questionnaire; (2) the words recorded during a focus group interview; (3) the tally of vehicles that pass through a specified intersection; (4) the list of purchases, by product type, recorded by an electronic cash register at a local supermarket.

All marketing information is derived from the following process: gather raw responses (or data); apply some form of data analysis to create data structures; and then have someone (researcher or decision maker) interpret those data structures.

Gather raw data ⟶ Create data structures ⟶ Provide interpretative meaning

---

Data structures represent the results of combining a group of raw data using some type of quantitative or qualitative analysis (e.g., content analysis, calculation of sample statistics). The results can reveal data patterns or trends, which in turn can be simple or

---

Margin notes:

Scientific method Formalized research procedures that can be characterized as logical, objective, systematic, reliable, valid, impersonal, and ongoing.

Raw data Actual firsthand responses obtained about the subject of investigation

Data structures Results of combining a group of raw data using some type of quantitative or qualitative analysis.

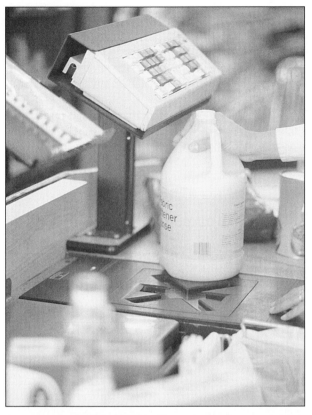

Recording an item's purchase with an electronic scanner is one type of raw data source.

complex. Take for example the data structures presented in Table 2.1. In this study, 880 people (440 first-time and 440 repeat patrons) were asked separately to indicate the importance they placed on each of seven criteria when selecting a hotel. The respondents used a six-point importance scale ranging from 6 ("extremely important") to 1 ("not at all important"). The individual responses (i.e., actual scale responses) by themselves would represent the raw data, but because the average importance value for each criterion was calculated through simple mean analysis, the resulting mean values (shown in the table) represent the data structures associated with each selection criterion. In fact, all the numbers displayed in Table 2.1 represent data structures.

Information is derived from data structures only when someone—either the researcher or decision maker—takes the time and effort to interpret the data structures and attach a narrative meaning to them. In the hotel selection criteria example, information might be derived from the data structures as follows:

> Among the total group of hotel patrons ($n = 880$), "cleanliness of the room" ($\bar{x} = 5.65$) and "good-quality bedding and towels" ($\bar{x} = 5.60$) are deemed to be two of the most important features that people consider in their process of selecting a hotel for overnight accommodations.

TABLE 2.1	Summary of Overall Importance Differences of Selected Hotel-Choice Criteria Used by First-Time and Repeat Business Patrons

	Total (n = 880)		First-Time Patrons (n = 440)			Repeat Patrons (n = 440)			
Hotel Selection Criteria	**Mean[a] Value**	**(SG)[b]**	**Mean Value**	**Standard Error**	**(SG)**	**Mean Value**	**Standard Error**	**(SG)**	**Z-Tests**
Cleanliness of the room	5.65	(A)	5.75	.06	(A)	5.50	.05	(A)	*
Good-quality bedding and towels	5.60	(A)	5.55	.06	(A)	5.62	.07	(A)	
Has preferred guest card options	5.57	(A)	5.42	.07	(A)	5.71	.06	(A)	*
Friendly/courteous staff and employees	5.10	(B)	4.85	.09	(B)	5.45	.07	(B)	*
Offers free VIP services	5.06	(B)	4.35	.10	(B)	5.38	.11	(B)	*
Conveniently located for business	5.04	(B)	5.25	.09	(B)	4.92	.10	(B)	*
In-room movie entertainment	3.63	(D)	3.30	.13	(D)	4.56	.11	(C)	*

[a]Importance scale: a six-point scale ranging from 6 ("extremely important") to 1 ("not at all important").

[b]Significant groupings (SG): (A) = Definitely strong factor; (B) = Strong factor; (C) = Moderately strong factor; (D) = Weak factor.

*Mean importance difference between the two patron groups is significant at $p < .05$.

Integrative Task Steps within the Research Process

Once decision makers recognize that they need assistance, they should turn their efforts toward executing a scientific research process. Exhibit 2.3 lists the interrelated task steps included within the four phases of the research process. An overview of the major activities within each phase is given in the next four sections of this chapter, and each step is discussed in detail in a later chapter.

Before proceeding, however, it is important for us to note that although researchers generally should follow the steps in order, the steps are interrelated and may be shifted or even left out. In fact, only in rare cases will all the steps be necessary. The complexity of the problem, the level of risk involved, and the clarification of management's information needs together will determine how many of the steps to take and in what order.

EXHIBIT 2.3	Phases and Task Steps in the Information Research Process

PHASE I: DETERMINATION OF THE INFORMATION RESEARCH PROBLEM

Task Step 1 :   Determine and Clarify Management's Information Needs

Task Step 2 :   Redefine the Decision Problem as a Research Problem

Task Step 3 :   Establish Research Objectives and Determine the Value of the Information

PHASE II: DEVELOPMENT OF THE APPROPRIATE RESEARCH DESIGN

Task Step 4 :   Determine and Evaluate the Reseach Design and Data Sources

Task Step 5 :   Determine the Sample Plan and Sample Size

Task Step 6 :   Determine the Measurement Issues and Scales

PHASE III: EXECUTION OF THE RESEARCH DESIGN

Task Step 7 :   Collect and Process Data

Task Step 8 :   Analyze Data

Task Step 9 :   Transform Data Structures into Information

PHASE IV: COMMUNICATION OF THE RESULTS

Task Step 10 :   Prepare and Present Final Report to Management

Note: Each of these research task steps are discussed in detail in later text chapters.

Phase I: Determination of the Information Research Problem

The main objective of Phase I is to explicitly identify the information research problem. To achieve this objective, researchers must focus on the first three task steps (see Exhibit 2.4).

Task Step 1: Determine and Clarify Management's Information Needs

The activities included in this first step tend to bring researchers and decision makers together under the notion that management has recognized the need for some type of information in order to deal with either a problem, an opportunity, or a critical question concerning a market performance symptom. Usually before the researcher becomes involved, the decision maker has made a formal statement of what she or he believes is the issue. At this point, the researcher's responsibility is to make sure management has clearly and correctly specified the problem, opportunity, or question. The researcher then assists the decision maker in determining whether the defined problem is really a problem or just a symptom of a yet-unidentified problem. To do so, the researcher might employ the iceberg principle or a situation analysis.[3] (See Chapter 3 for descriptions of these analysis techniques.)

It is important for the decision maker and the researcher to agree on the definition of the problem so that the research process produces useful information. Working with the decision maker, the researcher lists the factors that could have a direct or indirect impact on the defined problem or opportunity. Both parties must also agree on which type of information (subjective, secondary, primary, or a combination) is needed. The researcher leaves this step with enough knowledge of the situation to be able to enter Task Step 2. Chapter 3 elaborates further on the activities required in Task Step 1.

Task Step 2: Redefine the Decision Problem as a Research Problem

Once the researcher and decision maker have identified the specific information needs, the researcher must redefine the problem in scientific terms. In doing so, most decision makers use a pragmatic framework, whereas researchers feel more comfortable using a scientific framework.

Redefining the decision problem is the most critical step in the information research process. This is because the definition of the research problem so greatly influences many of the other steps. The researcher's responsibility is to restate the initial variables associated with the decision problem in the form of one or more key question formats (how, what, where, when, or why).

For example, several years ago management of Scotty's Inc. (a southern hardware/lumber retailer) was concerned about the overall image of Scotty's retail operations as well as

---

EXHIBIT 2.4   **Research Questions Used by Scotty's Inc.**

1. What store/operation aspects do people deem important in selecting a retail hardware/lumber outlet?
2. How do known customers evaluate Scotty's retail outlets on the basis of a prespecified set of store/operation aspects associated with Scotty's?
3. What are the perceived strengths and weaknesses of Scotty's retail operations?
4. How do customers and noncustomers alike compare Scotty's to other retail hardware/lumber outlets within the Atlanta metropolitan market?
5. What is the demographic/psychographic profile of the people who patronize Scotty's retail outlets within the Atlanta market?

---

about its image among known customers within the Atlanta metropolitan market. The initial question was, "What marketing strategies need to be either developed or modified to increase satisfaction among our current and future customer segments?" After Scotty's management met with consultants at Corporate Communications and Marketing, Inc., to clarify Scotty's critical information needs, the consultants transposed the problem factors into the specific questions displayed in Exhibit 2.4.

The consultants, with assistance from management, then identified the specific attributes to be included in each key research question. For example, the specific "store/operation aspects" included convenient operating hours, friendly/courteous staff, and wide assortment of products and services.

An example of the integratedness of the task steps is that the researcher might have had to employ some type of qualitative or exploratory research activities (Task Step 4) in the process of determining the key aspects of Scotty's retail operations. In addition, the researcher's activities might have focused on determining what specific information requirements (i.e., facts, estimates, predictions, relationships, or some combination) will be needed to answer the specific research questions as well as the quality requirements of the data structures.

Finally, this task step affords the researcher the opportunity to determine whether the information being requested by management is necessary or nice. Overall, the researcher must complete this step before going on to Task Step 3.

Task Step 3: Establish Research Objectives and Determine the Value of the Information

The research objectives should follow from the definition of the research problem established in Task Step 2. Formally stated research objectives provide the guidelines for determining which other task steps must be undertaken. The underlying assumption is that, if the objectives are achieved, the decision maker will have the information he or she needs to solve the problem.

In some ways, research objectives serve as the justification for management and researchers to undertake an information research project. Consider the Ford Foundation example in the Small Business Implications box. You should notice that the three information objectives listed at the end are different from the foundation's defined decision problem and the researcher's defined information problem. Before researchers move on from Phase I of the research process, they must make sure that a clear, complete definition is given to each factor or variable to be included in the study. There also must be clear justification to the relevancy of each factor. For example, what does the Ford Foundation really mean by "protection"? Protection from what—rain or cold or snow?

Phase II: Development of the Appropriate Research Design

The main focus of Phase II is to develop the most appropriate research design for a given set of research objectives. The three task steps in this phase are briefly outlined below.

Task Step 4: Determine and Evaluate the Research Design and Data Sources

The research design serves as a master plan of the methods and procedures that should be used to collect and analyze the data needed by the decision maker. Determining the most appropriate research design is a function of the information research objectives and the

A CLOSER LOOK AT RESEARCH   **Small Business Implications**

Several years ago, the Ford Foundation of the Performing Arts, located in Vail, Colorado, successfully completed a $5 million fund-raising drive for constructing an amphitheater to house performing arts events. The Foundation's Amphitheater Design Team faced some difficult decisions. They were not sure which design features should be included in the structure to handle different types of events (theatrical productions, music concerts, dance productions, etc.). They could not decide if the structure should accommodate indoor events, outdoor events, or a combination. They questioned the seating capacity and worried about ticket prices, parking requirements, availability of refreshments, and types of events most desired by local residents and visitors. The foundation hired a marketing research consultant to assist in the gathering of primary and secondary data needed to address the team's questions and concerns. After several meetings with the design team, the researcher presented his research proposal, which stated that the "*primary research objective* focused on the collection and interpretation of specific attitudinal and behavioral information to be used in addressing several questions posed by the Ford Amphitheater Design Team concerning selected performing arts events and possible design features for the proposed amphitheater structure." Three of the key questions were

1. What type of performing arts programs would residents and guests most prefer to see offered in the Vail Valley area?
2. What prices should be charged for the various types of events?
3. What type of summer-evening performing arts programs would people prefer attending at an indoor versus outdoor facility? If outdoors, what type of protection should be provided to the audience and the performers?

These questions were then transformed into the following research objectives:

1. To determine how often people attended performance arts events in the past 12 months and what three types of events (dance productions, theatrical productions, music concerts, etc.) they would be most interested in attending while staying in Vail Valley.
2. To determine, by event type, the average price range a person would expect and would be willing to pay for an adult-reserved-seat ticket to the events presented in Vail Valley.
3. To determine the extent to which people would prefer to attend a specific type of event at an indoor or outdoor facility and the specific type of protection that should be offered the audience if the event was held at an outdoor facility.[4]

specific information requirements. In this master plan, the researcher must consider the design technique (survey, observation, experiment, etc.), the sampling methodology and procedures, the schedule, and the budget. Although every research problem is unique, most research objectives can be met by using one of three types of research designs: exploratory, descriptive, causal.

Exploratory Research Designs

Exploratory research
Research that focuses on collecting either secondary or primary data and using an unstructured format or informal procedures to interpret them.

Exploratory research focuses on collecting either secondary or primary data and using an unstructured format or informal procedures to interpret them. Among the three types of research designs, exploratory research incorporates the fewest characteristics or principles of the scientific method. It is often used simply to classify the problems or opportunities and it is not intended to provide conclusive information from which a particular course of action can be determined. Some examples of exploratory research techniques are focus-group interviews, experience surveys, and pilot studies. Exploratory research may also use some forms of secondary data (e.g., online databases). Exploratory research can be somewhat intuitive and is used by many decision makers who monitor market performance measures pertinent to their company or industry.

Descriptive Research Designs

Descriptive research

Research that uses a set of scientific methods and procedures to collect raw data and create data structures that describe the existing characteristics of a defined target population or market structure.

Descriptive research uses a set of scientific methods and procedures to collect raw data and create data structures that describe the existing characteristics (e.g., attitudes, intentions, preferences, purchase behaviors, evaluations of current marketing mix strategies) of a defined target population or market structure. Descriptive research designs are appropriate when the research objectives include determination of the degree to which marketing (or decision) variables are related to actual market phenomena. Here, the researcher looks for answers to the how, who, what, when, and where questions concerning different components of a market structure.

Descriptive studies generally allow decision makers to draw inferences about their customers, competitors, target markets, environmental factors, or other phenomena of concern. For example, there is a growing trend among today's major chain restaurants to conduct annual studies designed to identify and describe consumers' attitudes, feelings, and patronage behavior toward their own restaurants as well as toward those of their main competitors. These studies, referred to as either image assessment surveys or customer service satisfaction surveys, partially describe how consumers rate different restaurants' customer service, convenience of location, food quality, overall quality, and so on. However, descriptive designs are not capable of addressing any of the why questions associated with a given research problem. Still, the data and information generated through descriptive designs can provide decision makers with evidence that can lead to a course of action. Descriptive designs will be discussed further in Chapter 9.

Causal Research Designs

Causal research

Research designed to collect raw data and create data structures and information that will allow the researcher to model cause-and-effect relationships between two or more market (or decision) variables.

Causal research is designed to collect raw data and create data structures and information that will allow the decision maker or researcher to model cause-and-effect relationships between two or more market (or decision) variables. Causal research is most appropriate when the research objectives include the need to understand the reasons why certain market phenomena happen as they do. That is to say, the decision maker may have a strong desire to understand which (independent) market or decision variables are the cause of the dependent phenomenon defined in the decision or research problem.

Causal research can be used to understand the functional relationships between the causal factors and the effect predicted on the market performance variable under investigation. This type of research design allows decision makers to gain the highest level of understanding in the research process. In addition, understanding the cause–effect relationships among market performance factors allows the decision maker to make if-then statements about the variables. For example, the owner of a small casual men's clothing store in Chicago might be able to say, "*If* I expand the assortment of brand-name shirts, increase my advertising budget by 15 percent, have an introductory 30 percent off sale on the new shirts, and keep the rest of my marketing mix strategies unchanged, *then* our overall sales volume will increase by 40 percent."

While causal research designs offer opportunity for identifying, determining, and explaining causality among critical market factors, they tend to be complex, expensive, and time-consuming. Among the different data collection techniques available, experimental designs hold the greatest potential for establishing cause–effect relationships because they allow researchers to investigate changes in one variable while manipulating one or two other variables under controlled conditions. Causal research designs are treated in more depth in Chapter 10.

Secondary and Primary Data Sources

The availability of data structures and information needed to resolve decision and informa- tion research problems are many and can be classified as being either secondary or pri- mary. Determination of membership is based on three fundamental dimensions: (1) the extent that the data already exists in some type of recognizable format, (2) the degree to which the data has been interpreted by someone, and (3) the extent to which the researcher or decision maker understands the reason(s) why the data was collected and assembled.

Secondary data Histor- ical data structures of vari- ables previously collected and assembled for some research problem or opportunity situation other than the current situation.

Building on earlier discussions, secondary data can usually be gathered faster and at less cost than primary data structures, but the data can be outdated or may not fit the researcher's information needs. **Secondary data** are historical data structures of variables previously collected and assembled for some research problem or opportunity situation other than the current situation. Sources for these types of data structures can be found inside a company, at public libraries and universities, on World Wide Web (WWW) sites, or purchased from a firm specializing in providing secondary information. Chapters 4 through 6 are dedicated to secondary data and sources.

Primary data Firsthand raw data and structures, and have yet to receive any type of meaningful interpretation.

In contrast, **primary data** represent "firsthand" raw data and structures, and have yet to receive any type of meaningful interpretation. Sources of primary data tend to be the output of conducting some type of exploratory, descriptive, or causal research project that employs either surveys, experiments, and/or observation as techniques of collecting the needed data. Primary data are raw data and structures of variables that have been specifically collected and assembled for a current information research problem or opportunity situation. Greater insights underlying primary data will be provided in Chapters 8 through 14.

Task Step 5: Determine the Sample Plan and Sample Size

For decision makers and researchers to be able to make inferences or predictions about market phenomena, they must understand who is supplying the raw data and how repre- sentative those data are. Normally, marketing decision makers are most interested in iden- tifying and resolving problems associated with their target markets. Therefore, researchers need to identify the relevant **defined target population.** In taking this step, researchers can choose between two basic procedures. The first is referred to as a census of the target population; this is the preferred action for a small population. In a **census,** the researcher attempts to question or observe all the members of a defined target population.

Defined target population A specified group of people or objects for which questions can be asked or observations made to develop required data structures and information.

The second procedure, which is preferred when the defined target population is large or unknown, involves the random selection of a subgroup, or **sample,** from the overall mem- bership pool of a defined target population. So that the resulting data structures and infor- mation are generalizable and reliable, researchers must ensure that the sample is representative of the population. In achieving this objective, researchers develop an explicit sampling plan as part of the overall research design. A sampling plan serves as the blueprint for defining the appropriate target population, identifying the possible respon- dents, establishing the procedural steps in drawing the required sample, and determining the appropriate size of the sample. Exhibit 2.5 displays some of the critical questions and issues that researchers normally face when developing a sampling plan.

Census A procedure in which the researcher attempts to question or observe all the members of a defined target population.

Sampling plans can be classified into two general types: probability and nonprobabil- ity. In a probability sampling plan, each member of the defined target population has a known, nonzero chance of being drawn into the sample group. Probability sampling gives the researcher the opportunity to assess the existence of sampling error.

Sample A randomly selected subgroup of people or objects from the overall membership pool of a defined target population.

In contrast, nonprobability sampling plans eliminate the true assessment of sampling error existence and limit the generalizability of any information to larger groups of people other than that group which provided the original raw data.

EXHIBIT 2.5	Critical Questions and Issues in the Development of a Sampling Plan

Given the stated decision problem, research objectives, and specific information requirements, *who* would be the best type of person (or best object) to question or observe?

What explicit demographic (e.g., gender, occupation, age, marital status, income levels, education, etc.) and/or behavioral traits (e.g., regular/occasional/rare/non shopper; heavy user/light user/nonuser; known customer/noncustomer) should be used to identify population membership?

How many population elements must be drawn into the sample to ensure the representativeness of the population membership?

How reliable does the resulting information have to be for the decision maker? *What* are the data quality factors and acceptable levels of sampling error?

What technique should be used in the actual selection of sampling units?

What are the time and cost constraints associated with developing and executing the appropriate sampling plan?

Sample size affects data quality and generalizability. Researchers must therefore think carefully about how many people to include or how many objects to investigate. Chapter 11 discusses sampling in more detail.

Task Step 6: Determine the Measurement Issues and Scales

After Task Step 2, in which the decision problem is redefined as a research problem, Task Step 6 should be considered the second most important step in the research process. Activities within this step focus on determining the dimensions of the factors being investigated and measuring the variables that underlie the defined problem. The measurement process determines how much raw data can be collected and thus also the amount of information that can be inferred from the resulting data structures.

Given the importance of measurement to the process of creating information, researchers must be able to answer questions like the following: (1) What level of information is needed from a variable (nominal, ordinal, ordinally interval, interval, ratio)? (2) How reliable does the information need to be? (3) How valid does the information need to be? (4) How does one ensure the development of reliable and valid scale measurements? (5) What dimensions underlie the critical factors being investigated (e.g., unidimensional vs. multidimensional structures)? and (6) Should single measures or multi-item measures be used to collect the data on the variables included in a study? For example, researchers must know what scaling assumptions or properties (e.g., description, order, distance, origin) must be built into a scale design to ensure that management's information needs are met. Chapters 12 and 13 discuss measurement and scale design procedures among other important measurement issues.

Phase III: Execution of the Research Design

In many ways, the execution phase is the heart of the marketing research process. The main objectives of this phase are to develop all necessary data collection forms, gather the actual raw data, process the data, analyze the data and create appropriate data structures, and interpret those structures into meaningful bits of information that can be used to address the initial problem. To achieve this overall objective, researchers have to focus on executing the next three specific interactive task steps of the research process: (7) data collection and processing of data, (8) data analysis procedures, and (9) interpret data structures into information. As in the first two phases, researchers here must operate with care to ensure that potential biases or errors are either eliminated or at least controlled.

Task Step 7: Collect and Process Data

Data Collection Methods

It is important to remember that there are two fundamental approaches to gathering raw data. One is to *ask questions* about variables and market phenomena using trained interviewers or questionnaires. The other is to *observe* variables and market phenomena using professional observers or high-tech devices. Self-administered surveys, personal interviews, computer simulations, telephone interviews, and focus groups are just some of the tools researchers can use to collect data (see Exhibit 2.6).

A major advantage that questioning techniques have over observation techniques is that they allow the researcher to collect a wider array of raw data. Raw data from a survey can pertain not only to a person's current behavior but also to his or her state of mind or intentions.

In turn, observation methods can be characterized as natural or contrived, disguised or undisguised, structured or unstructured, direct or indirect, or human or mechanical. For example, researchers might use trained human observers or a variety of mechanical devices such as a video camera, tape recorder, audiometer, eye camera, psychogalvanometer, or pupilometer to record behavior or events.

EXHIBIT 2.6	**Data Collection Tools Used in Marketing Research**
Observation Tool	**Description**
Trained observers	Highly skilled people who use their senses (sight, hearing, smell, touch, taste) to observe and record physical phenomena. *Examples:* mystery shoppers; traffic counters; focus-group moderators.
Mechanical devices	High-technology instruments that can artificially observe and record physical phenomena. *Examples:* security cameras; videotaping equipment; scanning devices; tape recorders; air-hose traffic counters.
Questioning Tool	
Trained interviewers	Highly trained people who ask respondents specific questions and accurately record their responses. *Examples:* face-to-face interviewers; telephone interviewers; group survey leaders.
Interviewer/mechanical devices	Highly skilled people who use high-technology devices during encounters with respondents. *Examples:* computer-assisted personal interviews; computer-assisted telephone interviews.
Fully automatic devices	High-tech devices that interact with respondents without the presence of a trained interviewer. *Examples:* on-site fully automatic interviews; fully automatic telephone interviews; computer-disk mail surveys; electronic-mail surveys; computer-generated fax surveys; Internet surveys.
Direct self-administered questionnaires	Survey instruments that are designed to have the respondent serve the roles of both interviewer and respondent. *Examples:* direct mail surveys; most group self-administered surveys.

Processing of Data

Once the raw data are collected, the researcher must perform several procedural activities before doing any type of data analysis. A coding scheme is needed so that the raw data can be entered into computer files. Normally, the researcher will assign a logical numerical descriptor (code value) to all response categories. After the raw responses are entered, the researcher must inspect the computer files to verify that they are correct and easy to locate. The researcher must then clean the raw data of either coding or data-entry errors. As part of the verification and data-cleaning processes, a simple tabulation is run on each variable's data structure. Chapter 15 will present more discussions on raw-data processing.

Task Step 8: Analyze Data

In Task Step 8, the researcher begins the process of turning raw data into data structures that can be used in generating meaningful and useful bits of information for the decision maker. Using a variety of data analysis techniques, the researcher can create new, complex data structures by combining two or more variables into indexes, ratios, constructs, and so on. Analysis procedures can vary widely in sophistication and complexity, from simple frequency distributions (percentages) to sample statistics measures (e.g., mode, median, mean, range, standard deviation, and standard error) to multivariate data analysis techniques. Different analysis procedures will allow the researcher to (1) statistically test for significant differences between two sample statistics and associations among several variables, (2) test hypothesized interdependence between two or more variables, (3) evaluate data quality, and (4) build and test complex models of cause–effect relationships. Chapters 16 through 18 are dedicated to data analysis procedures.

Task Step 9: Transform Data Structures into Information

Task Step 9 is where information is created for decision makers. It is in this step that the researcher or, in some cases the decision maker, takes the statistical testing results or the investigation's findings and creates a narrative interpretation. This does not mean a simple narrative description of the results. Narrative interpretation relates to integrating several pieces (variables) of the results into an understandable statement that the decision maker can use to answer the initial question. The data are analogous to colors that can be used to paint a comprehensive picture.

Phase IV: Communication of the Results

The last phase of the information research process focuses on reporting the research findings and newly created information to management. The overall objective is to develop a report that is useful to a non-research-oriented person.

Task Step 10: Prepare and Present the Final Report to Management

Task Step 10 is to prepare and present the final research report to management. The importance of this step cannot be overstated. While there are some sections that should be included in any research report (e.g., executive summary, introduction, problem definition and objectives, methodology, results and findings, and limitations of study), the researcher should ask the decision maker whether any other specific sections need to be included, such as recommendations for future actions, implications, or further information needs. In some cases, the researcher will be required not only to submit a well-produced written report but also to make an oral presentation to the decision maker or group of executives.

The presentation may include the use of overhead transparencies, PowerPoint slides, or displays on a flip chart. Chapter 19 describes how to write and present research reports.

Development of an Information Research Proposal

Research proposal

A specific document that serves as a written contract between the decision maker and the researcher.

Upon understanding the four phases and the 10 task steps of the research process, a researcher can logically develop a research proposal that communicates to the decision maker the overall research framework. A **research proposal** is a specific document that serves as a written contract between the decision maker and the researcher. It tells what activities will be undertaken to develop the needed information, and at what costs.

While a research proposal is not the same as a final research report, some of the sections appear similar. There is no one acceptable way to write a research proposal; Exhibit 2.7 presents our suggestions of the parts that should be included in most research proposals. Although the exhibit presents only a general outline, a complete illustration of an actual proposal is located in the Marketing Research Illustration at the end of this chapter.

EXHIBIT 2.7 **General Outline of a Research Proposal**

TITLE OF THE RESEARCH PROPOSAL

I. Purpose of the Proposed Research Project
Includes a clear expression of the decision problem, information research problem, and specific research objectives.

II. Type of Study
Includes discussions of the type of research design (i.e., exploratory, descriptive, causal), and secondary versus primary data requirements, with some justification of choice.

III. Definition of the Target Population and Sample Size
Describes the overall target population to be studied and determination of the appropriate sample size, including a justification of the size.

IV. Sample Design, Technique, and Data Collection Method
Includes a substantial discussion regarding the sampling technique used to draw the required sample, the actual method for collecting the data (i.e., observation, survey, experiment), incentive plans, and justifications.

V. Specific Research Instruments
Discusses the method used to collect the needed raw data; includes discussions of the various types of scale measurement requirements.

VI. Potential Managerial Benefits of the Proposed Study
Discusses the expected values of the information to management and how the initial problem might be resolved; includes a separate discussion on the possible limitations of the study.

VII. Proposed Cost Structure for the Total Project
Itemizes the expected costs associated with conducting the research project; includes a total cost figure and any pricing policy for changes, as well as appropriate completion time frames (of specific tasks and/or total project).

VIII. Profile of the Researcher and Company
Briefly describes the main researchers and their qualifications; includes a general assessment of the company.

IX. Optional Dummy Tables of the Projected Results
Offers examples of how the data might be presented in the final report.

Components of a Research Proposal

A research proposal should always begin with a section on the *purpose of the research,* which is a brief but clear statement of the decision problem or opportunity as viewed by management. Both the overall problem and its implications are emphasized. In addition, the research purposes and objectives must be clearly communicated, along with the project's scope and limits. More specifically, this section describes the areas of inquiry to be investigated, the project's goals and an idea of what it will take to achieve them, and the specific research questions or hypotheses.

The next section of the proposal, known as the *type of study,* includes discussions of the research methods that will be used to collect either primary or secondary data. For example, does the specific research problem require the use of either a qualitative or quantitative research design, or a more complex design that combines both types? It is in this section that the information requirements are clearly identified and justified.

The *target population and sample size* section clearly defines the specific population under investigation in both descriptive and quantitative terms. The researcher also projects the size of the sample needed to be representative of the defined target population, and includes a justification of that projection. Next, the *sample design, technique, and data collection method* section should discuss the appropriateness of using either probability or nonprobability sampling. The procedures necessary to correctly execute the drawing of the sample should be discussed in detail. Also included are discussions that identify and justify the most appropriate research design (i.e., observation, survey, or experiment).

The section on *specific research instruments* discusses the specific methods that will be used to collect the data (personal interviews, self-administered surveys, disguised/ nondisguised observations, focus groups, etc.). It is here that the researcher will discuss the types of data and appropriate scale measurement designs needed to achieve the stated information requirements. If interviewers are required, this section should explain the procedures that will be used to train them. The next section presents the *potential managerial benefits* of the study, along with the limitations that might exist. The focus should be on how the proposed information will help management solve the initial decision problem. In general, project limitations will normally be associated with the generalizability of the results beyond the sampled respondents, the data collection methods used, the sampling procedures, and time and financial constraints.

The *cost structure* section of the proposal allows the researcher and the decision maker to determine what activities in the research process will cost the most. This section should address the decision maker's overall budget concerns; the reader may make his or her final decision on whether to undertake the research endeavor based on the content of this section. Knowing the overall cost of doing research can also aid the decision maker in determining what value to assign the expected research information. There should be a statement about how long it will take to complete the research project.

The *profile of the researcher and company* should assist the decision maker in his or her efforts to assess the quality of the data and information the product will generate. By clearly presenting the researcher's qualifications and areas of expertise as well as the research firm's reputation, the researcher can quickly establish a comfort zone between himself or herself and the decision maker, thus enhancing the working relationship among all the parties involved in the research process.

The final section of any proposal consists of providing the decision maker with several *dummy data tables of the projected results.* The main benefit of this section is that it allows the decision maker to visualize the different ways in which data results can be displayed, thus helping him or her decide the best way to present the final results.

SUMMARY OF LEARNING OBJECTIVES

Describe the major environmental factors that are directly influencing marketing research, and explain some of their impact on the research process.

Three environmental factors have been changing the tasks, responsibilities, and efforts associated with marketing research. Advances in interactive marketing communication technologies, internal quality movements, and new global market structures are forcing researchers to balance their use of secondary and primary data to assist decision makers in solving decision problems. Researchers are being asked to improve their ability to use technology-driven databases. There are also greater needs for gathering, analyzing, interpreting, and sharing cross-functional data and information among decision-making teams within global markets.

Describe and discuss the four phases and the 10 integrative task steps involved with the research process, and explain some of the key activities within each step.

The information research process was discussed in terms of four major phases, identified as (1) determination of the research problem, (2) development of the appropriate research design, (3) execution of the research design, and (4) communication of the results. To achieve the overall objectives of each phase, researchers must be able to successfully execute 10 interrelated task steps: (1) determine and clarify management's information needs, (2) redefine the decision problem as a research problem, (3) establish research objectives and determine the value of the information, (4) determine and evaluate the research design and data sources, (5) determine the sample plan and sample size, (6) determine the measurement issues and scales, (7) collect and process data, (8) analyze data, (9) transform data structures into information, and (10) prepare and present the final report to management. The overview of the steps highlighted the importance of each step and showed how it was related to the other steps in the research process.

Explain the differences between raw data, data structures, and information, and explain the process by which raw data are transformed into information that managers can use.

Researchers and decision makers must understand that raw data, data structures, and information are different constructs. *Raw data* consist of the responses obtained by either questioning or observing people or physical phenomenon. *Data structures* are created by submitting the raw data to some type of analysis procedure. In turn, *information* is created only when either the researcher or decision maker narratively interprets the data structures.

Identify the most critical task step in the research process, and explain why it is so important.

While all the task steps are necessary, *Task Step 2, redefine the decision problem as a research problem,* is the most critical in the overall research process. How the information problem is stated in research terms directly influences many, if not all, of the other steps. It is in this step that researchers identify the variables of the decision problem and transform them into key how, when, what, where, and why questions. Without an accurate definition of the research problem, it is highly unlikely that the research process will produce the high-quality and pertinent information needed by the decision maker.

Distinguish between exploratory, descriptive, and causal research designs.

The main objective of exploratory research designs is to create information that the researcher or decision maker can use to (1) gain a clearer understanding of the decision problem; (2) define or redefine the initial problem, separating the symptom variables from the independent and dependent factors; (3) crystallize the problem and the objective; or (4) identify the specific information requirements (e.g., facts, estimates, predictions, variable relationships). Exploratory research designs are not intended to provide conclusive information from which a particular course of action can be determined.

Descriptive research designs focus on using a set of scientific methods to collect raw data and create data structures that are used to describe the existing characteristics (e.g., attitudes, intentions, preferences, purchase behaviors, evaluations of current marketing mix strategies) of a defined target population. The researcher looks for answers to how, who, what, when, and where questions. Information from this type of research design allows decision makers to draw inferences about their customers, competitors, target markets, environmental factors, or other phenomena of concern.

Finally, causal research designs are most useful when the research objectives include the need to understand why market phenomena happen. The focus of this type of research design is to collect raw data and create data structures and information that will allow the decision maker or researcher to model cause-and-effect relationships between two or more variables.

List the critical issues in the development of a sampling plan, and explain the basic differences between a probability and nonprobability sampling plan.

A sampling plan is a blueprint for correctly defining the appropriate target population, establishing the procedural steps needed to draw the required sample and determining the appropriate size of the sample. Some of the critical questions that researchers must address when developing a sampling plan are the following: *Who* would be the best type of person to question or observe? *What* explicit demographic or behavioral traits should be used to identify population membership? *How many* population elements must be drawn into the sample to ensure the representativeness of the population membership? *How* reliable does the resulting information have to be for the decision maker? *What* technique should be used in the actual selection of sampling units? *What* are the time and cost constraints associated with developing and executing the appropriate sampling plan?

Identify and explain the major components of a solid research proposal.

Once the researcher understands the different phases and task steps of the information research process, he or she can develop a solid research proposal. The proposal serves as a contract between the researcher and decision maker. There are nine specific content sections suggested for inclusion: (1) purpose of the proposed research project; (2) type of study; (3) definition of the target population and sample size; (4) sample design, technique, and data collection method; (5) specific research instruments; (6) potential managerial benefits of the proposed study; (7) proposed cost structure for the total project; (8) profile of the researcher and company; and (9) optional dummy tables of the projected results.

KEY TERMS AND CONCEPTS

Causal research 38	**Descriptive research** 38	**Raw data** 32
Census 39	**Exploratory research** 37	**Research proposal** 43
Data structures 32	**Information** 33	**Sample** 39
Decision opportunity 31	**Information research process** 30	**Scientific method** 32
Decision problem 31	**Market performance symptoms** 31	**Secondary data** 39
Defined target population 39	**Primary data** 39	

REVIEW QUESTIONS

1. Identify the significant changes taking place in today's business environment that are forcing management decision makers to rethink their views of marketing research. Also discuss the potential impact that these changes might have on marketing research activities.

2. As the business world enters the 21st century, will it be possible to make critical marketing decisions without marketing research? Why or why not?

3. How are management decision makers and information researchers alike? How are they different? How might the differences be reduced between these two types of professionals?

4. Explain the specific differences that exist between *raw data, data structures,* and *information.* Discuss how marketing research practices are used to transform raw data into meaningful bits of information.

5. Comment on the following statements:
   a. The primary responsibility for determining whether marketing research activities are necessary is that of the marketing research specialist.
   b. The information research process serves as a blueprint for reducing risks in making marketing decisions.
   c. Selecting the most appropriate research design is the most critical task in the research process.

6. Design a research proposal that can be used to address the following decision problem: "Should the Marriott Hotel in Pittsburgh, Pennsylvania, reduce the quality of its towels and bedding in order to improve the profitability of the hotel's operations?"

DISCUSSION QUESTIONS

1. For each of the four phases of the information research process, identify the corresponding task steps and develop a set of questions that a researcher should attempt to answer.

2. What are the differences in the main research objectives of *exploratory, descriptive,* and *causal* research designs? Which design type would be most appropriate to address the following question: "How satisfied or dissatisfied are customers with the automobile repair service offerings of the dealership from which they purchased their new 1999 Mazda Millenia?"

3. When should a researcher use a probability sampling method rather than a nonprobability method?

4. **EXPERIENCE THE INTERNET.** Using the Netscape browser and the Excite search engine, go to the Gallup Poll Organization's home page at www.gallup.com. Select the "Take poll" option and review the results by selecting the "Findings" option. After reviewing the information, outline the different phases and task steps of the information research process that might have been used in the Gallup Internet Poll.

ENDNOTES

1. See Alvin C. Burns and Ronald F. Bush, *Marketing Research* (Englewood Cliffs, NJ: Prentice Hall, 1995), p. 51; and also Carl McDaniel Jr. and Roger Gates, *Marketing Research Essentials* (St. Paul, MN: West Publishing, 1995), p. 25.

2. Some researchers portray the marketing research process as consisting of six continuous stages; see, e.g., William G. Zikmund, *Exploring Marketing Research,* 6th ed. (Fort Worth, TX: Dryden Press, 1997), p. 55. Others have discussed the process as having 11 major steps; see Alvin C. Burns and Ronald F. Bush, *Marketing Research* (Englewood Cliffs, NJ: Prentice Hall, 1995), pp. 49–50.

3. The iceberg principle and situation analysis techniques used to help determine and clarify management's initial information problems and/or needs will be discussed in detail in Chapter 3. For similar discussions see Richard D. Crisp, *Marketing Research* (New York: McGraw-Hill, 1957), p. 144; and William G. Zikmund, *Exploring Marketing Research,* 6th ed. (Fort Worth, TX: Dryden Press, Harcourt Brace College Publishers, 1997), p. 108.

4. This example has been adapted from a customized research consulting project by one of the text's authors that was conducted for the Ford Foundation's Amphitheater Design Team in Vail, Colorado, in 1984.

MARKETING RESEARCH ILLUSTRATION

WHAT DOES AN INFORMATION RESEARCH PROPOSAL LOOK LIKE?

The JP Hotel Preferred Guest Card Information Research Proposal

Purpose of the Proposed Research Project

The purpose of this proposed research project is to collect specific attitudinal, behavioral, motivational, and general demographic information to be used in addressing several key questions jointly posed by management of Louis Benito Advertising and W. B. Johnson Properties, Inc., concerning the JP Hotel Preferred Guest Card, a newly implemented marketing strategy within JP Hotel's overall marketing program. These key questions are as follows:

- To what extent is the Preferred Guest Card being used by cardholders?

- How do the cardholders evaluate the card on the basis of the specific privileges associated with it?

- What are the perceived benefits and weaknesses of the card, and why?

- To what extent does the Preferred Guest Card serve as an important factor in selecting a hotel?

- How often do the cardholders use their Preferred Guest Card?

- When do the cardholders use the card?

- Of those who have used the card, what privileges have been used? And how often?

- What general or specific improvements should be made regarding the card or the specific extended privileges?

- How did the cardholders obtain the card?

- Should the Preferred Guest Card membership be complimentary or should cardholders pay an annual fee?

- If there should be an annual fee, how much should it be? What would a cardholder be willing to pay?

- What is the demographic profile of the people who have the JP Hotel Preferred Guest Card?

Type of Study

To collect the data needed to address the above-mentioned managerial questions, the research should be of a structured, nondisguised design characterized as descriptive, exploratory, and explanatory. The study will be descriptive to the extent that most of the questions focus on identifying the perceptual awareness, attitudes, and usage patterns of the JP Hotel Preferred Guest Card as well as the demographic profiles of the current cardholders. It will be exploratory with regard to the investigation of possible improvements to the card and its privileges as well as the price structure considerations. Finally, the study will have explanatory elements incorporated regarding the reasons underlying the perceived benefits and weaknesses of the current card's features.

Definition of the Target Population and Sample Size

The target population to be studied in this research project consists of adults who are known to be current cardholders of the JP Hotel Preferred Guest Card. At present, this population frame is equal to approximately 17,000 individuals located across the United States. Statistically a conservative sample size representative of the defined target population frame would be 384, but realistically a sample of approximately 1,500 should be included in the total survey. The bases for this approximation are (1) the assessment of the likely response rate range that could be expected by using current methodological and control factors in the sampling and questionnaire designs, (2) a predetermined level of precision of not more than ± 5% sampling error and a desired confidence level of 95%, (3) general administrative costs and trade-offs, and (4) the desirability of having a prespecified minimum number of randomly selected cardholders included in data analyses.

Sample Design, Technique, and Data Collection Method

A probabilistic random sampling technique will be used to draw the needed sample for the project from W. B. Johnson Properties, Inc.'s central cardholder bank. Using a direct-mail survey method, those cardholders randomly selected as prospective respondents would be mailed a specifically tailored self-administered questionnaire. Attached to the questionnaire would be a carefully designed cover letter that explains the generalities of the study as well as inducements for respondent participation. Given the nature of the study, the perceived type of cardholder, the general trade-offs regarding costs and time considerations, and the utilization of updated incentives to induce respondent participation, the direct-mail design would be more appropriate than the alternative telephone interview or focus-group methods.

The Questionnaire

The questionnaire to be used in the proposed research project will be designed for self-administration. That is, the respondent will fill out the survey instrument in the privacy of his or her home and without the presence of an interviewer. The questionnaire will be designed, therefore, with the intended maximum self-administration, thus eliminating the costs and potential errors associated with interviews. All the questions in the survey will be pretested by a convenience sample to assess clarity of instructions, questions, and administrative time dimensions. Response scales to be used in the actual questions will conform to standard questionnaire design guidelines and industry wisdom.

Potential Managerial Benefits of the Proposed Study

Given the scope and nature of this proposed research project, the study's findings could provide JP Hotel's management informational insights into addressing the Preferred Guest Card questions of concern as well as other managerial implications regarding JP Hotel's current marketing strategies. More specifically, data and information gathered in this proposed study would provide JP Hotel with meaningful and useful insights toward

1. better understanding what type of people hold and use the Preferred Guest Card and the extent of that usage;

2. identifying specific feature problems that could serve as indicators for evaluating (and possibly modifying) current marketing/management strategies, policies, or tactics as they relate to the card and its privileges; and

3. identifying specific insights concerning the promotion and distribution of the card to expanded marketable segments.

Additionally, this proposed research project would functionally serve to initiate a customer-oriented database and collection system to assist JP's management in better understanding its customers' hotel service needs and wants in the 1990s. Customer-oriented data bases would prove vital not only in the firm's promotional strategy area but also in the important areas of pricing and service selection.

Proposed Cost Structure for the Total Project

Questionnaire/cover letter design and reproduction costs	$ 2,800	Coding and predata analysis costs	4,000
Development		Coding and setting of final codes	
Typing		Data entry	
Pretest		Tab development	
Reproduction (1,500)		Computer programming requirements	
Envelopes (3,000)		Computer time	
Sample design and plan costs	1,620	Data analysis and interpretation costs	6,500
Administration/data collection costs	3,840	Written report and presentation costs	2,850
Questionnaire packet assembly			
Postage and P.O. box			
Address labels		Total maximum proposed project cost*	$21,610

*Costing policy: Some of the costs included might actually be less than what is stated on the proposal. As such, those cost reductions would be passed on to the client. Additionally, there is a ± 10% cost margin associated with the pre- and actual data analysis activities depending on client changes of the original tab and analyses requirements.

Principal Researcher's Profile

The necessary research for this proposed project will be conducted by the Marketing Resource Group (MRG), a research firm that specializes in a wide array of exploratory, descriptive, and causal research designs and practices. MRG is located in Tampa, Florida, and has conducted numerous marketing research studies for many Fortune 1000 companies. The principal researcher and project coordinator will be Mr. Alex Smith, Senior Project Director at MRG. Mr. Smith holds a PhD in Marketing from Louisiana State University, an MBA from Illinois State University, and a BS from Southern Illinois University. With 25 years of marketing research experience, he has conducted numerous projects within the consumer packaging products, hotel/resort, retail banking, automobile, and insurance industries, to name a few. He specializes in projects that focus on customer satisfaction, service/product quality, market segmentation, and general consumer attitudes and behavior patterns as well as interactive electronic marketing technologies. In addition, he has published numerous articles on theoretical and pragmatic researching topics.

A Dummy Table Example of Data Results

In an effort to illustrate the potential types of data results that can be expected from this proposed research endeavor, the following dummy data results table is provided in this proposal (see Exhibit 1).

EXHIBIT 1	Summary of Overall Importance Differences of Selected Hotel-Choice Criteria Used by First-Time and Repeat Business Patrons								

Hotel Selection Criteria	Total (n = 880)		First-Time Patrons (n = 440)			Repeat Patrons (n = 440)			Z-Tests
	Mean[a] Value	(SG)[b]	Mean Value	Standard Error	(SG)	Mean Value	Standard Error	(SG)	
Cleanliness of the room	5.65	(A)	5.75	.06	(A)	5.50	.05	(A)	*
Good-quality bedding and towels	5.60	(A)	5.55	.06	(A)	5.62	.07	(A)	
Has preferred guest card options	5.57	(A)	5.42	.07	(A)	5.71	.06	(A)	*
Friendly/courteous staff and employees	5.10	(B)	4.85	.09	(B)	5.45	.07	(B)	*
Offers free VIP services	5.06	(B)	4.35	.10	(B)	5.38	.11	(B)	*
Conveniently located for business	5.04	(B)	5.25	.09	(B)	4.92	.10	(B)	*
In-room movie entertainment	3.63	(D)	3.30	.13	(D)	4.56	.11	(C)	*

[a]Importance scale: a six-point scale ranging from 6 ("extremely important") to 1 ("not at all important").

[b]Significant groupings (SG): (A) = "definitely strong factor"; (B) = "strong factor"; (C) = "moderately strong factor"; (D) = "weak factor."

*Mean importance difference between the two patron groups is significant at $p < .05$.

MARKETING RESEARCH CASE EXERCISE

UNITED PARCEL SERVICE: WILL BIG BROWN REMAIN THE DOMINANT PACKAGE DELIVERY SERVICE?

United Parcel Service (UPS) is one of the oldest and strongest companies in the United States, delivering over 5 percent of the U.S. gross domestic product yearly. UPS's daily delivery volume is 12 million parcels and documents, with air freight volume estimated at 2 million parcels and documents. UPS's customer base has grown from 500,000 in 1980 to over 1.46 million daily pickup customers in 1996. "Big Brown" (as the company is called, after the color of its trucks) employs over 336,000 people. Its 1996 revenues exceeded $22 billion.

The Strike of 1997

In early August of 1997, the teamster-organized couriers at UPS went on a nationwide strike, the first national strike in the history of UPS. The parcel post segment of the business—small and medium-size packages and documents—constituted 80 percent of the total market for UPS prior to the strike. Express delivery, or overnight package delivery, constituted 12 percent of the company's volume, with freight accounting for 8 percent of total volume. The August 1997 strike was directed at the parcel post delivery group, thus affecting the largest segment of UPS's business. UPS estimates that the strike resulted in a 10 to 15 percent market share loss in the parcel post delivery market, along with a total daily performance decrease of 90 percent. Of the 336,000 employees, the 180,000 who went on strike were employed in the parcel post delivery function of UPS.

Ramifications of the August 1997 Strike

The following factors were directly attributed to the 1997 UPS strike:

1. *Loss of dominance.* UPS lost 10 to 15 percent of its market share in its core business of standard parcel post delivery. Competitors (FedEx, Airborne, DHL,

USPS, etc.) gained valuable information on UPS customers who switched from UPS during the strike, allowing them to better position themselves to retain many of the UPS customers after the strike was settled. Customers were also exposed to a variety of competitive services that offered them new options for package delivery.

2. *A public relations challenge.* UPS now has the difficult task of restoring the image of cheerful "Big Brown" couriers hustling down Main Street U.S.A., delivering packages like clockwork. The strike created a negative perception of UPS among many small to medium-size businesses because it directly damaged many of these businesses.

3. *Loss of loyal customers.* Many traditional UPS customers vowed never again to depend on one carrier for their shipping needs. Following the strike, many businesses stated that they would diversify their package shipping business among several carriers so that they would never again be victims of such an uncontrollable force.

Using as a guide the marketing research proposal provided in the Marketing Research Illustration, prepare a research proposal for UPS, specifically concentrating on the following topics:

1. Illustrate how you will attempt to measure the effects of the August 1997 strike on the current situation UPS faces.

2. Explain how you would measure perceptions of small to medium-size businesses regarding their image of UPS, as well as competing package delivery services.

3. In your proposal, be sure to identify the appropriate target groups that you would consider when developing a sample for your proposed research.

CHAPTER 3

Learning Objectives

After reading this chapter, you will be able to

1. Distinguish types of pragmatic and scientific information needed to determine and resolve information problems or questions.

2. Describe the nature and purpose of a marketing research project.

3. Illustrate and explain the critical elements of problem definition in marketing research.

4. Determine the expected value of information obtainable through marketing research.

5. Identify and discuss both the procedural and methodological factors used in evaluating a marketing research project.

6. Discuss how price is determined and how it affects marketing research.

7. Identify and explain the characteristics used to evaluate a supplier of marketing research.

8. Discuss ethics in the marketing research industry.

Problem Definition, Research Objectives, and Marketing Research Ethics

❝ The passion for original Coke was something that just caught us by surprise. The simple fact is that all of the time and money and skill poured into marketing research on the new Coca-Cola could not measure or reveal the depth and emotional attachment to the original Coca-Cola felt by so many people. **❞**

DONALD R. KEOUGH
President
Coca-Cola Company[1]

"Can I Get a New Coke, Please!"

From 1980 to 1984, the Pepsi Cola Company conducted a series of blind taste tests and determined that soft-drink consumers preferred the sweetness of Pepsi to the crisper taste of Coke. Based on what was called the Pepsi Challenge, Pepsi developed a marketing program concentrating on younger soft-drink customers and labeling them the *Pepsi Generation.*

The Coca-Cola company's initial response was to increase its advertising budget and develop a claim of product superiority. Nonetheless, Coke's own taste tests validated Pepsi's claims that customers preferred a sweeter product. Using informational insights that were gained in the development of Diet Coke, Coca-Cola developed a new, sweeter Coke product and embarked on one of the most extensive marketing research programs in the history of the soft-drink industry.

Using an unparalleled test market research design lasting three years, the company asked over 200,000 customers to participate in blind taste tests that were conducted in shopping malls across the country. The information research question that guided Coca-Cola's research program was, What will the ultimate consumer reactions be to the taste of the new Coke product? The results of the marketing research indicated that when asked to compare unmarked beverages, consumers favored the new Coke formula over the original Coke product, by a margin of 55 percent to 45 percent. When both soft drinks were identified, 53 percent of those taking the test still preferred the new Coke formula over the original Coke.[2]

Using these marketing research results, Coca-Cola's management decided to introduce a new product. In April 1985, the sweeter-formula Coca-Cola product was introduced with the name New Coke and the original Coke was discontinued. In July 1985, however, old Coke was brought back into distribution, and by the end of 1985, the new Coke formula, the one marketing research showed to be preferred by drinkers, was discontinued. What happened? Where did Coca-Cola go wrong? What should have been measured? What if Coca-Cola had put the new product under the old label? These remain good topics of discussion within marketing research. From one perspective, Coca-Cola can be accused of being too narrow in the scope of its research question and defining the problem so that researchers investigated and tested only one aspect—consumers' preferences of taste associated with cola soft drinks.[3] In this situation, researchers can be criticized for not also investigating the extent to which consumers have emotional attachment and loyalty to existing brand names and the impact of such loyalty on purchase and consumption behavior. Coca-Cola's research failed to ask the respondents if the new Coke product should replace the original Coca-Cola.

Value of Determining the Research Problem

The story of the New Coke failure is not intended to show that marketing research is unimportant in new-product development and testing. Conversely, this example illustrates the importance of correctly determining the information research problem and the care needed in designing and evaluating the research project so that proper methodological research procedures are followed to ensure accuracy in the data being collected. As the opening quote of this chapter suggests, there are some things marketing research will never be able to uncover, much less explain. Yet the probability of making accurate decisions dramatically increases with a sound information research approach.

This chapter focuses on the development of such an approach. Using the overview discussions and insights presented in Chapter 2, this chapter details the journey through the information research process. Moreover, discussions will focus on Phase I, Determination of the Information Research Problem, and its three main task steps. The chapter is intended to provide an awareness of and appreciation for the importance of identifying and exploring the guidelines and criteria that can help both the research provider and client gain confidence in developing and executing marketing research projects. Nowhere does the saying "Garbage in, garbage out" apply more than in the field of marketing research. The raw data, structures, and information generated by the research process will only be as good as the research design used. Therefore, this chapter will discuss the critical topics that need to be considered in Phase I of the research process as well as creating and evaluating research objectives.

Given the importance of correctly identifying information problems, this text takes a unique approach by introducing the topic of ethics in marketing research within this early chapter rather than later in the text as a separate chapter. The discussion highlights the impact of unethical practices on the marketing research process. Examples regarding marketing research ethics will appear throughout the text as well.

Situations When Using the Information Research Process Might Be Inappropriate

We noted in Chapter 2 that the decision maker rather than the researcher holds the initial responsibility for deciding whether or not to use the marketing research process. Some experts believe that there are four situations in which the decision to commission a marketing research project is ill advised;[4] these are listed in Exhibit 3.1. One of the shortcomings

EXHIBIT 3.1	Times When Marketing Research Might Not Be Needed
Situation Factors	**Comments**
Information already available	When the decision maker has significant knowledge of the markets, relevant products and services, and competition, enough information may exist that allows for an informed decision without commissioning marketing research.[*] Some experts suggest that advancements in computer and information processing technology enhance providing the right information to the right decision makers in a timely fashion.[†]
Insufficient time frames	There are times when the discovery of a decision problem situation leaves an inadequate time frame for implementing the necessary research activities for properly conducting primary data and information. In competitive market environments, competitor actions/reactions might come so fast that they make it impossible to have formalized marketing research activities as a feasible option.
Inadequate resources	If there are significant limitations in money, manpower, and/or facilities, then marketing research activities tend to be discounted as being not feasible. When a firm is strapped for cash, there is a strong tendency to avoid marketing research practices.[‡]
Costs outweigh the value of information	In situations where the decision maker is viewing the market symptoms incorrectly as the decision problem, necessary marketing research costs can be seen as being too costly for the value (or quality) attached to the proposed information.

[*]R. K. Wade, "The When/What Research Decision Guide," *Marketing Research: A Magazine and Application*, 5, no. 3 (Summer 1993), pp. 24–27.

[†]William D. Perreault, Jr., "The Shifting Paradigm in Marketing Research," *Journal of the Academy of Marketing Science*, 20, no. 4 (Fall 1992), p. 369.

[‡]Richard F. Tomasino, "Integrate Marketing Research with Strategic Plan to Get Budget OK," *Marketing News*, January 4, 1985, p. 8.

of this typology is that in each situation it is assumed that the decision maker has either prior knowledge about the "true" availability of existing information, the necessary time and manpower, adequate resources, or clear insights into the value of the information that can be derived from the research process. In reality, the researcher must interact with the decision maker to assess whether conducting marketing research might be an infeasible option for resolving the business decision problem or opportunity at hand. The criteria for determining whether or not information research should be undertaken will be discussed later in this chapter.

Types of Information Used by Decision Makers
Pragmatic Forms of Information

Before discussing the information research problem definition process, we will identify and classify the different types of information used by decision makers and researchers to solve business and marketing problems. Many non-research-oriented decision makers (including consumers) simply classify the information they use to solve problems, answer questions, or evaluate opportunities as either *subjective, secondary,* or *primary.* This pragmatic classification system tends to be based on two fundamental dimensions: availability and degree of manipulation. *Availability of information* refers to the degree to which the information has already been collected and assembled in some type of recognizable format. *Degree of manipulation* refers to the extent to which data structures and results have been interpreted and applied to a specific situation. Within a decision-making framework, availability of information and degree of manipulation serve as two dominant factors that allow for easier classification of all types of information into three mutually exclusive categories used by decision makers and consumers alike to resolve their problems or opportunities. Exhibit 3.2 summarizes the different types of information and compares their availability and manipulation traits.

Subjective information
Information based on the decision maker's past experiences, expertise, assumptions, feelings, or judgments without any systematic gathering of facts.

SUBJECTIVE INFORMATION. Over time, subjective information has been given many different names, such as guestimation, intuition, gut reaction, seat-of-the-pants calculation, rumors, or even expert opinions. Regardless of the name, **subjective information** can simply be viewed as information that is based on the decision maker's past experiences, expertise, assumptions, feelings, or judgments without any systematic gathering of facts.[5] While such information is usually readily available, it often is not generalizable to the current problem situation. For the most part, relying on subjective information increases the risk of making a poor decision.

EXHIBIT 3.2 **Pragmatic Types of Information Used by Decision Makers**

Type of Information	Availability Factor	Manipulation Factor
Subjective	Very good availability, but based on individual's own experiences, feelings, or assumptions	Selectively interpreted
Secondary	Good availability, but extensive search time required	Information and data structures must be remanipulated and reinterpreted for at least a second time
Primary	Does not initially exist, must be created	Data structures must be manipulated and interpreted for first time

Secondary information

Information that was collected and interpreted at least once for some specific situation other than the current one.

SECONDARY INFORMATION. Secondary information is that which was collected and interpreted at least once for some specific situation other than the current one.[6] Basically, decision makers only need to locate such information and remanipulate (or reinterpret) it to apply it to their current problem situation. Availability is normally high, but there are great difficulties associated with applying secondary information to specific current situations because of how it was originally assembled or because the original reasons for collecting the information are unknown. Secondary information was initially primary. Some examples of secondary information are facts, estimates, and predictions published in *Consumer Reports* or *Time* magazine; sources include most TV commercials, marketing research textbooks, and online databases.

Primary information

Firsthand information derived through a formalized research process for a specific, current problem situation.

PRIMARY INFORMATION. Many decision makers refer to **primary information** as firsthand information derived through a formalized research process for a specific, current problem situation.[7] Some examples are data from a marketing research project or pilot study; statements from 500 randomly selected bank customers regarding the service features they consider most important; a count of the cars that travel through a particular intersection in one hour; or a tally of baseball fans who eat at least one hot dog when they go to the ballpark.

Beginning with the research problem definition process, it is important to remember that secondary and primary information do not exist until someone (the researcher or the decision maker) analyzes the raw data structures and provides interpretive meaning to the results.

Scientific Forms of Information

Researchers tend to categorize the information they gather during the research process into four types: facts, estimates, predictions, or modeled relationships. These information types are based on two fundamental dimensions—quality and complexity. *Quality of information* relates to the degree to which the information can be depended on as being accurate and reliable. *Complexity of information* refers to the degree to which the information is easily understood and applied to the problem or question under investigation. Exhibit 3.3 summarizes the different types of scientific information used by researchers and compares differences in their quality and complexity traits.

EXHIBIT 3.3   **Types of Information Used by Researchers and Decision Makers**

Type of Information	Quality Factor	Complexity Factor
Facts	Very high quality; are observable and verifiable bits of information; high in accuracy and reliability	Not complicated; easy to understand and use
Estimates	Degree of quality is based on the representativeness of the fact sources and the statistical procedures used to create them	More complex than facts due to the statistical procedures used to derive them and the possibility of error
Predictions	Lower quality than estimates or facts due to the perceived risk and uncertainty of future conditions	Greater complexity; forecasted estimates or projections into the future
Relationships	Quality is dependent on the precision of the researcher's statements of the inter-relationship between sets of variables	Highest complexity; interrelationships of several variables being simultaneously analyzed

Fact   Some piece of information that is observable and verifiable through a number of external sources.

FACTS. Facts serve as the most basic form of information. A **fact** is some piece of information that is *observable* and *verifiable* through a number of external sources. For example, it would be a fact that a salesperson has not met his quota this quarter, or that Procter & Gamble's Tide has captured 50 percent of the laundry detergent market, or that a dissatisfied consumer has written a letter of complaint to a given company. Facts are considered high-quality, uncomplicated bits of information. As long as a fact is timely, decision makers can place a great deal of reliance on it as they look for solutions to a specifically defined problem.

Estimate   A generalized application of a fact from a limited source to information about a larger source.

ESTIMATES. An **estimate** can be considered one step above a fact because it is a generalized application of a fact from a limited source to information about a larger source. For example, when a survey is conducted among a representative sample of customers, the results are facts as long as any references to them are restricted to just that sample. Here, the researcher could go back and verify each respondent's answers to the questions. These facts are transformed into estimates only when the researcher or decision maker suggests that they represent accurate information about the total market.

The quality of estimates is determined by the accuracy of measurement and their true representativeness of the whole group under investigation. Normally, estimates are somewhat less reliable than facts, yet they are more complex because of the statistical procedures by which they are derived. Correct definition of the research problem at the beginning of the research process will minimize (but never completely eliminate) the possibility of errors so that the estimates can be used to make good decisions.

Prediction   An estimate that is carried into the future.

PREDICTIONS. A **prediction** is an estimate that is carried into the future. Knowing what occurred in the past and what is happening in the present is extremely helpful to any decision maker, but their true concern is the ability to determine what will transpire in the future, because it is in the future that decisions will be tested. As such, information researchers are often called on to predict events given certain conditions. Consequently, predictions are less reliable than estimates. Since predictions are nothing more than projections of estimates into the future, they will automatically include (and probably magnify) whatever errors have been allowed to exist in the estimates.

Relationship   The existence of either a cause-and-effect or covariate interaction between two or more variables being investigated by the researcher.

RELATIONSHIPS. The last type of information supplied through the research process is a **relationship,** which is the existence of a cause-and-effect or covariate interaction between two or more variables being investigated by the researcher. For example, many decision makers have been taught to believe that cutting the price of a particular product or service will increase the demand for it, and there are many cases in which this relationship holds true, thus creating a downward-sloping demand curve. But relationship models can be built that can simultaneously compare sales to price changes, advertising expenditures, salesperson incentives, shorter warranty periods, and customers' occupation status. These models, which involve more complicated methods of combining and creating information, may show that the relationship between price cuts and demand is not so simple. The quality of the final information relies heavily on the precision of the researcher's statements of the relationships between several factors simultaneously affecting sales. These categorical types of information are integrated throughout the remainder of this book.

Importance of Determining the Information Research Problem

As illustrated by the New Coke example in the chapter opener, development and successful marketing of new products come about from understanding consumer decisions and from careful planning through a sound information research process. Once a business decision problem or opportunity is identified and acknowledgment made that some type of information (secondary or primary) is required, all the activities involved in planning and securing that information can be viewed as part of the research process. Consequently, it is important for decision makers and researchers to interact in initiating the first phase of the research process. This is true whether the situation requires that information be gathered periodically or only once. Any systematic attempt to gather or create information that can aid in a manager's decision-making practices will require activating the research process.

The first phase of the research process, Determination of the Information Research Problems, consists of three important task steps: (1) determine and clarify management's information needs; (2) redefine the decision problem as a research problem; and (3) establish research objectives and determine the value of the information. The researcher must achieve the task steps' objectives in order to reach the overall goal of identifying the information problems that underlie the decision problem or opportunity and to provide accurate statements of the research objectives.

Determine and Clarify Management's Information Needs

Decision problem The situation that exists when management has established a specific objective that may be achieved through any of several courses of action.

To ensure that appropriate information will be created through the research process, researchers must assist decision makers in making sure the problem or opportunity has been correctly defined and that the decision maker is aware of the information requirements. Remember that a **decision problem** exists when management has established a specific objective that may be achieved through any of several courses of action. The question becomes, Which is the best option? For researchers to gain clear understanding of the decision problem, they must employ an integrated problem definition process. There is no one best process, but any process undertaken should include the following activities: (1) determine the decision maker's purpose for the research, (2) understand the complete problem situation, (3) identify and separate out measurable symptoms within the problem situation, (4) determine the appropriate unit of analysis, and (5) determine the relevant variables. Being able to correctly define and understand the actual decision problem is an important first step in determining if it is really necessary to employ the research process. A poorly defined decision problem can easily produce research results that are unlikely to have any value, as in the New Coke example.

Integrated Decision Problem Definition Process

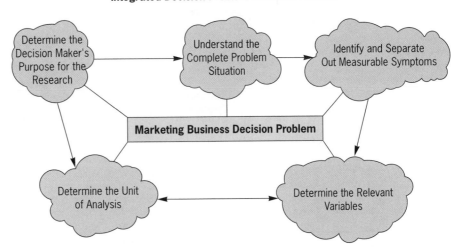

Purpose of the Research Request

Determining the purpose of the research begins any good problem definition process. As discussed in Chapter 2, the decision maker holds the initial responsibility of deciding that there might be a need for the services of a researcher in addressing a recognized decision problem or opportunity. Once brought into the situation, the researcher begins the problem definition process by asking the decision maker to express his or her reasons for thinking that there is a need to undertake research. Using this type of initial questioning procedure, researchers can begin to develop insights as to what the decision maker believes to be the problem. Having some basic idea of why research is needed focuses attention on the circumstances surrounding the problem. The researcher can then present a line of questions that can lead to establishing clarity between symptoms and actual causal factors. One method that might be employed here is for researchers to familiarize the decision maker about the **iceberg principle,** displayed in Exhibit 3.4.

Iceberg principle Principle that states that only 10 percent of most problems are visible to decision makers, while the remaining 90 percent must be discovered through research.

EXHIBIT 3.4   **The Iceberg Principle**

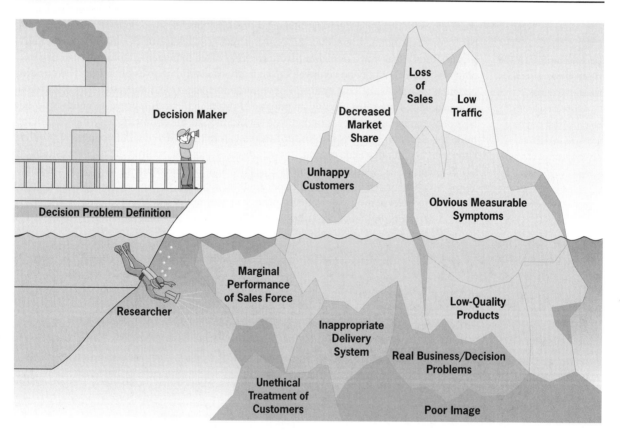

The iceberg principle states that in many business problem situations the decision maker is aware of only 10 percent of the true problem. Most of the time what is thought to be the problem is nothing more than an observable outcome factor or symptom (i.e., some type of measurable market performance factor), while 90 percent of the problem is neither visible to nor clearly understood by decision makers. The real problems are submerged below the waterline of observation. If the submerged portions of the problem are omitted from the problem definition and later from the research design, then decisions based on the research may be less than optimal.

Understand the Complete Problem Situation

Both the decision maker and researcher must understand the complete problem situation. This is easy to state but quite often difficult to execute. To gain such understanding, researchers and decision makers should perform a basic situation analysis of the circumstances surrounding the problem area. A **situation analysis** is a popular tool that focuses on the informal gathering of background information to familiarize the researcher with the overall complexity of the decision area. A situation analysis attempts to identify the events and factors that have led to the current decision problem situation, as well as any expected future consequences. Complete awareness of the problem situation provides better perspectives on (1) the decision maker's needs; (2) the complexity of the problem situation; and (3) the types of factors involved.

Situation analysis A tool that focuses on the informal gathering of background information to familiarize the researcher with the overall complexity of the decision area.

Conducting a situation analysis can enhance communication between the researcher and decision maker. It is the responsibility of the researcher to fully develop his or her knowledge of the client's overall business and daily activities. To objectively understand the client's domain (i.e., industry, competition, product lines, markets, and in some cases production facilities), the researcher cannot rely solely on information provided by the client, because many decision makers tend to be myopic within their own domain. Only when the researcher sees the client's business practices objectively can true problem clarification occur.[8] In short, the researchers must develop expertise in the client's business.

Identify and Separate Out Measurable Symptoms

Once the researcher understands the overall problem situation, he or she must work with the decision maker to separate the root problems from the observable and measurable symptoms that may have been initially perceived as being the decision problem. For example, many times managers view declining sales or reduction in market share as problems. After fully examining these issues, the researcher may see that they are the result of more concise issues such as poor advertising execution, lack of sales force motivation, or even poorly designed distribution networks. The challenge facing the researcher is one of clarifying the real decision problem by separating out possible causes from symptoms. Is a decline in sales truly the problem or merely a symptom of bad advertising practices, poor retail choice, or ineffective sales management?

Determine the Unit of Analysis

As a fundamental part of problem definition, the researcher must employ the objective yet visionary skill of determining the appropriate unit of analysis for the study. The researcher must be able to specify whether data should be collected about individuals, households, organizations, departments, geographical areas, specific objects, or some combination of these. The unit of analysis will provide direction in later activities such as scale measurement development and drawing appropriate samples of respondents. Take, for example, information problems that are investigated in typical automobile satisfaction studies. The researcher must decide whether to collect data from the known purchaser (i.e., individual) of a specific vehicle or from a husband-wife dyad representing the household in which the vehicle is driven.

Determine the Relevant Variables to the Situation

In this step, the researcher and decision maker jointly determine the specific variables pertinent to each defined problem or question that needs to be answered. The focus is on identifying the different independent and dependent variables. Determination must be made as to the types of information (i.e., facts, estimates, predictions, relationships) and specific

EXHIBIT 3.5	Examples of Constructs Routinely Investigated

Constructs	Operational Description
Brand awareness	Percentage of respondents having heard of a designated brand; awareness could be either unaided or aided.
Attitudes toward a brand	The number of respondents and their intensity of feeling positive or negative toward a specific brand.
Intentions to purchase	The number of people who are planning to buy the specified object (e.g., product or service) within a designated time period.
Importance of factors	What factors and their intensity influence a person's purchase choice.
Demographic characteristics	The age, gender, occupation status, income level, and so forth of individuals providing the information.
Satisfaction of experience	How people evaluate their postpurchase consumption experience of a specified object.

Construct Concepts or ideas about an object, attribute, or phenomenon that are worthy of measurement.

constructs that are relevant to the decision problem. Exhibit 3.5 provides several examples of marketing constructs that are routinely investigated through marketing research practices (though by no means is this a complete list of key constructs).

Redefine the Decision Problem as a Research Problem

Once the decision problem at hand is understood and specific information requirements are identified, the researcher must redefine the decision problem in more scientific terms. As discussed in Chapter 2, this second task step is the most critical step in the research process. The fundamental reason why it is necessary to reformulate most decision problems is that the decision makers use *pragmatic* frameworks and terminology in their efforts of initially defining a problem, whereas most researchers are trained to investigate problems and opportunities using *scientific* frameworks. In essence, marketing decision makers and researchers live in two distinct worlds. While the differences were discussed in Chapter 2, Exhibit 3.6 provides a summary of the fundamental differences between most decision makers and researchers as a reminder.

EXHIBIT 3.6	Fundamental and Philosophical Differences between Management and Researchers

Attribute Differences	Decision Makers	Researchers
Research motivation	To make symptoms disappear	To discover the true facts and relationships
Disposition toward knowledge	Want answers to questions	Want to ask questions
Orientation	Pragmatic, subjective	Scientific, objective
Responsibility	To make profits	To generate information
Use of the research	Political	Nonpolitical
Organizational position	Line/middle/top management	Supportive staff, specialist
Level of involvement	Highly involved, emotional	Detached, analytical
Training	General decision making	Scientific/technique application

In reframing decision problems and questions as information research questions, researchers must use their scientific knowledge and expertise. Information research questions are those specific how, what, which, where, when, and why statements about the problem areas that the research will attempt to investigate. Here, a decision problem is broken down into a series of more specific research questions. To illustrate this point, Exhibit 3.7 provides an example in which the management of a retail men's casual wear specialty store faced trends of low in-store traffic and sales figures. An objective analysis of the company's operations led the researcher to redefine the initial decision problem as a set of specific questions. Establishing information research questions specific to management's decision problem has a tendency to force the decision maker to provide additional information that is relevant to the actual problem.[9] In other situations, redefining decision problems as research problems can lead to the establishment of research hypotheses rather than research questions.

EXHIBIT 3.7	**Management Problem Expressed in Terms of Research Questions and Hypotheses**

Situation: A small retail specialty store featuring men's casual wear in Southern California was concerned about its trends in low traffic and sales figures. Management was unclear about what the store's retail image was among consumers.

Management's Initial Decision Problems

What store/product/service/operation strategies should be evaluated and possibly modified to increase growth in the store's revenue and market share indicators? What impact do merchandise quality, prices, and service quality have on customer satisfaction, in-store traffic patterns, and store loyalty images?

Redefined as Research Questions

What are the shopping habits and purchasing patterns among people who buy men's casual wear? That is,
    Where do these people normally shop for quality men's casual wear?
    When (how often) do they go shopping for quality men's casual wear?
    What types of casual wear items do they like to shop for (purchase)?
    Whom do they normally purchase men's casual wear for?
    How much (on average) do they spend on men's casual wear?

What store/operation features do people deem important in selecting a retail store in which to shop for men's casual wear?

How do known customers evaluate the store's performance on given store/operation features compared to selected direct competitors' features?

Redefined as Research Hypotheses

There is a positive relationship between quality of merchandise offered and store loyalty among customers.

Competitive prices have greater influence on generating in-store traffic patterns than do service quality features.

Unknowledgeable sales staff will negatively influence the satisfaction levels associated with customers' in-store shopping experiences.

Research Objectives

To collect specific attitudinal and behavioral data for identifying consumers' shopping behavior, preferences, and purchasing habits toward men's casual wear.

To collect specified store/product/service/operation performance data for identifying the retailer's strengths and weaknesses which could serve as indicators for evaluating current marketing and operational strategies.

To collect attitudinal data for assessing the retailer's current overall image and reputation as a retail men's casual wear specialty store.

A CLOSER LOOK AT RESEARCH   **Small Business Implications**

The Business Research Lab, available at www.busreslab.com, is a full-service market research company. Services provided by the Business Research Lab include customer satisfaction surveys, promotions testing, small-business solutions, employee satisfaction testing help, and sample surveys that individuals can download for personal use. The Business Research Lab prides itself on providing quality, detailed advice for its clients. An important area of budgetary concern for small-business owners or managers involves the allocation of resources for promotion. The sponsorship of events and promotion of other activities can quickly drain a small-business owner's promotion budget. The Busi-

ness Research Lab provides guidance for business owners seeking the right promotion strategy. For example, Pro-Sort, the promotions testing division of the Business Research Lab at http://spider.netrop olis.net/brl/prosort2.htm provides methodological guidelines for selecting the most profit-enhancing promotions. In three weeks, Pro-Sort will give you the data you need to have a meaningful, competitive edge. The goal of any promotion should be to eventually obtain increased sales. By contacting the Business Research Lab through its corporate e-mail address or dialing its toll-free telephone number, small-business owners can, at least, obtain experienced instructions for designing their promotions.

Hypothesis An unproven statement of a research question in a testable format.

A **hypothesis** is basically an unproven statement of a research question in a testable format. Hypothetical statements can be formulated about any variable and can express a possible relationship between two or more market factors. While research questions and hypotheses are similar in their intent to express relationships, hypotheses tend to be more specific and declarative, whereas research problem statements are more interrogative. Hypotheses can be tested empirically through the research process. Exhibit 3.7 illustrates the differences between interrogative research questions and hypotheses. Hypothesis development is discussed in greater detail in later chapters.

The task of redefining decision problems as information research questions or hypotheses serves as the point where the researcher rather than the decision maker becomes the more dominant player, the one with the most responsibility for the success or failure of a research project. Moreover, the activities in this task step play a critical role in preparing the researcher for the next task step, establishing the research objectives and determining the value of the information. Unless the research problem is defined accurately, the information that results from the research project is unlikely to have any value. See the Small Business Implications box (above) for how the Business Research Lab company claims to solve marketing research problems for small-business clients.

Establish Research Objectives and Determine the Value of the Information

Establishing Research Objectives

Research objectives are precise statements of what a research project will attempt to achieve. They also indirectly represent a blueprint of the research project's activities. Research objectives allow the researcher to document concise, measurable, and realistic events that either increase or decrease the magnitude of marketing management's problems. More important, they allow for the specification of information required to assist management's decision-making capabilities. In addition to illustrating how decision problems may be redefined as research questions and hypotheses, Exhibit 3.7 illustrates a set of research objectives (though by no means is this example meant to be representative of all decision problems facing today's marketing managers).

An example of L'eggs pantyhose new package design.

A major issue surrounding any research endeavor is to realize that research alone can never formulate solutions to a problem. Research can only facilitate the proper decisions from which solutions are examined. The objective underlying a research endeavor is to generate the necessary information to help management make decisions and hence formulate solutions. Thus, it becomes necessary to determine the value of acquiring information.

Determining the Value of the Expected Information

While undertaking problem definition activities, the decision maker and the researcher need to understand the potential worth of acquiring information. The major concern is whether the cost of generating the information will exceed its value. This may occur when the information must be at a very high accuracy level. For example, Hanes, maker of L'eggs pantyhose, conducted tests of alternative package designs for this product. Three alternative packages were developed and tested in a controlled test market situation. Results of the study indicated equal liking of all three packages. Hanes spent approximately $60,000 on this project and received only a limited amount of information relative to designing a truly effective package.[10] A possible alternative might have been to design a simple preference study focusing on the underlying dynamics that influence a customer's perception of various package designs. The study probably would have cost less yet revealed more data on what characterizes a good package design for this product. Hanes may have collected additional data, at no extra cost, that may have generated information useful for future decisions of this type. This simple example illustrates a fundamental principle in deciding whether or not to conduct research: *Market research should be conducted only when the expected value of the information to be obtained exceeds the cost of obtaining it.*

Although this principle sounds simple, it is extremely difficult to implement. The inherent difficulty is that of trying to predetermine the true value of the information. It is usually impossible to determine the cost-to-value ratio of most marketing research projects. Nevertheless, in Exhibit 3.8, we suggest some guidelines that should be given consideration in the process of approximating this critical ratio.

EXHIBIT 3.8	**Guidelines for Approximating the Cost-to-Value Ratio of a Research Project**

1. **Focus on the most important issues of the project.** Identify certain issues as important and others as peripheral to the problem. Unimportant issues are only a drain on resources and obscure the information that truly needs to be collected.

2. **Never try to do too much.** There is a limit to the amount of information that can be collected. Given this limitation, the researcher usually must make a trade-off between the number of issues that can be dealt with and the depth of each issue. Therefore, it is necessary to focus on those issues of greatest potential value.

3. **Determine whether secondary information, primary information, or a combination is needed.** Once the research objectives have been developed, the researcher must identify whether secondary or primary information would be most appropriate in addressing the stated decision problem. In some cases, it might be determined that a combination of both secondary and primary information is required.

4. **Analyze all potential methods of collecting information.** As we will see in the next phase of the research process, alternative data sources and research designs may be available that will allow detailed investigation of the issues at a relatively lower cost.

5. **Subjectively assess the value of information.** The researcher must ask some fundamental questions relating to the research objectives; for example:
   a. Can the information be collected at all?
   b. Can the information tell me something I don't already know?
   c. Will the information provide significant insights?
   d. What benefits will be delivered from this information?

Information for decision making will almost always be insufficient. It may be in short supply because additional information is simply not available at any cost. A worst-case scenario is that while additional information could be obtained, the cost to obtain it would be too high. Therefore, when specifying information requirements, either for an "as needed" or cost purpose, researchers should always evaluate the possibilites of collecting data from secondary sources (Chapters 4 and 5 discuss this issue in detail). If pertinent and accurate secondary forms of information are available, then the cost of securing the information is almost always significantly lower than the cost of collecting primary data. As we note throughout this text, with the proliferation of secondary information due to technological advances, many researchers are realizing that secondary information is an increasingly valuable source of marketing research information.[11]

Once the research objectives and information requirements have been determined, it becomes important for both decision maker and researcher to step back and again determine the necessity of actually performing marketing research. While the situation factors presented in Exhibit 3.1 (p. 55) may influence the evaluation process, there are other subjective criteria worthy of joint consideration at this point. For example, going forth with a research endeavor might prove inappropriate if

1. **Conducting the needed research would give valuable information to the firm's competition.** Many visible research procedures may give other companies an opportunity to formulate a competitive response before the research project is completed.

2. **The research findings cannot or will not be implemented.** Marketing research information has little to no value if management cannot afford to implement or refuses to act on it.

3. **The research design does not represent reality.** Many research designs, particularly experimental ones, may not adequately represent the true conditions of the market environment.

4. **The research results and findings are to be used as legal evidence.** This may occur in product liability or deceptive advertising lawsuits.

5. **The critical variables to the proposed investigation cannot be adequately designed or measured due to uncontrollable or ambiguous circumstances.**

6. **The research is being politically motivated.** Some managers may try to use research findings to advance their own career or to unethically elevate a company's standing in the community.

All of these situations must be evaluated prior to moving to the next phase of the research process, that of research design development. Remember, research conducted improperly or for the wrong reasons can do more harm than good.

In turn, many decision makers argue that they simply cannot afford to conduct properly designed marketing research projects. Yet most agree that survival in today's business environment depends directly on understanding, comprehending, and monitoring one's own operating environment. Acting in and reacting to a changing environment can best be executed by making sound decisions based on accurate information. Choosing not to conduct marketing research is in most cases simply a poor choice, given environmental realities. Therefore, the question should not be, How much marketing research can we afford to do? but rather, How much marketing research can we not afford not to do?

Procedural Considerations in Evaluating a Marketing Research Project

Although decision makers play a key role in determining the information problems, research objectives, and information requirements, rarely do they have the knowledge to effectively assess the value of the marketing research project from certain procedural or methodological dimensions. Here the researcher must teach the decision maker about the procedural and methodological criteria necessary to understand and evaluate a project. Some of the more critical criteria include pricing the project, objectivity, confidentiality, inaccurate data, and data validation.

Pricing the Research Project

Of special interest to both the decision maker and researcher is the cost of the recommended research project. Basically, the conventional wisdom that applies to any pricing decision also applies to determining the price of a given marketing research project. Most

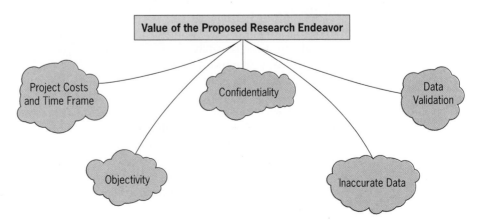

EXHIBIT 3.9	Research Activities Normally Itemized to Reflect Total Research Project Costs

1. Internal secondary data search
2. External secondary data search
3. Preliminary questionnaire design
4. Pretesting of questionnaire
5. Designing analysis procedures
6. Coding questionnaires for data analysis
7. Fees for data entry
8. Conducting data analysis
9. Outbound/inbound postage

10. Telephone/personal interview fees
11. Computer time charges
12. Copying and duplication
13. Word processing charges
14. Charge for graphics and overheads in final presentation
15. Mileage and travel expenses
16. Respondent incentives (if any)
17. Long distance tolls

projects involve direct costs, overhead costs, and a fee for professional service. In turn, the decision maker's confidence in the researcher's ability and the specifications of any given research project will also influence the price of the study.

One the best practices to employ when evaluating the cost of a research project is to request that an itemized list of activities appear in the research proposal with a dollar value assigned to each task. Some of the common research-related tasks are illustrated in Exhibit 3.9. The final price quoted by the researcher should be based on the collective costs of these activities. If any of the tasks or the related expenses change, then the decision maker should expect a change in the final negotiated price. The pricing structure should also include a specified agreement that explains the general responsibility for handling any cost overruns or underestimations due to unanticipated changes that may occur during the execution of the research project.

To understand this point more fully, revisit the research proposal displayed at the end of Chapter 2 and review the Proposed Cost Structure section (p. 50). Another factor that can complicate efforts in pricing any research project is the time frame in which the information needs to be delivered to the decision maker. In those situations where the overall time frame is short, the costs involved with collecting, analyzing, and preparing the report have a propensity to increase the price of the project. (Insights into the pricing differences of international marketing research projects can be gained from reading the Global Insights box on the next page.)

Objectivity

A second procedural criterion is to establish means by which to ensure that the information that results from the research project will be truly objective. The decision maker needs clear confirmation of how the sampling procedures that will be employed will avoid bias. For example, in the late 1980s, the Chrysler Corporation commissioned a study that indicated that people preferred Chrysler's cars over Toyota's. It was later revealed that none of the 100 respondents had ever owned a foreign auto.[12] The respondents in this sample were probably biased against foreign automobiles.

For any project, decision makers need to understand that statistics must be used and reported properly. If the level and type of analysis is not clearly specified at the start of a project, misuse of statistics can easily occur. Take, for example, the reported statistical fact that there exists a direct positive correlation between upturns and downswings in the stock

GLOBAL INSIGHTS · · THE COST OF CONDUCTING RESEARCH IN THE PACIFIC RIM · ·

In 1995, the Coca-Cola Company obtained price quotations for 10 different research studies, all relating to the category of soft drinks, to be performed in various Pacific Rim countries. The study was designed to get a relative comparison of research prices in the Pacific Rim region. While the actual cost of the studies were not revealed, an index was computed so as to rank countries on a relative cost basis. The ranks of the countries, from most expensive to least expensive, are as follows: (1) Japan, (2) Korea, (3) Singapore, (4) China, (5) Hong Kong, (6) Malaysia, (7) Australia, (8) Thailand, (9) Indonesia, (10) Philippines, (11) New Zealand, (12) Pakistan, and (13) Sri Lanka.

Through additional analysis, Coca-Cola was able to segment the 13 countries into three subgroups based on cost factors. Japan stood by itself as the *most expensive* place to do research. The next group, labeled *above average cost,* included Korea, Singapore, China, Hong Kong, Malaysia, and Australia. The third group, considered *below average cost,* consisted of Thailand, Indonesia, Philippines, New Zealand, Pakistan, and Sri Lanka.

market and the length of women's skirts. While this may be statistically accurate, the conclusions one may draw from it are worthless. A sound evaluation of the type of analysis and statistical representation can ensure objectivity of the research project.

Finally, researchers must avoid designing projects to achieve a predetermined outcome that will support some action or cause. For example, many critics speculate that the results of the marketing research for R. J. Reynolds' Premier cigarettes were the function of the research design.[13] Rather than a study that would determine the causes of consumers' product preferences, a descriptive study was employed because such a study would yield more positive results to support the marketing of the cigarette. Coincidentally, this occurred while the company was trying to increase its stock share price because of a leveraged buyout speculation.[14]

Confidentiality

A third criterion used in evaluating research projects is confidentiality. Due to the broad range of activities undertaken by many outside-the-company researchers, it is not uncommon for a researcher to perform studies for several firms in a given industry. This may or may not represent a conflict of interest if truly proprietary information is protected.[15] Therefore, before any research project is initiated, it becomes good practice for the decision maker to request from an outside researcher a statement of confidentiality and proprietary treatment of information. It should also be established at this time that any documentation generated by the research project (i.e., completed questionnaires, sampling frames, data analysis printouts) will become the property of the decision maker's company.

Inaccurate Data

Both controllable and uncontrollable factors can develop to cloud the accuracy of the data collected in a research project. While subsequent chapters will illustrate techniques to avoid data collection problems, data accuracy is still a prominent issue in project evaluation. One of the best safeguards for ensuring the accuracy of a researcher's data is evidence of past performance. Operating as part of the evaluation process, the decision maker

Most people are aware of the wealth of information available on the Internet. Even those with very little computer experience acknowledge that the Internet is the most widely used reference source in the world. And while many individuals debate the topic of whether the government should regulate information available on the Internet, few individuals realize the wealth of information available from the U. S. government via the Internet. One of the many sources of government information available through online connections is provided by the U.S. Department of Commerce, located at www.doc.gov. The information available through this host includes updated statistical information for the U.S. economy, business and trade figures for the United States and the world, and federal job openings.

One vital area of knowledge available at this site revolves around the Bureau of Export Administration (BXA). The BXA is a division of the U.S. Department of Commerce and provides rulings and clarifications for export legal issues. The BXA also enhances the nation's security and its economic opportunities by controlling exports for national security, foreign policy, and other supply-related factors. The BXA is in charge of developing export policies, issuing licenses for exporting, and punishing violators of export regulations. Updated information on export policies, entities that were denied export privileges, and press releases are all available from this Internet site. Individuals or business firms seeking more detailed information on regional or national trade policies now have access to such information online. For multinational companies facing uncertain exporting protocol, this Web site provides relevant, government-enforced rulings by which each company can and should abide.

Finally, the information provided by government Internet sites can be held in high regard. Often, individuals are skeptical of the information they retrieve online. With no governing body responsible for verification of the information transferred daily on the Internet, individuals are often able to transmit false or misleading information to the public. However, with few exceptions, individuals should be able to rely on the validity of the data the United States government provides through the Internet.

should ask any outside researcher to provide references. Those who give such references should be in the position to objectively assess a researcher's past performance with regard to type of projects conducted, realized outcomes, level of expertise, and knowledge of current marketing research practices. While it is difficult (if not impossible) to guarantee 100 percent accuracy for any marketing research project, evidence of a researcher's past performance and capabilities can increase the decision maker's confidence that the study or project will be accomplished professionally.

Data Validation

In the process of collecting data from respondents, it is customary to validate at least 20 percent of total responses,[16] to ensure that the data were collected and recorded accurately. As part of the total research package, it is the obligation of the researcher to perform this service for the decision maker. Researchers who balk at this service should be carefully scrutinized with regard to their ability to bring professionalism to the research project. As with all other project-related documents, validation forms should be returned to the decision maker upon project completion. Many clients will take this one step further and perform their own validation procedure beyond that of the researcher. This is just one additional criterion used to ensure that the research project will be conducted accurately. The Using Technology box above explains how business decision makers can obtain high-quality research data through U.S. government documents offered on the Internet.

Assessing the Quality of a Contracted Research Firm

As noted in the preceding discussion, decision makers should thoroughly evaluate the expected outcomes of the research before investing in a marketing research study. Of equal importance is the decision maker's ability to evaluate the characteristics required of a competent contracted marketing research provider. While this is indeed no easy task, the industry "best practices" suggest that the most important variables to use when evaluating research suppliers are (1) technical competency, (2) marketing knowledge, (3) reliable service, (4) conformance, and (5) reputation.[17]

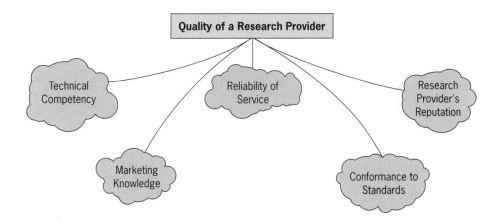

Technical Competency

Technical competency refers to whether the research provider possesses the necessary functional requirements to conduct the research project. Expertise, practical skills, and confidence are three requirements for any research provider. The contracted research provider must accurately diagnose problems, design appropriate techniques for dealing with those problems, and apply research findings to practical marketing actions that may lead to solutions. To assess this technical competence, the decision maker should request the name of several previous clients and call to verify the research provider's past performance. Alternatively, examples of other conducted studies might provide the needed validation of the research firm's technical competency.

Marketing Knowledge

Marketing knowledge complements a research provider's technical competency. Researchers must be able to assimilate diverse marketing environments and situations very rapidly. They must be able to quickly grasp enough of the decision maker's business background to devise and carry out a valid research project. To do so, the research provider must have a comprehensive knowledge of marketing theory; experience in application of the theory across a variety of areas (e.g., merchandising, pricing, advertising, consumer behavior, sales, customer satisfaction, service quality); and the ability to communicate that knowledge to the decision maker. Without this level of knowledge, a researcher will find it difficult, if not impossible, to understand the problem and find ways to overcome it. In many cases, the initial interaction between the decision maker and the research provider in the decision problem definition process described earlier should allow the decision maker to fairly assess this factor.

Reliability of Service

Reliability can be interpreted as the research provider's ability to be consistent and responsive to the needs of the decision maker. Operating under this characteristic, competent research providers assume the role of an employee within the decision maker's business. They expand their role from that of a mere researcher to that of a total consultant to the decision maker. They formulate all issues to benefit management's position on cost and revenue opportunities derived from the research project. Also, upon concluding the research project, the research provider does not abandon the decision maker. A reliable research provider will offer advice on program execution and recommended courses of action as suggested by the research findings.

Conformance to Standards

Conformance focuses on the research provider's ability to be accurate and on time with regard to performance standards. Conformance can be interpreted as following the old saying "Never promise what you can't deliver." High-quality research providers will adhere to projected timetables and will guarantee accuracy in all phases of the research project. More important, they will bring with them the highest degree of integrity and professionalism, from the initial meeting with the decision maker all the way through the presentation of the research results.

The Research Provider's Reputation

The reputation of a research provider is the aggregate of the four characteristics discussed above. In most contracted research situations, the true (or absolute) outcome of the research project can seldom be observed until the project is completed. Unfortunately, for the decision maker, this is too late. Therefore, quality of the finished research project usually must be inferred from various intangible aspects of the research provider. Reputation is the primary dimension of perceived quality outcomes. Its power comes from a nonslated image that the quality of the end product can be gauged in direct proportion to the level of expertise, trust, and believability of the researcher and the final results that are brought to the decision maker.

The above discussion suggests that there are many criteria to consider in assessing the value of the expected research information prior to moving into Phase II of the research process. While the actual criteria will vary from business to business, Exhibit 3.10 offers a summary of several generalized dimensions that are useful evaluative factors for judging most proposed research endeavors.

In addition to such evaluation criteria, many organizations will use a formal evaluation procedure when evaluating research suppliers. These procedures, employed at the completion of the project, use a formal rating scale. All individuals of the business who have been involved in the research project rate both the project and the research supplier on scales normally ranging from excellent to poor. These rating systems usually become the major standards the business uses when evaluating future research suppliers.

Ethics in Marketing Research Practices

Beginning in the first phase of determining the information research problem, the decision maker and researcher must address the ethical issues and practices that directly and indirectly affect the development and evaluation of any proposed research project as well as the overall research process. In research, as in any business situation, some ethical issues

EXHIBIT 3.10	General Criteria Used to Evaluate Research Suppliers

Evaluative Criteria	Description
Marketing knowledge	Shows ability to translate project objectives into a marketing perspective, and ability to implement recommendations into working marketing program action
Technical skills	Has ability to design research, questionnaire, and sample, and to use appropriate measurements and analysis techniques
Reliability	Provides consistent research-related performance over entire duration of project
Responsiveness	Shows willingness and readiness to provide designated tasks as indicated in research proposal
Access	Provides prompt replies on questions; is easily approachable
Communication	Keeps client informed of developments throughout the entire project
Credibility	Exhibits expertise in marketing research; is trustworthy with regard to project's goals; and performs activities in a professional manner
Understanding	Makes all efforts to keep project costs at lowest levels; understands true nature of client's problems, business, and daily activities
Quality of report/ presentation	Makes well-planned, concise, and accurate report; does not interject wasted information into presentation
Cost	Justifies and itemizes costs based on all necessary tasks to complete project
Timing	Completes project as promised within a reasonable time frame

are difficult or unclear. In such cases, decision makers and researchers must understand what constitutes ethical practices in marketing research.[18] This section provides an overview of ethical decision making and gives attention to ethical practices that may affect the decision to go forward with a research endeavor or to select a certain supplier of marketing research.

Overview of Ethics in Today's Business Environment

The need for all businesspeople to better understand business was highlighted by the insider trading scandals on Wall Street in the 1980s. These illegal practices made businesspeople realize that some individuals will do whatever it takes to secure the outcome they are seeking, be it money, power, promotion, or manipulation. New concerns about ethical business practices have forced the American business community to take a hard look at itself in the mirror. The conclusion of many observers was that we should not be too happy with the image that has appeared. While it was the major news stories from Wall Street that moved ethics to the forefront of business topics for this decade, and into business-school classrooms around the country, the hard truth is that the ethical crisis is not just the result of a few greedy people seeking to increase their wealth. The problem is much more widespread than many people might want to admit. For example, recent studies show that nearly one-third of all middle-level managers admit to submitting deceptive reports to their supervisors.[19] Major corporations like Firestone (the "500" tire), Dow Corning (breast implants), and Philip Morris (cigarettes) have admitted to marketing products they knew to be potentially harmful to their customers. Certainly not every company falls into the category of harming its customers, but ethical challenges and breaches of ethical conduct are as much managerial issues today as are employee recruiting, quality management, and production.

E T H I C S

While many companies would concur with Chemical Bank's position, the harsh realities of difficult and ever-changing business environments cause people to question if a solid ethical foundation is advisable. Most realize that just having "good people" is not enough to ensure that ethical breeches do not occur. For instance, one study on ethical practices within U.S. businesses found that managers believed that strictly adhering to business ethics can be a detriment to a successful business career. The study also uncovered that over half the colleagues known by the study's respondents were perceived as being rule-benders for their own personal advancement.[*] In another study that used a battery of psychological test measures given to business executives, the findings suggested that executives who were determined to be more emotionally healthy were also more likely to embrace higher ethical standards and practices. Yet the study also suggested that corporate pressures to produce results, irrespective of the means used, led to a higher level of stress than when appropriate ethical policies have been established.[†]

[*]Kenneth Labich, "The New Crisis in Business Ethics," *Fortune*, April 20, 1992, pp. 167–176.
[†]Patrick E. Murphy and Gene R. Laczniak, "Emerging Ethical Issues Facing Marketing Researchers," *Marketing Research: A Magazine and Application*, 4, no. 2 (June 1992), pp. 6–11; also see Margery S. Steinberg, "The 'Professionalization' of Marketing," *Marketing Research: A Magazine and Application*, 4, no. 2 (June 1992), p. 56.

Ethics The field of study that tries to determine what behaviors are appropriate under certain circumstances according to established codes of behavior set forth by society.

Business ethics takes a look at real-life issues that stand outside the often cut-and-dried distinctions between acceptable and unacceptable behavior that laws provide. Overall, the word **ethics** refers to the field of study that tries to determine what behaviors are appropriate under certain circumstances according to established codes of behavior set forth by society.[20] Ethics in marketing research looks at how firms can go about taking steps to increase the likelihood that individuals will make ethical decisions within the implementation of the research process. The principles and standards used to judge ethical practices are influenced by many different factors such as mass media, interest groups, culture, business organizations, and the personal morals and values of the people involved. These acknowledged standards apply to all the relationships addressed in the prior section of this chapter, specifically those between the users of research information (decision makers or clients) and the providers (researchers, research supplier, respondents).

As discussed earlier, decision problem situations encompass activities that place people in the position of selecting among several alternative actions. In most cases, decision situations implicitly require judgments of what is right and wrong, ethical or unethical. Moreover, decision makers may need to give careful consideration to the moral consequences of the different alternatives. Historically, many organizations have felt that the key to resolving ethical problems was to hire good citizens with solid attitudes and backgrounds. The Ethics box above describes Chemical Banking Corporation's philosophy that the reputation and integrity of its people are truly the firm's most valuable assets.[21]

In many of the ethical decisions marketing researchers face today, there is no clear distinction between those alternatives that are "right" and those that are "wrong." For example, should a research project manager terminate a problem employee when he or she learns that that person did not use the proper procedure for data validation? This is a question frequently faced by project managers trying to control the costs of a project. Should a researcher use a past marketing research report from a client's competitor as a secondary data source? Another ethical dilemma might arise if only 190 responses were collected from a sample requirement determined to be 200—is it appropriate to ignore the missing responses? These types of questions would likely produce different responses from different people.

Ethical Dilemmas in Marketing Research

There are many opportunities for both ethical and unethical behaviors to occur in the research process. The major sources of ethical dilemmas in marketing research are the interactions among the three key groups: (1) the research information user (e.g., decision maker, sponsoring client, management team, practitioner); (2) the research information provider (e.g., researcher, research organization or company, project supervisor, researcher's staff representative or employees); and (3) the selected respondents (e.g., subjects or objects of investigation). While the three main parties in any research situation can be described by a number of different terms, the following discussion will use, for the most part, *decision maker* to represent information user groups, *researcher* to denote the information provider groups, and *respondent* to represent the people who are asked to supply raw data.

Unethical Activities by the Researcher or Research Company

While there might be numerous opportunities for either the researcher, the research company, or its representatives to act unethically in the process of conducting a study, there are four major sources of unethical activities that can originate with the research company. First, a policy of unethical pricing practices is a common source of conflict. Research companies may bid an arbitrarily low project price from a fixed-cost basis to secure the client's business, then increase the amount of money received by manipulating variable project costs. For example, after quoting a set overall price for a proposed research project, the researcher may tell the decision maker that variable-cost items such as travel expenses, monetary response incentives, or fees charged for computer time are extra, over and above the quoted price. Such "soft" costs can be easily used to manipulate the total project cost.

Second, some research companies are often guilty of never fulfilling the promises they make to respondents and certain field workers. All too often research firms just simply do not provide the promised incentive (e.g., contest awards, gifts, even money) to respondents for completing the interviews or questionnaires. Also, many firms will delay indefinitely the fees owed to field workers (e.g., interviewers, data tabulators, data entry personnel). Normally, these parties are paid at the project's completion and thus lose any leverage they have with the research provider to collect on services rendered.

Third, it is not uncommon for the researcher or the organization to create respondent abuse. Research companies have a tendency to state that interviews are very short when in reality they may last up to one hour. Other situations of known respondent abuse include selling the respondents' names and demographic data to other companies without their approval, using infrared dye on questionnaires to trace selective respondents for the purpose of making a sales call, or using hidden tape recorders in a personal interviewing situation without the respondent's permission.

Finally, an unethical practice found all too often in marketing research is the selling of unnecessary or unwarranted research services. While it is perfectly acceptable to sell follow-up research that can aid the decision maker's company, selling bogus services is completely unethical. For example, the researcher convinces the decision maker that two or three forms of data collection methods are necessary when in fact only one method is appropriate. A similar unethical behavior is when the researcher sells two or three additional but unnecessary research projects or performs costly data analysis that is not consistent with the initial research design. There are several other researcher-related unethical practices that are worth separate attention.

Unethical Activities within the Execution of the Research Design

Researchers may act unethically while conducting the actual project. Three of the most important breaches of ethical conduct are (1) falsifying data, (2) duplicating actual response data, and (3) consciously manipulating the data structures inappropriately.

A practice of data falsification known to many researchers and field interviewers is called curbstoning (or rocking-chair) interviewing. This occurs when the researcher's trained interviewers or observers, rather than conducting interviews or observing respondents' actions as directed in the study, will complete the interviews themselves or make up "observed" respondents' behaviors. These unethical activities can occur in any of the data collection methods used to obtain raw primary data from randomly selected respondents (i.e., personal, telephone, or computer-assisted interviews or even observation techniques requiring trained human observers). Other falsification practices include having friends and relatives fill out surveys, not using the designated sample of sample respondents but rather anyone who is conveniently available to complete the survey, or not following up on the established call-back procedures indicated in the research procedure. These and other unethical practices are discussed in more detail in later chapters.

Another variation of data falsification is duplication of responses or the creation of the "phantom" respondents. This is a process whereby a researcher or field personnel (e.g., interviewer, field observer, or data entry personnel) will take an actual respondent's data and duplicate it to represent a second set of responses. This practice artificially creates data responses from people who were scheduled to be in the study but who for some reason were not actually interviewed. Let's take, for example, the research situation where the initial study requirements were to conduct and complete 100 telephone interviews, but the interviewer was only able to conduct and complete, say, 75 interviews and then takes the respondent's identification information from 25 telephone contacts where the prospective respondent was either not available or refused to participate and simply duplicates the responses from 25 of the completed surveys in order to gain the required 100 completed telephone interviews. To decrease the likelihood of data falsification, the research company can mandate that 10 to 15 percent of the interviews or surveys be randomly verified. Even so, some unethical field personnel report pay telephone numbers or neglect to account for phone numbers on the questionnaire in order to avoid the data validation process.

Finally, researchers act unethically when they either (1) consciously manipulate data structures from data analysis procedures for the purpose of reporting a biased picture to the decision maker or (2) do not report selected findings at all. A simple example of this type of unethical behavior is all the research conducted by the tobacco companies for 40 years that suggested cigarette smoking was not a direct link to certain types of cancer. Many companies manipulated the data or simply hid the truth about the relationship between smoking and cancer.

Unethical Activities by the Client

Decisions and practices of the client or decision maker also present opportunities for unethical behavior. One such behavior is when the decision maker requests a detailed research proposal from several competing research providers with no intention of selecting a firm to conduct the research. In this situation, companies solicit the proposals for the purpose of learning how to conduct the necessary marketing research themselves. Decision makers can obtain first drafts of questionnaires, sampling frames and sampling procedures, and knowledge on data collection procedures. Then, unethically, they can use the information to either perform the research project themselves or bargain for a better price among interested research companies.

Unfortunately, another common behavior among unethical decision makers is promising a prospective research provider a long-term relationship or additional projects in order to obtain a very low price on the initial research project. Then, after the researcher completes the initial project, the decision maker forgets about the long-term promises.

Unethical Activities by the Respondent

The primary unethical practice of respondents or subjects in any research endeavor is that of providing dishonest answers or of faking behavior. The general expectation is that when a subject has freely consented to participate, she or he will provide truthful responses, but truthfulness might be more difficult to achieve than one thinks. Some procedures are available to researchers to help evaluate the honesty of respondents' answers or actions. For example, when using a survey, researchers can build into their question/answer procedures internal consistency checks. These checks amount to asking for the same information using two different forms or approaches. Logic suggests that people should respond the same way to similar questions. Sometimes bipolar questions are used as consistency checks. Here the first question is framed in a positive way and the second question is framed in a negative way. The respondent's answers, if consistent, would be inversely related. More discussions on respondents' honesty are provided in later chapters.

Other areas of possible ethical dilemmas within a researcher-respondent relationship are (1) the respondent's right to privacy; (2) the need to disguise the true purpose of the research; and (3) the respondent's right to be informed about certain aspects of the research process, including the sponsorship of the research. Discussions on these and other ethical and unethical behaviors found within the information research process will be provided throughout this book.

Marketing Research Codes of Ethics

Of increasing importance to today's ethical decision-making processes is the establishment of company ethics programs. Special attention is provided here to such programs because they offer perhaps the best chance of minimizing unethical behavior. The fact is, today's marketing researchers must be proactive in their efforts to ensure an ethical environment, and the first step in being proactive is to develop a code of ethics. Many marketing research companies have established internal company codes of ethics derived from the ethical codes formulated by larger institutions that govern today's marketing research industry. Exhibit 3.11 displays the code developed by the American Marketing Association.[22] This code provides the framework for identifying ethical issues and arriving at ethical decisions in situations that sometimes suddenly and unexpectedly confront researchers in their jobs.

The development and distribution of the codes is only one step in an ethics program. It is certainly no guarantee against ethical problems in the company. The codes must be enforced. When violations of the code occur, they must be dealt with swiftly and consistently, no matter who the violator is, even if the requisite punishment is dismissal. If violations by top management are ignored, a major problem exists. Not only has the code been devalued, but top management has set a negative example for the entire firm. Marketing research organizations and researchers themselves must encourage employees to give evidence of code violation to counsel or some other designated individual. Ethics codes are not designed to encourage tattling, but they do depend on the integrity of the individuals in the firm to come forth to protect the ethical character of the business and research industry. Confidentiality must be assured where appropriate, and people must be able to present information regarding violations by a research project supervisor or any staff without fear of retaliation. It is the violator of the ethical code who must fear the consequences of the action. Approximately one-third of the Fortune 1000 firms have set up ethics committees to see that appropriate procedures are followed when ethical dilemmas are confronted.[23] Similarly, the marketing research industry has taken steps to ensure that ethical research practices become the norm rather than the exception.

EXHIBIT 3.11   Code of Ethics of the American Marketing Association

The American Marketing Association, in furtherance of its central objective of the advancement of science in marketing and in recognition of its obligation to the public, has established these principles of ethical practice of marketing research for the guidance of its members. In an increasingly complex society, marketing research is more and more dependent upon marketing information intelligently and systematically obtained. The consumer is the source of much of this information. Seeking the cooperation of the consumer in the development of information, marketing management must acknowledge its obligation to protect the public from misrepresentation and exploitation under the guise of research.

Similarly the research practitioner has an obligation to the discipline he practices and to those who provide support of his practice—an obligation to adhere to basic and commonly accepted standards of scientific investigation as they apply to the domain of marketing research. It is the intent of this code to define ethical standards required of marketing research in satisfying these obligations.

Adherence to this code will assure the user of marketing research that the research was done in accordance with acceptable ethical practices. Those engaged in research will find in this code an affirmation of sound and honest basic principles which have developed over the years as the profession has grown. The field interviewers who are the point of contact between the profession and the consumer will also find guidance in fulfilling their vitally important roles.

For Research Users, Practitioners and Interviewers

1. No individual or organization will undertake any activity which is directly or indirectly represented to be marketing research, but which has as its real purpose the attempted sale of merchandise or services to some or all the respondents interviewed in the course of the research.

2. If a respondent has been led to believe, directly or indirectly, that he is participating in a marketing research survey and that his anonymity will be protected, his name shall not be made known to anyone outside the research organization or research department, or used for other than research purposes.

For Research Practitioners

1. There will be no intentional or deliberate misrepresentation of research methods or results. An adequate description of methods employed will be made available upon request to the sponsor of the research. Evidence that fieldwork has been completed according to specifications will, upon request, be made available to buyers of research.

2. The identity of the survey sponsor and/or the ultimate client for whom a survey is being done will be held in confidence by the research organization or department and not used for personal gain or made available to any outside party unless the client specifically authorizes such release.

3. A research organization shall not undertake studies for competitive clients when such studies would jeopardize the confidential nature of client-agency relationships.

For Users of Marketing Research

1. A user of research shall not knowingly disseminate conclusions from a given research project or service that are inconsistent with or not warranted by the data.

2. To the extent that there is involved in a research project a unique design involving techniques, approaches or concepts not commonly available to research practitioners, the prospective user of research shall not solicit such a design from one practitioner and deliver it to another for execution without the approval of the design originator.

For Field Interviewers

1. Research assignments and material received, as well as information obtained from respondents, shall be held in confidence by the interviewer and revealed to no one except the research organization conducting the marketing study.

2. No information gained through a marketing research activity shall be used, directly or indirectly, for the personal gain or advantage of the interviewer.

3. Interviews shall be conducted in strict accordance with specifications and instructions received.

4. An interviewer shall not carry out two or more interviewing assignments simultaneously unless authorized by all contractors or employers concerned.

Members of the American Marketing Association will be expected to conduct themselves in accordance with provisions of this code in all of their marketing research activities.

Source: American Marketing Association, Chicago, IL.

EXHIBIT 3.12   **Marketing Research Association's Code of Ethics**

The Code of Professional Ethics and Practices of the
MARKETING RESEARCH ASSOCIATION, INC.
is subscribed to as follows:

1. To maintain high standards of competence and integrity in marketing and survey research.

2. To exercise all reasonable care and to observe the best standards of objectivity and accuracy in the development, collection, processing and reporting of marketing and survey research information.

3. To protect the anonymity of respondents and hold all information concerning an individual respondent privileged, such that this information is used only within the context of the particular study.

4. To thoroughly instruct and supervise all persons for whose work I am responsible in accordance with study specifications and general research techniques.

5. To observe the rights of ownership of all materials received from and/or developed for clients, and to keep in confidence all research techniques, data and other information considered confidential by their owners.

6. To make available to clients such details on the research methods and techniques of an assignment as may be reasonably required for proper interpretation of the data, providing this reporting does not violate the confidence of respondents or clients.

7. To promote the trust of the public for marketing and survey research activities and to avoid any procedure which misrepresents the activities of a respondent, the rewards of cooperation or the uses of the data.

8. To refrain from referring to membership in this organization as proof of competence, since the organization does not so certify any person or organization.

9. To encourage the observance of the principles of this code among all people engaged in marketing and survey research.

In recent years, numerous professional marketing research associations, such as the Council of American Survey Research Organizations (CASRO) and Marketing Research Association, Inc. (AMR), have been formed in attempts to bring higher integrity to the marketing research industry. Each has its own code of ethics to guide the behavior of its members. Exhibit 3.12 presents the code of ethics underwritten by the Marketing Research Association.[24]

While the codes of ethics advocated by marketing and survey research associations have given proactive guidance and the appearance of integrity to the marketing research industry, some researchers do not believe they are enough to guarantee continuous ethical behavior. Some have argued that all research practitioners should be required to be professionally certified, with certification granted on the successful completion of a four-part exam on the areas of (1) fundamentals of marketing, (2) secondary data, (3) research methods, and (4) data analysis.[25] It has been proposed that a professional designation of Certified Public Researchers (CPR) would enhance the overall integrity of the marketing research industry's image while ensuring that researchers undertake ethical practices.[26] Regardless of the proactive guidelines for dealing with ethics in marketing research, ethical dilemmas remain a never-ending concern for all the parties involved with research practices.

SUMMARY OF LEARNING OBJECTIVES

Distinguish types of pragmatic and scientific information needed to determine and resolve information problems or questions.

Today's decision makers are faced with new sets of challenges that directly influence their firm's competitive market structure, organization structure, and marketing mix strategies. Decision makers cannot rely strictly on subjective information to address and resolve those problems or to successfully exploit market opportunities. The need for additional information should be met by using scientific methods to generate secondary and primary information (i.e., facts, estimates, predictions, and relationships). Decision makers must concern themselves with both the complexity and the quality of the information, as well as the availability and degree-of-manipulation factors associated with the information they use to resolve identifiable problems and opportunities.

Describe the nature and purpose of a marketing research project.

A marketing research project involves activities designed to secure information for decision making. In order to ensure that the appropriate information is collected, a detailed research plan must be developed. Phase I of the information research process (Determination of the Information Research Program) must be successfully completed prior to developing the research design.

Illustrate and explain the critical elements of problem definition in marketing research.

Phase I of the research process consists of three important task steps: (1) determine and clarify management's information needs; (2) redefine the decision problem as a research problem; and (3) establish research objectives and evaluate the value of information. The most critical step to the success of any research endeavor is the second one. Before redefining the initial decision problem as a set of more specific research questions, the decision maker needs to work with the researcher to determine or clarify the true information needs of the situation. Defining the decision problem correctly requires the use of a five-step model that includes uncovering the decision maker's purpose, understanding the complete problem situation, separating out the measurable symptoms, determining the appropriate unit of analysis, and determining the most relevant factors of the situation. Defining decision problems as research questions allows the researcher to focus on the

how, what, which, who, when, where, and why questions needed to guide the formulation of the research objectives and clarify the pertinent information requirements. All the effort, time, and money spent to execute marketing research will be wasted if the true information research problems are misunderstood.

Determine the expected value of information obtainable through marketing research.

Marketing research should be conducted only when the expected value of information to be obtained exceeds the cost of obtaining it. While it is difficult to evaluate information, certain criteria can be used. First, focus on only the important issues of the problem. Second, never try to do too much in a single project; realize that limitations do exist. Third, explore all potentially available methods for collecting data—some are less expensive than others. Finally, subjectively assess the major benefits to be generated by the marketing research information.

Identify and discuss both the procedural and methodological factors used in evaluating a marketing research project.

It is always considered good practice for the client to have an understanding of various procedural and methodological issues for evaluating any proposed marketing research project. While these issues will certainly vary according to the type of project being performed, several general topics can be used to help the client understand project requirements: the cost of the study, maintaining objectivity, protecting client confidentiality, inaccurate data collection, and data validation.

Discuss how price is determined and how it affects marketing research.

While the cost of any marketing research endeavor is normally negotiated between the client and the researcher, direct costs and overhead associated with the project play an important role in pricing. In addition to knowing the fee for professional services, the client should request an itemized list of activities with assigned dollar values. Also, cost overruns and underestimates should also figure in to the project's final cost.

Identify and explain the characteristics used to evaluate a supplier of marketing research.

Industry best practices suggest the most important variables when evaluating a research supplier are technical competency, marketing knowledge, reliability of service, conformance to standards, and overall reputation. These variables can translate into the level of expertise, trustworthiness, and credibility that the research supplier brings the client.

Discuss ethics in the marketing research industry.
Ethical decision making affects all industries, including marketing research. Ethical dilemmas in marketing research are likely to occur among the research informa-

tion user, the research information provider, and the selected respondents. Specific unethical practices among research providers include unethical pricing practices, failure to meet obligations to respondents, respondent abuse, and selling unnecessary services. Unethical behavior by clients includes requesting research proposals with no intent to follow through and unethical practices to secure low-cost research services. The falsification of data and duplication of actual responses are unethical practices associated with the research firm.

KEY TERMS AND CONCEPTS

Construct 62

Decision problem 59

Estimate 58

Ethics 74

Fact 58

Hypothesis 64

Iceberg principle 60

Prediction 58

Primary information 57

Relationship 58

Secondary information 57

Situation analysis 61

Subjective information 56

REVIEW QUESTIONS

1. Why is determining the decision problem as a research problem the most critical task step in any research endeavor?

2. How does a decision maker's problem statement differ from the information research problem statement?

3. Discuss the activities or steps in the problem definition process. What should be the researcher's responsibilities in that process?

4. How can the iceberg principle be used to help decision makers gain a clearer understanding of their decision problem? What are the major differences between problem symptoms and decision problems?

5. How might a researcher or decision maker use the cost-to-value ratio to determine the value of expected research information? Identify and discuss three guidelines for assessing the value of research information.

6. Identify and explain four potential unethical practices within the marketing research process and their contribution to garbage-in, garbage-out situations.

DISCUSSION QUESTIONS

1. Using McDonald's as a case company, discuss how doing a situation analysis can help the researcher in determining an information research problem.

2. The program manager at Time Warner Cable would like to know how many viewers would tune in to a new proposed weekly TV show called "Leave It on the Table." Identify three situations in which doing a marketing research study to

address the program manager's question might prove to be inappropriate, and explain why.

3. What practical value do you believe a code of ethics in marketing research would have for a research supplier, like ACNielsen? A research user, like Wal-Mart? Actual respondents (e.g., students at your university)?

4. EXPERIENCE THE INTERNET. As the Internet continues to grow as a medium for conducting various types of marketing research studies, there is growing concern about ethical issues. Identify and discuss three ethical issues pertinent to doing research through the Net.

Now go to the Net and validate your ethical concerns. Using any browser and search engine go to the Internet Fraud home page, at www.fraud.org/ifw.htm. Click on the other links and browse the information. What unethical practices are plaguing the Net?

Using the information from the Net, write a three-page report on the unethical uses of the Internet, including those practices that researchers and decision makers alike must be aware of when conducting Internet research.

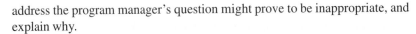

ENDNOTES

1. " Coca-Cola Company, Form 10-K" (Washington, DC: Securities and Exchange Commission, September 16, 1996).

2. Ibid.

3. Mitchell J. Shields, "Coke's Research Fizzles, Fails to Factor in Customer Loyalty," *Adweek,* July 15, 1985, p. 8.

4. John Martin and John Chadwick, "Factors Associated with Executive Decisions to Conduct Marketing Research: An Exploratory Study," in David L. Moore, ed., *Marketing: Forward Motion* (Proceedings of the Atlantic Marketing Association, 1988), pp. 698–709; also see Howard Schlossberg, "Cost Allocation Can Show True Value of Research," *Marketing News* 24 (January 8, 1990), p. 2.

5. See Lee Adler, "Systems Approach to Marketing," *Harvard Business Review,* May–June 1967, p. 110; and Lee Adler and Charles S. Mayer, *Managing the Marketing Research Function* (Chicago: American Marketing Association, 1977), p. 18.

6. This definition of secondary information has been commonly accepted by many marketing research experts over the past two decades. For example, see Paul E. Green and Donald S. Tull, *Research for Marketing Decisions,* 4th ed. (Englewood Cliffs, NJ: Prentice Hall, 1978), p. 76; also see Peter D. Bennett, *Dictionary of Marketing Terms* (Chicago: American Marketing Association, 1988), p. 156; or A. B. Blankenship and George Edward Breen, *State of the Art Marketing Research* (Chicago: American Marketing Association, 1992), p. 19.

7. This definition of primary information is standard and well accepted within the marketing research industry. See, for example, Bennett, *Dictionary of Marketing Terms,* p. 136; or Alvin C. Burns and Ronald F. Bush, *Marketing Research* (Englewood Cliffs, NJ: Prentice Hall, 1995), p. 133.

8. Vincent P. Barabba, "The Marketing Research Encyclopedia," *Harvard Business Review* (January–February 1990), pp. 7–18.

9. Randall G. Chapman, "Problem-Definition in Marketing Research Studies," *Journal of Marketing Research* 26, no. 1 (February 1989), pp. 51–59; also see Barabba, "The Marketing Research Encyclopedia," pp. 7–18.

10. David W. Cravens, *Strategic Marketing,* 4th ed. (Burr Ridge, IL: Irwin, 1994), pp. 128–30.

11. Susan Detneiller, "Second Hand Prose," *Marketing Tool* (January–February 1995), pp. 12–16.

12. Michael Hammer and James Champy, *Re-engineering The Corporation: A Manifesto for Business Revolution* (New York: Harper Business Publishing, 1993), pp. 169–76.

13. Ibid, p. 164.

14. Ibid, p. 168.

15. Joannine B. Evereth, "The Missing Link," *Marketing Research Magazine* (Spring 1997), pp. 33–36.

16. Todd Remington, "Rising Refusal Rates: The Impact of Telemarketers," *Quirks Marketing Research Review* (May 1992), pp. 8–15.

17. Ibid, pp. 8–15.

18. O. C. Ferrell and John Fraedrich, "Understanding Pressures That Cause Unethical Behavior in Business," *Journal of the Academy of Marketing Science* (Summer 1992), pp. 245–252.

19. O.C. Ferrell and John Fraedrich, *Business Ethics,* Boston: Houghton Mifflin, 1991, 5.

20. Ibid, p. 7.

21. "How All 306 Companies Rank," *Fortune,* February 11, 1991, pp. 75–80; "America's Most Admired Corporations," *Fortune,* February 10, 1992, pp. 40–72; also see "America's Most Admired Corporations," *Fortune,* February 8, 1993, pp. 44–72.

22. "AMA Adopts New Code of Ethics," *Marketing News,* September 11, 1987, pp. 1, 10.

23. "How All 306 Companies Rank," *Fortune,* February 11, 1991, pp. 75–80; "America's Most Admired Corporations" (February 10, 1992); also see "America's Most Admired Corporations" (February 8, 1993).

24. "The Code of Professional Ethics and Practices" (Chicago: Marketing Research Association, 1986).

25. Bruce L. Stern and Edward L. Grubb, "Alternative Solutions to the Marketing Research Industry's Quality Control Problem," in Robert L. King, ed., *Marketing: Toward the Twenty-First Century* (Proceedings of the Southern Marketing Association, 1991), pp. 225–29; also see Michael A. Jones and Roger McKinney, "The Need for Certification in Marketing Research," in David Thompson, ed., *Marketing and Education: Partners in Progress* (Proceedings of the Atlantic Marketing Association, 1993), pp. 224–29.

26. Terri L. Rittenburg and Gene W. Murdock, "Highly Sensitive Issues Still Spark Controversy within the Industry," *Marketing Research: A Magazine and Application* 6, no. 2 (Spring 1994), pp. 5–10; also see Alvin A. Achenbaum, "Can We Tolerate a Double Standard in Marketing Research?" *Journal of Advertising Research* 25 (June–July 1985), pp. RC3–7.

MARKETING RESEARCH ILLUSTRATION

DEVELOPMENT OF RESEARCH OBJECTIVES AND VALUE ASSESSMENT OF A PROPOSED RESEARCH ENDEAVOR

The JP Hotel Preferred Guest Card Study

This illustration of marketing research practices limits its intent to presenting the activities necessary to successfully complete Phase I (Determination of the Research Problem) of the information research process. The research proposal presented at the end of Chapter 2 is revisited and used to illustrate a framework for assessing the expected information value of a proposed research endeavor.

Marketing Management's Problem Situation

Several years back, JP Hotel's corporate management team implemented a new marketing strategy designed to attract and retain customers in their business-traveler market. The overall strategy consisted of marketing a VIP hotel card system to business-travel customers that provided benefits to the cardholder that were not offered to other hotel patrons. In some ways the initial system was similar to the airline industry's "frequent flier" programs. At the time, management thought the hotel card program, named "JP Hotel Preferred Guest Card," would help increase the hotel chain's market share of business travelers and create a sense of loyalty among those who were in the program. To become a member of the preferred guest program, a business traveler had only to fill out a simple application at any of the hotel's properties across the country. There was no cost to join and no annual fee. JP Hotel's corporate accounting records indicated that the initial implementation costs associated with the program were approximately $55,000 and annual operating costs about $85,000. At the end of the program's third year, records indicated that membership stood at 17,000.

At a corporate management team meeting, the CEO asked the following questions concerning the JP Hotel Preferred Guest Card program: How well is the guest card strategy working? Does it serve as a competitive advantage? Has the program increased the hotel's market share of business travelers? Is the company making money (profit) from the program? Is the program helping to create loyalty among our business customers? Taken by surprise by this line of questions, the corporate vice president of marketing replied by saying those were great questions but with no answers at that time. After having his assistants investigate corporate records to come up with the needed information, the vice president of marketing realized that all he had was a current membership listing and a total of the program costs to date (about $310,000). He did not have any good secondary information relevant to the attitudes and behaviors of cardholders, and his best guess at revenue benefits was about $85,000 a year. At best, the program was operating at close to a breakeven point.

Realizing he needed help, the vice president contacted his friend Alex Smith, the senior project director at Marketing Resource Group (MRG). MRG, located in Tampa, Florida, is a marketing research firm that specializes in a wide array of exploratory, descriptive, and causal research designs and practices. The vice president of marketing had previous dealings with Smith regarding several other researching projects for JP Hotel. An informal meeting was scheduled to discuss the decision problem situation and begin the necessary research process. The following discussions will highlight the important research activities or task steps necessary for determining the information research problem and setting the research objectives.

Task Step 1: Determine and Clarify Management's Information Needs

At the informal meeting, the vice president of marketing restated the questions asked by the CEO concerning the JP Hotel Preferred Guest Card program and added that the company does not have any solid secondary information that can address the attitudinal, behavioral, or motivational questions about current cardholders. In the vice president's words, "The company does not know whether the Preferred Guest Card program is a money maker or an unnecessary expense being accrued for the benefit of a few business patrons." In the discussions, it was mentioned that JP Hotel has been using an outside advertising agency to promote the card program. Alex Smith suggested that a representative of the ad agency should be included in these initial discussions, and a second meeting was then scheduled for two days later.

At the second meeting, Alex listened to the concerns of both JP Hotel and the ad agency's representative regarding the card program. Using such techniques as situational analysis and elements of the iceberg principle, Alex asked the following questions: What was the purpose of the Preferred Guest Card program? What were the factors that led to creating such a program? What were the short-term and long-term gains hoped for by offering such a program? What type of benefits were included in the program? How was the program being promoted to business travelers? Through which mediums was the program being advertised? What message about card membership was being communicated? To what extent were cardholders using the card? How important was being a cardholder in selecting hotel accommodations? This questioning approach helped in clarifying the decision problems for both hotel management and the ad agency. This first task step brought clarity and closure to the following two decision problems:

1. JP Hotel needed information that would aid in determining whether or not the company should continue the Preferred Guest Card program.

2.. The ad agency needed attitudinal, behavioral, motivational, and demographic information that would aid in fine-tuning promotional strategies that would attract new members, retain current cardholders, and increase the card usage.

Task Step 2: Redefine the Decision Problem as a Research Problem

After gaining clarification of the decision problems in the situation, Alex Smith's responsibility was to translate those decision problems into information research problems or specific research questions. Prior to doing this transformation, Smith collected some additional qualitative information by conducting several in-depth interviews with the general manager of three JP Hotel properties and a focus group session with 10 known JP Hotel Preferred Guest Card holders. Using all the collected background information, his research knowledge, and his training in scientific methods, he posed the following set of pertinent research questions:

> To *what* extent is the Preferred Guest Card being used by known cardholders?
>
> *How* do the cardholders evaluate the card on the basis of specific privileges associated with the card?
>
> *What* are the perceived benefits and weaknesses of the card? And *why?*
>
> To *what* extent does the Preferred Guest Card serve as an important factor in selecting a hotel?
>
> *How* often do the cardholders use their Preferred Guest Card? *When* do they use the card?
>
> Among those who have used the card, *what* privileges have been used? And *how* often?
>
> *What* general and/or specific improvements should be made regarding the card or the specific extended privileges?
>
> *How* was the card obtained? *How* did people become aware of the Preferred Guest Card program?
>
> *Should* the Preferred Guest Card membership be complimentary or should it carry an annual fee?
>
> If there should be an annual fee, *what* should it be? *What* price would people be willing to pay?
>
> *What* is the demographic/socioeconomic profile of the people who have a JP Preferred Guest Card?

Task Step 3: Establish the Research Objectives and Determine the Value of the Expected Information

In this task step, the researcher brings closure to the information research problems and sets forth the overall guidelines for conducting the proposed research. Using his knowledge of the decision and information research problems identified through the first two task steps, Alex Smith established the necessary research objectives. These objective statements basically explain why the research is being conducted and become a critical component in determining the most appropriate research design for collecting the needed primary data. Smith stated the research objectives in this situation as follows:

1. To determine the existing card usage patterns among known JP Hotel Preferred Guest Card holders, with focus on how often the cards are used and the frequency of use of the specific privileges associated with the card program.

2. To identify and evaluate the privileges associated with the card program, with particular emphasis on cardholders' judgments of the perceived benefits and weaknesses for making improvements to the overall program, as well as determining the importance of the card as being a factor in selecting a hotel for business purposes.

3. To determine business travelers' total awareness of the JP Hotel Preferred Guest Card program and their methods of obtaining a card.

4. To determine whether or not card membership should carry an annual fee and to determine the average fee range that a businessperson would expect and would be willing to pay for such a membership card.

5. To identify demographic/socioeconomic profile differences between heavy users, moderate users, rare users, and nonusers of the card.

By establishing the research objectives, Smith was in a solid position to determine what other task steps would be required in designing the appropriate research project, including the cost figures associated with each of those activities. Refer back to the "Proposed Cost Structure for the Total Project" section in the research proposal at the end of Chapter 2. Smith estimated the total cost of this proposed research project to be $21,610.

Once the cost of doing the research was determined, JP Hotel's management had to determine whether or not to go forward with the project. Basically, management had to decide whether the benefits of having the additional primary information were worth the costs of obtaining that information. One assessment technique available to the vice president of marketing was the cost-to-value ratio method discussed earlier in this chapter. Using in part the guidelines in Exhibit 3.7 and all the descriptive information presented in the actual research proposal, management responded positively to each guideline. In addition, management had to consider the following scenario: What if the research provided information that suggests the program might not continue to grow? Given that the total cost for doing the project is $21,610 and the dollar figure associated with the benefit of the card program was assumed to be at least $85,000 (current guess at annual revenue figure for the program), the cost-to-value ratio method would suggest that the increased revenue benefits would have to be above $106,610 (e.g., the current dollar revenue benefit estimate of $85,000 plus the cost of the research, $21,610). While Alex Smith could guarantee MRG's listed project costs, objectivity and confidentiality of the information, data validation processes, and solid research methodologies to avoid intentional data inaccuracies, he could not ethically guarantee that dollar revenues generated from the JP Hotel Preferred Guest Card program would automatically increase over the current estimated $85,000 solely on the basis of the additional information from the research project. Alex Smith left the research proposal with the vice president of marketing and was told a "go" or "no go" decision would be made in the next few days.

A POSTSCRIPT. Due to JP Hotel's management team's inability to more accurately determine the revenue dollar benefits associated with the Preferred Guest Card program, the proposed project was placed on hold indefinitely.

MARKETING RESEARCH CASE EXERCISE

PLANNING THE RESEARCH PROCESS: CORONA VERSUS HEINEKEN

Corona beer, produced by a Mexican-based company, is available in 124 countries around the world. Up to 1997, Corona had always been the second-best-selling import beer next to Heineken, a Netherlands-based beer sold in 170 countries around the world. Corona passed Heineken in total volume shipments in late 1997. In fact, over the past three years, Corona has been averaging a 35 percent increase in sales, while Heineken has been able to maintain only a 7 percent increase in the same period.

Why the sudden craze for Corona? Many experts in the field contend that it is more likely due to problems related to Heineken than to the success of Corona. Heineken has been the number one imported beer for two decades and thus the company may have forgotten how to compete. In a past news release, one of Heineken's managers was reported to have stated, "We are number one, we always have been number one, and we will always be number one." Today, however, Heineken is no longer number one, and the company is attempting to stage a comeback against Corona.

Aside from its complacency, Heineken has been experiencing some setbacks associated with competition from other beer producers. Some of these issues are as follows:

1. An advertising campaign by Anheuser-Busch announcing the labeling of freshness dates on its beer brands and suggesting that Heineken is not a "fresh" product and is considered "skunky" by many beer drinkers.

2. An increased level of consumption of microbrews and specialty beers, offering a variety of brands for a variety of consumer tastes. Heineken has a product mix of only two brands: the traditional brand and a dark amber variety.

3. Demographic changes in the traditional beer-drinking population. Beer drinkers are getting older and drinking less. The baby-boomer segment has declined in consumption of beer, while the Generation X segment has become a larger beer market. Heineken has admited that it has done a poor job in nurturing the Generation X segment as Heineken consumers.

4. Retailers' discomfort over Heineken's distributors' pricing. The overall price of Heineken charged to the point-of-sale retailer is approximately 15 percent higher than that of competing import beers. This, along with a strong point-of-sale promotion program by Corona, is prompting many retailers to reduce shelf space for the Heineken brand.

The strategic goal for Heineken is to recapture its number one postion in the beer-drinking market. In order to do so, Heineken must make some critical decisions in the near future.

1. Research the import beer industry from 1996 to the present and list several marketing decisions facing Heineken today.

2. Plan a research agenda that Heineken can use in order to successfully implement these decisions. Specifically, translate the decisions you have developed into specific research objectives for Heineken.

3. What are the central research questions that Heineken needs to address? Also, what information needs are critical in order for Heineken to implement its marketing decisions?

CHAPTER 4

Learning Objectives

After reading this chapter, you will be able to

1. Understand how secondary data fit into the marketing research process.

2. Demonstrate how secondary data can be used in problem solving.

3. List sources of traditional internal secondary data.

4. Demonstrate how to obtain external sources of secondary data.

5. List sources of external secondary data.

6. Understand the availability and use of syndicated sources of secondary data.

7. Understand the changing focus of secondary data usage.

Strategic Information Management: Secondary Data Sources

❝ In today's competitive environment, the key word is fast. Faster in obtaining results, faster in disseminating results. Therefore, we now conduct marketing research with priority given to secondary data. Why? Its faster. ❞[1]

ROBERT BENGEN
Director of Marketing and Research
Samsonite Corporation

Talking Turkey

Over the past 10 years, the top meal choices among Americans have remained very stable. Only the bologna sandwich has dropped off the list, replaced by the turkey sandwich. In 1987, the top 10 choices, in order of preference, were ham sandwich, steak, hot dog, cheese sandwich, peanut butter and jelly, hamburger, bologna sandwich, pizza, spaghetti, and macaroni and cheese. In 1997, the list was, in order, pizza, ham sandwich, hot dog, peanut butter and jelly, steak, macaroni and cheese, turkey sandwich, cheese sandwich, hamburger, and spaghetti.

Other facts about American consumption patterns indicate that 65 percent of Americans consume alcoholic beverages, up from 56 percent five years ago. The alcoholic beverage with the largest increase in consumption is red wine. Coke Classic continues to be the nation's most popular beverage, followed by tap water, coffee, beer, milk, buttermilk, tea, and juice. Additionally, in 1997, Americans consumed 63.7 pounds of beef per person, 49.5 pounds of pork, 48.2 pounds of chicken, 14.9 pounds of fish and shellfish, and 14.3 pounds of turkey. The information contained in this brief example comes from two sources, *Beverage Industry Magazine* and the U.S. Department of Agriculture. These data represent only a tiny fraction of the information available to anyone free of charge.

The Healthy American

We may remember 1997 as the year when beef came back, sweets and snacks in low-fat versions were consumed in record quantities, and American consumers looked at vegetables and collectively said, "I say it's spinach and I say the hell with it."

Never before in this country's history have so many food choices, or so much information on the relationship between diet and health, been available. Ironically, the bulk of the population is eating larger portions of nutrient-poor food, and consequently health problems are increasing. "After years of conducting marketing research on food consumption, the only constant is no change," says Harry Balzer, Vice President of National Purchase Diary (NPD).[2] NPD tracks the consumption patterns of 2,000 American households every year. The 1997 report indicates that the favorite lunch and dinner entrees are the same as in 1987. People are eating the same foods they have always eaten, only in low-fat versions.

NPD also publishes data pertaining to restaurant visits, food product preferences, major decision variables, and attitudes toward new-food-product introductions. The data are not compiled for any single company but are instead used by many competing firms in the food industry such as Nabisco, Frito-Lay, McDonald's, and Pizza Hut.[3] While no one company commissioned this study for any specific purpose, they have all secured the rights to specific industry information for a nominal charge.

The Value of Secondary Data

The information contained in the chapter opener is just one example of the vast array of available secondary data. These data were obtained free of charge from the trade association of the quick casual dining association. More and more companies are electing to use existing data as a major tool in their marketing research decisions. As more and more such data become available, many companies are realizing that they can be used to make sound marketing decisions. Data of this nature are more readily available, often more highly valid, and usually less expensive to secure than company-gathered primary data. This chapter focuses on the types of secondary marketing research data available, how they can be used, and what benefits they offer. The discussion here will concentrate on traditional sources of secondary data. Use of the Internet as a source for secondary data will be discussed in Chapter 5.

The Nature and Scope of Secondary Data

Secondary data Data not gathered for the immediate study at hand but for some other purpose.

Internal secondary data Data collected by the individual company for accounting purposes or marketing activity reports.

External secondary data Data collected by outside agencies such as the federal government, trade associations, or periodicals.

One of the basic tasks of competent marketing research is to obtain information that helps a company's management make the best possible decisions. Focusing on the particular marketing problem to be analyzed, the researcher needs to determine whether useful information already exists, how relevant the information is, and how it should be obtained. Existing sources of information are more widespread than one might expect, as illustrated in the chapter opener, and should always be considered first in any data collection procedure.

The term **secondary data** refers to data not gathered for the immediate study at hand but for some other purpose.[4] Secondary data exist in three forms. **Internal secondary data** is data collected by the individual company for accounting purposes or marketing activity reports. **External secondary data** consist of data collected by outside agencies such as the federal government, trade associations, or periodicals. External data may also be available through standardized marketing research services such as NPD Marketing Research's food consumption reports, store audits, or consumer purchase panels. Finally, secondary data may exist in computerized data sources. Computerized secondary data sources are usually designed by specific companies and include internal and external data combined with online information sources. These computerized information sources may include information vendors (America Online, Prodigy), private Web sites, mailing lists, or direct marketing clearing and fulfillment services.

The Role of Secondary Data in Marketing Research

The role of secondary data in the marketing research process has changed over the past several years. Traditionally, research based on secondary data was viewed as nonoriginal; it was often outsourced to a corporate librarian, syndicated data collection firm, or junior research analyst. The main functions of secondary data research were to provide historical background for a current primary research endeavor and to allow longitudinal trend analysis within an industry. In other words, secondary data research was viewed as the filler, attachment, or appendix to the formal primary research report. Today, with the increased emphasis on business and competitive intelligence (which will be discussed in Chapter 7), and the ever increasing availability of information from proprietary online databases, secondary data research is gaining importance in the marketing research process.

In today's marketing research environment, secondary research tasks are applied more often to specific marketing problems than are primary techniques due to the relative speed and cost-effectiveness of gathering secondary data. Many large corporations are redefining the role of the secondary research analyst to that of a business units information professional or specialist now linked to the information technology area for the purpose of creating contact and sales databases, preparing competitive trend reports, and developing customer retention strategies.

Secondary Data Research Tasks and the Marketing Research Process

In many areas of marketing research, secondary research will always play a subordinate role to primary research. In product and concept testing, focus groups, and customer satisfaction surveys, only primary research can provide answers to marketing problems. Yet when appropriately selected for specific situations, secondary data research can not only save time and money, but also provide the researcher with a broad avenue of answers. In many instances, secondary data can be used to directly assess the research problem at hand. For example, in many research situations, secondary data collection is the starting point of defining the actual research that needs to be conducted. If the problem can be solved based on available secondary data alone, then the company can save time, money, and effort. If the level of secondary data is not sufficient to solve the specific research problems, then primary data collection needs to be considered.

Exhibit 4.1 illustrates the functional roles of secondary data research. These roles are normally viewed in terms of their focus and value. If the focus of the research project is on external market dynamics, it will likely be a secondary research responsibility. One task of secondary research is trend analysis, which uses past market data to project future changes in a dynamic marketplace. Additionally, secondary data collection is a vital support task in providing business and competitive intelligence. Both tasks involve the acquisition of secondary data and information about all aspects of a competitor's marketing and business activities. In short, external market dynamics is an area that requires proactive secondary research.

If the research focus is on the external customer, secondary research adds value to the research process. Researchers may, for example, use internal company documents to profile the current customer base. This existing customer base can then be used to identify significant characteristics of potential new customers. Finally, needs analysis, which identifies critical problems or requirements of specific customer groups, is an additional secondary research task. The third category of secondary research tasks involves providing internal support data for the company. With these tasks the focus switches to providing support for primary research activities, support for sales presentations, and support for decision-making functions. It's important to realize that a marketing organization cannot survive without sales generated by professional presentations or decisions on product, price, place and promotion. Also, the organization cannot go without full knowledge of how markets are shifting and changing under its strategic planning process. Providing need-to-have planning tools is a primary task of secondary research.

To further characterize the role of secondary data research in the marketing research process, the Society of Competitive Intelligence Professionals conducted a survey among

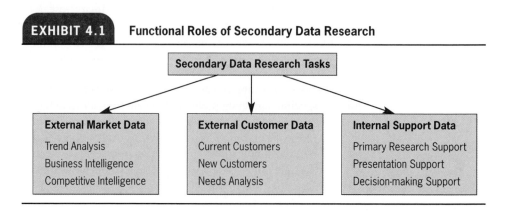

EXHIBIT 4.1   **Functional Roles of Secondary Data Research**

Secondary Data Research Tasks

External Market Data
Trend Analysis
Business Intelligence
Competitive Intelligence

External Customer Data
Current Customers
New Customers
Needs Analysis

Internal Support Data
Primary Research Support
Presentation Support
Decision-making Support

marketing research firms.[5] Sixty percent of the sample reported using secondary research tasks on a regular basis. The survey also revealed that, among the firms involved,

1. 82 percent report using secondary data for monitoring competitive and business intelligence.

2. 75 percent use secondary data to provide functional support for primary research projects.

3. 59 percent indicate using secondary data for managerial presentations.

4. 57 percent use secondary data for specific business decisions.

5. 48 percent use secondary research to validate internal data and primary data collection.[6]

As secondary research continues to increase its presence in marketing research, and as the required skills for acquiring new forms of data delivery continue to evolve, the importance and value of secondary data research within the research process will increase.

Use and Evaluation of Secondary Data Sources

As we noted earlier, the predominant reason for using secondary data is that they save the researcher time and money. Normally, secondary data collection involves simply locating the appropriate source or sources, extracting the necessary data, and recording the data relative to the research purpose in question. This usually takes only several days, and in some cases only a few hours. Primary data, in contrast, can take months to accurately collect. When you consider the process of designing and testing questionnaires, developing a sampling plan, actually collecting the data, and then analyzing and tabulating them, you can see that primary data collection can be a long and involved procedure.

In addition to taking a long time, primary data collection can cost thousands of dollars. In a 1997 survey among market research firms, the fees reported for services rendered by these firms ranged from $5,000 to $500,000.[7] Obviously, the scope and magnitude of the research study play significant roles in the fee a firm levies on a project.[8] Yet with any primary data collection project it is difficult to avoid wages and expenses, transportation and data collection costs, and clerical and field services charges. With many secondary data sources, such costs are nonexistent or, at worst, nominal. Expenses associated with secondary data are usually either incurred by the original data source, as with published secondary data sources (the U.S. census, corporate surveys of buying power, state and county demographic data), or shared between the user and the commercial provider of the data. Regardless, securing secondary data normally costs significantly less than securing primary data.

Because of time and cost savings, the first general rule of thumb associated with any research endeavor is to exhaust all potential sources of secondary data. If for some reason the particular research problem cannot be solved through the acquisition of secondary data, then serious consideration should be given to primary data collection procedures. Interestingly enough, in today's environment of information abundance, many firms, both consumer and industrial, are finding secondary data sources adequate for solving many of their marketing research problems. Consistent with this statement is the prediction of many marketing research firms that by the turn of the century almost half of all marketing research objectives will be accomplished through the acquisition of secondary data.[9]

As information becomes more abundant, and technology allows for greater refinement and categorization of the information, the emphasis on secondary data is likely to increase. In addition, secondary data are likely to become more accurate. Bar coding, optical scanning, and database development are beginning to generate point-of-purchase data banks. Already these data banks are providing companies with all the information they need for a majority of their marketing research.

If in fact the emphasis on secondary data will increase, researchers will need to establish a new set of procedures and evaluative criteria regarding the quality of information obtained via secondary data sources. Specifically, if secondary data are to be used to assist in a decision process, then they should be assessed according to six fundamental principles:[10]

1. **Purpose.** Since most secondary data are collected for purposes other than the one at hand, the data must be carefully evaluated on how they relate to the current research objective. Many times the original collection of the data is not consistent with a particular market research study. These inconsistencies usually stem from the methods and the units of measure employed. For example, most of the data regarding product consumption patterns in the *Survey of Buying Power* published by *Sales and Marketing Management* (discussed later in this chapter) are based on average expenditure patterns of a population. Each figure is assigned an arbitrary weight to account for environmental or situational differences. While the results may represent a good average, they may not provide the necessary precision for profiling a highly defined target market relative to actual dollars spent on some particular product category.

2. **Accuracy.** When assessing secondary data, researchers need to keep in mind what was actually measured. For example, if actual purchases in a test market were measured, were they first-time trial purchases or repeat purchases? Researchers must also assess the generalizability of the data. Were the data collected from certain groups only (e.g., men, women, children) or randomly? Were the measures for the study developed properly? For example, a specific question might be, "Were dichotomous forced-choice questions used instead of interval scales when attempting to measure attitudes toward foreign automobile imports?" Researchers must further evaluate the data relative to their classifications. Were the data presented as a total of responses from all respondents, or were they categorized by age, sex, or socioeconomic status?

    In addition to the above dimensions, researchers must assess *when* the data were collected. For example, a researcher tracking the sales of imported Japanese autos in the U.S. market needs to consider changing attitudes, newly imposed tariffs that may restrict imports, and even fluctuations in the exchange rate. Factors such as these not only can hamper the accuracy of the data but also may render the data useless for interpretation.

    With regard to the accuracy of secondary data, researchers must keep in mind that the data were collected to answer a completely different set of research questions than the ones at hand. As such, they may not accurately address all the aspects of a research issue, or flaws may exist in the research design and method that are not apparent in the secondary data result.

3. **Consistency.** When evaluating any source of secondary data, a good strategy is to seek out multiple sources of the same data to assure consistency. For example, when evaluating the economic characteristic of a foreign market, a researcher may

Unloading Japanese-made automobiles at a U.S. port.

try to gather the same information from government sources, private business publications (*Fortune, Business Week*), and specialty import/export trade publications.

4. **Credibility.** Researchers should always question the credibility of the secondary data source. Technical competence, service quality, reputation, and training and expertise of personnel representing the organization are some of the measures of credibility.

5. **Methodology.** The quality of secondary data is only as good as the methodology employed to gather them. Flaws in methodological procedures could produce results that are invalid, unreliable, or not generalizable beyond the study itself. Therefore, the researcher must evaluate the size and description of the sample, the response rate, the questionnaire, and the overall procedure for collecting the data (telephone, mail, or personal interview).

6. **Bias.** Researchers must try to determine the underlying motivation or hidden agenda, if any, behind secondary data. It is not uncommon to find many secondary data sources published to advance the interest of commercial, political, or other special interest groups. Many times secondary data are published to incite controversy or refute other data sources. Researchers should try to determine if the organization reporting the data is motivated by a certain purpose. For example, statistics on animal extinction reported by the National Hardwood Lumber Association or deaths attributed to handguns as reported by the National Rifle Association should be validated before they can be relied on as unbiased sources of information.

Traditional Internal Sources of Secondary Data

The logical starting point in searching for secondary data is the company's own internal information. Many organizations fail to realize the wealth of information their own records contain. Additionally, internal data are the most readily available and can be accessed at little or no cost at all. Yet, while this appears to be an overwhelming rationale for using internal data, researchers must realize that a majority of this information comes from past business activities. This is not to say that internal data is not usable for future business decisions. As will be evident in the following discussion, internal data sources can be highly effective in helping decision makers plan new-product introductions or new distribution outlets.

Types of Internal Secondary Data

Generally, internal data will consist of sales or cost information. Data of this type are commonly found in internal accounting or financial records. The two most useful sources of information are sales invoices and accounts receivable reports; quarterly sales reports and sales activity reports are also useful. Exhibit 4.2 lists key variables found in each of these internal sources of secondary data.

Sales Invoices

Sales invoices contain a wealth of data pertaining to both current and past customers. As a secondary data research tool, such invoices can provide customer profiles, sales trends, unit sales history, and other key items of information.

Accounts Receivable Reports

Accounts receivable reports contain information relative to both past and current customers, but in addition they can also provide information on relative profit margins on certain prod-

---

EXHIBIT 4.2

Common Sources of Internal Secondary Data Including Key Variables

1. Sales invoices
   - **a.** Customer name
   - **b.** Address
   - **c.** Class of product/service sold
   - **d.** Price by unit
   - **e.** Salesperson
   - **f.** Term of sales
   - **g.** Shipment point

2. Accounts receivable reports
   - **a.** Customer name
   - **b.** Product purchased
   - **c.** Total unit and dollar sales
   - **d.** Customer as percentage of sales
   - **e.** Customer as percentage of regional sales
   - **f.** Profit margin
   - **g.** Credit rating
   - **h.** Items returned
   - **i.** Reason for return

3. Quarterly sales report
   - **a.** Total dollar and unit sales by:

     Customer
     Customer segment
     Product

   Product segment
   Geographic segment
   Sales territory
   Sales rep.
   - **b.** Total sales against planned objective
   - **c.** Total sales against budget
   - **d.** Total sales against prior periods
   - **e.** Actual sales percentage increase/decrease
   - **f.** Contribution trends

4. Sales activity reports
   - **a.** Classification of customer account

     Mega
     Large
     Medium
     Small
   - **b.** Available dollar sales potential
   - **c.** Current sales penetration
   - **d.** Exiting bids/contracts by

     Customer location
     Product

ucts, reasons behind customer returns and charge backs, and revenues by industry, segment, or geographic location. With such information, accounts receivable reports can provide indirect measures of customer satisfaction/dissatisfaction, price tactics, and sales history.

Quarterly Sales Reports

Quarterly sales reports normally illustrate planned sales activities relative to actual sales results. These reports prove to be invaluable sources of information on sales territories, effective sales techniques, and competitive intelligence. This information is often useful in sales training and presentation planning.

Sales Activity Reports

Sales activity reports are usually prepared each month by individual sales representatives and normally contain data on sales, competition, territory activities, and changes in the marketplace. In general, most selling organizations require their sales personnel to include competitive activities on these reports, making them an excellent source of data for competitive intelligence.

Other Types

Other types of internal data that exist among company records can be used to complement the information thus far discussed. Exhibit 4.3 outlines other potential sources of internal secondary data.

As we said earlier, a wealth of information exists internally to a company for useful marketing research activities. If maintained and categorized properly, internal data can be used to analyze product performance, customer satisfaction, distribution effectiveness, and target market strategies. These forms of internal data are also useful for planning new-product introductions, product deletions, promotional strategies, competitive intelligence, or customer service tactics.

EXHIBIT 4.3   **Additional Sources of Secondary Data**

Source	Information
Customer letters	General satisfaction/dissatisfaction data
Customer comment cards	Overall performance data
Mail-order forms	Customer name, address, items purchased, quality, cycle time of order
Credit applications	Full and detailed biography (demographic, socioeconomic, credit usage, credit ratings) of customer segments
Cash register receipts	Dollar volume, merchandise type, salesperson, vendor, manufacturer
Salesperson expense reports	Sales activities, competitor activities in market
Employee exit interviews	General internal satisfaction/dissatisfaction data, internal company performance data
Warranty cards	Sales volume; names, addresses, zip codes, items purchased, reasons for product return
Past marketing research studies	A variety of data pertaining to the situation in which the marketing research was conducted

Using and Extracting External Sources of Secondary Data

Upon completion of an exhaustive search for internal secondary data, the next logical step for the researcher is to focus on potential sources of external secondary data. External secondary data can exist in one or more of three forms: (1) published data in periodicals, directories, or indexes; (2) data compiled by an outside (syndicated or commercial) agency that can be acquired on an as-needed basis for a nominal fee; or (3) data contained in online databases or available through computer-facilitating agencies or vendors. This section will focus on two forms of external sources of secondary data: published sources and syndicated/commercial sources. Chapter 5 will provide a complete discussion of technology-based sources.

Planning for the External Secondary Data Search

The major challenge associated with external data sources is not finding the right data to assist in the research process but rather finding and securing the appropriate source for extracting the data. Several top researchers at the U.S. Department of Defense have speculated that there is enough information available today to solve a majority of managers' questions and problems, but 90 percent of that information is not categorized in any particular form.[11] Therefore, the problem is not finding out whether information exists; it is finding out where the information resides.

When seeking out secondary data sources, it is best to follow some sort of plan or strategy. For most researchers, the fundamental reasons for seeking secondary data are time and money. Getting lost in a secondary data search can void both of these benefits. A simple procedure researchers can employ when searching for secondary data is referred to as the GO-CART approach (for *g*oals, *o*bjectives, *c*haracteristics, *a*ctivities, *r*eliability, and *t*abulation).

1. **Goals.** Focus your information search on topics and concepts relevant to the specific research question at hand. If the research question is how to develop market or target market profiles, seek out information relevant to this topic (demographics, socioeconomic data, SIC codes, etc.). If the research question is how to understand customer satisfaction as it relates to product usage, seek out information on the product—how it is manufactured, distributed, and transported. Let this information, if possible, unveil potential reasons for satisfaction or dissatisfaction.

2. **Objectives.** Many experts believe the best way of managing primary data is to initially gather a lot of it and then to categorize it into specific topics. Managing a secondary data source is very similar. Seek out as much information as you can on the topic, and then check all references and citations that may allow you to address more specific topics. Keep in mind that many sources of secondary data are compiled from specific categories of information and reported in a general format. Backtracking through references and citations will allow you to narrow down the information. For example, much of the data reported in the *Survey of Buying Power* (discussed later in this chapter) is general in reference to a standard metropolitan area. Yet analyzing how the data was compiled could lead one to specific information by city limits, areas of a city, even specific zip codes.

3. **Characteristics.** Always define the specific characteristics of information you are seeking. Write out a list of topics that need to be explored in your search. If you are

seeking psychographic data, identify the specific characteristics of this data you wish to uncover. Are you looking for activities, interests, opinions (i.e., lifestyles)? If so, relative to what topics? Television viewing patterns, product usage, political affiliations, etc.? Focus your data search on a list of characteristics you're seeking as an aid in answering the research question.

4. **Activities.** Specifically outline the places, people, events, and tasks that will be part of your secondary data search. You will probably need to visit libraries and speak with reference librarians. You may need to go to trade associations, state or county planning commission offices, newspaper file rooms, or even seminars. Document what needs to be done, where you need to do it, and who can help you along the way.

5. **Reliability.** As mentioned in an earlier section of this chapter, try to find several data sources on the same topic. This will allow you to establish some consistency and will lead to greater levels of reliable data.

6. **Tabulation.** Document all sources of your data search. If possible, cross-reference various sources to allow for more meaning of the data. More important, verify that what you have collected is indeed what needs to be collected to answer the research question at hand. If not, an additional data search may be necessary.

The GO-CART approach for planning a secondary data search is by no means the only way to collect secondary data. It does however, provide an agenda to follow in order to prioritize elements of the search process. Because the search for secondary data can be anything from very simple to highly complicated, a specific plan for a data search is necessary for each situation the researcher faces. Without any type of plan, the time and cost benefits normally associated with secondary data may not be realized.

Key Sources of External Secondary Data

When undertaking the search for secondary data, researchers must remember that the number of available sources is extremely large. While the amount of available information is indeed vast, the information needs of many researchers are connected by a common theme. The key variables most often sought by researchers are demographic dimensions, employment characteristics, economic characteristics, competitive characteristics, supply characteristics, regulations, and international market characteristics.[12] Exhibit 4.4 provides examples of selective variables within these categories.

Several key sources of secondary data allow the researcher to create a hierarchy of information sources to guide a secondary data search, regardless of the variables sought. Developing a hierarchy of secondary data sources is consistent with the second task of the GO-CART approach—initially seek volume and then work to tailor your data search to specific needs. Several broad to narrow data sources are presented below to help guide the researcher through the jungle of secondary information.

Standard Industrial Classification Codes

Standard industrial classification (SIC) codes Numerical industrial listings designed to promote uniformity in data reporting procedures for the U.S. government.

An initial step in any secondary data search is to use the numeric listings of the **standard industrial classification (SIC) codes.** SIC codes were designed to promote uniformity in data reporting by federal and state government sources and private business. The federal government assigns every industry an SIC code. Businesses within each industry report

---

EXHIBIT 4.4   **Key Variables Sought in Secondary Data Search**

Demographic Dimensions

Population growth: actual and projected

Population density

In-migration and out-migration patterns

Population trends by age, race, and ethnic background

Employment Characteristics

Labor force growth

Unemployment levels

Percentage of employment by occupation categories

Employment by industry

Economic Characteristics

Personal income levels (per capita and median)

Type of manufacturing/service firms

Total housing starts

Building permits issued

Sales tax rates

Competitive Characteristics

Levels of retail and wholesale sales

Number and types of competing retailers

Availability of financial institutions

Supply Characteristics

Number of distribution facilities

Cost of deliveries

Level of rail, water, air, and road transportation

Regulations

Taxes

Licensing

Wages

Zoning

International Market Characteristics

Transportation and exporting requirements

Trade barriers

Business philosophies

Legal system

Social customs

Political climate

Cultural patterns

Religious and moral backgrounds

---

all activities (sales, payrolls, taxation) according to their code. Currently, there are 99 two-digit industry codes representing everything from agricultural production of crops to environmental quality and housing. Within each two-digit industry classification code is a four-digit industry group code representing specific industry groups. All businesses in the industry represented by a given four-digit code will report detailed information and statistics about the business to various sources for publication. For example, as shown in Exhibit 4.5, SIC code 12 is assigned to coal mining and SIC code 1221 specifies bituminous coal and lignite, surface extraction. It is at the four-digit level where the researcher will concentrate the data search.

Government Documents

Detail, completeness, and consistency are major reasons for using U.S. government documents. More specifically, the U.S. Bureau of the Census reports are the statistical foundation for most of the information available on U.S. population and economic activities. Exhibit 4.6 lists some of the common sources of secondary data available from the U.S.

| EXHIBIT 4.5 | Sample List of Standard Industrial Classification Codes Numeric Listing |

10—Metal Mining

1011	Iron Ores
1021	Copper Ores
1031	Lead & Zinc Ores
1041	Gold Ores
1044	Silver Ores
1061	Ferroalloy Ores Except Vanadium
1081	Metal Mining Services
1094	Uranium, Radium & Vanadium Ores
1099	Metal Ores Nec

12—Coal Mining

1221	Bituminous Coal & Lignite—Surface
1222	Bituminous Coal—Underground
1231	Anthracite Mining
1241	Coal Mining Services

13—Oil & Gas Extraction

1311	Crude Petroleum & Natural Gas
1321	Natural Gas Liquids
1381	Drilling Oil & Gas Wells
1382	Oil & Gas Exploration Services
1389	Oil & Gas Field Services Nec

14—Nonmetallic Minerals Except Fuels

1411	Dimension Stone
1422	Crushed & Broken Limestone
1423	Crushed & Broken Granite
1429	Crushed & Broken Stone Nec
1442	Construction Sand & Gravel
1446	Industrial Sand

Source: Ward Business Directory of U.S. Private and Public Companies, 1995.

government. These include specific census data (e.g., censuses of agriculture or construction), census reports (e.g., the *County and City Data Book*), U.S. Department of Commerce data, and a variety of additional government reports.

There are two notes of caution when using census or other secondary data. First, census data is collected only every 10 years with slight periodic updates, so researchers always need to be aware of the timeliness issue of census data. Second, census data can be misleading. Not every person or household is reflected in census data. Those who have recently changed residences or were simply not available for contact at census time are not included in census data.

A final source of information available through the U.S. government is the *Catalog of Government Publications* compiled by Marcive, Inc. This catalog indexes major market research reports for a variety of domestic and international industries, markets, and institutions. It also provides an index of publications available to researchers from July 1976 to the current month and year.

Secondary Sources of Business Information

It is virtually impossible to document all of the sources of secondary data available from businesses. Most sources are, however, classified by some index, directory, or standardized guidebook, so it is well within the interest of the researcher to consult a directory of business information. Such directories identify statistical information, trade associations, trade journals, market characteristics, environmental trends, and so on.

EXHIBIT 4.6	**Common Government Documents Used as Secondary Data Sources**

U.S. Census Data

Census of Agriculture

Census of Construction

Census of Government

Census of Manufacturing

Census of Mineral Industries

Census of Retail Trade

Census of Service Industries

Census of Transportation

Census of Wholesale Trade

Census of Housing

Census of Population

U.S. Census Reports

Guide to Industrial Statistics

County and City Data Book

Statistical Abstract of the U.S.

Fact Finders for the Nation

Guide to Foreign Trade Statistics

U.S. Department of Commerce Data

U.S. Industrial Outlook

County Business Patterns

State and Metro Area Data Book

Business Statistics

Handbook of Cyclable Indicators

Monthly Labor Review

Measuring Markets: Federal and State Statistical Data

Additional Government Reports

Aging America: Trends and Population

Economic Indicators

Economic Report of the President

Federal Reserve Bulletin

Statistics of Income

Survey of Current Business

The following are some commonly used sources of business information:

Business Organizations, Agencies, and Publications Directory.

Directory of Corporate Affiliation.

Fortune Magazine Directory.

International Directory of Corporate Affiliations.

Million Dollar Directory.

F & S Index: Domestic, International, Europe.

Standard and Poor's Registry of Corporations.

Thomas' Register of American Manufacturers.

Marketing Economics Guide.

Business Index.

Business Periodical Index.

Gathering market information through business sources, in most cases, will lead the researcher to three widely used sources of data: *Sales and Marketing Management*'s *Survey of Buying Power, Editors and Publishers Market Guide*, and *Source Book of Demographics and Buying Power for Every Zip Code in the U.S.A.* Excellent sources of international secondary data are listed in the Global Insights Box.

GLOBAL INSIGHTS · SOURCES FOR INTERNATIONAL SECONDARY DATA

Marketing Survey Index (includes a variety of international multiclient reports).

Consumer Japan (examines most major product markets in Japan).

Consumer Europe (examines many major product markets for Europe).

International Marketing Data and Statistics.

European Marketing Data.

The Worldwide Government Directory (provides data and information on 100 international agencies).

Beri's Risk Service (provides data and information on international financial markets and risk).

Business Line France (300 financial databases throughout the world).

A.R.K. (illustrates data on 14 major industries in Europe and 2,000 public companies in Europe).

Sales and Marketing Management's Survey of Buying Power

One popular source of information on area buying power is *Sales and Marketing Management*'s *Survey of Buying Power.* Published annually, the survey covers all metropolitan statistical areas (MSA), counties, cities, and states in the United States. It provides data on retail sales by merchandise categories, total retail sales by area, population projections, and effective buying income. Exhibit 4.7 shows typical data from the survey for the auto market in three metropolitan areas in Tennessee. All such statistics are updated annually and include five-year projections.[13]

Effective buying income (EBI) A measure of personal income less federal, state, and local taxes.

Among the most useful data the survey provides are estimates of an area's effective buying income. **Effective buying income (EBI)** is a measure of personal income (wages, salaries, interest, dividends, and profits) less federal, state, and local taxes.[14] It is expressed as a total dollar amount.

Buying power index (BPI) A weighted average of population, retail sales, and effective buying income of an area.

When combined with retail sales and population size, the EBI is an overall indicator of an area's buying power, known as the **buying power index (BPI).** The BPI is expressed as a percentage of total U.S. sales. The higher the BPI, the greater the ability of the market area to generate spendable income. For example, in Exhibit 4.7, the BPI for Nashville (.4131) is greater than those of Memphis (.3692) and Knoxville (.2362), which indicates that Nashville has a greater market potential for new auto purchases.

The BPI actually is a weighted average of the population, retail sales, and effective buying income of an area. Each of these criteria is assigned a weight based on its importance to the study at hand. For example, if population is the most important variable, it should receive the highest weight. Using weights of 5, 3, and 2, the buying power index can be calculated as follows:

$$BPI = \frac{(\text{Population} \times 5) + (\text{Retail sales} \times 3) + (\text{Effective buying income} \times 2)}{10 \text{ (Sum of the weights)}}$$

A major drawback of the BPI is that it is useful only for estimating the potential for general merchandise categories sold at median prices. For specialized merchandise, such as men's shoes, a customized BPI must be constructed.[15]

Editors and Publishers Market Guide

An additional source of secondary information on buying potential is the *Editors and Publishers Market Guide.* This guide provides much the same information as the *Survey of Buying Power,* plus some unique city-by-city variables useful in making comparisons. As

EXHIBIT 4.7	Example of Effective Buying Income for Automobiles in Three Selective Cities

	Knoxville	Memphis	Nashville
December 31, 199X			
Total population	608,400	990,600	997,500
Number of people age 18 and over	467,860	712,421	745,132
Percentage of population age 18 and over	76.9	71.9	74.7
Number of households	239,300	360,930	380,500
Total effective buying income (EBI) (000)	$7,601,304	$12,106,512	$14,218,794
Medium household (EBI)	$23,564	$24,834	$38,687
Per capita (EBI)	$12,494	$12,221	$14,254
Percentage of households with $35,000–$49,999 EBI	15.3	16.3	18.5
Total retail sales (000)	$4,776,261	$7,055,066	$7,828,318
Buying power index	.2362	.3692	.4131
Percentage of U.S. EBI	.2172	.3460	.4063
Percentage of U.S. retail sales	.2643	.3904	.4337
Automobile retail sales 199X (000)	$1,203,682	$1,872,298	$1,982,461
Projections for December 31, 200X			
Total population	627,800	1,021,600	1,059,600
Percentage of change in population	3.0	3.6	7.3
Total EBI (000)	$11,088,408	$17,471,724	$21,218,110
Percentage of change in total EBI	54.5	55.5	61.0
Total retail sales (000)	$5,778,454	$8,682,189	$10,624,682
Percentage of change in retail sales	29.4	30.9	36.4
Buying power index	.2337	.3644	.4306

Source: Sales and Marketing Management, Survey of Buying Power, 1997.

Exhibit 4.8 shows, the guide includes information of infrastructure, transportation, principal industries, banks, and retail outlets. Such information provides the researcher with a detailed profile of economic activity within a given geographic area. These data are normally used for comparison purposes when selecting markets for new stores or product introductions.

Source Book of Demographics and Buying Power for Every Zip Code in the U.S.A.

The *Source Book of Demographics and Buying Power for Every Zip Code in the U.S.A.* provides the researcher with information on population, socioeconomic characteristics, buying power, and other demographic characteristics for zip code areas across the United States. Each zip code area is analyzed relative to its consumption potential across a variety of product categories, and a purchasing potential index is calculated. This index is based on a national average score of 100.[16] For example, if zip code 55959 generates a score of 110 for furniture consumption, then that zip code area has a 10 percent greater potential to purchase furniture than the U.S. average.

EXHIBIT 4.8 **Sample Listing of Available Data from *Editors and Publishers Market Guide***

KNOXVILLE

1-LOCATION: Knox County (MSA). E&P Map-2. County Seat. Industrial, wholesale, and energy center. At the juncture of the Holston and French Broad Rivers, which form Louden Lake of TVA System. (Tennessee River); 112 mi. from Chattanooga; 285 mi. S. of Cincinnati, OH; 198 mi. E of Nashville; 191 mi. N of Atlanta, GA: U.S. Hwys. 11, 25@, 70, 129, 441, I-40, I-75, I-81; State Hwys. 33, 71, 127, 139.

2-TRANSPORTATION: Railroads-Southern; Louisville & Nashville (L&N)
Motor Freight Carriers-39
Intercity Bus Lines-Knoxville Transit Corp. (City); Suburban; Greyhound; Trailways.
Airlines-United; Delta; Tenn. Airways; American Eagle; ComAir; Metro Express; USAir; TWE; United Press.

3-POPULATION
Corp. City 90 Cen. 165, 121; E&P 92 Est. 163, 139
CZ-ABC: (80) 252,539
JRTZ-ABC: (80) 739, 539
County 90 Cen. 335, 749; E&P 92 Est. 345, 679
MSA 90 Cen. 604, 816; E&P 92 Est. 624, 549
City & RTZ-ABC: (80) 992, 059
Demographic Information available from Newspaper. See paragraph 14.

4- HOUSEHOLDS:

City 90 Cen. 61, 727; E&P 92 Est. 69,987
CZ-ABC: (80) 95,466
RTZ-ABC: (90) 258, 192
County 90 Cen. 139, 896; E&P 92 Est. 144, 033
MSA 90 Cen. 245, 936: E&P 92 Est. 253, 932
City & RTZ-ABC: (80)

5-BANKS: NUMBER DEPOSITS

Commercial 7 $1,594,000,000
Savings & Loan 7 $788,719,000

6-PASSENGER AUTOS: Knox County 255,100

7-ELECTRIC METERS: Residence 140,685

8-GAS METERS: Residence 23,163

9-PRINCIPAL INDUSTRIES: Industry, No. of Wage Earners (Av. Wkly. Wage)-Textiles 3,200 ($225); Food 4,100 ($270); Stone & Clay Prods. 1,600 ($332); Apparel 7,600 ($261); Mach. 2,700 ($375).
Principal Industrial Pay Days-Fri, 1st, 15th, 26th.

10-CLIMATE: Min. & Max. Temp.-Spring 28-84; Summer 44-93; Fall 25-90; Winter 11-69. First killing frost, Oct. 20; last killing frost, Apr.14.

Nearby Shopping Centers

Name (No. of Stores)	Miles from Downtown	Principal Stores
Bearden (24)	6	
Broadway (28)	3	Kroger, Food City
Broadway Sq.	6	Revco
Black Oak	10	Kmart, Kroger
Chapman Hwy. (15)	12	Kmart, Kroger
Clinton Hwy. (15)	6	Kmart, Revco, Winn-Dixie
Plaza (18)	9	Kroger, Winn-Dixie
Holston (18)	4	Hall-Brown, Food City
Kingston (10)	4	Long's, Food City
Northgate (7)	5	Winn-Dixie, Revco, Food City
Southgate (12)	7	Food City
Suburban (27)	8	Toys "R" Us
West Haven (15)	7	
Western Piz. (33)	3	Hall-Brown
West Town (90)	8	Hess's, JC Penny, Proffit's, Sears
Walker Springs (8)	12	Kroger, SupeRx
Cedar Springs	10	Winn-Dixie, Revco
Cedar Bluff	10	Food City
Knox Piz.	4	Kroger, SupeRx
Halls (10)	10	
Halls Piz. (11)	10	Winn-Dixie, Revco
East Towne Mall	8	Hess's, Proffitt's, JC Penny, Sears, Serv. Mdse.

Principal Shopping Days- Department Stores-Sun, Mon., Fri., Sat; Foods-Thur., Fri., Sat.
Stores Open Evenings- Dept. -Mon., Thur.; Sears, Discount Stores and West Town- Mon. Through Sat.; Food-Every night until 9 p.m.
Stores Open Sundays-Some food & supermarkets: Kmart; West Town Mall; East Towne Mall.

13-RETAIL OUTLETS: Department Stores-Hess's 5; Sears 4; JC Penney 6; Ira A. Watson 2; Profitt's 5; Hills 3.
Discount Stores- Kmart 11; Service Mdse. 2; Target 2; Wal-Mart 5.
Variety Stores- Woolworth; Emery
Chain Drug Stores-Revco; SupeRx 7; Begleys; Walgreens 2; Rite Aid 2.

Chain Supermarkets- Kroger 15; Winn-Dixie 8; A&P; Inghles 5; Bi-Lo 3; Pilot 12; Red Foods 2; Food Lion 4; Food City 30.
Other Chain Stores-Firestone; Western Auto; Sterchi's Furn.; National Shirt; Lerner; Shoes: Hill Bros., Hardy, Jaman, Bell Bros. Kinney's, Baker's;Zales Jewelers; Richman Bros., General Nutrition; Hickory Farms; Merle Norman; Brooks Fashions; Casual Corner; Singer Co.; Lillie Rubin; Ups & Downs; Radio Shack.

14-NEWSPAPERS: NEWS-SENTINEL (m) 104,545; JOURNAL (e) 40, 9046; NEWS-SENTINEL (S) 172, 759; Mar. 31, 1991 ABC.
Local Contact for Advertising and Merchandising Data: Bruce Hartman, Adv. Dir., NEWS-SENTINEL and JOURNAL, PO Box 59038, Knoxville, TN 37950-9038; Tel. (615) 523-3131.
National Representative: Sawyer-Ferguson-Walker Co.

Source: Editors and Publishers Market Guide, 1995.

Statistical Sources of Information

Statistical sources of secondary data can lead the researcher to specific statistical publications or can provide actual reprints of data extracted from numerous other secondary data sources. If actual data are located in the sourcebook, rather than in indexed references, these sources can save considerable research time. The following are examples of statistical data sources:

> *Merchandising: "Statistical and Marketing Report."*
>
> *Standard and Poor's Industrial Surveys.*
>
> *Data Sources for Business and Market Analysis.*
>
> *American Statistics Index.*
>
> *Statistical Reference Index.*
>
> *Federal Statistical Directory.*

Commercial Publications and Newspapers

Newspapers and commercial publications (*Time, Newsweek, Forbes, Fortune*) are important sources of secondary information. Because these publications are circulated on a daily, weekly, or monthly basis, the information they contain is extremely recent. In addition, many publications are archived in some manner, allowing the researcher access to historical information. The problem with commercial publications and newspapers is volume. A recent estimation suggested that more than 700 business-related commercial publications are in circulation.[17] Many of these publications, especially newspapers, are not indexed in traditional reference books. Those that do provide indexing are usually associated with major metropolitan markets. For example, the following newspapers are indexed from 1979 to present:

> *The New York Times.*
>
> *The Wall Street Journal.*
>
> *Christian Science Monitor.*
>
> *Los Angeles Times.*
>
> *Chicago Tribune.*
>
> *Boston Globe.*
>
> *Atlanta Constitution.*

The *Business Periodical Index* (part of the list on p. 102) is the primary index for commercial publications.

Syndicated Sources of Secondary Data

A major trend in marketing research is that toward a greater dependency on what are called syndicated (or commercial) data sources. The rationale for this is quite simple. Companies can obtain a wealth of information across a variety of industries at a relatively low cost. Also, because most of the data contained in these sources were collected at point of purchase, the information represents actual purchase behavior rather than purchase intentions.

It is interesting to note that in the Society of Competitive Intelligence Professionals, mentioned earlier in this chapter, 81 percent of marketing research firms said they purchase and use secondary research reports from commercial vendors. In addition, they reported spending approximately 8 to 10 hours per week analyzing syndicated data. This suggests that, while traditional paper-based and networking information sources remain the norm, syndicated reports available for purchase online are rapidly gaining popularity. It is also reported that secondary researchers spend an annual average of $14,300 for commercial or syndicated data.[18]

Characteristics of Syndicated Data Sources

Syndicated (or commercial) data Data that have been compiled according to some standardized procedure; provides customized data for companies, such as market share, ad effectiveness, and sales tracking.

Syndicated (or commercial) data normally consist of data that have been collected and compiled according to some standardized procedure. In most cases these data are collected for a particular business or company, with a specific reason or purpose driving the data collection procedure. This information is then sold to different client companies in the form of tabulated results or reports communicated specifically for a client's research needs. Commonly, these reports are personalized and tailored to the client by reporting units. For example, reports can be organized by geographic region, sales territory, market segment, product class, or brand. In order for these data sources to be effective, suppliers of commercial/syndicated data must have in-depth knowledge of the industry and generate timely data. Suppliers have traditionally employed one of two methods of data collection: consumer panels and store audits. A third method that is gaining ground—optical-scanner technology—will be discussed in a later chapter.

Consumer Panels

Consumer panels Large samples of households that provide specific, detailed data for an extended period of time.

Consumer panels consist of large samples of households that have agreed to provide specific, detailed data for an extended period of time. Data provided by these panels usually consists of product purchase information or media habits. As they exist today, panels normally report information relative to the consumer package goods industry, but, as mentioned above, they are gradually being replaced by optical-scanner technology.

Panels are normally designed and developed by marketing research firms. As previously mentioned, panels follow a fairly rigorous and standardized data collection method. Panel respondents are required to record detailed behaviors, at the time of occurrence, on a highly structured questionnaire. This instrument will normally contain a large number of questions related directly to actual product purchases or media exposure. This is normally an ongoing procedure, whereby respondents report data back to the company on a weekly or monthly basis.

Panel data are then sold to a variety of clients, after being personalized and tailored to the client's research needs. There are a variety of benefits in using panel data as a source of marketing research information. These normally include (1) Lower cost than primary data collection methods; (2) Rapid availability and timeliness; (3) Accurate reporting of socially sensitive expenditure (i.e., products may include beer, liquor, cigarettes, generic brands); and (4) High level of specificity (i.e., data pertain to actual products purchased or media habits, not merely intentions or propensities to purchase).

When selecting a consumer panel data source, researchers should consider a number of issues. Reporting errors by respondents, inability to answer ambiguous questions, and forgetting brand names or product characteristics are inherent problems with these sources. More specifically, consumer panels tend to suffer from three primary weaknesses:

1. **Sampling error.** Most consumer panels underrepresent minorities. In fact, many panels report a sampling distribution that is highly skewed to white, middle-class respondents.

2. **Turnover.** No one panel member is obligated to stay on the panel for the entire duration. Many members leave the panel, have other family members perform the response activities, or simply don't respond at all. This feature seriously jeopardizes the representativeness and internal validity of the data.

3. **Response bias.** Many panel respondents have a tendency to answer questions in a socially desirable manner, knowing their purchases are being scrutinized. Leaving certain questions blank and recording wrong answers can lead to high levels of response bias among the panel data.

As suggested above, two types of panel-based data sources exist: those reflecting actual purchases of products and services and those reflecting media habits. The discussions below provide some examples of consumer panel data sources and then some examples of media panel data sources.

EXAMPLES OF CONSUMER PANEL DATA SOURCES. A variety of companies offer panel-based purchasing data. Two of the largest companies are National Family Opinion (NFO) and the National Purchase Diary (NPD) Group. NPD collects continuous data from a national sample consisting of approximately 15,000 members. Data collection centers on consumer attitudes and awareness of such products as toys, apparel, textiles, sporting goods, athletic footwear, automotive products, home electronics, and cameras.[19]

Three of NPD's most commonly used data sources are the Consumer Report on Eating Share Trends (CREST); National Eating Trends (NET); and a service which provides data on the food service industry in general. CREST is comprised of over 14,000 households that report data on restaurant habits. NET provides continuous tracking of in-home food and beverage consumption patterns. ISL, a Canadian subsidiary of the NPD Group, provides similar purchase data through the Consumer Panel of Canada.

NPD with U.S. custom service uses a 350,000-household data source for providing forecasting models, determining market structure and brand loyalty, and helping with concept and product development.

National Family Opinion (NFO) maintains a consumer panel of over 450,000 households, or 1.2 million people, to conduct product tests; concept tests; and attitude, awareness, and brand-usage studies. In connection with the panel, NFO offers a proprietary software program called Smart-System. This system allows clients to access and analyze complex information quickly, with easy cross-referencing on major data variables. In addition, NFO maintains highly targeted panels referred to as the Hispanic Panel, the Baby Panel, the Mover Panel, and SIP (Share of Intake Panel on Beverage Consumption).

The following list describes additional companies and the consumer panels they maintain:

- Market Facts, Inc., provides panel data for forecasting models, brand equity/loyalty models, and brand tracking information.

- The Bases Group specializes in new-product planning, evaluation, and forecasting using consumer panels and simulated test markets.

- J. D. Power and Associates maintains a consumer panel of car and light-truck owners to provide data on product quality, satisfaction, and vehicle dependability.

- Roper Starch Worldwide provides data on consumption patterns for the 6- to 18-year-old age market.

- Creative and Response Research Services, known primarily for maintaining a consumer panel called Kidspeak, provides advertising and brand tracking among children.

- Chilton Research Services conducts highly specialized research for the automotive, financial, and health care industries.

- Yankelovich Partners, Inc., maintains the Yankelovich monitor system used for monitoring values in the United States.

EXAMPLES OF MEDIA PANEL DATA SOURCES. Media panels and consumer panels are similar in procedure, panel composition, and design. They differ only in that media panels primarily measure media consumption habits as opposed to product or brand consumption. As with consumer panels, a multitude of media panels exist. The intent of this section is to provide examples of the more commonly used syndicated media panel data sources.

Nielsen Media Research is by far the most widely known and accepted source of media panel data. The flagship service of Nielsen is the National Television Index (NIT). Based on a 5,000-household sample, the NIT provides an estimation of national television audiences measuring "ratings" and "share." Ratings refer to the percentage of households that have at least one television set tuned to a program for at least 6 of every 15 minutes a program is aired. Share constitutes the percentage of households that have a television tuned to one specific program at one specific time.[20] Data are collected on television, cable, and home video viewing habits through an electronic device, called a people meter, connected to a television set. The people meter, electronically and continuously, monitors and records when a television set is turned on, what channels are being viewed, how much time is spent on each channel, and who is watching. The data are communicated back to the central computer by telephone.

The primary purpose of the NIT data is to assist media planners in determining audience volume, demographics, and viewing habits. This information is then used for calculating media efficiency by way of determining cost per thousand (CPM), that is, how much it costs to reach 1,000 viewers. CPM represents a program's ability to deliver the largest target audience at the lowest cost.

While a majority of data are collected by the people meter, Nielsen still maintains diary panels in 211 local markets measuring the same media habits. In addition, Nielsen also operates an 800-household sample of Hispanic TV viewers designed to measure Spanish-language media usage in the United States.

The Arbitron Company is primarily a media research firm that conducts ongoing data collection for the electronic media. Arbitron is organized into five media research business units.[21] Arbitron Radio provides radio audience data for 261 local market areas. Utilizing a 2 million–plus customer panel, Arbitron Radio collects over 1 million weekly listening diaries, which comprise the foundation for Arbitron Radio's station rating reports. The data are primarily used by media planners, advertising agencies, and advertisers. These facilitation agencies gain access to the data via two computer applications called Maximizer and MediaPro.

Scarborough Research was acquired by Arbitron in 1995 and provides syndicated data on local media, consumer listening habits, and retail advertising impact data across 58 of the major U.S. markets. Currently, 600 newspapers, radio stations, television stations, and cable systems are predominant users of this syndicated data source.

The following list describes media panels maintained by other companies:

- Local Motion Retail Ratings was introduced in 1994 and provides syndicated data on TV, radio, and cable systems. Data collection is a combination of media diary panels and telephone panels collected in 11 market areas across the United States.

- Arbitron Newmedia provides syndicated data on emerging market segments regarding electronic media usage, specifically interactive TV, online services, interactive cable systems, and direct broadcast satellites.

- Media Marketing Technologies, acquired by Arbitron in 1995, has designed a database known as Mediamaps. Based on a media diary panel of 100,000 listeners, Mediamaps profiles prospective radio station listeners, identified and profiled on geodemographic mapping dimensions.

- Macro International, Inc., offers four syndicated data sources developed on a consumer media/purchase panel of more than 100,000 respondents. Europinion is a database, begun in 1992, providing quarterly reports on consumption attitudes and behaviors in Eastern European countries.

- Simmons Marketing Research Bureau (SMRB) Group, Ltd., has been publishing its *Annual Report on Media and Markets* for the past 30 years. Simmons also offers syndicated reports tailored to teenage, child, and Hispanic markets.

- ASI Marketing Research, Inc., maintains two advertising copy syndicated data sources. Targeted Copy Testing (TCT) measures advertising recall and copy effectiveness. Kid Copy Testing (KCT) uses a touch-screen, multimedia, digital voice technology to capture moment-by-moment response measures on the creative content of advertising directed to children 6 to 11 years of age.

Store Audits

Store audits   Formal examination and verification of how much of a particular product or brand has been sold at the retail level.

Store audits consist of formal examination and verification of how much of a particular product or brand has been sold at the retail level. Based on a collection of participating retailers (normally discount, supermarket, and drugstore retailers), audits are performed on product or brand movement in return for detailed activity reports and cash compensation to the retailer. The audits then operate as a secondary data source; clients can acquire the data relative to industry, competition, product, or specific brand.

Store audits provide two unique benefits: precision and timeliness. Many of the biases of consumer panels are not found within the context of store audits. By design, store audits measure product and brand movement directly at the point of sale (normally at the retail level). Reflected in these measures are accurate, precise data regarding sales volume, sales of competing products, sales for new products, and other competitive activities.

Also, data collected through the store audit process can be made available and communicated on a moment-by-moment basis. Actual sales and competitive activities can be reported within hours after the store audit is completed, making the data timely and readily available to potential users.

One inherent problem of the traditional store audit is representativeness. In most audit situations only 75 to 85 percent of retail stores are involved in the process.[22] Rarely can any audit be performed at all stores in any given area. Therefore, what is normally reported can be somewhat misleading. Areas in which product sales are extremely high or low may be ignored for the audit process. While this may not affect inferences regarding national sales averages, it can clearly contaminate certain sales figures at the regional or local level. Despite this inherent problem, store audits do provide valuable data.

DATA GATHERING IN THE STORE AUDIT. Key variables being measured in the store audit normally include beginning and ending inventory levels, sales receipts, price levels, price inducements, local advertising, and point-of-purchase displays. Collectively, these data allow users of store audit services to generate information on the following factors:

1. Product/brand sales in relation to competition.

2. Direct sales and inventory levels at retail.

3. Effectiveness of shelf space and P-O-P displays.

4. Sales at various price points and levels.

5. Effectiveness of in-store promotions and point-of-sale coupons.

6. Competitive marketing practices.

7. Direct sales by store type, product location, territory, and region.

Two of the major providers of in-store audit services are AC Nielsen (Nielsen Retail Index) and Information Resources (Infoscan). Collectively, these two organizations conduct over 150,000 store audits in more than 40,000 separate retail locations. The Nielsen Retail Index provides information on a wide range of causal marketing factors that affect consumer responses to grocery, health and beauty, drug, and beverage products. Nielsen audits are developed on a stratified sampling procedure of store size, type, population, and geographic location. Actual stores used in the audit are randomly selected with the designed strata in which they reside. Audits are normally performed on a monthly basis at the point-of-sale level.

Information Resources, through Infoscan, provides census-based information rather than information based on a sample of representative stores. Through the Infoscan census, all stores within a particular retail chain (e.g., Wal-Mart, Kroger, Kmart) are audited. Information from the audit is then compiled and disseminated to each store within the chain for specific, store-level marketing applications. The data are also used within specific industries for the development of customer response programs at the manufacturer or wholesale level.

A variety of smaller audit services exist, such as Audits and Surveys, Inc., which provides syndicated product movement data in the automotive, sporting goods, home improvement, and entertainment industries. Through the audit service called National Total Market, Audits and Surveys provides a retail census of distribution for any specific company (AutoZone, Hand City, etc.) and in-store data on shelf-space availability, brand-name sales, mystery-shopper programs, and in-store promotional impacts.

The Future of Secondary Data Sources

Although this chapter has focused on traditional secondary data sources, 90 percent of the information referenced here currently exists online. As the technology of information management becomes more acceptable and accessible, more and more secondary data will be available at the push of a computer key. This is already happening, and is more fully described in Chapter 5. More important, as communication technology begins to merge with computer technology (interactive television and shopping, two-way satellite communications, at-home on-demand shopping), the amount of secondary data is expected to mushroom. Although this increase may not be the purpose of the technology, it will be the result of the interaction process. More actual purchase information than ever before will become available in a timely and cost-efficient manner.

As more and more organizations begin to realize the full value of database development and information systems management, they will be able to customize secondary data sources (see the In the Field box).

A CLOSER LOOK AT RESEARCH   **In the Field**

As computer technology continues to change and as more people become versed in Boolean search strategies for databases and learn to cope with a society rich in information, the role of secondary research will continue to change. Evidence suggests that secondary data researchers will become more involved with a company's internal technology department as they begin to tap into real-time inventory and client or production systems to add more customization of information to the secondary data that they also find online. Try it for yourself. Go to the Internet and contact www.freedgar.com. Here you will find hundreds of documents on U.S. companies that are not only updated daily but also highly customized from a secondary data perspective.

SUMMARY OF LEARNING OBJECTIVES

Understand how secondary data fit into the marketing research process.

The task of any competent marketing researcher is to solve the problem in which the marketing research task was undertaken in the shortest time, at the least cost, with the highest level of accuracy. Therefore, before any marketing research project is conducted, it is the obligation of the researcher to seek out existing information that may facilitate a decision or outcome for a company. Existing data are commonly called secondary data.

Demonstrate how secondary data can be used in problem solving.

If secondary data are to be used to assist the decision-making process or problem-solving ability of the manager, they need to be evaluated on six fundamental principles: (1) purpose (how relevant is the data to achieving the specific research objective at hand?); (2) accuracy (are the data collected, measured, and reported in a manner consistent with quality research practices?); (3) consistency (do multiple sources of the data exist?); (4) credibility (how was the data obtained? what is the source of the data?); (5) methodology (are the methodological procedures used to collect the data proper in that the quality of the data is high?); and (6) biases (was the data-reporting procedure tainted by some hidden agenda or underlying motivation to advance some public or private concern?).

List sources of traditional internal secondary data.

Secondary data are usually sorted into three categories. First are the internal accounting or financial records of the company. These normally consist of sales invoices, accounts receivable reports, and quarterly sales reports. Other forms of internal data include past marketing research studies, customer credit applications, warranty cards, and employee exit interviews.

Demonstrate how to obtain external sources of secondary data.

Because of the volume of external data available, researchers need to plan the steps of ensuring that the right data are located and extracted. A simple guideline to follow is called the GO-CART approach: define *goals* that the secondary data need to achieve; specify *objectives* behind the secondary search process; define specific *characteristics* of data that are to be extracted; document all *activities* necessary to find, locate, and extract the data sources; focus on *reliable* sources of data; and *tabulate* all the data that were extracted.

List sources of external secondary data.

Secondary data exist in a wide variety of sources. The most common forms of external data are standard industrial classification (SIC) codes, government documents (which include census reports), business directories, trade journals, statistical sources, commercial publications, and newspapers.

Understand the availability and use of syndicated sources of secondary data.

Syndicated (or commercial) data sources consist of data that have been systematically collected and compiled according to some standardized procedure. Suppliers of syndicated data have traditionally employed one of two approaches in collecting data: consumer panels and store audits. (A third approach, optical-scanner technology, will be discussed in a later chapter.) With most syndicated data sources, the objective is quite clear: to measure point-of-sale purchase behaviors or to measure media habits.

Understand the changing focus of secondary data usage.
The computerization of secondary data is revolutionizing the marketing research industry. Online services are making available more data that are more applicable to business needs than ever before. In addition, databases and information systems are bringing the use of secondary data to monumental proportions. Technology will make secondary data more customized and applicable for many businesses; therefore, the next chapter will focus on this new aspect of secondary data.

KEY TERMS AND CONCEPTS

Buying power index (BPI) 103

Consumer panels 107

Effective buying income (EBI) 103

External secondary data 91

Internal secondary data 91

Secondary data 91

Standard industrial classification (SIC) codes 99

Store audits 110

Syndicated (or commercial) data 107

REVIEW QUESTIONS

1. What characteristic separates secondary data from primary data? What are three sources of secondary data?

2. Explain why a company should use all potential sources of secondary data before initiating primary data collection procedures.

3. List the six fundamental principles used to assess the validity of secondary data.

4. List the three methods of data collection normally used by the suppliers of commercial data sources, and discuss the advantages and disadvantages associated with each.

5. How can information from a sales activity report be used to improve a company's marketing research efforts?

6. Briefly discuss the GO-CART approach of secondary data search management.

DISCUSSION QUESTIONS

1. **EXPERIENCE THE INTERNET.** Go online to your favorite browser (e.g., Netscape) and find the home page for your particular state. For example, www.mississippi.com would get you to the home page for the state of Mississippi. Once there, seek out the category that gives you information on county and local statistics. Select the county where you reside and obtain the vital demographic and socioeconomic data available. Provide a demographic profile of the residents in your community.

2. **EXPERIENCE THE INTERNET.** Go to the home page of the U.S. census, www.census.gov. Select the category Current Economic Indicators and browse the data provided.

3. What specific industry information could executives at Procter & Gamble obtain from the *Source Book of Demographics and Buying Power for Every Zip Code in the U.S.A.?* How would this information improve Procter & Gamble's marketing strategies?

4. You are planning to open a coffee shop in one of two areas in your local community. Conduct a secondary data search on key variables that would allow you to make a logical decision on which area is best suited for your proposed coffee shop.

ENDNOTES

1. "Good and Not So Good," *IAC Newsletter Database* 8, no. 15, April 21, 1997.

2. "Marketing Research Reports On Line," *Database,* April 1996.

3. Ibid.

4. American Marketing Association, *Definition of Marketing Terms.*

5. "The Dollar Sign: Secondary Data," *Database,* May 1997.

6. Ibid.

7. "Marketing Research Costs and Benefits," *Marketing Research Magazine,* Fall 1997.

8. Ibid.

9. "Secondary Research," *Marketing Research Magazine,* Fall 1997.

10. William Pride and O. C. Ferrell, *Marketing,* 7th ed. (Boston: Houghton-Mifflin, 1996).

11. Ibid.

12. Ibid.

13. "Survey of Buying Power," *Sales and Marketing Management,* 1995.

14. Ibid.

15. Ibid.

16. *Source Book of Demographics and Buying Power for Every Zip Code in the U.S.A.,* 1997.

17. *The Wall Street Journal Index,* 1997.

18. Ibid.

19. National Purchase Diary, 10 K Report, 1997.

20. AC Nielsen Media Research, annual report, 1997.

21. Arbitron, Inc., annual report, 1997.

22. Ibid.

MARKETING RESEARCH ILLUSTRATION

UNDERSTANDING THE METHODOLOGY FOR SECONDARY DATA COLLECTION— A RETAIL GAP ANALYSIS

The purpose of this study is to estimate the residential buying power of the Orange Mound neighborhood and to determine the potential for business creation in the neighborhood. The emphasis is on retail businesses and service firms that draw their market primarily from household expenditures. Orange Mound and the surrounding retail trade area are included in the study. New businesses serving existing neighborhood consumer demand, or attracting shoppers from a larger trade area, can help revitalize the neighborhood by keeping income circulating in the community and by providing entrepreneurial opportunities. New businesses can also serve as a catalyst for other redevelopment efforts.

Method

The regional economic development center developed current estimates for total income and consumer expenditures for the Orange Mound neighborhood based on a combination of census data and published economic data. The 1990 household income ranges were adjusted to 1998 estimates based on an estimate for inflation and real income growth for the city. Estimated 1998 income range midpoints were then multiplied by the number of households in the community to arrive at an estimated aggregate household income for each of 25 income ranges. Income ranges were sufficiently narrow such that the midpoints would likely be very close to the average income for the range. Aggregate incomes for each income range was then multiplied by the appropriate ratio of household expenditures to household income from the Bureau of Labor Statistics Consumer Expenditure Survey.

This technique allows for a more accurate estimation of consumer spending, especially for areas with high proportions of low-income households. The expenditure worksheet (Table 1) shows an example of the calculation of total consumer expenditures for the neighborhood.

A similar technique was used to estimate current expenditures for the neighborhood trade area. However, as the trade area did not conform with census boundaries, Census Bureau income ranges could not be used and nine income ranges from the EQUIFAX database were substituted for the trade area outside the primary neighborhood. While somewhat less accurate than the narrow Census Bureau income ranges, this method still provides an equally reasonable estimate of the trade area's aggregate consumer expenditures.

Total consumer expenditures were allocated to individual categories of retail trade and services based on expenditure patterns from the Consumer Expenditure Survey, and actual sales data by industry for the designated MSA (1992 Census of Retail Trade, 1992 Census of Service Industries). The MSA was the lowest level of geography where complete industry sales were available at the two or three digit Standard Industrial Classification (SIC) level.

TABLE 4.1 — 1997 Income Range Estimates, Aggregate Income, and Estimated Aggregate Household Expenditures, Orange Mound Neighborhood

1989 Income Ranges[1]		1989–97 Income Adjustment[2]	Estimated 1997 Income Ranges		Orange Mound Households			Est. 1997 Midpoint HH Income	Estimated Aggregate Income	CES Ratio of Expenditures to Income[3]	CES Reference Group[4]	Estimated Aggregate Expenditures
Lower Limit	Upper Limit		Lower Limit	Upper Limit	CT 67	CT 68	Total					
$ 0	$ 4,999	$1.382	$ 0	$ 6,909	503	306	809	$ 3,454	$2,794,536	4.770	Same expend. as $5K–10K	$13,329,937
5,000	9,999	1.382	6,910	13,819	478	236	714	10,364	7,400,117	1.590	Midpoint $5k–$15k	11,766,185
10,000	12,499	1.382	13,820	17,274	170	95	265	15,547	4,119,904	1.360	Midpoint $10K–$20K	5,601,010
12,500	14,999	1.382	17,275	20,729	119	107	226	19,002	4,294,409	1.286	$15,000 to $19,999	5,522,025
15,000	17,499	1.382	20,730	24,184	160	105	265	22,457	5,951,054	1.097	$20,000 to $29,999	6,528,307
17,500	19,999	1.382	24,185	27,639	101	79	180	25,912	4,664,126	1.097	"	5,116,546
20,000	22,499	1.382	27,640	31,094	56	75	131	29,367	3,847,052	1.097	"	4,218,458
22,500	24,999	1.382	31,095	34,549	101	48	149	32,822	4,890,450	0.948	$30,000 to $39,999	4,636,146
25,000	27,499	1.382	34,550	38,004	118	30	148	36,277	5,368,968	0.948	"	5,089,781
27,500	29,999	1.382	38,005	41,459	23	15	38	39,732	1,509,809	0.948	"	1,431,603
30,000	32,499	1.382	41,460	44,914	62	69	131	43,187	5,657,472	0.858	$40,000 to $49,999	4,854,111
32,500	34,999	1.382	44,915	48,369	21	5	26	46,642	1,212,687	0.858	"	1,040,485
35,000	37,499	1.382	48,370	51,824	22	49	71	50,097	3,556,873	0.858	"	3,052,991
37,500	39,999	1.382	51,825	55,279	22	16	38	53,552	2,034,969	0.837	$50,000 to $69,999	1,703,269
40,000	42,499	1.382	55,280	58,734	27	7	34	57,007	1,938,232	0.837	"	1,622,300
42,500	44,999	1.382	58,735	62,189	9	13	22	60,462	1,330,160	0.837	"	1,113,344
45,000	47,499	1.382	62,190	65,644	7	9	16	63,917	1,022,669	0.837	"	855,974
47,500	49,999	1.382	65,645	69,099	16	0	16	67,372	1,077,949	0.837	"	902,243
50,000	54,999	1.382	69,100	76,009	33	7	40	72,554	2,902,172	0.649	$70,000 and over	1,883,510
55,000	59,999	1.382	76,010	82,919	0	19	19	79,464	1,509,822	0.649	"	979,874
60,000	74,999	1.382	82,920	103,649	14	28	42	93,284	3,917,941	0.649	"	2,542,744
75,000	99,999	1.382	103,650	138,199	10	0	10	120,924	1,209,243	0.649	"	784,874
100,000	124,999	1.382	138,200	172,749	0	8	8	155,474	1,243,794	0.649	"	807,300
125,000	149,999	1.382	172,750	207,299	0	0	0	190,024	0	0.649	"	0
150,000	211,800	1.382	207,300	292,708	0	4	4	250,004	1,000,015	0.649	"	649,072
Totals					2,072	1,330	3,402		$74,454,422	1.156		$86,032,090

Mean household income $21,885

Mean expenditure per household $25,289

(1) Income ranges from 1990 Census of Population & Housing.   (2) Income adjustment to account for inflation and growth in real income.   (3) Calculated from 1995 BLS Consumer Expenditure Survey (CES).
(4) CES household income group most closely matching the estimated 1997 household income range.

MARKETING RESEARCH CASE EXERCISE

RESEARCHING THE OPPORTUNITY TO OPEN A TCBY FRANCHISE

TCBY Enterprises, Inc. is a Delaware-based corporation that was organized in May of 1982. Today, the company operates from the principal address at 11300 Rodney Parham Road, Little Rock, Arkansas. TCBY is a publicly traded company on the NASDAQ over-the-counter market. Currently, the franchise operation resides with TCBY Systems, Inc., located at the TCBY Tower, 425 West Capitol Ave., Little Rock, Arkansas.

Company Background

TCBY stores offer soft-serve premium frozen yogurt as a treat, dessert, snack, or light meal item. Yogurt, a cultured milk product, has become increasingly popular both domestically and internationally, due to its low calorie and cholesterol content and its high nutritional value. Traditionally, most forms of frozen yogurt have a somewhat tart taste with an icy texture. TCBY, which uses Americana as its primary supplier, produces a sweet-tasting, smooth-textured yogurt comparable to a premium ice cream, yet containing all the health benefits associated with yogurt.

Americana currently produces TCBY frozen yogurt in over 20 traditional and specialty flavors. Chocolate and vanilla are available daily in all TCBY stores, along with two to four specialty flavors. TCBY yogurt is also served in a variety of methods, including cups, cones, waffle cones, sundaes, and shakes. In addition, yogurt can also be complemented with such items as cookies, crepes, and Belgian waffles. Most of the menu items are also served with a variety of toppings, including M&M's, Oreo cookies, Reese's Pieces, hot fudge, and natural fruits. All TCBY products are also sold in hand-packed freezer containers for take-home convenience.

TCBY stores are established in a variety of locations, including strip shopping centers, freestanding buildings (with or without drive-up windows), and regional shopping malls. Stores are primarily located in cities and small urban areas, especially communities with colleges or universities. TCBY stores range from 1,200 to 1,600 square feet, seat 24 to 44 customers, and cater to both carry-out and eat-in business. Most stores are open year-round.

At the end of fiscal year 1996, TCBY had 2,696 locations worldwide. It also had several thousand point-of-sale kiosks, such as in airport locations, worldwide. At the beginning of 1997, 314 new TCBY locations were under agreement. Most of the new store locations under development were expected to operate out of co-branded locations in conjunction with fast-food, petroleum, and convenience-store locations.

For additional financial information and a rich history of TCBY Enterprises, Inc., consult the company's Web page at www.tcby.com.

1. Prepare a thorough market feasibility study for opening a TCBY location in your area. Specifically, gather data, such as that listed in Exhibit 4.4, to assess the possibility of opening a TCBY franchise in your city.

2. Once you have collected the necessary market data, provide an assessment of the possible success of the business. Be sure to justify your decision based on the data you have collected.

CHAPTER 5

Learning Objectives

After reading this chapter, you will be able to

1. Understand the concept of electronic marketing research media.

2. Understand the impact of new electronic technology on secondary marketing research methods.

3. Outline the dimensions of the resources available on the information superhighway.

4. Understand several of the online services available to market researchers.

5. Demonstrate how to obtain secondary marketing research data.

Technology and the New Information Age

❝ On the one hand, everything is available. But on the other hand, *everything* is available.❞ [1]

ALFRED GLOSSGRENNER
Expert on online databases

The Value of Internet Information

Ancient ROM, or It's All Greek to Me

In 1987 a budding classical scholar from the University of Lausanne in Switzerland completed four years of intensive labor. She had spent countless hours searching ancient Greek writings in an effort to identify the sources of some 2,000 fragments of text written in medieval Europe. In the course of her research, the scholar found 600 sources. Unfortunately, all of the work she had carried out in libraries and archives was eclipsed just as she was preparing to write her doctoral dissertation. In just a few hours of work with an online database, she was able to locate every one of her sources, along with 300 more she had missed during her previous four years of labor.

Northwest Airlines Surveys Net Surfers

> All the future up and coming economies will progress by means of knowledge and information rather than by investing in heavy machinery. The more society becomes based on information the more you have to be connected to that information source, you cannot gain information through isolation.[2]
>
> JOSEPH LUNG
> Managing Director, ATC Dataquest
> (a market research consultancy
> based in Hong Kong)

Like all large business enterprises, Northwest Airlines has long been familiar with the the typical tools of communication. Telephones, fax machines, direct mail, frequent-flier bonus programs, and even symbolic communication devices such as the red airplane tail are old hat. But a new communication tool is being employed at Northwest: the Internet.

The airline has created an Internet Web site in an effort to inform current and potential fliers about Northwest. A Web site is akin to an information booth. Internet users can access the site any time of day or night, every day of the year. Web pages allow people to see and, in some instances, hear information. Northwest created its site in response to a survey conducted electronically. The company had posted an invitation to several electronic bulletin boards for Internet enthusiasts, or Net surfers, to take part in a market research survey.

Northwest now knows what has come to be common knowledge: most Net surfers are financially well-off white males under 40. Northwest also learned that the surfers travel at Christmas, like beach vacations, and want all flights to be on time more than anything else.

The most important finding for Northwest was that the survey worked. Northwest now knows that it can reach people through the Internet—more than 800 people responded to this one survey.

Northwest also realizes that the Internet is different from other forms of communication. Direct mail (through the postal service or mass faxes), television or radio advertising, and telemarketing are all intrusive forms of communication that impose upon the recipient. Communication through the Internet is passive. The recipient chooses to be exposed or not. This means that respondents are self-selected and therefore comprise nonrandom samples.

Because nonrandom sampling can skew survey results, Northwest likely will not make any significant business decisions based on its Internet survey. But, since the company's main purpose was to try out the new medium, the result was a success. However, Jon Austin, a spokesman for Northwest, admits that though this first foray into the Internet was exciting, the company has no idea what to do next. But, he says, "If nothing else, now we have people around the company thinking about it."

Value of Internet Research Information

The database used by the scholar whose work was described in the chapter opener was the Thesaurus Liguane Grecae, one of the first electronic databases established for humanities research. As the expense of using computers decreases and sophisticated programming becomes commonplace, even arcane research in the humanities is being forced to reckon with the electronic revolution. Whole libraries are being transformed into electronic domains in which computerized scanning can produce exhaustive searches at rapid speeds.

While moving to an electronic format seems today to be inevitable, the digitization of ancient Greek tomes that began in the 1970s may have seemed innovative at the time. A group of classical scholars at the University of California, Irvine, began with an extraordinary concept. They wanted to produce a database that contained every word of the surviving ancient Greek literature. This database would include some 3,000 authors and 66 million words! In addition, the UC Irvine group wanted the entire database to be searchable, accessible, and printable. In short, the idea was to make classical Greek literature available and useful to all classical scholars. Private patrons and the National Endowment for the Humanities aided the efforts, each contributing about half of the $7 million required to produce Thesaurus Liguane Grecae. In more than 1,400 locations around the world, a classicist can search the accumulated works for allusions or references. In addition, the Thesaurus Liguane Grecae can be purchased on optical disk for around $300.

When computers were just fairly fast calculators, classical researchers and market researchers had little use for them as data collection tools. Now that vast literary heritages and vast market information have been digitized, computers can be harnessed to scan these databases at inhuman speeds. Classical researchers and market researchers have a need to catch up. It is now clear that the electronic revolution has arrived at marketing research's doorstep.

At present, electronic databases are better for secondary research than for primary research. As the Northwest Airlines example showed, using electronic primary data collection methods has drawbacks. Not only were the demographics skewed for Northwest, but usage patterns were also skewed. The average frequent flier for Northwest travels internationally once a year. Respondents to the electronic survey traveled internationally five times a year. However, with a little imagination and with a little more time, primary research, even one-to-one exchanges with customers, will be possible. A prelude to this is illustrated in the Using Technology box.

This chapter is divided into four main sections. First is an introduction to the Internet, a critical component of the elusive and much-hyped information superhighway. Second is a discussion of several of the largest online databases. CompuServe is featured because it has the largest number of subscribers. Third is a detailed discussion of Lexis/Nexis, a commercial electronic database. While Lexis/Nexis is not the only electronic database available for market researchers, it is a powerful tool skilled researchers can use to capture large amounts of information from many sources in a short time. Finally, the chapter closes with an analysis of the strengths and weaknesses of electronic secondary market research.

The Internet

To understand the Internet, one must first understand the concept of the information superhighway. The information superhighway is little more than a clever name for a combination of new media technologies that involve the interaction of computing and telecommunications.

Powerful low-cost computing has made exhaustive searches of vast databases possible for market researchers. Until the advent of powerful computers and inexpensive computer-readable data to access, secondary market research was principally performed by manual searches of printed documents in a library. Such manual searches are expensive and are subject to human error. People make mistakes as they tire or become bored. Extensive library searches do become tiring and can become boring. Thus, these searches are prone

A CLOSER LOOK AT RESEARCH   Using Technology

The use of surveys to conduct market research has become commonplace through online services. Companies utilize Internet capabilities to build massive online databases that can then be accessed by Internet browsers for marketing research use. The following summary, taken from www.ideapro.com/research.html#7th, provides individuals and businesses information concerning one particular online survey. The results, which can be accessed through the Graphic, Visualization & Usability Center at Georgia Tech University, provide detailed accounts of Internet usage and viability.

Subject: The Graphic, Visualization & Usability Center's (GVU) 8th WWW User Survey

This new survey may be the most comprehensive yet performed on the Internet. About one-in-1,500 actual users of the Web were expected to participate in this survey. Information was gathered on a voluntary basis. The surveys took each participant about one half-hour to complete, so several thousands hours were spent submitting data . . .

Among the top findings this time around, the gender ratio continues to move closer and closer to par, with 40 percent of the U.S. respondents reporting being female (compared to 5 percent back in January 1994). Privacy now overshadows censorship as the number one most important issue facing the Internet, maybe in response to the tremendous amount of media coverage privacy issues have received in the past several months. Electronic commerce is taking off both in terms of the number of users shopping as well as the total amount people are spending via Internet based transactions. Just the same, security remains the number one reason Web users report for not purchasing over the Web. Supporting the notion that the Web has become an important tool to access information, 84 percent of the users report that they consider access to the Web indispensable, nearly the same percentage as those who feel e-mail is indispensable. That a technology could become so vital in such a short period is truly an awesome statement of the impact of the Web on our society.

What future improvements will be necessary for the Internet to continue this impressive growth pattern? What possible implications will the World Wide Web have on business strategies in the next century?

---

to errors of omission. The market researcher can easily overlook informative sources. Computers do not become tired or bored and can search at very high speeds relative to human search speeds. Recall the classical scholar from the chapter opener who spent four years reading in libraries and still missed 300 of the references she was seeking. The tireless computer found them.

The second technology integral to the information superhighway is telecommunications. Inexpensive and reliable telecommunications systems allow the market researcher to access data at geographically remote sites. In effect, computers can, and quite often do, search all over the world via telephone lines to find the information market researchers are seeking.

Internet A network of computers and computer networks, and the technology linking these into an information superhighway.

The **Internet** is the network that allows market researchers access to the information superhighway. The Internet is a network currently consisting of more than 48,000 computers and computer networks all over the world and the technology to link these networks. The World Wide Web (WWW) constitutes specific pages or sites on the Internet. Many experts consider the Internet synonymous with the information superhighway.

The Internet is the result of 1960s cold war defense planning. The Pentagon needed to find a way for an unlimited number of computers to communicate without the need of one central computer to manage the process. The defense planners were worried that a centralized computer network would be destroyed in the event of nuclear attack—sort of network decapitation. In 1969, the Pentagon funded the Arpanet, a network that used a new technology called packet-switching to link four research laboratories. Universities soon were added to the network, while additional software and communications tools were developed. One of the most powerful innovations was the Internet protocol, a communication protocol that allows any number of computer networks to join and act as one network. Thus, there is no need for a user to worry about which of the numerous independent specialists carry the information or what route the information will travel. This protocol gave its name to the Internet.[3]

Currently, the computer networking systems and subsystems cover the world. It is possible to browse through a remote library (even as far away as Japan) as easily as browsing through your own campus electronic directory. There is a delay in response as the electronic messages move across the myriad of networks from one computer to another, but usually this is negligible.

To a remarkable extent, much of this modern networking came about spontaneously, in some cases even accidentally. No single organization, business, institution, government, or individual owns the Internet. In fact, the Internet is so vast that no single company or institution even guides it. Thus, it a technical, social, and cultural phenomenon. Individuals commonly experiment with their best ideas on the Internet. There is a good deal of cultural resistance to using the Internet as an advertising or selling medium. The Internet is, however, an exciting source of information for almost any subject imaginable.

There are three features of the Internet that will ensure its usefulness to market researchers for the foreseeable future. First, by prior arrangement, all Internet subnetworks move and process information at no charge to any other subnetwork, nor do the subnetworks charge the network as a whole. The result is that market researchers, like all other users, pay a flat rate based on connecting time and bandwidth capacity of the Internet gateway host system. In comparison, other online systems charge a fee to access most types of data of interest to market researchers.

Second, the Internet's unique technology allows information to move over a wide variety of physical channels. It is quite possible for Internet traffic to flow through telephone lines, satellite links, television cables, wireless devices, and very high speed fiber-optic lines. As a result, the communication flexibility and capacity of the Internet are virtually unlimited.

Third, the Internet is not tied to any single computer technology. At the outset, the Internet nodes were very large mainframe computers. As the processing power of microcomputers has increased, the Internet has been able to make use of them as well.

The Internet does have limitations, however. As a practical matter, it offers little real security. The original designers were concerned with survival from a nuclear attack and thus did not really concern themselves with the security features that modern businesses need. Businesses that sell through the Internet are concerned that someone will enter their information flow and copy sensitive information such as customers' credit card numbers. Businesses and Internet service providers are keenly aware of this limitation. There is much activity focused on plugging this particular gap.

There are hundreds, if not thousands, of Web pages of interest to market researchers. A **Web page** is simply a source of information that is likely to be linked to other areas of the Internet with complementary information. Searching through the millions of Web pages became much easier with the advent of search engines. A search engine is a program that sorts through the millions of pages of information on the Internet at very high speed and selects those pages that meet the search criteria specified by the market

Web page Source of information that is likely to be linked to other, complementary pages.

researcher. (Exhibit 5.1 provides some commonly used terms a researcher may find in searching the Internet.) Of all the Web pages available to market researchers, three of the most highly used are the home pages for the U.S. government census, WilsonWeb, and Internets.

The U.S. Census Bureau collects demographic, social, and economic data in great detail. Much of the resulting collection is of interest to market researchers. For example, population data can be useful in locating a business, such as a shopping center, sensitive to the number of people in an area. The Census Bureau also provides information regarding economic activity and housing. In an effort to aid dissemination of census data, the Census Bureau has set up a home page that leads to its main data-bank Web page. At the Main Databank menu, users can choose from the following tools and sites.

EXHIBIT 5.1   **Commonly Used Terms on the Internet**

The individuals who frequently "surf the Net" (see below for translation) have developed their own richly descriptive language. Failure to adhere to the slang and appropriate "Netiquette" "immediately identifies one as a "newbie" and may be considered grounds for "flames." The following glossary is an abbreviated listing that should be considered a launch point into "cyberspace" for those who wish to "cyber-surf" the "infobahn."

Bandwidth The amount of traffic that can be handled by the news reader or other gateway. Using bandwidth means to send or receive over the net. Having your input labeled "Wasting bandwidth" is akin to calling your communication worthless.

BTW An acronym used by experienced electronic system users for "by the way." BTW and other acronyms are commonly used to save bandwidth (a very small savings), but primarily are a sort of shorthand.

Cyberspace The computer-generated "space" where it all happens. The Internet resides in cyberspace.

Cybersurfing (also Net surfing) The act of searching the Internet for items of interest. Generally used to describe a walk through cyberspace rather than an extended stay at any single site.

Download The process of transferring files from the online service provider or some other computer and transferring it to your computer. Typically, market researchers will download data from a site on the Internet to their own computer, where the data will be analyzed.

E-mail Messages that are sent via electronic means. Usually, messages are typed into a computer, sent through an electronic system such as one of the online services, and received at the addressee's location. The electronic address of an individual is termed an e-mailbox.

E-zines Magazines that are published only on the Internet or other electronic systems. Sometimes shortened to simply "zines."

FAQs An acronym for "frequently asked questions." Discussion groups generally have a file that contains answers to the commonly asked questions within the group's discussion domain. Not reading the FAQs and using bandwidth asking questions answered in the FAQs may be considered grounds for flames.

Flames Those nasty e-mail messages that Net surfers will send you filling your e-mailbox to overflowing when you breach the Netiquette. Try to avoid flames.

FTP File transfer protocol. In the verb form, "to FTP" means to download information, to copy a file from one computer to your own computer.

IMHO In my humble opinion. Another acronym used by experienced Netters.

Infobahn Another name for the information superhighway.

Net Another name for the Internet.

Netiquette The generally accepted and largely unwritten code of conduct governing communications on the Internet. Failure to adhere to proper Netiquette can result in flames.

Newbie A novice Internet user.

Surfing See *cybersurfing.*

World Wide Web (WWW or Web for short). The Web is a graphical interface (picture/icon-oriented menu system) that has the ability to link text from different locations on the Internet. The Web also has audio capabilities. Thus, a marketing researcher can use a Web site to track down detailed information without realizing that the information resides elsewhere. The system also allows for integration of text and graphics such as charts and pictures. The WWW technology was developed in Switzerland by the European Institute for Particle Physics.

Sources: Sophie Littlefield, "A World Gone Web," *Online Access* 10, no. 2 (February 1995), pp. 40–45; Jim Romenesko, "Internet Relay Chat: The New Wild West," *Online Access* 10, no. 2 (February 1995), pp. 71–73; and "Get the Picture," *NetGuide* 2, no. 2 (February 1995), p. 73.

DOCUMENTS AND PUBLICATIONS. This section of the Census Bureau Web site contains two- to four-page briefs that provide timely data on specific issues of public policy. The reports are in a narrative format and generally contain graphs. The briefs summarize the demographic data or economic activities within the United States.

DATA ACCESS TOOLS. The Data Access Tools menu allows market researchers to create custom extracts and tabulations from the Census Bureau's extensive data sets relating to the 1990 Census of the Population. The data set can be accessed a number of ways. The two easiest are DataMap and 1990 Census Lookup.

DataMap provides an easy way to view profiles of states and counties. Data collected in the 1990 census are presented in tabular and graphical form. The user can select which state to display by simply clicking on the map. County information is being made available.

For more flexible geographic data retrieval, the 1990 Census Lookup option allows market researchers to create customized extracts of the 1990 summaries. With this tool, researchers can examine geographic segments such as states, counties, places, and urban areas in excruciating detail.

CENTER FOR ECONOMIC STUDIES. This segment contains research and discussion papers. Topics are varied, although all have a decidedly economic bent. Common issues discussed in these papers are productive capacity, modeling techniques such as linear dynamic modeling, measurement issues, pricing issues, and the effects of many factors on employment, wages, and productivity.

CONTINUOUS MEASUREMENT PUBLIC USE MICRODATA. The Census Bureau is considering replacing the traditional census taken every 10 years with a program that continuously measures a sample of the nation. The program as currently envisioned would sample 400,000 households each month for three years. After three years, the sample would decrease to 250,000 per month. The anticipated start date of the continuous measurement model is in 2000. This menu choice provides an introduction to these changes and invites interested persons to gain further information on the continuous measurement program.

FINANCIAL DATA. This is financial data for government units such as cities and school districts. Information is presented on the sources and expenditures of these government units.

POPULATION DATA. This is a small segment that provides information on the size, structure, distribution, and social characteristics of the population of the United States. Data are from the various census surveys and other sources.

STATISTICAL ABSTRACT OF THE UNITED STATES. The *Statistical Abstract of the United States* is a valuable reference source for demographic information. There are more than 1,400 tables in the reference book on social characteristics, economic issues, and international subjects.

TIGER A Census Bureau tool that allows researchers to prepare detailed maps of the United States.

TIGER. The Topographically Integrated Geographic Encoding and Referencing System **(TIGER)** is a new and major innovation from the Census Bureau. TIGER gives a market researcher the ability to prepare a detailed map of the entire United States. Information is becoming available on geographic entities and census blocks based on topographical features such as streets, rivers, and railroads. In effect, market researchers will be able to generate finely detailed demographic structures of the entire United States and its territories, street by street, block by block, or other polygonal geographic areas defined by recognizable landmarks. TIGER should be a useful aid to locating retail establishments and fine-tuning mass mailings of direct advertising.

The home page for WilsonWeb, www.wilsonweb.com/webmarket, provides an extensive listing of articles and database links for the market researcher. WilsonWeb also provides an extensive database for research in electronic commerce, referred to as the Electronic Commerce Research Room.

Finally, the home page for Internets, www.internets.com, provides access to all major search engines, over 500 databases covering business, economics, and international trade, and current news publications such as *Forbes, Standard and Poor's,* and *Business Week,* just to name a few.

World Wide Web (WWW) Search Engines

There are several Web search engines available to the marketing researcher. When using Netscape, simply clicking on the "N" or the "Search" button will send you to a search engine. A **search engine** is a tool that allows the market researcher to enter a word or words as search criteria and then sifts through the millions of sites on the Web for matching words. (Search engines are sometimes called spiders or crawlers.) This sifting and sorting makes the Web accessible. Without the power of the search engine, the size and complexity of the Web would preclude finding all but a very few sites.

Search engine A tool that allows the researcher to enter words as search criteria and then sifts through the millions of sites on the Web for matching words.

There are several search engines available. Excite, Infoseek, Lycos, and Yahoo! are only a few of the growing number. All are modestly different from each other, yet all have some capabilities in common. The following operators generally can help the market researcher narrow a given search and produce a manageable number of hits. Note that not all operators work, or even work in the same way, in all search engines. The researcher should be sure to check the specific search engine's instructions to get the best results.

QUOTATION MARKS. Some search engines allow the researcher to add quotation marks to more accurately define the search string. Enclosing several words within quotation marks tells the search engine to list only those Web sites that contain the specified words in the specified order. For example, "Chicago Illinois restaurants" will return only those sites with all three words in the exact order specified. This search is likely to produce a much smaller (but more relevant) number of hits than it would without the quotation marks.

PLUS (+) AND MINUS (−) SIGNS. Adding a plus sign before a search word instructs the search engine to list only those sites containing the specified word or phrase. Adding a minus sign before the search word instructs the search engine to list only those sites that do not contain the specified word or phrase. For example, *restaurant Chicago Illinois* will return sites with any of the words *restaurant, Chicago,* or *Illinois.* This is likely to return an impossibly large number of sites. Entering + *restaurant − Chicago + Illinois* will return a smaller number of sites, primarily restaurants in Illinois but not in Chicago.

Boolean operators Words that form a logic string to sort through huge numbers of sites on the Web.

BOOLEAN OPERATORS. **Boolean operators** are words that form a logic string to sort through the huge number of sites on the Web. Boolean operators include the words *AND, OR, AND NOT,* and, in some instances, parentheses. The operators work in a similar fashion to the Boolean operators in electronic spreadsheets. However, in the Web search engines, the operators must be in capital letters and separated by a space on either side of the operator word.

- **AND.** This operator functions in a manner similar to the plus (+) sign. AND indicates that the words entered in the search field must all be contained in any documents found. For example, to find sites containing the words *restaurant* and *Chicago,* enter the search as *restaurant AND Chicago.*

- **OR.** The OR operator instructs the search engine to return sites that contain at least one of the words linked by the operator. For example, to find sites that contain either *restaurant* or *Chicago,* enter *restaurant OR Chicago.*

- **AND NOT.** Using the AND NOT operator is similar to using the minus (–) sign. AND NOT instructs the search engine to return sites that do not include any of the words entered in the search field. For example, to find sites that contain the word *restaurant,* but not the word *Chicago,* enter *restaurant AND NOT Chicago.*

- **Parentheses.** Parentheses may be used to group segments of the search terms and form complex queries. Using parentheses is sometimes an exercise in logical thinking, but the results can be very specific and thus very useful to the market researcher. For example, to find sites that contain the word *restaurant* and either the word *Chicago* or the word *Illinois,* enter *restaurant AND (Chicago OR Illinois).*

TITLE SEARCH. This handy feature allows the researcher to select only those sites that have the specified search word or words in the title of the Web site. This search feature is activated by using the word *title* or the letter *t,* followed by a colon. For example, entering *title:restaurant* or *t:restaurant* will return only those sites with the word *restaurant* in the title of the document.

WILDCARD SEARCH. Attaching a wildcard character (*) to the right-hand side of a word will return all left-hand-side partial matches. This feature allows the researcher to broaden the scope of the search and include all partial matches of the search term. To illustrate how this wildcard search broadens the scope of the search, compare the results of using *Chicago* and using *Chi*.*

URL SEARCH. Another handy search feature instructs the search engine to list only those documents with the specified search terms in the Web address, known as the uniform resource locator (URL). This search feature is activated by entering *url:* or *u:.* For example, entering *url:restaurant* or *u:restaurant* will return only those documents with the word *restaurant* in the URL.

When the search engine is finished sifting through the documents, it will return a list of sites that meet the specified search criteria. The list will be in a nonrandom sequence; that is, the search engine lists the sites in order, from the most to the least relevant. As a result, the sites that best match the search criteria are generally the first few returned. The list will include a title of the document and a brief description of the site. The researcher scrolls down the list and selects the site that seems to best meet his or her needs. Clicking on the underlined word or phrase links the researcher to the selected Web site.

For example, the Census Bureau has designed Web pages to disseminate information collected in the 1990 census. The first page, called the home page, serves as an index, or table of contents. Usually, the home page is what will be returned by the search engine. The home page contains links to other Web pages that contain specific information that the researcher may wish to access. The researcher simply clicks on the highlighted areas and follows the site instructions.

Major Search Engines for Marketing Research

Which of the many search engines really matter? Usually, it's the search engines that are well known and well used. For researchers, using well-known, commercially backed search engines generally means more dependable results. These search engines are more likely to be well maintained and upgraded when necessary, to keep pace with the growing Web.

Search engines constantly visit Web sites to create catalogs of Web pages. Because they run automatically and index so many Web pages, search engines may often find information not listed in directories.

Directories, unlike search engines, are created by individual researchers. Sites are submitted and then are assigned to an appropriate category or categories. Because of the human role, directories can often provide better results than search engines. Yahoo! is an example of a directory.

Hybrid search engines contain directories or sites that have been reviewed or rated. For the most part, these reviewed sites do not appear as the default when a query is made to a hybrid search engine; instead, a user must consciously choose to see the reviews.

- **AltaVista.** This is one of the largest search engines on the Web, in terms of pages indexed. Its comprehensive coverage and wide range of powerful searching commands make it a particular favorite among researchers. It also offers a number of features designed to appeal to basic users, such as "Ask AltaVista."

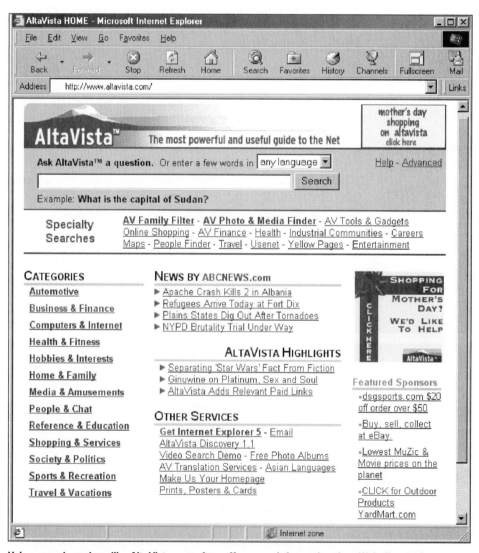

Using search engines like AltaVista can often offer more information than Web directories.

- **Ask Jeeves.** This is a human-powered search engine that aims to direct you to the exact page that answers your research question. If it fails to find a match within its own database, then it will provide matching Web pages from other search engines.

- **Excite.** Excite is currently the most popular search service on the Web. It offers a medium-sized index and integrates non-Web material, such as company information, sports scores, and weather into its results. It also offers one of the best "news search" services available, Excite NewsTracker.

- **HotBot.** Like AltaVista, HotBot is another favorite among researchers due to its large index and many powerful search features. HotBot is powered by the Inktomi search engine, which is also used by other search services.

- **Infoseek.** Infoseek is another popular search service on the Web. It has a small to medium-sized index, so it may not be the best place for anyone doing a comprehensive search of the Web. However, it consistently provides quality results in response to many broad or general searches, thanks to its Electronic Search Program (ESP) algorithm. It also has an impressive human-compiled directory of Web sites.

- **LookSmart.** This is the closest rival to Yahoo! in terms of being a human-compiled directory of the Web. In addition to being a stand-alone service, LookSmart provides directory results to both AltaVista and HotBot.

- **Lycos.** This service uses a small index that is more out-of-date than the previously listed services. Although its search listings are weak, Lycos does feature an impressive directory of Web sites called Lycos Community Guides.

Does the world come to an end if your information can't be found in any of these search engines? Not necessarily. If you want to research apple farmers, then getting a link to your site from an obscure apple farming Web site may bring you much more meaningful information than by being indexed by all the general search engines. Industry best practices suggest that when researching an issue on the major search engines, you should use those engines that are well maintained and current. To keep abreast of search engine changes, consult www.searchenginewatch.com/facts/major.html before conducting your research endeavor.

Online Services

Online services, which have been dubbed the fifth medium,[4] offer individuals access to an enormous number of information services. Many of these services are, or soon will be, interactive. Marketing researchers can use online services to access information formerly too time-consuming or inconveniently located to be useful. Until recently, mass communication had been only through radio, television, newspapers, or magazines. The newest medium, said to have revolutionized data retrieval, consists of a potent mix of telecommunications and computer technology. There are a variety of names for this newest medium, including *telecomputing, electronic publishing,* and simply *online.* No matter what the name, the services consist of high-speed (relative to manual searches) computer-assisted information retrieval systems (see Exhibit 5.2).

There are several large online services commonly available. CompuServe (now a part of America Online), Prodigy, Microsoft Network, and America Online are commonly regarded as the largest in the United States. CompuServe is profiled here because it is commonly available, well known, and fairly typical of the online services. While each has its own strengths and weaknesses, all the major services share similarities.

EXHIBIT 5.2   **A Fifth Medium?**

The evolving marriage of telecommunications and computing technologies allows marketing researchers access to a huge and growing number of interactive and informative sources. Marketing researchers are able to customize searches of electronic "libraries" at very high speeds. The computers can scan very large amounts of data in a short time. The results of a search are based on search terms the researcher deems appropriate to the task at hand. And the researcher may never have to leave home to accomplish all this! Currently, a limit to the technology is the infrastructure of existing telecommunications systems. A fiber-optics system or other high-speed highway to the researcher's computer needs to become widely available.

But the fifth medium is not a seamless cloth. Advertisers, major users of marketing research, describe the newest medium in terms of six functional areas, as follows:

1. **The household database provider.** Companies in this functional area provide information regarding households segmented by demographic variables and by purchase behaviors of the household.

2. **An information provider.** These are firms that actually generate the information and entertainment that are transmitted through the fifth medium. Examples of information provider firms are moviemakers Paramount and Columbia Studios and other entertainment giants like Nintendo.

3. **A programmer.** Just as in other media, in the fifth medium there is a need to group entertainment into packages for delivery through the medium. Examples of programmers include MTV and Turner Broadcast Systems. Online service providers such as America Online, CompuServe, and Prodigy fall into the category of programmers.

4. **Facility providers.** These are the companies that actually provide the fiber-optic technology that carries the information produced and packaged.

5. **Equipment providers.** These firms provide individuals and researchers with the terminal hardware and switching equipment that bring the fifth medium to the researcher. Examples include computer firms such as IBM and Apple, as well as telecommunications firms like AT&T.

6. **The advertisers.** These are the firms that create customized messages targeted to individual households. Advertisers are important because the clients of these firms (Procter & Gamble, Ford, Miller Brewing, etc.) will be major sources of revenue for the fifth medium. These revenue sources will subsidize the cost of the new medium and hold down prices. These are the same firms that purchase marketing research as well.

Source: Adapted from David Russell and Blyane Colter, "The Fifth Medium," *American Demographics,* June 1990, pp. 24+.

CompuServe

In 1994, CompuServe was the largest company in the online services industry, with, it claimed, 2.4 million subscribers and an average of two users per subscription.[5] The current rate for a CompuServe subscription that includes unlimited access to the company's basic services is $24.95 per month. Those who will not use as many hours can choose a plan for $9.95 per month that includes five hours of connect time and charges for additional time at the rate of $2.95 per hour; there are further charges for accessing extended services. In addition to the basic service fees, fees are charged for extended services. Within the CompuServe environment, those extra-fee services are marked with a plus sign (+) so that market researchers will know they are paying an additional fee for the time used.

Among the divisions it offers, CompuServe is well known for its electronic mall shopping. Within this electronic mall, users can select merchandise from suppliers as varied as compact disc music clubs, clothiers, and travel agents.

Areas of interest for marketing researchers include small-business forums and research areas. The business forums include discussion groups and information services that specialize in such topics as working in a home office or issues important to entrepreneurs. For example, discussion groups exist that focus on microcomputer equipment and software that marketing researchers commonly use.

Discussion groups are made up of interested parties whose accumulated messages are posted to an electronic bulletin board. Others interested in the topic respond with their own questions and answers. In this manner, issues are discussed among those concerned, and information and thoughts are shared and explored. There can be a substantial amount of group synergy in an electronic discussion group. Discussion groups can be found for a very large and diverse group of issues or topics. The questioning of others and sharing of information with others familiar with the topic at hand can be a valuable source of insight for the marketing researcher.

Sources of Secondary Market Research Data within CompuServe

The following are brief descriptions of sources of secondary marketing information available in the research section of CompuServe and should be considered a partial list.[6] CompuServe is a source of extensive data, and any listing such as the following is at best only indicative of the vast amount of information available. Nearly all of the following services are provided by CompuServe at additional charges. These databases are sources of information on U.S. and international companies, whole industries, management, markets, and international trade. The databases listed in the following table are all incorporated in the Business and Company Information segment of CompuServe's Iquest, an information retrieval service that covers a multitude of databases. In effect, Iquest provides access to many databases under one umbrella section of CompuServe. Information is available in bibliographic and full-text formats. Typical sources of information for the databases include newspapers, magazines, trade journals, scholarly journals, popular press publications, government documents, conference proceedings, directories, encyclopedias, and patent records. Because of the complexity of Iquest, three methods of searching are available to the market researcher: (1) Iquest will select the appropriate database once the researcher has chosen the research topic; or (2) the researcher can elect a specific database; or (3) the researcher may elect to search multiple databases.

Specific Database	Description of Databases Searched
Accounting and Tax MegaSearch	Accounting and Tax Database, BNA Daily News from Washington, and Tax Notes Today
Business Management MegaSearch	ABI/INFORM, Business and Management Practices, Management Contents, Harvard Business Review, and IAC Trade and Industry Database
Business News MegaSearch	Business Wire, Business & Industry, PROMT, Knight-Ridder/Tribune Business News, and PR Newswire
Employee Benefits	Abstracts from Employee Benefits Infosource dating back to 1986
Experian (TRW) Canadian Business Credit Profiles	Credit and business information on 1.5 million Canadian businesses
Experian (TRW) U.S. Business Credit Profiles	Credit and business information on over 13 million U.S. businesses
Exports	Manifests of ships loading international cargo at 62 continental U.S. seaports
Human Resource Management MegaSearch	ABI/INFORM, Management Contents, BNA Daily News, ERIC, and Occupational Safety and Health
Imports	Manifests of ships unloading international cargo at 62 continental U.S. seaports

Specific Database	Description of Databases Searched
Industry News MegaSearch	ABI/INFORM, Business & Industry, IAC Industry Express, Journal of Commerce, Knight-Ridder/Tribune Business News, McGraw-Hill Publications Online, PTS Product Announcements, Prompt, PTS Newsletter Database, Trade and Industry Database Fulltext
Journal of Commerce	Full text of articles from *Journal of Commerce*
Market and Product News MegaSearch	Prompt news search (fast), Marketing and Advertising Reference Service, Business & Industry, PTS News Product Announcements
Market Intelligence MegaSearch	Datamonitor Market Research, Euromonitor Market Research, BCC Market Research, Frost & Sullivan Market Intelligence, FIND/SVP Market Research Reports
Media General Plus	Financial and price statistics regarding New York Stock Exchange (NYSE), American Stock Exchange (ASE), and selected over-the-counter (OTC) stocks
Trade Newsletters	A full-text database covering over 800 business and trade newsletters covering 50 industries since 1988
U.S. Company MegaSearch	Moody's Corporate News, S&P Daily News, PR Newswire, Business Wire
Worldwide Company Newswire MegaSearch	Business Wire, Japan Economic Newswire Plus, PR Newswire, Canada Newswire, South American Business Information

Source: CompuServe Web site www.iquest.n2k.com/mbus.html.

While much information is available in Iquest, there is a drawback. With so much available, the researcher can have a difficult time finding exactly what he or she needs without sorting through a mountain of useless babble. Efforts to reduce the irrelevant material can result in loss of important information. Later in this chapter, we will provide a strategy for finding the information you need with less babble and less loss of information.

It is apparent that CompuServe is a potent reference source of secondary marketing research data. However, there are some criticisms of CompuServe that should be noted.

CompuServe has been criticized for its focus on consumer-oriented services such as entertainment and multimedia offerings. It has promoted the home and leisure-time value, leaving some corporate managers to worry about how committed CompuServe is to maintaining corporate services. As other online services come to market, the technical discussion groups may move to another service provider, leaving CompuServe with an even more consumer-oriented product.

Second, CompuServe has struggled with its old style of operations. CompuServe was started in the 1970s, and some of the decisions made then are haunting operations to this day. CompuServe has operated as a highly simplistic, instruction-driven terminal user interface, and a frequent complaint is that overloaded computers make business-to-business transactions difficult. Security and support of the rich text and graphics required for newer applications are also weaknesses in CompuServe. AOL has promised to improve CompuServe, but weak spots still exist for the present.

Pricing is a sensitive issue for many corporate managers. CompuServe bills individual customer's credit card accounts and currently does not have a method to aggregate all of a corporation's billings into an umbrella account. The credit card statement says, simply, CompuServe, Columbus, Ohio, and no additional information is available. Thus, corporate managers have no easy way to monitor usage or to itemize account activity. Corporate managers worry about paying for noncorporate use of the service.

In addition to nonauthorized service use, corporate managers have expressed concern with CompuServe's entire pricing structure.[7] As noted in the discussion introducing the reference sources, many of CompuServe's services are not included in the basic monthly rate.

This means that accessing these services can be very costly to marketing researchers. A search on some databases can cost up to $100 per record retrieved. In a corporate setting with multiple users working on several difficult projects, charges can mount rapidly. Adding search costs to the researcher's overhead can negate the benefits of an electronic research.

While pricing is an issue of immediate concern, CompuServe does offer access to the Internet and the cheap resources available there. CompuServe has supported Internet e-mail for some time, but support for the technically advanced features on the Internet is not possible with the dumb terminal operation. CompuServe is accused not only of slow Internet service, but also of deficient support for the World Wide Web text, graphics, and audio. Other service providers such as America Online, Prodigy, and Microsoft utilize a different technology to make faster, more error-free exchanges between computers.[8] Exhibit 5.3 provides an example of some of the difficulties one may encounter when searching for secondary data.

EXHIBIT 5.3 **Potholes in the Infobahn?**

Connecting to the Internet to collect secondary marketing research data is not as simple as some would have you believe. The connections required are commonly available, but there is a substantial amount of new high technology at work. From the user's perspective, the requirements do not seem severe. A personal computer equipped with a modem and a working telephone line are all that are immediately apparent. However, from that point, connecting to, and making use of, the Internet can be a daunting task.

Recently, an *Inc.* magazine reporter, Susan Murphy, described her experiences trying to hook up to the Internet and do research for a new business to start up. The editors noted the reporter's frustrations in the opening teaser paragraph by saying "Here, expletives deleted, is her report."

Murphy is apparently no newbie. She notes within the article that she had prior experience using America Online and CompuServe. Still, she had significant difficulties from the first day of her efforts.

Day one started with the frustrations of making four attempts and waiting 20 minutes for access through her Internet gateway provider. Two days later, after much reading of helpful books and manuals, Murphy was connected. She was then faced with the task of selecting which electronic news groups she wanted to participate in. Unfortunately, the process degenerated into declining or accepting subscriptions to each of the 3,500 or so available news groups, one at a time. The experience resulted in Murphy's Virtual Rule Number One: When in doubt, log out.

After the intrepid reporter found her way through the news-group maze, she wandered into gopherspace, one method of Net surfing. "Gopher" is a method of window-shopping the Internet. Because the Internet domain is so vast, a curious individual easily becomes sidetracked by useless, although sometimes interesting, information—cyberchaff, so to speak. This led to Murphy's Virtual Rule Number Two: If you don't know exactly what you want and where to get it, it's no big deal. The Net is way cool.

By day number 17, Murphy was becoming exceptionally frustrated. The wealth of information she found was overwhelming, the complexity exasperating. She was apparently progressing along the learning curve far enough to realize that she was in need of help with her endeavor. She developed Virtual Rule Number Three: Don't try to conquer the Internet alone; seek professional help.

Murphy enlisted the aid of her gateway host by asking about a software package called Mosaic that helps users navigate the infobahn. Help responded with the news that the program could be acquired via FTP from the site ftp.ncsa.uiuc.edu. After some deciphering and much consternation, the program was obtained. Unfortunately, Murphy discovered that software was needed in addition to Mosaic. This led to a comedy (for all but Murphy) of experiences as the reporter tried and eventually succeeded in acquiring the necessary software. The process led to Virtual Rule Number Four: The Internet is tautological; to master it, all you have to know is how to master it. The best recommendation is a pet geek.

Murphy ended her report by saying that she may start an electronic bulletin board for survivors of similar experiences, perhaps even an organization complete with books, videos, and CD-ROMs. She envisioned a feature-length film about cruising the information superhighway with the title *Revenge of the Roadkill.*

Source: "Potholes in the InfoBahn," *Inc.*, July 1997.

Despite these shortcomings, CompuServe remains a potent secondary data research tool. There is a wealth of information regarding firms and industries available and a proven, if aging, method of accessing the data. However, because of the limitations of the CompuServe system, the following section uses Lexis/Nexis to illustrate how to search an online database.

Searching an Online Database

In this section, the Lexis/Nexis database will be used to illustrate a technique that locates pertinent information and reduces the amount of irrelevant information retrieved in an Internet search. Lexis/Nexis was selected because it is a full-text database widely available to marketing researchers. A **full-text database** is one that contains entire news stories, articles, or numerical information rather than summaries. As a large and complex database, Lexis/Nexis exhibits the major strengths of electronic databases as well as the weaknesses. The marketing researcher can gain access to Lexis/Nexis in a number of ways. The following discussion assumes the researcher is connected directly to the Lexis/Nexis computers and that the researcher is not using the Web access mode.

Full-text database   An electronic database that contains entire news stories, articles, or numerical information rather than summaries.

The Lexis/Nexis database is actually a collection of databases. In general terms, Lexis is primarily a source of legal information such as cases, opinions, and legal research. Nexis is primarily a news, business, and financial database. Nexis collects information from 4,500 sources.[9]

Services offered within the Lexis/Nexis database include the following.

- **Lexis Public Records Online Service.** Public Records Online is a service that allows the marketing researcher access to property-related information such as real estate assessment records and transfers of deeds. In addition, this service provides docket information for California, New York, and Pennsylvania state courts. Information regarding liens is also online here. The information is updated daily or weekly. Marketing researchers interested in demographic data related to real estate, real estate transactions, or the status of liens will find Lexis Public Records Online useful.

- **Nexis Service.** Nexis is a very powerful data-collection tool for marketing researchers. Nexis contains the full text of newspapers, magazines, trade journals, and wire services from the United States and abroad. The Nexis service even includes some broadcast transcripts. The wide-ranging Nexis database is growing rapidly as more publishers put their printed documents online. For example, the American Marketing Association journals (*Journal of Marketing, Journal of Marketing Research, Journal of Consumer Marketing,* etc.) are available on the Nexis service. The range of the Nexis service is virtually unlimited.

- **Associated Press Political Service.** Through this service, marketing researchers can access data related to election campaigns and politicians' stances on various issues, as well as events associated with past, present, and future elections. This service allows marketing researchers to understand the context of political decisions made by elected officials and candidates.

- **Lexis Country Information.** By using the Lexis Country Information service, marketing researchers can stay current, or catch up, on economic conditions and political events around the world. Economic and political news from Europe, the Far East, Africa, the Middle East, South America, and North America is included in this service.

- **Lexis Financial Information Service.** The Lexis Financial Information Service contains information regarding corporate mergers and acquisitions. Analytical reports regarding industries and companies are available as well.

- **National Automated Accounting Research System Service (NAARS).** NAARS is a service providing marketing researchers with access to the financial statements and annual reports of many corporations.

Because the Lexis/Nexis database contains a remarkable amount of information, the challenge is to find only that which is needed. Perhaps the most difficult part of an electronic database search is formulating the commands that ferret out the few sources that are pertinent and discard the many thousands that are not. However, there are some techniques that, when mastered, will reduce the cyberchaff and find the cybergrain.

The most potent tool available to a user of a large and complex electronic database such as Lexis/Nexis is a good search strategy. To formulate a search strategy for using Nexis, the marketing researcher needs to know how to:

1. Choose appropriate search words.

2. Simplify the search words.

3. Connect the search words.

4. Choose a library and file.

Choose Appropriate Search Words

Choosing appropriate search words gets at the heart of the information needed as quickly as possible. It is probably wise for a researcher to set down a few words that describe the event or data desired before logging onto the database. Just as it is important to avoid using words that are too general, it is important to include alternative words so that additional information can be located.

Usually people start with broad search terms and thus locate too many documents that are not germane to the topic. Then the search terms are narrowed in scope generating fewer and fewer **hits,** or documents that meet the search criteria. CompuServe recommends the opposite approach: start with a highly focused search and, if necessary, expand from there.[10] This approach is likely to save the researcher time and money.

Hits Documents that meet the search criteria.

Simplify Search Words

A second suggestion regarding search words is to use the root forms of the words. Using the root form will generally locate variations of the term. For example, suppose the marketing researcher wants to know how much fast-food restaurant packaging is recycled. Possible search words are *recycle, recycling, recyclable; package, packaging, packages; container, containers;* and *fast food.*

In most cases Lexis/Nexis, like other electronic databases, will find plurals and possessives of the search words. That means that Nexis will locate documents that have the words *container* and *containers.* But the user can aid the process a bit. Lexis/Nexis allows the use of wildcard characters. In Nexis, the wildcard character is the exclamation point (!). In some instances, the researcher may want to locate all forms of the root with only one character added. In those unusual instances, an asterisk (*) is added to the end of the search word. For example, searching for *recyc!* will locate recycle, recycling, recyclable, and any other variations on the root *recyc.* Using the root form of the search term with a wildcard character allows the computer to expand the search enough to find slight variations that the researcher may not think of. In addition, even if the term is on the researcher's list, letting the computer do the work is always easier.

Connect Search Words

Connectors Special words that allow search terms to be linked together in a Boolean logic form.

The Lexis/Nexis database contains special words called **connectors.** Connectors allow search terms to be linked together in a Boolean logic form. In addition to the Boolean operators listed on pp. 126–27, these connectors include *w/n* (where *n* is a specified number of words), *pre/n* (where the first search word must precede the second search word by a specified number of words), and *w/seg* (within a segment of words).

Thus, entering *recyc! AND w/15 container* will locate all documents in which both search words appear and in which the terms are separated by 15 words or less. Generally, setting *n* to 3, 4, or 5 links words within a phrase, setting *n* to 10 to 15 links words in the same sentence, and setting *n* to 25 to 100 links words in the same paragraph. Searching within specified ranges helps to limit the number of hits. Many times, the search terms can be within the same document but so far apart that they are not logically connected.

Another type of connector in Nexis allows the marketing researcher to select the time frame to scan. For example, the researcher may not be interested in the recycling efforts of fast-food restaurants before 1990. In that case, he or she would enter the search terms followed by *And date aft 1989* to find hits from 1990 to the present. Nexis also has a *date bef* connector, which finds hits occurring before a specified date, and *date is,* which locates hits with a specific date.

Choose a Library and File

It is just as important to plan where you will search as it is to plan what to search. Without careful planning of where to search, the researcher can waste a lot of time sorting through hundreds of completely useless hits.

Library A large group of related information, categorized by topic, news event, and source.

A **library** is a large group of related information, categorized by topic, news event, and source. The News Library within Nexis consists of news clippings and articles from many sources such as trade journals, business periodicals, consumer magazines, and scholarly journals. If the News Library is selected, these articles will be scanned for the search terms. In comparison, the Company (SEC) Library contains financial data gleaned from sources such as forms 10K, which are filed with the Securities and Exchange Commission.

Libraries are further segmented into files. Files contain information from groups of similar sources or individual periodicals or newspapers. For example, if the Papers file is scanned, no articles from wire services will be located. Searching the JMR file will produce only articles from the *Journal of Marketing Research.*

Strengths and Weaknesses of Electronic Databases

Secondary data are frequently used to monitor a company's business environment. Attitudes, fashions, and fads change so rapidly that primary data collection does not always provide information that is current or wide ranging enough. When competitors change their stance in the marketplace, the firm needs to know so it can react effectively. Business environment forces such as regulation are also a concern. To stay current and to attempt to anticipate the future, firms monitor newspapers, magazines, trade journals, and many other sources of environmental information. Electronic databases can contribute to effective monitoring.

Regardless of the strengths or weaknesses of electronic databases, the researcher must always be aware of the ethical concerns associated with Internet research. Invasion of pri-

E T H I C S

As the Internet grows as a method of conducting marketing research studies, there is increased concern about the ethical issues that need to be addressed. Identify and discuss three ethical issues associated with doing research on the Internet. Now, validate your concerns by going to the National Fraud Information Center at www.fraud.org. Click on Internet Fraud Watch and browse the information available. What unethical practices are plaguing the Internet today?

vacy (e.g., tracking individual purchases) and fraud are just two items of concern when conducting Internet research. The Ethics box provides a good start for dealing with ethical situations on the Internet.

Electronic databases have at least four major strengths. First is the broad scope of information available. Many databases, such as Nexis, consist of a multitude of information sources from the United States and internationally. A second strength of electronic databases is their speed. Computers can search through a mountain of information at very high speeds relative to human search speeds. The computers don't miss sources due to fatigue or boredom either. Third, electronic sources are frequently available before printed documents are. Often, the data will be loaded in the computers before it is officially published due to delays in printing and distribution of the tangible document. It is common for a magazine, for example, to be available online a short time before a subscriber receives it in the mail. Fourth, electronic database searching allows the user to specify multiple search criteria. This provides flexibility and narrow targeting of data retrieval. It is easy, generally, to specify criteria that are relevant to the search, but not within the same context. For example, the Lexis/Nexis fast-food container recycling search example could have been for a specified geographic region or for specific packaging materials.

Electronic databases also have disadvantages that need to be considered. Whether accessed through a search engine, an online service such as CompuServe, or a private provider such as Lexis/Nexis, all databases have some limitations. Note that electronic sources of secondary information are also subject to the same weaknesses as traditional sources of secondary information. For example, all secondary information has the drawback of dependence upon the accuracy and reliability of the author. If an abstract is used, the researcher is dependent on the abstracting author as well. However, electronic databases have some unique disadvantages that marketing researchers should weigh in their decisions regarding where and how to find information.

With so much information available online and the quantity growing at dizzying rates, it is easy to fall into the trap of believing that everything and anything is available with just a few simple keystrokes. That so much information is available can actually be considered a drawback. As the opening quotation of this chapter succinctly points out, having massive amounts of information is a double-edged sword. Having too much information is overwhelming and can be just as problematic as having too little information. A good search strategy will help reduce the potential overload. Simply accessing the database, entering search terms as they are thought of, and expecting productive results is unrealistic.

Second, the cost of data retrieval can be high. Access-time charges can become expensive. Again, having a good strategy before sitting down at the terminal can prove to be valuable, but the charges can still mount up rapidly (though it should be noted that secondary research, even with the access charges, is still likely to be much less expensive than primary research).

A significant weakness of electronic databases is that their quality depends on the journal and article selection policy of the database provider. Because many of the electronic databases are so large, users sometimes assume that they contain all the relevant data sources available. That may not be the case. A highly pertinent source may be missing, and thus important information may not be located in the search. A poor decision may result from having incomplete information. Note that this weakness is the flip side of the scope advantage. While it is important to understand what is in the database, it is equally important to understand what is *not* in the database. There is no substitute for knowing the database.

The final limitation of electronic databases discussed here relates to idiosyncracies of the search process. The results of a search are very dependent on the search terms used. Using terms that are not germane to the topic produces unpredictable results. Mountains of useless data can be generated and mountains of useful data can be missed by using ineffective search terms. In addition, many databases include only abstracts of articles. If the search terms are not in the abstract, the entire article may be missed. For example, the marketing researcher interested in the market for microcomputers would not be interested in retrieving the entire database on computers. However, an abstract may contain the word *computer* without specifics as to the size of the computer. Searching on *minicomputer* or *microcomputer* would produce more useful results.

The best way to combat the limits of secondary marketing research with electronic sources is to understand the issue being researched, formulate a good search strategy, and understand the limitations of electronic databases.

SUMMARY OF LEARNING OBJECTIVES

Understand the concept of electronic marketing research media.

Electronic marketing research media are merely libraries in a new format. Instead of books, journals, newspapers, and other sorts of paper media, the electronic medium consists of a marriage of telecommunications and computing technology. Marketing research is responsible for producing information that can be used to make decisions. For the researcher, the medium used to develop the information is a matter of convenience, as well as cost versus benefits. Frequently, the marriage of telecommunications with computer power can produce satisfying information in a timely and cost-effective manner.

Understand the impact of new electronic technology on secondary marketing research methods.

The impact of the new technology on secondary marketing research is growing as more and more information becomes available in an electronic format and as more researchers become aware of electronic resources. Electronic searches are powerful and very fast relative to manual searches. A great deal of information can be located from a wide variety of sources and from widely divergent geographic locations. However, the limitations of electronic searching also need to be understood. Careful planning of the electronic search is a critical phase of any marketing research project.

Outline the dimensions of the resources available on the information superhighway.

The number of sources available electronically is growing very rapidly. Commercial services such as CompuServe, America Online, Lexis/Nexis, and many others provide access to a wide range of information sources. A skilled researcher can access detailed demographic information from the Census Bureau, financial reports regarding competitors, and trade journal reports of new products in the marketplace; he or she can even tap into the synergy generated by groups of individuals with similar interests. The quantity as well as the quality of marketing research information available electronically is increasing so quickly that a list of what is available is likely to be obsolete by the time it is published. However, because so much is available, the researcher must be especially careful to plan the electronic search to limit the amount of useless data and, at the same time, maximize the amount of useful information.

Understand several of the online services available to market researchers.
CompuServe, America Online, and Prodigy are three of the most commonly used services providing marketing researchers with access to electronic databases. The Internet is a vast and unruly amalgamation that is currently disorganized and difficult to navigate without specialized software. Stand-alone databases such as Lexis/Nexis are also available. Much information is available on all of the major services. As a result, the researcher should consider the service provider's ease of use as an important selection criterion.

Demonstrate how to obtain secondary marketing research data.
The most effective electronic marketing research is based on a carefully developed search strategy. Steps in the strategy include choosing appropriate search words, simplifying the search words, connecting the search words, and selecting the appropriate place to search. Having a good search strategy reduces the amount of useless trivia captured while maximizing the amount of useful information captured.

KEY TERMS AND CONCEPTS

Boolean operators 126	**Hits** 135	**Search engine** 126
Connectors 136	**Internet** 122	**TIGER** 125
Full-text database 134	**Library** 136	**Web page** 123

REVIEW QUESTIONS

1. What are the strengths and weaknesses of electronic databases relative to marketing research?

2. Suppose you needed demographic information about a particular geographic area. Where would you start looking for this information? How would you write the search terms?

3. Suppose you needed information regarding other firms in a given industry as a part of the competitive environment analysis so common in marketing research reports. How would you find information related to the firms in a particular industry? How would you write the search terms?

4. Suppose you needed background information as part of a preliminary situation analysis. If industry experts are not available for interviews, where would you start looking for this type of information? Of the databases described in this chapter, which do you think would be most useful? How would you write the search terms?

5. One of the drawbacks of electronic databases is their ability to find so much information that the marketing researcher simply can't work with all of it. How would you write the search terms to gather information regarding breeders of black Labradors in an Internet search? In a Lexis/Nexis search?

6. Because of the speed and comprehensiveness of online databases such as Lexis/Nexis, many people have become concerned over what they see as an invasion of privacy. What are your feelings regarding the privacy issue? How would you convince someone with an opposing view that you are correct?

DISCUSSION QUESTIONS

1. Discuss the future of the Internet with regard to its capacity as a marketing research tool.

2. Find three potential sources of marketing research data on the Internet. Document the sources and briefly describe the content of the data provided.

3. **EXPERIENCE THE INTERNET.** Go to the U.S. Census Bureau's Web site at www.census.gov and access the Topographically Integrated Geographic Encoding and Referencing System (TIGER). Comment on TIGER's value as a marketing research tool.

4. **EXPERIENCE THE INTERNET.** While at the Census Bureau Web site, access U.S. International Trade Statistics and report the level of trade occurring between the United States and Japan.

5. **EXPERIENCE THE INTERNET.** Go to http://webopinion.com and access the research survey template located at that site. Suggest ways in which you would attract respondents to the site to achieve a high response rate among a particular population of interest.

ENDNOTES

1. Quoted by Douglas G. Branstetter, "Dear Reader," *CompuServe Magazine* 12, no. 9 (September 1993), p. 3.

2. Sharma, Yojana, "China-Communications: Netting the Internet," Inter Press Service, January 16, 1995.

3. Ibid.

4. David Russell and Blyane Colter, "The Fifth Medium," *American Demographics,* June 1990, pp. 24+.

5. Doug Van Kirk, "CompuServe's Electronic Kingdom," *Info World,* December 5, 1994, p. 25.

6. The information for this list is taken from "I Didn't Know I Could Do That, O CompuServe!" CompuServe Incorporated, 1994, pp. 73+.

7. Van Kirk, "CompuServe's Electronic Kingdom," pp. 65+.

8. Ibid.

9. *State Journal-Register* (Springfield, IL), October 6, 1994, Business section, p. 22.

10. Robert Lauriston, "Search Words of Wisdom," *Compu-Serve Magazine* 13, no. 9 (September 1994), pp. 28+.

MARKETING RESEARCH ILLUSTRATION

SECONDARY DATA ON THE RESTAURANT INDUSTRY

This Marketing Research Illustration demonstrates secondary data available on the restaurant industry. These data were accessed directly from www.restaurant.com and illustrate the type of information that would be useful in a marketing research study on restaurant trends.

1999 Restaurant Industry Forecast: Full-Service Outlook

After posting strong growth in 1998, sales at fullservice restaurants should exceed $117 billion in 1999—a gain of nearly $5.5 billion, or 4.9 percent, over sales in 1998. Real growth in 1999 is expected to be roughly 2.1 percent, similar to gains experienced in 1995 and 1996 but a full percentage point below the 3.1 percent real gain in 1997.

As in the quickservice sector, this expected slowdown in sales growth at fullservice restaurants should come as a result of a less robust economy. Although the fullservice sector should continue to cash in on the relative stability of the economy and the continuing financial comfort of consumers, growth is not likely to reach the heights it did in 1998.

Booming Economy and Consumer Sentiment Drove Growth in 98

Strong economic growth was the foundation of fullservice restaurants' excellent sales performance in 1998, especially during the first half of the year. But there is more to the strong showing than simple economic statistics—consumers' emotions and desires also played vital roles.

During 1998, consumer sentiment soared. After years of worrying about their jobs, consumers found that jobs were plentiful; even if a job was lost, it would not be hard to find a new one. Those in the financial community, particularly stockbrokers, enjoyed the effects of astronomical bonuses not seen in years, and many high-tech employees reaped the benefits of accumulated stock options. After three years of extraordinary gains in the stock market, many consumers felt the "wealth effect," so when the slowdown came, they sensed that some of their money should be taken out of the market and enjoyed. In addition, many consumers found themselves with more spendable cash, thanks to home mortgages that were refinanced at near-historic-low rates. Even gasoline prices declined from the previous year.

Taken together, all of those factors helped drive stronger-than-expected growth in the fullservice sector in 1998. Fine dining fared particularly well in this restaurant-friendly climate. The Association's 1998 Tableservice Operator Survey shows that tableservice operators with higher check averages—$15 per person or higher—were more likely than those with lower check averages to report that business in 1998 was better than in the previous year. Ethnic concepts were also especially likely to report a strong 1998 compared with a year earlier.

Maintaining the Momentum

But even in such a positive picture, there were still signs of struggle. For example, competition remained intense in 1998 and is likely to continue to be in 1999. Today's consumer is well aware that restaurant choices abound. Nearly four out of five adults report that they have a larger selection of restaurants available to them today compared with several years ago—and restaurateurs feel that competitive pressure every day, according to the 1998 Consumer Survey.

The Association's 1998 Tableservice Operator Survey confirms that competitive intensity is on the rise in the fullservice sector. When restaurateurs were asked to use a thermometer scale to evaluate the intensity of the competition in 1997, 1998, and 1999, they reported no letup in the past and expect none in the future. Competition is especially high at restaurants with higher check averages.

After considerable growth in the past few years, high-end restaurants will likely feel increased pressures in addition to increased competition in 1999. For example, value perception is less favorable in the higher-check-size category. Although in general consumers voice satisfaction with their experiences at fullservice restaurants, roughly one-quarter of adults say that the value they receive for the price they pay at higher-priced restaurants falls below their expectations. In contrast, nearly 90 percent of adults say that the value they receive for the price they pay at moderately priced fullservice restaurants meets or exceeds their expectations. Such satisfaction should work in moderately priced fullservice restaurants' favor in 1999, according to the 1998 Tableservice Operator Survey.

The less-robust economy is also likely to have a greater impact on higher-check restaurants in the coming year, because growth in fine dining has been driven by strong employment gains in the financial-services sector of the economy. U.S. and global events in the second half of 1998 point to a moderation in this critical driver in 1999.

Catering to Value-Conscious Consumers

Restaurateurs across all check-size categories are well aware of how value-conscious their consumers are and realize that although they are enjoying good economic times, customers are more discerning than ever. In fact, most restaurateurs agree that their customers are even more value-conscious today than they were two years ago.

But the increase in customers' expectations doesn't end at value. As more Americans move into their peak earning years, they are becoming increasingly demanding about flavor, plate presentation, and the entire dining experience—an attitude that is pushing fullservice operators to improve their offerings from the time customers make reservations to the time they pay their checks. Consumers have raised the bar and have increased their expectations for food quality, food safety, and service.

Today's customers, for example, often forgo the hassle of carrying cash by using credit cards. In the 1998 Tableservice Operator Survey, a substantial majority of tableservice restaurants reported increased use of credit cards compared with two years before. Operators of establishments with an average per-person check of $15 or more indicated that at least 50 percent of their sales were paid for with credit cards.

Discerning diners have also developed a taste for wine and beer. A majority of operators with per-person checks of $15 or more who responded to the 1998 Tableservice Operator Survey reported that customers were buying more wine. Approximately one-third of operators in that category reported more beer sales than before, due in part to the popularity of microbrews.

Reworking Workplace Cultures

Confronted with higher customer expectations, greater competitive intensity, and ongoing difficulty finding and motivating workers, tableservice-restaurant operators are reevaluating and reinventing their businesses. As previously discussed, they are recognizing that enlightened management, or a caring culture, is necessary to increase employee satisfaction and maximize their profit potential.

Caring for Customers

Of course, customers have their own requirements when seeking satisfaction, and operators must meet and exceed those needs, too. Operators who are maximizing their profit potential recognize that they must do more than just deliver on the basics—food and service—and consider customers' other concerns. Those operators are more likely to rank an "excellent reputation among customers," and "excellent location" and "competitive pricing" among their top three competitive advantages, according to the 1998 Tableservice Operator Survey.

MARKETING RESEARCH CASE EXERCISE

DATA DEVELOPMENT ON THE INTERNET

This Case Pertains to the Video Entitled Data Development

While watching the video entitled *Data Development*, pay particular attention to the various ways in which marketing research data are collected. Also pay specific attention to the approaches, problems, and outcomes associated with the various data collection methods.

Using this information, formulate a list of data that can be collected via the Internet. Specifically, address the types of data (both secondary and primary) that can be collected on the Internet, and how you would go about physically collecting that data. Finally, develop a list of some of the inherent problems of collecting data on the Internet. In your list be sure to address several of the ethical issues that may arise in collecting marketing research data through the Internet.

PART II

Designing the Marketing Research Project

Learning Objectives

After reading this chapter, you will be able to

1. Illustrate and define a marketing research database.

2. Explain the interactive nature of marketing research and data enhancement.

3. Describe the dynamics of database development.

4. List the general rules of thumb in database development.

5. Demonstrate understanding of technology in a database context.

6. Understand the role of modeling in database analysis.

Marketing Research and Database Development

❝ A lot of senior managers think database development is a marketing toy rather than a management tool . . . once they understand what the system is capable of doing, they ask themselves how they could have ever made a product or pricing decision without it. ❞[1]

**ROGER K. ATCHLEY
Database Consultant**

Using Databases for Customer Retention

Samsonite Corporation

A combination of traditional marketing research methods and new database-oriented approaches is reshaping the marketing research process at Samsonite. The development of a customer-oriented database provides Samsonite with unique marketing research tools to aid in decision making and help position Samsonite to cope with challenges of retail consolidation, blurring channel leadership, development of new distribution systems, and well-informed, proactive consumers.

The mission of marketing research is still to provide management with information regarding consumers and sales. Research is known as the key element in achieving Samsonite's primary goal, namely, establishing leading-edge capabilities in product, communication, customer service, and strategic planning. While the information managers need in order to achieve this goal is the same now as in the past, the approach to generating the information is different. Samsonite uses project teams made up of personnel from marketing research, marketing, engineering, and production—all of whom contribute to the solution of the research problem. The result of this team approach has led to dramatic changes in how research is conducted. According to Robert Bengen, Director of Marketing and Research, "the emphasis is now to use smaller sample sizes, shorter, more targeted questionnaires, and the examination of actual behavior over intentions (attitudes) because actions speak louder than words and more truthfully."

A consumer database is now the main source of market information for Samsonite. The database is driven by short, targeted questionnaires requesting demographic, lifestyle, and purchase information inserted into all Samsonite products. Marketing research then applies the data to several areas.[2]

1. **Market planning.** By analyzing the characteristics of various purchasers, Samsonite has been able to target its products more exactly. After examining customers against the population as a whole, the company has produced new products for neglected segments, mainly esteem luggage targeted toward professional women.
2. **Sales.** The consumer database also allows better planning for the sales force regarding retail account activity. The analysis of Samsonite purchasers in different retail accounts has enabled the sales force to understand how different retailers operate and has shown various retailers how taking on additional Samsonite luggage can effectively reach different shoppers.
3. **Customer satisfaction.** Samsonite has been able to conduct customer satisfaction studies for new and existing products quickly and efficiently. Because the incidence of luggage repurchase is relatively low, use of the database allows for a quick, targeted, cost-efficient approach for data generation. Samsonite currently conducts quarterly customer satisfaction studies for all new products as well as existing luggage items. The database allows marketing research to interact more closely and directly with customers. This interaction helps Samsonite understand its markets, develop and improve products, and involve consumers in the delivery of quality products with distinct value.

North County Bank of California: Relationship Marketing

Understanding who your customers are is a top priority in most businesses, especially North County Bank of California. According to Janet Marinello, Vice President of Marketing, "When I asked our eight branch managers who our VIP customers were, I got eight different answers." The criteria for determining the bank's best customers were so subjective that a "best customer" could have been a high-volume investor or the branch manager's best friend. Frustrated with having access to only generic attitudinal data, Marinello lobbied bank management to allow the marketing research department to establish a budget that could fund the development of a market-driven database.[3]

Ten months later, marketing research compiled a database of bank customers that included data on both profitability and product mix preferences. In addition, the database provided standardized customer profiles and a communications tracking system to evaluate promotional effectiveness. According to Marinello, "The bank now has the ability to make customer-related decisions based on actual purchase data, not vague attitudinal intentions."

Value of Database Information

Responding to the individual needs of customers in order to nurture customer relationships is becoming a major objective behind many marketing research endeavors. Known in the past as database marketing, the process of systematically categorizing timely customer data is now becoming a critical function of marketing research. Simply stated, the roles and responsibilities of the marketing research function are evolving from a process of merely collecting data to one of generating information through shared dialogue with the customer. Developing the ability to identify individual customers, ranking those customers' transactions over time, and knowing what those customers might or will buy together form the new agenda in many marketing research practices. This agenda, as illustrated in the chapter opener, requires a blending of traditional marketing research practices with procedural database development.

What Is a Database?

Database Collection of information indicating what customers are purchasing, how often they purchase, and the amount they purchase.

A marketing research database is a central repository of all relevant information concerning a company's customers. More specifically, a **database** is a collection of information indicating what customers are purchasing, how often they purchase, and the amount they purchase. A well-designed database incorporates information from a multitude of diverse sources, including actual transactions, history of promotional effectiveness, consumer surveys, secondary data, and other past marketing research project data. Unlike operational databases that reflect accounting and financial data, a true research database allows users to analyze purchase behavior, not intentions, over some predetermined time frame, event, or business situation.[4]

A typical database is structured around actual transactional information, which is then chronologically arranged to reflect each purchase occasion. Then, through a series of "marketing" techniques, additional information (demographics, lifestyles, media habits) are woven into the transactional data so a company can obtain a complete picture of who its customers actually are. The outcome is a complete customer profile based on actual purchase data, frequency of purchase, and amount of purchase at any given point in time. When categorized effectively, this information provides a company with a total customer portfolio to be used in making product or brand decisions, resource allocations, and decisions on communication tools and distribution channels.

More specifically, the information in a marketing database is generated by the customer via sales invoices, warranty cards, telephone calls, market research projects, and various other applications of customer data such as those illustrated in Chapter 1. This information is then logically arranged to allow for instant access whenever the customer contacts a company or vice versa.

Such databases are normally linked to an interactive computer and telephone system that can automatically provide a customer profile on demand. This enables the user of the database to recognize customers by name, purchase history, general interests, and product uses, as well as future product needs.

In addition, most marketing databases are complemented with information pertaining to a company's total product mix. This tells the user of the database exactly what a company makes or sells, which items are the most popular, and which items are most suitable for certain customer needs.

At the core of the database is a network that provides specific information on each and every product or service provided by the company. With such information companies can tell customers which replacement parts to order for their dishwasher, how to change a filter on their air conditioner, what games are available for their Nintendo system, and what each would cost. Even technical questions, such as those regarding installation of a home television satellite system, can be routed to a company expert.

A travel agent books a client's trip using a networked database.

Airlines and travel agencies provide excellent examples of marketing database development and usage. These service providers can book customers on complicated tours around the world, have hotel rooms and rental cars waiting at each destination, and deliver tickets, boarding passes, and itineraries overnight. This happens because of a networked database that links airlines, hotels, car rental services, and express delivery systems. The enhanced marketing database takes this concept one step further. With database information, the service provider knows that a particular customer prefers a window seat, usually travels with Northwest Airlines, always flies first class, is a World Club member, and uses Hertz Number One Gold Club Auto Rentals. The service provider knows the address to which the tickets are to be delivered, the spouse's name, and the home and office phone numbers. All of the customer's information is stored on the database and can be accessed instantly anytime the service provider needs it.[5]

Purposes of a Customer Database

In the broadest sense, the purpose of any customer database is to help a firm develop meaningful, personal communication with its customers. This level of communication deals with the proper products or brands, the various prices of the product offering, the level of customer service to be built into the total offering, and how much access customers have to the product. In short, a customer database allows a company to communicate at the right place, at the right time, with the right product, to the right customer.

More specific purposes of the customer database are (1) to improve the efficiency of market segment construction, (2) to increase the probability of repeat purchase behavior, and (3) to enhance sales and media effectiveness. To fulfill these purposes, the successful customer database must allow users to measure, track, and analyze customer buying behaviors. The role of marketing research, then, becomes one of generating, developing, and sustaining the database. The remainder of our discussion will focus on these responsibilities. Database construction, data collection procedures, and testing and evaluating information outcomes are three main areas of database implementation.

All marketing research databases are constructed to achieve or enhance customer relationships. Such databases bring back the level of individual service lost due to mass merchandising. In the past, local retailers knew each customer and his or her family members. They established a bond with customers that included two-way communication, instilled customer loyalty, increased customer satisfaction, and fostered the growth of the business. Mass merchandising and discount retailing ended this relationship. Price, not loyalty, began to drive customers' purchase decisions. While quality of merchandise went up, personal service went down. Today the situation is reversing itself. By giving a firm access to information on each customer's family demographics, leisure activities, purchase history, media interests, and personal socioeconomic factors, the modern database can help that firm re-create personal service.

More specifically, four fundamental areas in which the database benefits the firm are (1) exchanging information with customers, (2) determining heavy users, (3) determining lifetime customer value, and (4) building segment profiles.

One of the most valuable benefits of a database involves the exchange of information between a firm and its customers. Information on product availability, special features, competitive product comparisons, repairs, and warranties are critical information requirements for customer service. Most businesses, through internal secondary data, have this information available. The task becomes providing it to customers to allow them better decision-making capabilities.

At the same time, customers possess a wealth of information absolutely essential for any business. Why did customers buy a certain product? What features and benefits did they seek? What other products are they likely to purchase? Successful databases constantly provide such exchange of information. Every contact with a customer becomes an occasion to provide more information to a database. Also, as a business learns more about its customers, it will begin to understand what information customers want from it.

Information exchange will usually tell a business that all customers are not alike. With a database, businesses can distinguish heavy, medium, and light users of their product or service and adjust their strategy accordingly. The database's ranking system for all customers can help the business tailor products, benefits, and services to each class so as to keep heavy users loyal, and stimulate medium and light users to buy more.

Within each user class, the business can also determine the expected lifetime value per customer. When a customer is acquired, the database allows the business to determine what it can expect from that customer. Calculating contribution to profit and overhead for a customer's lifetime with the company is a major task for the database. Using this lifetime value, the company can easily calculate how much to spend on marketing activities to keep the customer satisfied and loyal.

Finally, a marketing research database allows the business to answer the crucial question, Why do some consumers buy our products or services regularly, while others do not? The simple premise behind the database is that the consumers themselves can provide the information necessary to answer this question. Further questions contributing to the overall answer include the following:

1. How do our products compare with the competition?

2. What is the relationship between perceived value and price of the product?

3. How satisfied are customers with the service level and support for the product?

4. What are the comparisons among lifestyles, demographics, attitudes, and media habits between heavy, medium, and light users of the product?[6]

Through various modeling techniques, the database can profile individuals based on selective characteristics or attributes that appear to distinguish buyers from nonbuyers. The remainder of our discussion will focus on the responsibilities involved in database development.

Marketing Research and Data Enhancement

Data enhancement The overlay or partitioning of information about new or existing customers for the purpose of better determining their responsiveness to marketing programs.

The primary role of a database is to serve as an information and intelligence resource for a company. Central to this objective is the process of **data enhancement,** which can be defined as the overlay or partitioning of information about new or existing customers for the purpose of better determining their responsiveness to marketing programs. As such, data enhancement can allow organizations three distinct advantages:

1. **More knowledge of customers.** Knowing exactly who buys products or services is extremely valuable in adjusting the strategic function of a company's marketing plan. Most databases are built with this purpose, concentrating on internal company data limited to current users of a product or service. Data enhancement allows for external primary data to be woven into current internal data to gain a more accurate categorization of customers relative to their true value to the company. The external data normally contain, but are not limited to, demographic, psychographic, behavioral, and motivational data about various consumers.

2. **Increase the effectiveness of marketing programs.** Through data enhancement, the marketing function of an organization can gain greater insights into communications, distribution, and new-product development. When internal data about customers are enhanced with external data, usage profiles by consumer can be tailored to reflect the unique desires of various customer groups.

3. **Predicting responsiveness to changing marketing programs.** Having concise information on various customer groups allows for increased targeting efficiency. Efficiency is increased when current customer profiles are used to predict the probability of targeting new yet similar customers with a new marketing plan. In short, the probability of success regarding new programs and procedures can be calculated according to the enhanced data.

Effective Development of the Enhanced Database

A typical database contains three critical data units that can be interactively categorized for unique customer profile reports: geodemographic factors, attribute data, and target market dimensions. Exhibit 6.1 shows the interactive properties of these data units.

Geodemographic factors are generally sourced at one of two levels: geographic market and residential area. At the residential level, information requirements center on the individual, the household, and the zip code where current customers reside. The geographic

EXHIBIT 6.1   **Three Dimensions of a Typical Database**

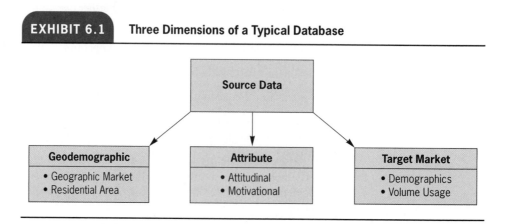

market level requires data at a more aggregate level representing metropolitan or regional market areas.

Typically, attitudinal data reflect an individual's preferences, inclinations, views, or feelings toward a particular product or service offering. Attitudinal data are one of the most important topics in database development because of their relationship to purchase behavior. In the context of the database, attitudinal data reflect a person's overall attitude toward the product itself, specific brands, and specific product features. When individuals prefer a product or brand, they are more inclined to buy it than when they have no preference. In essence, attitudinal data represent the prerequisites of purchase behavior.

Motivational data refer to the drive, urge, desire, or impulse that channels an individual's behavior toward a goal. Motivational data typically involve those factors behind why people behave as they do. Seeking particular product benefits, shopping at stores that are convenient and comfortable, or simply enjoying the interaction with certain salespeople may all constitute motivational characteristics that drive a purchase decision. In short, motivational data reflect the activities behind the purchase. Whether the issue is brand loyalty, store loyalty, or media influence, motivational data describe those circumstances that direct a customer's behavior toward a goal.

Target market characteristics describe heavy product users versus light users on such dimensions as demographics, purchase volume, and purchase frequency. Other data would reveal household consumption patterns, shopping patterns, advertising effectiveness, and price sensitivity information.

The key to database enhancement, of course, is the availability of data for increasing the interactive efficiency of the three data units. In most database development, the geodemographic unit is called the driver dimension because it determines (or *drives*) the type and amount of additional data (attribute and target market) that can be generated or solicited for cross-reference purposes. For example, Company A maintains a slim database of its current customers. It wants to develop a promotional campaign to increase awareness of its product offering among potential new users. Analysis of its current database based on geodemographic factors reveals useful information on where current customers reside; however, it provides little value regarding the targeting of new customers except for similar residential locations. Therefore, the data requirement shifts to soliciting external data on attributes and target market characteristics of current users in order to enhance the transferability of current customer profiles to potential new customers.

In this simple example, geodemographic data served as the driver for determining additional data requirements. Depending on the level and amount of information available on a geodemographic level, additional data requirements are then determined. Electronic databases are also effective tools for data enhancement, as discussed in the Using Technology box.

The Dynamics of Database Development

The basic definition of a database is "a comprehensive collection of interrelated data." The data may come from a variety of sources both internal and external to the company. Regardless of where the information comes from, it's important to realize that a database is only as good as the information it contains. If the information required to make marketing decisions is not in the database, the database is useless. From a marketing research perspective, it becomes critical that the information generated for a database possess four characteristics:

1. **Affinity.** Data must reflect prior usage of the product or service in question. Data reflecting past usage by current customers is one of the best predictors of future product needs.

A CLOSER LOOK AT RESEARCH   Using Technology

As detailed in Chapter 5, electronic databases have become extremely important for individuals needing immediate access to quality research information. Many Web sites offer access to electronic databases, usually for a fee. A site maintained by the University of Pennsylvania Library, at www.library.upenn.edu/dialog/subjlist.html, provides database links for a variety of interests. In most instances, each individual link will provide information on database contents and coverage available.

Often, researchers have great difficulty determining where to actually initiate the search for information to use in a study. Background information is often obscure and can only be uncovered after many arduous hours of searching.

Electronic databases, while not a panacea, often provide researchers with relatively easy access to much-needed information. For example, most databases are subdivided to allow greater research potential and a more user-friendly atmosphere. Electronic databases usually eliminate much of the costly waste of time that results from manually searching through volumes of written text.

As the process of electronic information transfer through databases improves, the ability to obtain pertinent market research data will be enriched.

2. **Frequency.** Information reflected in a database must give users the ability to categorize customers by frequency of purchase. Available information should reflect the amount of business any individual has conducted with the company.

3. **Recency.** Length of time between purchases is a very powerful predictor of future purchases. Because of this, recency of purchase is a critical factor in database dynamics. Recency assumes that a customer who purchased from a particular business last month has a greater probability of repurchase than a customer whose last purchase occurred six months ago.

   Recency and database development operate to profile all customers based on their most recent purchase, the most recent having the highest probability and the least recent having the lowest probability of repurchase. Each customer is assigned a recency code (1 = most recent, 5 = least recent, for example) and sorted into groups based on the assigned codes.

   Once these profiles are established, decision makers may view these customers in a totally different light. Certain customer groups can receive new-product promotions, while others may be targeted with specially designed marketing efforts to increase repeat purchases. Recency allows the business to build better relationships with different customer classes. It allows the researcher to determine which ones are most important and which groups need additional cultivation.

4. **Amount.** How much an individual consumes from any one company is a good predictor of future usage status. Therefore, the data must allow for the categorization of customers into specific usage groups (light, medium, heavy users).[7]

While it is important to realize that the information for a database must contain certain characteristics, researchers must also never lose sight of the fact that database development is unique to each company. The amount and type of information relevant to one marketing organization may not be relevant to another. Database development is highly specific, yet within this specificity lies the art of maximizing the relevancy of the information.

Exhibit 6.2 illustrates the steps in the database development process. The first step requires that the researcher determine the value of the information to be included in the database. Next is to identify the specific research needs that will govern the gathering of

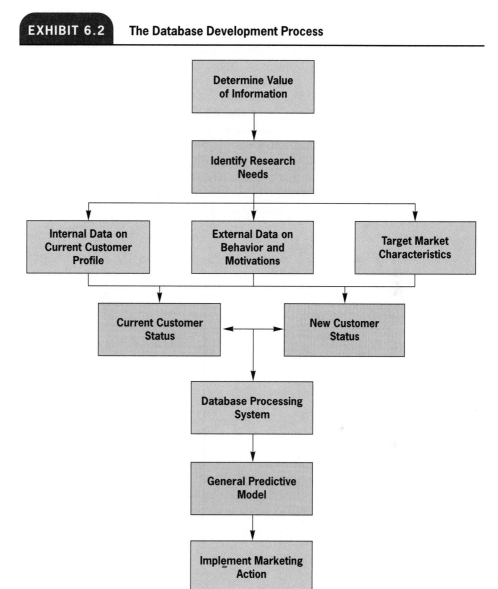

EXHIBIT 6.2   The Database Development Process

the information. The information should come from internal sources, external sources, and the target market. This information must then be customized for profiling existing customers across a variety of purchase categories. These categories will eventually become the means for generating new customer profiles. The information must then be processed through a particular database management system whereby predictive models are generated to estimate the total lifetime value certain customers represent to the company. Following these procedures, specific marketing programs can then be tailored to the various groups that are identified as potential new customers.

Determining the Value of Information

The first step in database development is to determine the value of the information that could be captured in the database, and the benefits such data will confer on all potential users. The value of the data is directly related to the variety of functions the database is intended to serve. Advertising, sales, product development, and customer service are just a few areas in which the database may be applied.

Given the range of applications in any given business, researchers must evaluate each application according to the level of data interaction that may occur. For example, Exhibit 6.3 illustrates a **data interaction matrix,** which lists all marketing applications across each functional area where the database will prove beneficial. The purpose of this matrix is to show the type and amount of data required by each functional area regardless of the cost of data collection. Once all the data needs are itemized, those areas indicating shared data needs can then be identified. The fundamental idea is that as more functional areas share data and database applications, the less it will cost to develop the total system. Once the shared data requirements have been determined, the next task is to see if the level and type of the required data exist internally in the company.

Data interaction matrix
A matrix that itemizes the type and amount of data required by each functional area regardless of the cost of data collection.

EXHIBIT 6.3   A Data Interaction Matrix

Marketing Action	Marketing Research Task				
Product mix					
Advertising					
Sales promotion					
Media					
Sales force					
New-product development					
Pricing					
Customer service					
Distribution					
Packaging					
Transportation					

Research Area	Source of Data		
	Historical/Secondary Data	Primary Data	Data Integration
Customer/segment profiles	X	X	X
Purchase volume	X		X
Purchase behaviors	X	X	X
Product preferences		X	X
Lifestyle profiles		X	
Shopping behaviors		X	X
Advertising effectiveness	X	X	X
Promotional preferences	X	X	X
Sales tracking		X	X

Evaluating Internal Data Sources

The best way to determine how much internal data is available is to evaluate all ways in which the company is currently communicating with customers or has done so in the past. The key is to be creative—the company may be communicating with customers in more ways than it first appears.

Exhibit 6.4 shows several key variables in a typical database developed solely from internal information on a particular customer. In this particular example, the customer's job number, company name, address, and phone and fax numbers are indicated, along with the key contact person. Added to this are the SIC code, number of employees, and quote and order dates. As a complement, the primary business is identified, with spaces left to add information on the customer's production factories, projected growth, and depth of product lines. Finally, there is room for the sales price, profit, salesperson (identified by a number), industry, segment, and product. The unique aspect of this example is that all the information on this customer profile exists internally to the organization.

Once all possible sources of internally available data have been identified, several key questions need to be asked. First, what is the "shelf life" of the internal data? For example, in Exhibit 6.4, is Mr. Sepulveda still the key contact person, or has he left the company? Or has the number of employees increased or decreased? In short, are the internal data timely,

EXHIBIT 6.4   **Key Current Customer Profile Attributes**

SOLD TO:	Bristol Myers Squibb		Job No:	6732
	PO Box 897	Mayzguez	PR	00708-0
PHONE:	8098001095		FAX:	20464
DELIVERY:	Bristol Myers Squibb			
		PR	00709	80983401
Key Contact Person:	Ben Sepulveda			

SIC Code	2834	**Quote Date**	11/14/90
Volume		**Order Date**	12/14/90
Employees	52600	**Ship Date**	

Business:	pers care
Production Factories:	
Projected Growth:	
Depth of Customer Product Line:	

Sales Price		**Industry**	
Profit		**Segment**	Pharma Powder/
Salesman	2	**Product**	Y

accurate, and up-to-date? Second, are there any key variables missing that could be obtained internally to enhance the database? For example, personal-level buying demographics such as the secretary's name, decision influencers, or key birth dates could be added to this profile.

When all information has been identified, and all relevant questions asked, the internal data sources should be compared to the data interaction matrix discussed earlier. The matrix should be revised according to the collected internal data.

Evaluating External Data Sources

External data for a database can come from many sources. In Chapters 4 and 5 we identified external secondary data sources available from syndicated marketing research suppliers and the Internet. A brief review of data available from such sources includes

- Competitive sales data.

- Industry surveys.

- Surveys of competitors.

- Government reports.

- Historical projections.

Also available are data collected on the purchase behavior of a customer that can indicate that customer's propensity to purchase a complementary product or service. For example, if a company purchases a heavy volume of computer printing paper, then that company may have a long-term need for computer printers. Data of this type would normally include

- Demographics.

- Lifestyle indicators.

- Financial data.

- Product purchase data.

- Promotional and sales data.

Again, after all relevant external data has been reviewed, the researcher must then revise the data interaction matrix by indicating what data are in fact available through external data enhancement.

Evaluating Custom-Designed Data Sources

Even after both internal and external sources have been evaluated, the data interaction matrix probably indicates data elements that have not been fulfilled. The only way to capture such data would be to develop a source of custom data. Custom data are commonly treated as primary data because of their limited distribution (sampling) and limited communication ability (disguised). Primary research from a database perspective is many times limited to gaining information on current customers. Casinos, for example, are very successful at enhancing internal data sources through the use of primary research techniques. From the moment a customer enters, a casino will attempt to track that person's every move. From restaurants to shows to gaming tables, information is collected and then fed back to the internal database. Many casinos use special credit or debit cards to track all customer spending. There are even slot-machine cards used to record the number of pulls on the lever a customer makes, and to bill the individual at the end of a set time period.

Some casinos complement this information with exit interviews on satisfaction/dissatisfaction issues. However, no matter how good these techniques are at tracking movements inside the casino, they cannot track customers at competing casinos.[8] From a database perspective, a major limitation of custom data sources is their inability to track or measure actual purchase behavior outside the company-controlled environment.

Evaluating the Source Data Mix

At this time the data interaction matrix should identify all levels of data available to capture. All the data that will be used to construct and develop the database, whether internal, external, or custom, should be delineated and appropriate variables confirmed for inclusion. Now a reassessment of information needs is necessary. It would be ideal to include all possible data that would classify both current customers and potential customers, but collection of such data would cost a great deal of money, time, and effort. Someone in the company will always say, "Prove to me that the database will be an asset that will offset the time, money, and effort needed to develop it."

The two real tests of a database's contribution to the bottom line are whether it provides relevant data and whether the data can be enhanced. To test data relevancy, the researcher needs to answer six simple questions:

1. Will the information contained in the database allow you to learn more about the company's customers and markets than you would know without it?

2. Will the database allow the company to develop better products and promotional programs?

3. Will the database increase the likelihood of selling or cross-selling existing goods and services?

4. Does the information in the database have the capacity to identify new customers?

5. Does the information in the database have the capacity to increase penetration of new or existing markets?

6. Will the database lend greater information to the sales force for selling purposes?

If the answers to these questions are all yes, then the database will ultimately be a significant asset that will contribute to the profitability of the company.

The second test of the worthiness of a database is its ability to overlay data to provide data enhancement. To put this more simply, will the interaction of various data elements increase the predictive power of the database, more so than if each data element were used alone? Because each specific data field has its own specific purpose and implication, various combinations of the fields should be examined to determine if more knowledge can be obtained. For example, one significant test is to combine selling region with account classification. Simply exploring selling region by itself may illustrate, for example, that the northeast has the greatest sales volume. But, when this is combined with account classification, the database may show that 90 percent of "A" accounts (the ones that generate high profit, at a low selling cost per contract) reside in the South. The combination of the two data fields may thus result in a greater enhancement of the entire data set, increasing the predictive power of the database.

Finally, by testing various combinations of data fields, the researcher is in a better position to eliminate data that would not serve any enhancement purposes. For example, adding "key contact person" to the "account classification and region" combination does not enhance the predictive ability of the database. In this case the cost of collecting key contact data would outweigh the benefit.

General Rules of Thumb in Database Development

Given the value a well-developed database can add to a company, management should view the total process of database development as a commitment to a long-term data acquisition plan. As such, they should budget the development of a database as a multiyear process. Researchers should begin with collecting the data that will have the greatest amount of predictive power.

Depth The overall number of key data fields or key variables that will comprise the data record.

Second, management should view the data acquisition process in terms of the width and the depth of the database. **Depth** refers to the overall number of key data fields or key variables that will comprise the data record; for example, look back to Exhibit 6.4 and note that each attribute in this customer profile is considered a data field or key variable. The profile thus has a total depth of 21 variables. Depth represents the density, volume, or key variables contained in each record. **Width,** in contrast, refers to the total number of records contained in the database. In more common market research terms, width is usually referred to as *sample size,* or the actual number of responses collected. Due to the fact that a single customer or potential customer may be represented in multiple records, researchers should not be concerned if they don't obtain a 100 percent depth for each record. Remember, the value of a database lies in its ability to interact or interchange data. If one record is not 100 percent complete, an additional record may compensate for it. For example, for the data record collected internally for Bristol Myers Squibb, two variables (e.g., sales volume and projected growth) may be missing. A second record on Bristol Myers Squibb, collected externally, may be missing, say, the job number while containing the sales volume and projected growth figures. The ability of the data to be overlaid is a key enhancement value in database development.

Width The total number of records contained in the database (also referred to as *sample size*).

Finally, companies should avoid jumping onto the database bandwagon (i.e., developing a database just because everyone else is) and then failing to commit the resources necessary to fully use it. A marketing research database, by design, is a constant and ongoing process. A database will not succeed unless the company makes a commitment to long-term data acquisition and enhancement.

Technology: Turning Data into Information

Most companies have data on almost every aspect of their operations. Many companies even have data on how much data they have. What are data? Data are verbal or numerical facts that can be used for reasoning or calculating. In database terminology, a data item or **data field** is a basic characteristic about a customer or client (e.g., sex, age, name, address). As we discussed in previous sections, data fields have little value when treated individually. When they are combined in a manner that makes them useful for making decisions, then they acquire value and can be regarded as information.

Data field A basic characteristic about a customer.

An important step in the database development process is transforming data into information. Technology provides the engine that powers this step.

Database Technology

Database technology The tools that are used to transform data into information.

Database technology refers to the tools that are used to transform data into information. While in definition database technology appears simple, in application it can be somewhat complicated. A brief overview will allow for a clearer understanding of what really drives a database.

Database technology allows data to be processed and stored in a single bank. It consists of two unique features: a database management system and a data dictionary. A database management system is a computer program that creates, modifies, and controls access to the data in the database. Users of these programs simply follow basic instructions to combine data to produce some desired output. A commonly used database management system is ACCESS.[9] Exhibit 6.5 on pp. 162–63 is an example of the use of this program. A data dictionary provides descriptions of the data in the database. It formats the data and assigns meaning to the data fields or variables. Together, the database management system and data dictionary comprise what is called the database processing system.

Sequential database system Data in a very simple pattern, that is, a simple path, linkage, or network.

Two types of database processing systems exist: sequential and relational. A **sequential database system** organizes data in a very simple pattern, that is, a simple path, linkage, or network. In a sequential database only two single data fields can be paired. Once paired, they can be linked to a third data field. Once this group is connected, it can then be linked to a fourth, that group to a fifth, and so on, as illustrated in Exhibit 6.6.

Many companies choose to develop sequential databases because they allow users to easily access detailed data linked to a specific data field or variable (e.g., region of country). Also, database systems are commonly used in companies that require reports based on consistent data in a given format.

Relational database system A system that structures a database in tables with rows and columns, with the tables (not data fields) being linked together depending on the output desired.

A **relational database system** operates somewhat differently from a sequential database system. The major difference is that relational databases require no direct relationship between data fields or variables. Data are structured in tables with rows and columns, with the tables (not the data fields) being linked together depending on the output desired. With a relational database system, the table becomes an individual file, rows correspond to records (width), and columns represent data fields or variables (depth) within each record.

In Exhibit 6.7, for example, each row represents the number of customers for that particular field; the primary market attribute, for example, is divided into regional, national, and international fields. Each column contains the breakdown of each customer by primary business (bakery, chemical, pharmaceutical, etc.). The rows and columns together constitute the table, which profiles customers by industry segment.

EXHIBIT 6.6 | An Example of a Sequential Database

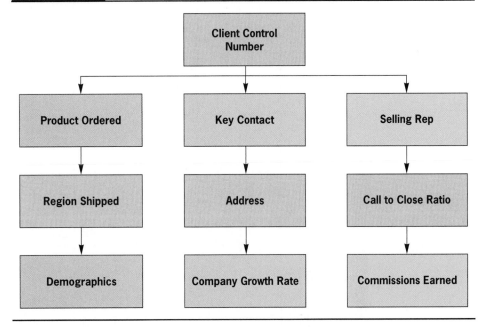

EXHIBIT 6.5 An ACCESS Example

PRIMARY BUSINE	KEY CONTACT PE	DELIVERY STREET	DCITY	DSTATE	DZIPCODE	PHONE	FAX	CUSTPO
	Douglas				2882231	0	100541	52117
banks	Ernest Stevens		AL	35203-	2052521161	2053266220	020890-2	299568
snack food	DENNY TAVERES				7176324477	7176327207	VERBAL PER DEN	572117
	Richard Trotter						2179	342422
food	John Lock		W	54467	7153415960	7153415966	21259	59571
food			W	54467	715341596	7153415566	29060	127397
	DALE COWART				5014245403	5014245228	MH51114	376271
			OR	97220-	5036664545	5036692223	DM9099	222620
pers care			PR	00709	3154322287	0	BM00030	54200
pers care			PR	00709	0	0	BM	109800
pers care	FRANCK		PR	00709	3154322287	315432411	VERBAL	96175
pers care	Ben Sepulveda		PR	00709	8098340185	8098331095	20464	48541
pers care	Ben Sepulveda		PR	00709	8098340185	8098001095	20464	48541
pers care	JERRY WOOSTER		VA	22021	2019266786	2019266782	M-01202	60067
	MILLOS CIKASA				8185494	8185496638	101071	53582
	OLIVIER DULAUN				6096632260	6096650474	5586	407602
					6096632260	0	1187	780000
building products					2154858959		72748	74000
					2068728400	2063957701	F-35580	145560
	MARK MIKA		WA	98032	2063957596	2063957591	D67428	3977000

							84007	194076
	CAROL COLLINS		MI	48043	6144386312	0	LMT104737	48897
			PA	19363	7088332900	7088331025	K-53167	43188
	PAUL MORGAN				6155976700	6155975243	13362	42009
	ALLEN RANSOM		IN	46041	8032815292	0	B883D150061	312743
snack foods			IN	46041	2143534893	0		375954
snack foods					0	0	U9914	383478
snack foods			NC		0	0		360140
snack foods			MD		0	0	EU10443	403937
snack foods	Royce Shafer							957600
snack foods					0	0	U9914	383478
snack foods								42960
snack foods	Engineering Accou		IN	46041-	2143534893	0	EU-7308	375954
snack foods	BRUCE FISHER/JI		MD		2143344940	2143345175	EU-14060	997554
snack foods	DAN PREMUS		OR	97005	2143344940	2145345175	EV14247	596553
snack foods	Bruce Fisher	Aberdeen	MD	21001			EV15168	325766
food	ED CASSATERI		IL	60185	7082311140	7082316968	WC-072810	189319
	D. WHEL		KS	66031	9137648100	9137646520	VERBAL	550691
	NANCY HOLLAND				8002556837	0	H2924	56861
		Burlingame	CA	94010			1717	222430
	Roland Gage						1717	787745
snack food					2159329330	2159325698	SM12067	98481
food	CHRISTINE ALLEN	HERSHEY	PA	17033			2R5076221	49428

EXHIBIT 6.7	A Relational Database That Shows a Customer Profile by Industry Segment				
	Bakery (15)	**Chemical (7)**	**Pharmaceutical (35)**	**Snack food (42)**	**Other (11)**
Primary Market Served					
Regional	1(6.7)	1 (14.3)		3 (7.1)	1 (9.1)
National		2 (28.6)	7 (20)	37 (88.1)	3 (27.3)
International	3 (20)	2 (28.6)	8 (22.9)		5 (45.5)
No. of Product Lines					
One	(6.7)	1 (14.3)	1 (2.9)		3 (27.3)
Two	6 (40)		2 (5.7)	2 (4.8)	2 (18.2)
Three		1 (14.3)	5 (14.3)	1 (2.4)	1 (9.1)
Four	1 (6.7)	3 (42.9)	4 (11.4)	4 (9.5)	—
Five		1 (2.9)			—
Six	1 (6.7)				1 (9.1)
Seven					
Region					
N.E.	5 (33.3)		13 (37.1)	9 (21.4)	2 (18.2)
S.E.	1 (1.7)	6 (85.7)	4 (11.4)	1 (2.4)	5(45.5)
M.W.	4 (26.7)	1 (14.3)	3 (8.6)	23 (54.8)	2 (18.2)
West	5 (33.3)		1 (2.9)	2 (4.8)	2(18.2)
CAN/Other			13 (37.1)	7 (16.7)	

Exhibit 6.8 shows the result of relating primary business to region of the country. If the analyst is concerned with one particular customer in this table, he or she needs only to isolate a job number that corresponds to that customer and request the relevant output.

Relational databases offer greater flexibility than sequential databases in examining many complex data relationships. In addition, relational databases allow the analyst to look at all variables or data fields simultaneously rather than one variable at a time. Overall, relational databases are best for dynamic situations in which the database must expand over time and in which multiple variable applications are needed.

While this discussion has only touched the tip of the iceberg on database technology, it should provide a basic understanding of the kinds of database systems that are available. We will now turn our attention to the main reason behind database development: database modeling.

Database Modeling

Before conducting any statistical modeling procedure, the researcher needs to review, refine, and format the raw data within the database so it can be easily processed by available statistical packages. This data interface process is necessary for successful query and modeling activities.

Database analysis and modeling are designed to summarize what companies already know about their best customers and at the same time indicate what they need to learn about these individuals. When a database model fails to predict a customer's future behavior, the database analyst needs to ask whether the company truly knows enough about its customers. (The In the Field box highlights one of the largest database firms in the world.)

| EXHIBIT 6.8 | A Relational Database That Shows Industry Profile by Region |

	Northeast (29)	Southeast (17)	Midwest (38)	West (9)	Canada/Other (23)
Primary Market Served					
Regional	3 (10.3)	1 (5.9)	1 (2.6)	1 (11.1)	
National	6 (20.7)	7 (41.2)	25 (65.8)	2 (22.2)	10 (43.5)
International	6 (20.7)	4 (23.5)	4 (10.5)	2 (22.2)	3 (13)
No. of Product Lines					
One	3 (10.3)	1 (5.9)		2 (22.2)	
Two	3 (10.3)	2 (11.8)	3 (7.9)	4 (44.4)	
Three	3 (10.3)	1 (5.9)	3 (7.9)		1 (4.3)
Four	5 (17.2)	3 (17.6)	1 (2.6)	1 (11.1)	3 (13)
Five		1 (5.9)	—		
Six			2 (5.3)		
Seven			1 (2.6)		
Selling Rep					
Cavendor	2 (6.9)	3 (17.6)	—	—	2 (8.7)
Moore	—	2 (11.8)	1 (2.6)	—	—
HWN	16 (55.2)	2 (11.8)	—	—	2 (8.7)
CAC	—	2 (11.8)	12 (31.6)	6 (66.7)	8 (34.8)
RBW	5 (17.2)	1 (6.3)	14 (36.8)	—	—
JMC	1 (3.4)	—	—	—	1 (4.3)
Emond	—	2 (11.8)	—	—	1 (4.3)
Nesti	2 (6.9)	—	1 (2.6)	—	1 (4.3)
CJE	—	3 (12.6)	—	—	3 (1.3)
Cherry	—	—	1 (2.6)	1 (11.1)	—
TC	1 (3.4)	1 (6.3)	1 (2.6)	—	—
WHHE	—	—	1 (2.6)	—	—
Roger	—	—	3 (7.9)	—	—
MN	—	—	2 (5.3)	—	1 (4.3)
CC	—	—	1 (2.6)	—	—
VS	—	—	—	—	1 (4.3)
Nichols	—	—	—	—	1 (4.3)

A CLOSER LOOK AT RESEARCH   In the Field

Database America Companies Introduces SalesLeads™— First Web-Based Lead Generating Service for Consumers and Small Businesses

Montvale New Jersey, Oct. 28, 1996—The Database America Companies today announced Sales-Leads™, a Web-based direct marketing database designed to generate sales leads for small to medium-sized businesses. SalesLeads provides anyone with access to the World Wide Web a cost-effective means of building targeted prospect lists from Database America's file of in-depth information on more than 11 million U.S. businesses. Visitors to Database America's Web site may develop highly customized mailing or telemarketing lists, paying a minimal charge for only the names they download. With the introduction of SalesLeads, Database America makes direct marketing an accessible, affordable, easy-to-use sales tool for consumers, hobbyists, small to mid-sized businesses and cottage industries.

Anyone with a personal computer and an Internet connection can access SalesLeads *via* the Database America Web site (http://www.databaseamerica.com). The system provides an easy interface for selecting marketing criteria such as geographic and demographic attributes and honing the list to specify details

such as sales volume or employee size. Uses for SalesLeads can range from students researching employment prospects, to hobbyists building a list of regional churches or associations sponsoring craft fairs, to commercial real estate agents generating leads for sale properties. There is no charge for looking and no minimum requirements. Customers pay only a few cents for each prospect they download and may pay *via* a secure credit card transaction on the system.

"Database America is drawing on more than 40 years of expertise in business-to-business direct mail marketing. We pride ourselves on leading the market with the latest technology," said Al Ambrosino, president of the Database America Companies. "With SalesLeads designed as an online service, we can now provide the small office and home office audience access to the identical, accurate database information previously geared towards much larger organizations."

SalesLeads is the first lead-generating product of its kind on the Web offering real-time delivery of information that can be easily updated. Users can conduct their searches by filling in criteria in an easy-to-use graphical form on the Database America Web page. These criteria include business name, business type *via* SIC (Standard Industrial Classification) codes, geography, ZIP code, number of employees, and sales volume.   *(continued)*

Many companies find themselves data rich and information poor. The process of customer modeling can often point to a company's information shortage and trigger new ideas for future marketing research endeavors.

An effective approach to handling database modeling is to begin with the end in mind. Andreasen described this as backward marketing research.[10] He states that the best way to design usable research is to start where the process will end and then work backward. The question then becomes, How will the information that is gathered be used? Or, What should this information allow us to do? Backward planning allows the researcher to better understand how the modeling output will be usable for the decision maker.

Among the many modeling procedures that exist in database analysis, two of the more traditional are scoring models and lifetime value models.

Scoring models Database models used to predict consumption behavior; each individual in the database is assigned a score based on his or her propensity to respond to a marketing variable or make an actual purchase.

Scoring Models

Scoring models are used to predict consumption behavior. Each individual in the database is assigned a score based on his or her propensity to respond to a marketing variable or

(concluded)

Once users have determined their search criteria and built a mailing or telemarketing list, they can download the file to their computers. The list is created in a standard character file format that is compatible with virtually all desktop word processing and spreadsheet programs. The list includes business names, addresses and phone numbers for printing out as address labels. Database America will also offer users the option of purchasing the data for shipment in hardcopy labels.

Once a search has been completed, the system creates and stores a record of the list, which can be downloaded over and over at no additional charge. This features helps users keep track of whom they have targeted, to avoid unintentional duplicate mailings as well as to manage sequential mailings or telemarketing campaigns. Updates to the list are available.

In June 1996, Database America launched an Interactive Media Division, created to bring its high-quality business and consumer information and direct marketing techniques to users of the Internet, the World Wide Web, corporate intranets and other types of electronic media. The company is among the first data providers to enable online search vehicles such as SalesLeads with direct marketing information for use by Web site visitors.

Availability

Database America will roll out two versions of Sales-Leads. A consumer or small office/home office (SOHO) version is being introduced at this week's Direct Marketing Association tradeshow in New Orleans (Booth #1901). A test demo of some of the product features is present on Database America's Web site. An industrial version of SalesLeads, targeting the more traditional business marketing manager and offering more in-depth features such as credit reports, will be introduced at the upcoming COMDEX tradeshow in November.

Database America

Database America specializes in compiling, updating and distributing business and consumer marketing information and services to increase sales and marketing advantage for companies. Headquartered in Montvale, New Jersey, with regional sales offices nationwide, Database America has been a marketing information leader for more than 40 years. In addition to creating a comprehensive database of more than 11 million businesses and 97 million households in the U.S., the company also supplies value-added computer and interactive media services. Database America can be reached at (800) 223-7777.

Source: Montvale, NJ, 1996 [cited 28 October 1996]. Available from http://www.databaseamerica.com; INTERNET.

make an actual purchase. High scores are indications of very desirable customers; low scores represent less desirable segments. The initial objective is to rank customer segments based on their potential profitability to the company. The primary feature of score models is called the gains table. An example of a gains table is presented in Exhibit 6.9.

Using a gains table, a database analyst can project and manage the profitability of various customer segments. For example, according to the data in Exhibit 6.9, the customer base is comprised of 500,000 persons. They are divided into five equal segments of 100,000, or five segments of 20 percent of the market. The gains table ranks each of these segments based on its profit potential. Group 1 customers have the highest profit potential, and group 5 the lowest. Group 1 is estimated to draw approximately $2 million to future profit, or an estimated $20 per customer, and so on. Aggregately, groups 1, 2, and 3 are estimated to generate $4.5 million in total future profits, or an estimated $20, $17.50, and $3.50, respectively, per customer. As one descends through the gains table in Exhibit 6.9, the percentage of profitability per segment begins to decrease. This table thus reinforces the basic marketing principle that customers are not homogeneous and, more specifically, the conventional wisdom that 20 percent of customers represent 80 percent of a company's revenue.

EXHIBIT 6.9   **An Example of a Gains Table**

Group Number	Number of Customers	Percentage of Customers	Cumulative Number of Customers	Cumulative Percentage	Average Profile per Customer	Predicted Total Profit	Cumulative Total	Cumulative Average per Customer
1	100,000	20%	100,000	20%	$20	$2,000,000	$2,000,000	$20.00
2	100,000	20	200,000	40	15	1,500,000	3,500,000	17.50
3	100,000	20	300,000	60	10	1,000,000	4,500,000	3.50
4	100,000	20	400,000	80	5	500,000	5,000,000	1.25
5	100,000	20	500,000	100	1	100,000	5,100,000	.20

Key Variables in Scoring Models

Key variables in the scoring model allow a researcher to demonstrate which factors can be combined to separate customers into purchase groups or categories. Scoring models use a series of weights that can be multiplied by assigned values in each customer's record on the database.[11] For example, let's suppose that we discovered five factors that are useful in separating heavy users from light users of hair spray: age, income, occupation, number of children under 18, and home value. Based on the analysis of customer characteristics in the database, the scoring model determines that for heavy users of hair spray, the variables are arranged in the following order and assigned a corresponding weight: home value, .130; age, .050; occupation, .042; number of children under 18, .022; and income, .012. Obviously, the real weights produced by the model would be quite different, since they are to be multiplied by numbers (e.g., age in years, occupation in assigned coded value, income in thousands). For the sake of our discussion, however, let's assume these are real values.

In this example, home value is a very important factor, with income being a less important factor, for classifying customers into a heavy user group. The model permits a researcher to run a program that takes each of the relevant factors in the customer record on the database and multiplies it by the appropriate weight. The weights are then added together to get an overall score. The score represents the likelihood of a customer's being a heavy user (or a medium user, etc.) of the product.

As in most database techniques, variables used to generate scoring model gains tables should be from actual purchase behavior data. Key variables would include demographics, psychographics, lifestyle data, and purchase habits including frequency, volume, and amount spent at a given time. These variables would then be assigned weights or scores depending on their ability to predict purchase behavior. For example, men may purchase more power tools than women; therefore, based on the single demographic variable of sex, men would be assigned a 10, women a 4. Each variable classification would be assigned a weight or score. The scoring weight structure for two customer groups may look like the following:

Customer Group A		*Customer Group B*	
Female	2 pts	Male	10 pts
Volume: $100	5 pts	Volume: $50	10 pts
Frequency: 2 weeks	4 pts	Frequency: 1 month	8 pts
Product purchased: dry cleaning	6 pts	Product purchased: dry cleaning	6 pts
Total:	17 pts	Total:	34 pts

Based on actual customer data, consumer Group B (with 34 points) has better matching variables than consumer Group A (with only 17 points). When all customers are aggregately identified, those having the highest scores would form Group 1 (20 percent of the customer base) in the gains table. The next highest group in the customer base would form Group 2 (an additional 20 percent), and so on.

The total scores for each customer per group would then be converted to dollars. So 34 points would become $34, and 17 points would become $17. This conversion becomes the foundation for predicting future profitability in gains table analysis.

Scoring models need to be designed with the consideration that they have a limited period of effectiveness. The life of the model is directly related to changes in customer demand. Therefore, scoring models need to be revised and changed as the market changes. Many analysts contend that once a scoring model has been developed, it automatically becomes obsolete. The Marketing Research Illustration at the end of this chapter discusses the value of scoring models for financial institutions.

Lifetime Value Models

Lifetime value models
Database models developed on historical data, using actual purchase behavior, not probability estimates, to predict future actions.

The fundamental premise behind **lifetime value models** is that customers, just like physical and tangible machinery, represent company assets. More important, customers represent a continuous stream of cash flow based on transactions they conduct with the business. All too often, the outcome of many marketing research projects is to obtain information that can be used to generate new customers only. Lifetime value models demonstrate that it is more valuable for businesses to concentrate on qualified customers first, then focus on refining them rather than constantly seeking out new customers.

Three research objectives are essential for lifetime value models:

1. To acquire information that establishes variables for prequalifying or selectively screening customers.

2. To obtain information on customer satisfaction. (In fact, data must be obtained on satisfaction beyond the product or service and must include satisfaction measures based on total customer expectations.)

3. To generate information that allows the business to build relationships with repeat customers.[12]

In most lifetime value models, information extracted from the database designed to achieve these objectives would include the following:

1. **Price variables:** The initial product or service cost and any price changes that occur.

2. **Sales promotional variables:** Type used, cost of the incentive, value to the customer.

3. **Advertising expenditures:** Direct costs of advertising expenses.

4. **Product costs:** Direct costs, plus quality of goods/services.

5. **Relationship-building efforts:** Type and costs of relationship-building devices; value of building long-term relationships.

The database, if properly designed, can channel information into what can be called a complex customer road map. Exhibit 6.10 represents the output from a hypothetical lifetime value model for a fast-food restaurant. In this example 10,000 new customers are targeted for the marketing effort. The average amount spent by customers is about $4.30, and a free sandwich (with a cost of 90 cents) is the incentive to attract the customers. There-

EXHIBIT 6.10	A Hypothetical Lifetime Value Model for a Fast-Food Restaurant

PERIOD	1	2	3	4
CUSTOMERS	10,000			
REPEAT		3500	1225	428
REPEAT %		%35	%35	%35
REVENUE				
AVE. TICKET	$4.30	$4.50	$4.75	$4.75
PRICE INC.	.90			
TOTAL	34,000	15,750	5818	2033
EXPENSES				
DIRECT COSTS	%60	%60	%60	%60
TOTAL	20400	9450	3491	1219
REPEAT EFFORT				
TARGET	10,000	3500	1225	428
REPEAT%	%35	%35	%35	%35
RATE	3500	1225	428	150
TOTAL MAIL	10,000	3500	1225	428
COST	$3800	$1330	$465	$162
TOTAL				
EXP.	$24200	$10780	$3956	$1381
CONTRIB.	9800	4970	1862	652
INVEST.	3800	1330	465	162
TOTAL				
LIFETIME				
VALUE	$6000	$9460	$11,037	$11,527
CUSTOMER				
VALUE	$.60	$.96	$1.10	$1.15

fore, the estimated revenue is about $34,000. Expenses amount to approximately 60 percent of total revenues, for a total expense of $20,400.

This business averages a 35 percent return rate of its customers. Therefore, mailing out 10,000 free sandwich coupons should yield 3,500 responses at a cost of $3,800. Total expenses for this planned effort are now estimated at $24,200. With an initial investment of $3,800, the total contribution should result in a $9,800 return to the business. This, in turn, equates to a total lifetime customer value of $6,000, or 60 cents per customer during the first period of the promotion. Given expected rates of return customers over the next three promotional periods, total contribution would fall to $652, with investment costs down to $162. Total lifetime value over four periods would increase to $11,527, or $1.15 per customer. The four-period lifetime value for an individual customer is $1.15.

To summarize, as a database analysis tool, lifetime value models equate the asset value of customers. In contrast to purchase intention data, lifetime value models can be based only on actual purchase data. The value of the technique is that it is based not on probability estimates but rather on actual purchase behavior and is therefore a good predictor of consumer behavior.

Databases, Marketing Research, and the New Millennium

Over the next 10 to 20 years, the environment in which marketing researchers operate will face dramatic changes. Businesses will demand from the marketing research industry higher-quality information, more quickly and more accurately than ever before. They will also expect this information to be founded on actual purchase data rather than purchase intentions. These changes will require more emphasis on database development by marketing research personnel. Traditional marketing research, as a business practice, will have to reexamine and reassess the value it brings to the business decision maker. In order for relationship marketing practices to be truly successful, marketing personnel will base their ability to make sound decisions on data-driven marketing techniques supplied by the marketing research arm of the business. Three important ingredients will force the marketing research industry to change its approach: technology, data, and data analysis.

Technology

Many of the upcoming technological changes will affect marketing research more than other marketing applications. There will be volumes and volumes of both internal and external source data to consider in database development. Extraction of this data will be the key focus of the marketing research industry. It is safe to say that marketing researchers will need to be able to access, manipulate, graphically format, and present database information from any possible location, be it the office, the poolside, the airplane, or the sales-call site. Technologies that will allow this to happen include

- Flash memory storage technology.

- Matchbox-sized data storage space.

- Wireless PC and fax modems.

- Hand-sized data processors designed to handle more information than today's PCs and to interact with databases all over the world at any time of day.

Already, the marketing research department at American Airlines, for example, has developed an information management database to support marketing strategy and planning activities. The system allows for 24-hour access of historical data on the entire airline industry. It also allows managers the ability to interactively access, analyze, compute, and display historical and future data. This database is used to forecast passenger load factors, market share, aircraft utilization, and customer satisfaction.

Data

The keys to data collection for marketing research will be timeliness and relevancy combined. The role of marketing research will be to collect data that allows companies the ability to track product purchases, promotions, communications, and distribution costs and relate them directly to the individual customer. This data collection method has already been designated as "transactional data collection." Today, Anheuser-Busch tracks purchases of products, frequency of purchase, in-store promotion effects, and purchase incentives on a weekly basis among certain large grocery retailers. With added value, a transaction made with a credit or debit card can be directly related to the customer. With this data, Anheuser-Busch can alter in-store promotional programs, change display space, and test the impact of price discounting at store level. Robert Signerelli, an executive vice president with Anheuser-Busch, says, "In our business we need data that tells us what's working today. We need data on what customers are buying on Monday, Tuesday, and Wednesday and what they will buy on Friday and Saturday. Data that is anything less than actual purchase data, more than one week old is irrelevant for our marketing research purposes."[13]

Data Analysis

As we have stressed throughout this chapter, the success of any database lies in its ability to predict customer responses. Therefore, predictive models will become commonplace in database analysis. These modeling techniques will lose much of the black-box mystique they currently hold. More specifically, modeling as an analysis tool will take on a learning systems paradigm similar to that of human thinking. Database modeling systems will actually "learn" from their own results. Such data analysis techniques will not only increase the accuracy of prediction but also provide new levels of capabilities for databases.

Summary on Marketing Research Databases and the New Millennium

"My research department tells me my customer is female, 18 to 34 years old, married with two kids. She and her husband live in suburban America, own their own home, and have an income of $40,000 per year. Unfortunately, though, when I visit retail stores and observe who takes my product off the shelf, they never look the same as my research suggests."

This anonymous quote is indicative of many businesses working with data and information today. Marketing research today stands at a crossroads of change. Many companies will continue to disseminate surveys directed at large samples of people. In doing so, they will continue to face the same problems they face today, the most serious of which is dealing with limited generalizability of purchase intentions rather than specific profiles of customers generated by actual purchase patterns. For marketing research, the future lies in the ability to provide information based on events as they actually occur. Many marketing research providers, and users, are recognizing that the database is becoming the tool of the future.

In today's business environment, slow and steady does not necessarily mean success. In fact, gathering data at a slow and steady pace will most likely produce results that are outdated even before they can be interpreted. Marketing research must be willing to change as new techniques emerge. Database applications have the potential for transforming marketing research from a data collection task into an information resource laboratory.

SUMMARY OF LEARNING OBJECTIVES

Illustrate and define a marketing research database.
A marketing research database is a central repository of information on what customers are purchasing, how often, and in what amount. The fundamental purpose of any customer database is to help a firm develop meaningful, personal communication with its customers. Other, more specific purposes of this database are to improve efficiency of market segment construction, increase the probability of repeat purchase behavior, and enhance sales and media effectiveness.

Explain the interactive nature of marketing research and data enhancement.
A database is designed to serve as an information and intelligence resource for the company. Data enhance-

ment allows a company to gain more knowledge of its customers, increase the effectiveness of its marketing programs, and predict responsiveness to changing marketing programs. Marketing research plays the critical role of gathering and collecting data relating to geodemographic factors, customer attributes, and target market characteristics.

Describe the dynamics of database development.
The development of a marketing research database takes into account numerous steps, including (1) assessing what information needs are required by the company; (2) identifying specific research needs; (3) collecting internal, external, and target market data; (4) profiling customers into purchase categories; and (5)

developing predictive models to estimate the total life-time value each customer represents to a business.

List the general rules of thumb in database development.

Three general rules of thumb exist in database development. First, collect data that will have the greatest amount of predictive power. Second, view the data acquisition process in terms of the width and depth of the database. Third, make a commitment to long-term data acquisition and enhancement.

Demonstrate understanding of technology in a database context.

Database technology refers to the process of transforming data into predictive information. This is accomplished through a database management system which creates, modifies, and controls access to the database. The two most commonly employed database management systems are relational and sequential database systems.

Understand the role of modeling in database analysis.

The purpose of database modeling is twofold: (1) to summarize what companies already know about their customers, and (2) to show companies what they need to learn about their customers. Two common modeling techniques exist in database analysis. A scoring model, using a gains table, is designed to predict consumption behavior. The lifetime value model is designed to measure the value customers represent to the firm. Both models rely on actual purchase behavior, not probability estimates based on purchase intentions.

KEY TERMS AND CONCEPTS

Database 149

Database technology 160

Data enhancement 152

Data field 160

Data interaction matrix 156

Depth 160

Lifetime value models 169

Relational database system 161

Scoring models 166

Sequential database system 161

Width 160

REVIEW QUESTIONS

1. How does a marketing research database differ from an operational database? How does a firm's strategic market plan benefit from the use of a marketing research database?

2. List the three advantages that data enhancement provides and explain how a manufacturer of office furniture could use each one.

3. When using internal data sources, what are two possible disadvantages that have to be considered? Identify possible solutions to overcome the problems associated with these disadvantages.

4. Should a company forsake the use of a database if it is not 100 percent complete? Why or why not?

5. Explain the differences between a sequential database and a relational database. What advantages are associated with each?

6. What three factors will have the greatest impact on future methods used to provide information in marketing research?

DISCUSSION QUESTIONS

1. Why have transactional data collection techniques become of utmost importance to Anheuser-Busch and other companies?

2. Briefly describe the differences between lifetime value models and scoring models. In what situations would each modeling procedure be most appropriate?

3. **EXPERIENCE THE INTERNET.** Visit the following Web site: www.internets.com. Search the business and finance databases available. See if you can locate market information pertaining to the Republic of China; once you have access to the data, provide a brief description of the demographics in that country.

4. **EXPERIENCE THE INTERNET.** Go to the Web site www.lawhk.hku.hk/dbmenu/economics.shtml. Obtain the category Asian Statistics, and do a search on the economic profile of a country of your choice.

ENDNOTES

1. David Reed, "Team Spirit," *Marketing Week,* September 15, 1995, pp. 73–76.

2. Ibid.

3. Katherine Morrall, "Database Marketing: Leaves Marketing to the Branches," *Bank Marketing,* November 1994, pp. 22–30.

4. Don Schultz, "Losing Attitude," *Marketing Research Magazine,* Fall/ Winter 1995.

5. Ibid.

6. Phyllis Ezop, "Database Marketing Research," *Marketing Research Magazine,* Fall 1994, pp. 34–41.

7. Ibid.

8. Martin Croft, "Record Makers," *Marketing Week,* September 29, 1995, pp. 73–76.

9. David Cohen, "Database of Marketing Research, Search Software," *Journal of Marketing Research,* May 1994, pp. 316–317.

10. Schultz, "Losing Attitude."

11. John Russell, *Strategic Database Management* (New York: Wiley, 1996).

12. Ibid.

13. Robert Signerelli, keynote speech at the 1995 Southwestern Marketing Association, March 1995.

MARKETING RESEARCH ILLUSTRATION

THE FUNCTION OF DATABASES WITHIN THE FINANCIAL INDUSTRY

This Marketing Research Illustration was provided by permission from Acxiom Database Management. The application is a *Case-in-Point* Report taken from the client files of Acxiom Database Management. It illustrates an actual development, use, and manipulation of a major service industry database.

Leading with Data

Credit card issuers and retail bankers have big appetites for customer data, and are using it to derive their businesses. As Gwen Dudley of Jackson, MS-based Trustmark National Bank recently explained at the Chicago conference of the National Center for Database Marketing (NCDM), "If we don't know our customers and their behavior patterns, we can't make decisions that harness those behavior patterns into desired actions."

Never has such knowledge been more crucial. The banking industry is in transition, with new electronic delivery channels rupturing traditional banker-client relationships, replacing them with a fluid market system in which consumers can shop for products and services on price. Loyalty is difficult to come by, as products become increasingly commoditized, and channels of delivery more abundant. In this environment, banks are grooming a new breed of data-savvy executives who can lead by following the data trail.

Courting Profitable Customers

According to Deane Conklin, business development executive with the financial services group of Acxiom Corporation in Conway, AR, bankers are at different levels in their mastery of the data basics of segmentation and data enhancement (see "Mastering the Basics"). But competition is forcing quick transformations of those who are not on board.

"The collection, integration, enhancement, and analysis of customer data have become must-do disciplines for improving marketing efficiency," he said.

According to Conklin, major credit card issuers have been using advanced database techniques for years. But other financial services businesses are just beginning to use such information technology. Mutual fund issuers are just beginning to take advantage of consumer data sources. Retail bankers are very involved in customer databases (called master customer information files or MCIFs), while work in commercial banking is only beginning. (For a comparison with 1995, see the *Case-in-Point* Report "Profiting from Banking's Data Riches" by calling 800-332-6391.)

Conklin noted that most banks are very concerned now with the warehousing of multiple streams of customer and prospect data, and with providing analytical tools to their executives to support customer acquisition and retention efforts. Some of this work is being outsourced to service bureaus and consultants to help bring projects to rapid completion. And new data service providers are cropping up in unexpected places. MasterCard International, for example, announced this year that its 22,000 member banks can now access consumer transaction data by account number using a system provided by MasterCard.

While data is driving more and more acquisition and retention programs, New York City–based research firm First Manhattan Group reports that only 10 percent of America's top 50 banks use data for the more sophisticated profitability analysis at the account or household level. Profitability analysis involves obtaining operating costs, by product, identifying profit components from each transaction file, creating a formula for each product, and validating the accuracy of the calculated data.

For example, CoreStates Bank, a Philadelphia multi-bank holding company with $30 billion in assets, uses profitability analysis to directly measure a customer's return. CoreStates' initial profitability analysis showed that 20 percent of customers are very profitable, 20 percent are very unprofitable, and 60 percent are marginal. Going further, CoreStates analyzed two of its branches. Branch "A" was in an affluent neighborhood and very profitable, while Branch "B" was in a blue-collar area and losing money.

To management's surprise, the two branches were comparable in loan ratios and all other areas except one: no-fee checking. That product alone pushed Branch "B" into the red. Claudia McElwee, vice president of database marketing for CoreStates, explaining what happened after that revealing look at data, said: "This knowledge allowed the product manager to change the minimum balance, raise fees and use other alternatives to improve the profitability of both the accounts and the branch. Conventional wisdom holds that the blue-collar customer is a bank's bread and butter because affluent customers tend to establish more than one banking relationship, but analysis showed that wasn't the case. In our situation, because the affluent customers' balances are so much higher—double that of unprofitable households, even without the total banking relationship, they produce a much better return for us."

Mastering the Basics

Tom Cloninger, business unit executive for Acxiom's data group, describes a basic set of data practices that all banks should master:

- **RFM Segmentation.** Segmenting your customer file by the three key variables of behavior: recency, frequency, and monetary value (RFM). Transaction data remains the most powerful predictor of future behavior, and can help banks identify best prospects and possible defectors.

- **Data Enhancement.** Appending demographic and geographic data elements to customer records permits various modeling and mining efforts to be undertaken, including:

  1. **Profiling.** Create a profile of individual customers and households in each of your key segments, comparing the incidence of a particular type of buyer in your customer universe to the larger marketplace.

  2. **Cross-selling within your existing customer base.** Identify best customers and target those who are prime candidates for additional products and services. Analytical models can pinpoint the variables that will lift response—which means you can mail to fewer people and get a greater response on what you do mail.

  3. **Upselling or reactivating customers.** Low-balance depositors and non-credit customers can be upgraded to more profitable status with appropriate product targeting. Inactive customers may likewise be viable prospects for other offerings. Inform your product strategy with appropriate data, including age, income, property ownership, auto ownership, lifestage, and lifestyle variables.

  4. **Retention.** Reduce churn in your customer base by identifying factors predictive of defection and testing programs to turn likely defectors into your most loyal customers.

  5. **Acquisition.** Data can be used in various ways to improve acquisition. Your profile of your best customers points the way to the prospect most likely to respond, to activate, and to be profitable over time. This data can drive your offer, your creative, your media selection, and your fulfillment approach. Large mailers or telemarketers can also screen prospect lists by running them through a regression model, since they have considerable bargaining power in the list rental marketplace.

At the other end of the spectrum is a small, 15-branch community bank based in Garden City, NY. The Roosevelt Savings Bank, with $3 million in assets in 1996, has become very proficient at identifying the most profitable branch portfolios. Marketing manager Peter Labenburg uses an MCIF system developed by Tampa, FL–based OKRA to determine who the most profitable customers are in each branch, and to evaluate product profitability by customer. This analysis has enabled the bank to generate multimillion dollar returns in customer acquisition and retention campaigns over the past two years (see "Eyes on the Profit Prize," a *Case-in-Point* Case Study available by calling 800-332-6391).

The Loyalty Connection

Developing deeper customer loyalty is an ongoing challenge for every financial institution. It is compounded by the industry's increasing reliance on technology, both for developing products and executing transactions. As reliance on brick-and mortar branch infrastructures and personal relationships lessens, Kurt Peters, publisher of Faulkner & Gray's *Home Banking and Financial Services* newsletter, ponders the impact that financial planners, insurers, and even brokers will have on banks' territories. Peters notes that low-cost, high-tech options such as automated teller machines (ATMs) and on-line banking are increasingly homogenizing product offerings, and suggests that banks may lose the opportunity to cross-sell and up-sell to their own customers because newcomers, not tied to banking's traditional branch infrastructure, can deliver services more cheaply.

While for most of us it's hard to think of bank products and services as commodities that we can shop around for like bread or a container of milk, that mindset is changing, spurred by companies such as FINdex. FINdex of West Palm Beach, FL, is marketing an interactive financial directory of over 500 banks and other financial services providers. At

FINdex's Internet site consumers can compare rates, gather information on product offerings, find banks near them, and purchase products. According to Stanton Freeman, FINdex's chairman, such tools will enable consumers to compare the products of as many suppliers as they choose. "If they find a product they like, they will be able to purchase it right on the spot, he explained. "It won't matter where the financial institution is located."

While newcomers to banking may make some inroads with Internet-happy customers, there is an upside for those established players who are expanding their own on-line offerings. Electronic transactions generate transactional data which, when handled proactively, can help banks stand out from the crowd. For example, data captured on which ATM locations a customer uses, where the ATM is located in relation to the consumer's home and work, and what type of transactions each consumer conducts by time of day, week, or month, can be very illuminating. Banks can use such data resources to increase overall ATM usage, to redirect traffic to under-utilized sites, to increase usage during low-peak evening and weekend hours, or to promote vacation usage.

Designing Win-Win Situations

Leading with data in financial services is not without its challenges. One of the key problems is that a model profitable customer—one who runs high balances on credit cards or other revolving loan programs—is also a model candidate for bankruptcy. That problem has been worsened by industry practices in issuing pre-approved credit cards, which has contributed to rising bad debt for both consumers and issuers. Noting the all-time delinquency rates of the first half of 1996, James Chessen, chief economist of the *Consumer Credit Delinquency Bulletin,* put the blame squarely at bankers' doorsteps. "The delinquencies being seen today are the result of lending decisions made by banks 18 to 24 months ago," he said.

Rising delinquency rates may turn out to be a boon for financial institutions that use data wisely. Peggy Scully, team leader of Acxiom's data group sales office in New York City, sees banks and credit card issuers taking corrective actions already. Their chief strategic response has been to shift from pre-approved to non-pre-approved card offers to qualify prospects on their lists, she noted. In this shift, demographic data takes a much stronger role than in the pre-approved environment, since credit information, usually the best predictor of customer behavior, is off limits because of legal restrictions.

Says Scully, "When a financial services company faces a squeeze, careful segmentation and list qualification helps because it cuts out additional mailing costs. Enhancement data supplies additional information that the financial institutions don't already have about their prospects and customers."

The delinquency crunch has attracted some non-bank innovators to the marketplace. Merchandise cataloger Fingerhut of Minnetonka, MN, for one, decided to pursue high risk customers as a lucrative credit card market. Using the company's catalog database, which contains 500 pieces of information on the cataloger's 50 million-name file, Fingerhut opened 670,000 credit card accounts with $500 million in receivables in less than a year, making it the twenty-third largest card issuer in the U.S. Factoring in the inherent risk of extending credit to low to middle income families, Fingerhut allows a six percent write-off for bad debt, and an interest rate of two percent on its co-branded Visa and MasterCards. Fingerhut's chief executive officer Theodore Deikel attributes the company's success to data. "It all goes back to the database," he said.

Sensitivity Prevails

Another sophisticated use of data is segmented pricing based on customers' and prospective customers' risk and return profiles. Such customization, however, while used successfully in the insurance industry, faces great consumer resistance when it comes to accessing credit. In fact, some issuers have raised consumer ire by offering pre-approved cards without revealing all of the facts about the offered rate. Variable rates and "as low as" offers are clearly on shaky ethical and legal ground (federal law requires issuers to disclose in writing the interest rate in pre-approved offers). And recent amendments to the Fair Credit Reporting Act will soon require all companies using credit bureau lists to inform consumers of their opt-out rights. Issuers must factor in these business realities as they experiment with data-driven programs.

Data can also help bankers to think about customers in fresh ways. Data helps banks to develop traditional or emerging channels and to glean all the information they possibly can. Trustmark National Bank, for example, offers senior citizens, who generally appreciate high-touch over high-tech service, the opportunity to have someone reconcile their check registers with their bank statements. Sound time consuming and unprofitable? To the contrary; Trustmark added a relational database field to track which seniors opened savings accounts for their grandchildren, and markets to them accordingly.

As banks head into the twenty-first century, they are poised to enter a new era of relationship-oriented strategies. Intensely transaction-driven, they have realized that product-oriented strategies will give way to more targeted and focused marketing efforts. William Geiger of Gemini Consulting, based in Cambridge, MA, outlines the benefits that banks will derive as they adopt relationship-building strategies that lead with data:

- They will efficiently sell the maximum amount of the banking products targeted to the right segments of their databases.

- Basic segmentation and cross-selling will become easier, as preferred pricing and service strategies emerge for customers who buy multiple products and keep their business close to home.

- They will build multiple product relationships with targeted customer segments, as sophisticated modeling techniques and profitability analysis at the account level allow customized value offerings and pricing.

- To overcome the increasing homogenization of banking products via Internet banking and other on-line services, banks must position and distribute distinct initiatives associated with a bank's brand identity.

MARKETING RESEARCH CASE EXERCISE

UNDERSTANDING A CUSTOMER DATABASE FOR GROCERY STORE RETAILERS

Few grocery retailers have yet amassed much capability for targeting their marketing to consumers based on known buying behaviors. Even though checkout scanners are widely used to capture purchase data, only a handful of retailers, such as Safeway, Von's, and Ukrop's, have built a database that links product data to purchases by individuals or households. Safeway is the largest company to have done so. The division operates 120 stores in Washington, D.C., Maryland, and Virginia. It functions as an autonomous business within the 1,057-store nationwide chain that produces annual sales of $16 billion. The division began the database effort in 1993, tying scanner purchases to consumer households with a frequent buyer program called Safeway Savings Club. Consumers were invited to join the club through acquisition mailings and in-store promotions. Upon completion of an enrollment form that captures important demographic information, participants are issued an encoded scanner card to present at the checkout counter. Presentation allows them to reap discounts on advertised items and take advantage of in-store promotions throughout the store. This electronic discounting gives the consumer hassle-free access to savings while ensuring that Safeway can amass detailed history on consumer purchases.

There are a number of critical success factors that Safeway had to consider in this database venture. One is protecting consumer privacy. Safeway does not release actual names of its retail customers to any of its distribution partners. Detailed analysis and modeling reports are provided to package-goods manufacturers for a fee. For more history on Safeway consult the company's Web page at www.safeway.com.

1. Identify several reasons why Safeway would develop such a sophisticated database for grocery store consumers. What do you think is the primary value of such a database for Safeway?

2. What is the value that this database can provide to package-goods manufacturers like Nabisco, Procter & Gamble, and Hershey?

3. If given the task to develop a similar database for a local grocer, what key variables would you use?

Learning Objectives

After reading this chapter, you will be able to

1. Understand the purpose of a marketing decision support system (MDSS).

2. Describe the various information requirements used to design an MDSS.

3. Understand the role of transactional data in the MDSS.

4. Explain the relationship between information processing and the MDSS.

5. Understand the various models used in an MDSS.

6. Provide examples of output from an MDSS.

7. Discuss the relationship between an MDSS and an expert system.

Marketing Decision Support Systems

❝ Successful businesses of the next decade will be the organizations that integrate information-driven technology in all functional areas. The decision support system we see today will be taken at least three generations further, giving business people more usable information than ever before. ❞ [1]

RON MCINTYRE
Director of Information Systems
Fox Retail Group

A New Generation of Marketing Decision Support Systems

In 1995, Fred Meyer Stores, a Portland, Oregon, based discount store chain, focused on four areas: (1) store redesign and geographic expansion, (2) reorganization of the store/department structure, (3) long-term employee training and morale building, (4) generation of a customer database to reflect changing tastes and preferences. This plan was devised in response to customer information that revealed two major problem areas: (1) unappealing merchandise and (2) inconvenient checkout procedures. Fred Meyer reorganized its management so that one manager in each department was totally responsible for the sales performance in that department. This allowed individual department managers to focus on their specific departments without interference from central headquarters. Each department was now in a position to better match merchandise with customer preferences. A department-by-department targeting of the specific needs of the cus-tomer was so successful that new stores followed in the evaluation. To overcome the inconvenient checkout problem, all merchandise was inventoried according to standardized codes and central (rather than departmental) checkout procedures were implemented.

Finally, Fred Meyer store expansion into California and Washington was fueled by information technology. Information shared by vendors, distributors, and store management revealed that customer buying habits differed dramatically in the two new states. Merchandising, store location, and even promotional decisions had to be modified to adapt to the market. All of the problem-solving factors that went into the decision to implement this strategic plan were generated by a marketing decision support system referred to as the Partnership, Accountability, Commitment, and Teamwork (PACT) system.[2]

Value of the Marketing Decision Support System

Fred Meyer's situation is similar to that of many other businesses. When businesses find themselves in uncertain competitive situations, they must make a series of strategic decisions. Such decisions may involve changing personnel, implementing new pricing policies, introducing new products, or exploring new promotional methods. The task then evolves to selecting the best action to solve the problem and generate the desired outcome. For example, if a change in price policy is recommended, a manager must know what prices to set, how the new pricing will affect customer perceptions, and how the competition will react. Similarly, if a new promotional method is recommended, what method should be used? How much will it cost? How effective will the new method be? Questions such as these can be answered only by properly interpreting the most appropriate information available.

The rapid advancement of technology over the past decade has made it possible for businesses to collect, condense, and categorize information in a highly efficient manner. But while this has produced an unprecedented level of information availability, it has not generated much improvement in managers' ability to correctly interpret information. Interpretation requires more than the ability to correctly read rows and columns of numbers, percentages, and absolute values. It begins with an understanding of where the information comes from, how the information is obtained, and what relevance the information has to the business situation being examined. Decision makers must anticipate the kinds of information that will be required to reduce uncertainty in the decision-making process. This involves selecting the proper information sources and knowing how to obtain information from those sources.

Correct interpretation of information is also affected by time. Information that was collected yesterday may be outdated today. In order for information to be correctly interpreted it must be collected in a timely, ongoing manner. A systematic gathering of longitudinal information reinforces a manager's ability to correctly interpret that information ahead of foreseeable decisions.[3]

Finally, the ability to correctly interpret information centers on its accuracy. Even if researchers establish careful criteria for information collection, it is inevitable that biases will arise out of personal or environmental factors. In order to reduce such biases, researchers should collect information from several sources or use several different approaches. Different information sources relevant to the decision problem can enhance accuracy in the interpretation process.

The Marketing Decision Support System

Marketing decision support system (MDSS) A computer-based system intended for use by particular marketing personnel at any functional level for the purpose of solving semistructured problems.

A **marketing decision support system (MDSS)** is a computer-based system intended for use by particular marketing personnel at any functional level (sales, product or brand management, advertising) for the purpose of solving semistructured problems. The output occurs in the form of special reports, mathematical simulations, or tracking devices.

The MDSS and the marketing information system (MIS) have been viewed as almost identical. Based on the emergence of new technology, however, the two systems have evolved into unique research tools. The MDSS, in contrast to the MIS, possesses the following unique characteristics:

1. It is designed for specific research problems to support individual marketing personnel.

2. It provides information designed to facilitate a specific decision (new-product planning, advertising effectiveness, distribution alternatives).

3. Its primary purpose is to evaluate alternative solutions to marketing-related problems and to identify the best course of action.

4. It is designed to focus on narrow (semistructured) problems such as facilitating the design of sales territories, evaluating outcomes of new-product or brand launches, or even profiling specific target markets for marketing actions.

5. Its emphasis is twofold: information storage and categorization, and resultant solutions.[4]

A Marketing Decision Support System Diagram

Exhibit 7.1 illustrates how an MDSS supports marketing personnel in various capacities. The MDSS stores and categorizes three groups of marketing information: environmental, transactional, and competitive. This information is contained within an information-processing system consisting of a computer, a marketing research database, and specialized software. This information-processing system enables the user to manipulate information and provide output in the form of specialized reports, responses to database queries, and model simulations. Reports and database queries are used most often to identify market-related problems. Simulations prove to be invaluable for planning alternative solutions for the marketing decision maker.

The purpose of this chapter is to acquaint the reader with how an MDSS is used. Chapters 4, 5, and 6 provided discussions of secondary data, information technology, and database development, which together form the foundation for understanding the MDSS. Therefore, just a brief discussion on these topics is considered.

A Marketing Decision Support System

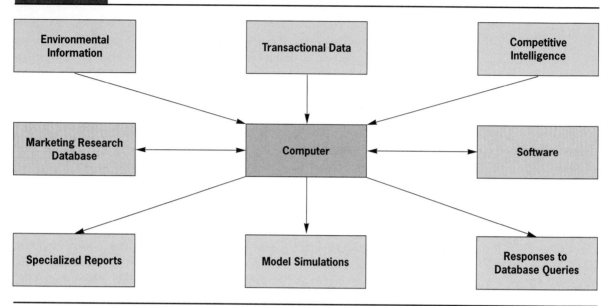

Information Requirements

The bulk of the information contained in the MDSS is secondary. Because the MDSS is designed to provide solutions to current problems in the marketplace, it contains actual market data, not intentions or attitudes. Information used in the MDSS must provide marketing personnel with a picture of what really has happened in the past, so that the present and the future can be put in perspective.[5] Present market activities must be reported quickly, as they actually happen, so that marketing personnel can act accordingly. For example, when Miller Brewing Company introduced its new Miller Red Beer into the market, managers needed to know how the beer was selling at different stores, at different price points, under different promotional campaigns. Any corrective actions to change or enhance the marketing effort had to take place immediately. Therefore, the only valuable data existing were the direct, point-of-sale, transactional data linked into the MDSS from various store locations. Transactional data revealed that sales were less than estimated at convenience stores in the southwestern United States. It happened that Budweiser was doing a massive point-of-sale campaign for its Michelob brand, undermining all marketing efforts by Miller. Within 24 hours, Miller distributors were instructed to contact convenience store managers in the Southwest and offer them a $1 buydown per case if they would remove all Michelob promotions and exclusively promote Miller Red.[6]

Based on a simulation of transactional data, Miller estimated sales to increase by 40 percent, which would more than offset the lost revenue resulting from the $1 buydown given to store management. In addition, the model estimated that individual store units would average 700 cases sold per week, resulting in $700 extra revenue for the store. Armed with these data, distributors found it easy to persuade convenience store managers to change their emphasis to Miller Red. This rapid reaction would not have been possible without point-of-sale data and MDSS simulations. The key to the success of this decision was showing managers at Miller what happened in the past, what was happening today, and what would happen tomorrow.

Environmental Information

Environmental information Information pertaining to suppliers and distributors.

Within the context of the MDSS, **environmental information** is that which pertains to suppliers and distributors. Information on suppliers is particularly important, because cooperation and coordination of activities with these firms ensure that a company has the necessary raw materials and services to react to changes in the market. Specifically, companies must have reliable information on supply considerations such as cost, quality, and product reliability.

In an MDSS, suppliers are ranked by the dollar volume of business they do with a company. A series of related criteria is then established and stored within the information processing unit of the MDSS. This information can then be analyzed using software that evaluates all suppliers on the following dimensions:

1. Dollar volume by season and year.
2. Growth or shrinkage of annual dollar volume.
3. Accuracy of shipping and billing.
4. Timeliness of deliveries.
5. Price terms and allowance.
6. Returns and procedures.

A sample output of supplier processing software is shown in Exhibit 7.2. Perhaps the greatest advantage of such a system is that a supplier can be selected or replaced immediately so that the company can avoid shortages or excessive inventory and, ultimately, customer dissatisfaction.

EXHIBIT 7.2   **Example of Output from Supplier Processing Software**

Dept. No.

Date

Resource

Merchandise   Top Grade _____   Medium _____   Low-End _____

Activity (Mfr., Jobber, Importer, etc.)

Sales Office Address   Telephone _____

Factory or Warehouse Address

Company Officers and Titles

Buyer Contacts—State peculiarities or special handling required by

    a. Sales Office   b. Factory

Rating—Dun & Bradstreet

Ethics of Firm

Ranking in Industry

Vendor Importance to Store

Store Importance to Vendor

Record of All Arrangements (Terms, Trade Discounts, Cash Discounts, Cooperative Advertising, etc.)

Remarks (State clearly any additional information not covered above that will guide any member of our organization who may have to deal with this vendor.)

Semiannual

Date   By Whom

Distribution Partners

Distributors are typically referred to as service wholesalers. They are businesses that secure products from the manufacturer and sell them to retailers. Service wholesalers are widely used because they offer many advantages over selling direct to retail. For example, they offer packaging and shipping services, reduce inventory carrying needs, reduce credit risks, and simplify bookkeeping. Many businesses, such as grocery stores and convenience stores, have no choice but to use wholesalers due to the vast level of merchandise variety they must maintain. As such, service wholesalers are entities whose contribution to a company's profits must be continually evaluated. Hard data related to wholesalers should include

1. Levels of inventory carried by various wholesalers.

2. On-time delivery performance.

3. Minimum ordering requirements.

4. Transportation costs.

5. Repairs, allowances, and adjustments.

6. Level of service (e.g., automatic merchandise replacement, markup, inventory management).[7]

Exhibit 7.3 shows a document from a wholesaler evaluation system (WES), included in many marketing decision support systems. As you can see, the system allows for quick, efficient comparative evaluation among wholesalers. Here again, the accuracy and timeliness of data are necessary in order for the system to be effective in the decision-making process.

EXHIBIT 7.3   **Example of Wholesaler Evaluation System**

```
VENDOR  INQUIRY                            PROGRAM-NAME: 201U5031
                                           PFKEY  1 - RESTART
   DEPT  20    LADIES SPORTSWEAR           PFKEY 16 - EXIT
 VENDOR  437801  LONGSTREET INDUSTRIES, LTD.
   DATE  06/8-

 RECEIPTS:              MARKDOWNS:

   UNITS     420          UNITS     56     ADV CONTRIBUTIONS:   .00
   @ RTL    6715.80       @ RTL    280.23
   @ COST   3156.45                        # P.O.'S PLACED:  6

                         PURCHASES:

 SALES:                                    # SHIPMENTS: 5

                          @ RTL    7438.20
   UNITS     324          @ COST   4462.92    OVER SHIPMENTS:  0
   @ RTL    5389.77
   @ COST   3108.45    INVOICED AMTS:         UNDER SHIPMENTS: 1

 RETURNS:                 INVOICE  3782.40
                            DISC    231.18
   UNITS      23         FREIGHT    45.20
   @ RTL     367.77       RETAIL  6715.80

                                      Press "ENTER" to continue *
```

Competitive Intelligence

Competitive intelligence
A procedure for collecting daily operational information pertinent to the company and the markets it serves.

An additional informational requirement of a marketing decision support system is **competitive intelligence.** Competitive intelligence activities lack the structure and rigor of more formal information-gathering practices associated with suppliers or distributors, but they do represent an important informational input into the MDSS. Competitive intelligence involves a procedure for collecting daily operational information pertinent to the company and markets it serves. Competitive intelligence information is usually collected by reading trade publications, books, and newspapers, as well as by talking to customers, suppliers, wholesalers, and other personnel within the company.

A major source of competitive intelligence data is the salesperson. Salespeople are in a position to pick up information missed by other means. Many companies, such as Procter & Gamble, sell their sales force on the importance of gathering information. To emphasize their importance as intelligence gatherers, P&G sales reps are asked to provide reports concerning customer service, competitive activities, customer complaints, and customer reactions to various pricing and merchandising policies. In addition, P&G ties quality of information collection to sales bonuses.

Another organization that directly links competitive intelligence information to its MDSS is the Men's Wearhouse. This organization operates over 104 stores nationwide, with an annual sales volume of more than $100 million. Henry Levy, who heads the decision support system at the Men's Wearhouse, considers the information system a critical link in the company's success. Again, salespeople are the key element in collecting competitive intelligence data. Through its sales staff, the Men's Wearhouse has developed a customer polling environment. Based on their contacts with customers, salespeople submit weekly activity reports that include demographic data, customer reactions to store layouts and merchandise, names of other stores where customers shop, and purchase history. In addition, salespeople are encouraged, on a weekly basis, to visit competitive stores and evaluate them relative to the Men's Wearhouse. All this information is then documented in the MDSS.[8] By means of a point-of-sale terminal, salespeople can access information indicating what competitors are selling and at what price, what the high-demand items are, and what type of customer buys particular merchandise. They can also view complete demographic profiles of customers that include names, addresses, sizes, past purchases, dollar amount of past purchases, and competing stores shopped. While the profiles are based on averages, they still provide valuable intelligence to the organization.

An additional source of competitive intelligence can be obtained from outside information suppliers, as discussed in Chapter 4. A wide variety of standardized information sources are available for purchase. Companies that offer such sources as ACNielsen, Moody's Investor Service, and Dun & Bradstreet. An example of competitive intelligence information on the food and drug industry provided by ACNielsen is shown in Exhibit 7.4.

Transactional Data

Transactional data
Information resulting from a transaction usually between a consumer and a retailer.

As the term implies, **transactional data** is information resulting from a transaction usually between a consumer and a retailer. Revolutionary new methods of collecting transactional data will emerge in the next decade and bring significant changes to the practice of marketing research. Presently, five technologies interact to help researchers collect and maintain transactional data: bar coding, optical scanning, automatic replenishment, electronic data interchange, and reader sorters. A brief discussion of each technology follows.

Bar coding A pattern of varied-width bars and spaces which represent a code of numbers and letters.

Bar coding consists of a pattern of varied-width bars and spaces, which represent a code of numbers and letters. When decoded through an optical scanning device, the code points to important product information. Brand name, style, size, color, and price are some of the data represented by bar codes. Bar codes also provide data on inventory levels, percentage

EXHIBIT 7.4	Nielsen Information on Competitive Intelligence

Nielsen Food and Drug Retail Index System

Health and beauty aid/drug products marketing applications

With HBA/drug products being sold through food, drug, and mass merchandiser stores, the marketer must continually evaluate his sales and distribution in each of the outlet types since the results can vary dramatically. In general terms, larger sizes are more acceptable to the trade in drug and mass merchandisers, while food stores prefer smaller package sizes. Such is clearly the case in the example where Brand A's large size is found in only 12 percent of all food stores.

Distribution—Large Size Brand A

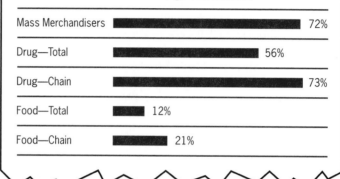

Mass Merchandisers	72%
Drug—Total	56%
Drug—Chain	73%
Food—Total	12%
Food—Chain	21%

Source: ACNielsen Company.

An example of transactional data in a retail environment.

of markup on the item, stock turn rate on merchandise, and quantity levels necessary for reordering.

Optical scanner   A light-sensitive device that "reads" bar codes; that is, captures and translates unique bar code numbers into product information.

Bar coding operates in conjunction with optical scanners. An **optical scanner** is a light-sensitive device that "reads" bar codes; that is, it captures and translates unique bar code numbers into product information and thus facilitates data entry into the MDSS. Two scanning techniques are commonly employed. First, the universal product code (UPC) is a generally accepted bar code for the retail industry. A UPC is a 12-digit number used for merchandise identification. Second is the shipper container marking (SCM). An SCM is a bar code that facilitates the identification and shipping of containers between manufacturers, distributors, and retailers. UPCs and SCMs can be read by a variety of optical scanners. A majority of discount stores like Target and Wal-Mart use handheld scanners, or laser guns, for speed and convenience. Optical scanning wands are used predominantly by department stores like Dillard's and Macy's because of loosely attached price tags. Flatbed scanners or in-line conveyers are used mainly by supermarkets due to the volume of items and coupons that need scanning.

Every time an optical scanner reads a bar code, it electronically records what was bought, the manufacturer and vendor, the size and price. This information is then archived in a database and enhanced with market intelligence and other research-related information. The resulting database has the potential to reveal what consumers watch on television, what type of neighborhood they live in, and what kinds of stores they shop at. Exhibit 7.5 not only describes how scanner data can be cross-referenced but also the value they hold for marketing researchers.

EXHIBIT 7.5   **HomeScan: Scanner Data for Decision Making**

Men are more active buyers of products in many categories than had been thought, according to new data from NPD/Nielsen's Advertising Services division.

The first data released from Nielsen's HomeScan database cover a year of magazine reading and product purchases in 18,000-plus households nationally, part of Nielsen's household panel.

While HomeScan's single-source information service is similar to annual surveys from Mediamark Research Inc. (MRI) and Simmons Market Research Bureau, HomeScan gathers purchasing information electronically, via a scanning wand. MRI and Simmons respondents record purchase information in response to a written questionnaire or interview.

HomeScan tracks magazine readers' use of 1,500 brands in 1,000 product categories. Among initial findings is the high number of package-goods purchases made by men.

"We are finding that men are a lot more important [as consumers]. Overall, about 30 percent of the dollars recorded by package goods were purchased by men," said Steve Coffey, vice president of NPD/Nielsen.

For example, among mouthwash brands, men bought 52 percent of all Viadent purchased and 22 percent of Colgate Tartar in the year ended June 1.

Nielsen isn't sure why HomeScan shows more purchases by men than previous estimates. But Coffey said it may be because other surveys typically designate a single member of each household as a homemaker who provides information about product purchases, while HomeScan distinguishes between household members and records their age and sex.

Another finding is that magazine audience levels are higher than those recorded by MRI and Simmons. Overall, HomeScan shows 44 percent higher audience levels than MRI and 86 percent higher than Simmons in the 140 magazines HomeScan tracks.

This disparity may be caused by interviewer bias in other surveys, Coffey said. Unlike MRI and Simmons, HomeScan collects readership information electronically, not through an interviewer.

As a result, some magazines—particularly those responders might feel awkward reporting they read, such as *The National Enquirer* and *Playboy*—post higher audience levels than in other surveys. Other categories, including newsweeklies, post audience levels similar to those reported by MRI and Simmons.

HomeScan subscribers can access the database, updated in October and April, via an online service or compact disc. Subscribers include *Parade; Reader's Digest; USA Today;* Kraft; General Foods; Leo Burnett Co.; Foote, Cone Belding Communications; and Walter Thompson USA.

**Automatic replenish-
ment system (ARS)** A
continuous automated sys-
tem designed to analyze
inventory levels, merchandise order lead times, and
forecasted sales.

The **automatic replenishment system (ARS)** is a continuous, automated system designed to analyze inventory levels, merchandise order lead times, and forecasted sales. It also generates purchase orders for merchandise that needs quick replenishment. ARS is designed to help firms carry the lowest possible levels of inventory while still maintaining a sufficient quantity to avoid stock-outs. The inventory levels can be optimized because order quantities are smaller and more frequent. In addition, inventory movement is enhanced because reordering is automatic, stock turn rates are higher, and the cost of spoilage and shrinkage is decreased dramatically.

**Electronic data inter-
change (EDI)** A com-
puterized system
designed to speed the
flow of information and
products from producer to
distributor to retailer.

Electronic data interchange (EDI) is a computerized system designed to speed the flow of information and products from producer to distributor to retailer. This, in turn, contributes to increased sales, reduced markdowns, and lowered inventory carrying costs. EDI differs from the automatic replenishment system (ARS) in that benefits are derived from reductions in costs of clerical and administrative activities associated with merchandise ordering. EDI centers mainly on the electronic exchange of information such as purchase orders, invoices, advanced shipping notices, and product return notices. In essence, EDI is the information arm of an automatic replenishment system.

EDI is available in two formats: direct data interchange (from retailer to vendors or distributors) and third-party networks, which operate as clearinghouses or electronic mailboxes for retailers. While slight differences exist between these two formats, their benefits are much the same. EDI reduces the costs of clerical work and data entry, postage, handling, and form printing. The speed of communication reduces inventory carrying costs, improving the efficiency of vendor and retailer.

Automatic replenishment systems and electronic data interchange are keys to the MDSS. Toys "R" Us, for example, which has 451 stores nationwide and 97 in foreign countries, attributes its growth and profitability to its inventory and information component of the MDSS. Being a highly seasonal company (60 percent of sales occur between Thanksgiving and Christmas), Toys "R" Us depends on inventory control for its survival. To date, Toys "R" Us is networked to over 500 vendors. Transmitted data include orders and shipment confirmations. Sales and inventory records are also transmitted, allowing buyers and vendors knowledge of which toys are sold at which stores worldwide, and when the items need to be replenished. More specifically, through EDI, Toys "R" Us can monitor sales trends and communicate with vendors automatically. Toys "R" Us stores in California, for example, sell more trend and fad merchandise than other stores. EDI allows buyers to create a balanced product mix of these goods with other, less seasonal goods.[9]

Reader-sorter A com-
puterized device located
at the point of sale that
resembles a miniature
automated teller machine
(ATM); it enables
consumers to pay for
transactions with credit
cards, ATM cards, or
debit cards.

The final element used in generating transactional data is the **reader-sorter.** The reader-sorter is a computerized device located at the point of sale that resembles a miniature automated teller machine (ATM). It enables consumers to pay for transactions with credit cards, ATM cards, or debit cards. The magnetic strip on the back of each card contains a wealth of consumer data. On this tiny strip an individual's personal, historical data are housed, along with other relevant data such as at which store the card was used, what was actually purchased, and when, along with significant demographic and lifestyle data.

At the point of sale, when a consumer uses the reader-sorter as a payment method, data from both the magnetic strip and the current purchase are automatically collected. The optical scanner (via a bar code) is collecting and recording product purchases while the reader-sorter (via the credit, ATM or debit card) is collecting and recording information on who is making the purchase. Both groups of information are then stored in the central database of the MDSS. When compiled with other consumer purchases, a specific product-related profile can be generated based on weekly, even daily, store activities.

Exhibit 7.6 contains a sample MDSS report output on individuals who have purchased Pepsi products at a particular chain supermarket. Based on the information revealed by the reader-sorter, these individuals also listen to contemporary rock music, visit theme parks, drink

EXHIBIT 7.6	Sample MDSS Report on Pepsi Buyers

Target Lifestyles/Mediastyles/Demographics for Pepsi

Target: South AO DDT Heavy User

Demographics	Penetration		Index	Demographics	Penetration		Index
	Total	Target			Total	Target	
Bought Heavy Rock Music	7.76	13.11	109	Go Power Boating	4.83	5.82	120
Bought Cntmpry Rock Music	15.90	24.85	156	Professional Wrestling Fans	10.95	13.17	120
Attended Pop/Rock Concerts	8.91	13.53	152	Drink Vodka	18.74	22.24	115
Ride Motorcycles	3.71	5.46	147	Go Bicycling	16.77	19.63	117
Bought Soul/R&B/Black Music	8.13	11.65	143	First Time Truck Buyers	7.12	8.31	117
Play Racquetball	4.53	6.45	143	Bought Pre-Rec Audio Csstte Tapes	23.44	27.26	116
Downhill Skiiers	3.98	5.65	143	Rented Video Cassettes lst yr	48.06	35.70	115
Bought Cntmpry Pop Vcl Music	17.10	24.18	141	Bought Traditional/Cntmpry Jazz	5.97	6.81	114
Do Weight Training	9.84	13.87	141	Bought 3-Door/Hatchback New	2.70	3.05	113
Water Skiiers	3.94	5.53	140	Bought Foreign Car New	12.28	13.85	113
Joggers/Runners	9.16	12.61	138	Smoke Menthol Cigarettes	9.15	10.26	112
Go Horesback Riding	4.26	5.35	137	Bought Country Music	17.70	10.82	112
Bought 1960's Rock Music	6.48	8.37	137	Take Adult Education Courses	7.13	7.98	112
Visited Theme Park pst yr	20.08	27.39	136	Attended Theatre/Concerts	21.49	23.55	120
Go Overnight Camping	9.41	12.62	134	Go Sailing	2.74	3.00	118
Bought CD Player pst year	6.34	8.24	130	Spent $10+ Tupperware party	7.23	7.83	108
4+ Movies in lst 90 days	15.10	19.51	129	Give Cookouts/Barbecues	36.62	39.65	108
Drink Rum	17.43	22.36	128	Professional Football Fans	41.47	44.27	107
Played Tennis 10+ times lst yr	3.35	4.30	128	Professional Basketball Fans	26.00	27.59	106
Went Swimming 20+ times lst yr	8.75	11.16	128	Go Salt Water Fishing	4.41	4.67	106
Go Target Shooting	4.49	5.71	127	Use Chewing Tobacco	1.83	1.92	105
Bought Blank Audio Csstte Tapes	17.78	22.25	125	Drink Imported Brandy or Cognac	7.28	7.64	105
Go Hiking/Backpacking	8.84	10.77	121	Own a PC at Home	22.36	23.26	101
Belong to a Health Club	4.37	5.28	121	College Basketball Fans	21.27	21.98	103
Go Fresh Water Fishing	11.83	14.28	121				

vodka, rent videocassettes, give cookouts and barbeques, are pro football watchers, and use a personal computer at home. While this is only a small amount of the data it would be possible to gather on Pepsi drinkers, it represents actual data collected and stored at the point of sale.

Armed with this information, Pepsi can anticipate daily sales, plan in-store promotional activities, anticipate reactions to price and packaging changes, and maintain an accurate description of its target market. The value of this information is in its predictive capability, being that it was generated on actual product purchases, not propensity or probability to purchase Pepsi. Therefore, it becomes obvious that the benefit of the MDSS is its ability to collect and categorize relevant customer information. Yet, recall that the key to interpreting this information remains in the information-processing element of the MDSS.

Information Processing and the MDSS

The three key elements of the information-processing component of the MDSS are the database, the computer facilities, and the software system. Given the extensive discussion on database development in Chapter 6, our discussion here will concentrate on the computer and the software system.

The computer and the software system serve one primary function in the MDSS: to produce reports that are valuable to the decision maker. The computer and software system of the MDSS should adhere to the following guidelines:

1. Report design should reflect the needs for the user, not the analyst.

2. The software system must be able to provide reports for the user within minutes.

3. The system must have the ability to sort and print highly specific report data.

4. The data must be easy to read, use, and manipulate.

5. The system should be custom-made versus prewritten systems. While a prewritten software system is less expensive, if the system does not meet the user's needs, it is useless.[10]

Two general types of software systems exist for MDSS: statistical software systems and managerial function software systems.

Statistical Software Systems

Statistical software systems MDSS systems that analyze large volumes of data and compute basic statistics such as means and standard deviations.

Statistical software systems have been available for performing basic statistical analysis since the early years of the computer. These systems analyze large volumes of data and compute basic statistics such as means and standard deviations. They also compare sets of numbers and use such tests as t-tests and chi-square tests to determine how similar or different the number sets are. More sophisticated routines like multiple regression and analysis of variance are also included. Statistical techniques are fully discussed in Chapters 17 and 18.

While a variety of statistical software systems exist, SAS and SPSS-X are the most robust packages for the MDSS. Due to the vast knowledge of mathematical and statistical background needed to use these systems, however, they are usually the favorite choice for the research analyst, not the manager. Therefore, managerial function software systems are also incorporated into the MDSS.

Managerial Function Software Systems

Managerial function software systems MDSS systems used by managers; these include forecasting systems, product/brand management systems, and promotional budget systems.

In the MDSS environment, three **managerial function software systems** are commonly employed: forecasting systems, product/brand management systems, and promotional budget systems.

Many forecasting systems exist that enable sales or marketing managers to project future occurrences. They all use the types of data described earlier in this chapter as a basis for predicting sales. For example, if transactional data indicate that purchases increase with increased presence of the product at retail, the exact relationship could be stated in mathematical (i.e., modeled) terms. Forecasting systems usually produce sales or profitability projections in a report form, such as the one in Exhibit 7.7.

Product/brand management software systems enable managers to plan for new-product introduction. One such package, called brand planning, is based on a critical path analysis and displays the output in the form of a Gantt chart. The brand-planning package plans the sequencing of activities (production, sales, packaging, etc.) that must be performed simultaneously in order to have a successful product launch.

A promotional budget system enables managers to predict and control promotional expenditures. Limits are set for each element of the promotional budget—sales, advertising, sales promotion, and media spending. Reports are issued on a monthly basis indicating how actual expenses relate to budget projections. An example of a promotional budget system is the ADBUG.[11] This model procedure provides evaluation of sales response to advertising. Conceptually, the system is quite simple in that it evaluates what is happening to an entire industry, product class, or even brand within the class, with respect to the brand's market share. The system operates on a very fundamental basis; using a what-if assumption, ADBUG performs a series of sensitivity analyses to measure sales response based on the effects of share advertising, media effectiveness, product seasonality, trends, competition, and price.

In order to develop the sales response function, the ADBUG user places a number of other assumptions into consideration:

1. A certain level of advertising expenditures will maintain brand share at some given level.

2. A floor exists where brand share will fall by a fixed amount with zero advertising.

3. A ceiling exists where brand share will increase given large advertising expenditures.

The ADBUG system has two main objectives: (1) to determine the optimum level of advertising expenditure to achieve a desired level of sales, and (2) to determine how to change advertising expenditure over time in order to maximize profits.

Regardless of which MDSS software system is used, the goal is to produce information from data in order to facilitate decisions. The common denominator of all MDSS software systems is that modeling capabilities are used to provide direct support to the manager for solving problems. Therefore, before we engage in a discussion on MDSS output, we will present a brief discussion on models.

Types of MDSS Models

When the information contained in the MDSS is categorized and classified by the appropriate software system, the result is some form of output for the decision maker. When the purpose of the output is to provide a solution to the problem, the solution effort was most likely generated by some modeling technique.

A model is an abstraction that represents some phenomenon or activity associated with an entity. If a model is to represent why a company's sales fluctuate, for example, then sales fluctuation becomes the entity. Models can be classified as static or dynamic, probabilistic or deterministic, and optimizing or suboptimizing.

Static models do not consider time as a major variable. They deal with events at one particular time. An advertising allocation model that computes the optimum dollar amount to spend on advertising using current spending is a static model. When time is added, the model becomes dynamic. Dynamic models illustrate behavior over time. A traditional sales forecast over a one-year period is a dynamic model.

EXHIBIT 7.7   Illustration of Output from Sales Forecasting System

PROJECTS QUOTED RECAP: September

RECAP BY INDUSTRY:

		Total w/Revisions by Indus. & Type	Total w/Revisions by Indus.	Total Complete By Indus. & Type	Total Complete by Indus.	No Quotes
BAKING:	Systems (S)	$550,004.00		$2,398,425.00	$2,398,425.00	3
	Screeners (CS)	$38,761.91		$38,761.91		1
	Rotary Valves (CV)	$0.00		$0.00		0
	Miscellaneous (M)	$0.00	$588,765.91	$0.00	$2,437,186.91	0
PLASTIC:	Systems (S)	$0.00		$0.00		0
	Screeners (CS)	$0.00		$0.00		0
	Rotary Valves (CV)	$0.00		$0.00		0
	Miscellaneous (M)	$0.00	$0.00	$0.00	$0.00	0
CHEMICAL:	Systems (S)	$314,980.00		$559,519.00	$559,519.00	4
	Screeners (CS)	$19,140.00		$19,140.00		3
	Rotary Valves (CV)	$10,860.00		$10,860.00		2
	Miscellaneous (M)	$0.00	$344,980.00	$0.00	$589,519.00	0
PHARMACEUTICAL:	Systems (S)	$69,918.00		$129,918.00		4
	Screeners (CS)	$0.00		$0.00		0
	Rotary Valves (CV)	$0.00		$0.00		0
	Miscellaneous (M)	$200,000.00	$269,918.00	$252,000.00	$381,918.00	2
FOOD:	Systems (S)	$13,670,547.00		$22,409,527.00	$22,910,514.00	12
	Screeners (CS)	$155,667.00		$155,667.00		6
	Rotary Valves (CV)	$28,120.00		$28,120.00		3
	Miscellaneous (M)	($67,100.00)	$13,787,234.00	$317,200.00		1

DAIRY, PARTS, and Powder paint breakdown

Category	Total w/Revisions	(subtotal)	Total Complete	(subtotal)	No. Quotes
DAIRY:					
Systems (S)	$0.00				0
Screeners (CS)	$13,374.00		$13,374.00		1
Rotary Valves (CV)	$0.00				0
Miscellaneous (M)	$0.00	$13,374.00	$0.00	$13,374.00	0
PARTS:					
General (Parts)	$0.00	$0.00	$0.00	$0.00	0
Powder paint: (PP)					
Systems (S)	$0.00				0
Screeners (CS)	$46,065.00		$97,584.00		3
Rotary Valves (CV)	$0.00				0
Miscellaneous (M)	$0.00	$46,065.00	$0.00	$97,584.00	0
	$15,050,336.91	$26,430,095.91			45

Total w/Revisions	Total Complete	No. Quotes
$311,987.91	$363,506.91	19
$0.00	$0.00	0
$138,918.00	$138,918.00	3
$13,485,890.00	$21,758,234.00	7
$655,000.00	$655,000.00	2
$458,541.00	$3,514,437.00	14
$0.00	$0.00	0
$0.00	$0.00	0
$0.00	$0.00	0
$15,050,336.91	$26,430,095.91	45

Another way to classify models is whether or not they include probabilities. A probability is a chance that some event is likely to occur. Probabilities can range from 0.00 (no chance of occurrence) to 1.00 (a 100 percent certainty of occurrence). A probability statement would be, "There is a 75 percent chance that customers will buy Pepsi for $1 a can." Models that include probabilities are called probabilistic models. Models that do not include probabilities are called deterministic models. Many sales forecasts are deterministic.

An optimizing model is one that selects the best solution among alternatives, and a suboptimizing model is one that will project an outcome on its own. Most models employed in distribution and logistical efficiency are either optimizing or suboptimizing.

Modeling capabilities allow the MDSS to produce output, which is the major concern for the manager or user. The most common types of MDSS output are reports, simulations, and queries.

An MDSS Sales Analysis Output Example

An example of MDSS output is a series of sales analysis reports produced from accounting and sales transaction data. The data used in preparing the records are sorted into various sequences to provide a sales manager with information describing the firm's sales by customer, region, and salesperson. A sales-by-customer report appears in Exhibit 7.8. The customers are listed in a descending order based on year-to-date sales and percentage contribution to total sales. This technique allows the sales manager to analyze customers on a percentage-of-sales basis. The same technique is used in the sales-by-region report in Exhibit 7.9. This allows the sales manager to analyze sales made by salespeople within their region.

Geographic Information Systems

When a model is said to simulate the entity, the model is the *simulator,* and the process of using the tool is *simulation*. A commonly employed MDSS simulation is referred to as a geographic information system (GIS). In its present form, GIS uses a spatial modeling technique in conjunction with data drawn from the MDSS. It enables users to capture, encode, edit, analyze, compose, and display spatial data organized as map layers. Each map layer represents a geographic theme conceptualized as a stack of floating maps tied to a common base. Each map layer can be independently accessed. Combined information and related attributes from each layer can be referenced to one another in a spatial perspective.

With the GIS, it is now possible to analyze market areas and learn where certain defined demographic characteristics overlap. Individual neighborhoods are even clustered into categories and defined by both demographic and lifestyle data. Such data are now being linked to household information to produce sophisticated neighborhood profiles that are invaluable for sales planning. A simple example of GIS use is described in the Marketing Research Illustration at the end of this chapter.

Within the context of the GIS, sets of geographic parameters are manipulated to identify regions or locations based on spatial coincidence of factors that are relevant for a given entity. For example, in a store location issue, GIS may be employed to provide output on interactions of developmental objectives with environmental, economic, and political factors to determine potential sites as well as the environmental impact of the proposed development. The main advantage of the GIS is its ability to pose what-if scenarios.

Hilton Corporation, for example, uses the GIS output to help reduce the gamble of locating new casinos. Hilton used the GIS to create what-if scenarios when considering whether or not to enter the casino market on the Mississippi Gulf Coast. Demographic, socioeconomic, and psychographic features were considered, along with the location of

| EXHIBIT 7.8 | Output of Sales-by-Customer Report for System Products |

Customer	Region	Sales $	% of Sales	% of System Sales
Emerald Industries	mw	$3,272,428	21.6%	31.2%
Keebler	mw	1,067,051	7.0%	10.2%
Merck Sharp & Dohme	ot	1,038,019	6.8%	9.9%
Pretzels Inc	mw	776,218	5.1%	7.4%
Snyders of Hanover	ne	632,505	4.2%	6.0%
Syntex	ot	590,717	3.9%	5.6%
Floor Daniel (Frito)	w	330,270	2.2%	3.1%
Ore-Ida Foods	w	300,830	2.0%	2.9%
Schultz Foods	ne	252,122	1.7%	2.4%
Sterling Drug	ne	233,028	1.5%	2.2%
Golden Flake	ne	178,000	1.2%	1.7%
M&M Mars	ne	172,725	1.1%	1.6%
Glaxo	ne	147,868	1.0%	1.4%
Continental Mills	w	145,560	1.0%	1.4%
Marion Merrell Dow	mw	125,688	0.8%	1.2%
Reading (troyer)	ne	117,644	0.8%	1.1%
Warner Lambert	ot	106,678	0.7%	1.0%
Reading (keystone)	ne	98,806	0.7%	0.9%
United Catalyst	se	75,957	0.5%	0.7%
Searle	ot	71,745	0.5%	0.7%
Ore-Ida Foods	w	70,566	0.5%	0.7%
Hershey Chocolate	ne	66,939	0.4%	0.6%
IFF	ne	63,801	0.4%	0.6%
Nutrasweet	se	60,476	0.4%	0.6%
Brystol Meyers	ne	59,667	0.4%	0.6%
Procter & Gamble	mw	53,500	0.4%	0.5%
Ferodo America	se	36,288	0.2%	0.3%
Syntex	ot	34,307	0.2%	0.3%
Procter & Gamble	se	33,418	0.2%	0.3%
Ferodo America	se	33,016	0.2%	0.3%
Kline Process	ne	31,050	0.2%	0.3%
M&M Mars	se	24,987	0.2%	0.3%

EXHIBIT 7.9   **Output of Sales-by-Region Report for Northeast Region**

Customer Name	Product	Sales $	% of Sales	% of System Sales
Snyders of Hanover	sys	$632,505	4.2%	26.6%
Schultz Foods	sys	252,122	1.7%	10.6%
Sterling Drug	sys	233,028	1.5%	9.8%
Golden Flake	sys	178,000	1.2%	7.5%
M&M Mars	sys	172,725	1.1%	7.3%
Glaxo	sys	147,868	1.0%	6.2%
Reading (troyer)	sys	117,644	0.8%	4.9%
Reading (keystone)	sys	98,806	0.7%	4.2%
Congoleum Corp	engr	74,000	0.5%	3.1%
Hershey Chocolate	sys	66,939	0.4%	2.8%
IFF	sys	63,801	0.4%	2.7%
Schultz Foods	inst	60,850	0.4%	2.6%
Brystol Meyers	sys	59,667	0.4%	2.5%
Kline Process	sys	31,050	0.2%	1.3%
Union Carbide	vlv	30,050	0.2%	1.3%
Wasca Foods	vlv	18,982	0.1%	0.8%
Glatt Air Technology	vlv	18,523	0.1%	0.8%
A & G Machine	scr	15,073	0.1%	0.6%
M&M Mars	vlv	15,062	0.1%	0.6%
Union Carbide	vlv	15,025	0.1%	0.6%
McNeil Consumer	vlv	14,672	0.1%	0.6%
McCormick	vlv	10,264	0.1%	0.4%
Harley-Davidson	scr	8,942	0.1%	0.4%
Deitrich Milk	vlv	8,890	0.1%	0.4%
L D Cauck	scr	6,805	0.0%	0.3%
Technik Inc	scr	5,325	0.0%	0.2%
McCormick	vlv	5,196	0.0%	0.2%
Ames Goldsmith	scr	5,028	0.0%	0.2%
MRA	scr	4,540	0.0%	0.2%
Providence Metal	scr	4,221	0.0%	0.2%
M&M Mars	vlv	2,680	0.0%	0.1%
Total		$2,378,283	15.7%	100.0%

competing sources of entertainment in the area. After the GIS output indicated saturation on the Mississippi Gulf Coast but a highly opportune environment in New Orleans, Hilton decided to open its casino in New Orleans. Exhibit 7.10 indicates how the GIS operates to provide companies with crucial location information and hence actual location decisions.

EXHIBIT 7.10 | **How a GIS Works**

GIS at Work

A vinyl siding company wants to identify for its local distributor the areas in Shelby County that hold the greatest potential for sales. Its target is based on (*a*) the location of homes 15 years and older that are (*b*) owned by people with annual median household incomes of at least $35,000. Using the query capability of GIS software, along with census data coded in the GIS database, the user can categorize census tracts based on age of homes (A) and annual median income (B). By overlaying the two map layers, a final layer that identifies various categories of needs and affordability can be quickly isolated (C).

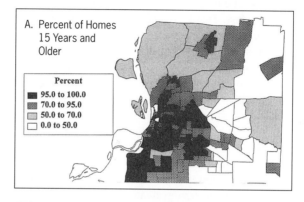

A. Percent of Homes 15 Years and Older

Percent
- 95.0 to 100.0
- 70.0 to 95.0
- 50.0 to 70.0
- 0.0 to 50.0

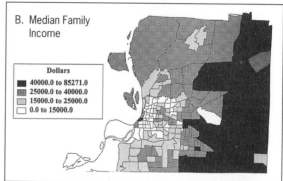

B. Median Family Income

Dollars
- 40000.0 to 85271.0
- 25000.0 to 40000.0
- 15000.0 to 25000.0
- 0.0 to 15000.0

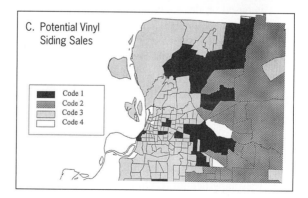

C. Potential Vinyl Siding Sales

- Code 1
- Code 2
- Code 3
- Code 4

Code 1 = Over 60% of homes 15 years old or older; median family income above $35,000
Code 2 = High median income, less than 60% of homes 15 years old or older
Code 3 = Low median income, over 60% of homes 15 years old or older
Code 4 = Low median income, less than 60% of homes 15 years old or older

The future of GIS will likely see expanded use of satellite imagery. The increased use of satellite images as a data source will lead to greater integration and more sophisticated use of global positioning regarding site locations along with advanced data exchange.

MDSS and Queries as an Output Resource

Query A segment of the MDSS that enables the user to retrieve information from the system without having to have special software.

A **query,** many times referred to as *query language,* is another segment of the MDSS that facilitates data retrieval. It enables the user to retrieve information from the system without having to have special software. The response, either on screen or in hard-copy form, has the same general appearance as a regular MDSS report.

The unique feature of MDSS queries is that they arise after data are presented to the analyst. That is, the need to use query operations arises after the results of another report are presented to the analyst. Thus, queries are specifiable in the context of MDSS output. For example, a loan manager interested in cross-selling bank services can request a display of customer use of banking products (e.g., loans, credit cards, savings accounts), which he would then use to formulate detailed queries about the customer's financial information without having to switch context or reports. This would allow the manager to view various services that the customer may not be using, hence providing a cross-selling opportunity for the bank. Query language would allow the analyst to combine input and output forms, so that inputs (new bank services to cross-sell) are always given in the context of the previous output (current product use) from the MDSS. Additionally, the analyst can fill in or select inputs that can modify the current output or result in different output altogether, such as new selection/evaluation criteria for new-product offerings.

The MDSS and Expert Systems

Expert systems Computer software programs that function in the same manner as a human expert, advising the analyst on how to solve a problem.

Artificial intelligence (AI) is the capability of a computer to display behavior that would be regarded as intelligent if it were observed in a human being. A major subset of AI research deals with software programs referred to as **expert systems.** Expert systems are designed to function in the same manner as a human expert, advising the analyst on how to solve a problem. The In the Field box looks at a version of an expert system called marketing automation.

The appeal of the expert system centers on the fact that certain tasks require specialized research knowledge that only an expert would have. Unfortunately, not every manager can afford a staff of full-time marketing research specialists. The concept of the expert system is based on the assumption that an expert's knowledge can be captured in a database and made available to others who have a need to apply that knowledge. The expert's knowledge enables the expert system to assume a large portion of a problem-solving task.

The expert system and the MDSS, while conceptually similar, differ in respect to problem solving. As previously discussed, an MDSS consists of routines that reflect how the manager believes a problem should be solved. The decisions produced by the MDSS therefore reflect the manager's style and capabilities. An expert system offers the opportunity to make decisions that exceed the manager's capabilities. For example, sales representatives for a particular business may use an expert system designed by a sales manager or vice president of sales when decisions or problems need to be considered when on the trade or in the field.

The expert system and MDSS also differ in their ability to explain a particular line of reasoning behind reaching a particular solution. Expert systems operate on both forward and reverse reasoning. With forward reasoning, decision rules are examined in sequential order. As each rule is examined, the system evaluates whether the rule is true or false. If true, the next rule in the sequence is examined. If false, the rule is deleted and the next rule is examined. In reverse reasoning, the problem is first identified and then divided according to its symptoms. A path of decision rules is then established and followed until the

Marketing Automation: Beyond Decision Support

Technology is finally coming to the rescue of the marketing executive. In April 1998, Rubric, Inc., will launch an application designed to automate and improve the marketing activities such as advertising campaign management, sales lead qualifications, and online analysis and reporting. Right now there are strategic applications for almost all parts of an organization, including sales and manufacturing, notes Rubric CEO, Anu Shukla. She claims marketing is the missing link to getting a full 360-degree view of the customer. Rubric's marketing automation package, called Rubric EMA 1.0, is designed to address this gap.

Rubric's product measures the impact of marketing activities by tracking marketing dollars spent against actual revenues generated. The key benefits, according to Shukla, are increased sales due to improved sales lead generation and tracking, as well as reduced costs through streamlined marketing operations.

N.E.T., Inc., $324 million provider of networking hardware, is testing the Rubric application. Technically, Rubric takes all the different functions of the marketing department and rolls them into one decision support application. With this application N.E.T. will be able to better classify sales leads, and then further engage prospects with information about the exact products or services they are interested in. The major benefit is that the time it takes to do this is only a matter of seconds.

There are several other vendors with decision support software products aimed at the same market, including Marketfirst and Epiphany software. According to Scott Nelson, research director for the Gartner Group, this is a new area of decision support technology that will grow astronomically in the next decade.

Source: Tom Stein, "Marketing Automation," *Informationweek*, April 13, 1998.

problem is solved or until it is determined that no solution is possible. In this case, a new problem scenario is analyzed.

Expert Systems and the Marketing Researcher

In the context of marketing research, expert systems are used predominantly for developing strategic and tactical models. Pricing models, sales territory assignments, media selection models, and store location models are considered tactical. They are developed to help managers allocate and control resources. These models are normally short term, ranging from several months to several years.

New-product evaluation and product deletion models are generally strategic models. They are used predominantly for executing strategic planning functions, and are therefore long term (several years rather than several months).

There is no question that with advances in database and computer technologies, the ways in which marketing information is obtained and utilized have changed dramatically. More and more companies are developing and using MDSSs and expert systems in organizing their marketing research efforts. With the rapid advancement of these systems, the need for traditional marketing research projects has diminished somewhat. A general industry trend has seen the expert systems and MDSSs proliferate in combination as a strategic planning research tool. Both systems are used extensively for monitoring occurrences among external environmental variables. Yet, under certain situations, these systems are unable to provide enough information for tactical decisions such as those involving changing in media selection, distribution systems, or packaging. When specific tactical information is required, the traditional research project is usually deemed more appropriate.

SUMMARY OF LEARNING OBJECTIVES

Understand the purpose of a marketing decision support system (MDSS).

The MDSS is designed to help marketing personnel with decision-making activities. These activities are highly focused on a specific problem and the information required to solve that problem. With proper information, the MDSS allows the manager to identify and evaluate the best course of action in solving market-related problems. Therefore, the primary purpose of the MDSS is to manipulate information to provide problem solutions.

Describe the various information requirements used to design an MDSS.

The bulk of the information contained in the MDSS comes from secondary data. The common forms of information used in the MDSS are environmental information, transactional data, and competitive intelligence. The primary purpose of the data is to provide managers with the information they need for making immediate market-reaction decisions.

Understand the role of transactional data in the MDSS.

Considered the most important information requirement, transactional data provide information resulting from point-of-sale transactions. This information allows managers to track and react to daily sales fluctuations, evaluate the effectiveness of point-of-sale marketing activities, and develop predictive models based on actual product sales data.

Explain the relationship between information processing and the MDSS.

The key elements of the information-processing components of the MDSS are the database, the computer facilities, and the software system. Collectively, these elements must provide the manager or user with the capability to produce timely and accurate reports. The driving force behind report generation is the specific software system employed by the MDSS. The two most common forms of software systems are statistical software systems and managerial function software systems.

Understand the various models used in an MDSS.

There are several different ways to classify MDSS models. Most are static or dynamic, probabilistic or deterministic, or optimizing or suboptimizing. Regardless of the model employed, the objective is to provide the manager with a set of usable outputs. These outputs most commonly include reports, simulations, and queries.

Provide examples of output from an MDSS.

The most common forms of MDSS output are reports, simulations, and queries. The reports are normally generated around the marketing elements and attempt to determine profitability or performance measures on the mix. Simulations are used to produce what-if scenarios. A valuable simulation for many MDSS users is the geographic information system (GIS). Finally, queries enable users to retrieve information from the system without having to have a unique software program.

Discuss the relationship between an MDSS and an expert system.

The expert system is considered to be one generation beyond the traditional MDSS. The decisions produced by the MDSS normally reflect a particular manager's style and capabilities. An expert system offers the opportunity to make decisions that exceed a manager's capability, decisions that would be more reflective of an expert rather than of an individual manager.

KEY TERMS AND CONCEPTS

Automatic replenishment system (ARS) 190

Bar coding 187

Competitive intelligence 187

Electronic data interchange (EDI) 190

Environmental information 185

Expert systems 200

Managerial function software systems 192

Marketing decision support system (MDSS) 183

Optical scanner 189

Query 200

Reader-sorter 190

Statistical software systems 192

Transactional data 187

REVIEW QUESTIONS

1. What distinct advantages of a marketing decision support system are not present in a management information system?

2. Why is it important to use secondary marketing information in a marketing decision support system?

3. Why do companies use service wholesalers? How do service wholesalers affect a company's use of a marketing decision support system?

4. List the five methods of collecting and maintaining transactional data, and provide an explanation of how each method can affect a company's marketing strategy.

5. What ethical implications are associated with the use of electronic scanning devices and electronic information storage procedures?

6. What are three key elements that comprise the information processing component of the MDSS?

DISCUSSION QUESTIONS

1. EXPERIENCE THE INTERNET. Go to the following Web site: www.internets.com. Select Business from the pop-up list category. Once there, select Business Databases, and select BizWiz. In the search instructions, type in *marketing decision support systems.* Once there, review some of the classified positions that require knowledge of the MDSS, and how they are used in those positions.

2. EXPERIENCE THE INTERNET. Go to www.yahoo.com and search for companies that use and develop MDSSs. Provide a brief report on the number of companies that develop the systems, and the applications for which they are used.

3. Discuss the differences associated with statistical software systems and managerial functional software systems. Why are managerial functional software systems used more frequently in actual business situations?

4. What is the most important advantage of a geographic information system (GIS)? What information would a GIS provide for a professional sports franchise seeking to relocate? Explain.

ENDNOTES

1. S. Ghose and Derek L. Nazareth, "Selecting the Appropriate Support for Marketing Decisions," *Omega,* September 1994.

2. Brian McWilliams, "Delighting the Marketer," *Computerworld,* November 1994.

3. Alan Buttery and Rick Tamaschke, "Marketing Decision Support Systems in a Small Trading Nation: A Case Study," *Marketing Intelligence and Planning* 13 (1995).

4. Boris Gendelev, "MIS and Marketing: Secrets of Strategic Information Mining," *Chief Information Officer Journal,* Summer 1992.

5. Ibid.

6. Louis Parks, "Using Advanced Customer Asset Management Systems to Automate Sales, Marketing, and Support Operations," *Telemarketing and Call Center Solutions,* March 1997.

7. W. Baets and V. Venugopal, "Neural Networks and Their Applications in Marketing Management," *Journal of Systems Management,* September 1994.

8. Kevin Higgins, "The Young Turks Leave Their Mark," *Credit Card Management,* May 1996.

9. Ibid.

10. Bernadette Szajna, "Software Evaluation and Choice: Predictive Validation of the Technology Acceptance Instrument," *MIS Quarterly,* September 1994.

11. Leonard Lodish, "On Measuring Advertising Effects," *Journal of Advertising Research,* September/October 1997.

MARKETING RESEARCH ILLUSTRATION

USING A GEOGRAPHIC INFORMATION SYSTEM

The following illustration details the construction and research use of a geographic information system (GIS). This application was provided by Dr. Devlin Fung.

Managing by the Map

Attend a seminar or read an article on modern marketing research, and one invariably encounters the term "GIS."

Geographic Information Systems (GIS), one of the most important tools in this age of "niche" marketing, has significant applications in a wide variety of industries. In fact, GIS has become a buzz word that represents to many a panacea to problem solving and decision making in marketing, resource management, planning, and environmental monitoring.

However, like most tools, GIS technology is only as good as the person using it, just as merely using a word processing software such as WordPerfect does not necessarily make one an accomplished writer. This is a pitfall too often overlooked by those who are fervently trying to embrace the technology. Effective use of GIS requires an understanding of the fundamental concepts of geographic data, map coordinate systems and registration, data integrity and accuracy, overlay analysis, and database manipulation. Applying GIS therefore involves more than merely investing in the necessary hardware/software system, and mastery of GIS software should not be equated with expertise in GIS. This article is intended to provide the reader with an understanding of the technology and demonstrate its potential as a valuable tool for business applications.

The concept of geographic information systems (GIS) evolved in the late 1950s from the traditional manual procedures for registering and overlaying individual layers of maps onto one another (giving rise to the term "light-table gymnastics.") This innovative use of maps as an analytical tool provided an entirely new facet in map usage, from mere physical description of geographic phenomena to spatial modeling applications (Berry, 1987; Parker, 1987).

Today, the evolution of GIS technology is intimately linked to the advent and development of computer technology. In its present form, GIS technology integrates spatial modeling, database management, and computer graphics in a hardware/software system for managing and manipulating geographic data. Typical GIS sofware, therefore, will provide the mechanisms to capture, encode, edit, analyze, compose, and display spatial data organized as map layers in a GIS database. In effect, these functions are categorized (Figure 1) as the four major components of a GIS: data input, data analysis, data management, and data output (Aronoff, 1989; Star and Estes, 1990).

At the Core, a Database

The key to proper application of GIS technology is the database. A GIS application today most probably will incorporate a relational database management system for the manipulation of feature attribute information.

FIGURE 1 **Components of a GIS include data input, data analysis, data management, and data output.**

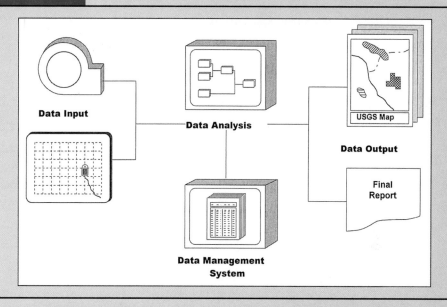

A GIS database contains map layers representing geographic themes organized in a digital format (Marble and Peuquet, 1983). These map layers, which are geocoded to a standard coordinate system such as the Universal Transverse Mercator (UTM) or State Plane Coordinate systems in use today, may be conceptualized (Figure 2) as a stack of floating maps tied to a common map base (Avery and Berlin, 1992). Each map layer can be independently accessed. When combined, information and related attributes from individual layers can be referenced to one another from a spatial standpoint.

In addition to the map layers, a GIS database also will include a data file or files containing attribute information about features indicated on each map layer and stored in a database file. For example, the data for a map layer of the road network of Shelby County may include such information as road name, road type, physical distance, class type, and address range. Through a relational database management system, the attribute information for each map feature in the database can be directly accessed as part of the input for analysis.

GIS and Spatial Analysis

In a GIS, the analysis component represents the crux of the system. Spatial analysis essentially involves the manipulation of map layers, individually or in combination, to derive solutions to spatial problems that assist the user in decision making. Geographic information systems may be categorized as (a) map reclassification, (b) map overlay, (c) neighborhood characterization, and (d) connectivity (or network) analysis (Berry, 1987). In any GIS software, a number of

FIGURE 2

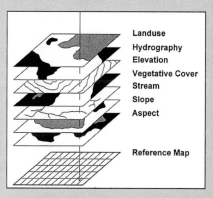

A GIS database may be conceptualized as a stack of floating map layers registered to a common map base.

operational commands are included to perform these functions. Through the combined use of these functions, various analysis models may be implemented.

Marketing Applications

In the 1980s, when niche marketing made it essential to consider demographic and other consumer information in relational ways, GIS provided marketers with a way to "layer" information within a neighborhood or larger geographic areas.

With GIS, it became possible to look at a market area and learn where certain defined demographic characteristics—age, sex, income, and race, for example—overlapped. Neighborhoods could be "clustered" into categories and defined by demographic data and lifestyle surveys.

Increasingly, geodemographic information is being linked with other types of household information to produce sophisticated profiles of neighborhoods that are a valuable tool for direct mail and other forms of target marketing. Some marketing research firms now offer databases that allow businesses to look at their market area in levels as fine as several blocks.

Which Data Structure?

In designing a GIS, the choice of the data structure is an important decision. The two most commonly used data formats are the *raster* and *vector* data structures (Burrough, 1989). In each map layer, spatial data are represented using the three geometric primitives: points, lines, and polygons. These primitives are defined differently in the raster and vector formats (Star and Estes, 1990).

Raster Format

In a raster format (A), each map layer is represented by a matrix of grid cells, with horizontal rows usually aligned in an east-west direction and the vertical columns aligned in a north-south direction (Aronoff, 1989). The origin of the matrix is normally at the top left corner (row 1, column 1) which corresponds to the northwest corner of the map layer (Star and Estes, 1990). Each cell is coded to represent a feature or value on the map layer.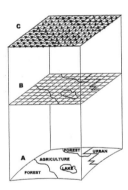

Perhaps the most salient feature of the raster format is the representation of spatial information using a uniform cell unit which defines the minimum mapping size (Avery and Berlin, 1992). A point feature, for instance, is represented by a cell which in effect indicates its existence within the cell. Similarly, a line feature is represented as a string of contiguous cells, and a polygon feature is represented by a group of contiguous cells.

Vector Format

A vector format provides a more precise approach to feature representation through the use of X,Y coordinate strings (B). A point feature is represented by a single X,Y coordinate pair that indicates its exact location on the map. A line feature is represented by an ordered string of consecutive X,Y coordinates where the beginning and end points (or nodes) are the starting and ending coordinates. A polygon feature is similarly represented, except that the beginning and the end nodes have the same X,Y coordinates to indicate an enclosed entity (Aronoff, 1989; Star and Estes, 1990).

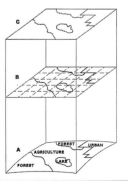

In a vector database, each of the point, line, and polygon features is usually topologically organized. In the topological organization, information about neighboring polygons, common boundaries, and nodes is also stored. This allows the relationships among entities to be maintained and reduces redundancies of commonly-shared points or linear features (Aronoff, 1989). Another characteristic of the vector format is its use of a relational database management system (RDBMS). Each feature (point, line, or polygon) is also uniquely identified and tied to a datafile in the database. This provides the means for storing the feature attribute information. Through the relational database management system, information about each feature can be accessed for editing and updating as each feature is identified (Antennucci, *et al.,* 1991; Avery and Berlin, 1992).

GIS Analysis and Business-Related Applications

The potential use of GIS as a research and planning tool has long been recognized by environmental scientists, planners, and resource managers for applications such as resource inventory surveys, change analysis, resource routing, and predictive modeling (Goodchild, 1987; Burrough, 1989; Antennucci, *et al.,* 1991). A great advantage of GIS technology is its ability to pose "what if" scenarios. Today, this potential has been increasingly recognized and capitalized on in the business world. Among these applications, predictive modeling appears to be the most appropriate GIS analysis strategy for business applications.

In GIS predictive modeling, sets of geographic parameters are manipulated to identify regions or locations based on spatial coincidence of factors that are relevant for a given scenario. In urban landuse planning, for instance, predictive modeling may be employed to analyze the interactions of developmental objectives with environmental, economic, and political factors to determine potential sites as well as the environmental impact of the proposed development (Gahegan and Roberts, 1988), or to detect urban development and its impact on the environment (Lo and Shipman, 1990).

The Hilton Corporation is now employing GIS technology to help reduce the gamble of locating new casinos. Hilton used mapping software, company-collected data, and data purchased from various sources when considering whether to enter the casino market on the Mississippi Gulf Coast. Demographic, socio-economic, and psychographic features were considered, along with the location of competing sources of entertainment in the area. Because of its marketing research, Hilton decided to postpone development on the Gulf Coast (except in New Orleans) due to saturation.

In another successful use of the technology, SYLVANIA employed GIS to help Stuart C. Irby Company, an electrical goods supplier based in Jackson, Miss., increase sales of SYLVANIA products. The Irby company provided SYLVANIA with information about the types of products it sells to customers and their geographic locations: SYLVANIA developed a plan of action to help Irby increase its SYLVANIA business (Wendelken, 1994).

Lichliter, Jameson & Associates (L/JA), a Houston-based consulting engineering firm, has effectively employed GIS to assist in their transportation planning and engineering projects. In one such project, GIS was used to assess environment impacts, manage asset data, and analyze effects of project alternatives in the company's endeavor to construct a 200 m.p.h. passenger rail system serving Houston, Dallas, Austin, and San Antonio.

These are but a few of the applications of predictive modeling as a planning tool by resource scientists, managers, and landuse planners. In essence, GIS has become a vital tool capable of providing solutions to land and resource-planning problems to help formulate developmental policies in private organizations and public planning agencies.

GIS Database Development

The development of a GIS database is the most fundamental, and perhaps the most critical, stage in a GIS operation. It is a very time-consuming task and represents the bulk of the effort in any GIS operation. The task involves the generation of map layers that are required for the analysis. Map layers in the GIS database must be encoded into a digital format compatible with the GIS software to be used. These map data may have to be digitized off available maps or aerial photographs, or they may be obtained from commercial or government sources.

Two commonly used street and highway databases are produced by the U.S. government. These are the Digital Line Graphs (DLGs) produced by the U.S. Geological Survey, and the Topologically Integrated Geographic Encoding and Referencing (TIGER/line) files from the U.S. Bureau of the Census (USBC). Additionally, attribute information has to be input into the datafile as the relational database component of the GIS database. Census/demographic data based on county and census tracts are also available from USBC.

GIS at Work

A vinyl siding company wants to identify for its local distributor the areas in Shelby County that hold the greatest potential for sales. Its target is based on (*a*) the location of homes 15 years and older that are (*b*) owned by people with annual median household incomes of at least $35,000. Using the query capability of GIS software, along with census data coded in the GIS database, the user can categorize census tracts based on age of homes (A) and annual median income (B). By overlaying the two map layers, a final layer that identifies various categories of needs and affordability can be quickly isolated (C).

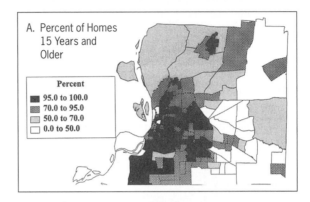

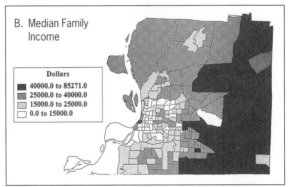

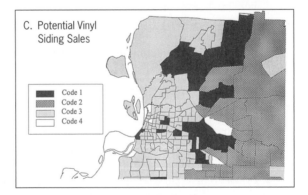

Code 1 = Over 60% of homes 15 years old or older; median family income above $35,000
Code 2 = High median income, less than 60% of homes 15 years old or older
Code 3 = Low median income, over 60% of homes 15 years old or older
Code 4 = Low median income, less than 60% of homes 15 years old or older

GIS at Work

An investment enterprise interested in constructing a large shopping mall within the perimeter of the town of Anysville has decided that the potential location should meet the following requirements:

a. Must be within a half-mile zone outside the urban area.

b. Should be located no more than 200 yards from existing high-traffic roads or no more than 100 yards from medium- or light-duty roads.

c. Should be located in an area that does not infringe on existing forested lands.

d. Selected parcels must be at least 12 acres in size.

From map layers of Anysville, a half-mile buffer zone surrounding the town is identified (A); 200-yard and 100-yard buffer zones are generated along existing heavy-duty and medium/light-duty roads (B). By overlaying these two map layers, the desired areas are identified (C). The forested areas are introduced and "removed" from the selected areas (D). Areas below the required size of 12 acres are eliminated to provide the potential mall sites (E).

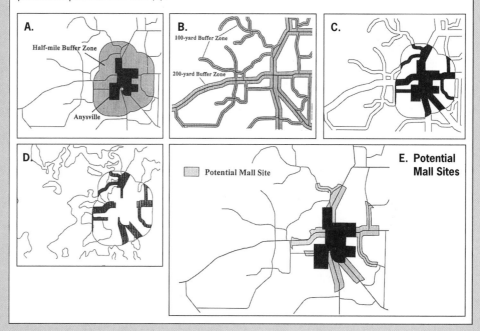

Commercial Data Sources

Commercial companies are important sources for geographic, demographic, business, and natural resource and environmental data. EtakMAP, for instance, provides highly-accurate, large-scale digital base maps of roads, addresses, ZIP codes, Metropolitan Statistical Area (MSA) boundaries, and related map features. Other commercial sources include Claritas, Geographic Data Technology, DataMap, SMI, EarthInfo, and MapInfo.

For the data to be useful, they must be transformed or encoded to the format required by individual GIS software. Most data sources will provide the necessary interface for the transformation. Likewise, most GIS software also provides the function to capture data from a variety of recognized formats. This not only provides an avenue for capturing data from such data sources, but also the possibility of acquiring data output from other GIS software.

21st Century GIS

While GIS software has grown increasingly sophisticated in the first half of the 1990s, greater strides are expected in the years ahead, both in the hardware component and, even more so, in the software component of GIS technology.

GIS at Work

A.

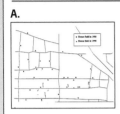

A real estate company wants to investigate the average cost of houses sold in Shelby County in 1980 and 1990, and the change within that period. Data needed includes houses sold during the two periods, the street/road map, and the housing zones based on the Multiple Listing Service (MLS). The location of each house can be identified on the street map, using the address-matching function of the GIS software (A). The average prices of houses for the two respective years are summarized, based on the MLS zones (B and C). Finally, by overlaying the two maps, the changes in price for each zone can be computed and displayed (D). The resulting map helps identify the spatial distribution and the magnitude of changes in average home prices within the period in Shelby County.

B.

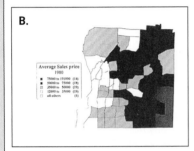

D.

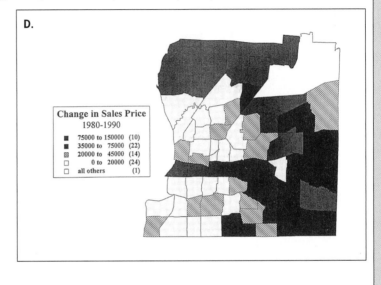

C.

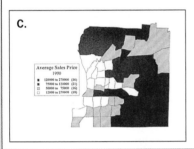

Presently, a majority of the most sophisticated GIS software makes use of vector data structure. Recently, software employing raster-based GIS has re-emerged, made possible by advances in computer systems that are more efficient in data storage, retrieval, and the display of voluminous datasets. These raster-based applications will greatly complement existing vector-based systems, with the future witnessing a complete integration of both vector-based and raster-based GIS, allowing the user to capitalize on the strengths of both systems in a single software.

The availability and expanded use of satellite imagery for GIS applications will have a marked effect on GIS technology. There will be increasing use of satellite images as GIS data sources, which in turn will lead to greater integration of GIS applications with remote sensing technology. Undoubtedly, there will be expanded and more sophisticated use of the Global Positioning System (GPS) in data location and registration. In addition, new standards and protocol to facilitate information/data exchange will have to be implemented.

On the horizon is the introduction of artificial (AI) and expert systems techniques to individual components of GIS applications. Artificial intelligence techniques will be increasingly employed to assist in data conversion (particularly raster-vector conversion), relational database management systems, feature recognition/extraction, and cartographic design. There already is a trend toward the introduction of knowledge-based experts systems to assist GIS modeling analysis. An all-encompassing system that will automate data capture, modeling analysis, and design cartography in a single GIS software is still a dream. However, the technology is certainly headed in that direction, and the dream is likely to become reality in the not too distant future.

REFERENCES

Antenucci, J.C., K. Brown, P.L. Croswell, M.J. Kevany, and H. Archer, 1991. *Geographic Information Systems: A Guide to the Technology.* Van Nostrand Reinhold, New York, New York, 301 pp.

Aronoff, S., 1989. *Geographic Information Systems: A Management Perspective.* WDL Publications, Ottawa, Canada, 294 pp.

Avery, T.E. and G.L. Berlin, 1992. *Fundamentals of Remote Sensing and Airphoto Interpretation.* Macmillan Publishing Co., New York, New York, 472 pp.

Berry, J., 1987. Computer-Assisted Map Analysis: Potential and Pitfalls. *Photogrammetric Engineering and Remote Sensing,* Vol. 52, No. 10, pp. 1405–1410.

Burrough, P.A., 1989. *Principles of Geographic Information Systems for Land Resources Assessment.* Oxford University Press, New York, New York, 193 pp.

Gahegan, M.N. and S.A. Roberts, 1988. An Intelligent, Object-Oriented Geographical Information System. *International Journal of Geographical Information Systems,* Vol. 2, No. 2, pp. 101–110.

Goodchild, M.F., 1987. A Spatial Analytical Perspective on Geographic Information Systems. *International Journal of Geographical Information Systems,* Vol. 1, No. 4, pp. 327–334.

Lo, C.P. and R.L. Shipman, 1990. A GIS Approach to Landuse Change Dynamics Detection. *Photogrammetric Engineering and Remote Sensing,* Vol. 56, No. 11, pp. 1483–1491.

Marble, D.F. and D.J. Peuquet (Eds.), 1983. Geographic Information Systems and Remote Sensing. *Manual of Remote Sensing, Second Edition.* American Society of Photogrammetry, Falls Church, Virginia, pp. 923–957.

Parker, H.D., 1987. What is Geographic Information System? Proceedings, Sixth Annual GIS Conference, October 26–39. San Francisco, California, pp. 72–80.

Star, J. and J. Estes, 1990. *Geographic Information Systems: An Introduction.* Prentice Hall, Englewood Cliffs, New Jersey, 303 pp.

Schultink, G., 1992. Integrated Remote Sensing, Spatial Information Systems, and Applied Models in Resource Assessment, Economic Development, and Policy Analysis. *Photogrammetric Engineering and Remote Sensing,* Vol. 58, No. 8, pp. 1229–1237.

Welch, R., M. Remillard, and J. Alberts, 1992. Integration of GPS, Remote Sensing, and Geographic Information System Technologies for Coastal Resource Management. *Photogrammetric Engineering and Remote Sensing,* Vol. 58, No. 11, pp. 1571–1578.

Wendelken, 1995. Hilton Beats the Odds. *Business Geographics,* Vol. 3, No. 1, pp. 28–32.

Wendelken, 1994. SYLVANIA Lights Up Sales. *Business Geographics,* Vol. 2, No. 1, pp. 22–25.

Source: Dr. Devlin Fung, "Managing by the Map," *Business Perspectives* (The University of Memphis) 8, no. 2 (Spring 1995).

MARKETING RESEARCH CASE EXERCISE

MARKETING RESEARCH FOR AN EXPORT OPERATION

Most of the time marketers have to make daily decisions for which there is neither time nor money for special research. To provide the decision maker with data to support ongoing decisions, there must be an information system already in place. Information and data management is more complex for international markets than for the domestic market because of separation of time and space as well as wide differences in cultural and technological environments.

Qualities of a Useful System

Corporations have responded by developing marketing decision support systems. To be truly useful to the decision maker, the chosen system must be relevant, timely, flexible, accurate, exhaustive, and convenient.

- **Relevant.** The data gathered must have meaning for the decision-making process. Few companies can spend a lot of money collecting facts that are nice to know. So the system cannot be an electronic grapevine or Christmas tree on which to hang anything that comes to mind. There must be a well-understood and widely disseminated set of guidelines about what goes in, as well as a gatekeeper controlling the supply.

- **Timely.** When managers need to know something right away, it might be acceptable if the answers arrive in a couple of days, but not in a month. Conversely, when information becomes outdated, it should be replaced, deleted, or at least clearly labeled as being possibly erroneous.

- **Flexible.** Information must be available in the forms needed by management. A marketing decision support system should therefore permit manipulations of the format and combination of the data.

- **Accurate.** Accuracy is of primary importance in the international field. Information that is available one day may be invalid the next because of major changes taking place in the world.

- **Exhaustive.** The systems data bank should be reasonably exhaustive. Because of the interrelationships among variables, all the factors that can influence a particular decision ought to be appropiately represented in the system. Because international marketing can be affected by many issues that do not come into play domestically, the necessity for an ample reservoir of pertinent data is apparent.

- **Convenience.** The system must be convenient to access and use. Time-consuming systems will not be used enough to justify their cost.

Conclusions

There are various reasons why international marketing decision support systems are being developed successfully. These reasons include technological advances in hardware and software, increased familiarity with technology, and acknowledgment by managers that acting without a sound basis is disastrous in the international arena.

1. Why is it so important to develop and maintain a decision support system for international marketing operations? What are some problems the system can overcome for the marketer?

2. When planning for the development of a decision support system for international marketing operations, what critical data or information would you design into the system? How would this data be helpful for understanding international markets?

Learning Objectives

After reading this chapter, you will be able to

1. Identify the fundamental differences between qualitative and quantitative research methods and explain their appropriateness in creating useful managerial information.

2. Describe and explain two popular qualitative techniques used in gathering raw primary data.

3. Explain the basic pros and cons of using qualitative methods of developing data structures.

4. Explain what focus groups are, the importance of a moderator, and how the resulting data are transformed into information.

Exploratory Designs: In-Depth Interviews and Focus Groups

❝ What new banking services or changes in existing service offerings does Barnett Bank need to consider to assure customer service quality and satisfaction? ❞

LAURA W. GAUTHIER
Vice President and Sales Manager
Barnett Bank of Pasco County

Using Focus Group Interviews to Gain Insights into Bank Customer Satisfaction

The Barnett Bank of Pasco County (BBPC) found itself in a position of declining market share among the senior citizen market structure for the fourth consecutive quarter. Although the bank conducted quarterly satisfaction surveys and the results indicated strong satisfaction among its senior customers, bank records indicated that an increasing number of senior customers were switching their accounts to BBPC's competitor banks. Not understanding this trend, BBPC's management called on the marketing research department to gather information among BBPC's senior customers regarding their attitudes, perceptions, and behaviors toward the bank's service offerings and current service delivery methods as well as how the bank might improve its service quality and ensure customer satisfaction.

A series of moderated small-group discussions was conducted among both current and past BBPC senior banking customers to determine their expectations and attitudes about BBPC's service. To assist the researcher in later in-depth analysis, each of the focus group sessions was videotaped. The findings revealed that these particular current and past customers wanted (1) very friendly and courteous treatment by BBPC's staff and management; (2) a personalized relationship with someone who demon-strated trust, diagnostic competence, reliability, credibility, and understanding of their banking needs; and (3) clear and correct answers to their questions. In turn, the discussions indicated that those senior customers who switched banks had experienced (1) their "favorite" teller losing his or her job or being transferred to another location; (2) a lack of empathy and concern on the part of the bank's employees; and (3) difficulty with the loan department.

The research afforded BBPC's management insights into potential problems in the delivery system used to service the senior customer market. BBPC learned that its methods of dealing with customers were too inflexible to handle attitudinal differences among demographic market segments. Front-line service personnel were being trained to treat all customers the same way. As a result of the additional insights gained through the focus group interviews, BBPC modified its training programs to teach its employees that demographically different customers hold different perceptions about banking services and delivery methods. New training programs stressed the need for more flexibility among its customer service and teller staff. Staff members were retrained to exhibit patience and extra politeness toward senior customers.

Value of Qualitative Research Information

The BBPC example in the chapter opener illustrates several important issues that business decision makers must be aware of in their process of resolving marketing problems and questions. First, management is quite often faced with problem situations where important questions cannot be adequately addressed or resolved merely with secondary information. Meaningful insights into some problem situations will be gained only through the collection of pertinent primary (or firsthand) data. Recall that primary data are normally collected by a set of formalized procedures in which researchers ask selected individuals questions or observe and record their behavior. Second, collecting only quantitative data structures does not guarantee that management will gain a complete understanding of the problem situation. Collecting qualitative data might be necessary as well.

As the journey through Phase II of the research process (Determine and Evaluate the Research Design) continues, attention turns away from research activities that focus on secondary data and information. This chapter begins a series of three chapters that discuss *exploratory, descriptive,* and *causal* research designs used to collect primary data and create data structures and information. As discussed in earlier chapters, the research objectives and information requirements are the keys to determining which type of research design will be the most appropriate to use in collecting raw data. At the heart of any research design are the methods and techniques actually used to collect the required data. In recent years, the methods available for collecting data have been generally classified into two very broad categories: *qualitative* and *quantitative.* This chapter introduces several popular research methods used mainly in exploratory research designs to collect qualitative, or "soft," data structures. Chapters 9 and 10 focus on the quantitative methods (e.g., surveys, experiments, test marketing) used by researchers in descriptive and causal research designs.

An Overview of Qualitative and Quantitative Research Methods

Prior to discussing the popular qualitative data collection techniques used in exploratory research designs, we will identify some of the fundamental differences between qualitative and quantitative research methods. Although there are vast differences in the two approaches, there is no single agreed-on set of factors that distinguishes them as being mutually exclusive. The dimensional factors listed in Exhibit 8.1 offer some insights on the general differences.

EXHIBIT 8.1   **Differences between Qualitative and Quantitative Research Methods**

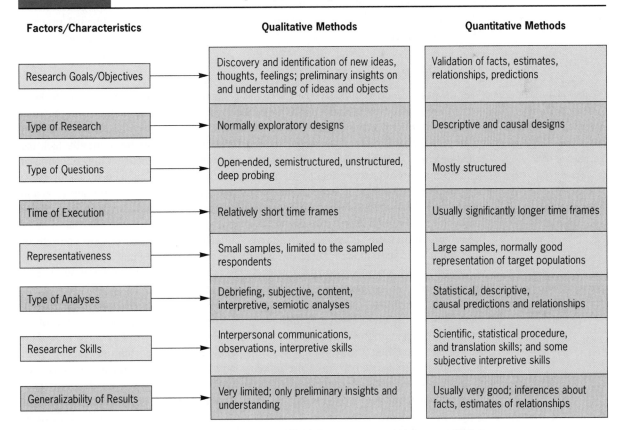

Factors/Characteristics	Qualitative Methods	Quantitative Methods
Research Goals/Objectives	Discovery and identification of new ideas, thoughts, feelings; preliminary insights on and understanding of ideas and objects	Validation of facts, estimates, relationships, predictions
Type of Research	Normally exploratory designs	Descriptive and causal designs
Type of Questions	Open-ended, semistructured, unstructured, deep probing	Mostly structured
Time of Execution	Relatively short time frames	Usually significantly longer time frames
Representativeness	Small samples, limited to the sampled respondents	Large samples, normally good representation of target populations
Type of Analyses	Debriefing, subjective, content, interpretive, semiotic analyses	Statistical, descriptive, causal predictions and relationships
Researcher Skills	Interpersonal communications, observations, interpretive skills	Scientific, statistical procedure, and translation skills; and some subjective interpretive skills
Generalizability of Results	Very limited; only preliminary insights and understanding	Usually very good; inferences about facts, estimates of relationships

Quantitative Research Methods

Quantitative research

Research that places heavy emphasis on using formalized standard questions and predetermined response options in questionnaires or surveys administered to large numbers of respondents.

Today, quantitative research is commonly associated with surveys or experiments and is still considered the mainstay of the research industry for collecting marketing data. **Quantitative research** places heavy emphasis on using formalized standard questions and predetermined response options in questionnaires or surveys administered to large numbers of respondents. For example, when you think of quantitative research, think of J. D. Powers and Associates conducting a nationwide mail survey on customer satisfaction among new car purchasers or American Express doing a nationwide survey on travel behaviors with telephone interviews. Normally in quantitative research, the information research problems and opportunities are specific and well defined, and the decision maker and researcher have agreed on what the precise information needs are. Quantitative research methods are more directly related to descriptive and causal research designs than to exploratory designs. Success in collecting primary data is more a function of correctly designing and administering the survey instrument than of the communication and interpretive skills of an interviewer or observer.

The main goal of quantitative research is to provide specific facts decision makers can use to (1) make accurate predictions about relationships between market factors and behaviors, (2) gain meaningful insights into those relationships, and (3) verify or validate the existing relationships. In quantitative research practices, researchers are well trained in construct development, scale measurement, questionnaire design, sampling, and statistical data analysis skills. In addition, researchers must have a solid ability to translate numerical data structures into meaningful narrative information. Data reliability and validity issues are serious concerns within quantitative research procedures. Descriptive research methods and procedures will be discussed in detail in Chapter 9 and experimental research designs in Chapter 10.

Qualitative Research Methods

Qualitative research

Research used in exploratory designs to gain preliminary insights into decision problems and opportunities.

Over the past decade, **qualitative research** has come to refer to selected research methods used in exploratory research designs. One of the main objectives of qualitative research is to gain preliminary insights into decision problems and opportunities. On the surface, qualitative research methods incorporate some scientific elements but normally lack the critical elements of true reliability. Qualitative research tends to focus on the collection of detailed amounts of primary data from relatively small samples of subjects by asking questions or observing behavior. Researchers well trained in interpersonal communication and interpretive skills use either open-ended questions that allow for in-depth probing of the subjects' initial responses or specific observational techniques that allow for analysis of behavior. In most cases, qualitative data can be collected within relatively short periods of time, but it is difficult to summarize or quantify the data structures into meaningful forms or numbers. Data analysis is normally restricted to very subjective content, interpretive, or semiotic analysis procedures.

Among the dimensional factors, the nonstructured format of the questions and the small sample size tend to severely limit the researcher's ability to generalize the qualitative data to larger segments of subjects. Nevertheless, qualitative data have important uses in understanding and resolving business problems and opportunities, especially in the areas of initial discovery and preliminary explanation of marketplace or consumer behavior and decision processes. For example, qualitative data can be invaluable in providing decision makers and researchers with initial ideas about specific problems or opportunities; theories, models, or constructs; or the designing of new, specific scale measurements. Yet these data structures are generally not meant to be used in recommending a final course of action.

| **EXHIBIT 8.2** | **Guidelines for Using Qualitative Research Methodologies** |

Qualitative research methods are appropriate when decision makers or researchers are

- In the process of correctly identifying a business problem or opportunity situation or establishing information requirements.

- Interested in obtaining some preliminary insights into the motivation, emotional, attitudinal, and personality factors that influence marketplace behaviors.

- In the process of building theories and models to explain marketplace behaviors or relationships between two or more marketing constructs.

- Attempting to develop reliable and valid scale measurements for investigating specific market factors, consumer qualities (e.g., attitudes, emotional feelings, preferences, beliefs, perceptions) and behavioral outcomes.

- Trying to determine the preliminary effectiveness of their marketing strategies on actual marketplace behaviors.

- Interested in new-product or service development or repositioning current product or service images.

When to Use Qualitative Research Methods

In most exploratory research endeavors, the raw data will be gathered through qualitative data collection practices. Exhibit 8.2 lists some guidelines for determining when it is appropriate to use qualitative research methods for collecting and creating additional information. These guidelines are by no means exhaustive.

Advantages and Disadvantages of Qualitative Research Methods

Like other primary data collection techniques, qualitative research methods offer several advantages to today's researchers. Exhibit 8.3 summarizes the main advantages and disadvantages.

Major Advantages

One general advantage of qualitative research methods is that they are both economical and timely. Due in part to the use of small samples, researchers can complete their investigations quicker and at a significantly lower total cost than they can with other types of methods. Another advantage is the richness of the data. The unstructured nature of qualitative techniques allows the researcher to collect in-depth data about the subjects' attitudes, beliefs, emotions, and perceptions, all of which may strongly influence their observable market behaviors. Such in-depth data can be invaluable to gaining a preliminary understanding of

---

| **EXHIBIT 8.3** | **Advantages and Disadvantages of Using Qualitative Research Methods** |

Advantages of Qualitative Methods	Disadvantages of Qualitative Methods
Economical and timely data collection	Lack of generalizability
Richness of the data	Inability to distinguish small differences
Accuracy of recording marketplace behaviors	Lack of reliability and validity
Preliminary insights into building models and scale measurements	Difficulty finding well-trained investigators, interviewers, and observers

those behaviors. Some qualitative techniques allow decision makers to gain firsthand experiences with flesh-and-blood consumers and can provide very revealing information about consumers and their thinking patterns. The richness of the qualitative data can often supplement the facts and estimates gathered through other primary data collection techniques. Some qualitative methods allow the investigator to accurately record actual behaviors, not just reported behaviors.

Some qualitative research methods can provide researchers with excellent preliminary insights into building marketing models and scale measurements. In addition, qualitative data play a critical role in identifying marketing problem or opportunity situations. The in-depth information enhances the researcher's ability to predict consumer behavior in the marketplace, as well as to develop better marketing constructs and more reliable and valid scale measurements of those constructs.

Major Disadvantages

Although qualitative research can, and does, produce helpful and useful information, it has two main potential disadvantages: sample size limitations and the need for well-trained interviewers, observers, and investigators. First, qualitative data normally lack generalizability. Due to the use of small, nonstatistically drawn samples, the information generated by qualitative research techniques cannot be generalized to larger groups of individuals. This lack of representativeness of the defined target population severely limits the use of qualitative information in helping decision makers select and implement final action strategies. For example, one would be hard pressed to demonstrate that the attitudes and behaviors of a group of 8 to 12 college students is representative of all college students in the United States, of college students at a particular university, of business majors at that university, or even of marketing majors. Small sample sizes make it impossible for researchers to test inferences about the groups' attitudes, beliefs, feelings, motivations, and perceptions, as well as their behavior beyond the group.

Another disadvantage is that the data generated through qualitative methods are limited by their inability to distinguish small differences. Many times marketing successes and failures are based on small differences in marketing mix strategies. Using small samples of subjects to provide critical data and information does not allow researchers to be in a position to evaluate the impact of small differences. Moreover, researchers are forced to analyze qualitative data at aggregate, not disaggregate, levels. Aggregation of the findings eliminates the opportunity to discover small differences and their impact. In most cases, qualitative research methods collect data that cannot be adequately assessed as being reliable. In most situations that require primary information, decision makers become uncomfortable if that information cannot be determined reliable.

Finally, the difficulty of finding well-trained investigators, interviewers, and observers to conduct qualitative research can be a potential disadvantage. Due to the informal, unstructured nature of obtaining qualitative data, there tends to be a significant number of people who without extensive formal training profess to be experts in the qualitative field. It is somewhat difficult for the unsuspecting practitioner to discern the researcher's qualifications or the quality of the research. Given all of these disadvantages, researchers should integrate both qualitative and quantitative techniques in order to make the research program complete.

Questioning Techniques in Qualitative Research

In today's business environment there are many marketing problem situations that need to look beyond current market behavior. Quite often decision makers need information that can be obtained only by directly asking people questions. Interviewing therefore plays an important role in qualitative research. While there are many kinds of interviews that could be used to collect qualitative data, we will focus on two: in-depth interviews and focus group interviews. Besides interviews, some other qualitative questioning techniques, known as projective techniques, are (1) word associations, (2) sentence completion tests, (3) picture tests, and (4) cartoon or balloon tests.

In-Depth Interviews

In-Depth Interviewing Techniques

In-depth interview

A formalized process in which a well-trained interviewer asks a subject a set of semistructured questions in a face-to-face setting.

As a qualitative technique, an **in-depth interview**, commonly referred to as a depth interview, represents a formalized process in which a well-trained interviewer asks a subject a set of semistructured, probing questions usually in a face-to-face setting. Depending on the research objectives, the normal setting for this type of interview would be either the subject's home or office, or some type of centralized interviewing center that is fairly convenient for the subject. In special situations, in-depth interviews can be conducted by telephone or through a high-tech telecommunication system that allows face-to-face interchanges through a television or computer. Exhibit 8.4 lists several of the main objectives of in-depth interviewing methods.

In-depth interviewing allows the researcher to collect both attitudinal and behavioral data from the subject that spans all time frames (past, present, and future). Let's say, for example, that corporate management of Marriott Hotels wants to understand how to deliver better on-site services to business customers. Marriott's researchers can conduct on-site, in-depth interviews with selected business travelers that include the following semistructured questions:

> What were the specific factors you used in selecting Marriott for overnight accommodations during your business trip to San Diego, California? (Motives.)
>
> What hotel services have you used during your stay? (Behavior.)
>
> How satisfied or dissatisfied are you with those services? (Current feelings.)
>
> How likely are you to stay at a Marriott Hotel next time you are in San Diego for business, and why? (Future intended behavior.)

Probing questions

Questions that result when an interviewer takes the subject's initial response to a question and uses that response as the framework for the next question (the probing question) in order to gain more detailed responses.

A unique characteristic of this data collection method is that the interviewer uses **probing questions** as the mechanism to get more data on the topic from the subject. By taking the subject's initial response and turning it into a question, the interviewer encourages the subject to further delineate the first response and creates natural opportunities for a more detailed discussion of the topic. The general rule of thumb is that the more a subject talks about a topic, the more likely he or she is to reveal underlying attitudes, motives, emotions, and behaviors. To illustrate the technique of using probing

EXHIBIT 8.4   **Main Research Objectives of In-Depth Interviewing**

1. To discover preliminary insights of **what** the subject thinks or believes about the topic of concern or **why** the subject exhibits certain behaviors.

2. To obtain unrestricted and detailed comments that include feelings, beliefs, or opinions that can help better understand the different elements of the subject's thoughts and the reasons why they exist.

3. To have the respondent communicate as much detail as possible about his or her knowledge and behavior toward a given topic or object.

This telephone interviewer conducts an in-depth interview survey.

questions, let's use one of the questions from the above Marriott example. The dialogue might go as follows:

Interviewer: "What hotel services have you used during your stay?"

Subject: "I have used the front desk, restaurant, and the hotel's fitness center."

Interviewer: "With regard to the front desk, what were some of the actual services that you requested?"

Subject: "Well besides checking in, I inquired about the availability of a fitness room and car rental."

Interviewer: "Why were you interested in information about the hotel's fitness center and car rental service?"

Subject: "When I am away on business, I enjoy a good workout to help relieve stress buildup and I find my energy level improves."

Interviewer: "While at the hotel, how does renting a car fit into your plans?"

Subject: "I have a business meeting tomorrow at 9:30 A.M. across town; afterward I plan to play a round of golf."

Interviewer: "Which rental car company do you usually prefer to use when renting a car?"

Subject: "Hertz—they are the best! I have Gold VIP status with them and I receive frequent flier miles."

Interviewer: "Besides using the fitness center and renting a car, what other hotel services might you request during your stay?"

Subject: "I will probably rent a movie tonight."

Interviewer: "Renting a movie? Please elaborate on your interest in renting movies."

Subject: "When away from home, I enjoy watching action-oriented movies as a means to relax after a long day on the road. I do not get much of a chance when I am at home with the wife and the kids."

Interviewer: "Are there any other services that you would consider using?"

Subject: "No." (With this response, the interviewer would move on to the next topic.)

A word of caution about probing questions: it is critically important that the interviewer avoid framing questions that allow the subject to reply with a simple but logical *no*. Unless the interviewer intends to bring closure to the discussion, probing questions should not be framed in formats like "Can you tell me more about that point?," "Could you elaborate on that?," "Do you have some specific reasons?," or "Is there anything else?" All these formats allow the subject to logically say no. Once a *no* response is given, it becomes very difficult to continue probing the topic for more detailed data.

Skills Required for Conducting In-Depth Interviews

For in-depth interviewing to serve as an efficient and valuable data collection tool, interviewers must have excellent interpersonal communication skills and listening skills. **Interpersonal communication skills** relate to the interviewer's ability to articulate the questions in a direct and clear manner so that the subject understands what she or he is responding to. **Listening skills** include the ability to accurately hear, record, and interpret the subject's responses. Depending on the complexity of the topic and the desired data requirements, most interviewers will secure prior permission from the subject to record the interview using either a tape recorder or possibly a video recorder rather than relying solely on handwritten notes.

As mentioned above, without excellent probing skills, the interviewer may inadvertently allow the discussion of a specific topic to end before all the potential data are revealed. Probing questions need to be precise and to incorporate the subject's previous reply. Interpretive skills relate to the interviewer's capabilities to accurately understand and record the subject's responses to questions. These skills play a critical role in the process of transforming the actual raw data into data structures and information. An interviewer's weak interpretive skills will have a negative impact on the quality of the data collected. For example, if the interviewer does not understand the subject's response, he or she is not likely to follow up with a probing question that will move the dialogue where it was intended to move. The resulting data may not be meaningful to the initial area of inquiry. Finally, the personality of the interviewer plays a significant role in establishing a "comfort zone" for the subject during the question/answer process. Interviewers should be easygoing, flexible, trustworthy, and professional. Respondents who feel at ease with a person are more likely to reveal their hidden attitudes, feelings, motivations, perceptions, and behaviors to that person.

Advantages of In-Depth Interviews

As a qualitative data collection method, in-depth interviewing offers researchers several benefits. First is flexibility. One-on-one personal interviews allow the researcher to ask questions and collect data on a wide variety of topics. The question-and-answer process gives the researcher the flexibility to collect data not only on the subject's activities and behavior patterns, but also on the attitudes, motivations, feelings, and opinions that underlie those reported behaviors. Another benefit relates to the large amount of detailed data that can be collected from each subject. Probing questions allow researchers to collect highly detailed data from the subject regarding the topic at hand. Once a certain comfort zone is reached in the interviewer-subject relationship, subjects willingly reveal their inner thinking.

Interpersonal communication skills The interviewer's ability to articulate questions in a direct and clear manner.

Listening skills The interviewer's ability to accurately interpret and record the subject's responses.

Disadvantages of In-Depth Interviews

As discussed earlier in the chapter, the data collected by in-depth interviews are subject to the same general limitations as in all qualitative methods. Although in-depth interviews can generate a lot of detailed data, the data structures tend to lack generalizability, reliability, and the ability to distinguish small differences. The researcher must be concerned with the issue of accuracy due to potential biases from interviewer–respondent artifacts (e.g., interviewer illustrates empathy toward the respondent's answers); respondent bias (e.g., faulty recall, concern with social acceptability, fatigue); or interviewer errors (e.g., inadequate listening, faulty recording procedures, fatigue). Other factors that limit the use of this questioning approach are the costs for both setup and completion and the extensive length of time required.

Focus Group Interviews

Nature of Focus Group Interviews

Focus group research

A formalized process of bringing a small group of people together for an interactive, spontaneous discussion on one particular topic or concept.

The second, and most popular, qualitative research method we will discuss in this chapter is focus group research. **Focus group research** involves a formalized process of bringing a small group of people together for an interactive and spontaneous discussion of one particular topic or concept. Focus groups normally consist of 6 to 12 participants who are guided by one or two professional facilitators, called moderators, through an unstructured discussion that typically lasts between 90 minutes and two hours. By getting the group members to talk at length and in detail about a topic, the moderator draws out as many ideas, attitudes, feelings, and experiences as possible about the specified issue.

The overall goal of focus group research is to give researchers, and ultimately decision makers, as much information as possible about how people regard the topic of interest. That topic is, typically, a product, service, concept, or organization. Unlike many other types of questioning techniques, focus group research is not restricted to just asking and answering questions posed by an interviewer. Its success relies heavily on the group dynamics, the willingness of members to engage in an interactive dialogue, and the professional moderator's ability to keep the discussion on track. The fundamental idea behind the focus group approach is that one person's response will spark comments from other members, thus generating a spontaneous interplay among all of the participants. The overall cost of conducting a focus group can vary from $2,000 to $5,000 per session.[1]

Focus Group Research Objectives

There are many reasons focus group research is the most popular qualitative research method. As we noted earlier, the data collected in focus groups can offer preliminary insights into hidden marketing phenomena. Exhibit 8.5 lists some other pertinent objectives of focus group research. Each of these is described in more detail below.

TO PROVIDE DATA FOR DEFINING AND REDEFINING MARKETING PROBLEMS. In those situations where managers or researchers experience difficulties in identifying and understanding a specific marketing problem, focus groups can help in distinguishing the differences between symptoms and root problem factors. For example, the marketing department chairperson at a major southwestern university was not sure why undergraduate enrollment levels were continually declining. The chairperson therefore called for a departmental faculty meeting using a focus group format. The discussion revealed several unexpected factors that provided the marketing department preliminary insights into why enrollment levels were declining. One of these had to do with whether the current marketing curriculum was offering marketing majors the kinds of skills currently demanded by businesses. The marketing department investigated this issue and found significant gaps

| EXHIBIT 8.5 | Main Focus Group Research Objectives |

1. To provide data for defining and redefining marketing problems.
2. To identify specific hidden information requirements.
3. To provide data for better understanding the results from other quantitative survey studies.
4. To reveal consumers' hidden needs, wants, attitudes, feelings, behaviors, perceptions, and motives regarding services, products, or practices.
5. To generate new ideas about products, services, or delivery methods.
6. To discover new constructs and measurement methods.
7. To help explain changing consumer preferences.

between the two perspectives as to which skills undergraduate marketing majors needed to acquire. The department began a reassessment of its own curriculum in an attempt to realign the skills being taught to those being mandated by the real business world.

TO IDENTIFY SPECIFIC HIDDEN INFORMATION REQUIREMENTS. In some situations decision makers and researchers are not totally sure what specific types of data or information should be investigated. In these situations, focus groups can reveal unexpected components of the problem and thus can directly help researchers determine what specific data should be collected. For example, as described in Chapter 2 (see the Small Business Implications box, p. 37), the directors of the Ford Foundation of Performing Arts in Vail, Colorado, were faced with the difficulties of deciding what design features should be included in the construction of a new $5 million Performing Arts Center. The foundation's research team conducted several focus groups consisting of local residents and seasonal visitors. From the groups' spontaneous, unstructured discussions, specific features and concerns such as different types of indoor and outdoor events, parking requirements, availability of refreshments, seating design and capacity, pricing of tickets, and protection from bad weather were revealed as being important factors that needed further understanding.

TO PROVIDE DATA FOR BETTER UNDERSTANDING RESULTS FROM QUANTITATIVE STUDIES. There are situations where quantitative research investigations leave the decision maker or researcher asking why the results came out the way they did. Focus groups can be conducted to help explain the findings of other surveys. For example, corporate management of JP Hotels, Inc., conducted a survey among business guests at its hotels concerning free in-room entertainment services. The results suggested that 85 percent of the business guests were aware of the availability of the entertainment services but only 15 percent actually used them. Not understanding this gap between awareness and actual use, JP Hotels conducted several focus groups among its business guests regarding these services. The focus group discussions revealed that business travelers were either too busy doing necessary paperwork or too exhausted to watch any type of TV at night. They preferred to read or listen to music as a means of relaxing after a long workday.

TO REVEAL CONSUMERS' HIDDEN NEEDS, WANTS, ATTITUDES, FEELINGS, BEHAVIORS. Focus group interviews provide researchers with excellent opportunities to gain preliminary insights into what consumers really think or feel about a wide array of products and services. For example, a manufacturer like Procter & Gamble uses focus groups to obtain data that reveal consumers' attitudes for and against using Crest toothpaste. These data help the company understand how consumer brand loyalty is developed and what marketing factors are necessary to reinforce it.

TO GENERATE NEW IDEAS ABOUT PRODUCTS, SERVICES, OR DELIVERY METHODS. This particular objective of focus group interviews has long been a mainstay among decision makers and researchers. Here, focus groups generate interactive discussions about new or existing products and services. Data collected through these moderated discussions can provide valuable preliminary insights into new-product development, new usages of existing products and services, possible changes for improving products or services, or identifying better delivery systems. A classic example is how Arm & Hammer, a division of Church and Dwight Company, Inc., has discovered new in-home uses for baking soda. Periodically, the company conducts focus group interviews among known users of Arm & Hammer baking soda. Data generated from these discussions have revealed that baking soda is used for such things as cleaning kitchens and bathrooms, cleaning around babies, deodorizing everything from carpets to cat litter boxes, freshening laundry, soothing and conditioning skin, and cleaning teeth. Today, Arm & Hammer baking soda is marketed as a natural product with "a houseful of uses."

TO DISCOVER NEW CONSTRUCTS AND MEASUREMENT METHODS. For academicians and practitioners alike, focus group interviews play a critical role in the process of developing new marketing constructs and creating reliable and valid construct measurement scales. In the exploratory stage of construct development, researchers might conduct sets of focus groups concerning a particular marketing idea to reveal additional insights to the underlying dimensions that may or may not make up the construct. These insights can help researchers develop scales that can be later tested and refined through larger survey research designs. Take the important construct of *service quality,* for example. Researchers have been trying to refine the measurement of this construct for the past 15 years. They continue to ask such questions as "What does service quality mean to consumers, practitioners, and academicians?," "What is the underlying dimensionality of the construct—is it unidimensional or multidimensional?," and "What is the most appropriate way of measuring service quality?" Read the In the Field box to see how these questions have been investigated.

TO HELP EXPLAIN CHANGING CONSUMER PREFERENCES. This objective refers to the use of focus group interviews to collect data that can be useful in understanding how customers describe their experiences with different products and services. This type of qualitative data can be valuable in improving marketing communication as well as in creating more effective marketing segmentation strategies. For example, a manufacturer of a brand-name line of lawn care products may be interested in such questions as "What do consumers like about lawn care and gardening?," "What words or terms do they use in describing lawn care/gardening products and their use?," "Why do they do their own lawn work?," and "How do they take care of their lawns and gardens?"

Conducting Focus Group Interviews

While there is no one particular approach acceptable to all researchers, focus group interviews can be viewed as a process divided into three logical phases: planning the study, conducting the focus group discussions, and analyzing and reporting the results (see Exhibit 8.6).

A CLOSER LOOK AT RESEARCH   **In the Field**

Recently, several researchers at the University of South Florida undertook an exploratory research endeavor in an effort to bring clarity to the dimensionality controversy that continues to plague the "service quality" construct. Using available secondary information from earlier research on service quality reported in the literature, several focus group interviews were conducted among known patrons of retail commercial banking services. A trained professional moderator led the participants through unstructured and spontaneous discussions using a predetermined series of topical questions relating to the generic aspects of service quality. The qualitative data resulting from the discussions revealed seven possible sets of interpersonal behavior activities that consumers relied on when assessing the existence of service quality. These activities were subjectively described as service provider's communication/listening capabilities; diagnostic competence—understanding customers' needs/wants; empathy with customers' needs/wants; tactful responsiveness to customers' questions; reliability/credibility of the service provider; technical knowledge; and interpersonal social skills. In addition, the data supplied the researchers with preliminary insights into specific behavioral interchanges between service providers and customers. In turn, the interchanges were useful in building a 75-item inventory of interpersonal behavior activities and were used in a quantitative survey designed to test which behavioral interchanges were associated with these behaviors.

Source: David J. Ortinau and Ronald P. Brensinger, "An Empirical Investigation of Perceived Quality's Intangible Dimensionality through Direct Cognitive Structural (DCS) Analysis," in *Marketing: Perspectives for the 1990s*, ed. Robert L. King (Richmond, VA: Southern Marketing Association, 1993), pp. 214–19.

EXHIBIT 8.6   **The Three-Phase Process for Developing a Focus Group Interview**

Phase 1: Planning the Focus Group Study

This is the most critical phase. Researchers must have an understanding of the purpose of the study, a precise definition of the problem, and specific data requirements.

Key decisions focus on who the appropriate participants would be; how to select and recruit respondents; what size the focus group should be; and where to have the sessions.

Phase 2: Conducting the Focus Group Discussions

One of the key players in this phase is the focus group moderator. To ensure a successful interactive session, the moderator's role and pertinent characteristics must be clearly understood by everyone involved.

A necessary activity in this phase is the development of a moderator's guide that outlines the topics, questions, and subquestions that will be used in the session. The actual focus group session should be structured with beginning, main, and closing sections.

Phase 3: Analyzing and Reporting the Results

After the actual session is completed and if the sponsoring client's representatives are present, the researcher should conduct a debriefing analysis with all the key players involved to compare notes.

The researcher should conduct a content analysis on the raw data obtained from the participants during the interviewing session and write a formal report that communicates the findings. Key to the researcher here is to remember who will be the reading audience, the purpose of the report, and the nature of reporting the results as well as an appropriate report style format.

Phase 1: Planning the Focus Group Study

As with most other types of marketing research, the planning phase is most critical for successful focus group interviews. In this phase, researchers and decision makers must have a clear understanding of the purpose of the study, a precise definition of the problem, and specific data requirements. There must be agreement to such questions as the following: "Why should such a study be conducted?" "What kinds of information will be produced?" "What types of information are of particular importance?" "How will the information be used?" and "Who wants the information?" Answers to these types of questions can help eliminate the obstacles (organizational politics, incomplete disclosure, and hidden personal agendas) that can delay agreement and create problems between decision makers and researchers. Other important factors in the planning phase relate to decisions about who the participants should be, how to select and recruit respondents, what size the focus group should be, and where to have the focus group sessions.

Focus Group Participants

In deciding who should be included as participants in a focus group, researchers must give strong consideration to the purpose of the study and think about who can best provide the requisite information. While there is no one set of human characteristics that can guarantee the right group dynamics, the focus group must be as homogeneous as possible but with enough variation to allow for contrasting opinions. Central factors in the selection process are the potential group dynamics and the willingness of members to engage in dialogue. Desirable commonalities among participants may include occupation; past use of a product, service, or program; educational level; age; gender; or family structure. The underlying concern is the degree to which these factors influence members' willingness to share ideas within group discussions. Having a homogeneous focus group in which participants recognize their common factors and feel comfortable with one another is likely to create a more natural and relaxed group environment than having a heterogeneous group. Furthermore, participants in homogeneous focus groups are less likely to be eager to present contrived or socially acceptable responses just to impress other group members or the moderator. Researchers need to remember that in most cases, focus group participants are neither friends nor even acquaintances but typically strangers. Many people can feel intimidated or hesitant to voice their opinions, feelings, or suggestions to strangers.

A factor that is often overlooked in the selection of focus group participants is that of individuals' existing knowledge level of the topic. Researchers must determine whether prospective participants have some prior knowledge about the topics to be discussed in the interview. Lack of knowledge on the part of participants severely limits the opportunities for creating spontaneous, interactive discussions that will provide detailed data about a specific topic. For example, bringing together a group of people who sell women shoes for a discussion about the operations of a nuclear power plant is likely to produce very few meaningful insights pertinent to that topic.

Selection and Recruitment of Participants

Selecting and recruiting appropriate participants are keys to the success of any focus group. We have already noted the necessity for homogeneous groups. Now it becomes critical to understand the general makeup of the target audience that needs to be represented by the focus group. Exhibit 8.7 lists some general rules for the selection process.

SELECTION OF PARTICIPANTS. To select participants for a focus group, the researcher must first develop a screening form that specifies the characteristics that respondents must have to qualify for group membership. Researchers must also choose a method for reach-

EXHIBIT 8.7	General Rules for the Selection of Focus Group Participants

General Rule Factors	Description of Rule Guidelines
Specify exact selection criteria	Interacting with the decision maker, the researcher needs to identify, as precisely as possible, all the desired characteristics of the group members.
Maintain control of the selection process	The researcher must maintain control of the selection process. A screening mechanism that contains the key demographic or socio-economic characteristics must be developed and used to ensure consistency in the selection process. In those situations where the researcher allows someone else to do the selection, precise instructions and training must be given to that individual.
Beware of potential selection biases	Selection bias tends to be overlooked by researchers and decision makers alike. Biases can develop in subtle ways and seriously erode the quality of the data collected. Beware of participants picked from memory, or because they expressed an interest or concerns about the topic, or because they are clones of the person doing the selection.
Incorporate randomization	Whenever possible, randomize the process. It will help ensure a non-biased cross-section of prospective participants. This will work only if the pool of respondents meets the established selection criteria.
Check respondents' knowledge and experience	For any given topic, prospective participants may differ in knowledge and experience. Lack of knowledge may directly affect respondents' abilities to engage in spontaneous topical discussions.
Keep in mind that no process is perfect	Researchers have to make the best choices they can with the knowledge they have at the time of selection. The process may overlook certain aspects of the problem and inadvertently neglect individuals with unique points of view.

Source: Adapted from suggestions offered in Krueger, *Focus Groups, A Practical Guide for Applied Research,* 2nd ed. (Thousand Oaks, CA: SAGE Publications, 1994), pp. 79–82; also see Joe L. Welch, "Research Marketing Problems and Opportunities with Focus Groups," *Industrial Marketing Management* 14 (1985), p. 248.

ing prospective participants. They can use existing lists of potential participants supplied by either the company sponsoring the research project, a specialty screening company that specializes in focus group interviewing, or a direct mail list company. Other methods are piggyback focus groups, on-location interviews, snowball sampling, random telephone screening, and placing ads in newspapers and on bulletin boards. Regardless of the method used to obtain the names of prospective participants, the key to qualifying a person is the screening form. A hypothetical telephone screening form is displayed in Exhibit 8.8; this form illustrates a sample format, key information questions, and screening instructions.

SAMPLING PROCEDURES FOR FOCUS GROUPS. The issue of sampling requires some special thought when planning focus group interviews. Traditionally, researchers try to randomize the process of identifying prospective subjects. While randomization is critical in quantitative surveys, it might not be necessary in qualitative studies. Focus groups tend to require a more flexible research design; while a degree of randomization is desirable, it is not the primary factor in selection. Participant credibility during the focus group discussions is one of the key factors that researchers want to achieve. Randomization can help reduce the selection bias inherent in some forms of personal recruitment, but there is never total assurance.

EXHIBIT 8.8   **Telephone Screening Questionnaire to Recruit Focus Group Participants: Performing Arts Programs among Adults in Vail, Colorado***

Respondent's Name: _____   Date: _____

Mailing Address: _____   Phone #: _____

_____   Fax #: _____
(City)   (State)   (Zip Code)

Hello, my name is _____, and I'm calling for the Marketing Resources Group in Tampa, Florida. We are conducting a short interesting survey in your area and would like to include your opinions. The Marketing Resources Group is conducting a study on performing arts programs offered in your metropolitan area and I would like to ask you a few questions. The questions will take less than two minutes. Let me begin by asking . . .

1. Do you or any member of your immediate household work for a research firm, advertising agency, or a firm that produces or markets performing arts programs or events?
   (____) Yes **[THANK THE PERSON AND TERMINATE AND TALLY]**
   (____) No **[CONTINUE]**

2. Have you attended a performing arts event in the past month?
   (____) Yes **[CONTINUE]**
   (____) No **[THANK THE PERSON AND TERMINATE AND TALLY]**

3. Are you a permanent resident of Summit County?
   (____) Yes **[CONTINUE]**
   (____) No **[THANK THE PERSON AND TERMINATE AND TALLY]**

4. Are you currently employed full-time or part-time outside the home?
   (____) Full-time **[CONTINUE]**
   (____) Part-time **[THANK THE PERSON AND TERMINATE AND TALLY]**
   (____) Not currently employed **[THANK THE PERSON AND TERMINATE AND TALLY]**

5. Please stop me when I come to the age category to which you belong.
   (____) Under 20 **[THANK THE PERSON AND TERMINATE AND TALLY]**
   (____) 21 to 35 **[RECRUIT AT LEAST 12]**
   (____) 36 to 50 **[RECRUIT AT LEAST 12]**
   (____) 51 to 65 **[RECRUIT AT LEAST 12]**
   (____) Over 65 **[THANK THE PERSON AND TERMINATE AND TALLY]**

[PARTICIPANT RECRUITMENT PART—READ BY INTERVIEWER]

(Mr., Mrs., Ms.) **(Person's Last Name Here)**, the **Marketing Resources Group (MRG)** is sponsoring a meeting with people, like yourself, to discuss performing arts programs and events. We understand that **many people are busy yet enjoy attending performing arts events and have opinions about different topics concerning the arts.** We would like you to join a group of people, like yourself, to **discuss** and **get your opinions** about some performing arts topics. This **is not** a sales meeting, **but strictly a research project.** The group will meet on **Wednesday evening, August 15th, at the Vail Chamber of Commerce Office,** in downtown Vail. We would like you to be our guest. The **session will start promptly at 7:00 P.M.,** there will be refreshments and the **session will be over by 9:30 P.M.** Those people **who participate will receive $100** as our token of appreciation for participating in this important discussion session. Will you be able to attend?

(____) Yes **[CONFIRM NAME, ADDRESS, PHONE, AND FAX NUMBERS]**
(____) No **[THANK THE PERSON AND TERMINATE AND TALLY]**

[If YES], I will be sending you a **letter and information packet in a few days confirming the meeting and your participation.**
If you have **any questions or need to cancel,** please telephone our office at **[GIVE OFFICE PHONE NUMBER].** On behalf of MRG, **thank you and have a pleasant (day or evening).**

Author's note: The items that absolutely must be included in a screening/recruitment form are in boldface type for identification purposes.

RECRUITMENT OF PARTICIPANTS. Once a prospective participant is identified, contacted, and qualified for group membership, the task becomes one of securing that person's willingness to actually join the group. Securing the respondent's willingness to participate is not an easy process. The researcher must invite the respondent to participate in the discussion of an interesting and important topic. There is no one best method of achieving this task, but there are some key factors that must be incorporated in the process. The researcher should use only professionally trained people as recruiters. They must have good interpersonal communication skills, as well as such characteristics as a positive, pleasant voice, a professional appearance, polite and friendly manners, and a "people-to-people" personality. The recruiter must establish a comfort zone with the respondent as quickly as possible.

To bring legitimacy to the research project, the recruiter must be able to clearly articulate the general interest and importance of the topic. It must be made clear to the respondent that because of the small group size, his or her opinions and feelings on the topic are very important to the success of the project. The recruiter must make it clear that the group meeting is not a sales meeting, but strictly a research project. Other information factors that must be included are the date, starting/ending times, location of the focus group, the incentives for participating, and a method of contacting the recruiter if the prospective participant has any questions or problems concerning the meeting. Exhibit 8.8 displays an example of the recruitment part of a screening form for a focus group session.

After the respondent commits to participating in the focus group, the researcher must send out a formal confirmation/invitation letter that includes all the critical information about the focus group meeting. The main purpose of this type of letter is to reinforce the person's commitment to participate in the focus group. Exhibit 8.9 displays a hypothetical confirmation letter. The last activity in the recruiting process is that of calling the respondent the day before (or the morning of) the actual focus group session to further reinforce his or her commitment to participate in the session.

Size of the Focus Group

Most experts agree that the optimal number of participants in any type of focus group interview is from 6 to 12 (or 6 to 10 if using professional experts). Any size smaller than six participants is not likely to generate the right type of group dynamics or energy necessary for a beneficial group session. Too few participants create a situation where one or two people can dominate the discussion regardless of the efforts of the moderator. Also there is the increased probability of the moderator having to become too active and talkative to keep the discussions flowing. In contrast, having too many participants can easily limit each person's opportunity to contribute insights and observations.

One of the reasons for the wide range of members (6 to 12) directly relates to the fact that it is difficult to predict just how many respondents will actually show up at the focus group session. It is not uncommon for 12 people to agree to participate but only 6 to show up. Some researchers may try to hedge on actual response rates by inviting more people than necessary, in hopes that only the right number will show up. In cases where too many respondents show up, the researcher is forced to decide whether or not to send some home. The greatest fear of a focus group researcher is that no one will show up for the session, despite promises to the contrary.

FOCUS GROUP INCENTIVES. While using screening forms, professionally trained recruiters, personalized invitations, and follow-up phone calls can help secure a person's willingness to participate, incentives are also needed because participation requires both time and effort. Participants usually must reserve time out of a busy schedule and are likely

**Sample of Confirmation/Invitation Letter
to Focus Group Members***

[USE OFFICIAL LETTERHEAD]

[Date]

[Name of the Participant]
[Mailing Address]
[City, State, Zip]

Dear **[First Name of Participant]:**

**Thank you for accepting our invitation to attend the discussion on Performing Arts
Programs and Events at the Vail Chamber of Commerce Office in Vail, Colorado, on
Wednesday evening, August 15.** The Chamber of Commerce Office is **located** at 1240 Windsor
Pine Drive in downtown Vail. For your convenience, **please find the enclosed map and specific
directions to the Commerce Office,** if needed. We would like **you to be at** the office **between
6:45 P.M. and 7:00 P.M.;** the discussion session **will begin at 7:00 P.M.** There will be
refreshments and the **session will end by 9:30 P.M.**

Since we are talking to a limited number of people, **the success and quality** of the discussion **will
be based on the cooperation and participation of the people who attend.** Your opinions and
feelings are **very important, and attendance** at the session will help **make the research project
a success.**

As mentioned during our earlier telephone conversation, the discussion will focus on several critical
issues and topics concerning Performing Arts Programs and Events, and **we would like to get
your opinions and feelings on these topics.** Your **candid thoughts on the topics** will be **very
important to the success of the study.** Remember, this session is **strictly a research project,**
and **no sales or solicitations** will be made. At the **conclusion** of the discussion session, we will be
giving you $100 to cover your expenses in attending. If necessary, child care will be provided.

If **by chance you find you are not able** to attend the session or **have any questions,** please call
us to let us know **as soon as possible** at our office. That **phone number is (813) 974-6236.**

**Again, on behalf of MRG I thank you for your willingness to participate in the study. I am
looking forward to meeting you on August 15 and sharing your important thoughts and
feelings on the performing arts topics and events.**

Sincerely,

**Thomas G. Smith
MRG Moderator**

Author's note: All parts that are in boldface type are information that must be included in the letter.

to incur expenses such as for child care, travel, and meals. Finally, participants will typically spend time (between 90 minutes and two hours) in the actual session. In some cases
the total time is three hours—two hours for the session and an additional hour for pre- and
postinterviewing activities.[2] Consequently, group members need to be compensated for
their "investments" associated with their willingness to participate.

The incentive should not be viewed as a reward, honorarium, or salary, but rather as a
stimulus to get prospective participants to attend the scheduled session on time. Focus
group incentives can help remind people that their commitment to participate is worth the

effort, keep the promised time slot from being preempted by other factors, and communicate to the participants that the discussion session is important. While different types of incentives have different effects on the participation ratio, money tends to be by far the best incentive choice. The advantages of using money as an incentive are that (1) it is immediately recognized and understood by the participants, (2) it is portable and fits into small spaces, (3) most people like to receive immediate cash, and (4) it has a proven track record of working. The dollar amount per participant will vary from project to project, with most ranging between $50 and $200.

NUMBER OF FOCUS GROUP SESSIONS. Depending on the complexity of the information problem and decisions concerning the structures of the pertinent target audiences, there are many situations that require conducting a series of focus group interviews or sessions. "Just how many sessions should be conducted?" is an elusive question. There is no set standard. About the best advice that can be offered is that there should be a minimum of two sessions but that sessions should continue until no more new ideas, thoughts, or feelings are offered by different groups of respondents.

Focus Group Locations

The last element in the planning phase is where to hold the focus group session. This component is important because of the length of the discussions. Since a focus group session can last between 90 minutes and two hours, it is necessary to ensure that the setting is comfortable, uncrowded, and conducive to spontaneous, unrestricted dialogue among all group members—such as a large room that allows for a roundtable format and is quiet enough so that at least audiotaping can take place with minimum disturbances. Depending on the researcher's budget constraints, focus groups can be held in such locations as the client's conference room, the moderator's home, a meeting room at a church or civic organization, a respondent's home, and an office or hotel meeting room, to name a few.

While all of the sites listed above are adequate, today the ideal location is a professional focus group facility. Such facilities offer a set of specially designed rooms for conducting focus group interviews. Normally, each room has a large table and comfortable chairs for up to 13 people (12 participants and a moderator), a relaxing atmosphere, built-in audio equipment, and usually a one-way mirror so that researchers or decision makers can view and hear the discussions without being seen. Also available is videotaping equipment used to capture the participants' nonverbal communication behaviors that transpire during the discussions. Using a professional focus group facility usually adds to the overall data collection costs. Depending on which services are used, extra costs can range between $800 and $2,000 per focus group session.[3]

Phase 2: Conducting the Focus Group Discussions

The success of the actual focus group session depends heavily on the moderator and his or her communication, interpersonal, probing, observation, and interpretive skills. The moderator must be able not only to ask the right questions but also to stimulate and control the direction of the participants' discussions over a variety of predetermined topics.

The Focus Group Moderator

Focus group moderator
A special person who is well trained in interpersonal communication skills and professional manners.

The **focus group moderator** is a special person who is well trained in interpersonal communication skills and professional manners. Moderators draw from the participants the best and most innovative ideas about the assigned topic or question. The moderator's objectives are to seek the best ideas from each group member and to stimulate spontaneous interactive and detailed discussions. The moderator is responsible for creating positive group dynamics and a comfort zone between himself or herself and each group member as well as among the members themselves. Although there is no one set of traits or characteristics that describe the type of person who would make the best focus group moderator, Exhibit 8.10 lists some of the agreed-on traits that researchers have used in selecting focus group moderators.

MODERATOR'S CHARACTERISTICS AND ROLE. Moderators must be comfortable and familiar with group dynamics and processes. The moderator must exercise mild, unobtrusive control over the participants and be able to guide them from one topic to the next while maintaining group enthusiasm and interest for the topic. Successful moderating requires knowing when to bring closure to one topic and move on to the next. The moderator should not only have a good understanding of the specified topics and questions but also demonstrate a curiosity toward each topic and each participant's response. This curiosity may result in follow-up probing questions that uncover ideas, avenues, or connections that shed new light on the topic. Another important trait is that of demonstrating respect and sensitivity for participants and their expressed opinions and feelings on the topic. Showing respect for the group members can directly affect the value and quality of the data collected.

The moderator must have enough background knowledge of the topic to place all comments in perspective and follow up on critical areas of concern.[4] Furthermore, the moderator must be able to communicate clearly and precisely both in writing and verbally. Moderating the session requires objectivity, self-discipline, concentration, and careful listening on the part of the moderator. She or he must guard against interjecting personal

---

EXHIBIT 8.10   **Important Traits of a Focus Group Moderator**

The following descriptions represent some of the important traits that a researcher must consider in the selection of an excellent moderator for the focus group session:

1. The person must be well trained in *interpersonal communications* and have excellent *listening, observation, and interpretive* skills.

2. The moderator must display *professional mannerisms* and *personality,* have a *good memory for names,* create positive *group dynamics* and a *comfort zone* for spontaneous and interactive dialogue.

3. The moderator must be *comfortable* and *familiar* with group dynamics and processes, and must be able to exercise mild, *unobtrusive control* over participants.

4. The moderator must have *good understanding* and *background knowledge* of the specified topics and questions and the *ability to guide* the participants from one topic to the next.

5. The person must be *well trained* in asking *follow-up probing questions,* and must demonstrate *respect* and *sensitivity* for the participants and their expressed opinions and feelings.

6. The moderator must be able to *communicate clearly* and *precisely* both in *writing and verbally,* and must be *objective, self-disciplined,* and *focused.*

7. The person should exhibit a *friendly, courteous, enthusiastic,* and *adaptive personality,* along with a *sense of humor.*

8. The person should be *experienced* in focus group research.

9. The moderator must have a *quick mind* capable of noting new ideas that come from the group.

10. The moderator must *know how and when to bring closure* to one topic and move the discussion to the next.

opinions about the topic or a participant's response and must instead focus on seeking out the perceptions of the group members. In addition, the moderator must be mentally prepared and completely familiar with the questioning route, yet flexible enough to allow follow-up probing questions.

Moderator's guide

A detailed outline of the topics, questions, and subquestions used by the moderator to lead the focus group session.

PREPARING A MODERATOR'S GUIDE. To ensure that the actual focus group session is productive, it is necessary to prepare a detailed moderator's guide. A **moderator's guide** represents a detailed outline of the topics, questions, and subquestions that will serve as the basis for generating the spontaneous interactive dialogue among the group participants. (The Small Business Implications box displays a moderator's guide that was incorporated in the Vail Performing Arts example, mentioned earlier.) Using a structured outline format, an order is established for asking a series of opening, introductory, transition, critical, and ending questions. *Opening questions* are asked at the beginning of the focus group and are designed to be answered rather quickly to identify characteristics that participants have in common. These questions are normally factual and are important in establishing the group's comfort zone and internal dynamics. *Introductory questions* are used to introduce the general topic of discussion as well as provide group members with the opportunity to reflect on past experiences and their connection with the overall topic. Normally, these questions are not critical to the final analysis but are important in creating spontaneous, interactive discussions. The main objective of *transition questions* is that of directing the conversation toward the main topics of interest. They help the group members envision the topic in a broader scope and let the participants know how others feel about the topic. In general, these questions serve as the logical link between introductory and critical questions. From a content perspective, *critical questions* drive the overall study. The moderator uses these questions to get to the heart of discussing the critical issues underlying the topics of interest. Finally, *ending questions* are asked to bring closure to the discussion. They allow the participants to reflect on previous comments and feelings, and encourage members to summarize any final thoughts.

The Actual Focus Group Session

BEGINNING THE SESSION. As the participants arrive for the session, they should be warmly greeted by the moderator and made to feel comfortable. If name cards have not been prepared in advance, participants should be instructed to write their first names, in large letters, on the cards. Before the participants sit down, there should be an opportunity (about 10 minutes) for sociable small talk, coupled with refreshments. The purpose of these presession activities is to create a friendly, warm, comfortable environment in which the participants feel at ease. During the socializing period, the moderator should use his or her observation skills to notice how well group members interact and converse with one another. If the moderator can identify dominant talkers and shy listeners, he or she can use this information to place members strategically around the table.

If consent forms are required, participants should sign them and give them to the moderator before the session begins. The moderator should briefly discuss the ground rules for the session: only one person should speak at a time, everyone should understand the purpose of the session and act accordingly, and so on. In some cases, a brief mention of the sponsoring client is in order (e.g., the sponsoring client looks forward to the group's discussion on the topic as a way to decide on a crucial matter). If the situation requires the use of a one-way mirror or audio/video equipment for taping purposes, the moderator must bring these facts to the attention of the participants and briefly explain their logical use in the session. After completing the ground rules, the moderator asks the first question using an opening question format. This question is designed to engage all participants in the discussion. Normally,

A CLOSER LOOK AT RESEARCH   Small Business Implications

Moderator's Guide for Vail Performing Arts Program Focus Group Interview Sessions

I. INTRODUCTION

a. Welcome the participants.

b. Briefly highlight the focus group format . . . get consent forms signed and turned in (if necessary).

c. Explain ground rules for session:

> No correct answers—only your opinions and feelings . . . you are speaking for other people like yourself . . . want to hear from everyone.
>
> Briefly explain the audiotaping of the session and why . . . so I don't have to take many notes. If necessary, mention the one-way mirror and that some of my associates are observing the session . . . because they are extremely interested in your opinions.
>
> Only one speaks at a time . . . please no side discussions . . . I do not want to miss anyone's comments.
>
> Do not worry if you do not know much about a particular topic we talk about . . . it is OK and important for me to know . . . if your views are different from someone else's that's all right . . . it is important for me to know that too . . . please do not be afraid of having different opinions, just express them . . . remember there is no one right answer.
>
> This is an informal discussion . . . a research project, not a sales meeting . . . I will not be contacting you later on to try to sell you anything . . . I want you to be comfortable and relax . . . just express your opinions and feelings.

d. Any questions? **[Answer all questions of participants.]** Let's begin.

II. WARMUP [Use opening question format.]

Tell us your name and one or two things about yourself. **[Ask this of each participant.]**

(Build group dynamics and comfort zone among group members.)

III. INTRODUCE FIRST TOPIC

[Use an introductory question format.]

"FROM YOUR VIEWPOINT, TO WHAT EXTENT DO YOU ENJOY ATTENDING PERFORMING ARTS PROGRAMS AND/OR ENTERTAINMENT EVENTS?"

Probe for:

a. *Types of programs and events* that have been attended in past and would attend in the future.

b. Types of programs and events *most preferred to see offered* in the Vail Valley area.

[Use transition question format to move to next topic.]

IV. SECOND MAJOR TOPIC

[Use a critical question format.]

Now I want you to think about how people make their decisions to attend performing arts events.

"WHAT PERFORMING ARTS/ENTERTAINMENT FEATURES DO PEOPLE DEEM IMPORTANT IN DECIDING TO ATTEND A PROGRAM OR EVENT?"

Probe for:

a. *Detail* and *clarification* of features.

b. Understanding of *importance of identified features*.

[Use transition question format to move to the next topic.]

V. SPECIFIC DESIGN FEATURES [Use a critical question format.]

Now think about the facilities used to present performing arts programs and events.

"WHAT FACTORS SHOULD BE INCLUDED IN FACILITY STRUCTURE DESIGN?"

Probe for:

a. Specific *design features* and *why*.

b. Thoughts and feelings about *indoor versus outdoor* event capabilities.

c. *Types of protection features* for outdoor events for the *audience*, the *performers*.

(continued)

(concluded)

[Use transition question format to move to closure of session.]

VI. CLOSE SESSION WITH SUGGESTIONS AND FINAL THOUGHTS
[Use ending question format.]
"TAKING INTO CONSIDERATION OUR DISCUSSIONS, WHAT SPECIFIC ACTIONS WOULD YOU SUGGEST OR RECOMMEND TO THE DESIGN TEAM TO HELP MAKE VAIL'S NEW PERFORMING ARTS FACILITY THE BEST POSSIBLE?"

Probe for clarity of *specific ideas* and *details as to why.*

Features: ___ structure designs
___ seating requirements
___ theater style vs. auditorium style
___ quality of sound system/acoustics
___ outdoor event protection features

"ANY LAST THOUGHTS, FEELINGS, OR COMMENTS?"
[Ask and probe for each participant.]

VII. END THE FOCUS SESSION
a. *Thank* the participants for their cooperation and input.
b. *Give* each participant his or her *gift of appreciation.*
c. Extend a warm wish to *drive home carefully.*

group members are asked to introduce themselves with a few short remarks. This approach breaks the ice, gets each participant to talk, and continues the process of building positive group dynamics and comfort zones.

MAIN SESSION. Using the moderator's guide, the first topic area is introduced to the participants. As the discussion unfolds, the moderator must be able to use probing techniques to gain as many details as possible. If there is a good rapport between group members and the moderator, it should not be completely necessary for the moderator to spend a lot of time merely asking selected questions and receiving answers. Because there are no hard-and-fast rules on how long the discussion should last on any one particular topic, the moderator must use his or her judgment in deciding when to bring closure to one topic and move on to the next. In general, the session should move toward the study's critical questions at a pace that ensures enough time for depth probing of as many details, ideas, thoughts, and feelings as possible.

CLOSING THE SESSION. After all of the prespecified topics have been covered to the moderator's satisfaction, the participants should be asked an ending question that encourages them to express final ideas, thoughts, or feelings. To enhance this closure process, the moderator should briefly summarize the group's main points and ask if these are accurate. During the summary activities, the moderator should observe the body language of the participants for signs of agreement, disagreement, hesitation, or confusion. For example, it would be appropriate for the moderator to present a final overview of the discussion and then ask the participants, "Have we missed anything?" or "Do you think we've missed anything in the discussion?" Responses to these types of closing questions may reveal some thoughts that were not anticipated. Upon final closure, the participants should be given a short debriefing of the session, thanked for participating, given the promised incentive gift or cash, and wished a safe journey home.

Phase 3: Analyzing and Reporting the Results

Analysis Techniques

DEBRIEFING ANALYSIS. If the researcher or the sponsoring client's representatives are present, they and the moderator should conduct a **debriefing analysis** and wrap-up activities immediately after the focus group members leave the session. These activities give the researcher, client, and moderator a chance to compare notes. The key players who have heard the discussion need to know how their impressions compare to those of the moderator. Insights and perceptions can be expressed concerning the major ideas, suggestions, thoughts, and feelings from the session.

> **Debriefing analysis** An interactive procedure in which the researcher and moderator discuss the subjects' responses to the topics that outlined the focus group session.

Ideas for improving the session can be uncovered and applied to further focus group sessions. For example, strong points can be identified and emphasized, and errors noted, while they are fresh in everyone's mind. Some researchers like to use debriefing analysis because it (1) provides an opportunity to include the opinions of marketing experts with those of the moderator; (2) allows the sponsoring client's representatives or researcher to learn, understand, and react to the moderator's top-of-mind perceptions and feelings about what was said in the group discussion; and (3) can offer opportunities for brainstorming new ideas and implications of the main points expressed in the discussion. In contrast, potential shortcomings of debriefing include (1) a clear possibility of creating interpretive bias; (2) faulty recall on the part of the moderator due to recency or limited memory capabilities; and (3) misconceptions due to lack of time for reflecting on what was actually said by the participants.[5]

> **Content analysis** The systematic procedure of taking individual responses and grouping them into larger theme categories or patterns.

CONTENT ANALYSIS. Content analysis is probably the most widely used formalized procedure by qualitative researchers in their efforts to create data structures from focus group discussions. This procedure requires the researcher to implement a systematic procedure of taking individual responses and categorizing them into larger theme categories or patterns.

Depending on how the group discussion was recorded and translated (e.g., transcript, audiotape, videotape, session notes), the researcher reviews the participants' raw comments and creates data structures according to common themes or patterns. This process requires the researcher to consider several analysis and interpretive factors (see Exhibit 8.11).

Reporting Focus Group Results

In situations where some type of final report is requested, the researcher must understand the audience, the purpose of the report, and the expected format. The researcher must have a strong understanding of the people who will be using the results—their preferences in receiving information and their demographic profile, including educational level, occupation, and age, to name only a few factors. Overall, the report should stress clarity and understanding and should support the findings. In many cases, the writing style can be informal and the vocabulary familiar. The researcher should use active rather than passive voice and incorporate quotations, illustrations, and examples where appropriate.

In writing the report, the researcher must be aware of its basic purpose. First, the report should communicate useful insights and information to the audience. It should be a clear and precise presentation tailored to the individual information needs of the specific users. It must offer a logical sequence of findings, insights, and recommendations. The researcher should also keep in mind that the report will serve as a historic record that may be subjected to examination at some point in the future.

Format of the Report

Traditionally, focus group reports have been presented in a narrative style that uses complete sentences supported by direct quotes from the group discussion. An alternative is to use an outline format supported with bulleted statements that use key words or phrases to highlight the critical points from the group discussion. Regardless of the style, the report

EXHIBIT 8.11	Important Analysis and Interpretive Factors When Analyzing Focus Group Data

Analysis/Interpretive Factors	Description and Comments
Consider the words	Thought must be given to both the words used by the participants and the meanings of those words. Because there will be a variety of words and phrases used by the group members, the researcher will have to determine the degree of similarity and classify them accordingly. It should be remembered that editing messy quotations is a difficult but necessary task.
Consider the context	The researcher will have to gain an understanding of the context in which participants expressed key words and phrases. The context includes the actual words as well as their tone and intensity (voice inflection). It must be remembered that nonverbal communication (body language) can also provide meaningful bits of data worth analyzing.
Consider the frequency of comments	In most situations, some of the topics presented in the session will be discussed by more participants (extensiveness) and some comments made more often (frequency) than others. The researcher should not assume that extensiveness and frequency of comments are directly related to their importance.
Consider the intensity of comments	Sometimes group members will talk about specific aspects of a topic with passion or deep feelings. While left undetected in transcripts alone, audio- or videotapes can uncover the intensity factor by changes in voice tone, talking speed, and emphasis placed on certain words or phrases.
Consider the specificity of responses	Those responses that are associated with some emotional firsthand experience probably are more intense than responses that are vague and impersonal. For example, "I feel that the new McDonald's McArch burger is a ripoff because I ate one and it tasted just terrible, especially at the price they are charging," should be given more weight than "The new McArch burger does not taste very good, considering what it costs."
Consider the big picture	Because data from focus groups come in many different forms (words, body language, intensity, etc.), the researcher needs to construct an aggregate theme or message of what is being portrayed. Painting a bigger picture of what group members are actually saying can provide preliminary insights into how consumers view the specified product, service, or program. Caution should be used when trying to quantify the data. Use of numbers can inappropriately convey the impression that the results can be projected to a target population, which is not within the capabilities of qualitative data.

Source: Adapted from Richard A. Krueger, *Focus Groups: A Practical Guide for Applied Research,* 2nd ed. (Thousand Oaks, CA: Sage Publications, 1994), pp. 149–51.

must be written in a clear, logical fashion and must look professional. Although there is no one best format, Exhibit 8.12 describes the essential components of a typical report.

Advantages of Focus Group Interviews

First, the spontaneous, unrestricted interaction among focus group members during the discussion can stimulate ideas, thoughts, and feelings that may not be raised in one-on-one interviews. Focus groups allow researchers to collect detailed data about the underlying reasons people act as they do in different market situations. Another advantage is that the energetic atmosphere of focus group discussions allows the client's representatives and researchers to observe firsthand (from behind a one-way mirror) some flesh-and-blood consumers respond

EXHIBIT 8.12	Components of a Written Focus Group Research Report

Components of the Report	Description and Comments
Cover page	The front cover should include the title, the names of people receiving or commissioning the report, the names of the researchers, and the date the report is submitted.
Executive summary	A brief, well-written executive summary should describe why the focus group session was conducted and list the major insights and recommendations. It should be limited to two pages and be able to stand alone.
Table of contents	This section provides the reader with information on how the report is organized and where various parts can be located. (It is optional for short reports.)
Statement of the problem, critical questions, and methods	This section describes the purpose of the study and includes a brief description of the focus interviews, the number of focus group sessions, the methods of selecting participants, and the number of people included in each session.
Results and findings	The results are most often organized by critical questions or overall ideas. The results can be presented in a number of ways using bulleted lists or narrative formats, listing raw data, summarizing the discussion, or using an interpretative approach.
Summary of themes	Statements in this section are not limited to specific questions but rather connect several questions into a larger picture.
Limitations and alternative explanations	This section can be placed within the results section, if it is brief. Limitations reflect those aspects of the study that reduce the application of the findings or affect different interpretations of the findings.
Recommendations	This optional section is not automatically included in all focus group reports. The recommendations suggest what might be done with the results.
Appendix	The appendix should include any additional materials that might be helpful to the reader. Most often a copy of the moderator's guide, screening form, or other relevant material would go into the appendix.

Source: Adapted from R. A. Krueger, *Focus Groups: A Practical Guide for Applied Research,* 2nd ed. (Thousand Oaks, CA: Sage Publications, 1994), pp. 165–66.

to information about products, services, or programs. Another advantage is the technique's unique ability to bring together groups of individuals, such as doctors, lawyers, and engineers, to name a few, who might not otherwise be willing to participate in a study.

Disadvantages of Focus Group Interviews

As with in-depth interviews, the data structures developed from focus group interviews tend to lack representativeness with regard to the target population and thus do not allow the researcher to generalize the results to larger market segments. Also, focus groups do not allow researchers to substantiate data reliability or to distinguish small differences. There is also the possibility of moderator interpretation bias, which can quickly reduce the credibility and trustworthiness of the data, data structures, and information being supplied to marketing decision makers.

As focus group methods become more popular among marketing researchers, it is useful to understand the differences in their application on a global basis. The Global Insights box describes focus group research practices in other countries.

GLOBAL INSIGHTS *UNDERSTANDING FOCUS GROUP RESEARCH ABROAD*

As more companies enter the global market, there is an increasing need for qualitative research information, both to help assess the demand for items and to identify the optimal way of marketing in foreign countries. Many U.S. companies are expanding their use of focus group research to their overseas markets. There are some major differences in doing focus groups outside the United States and Canada, according to Thomas L. Greenbaum, President of Groups Plus, Inc., in Wilton, Connecticut. One cannot simply take the same materials used to conduct focus groups in the United States and send them to a research organization in a foreign country and expect to get comparable, or even reliable, results. The following insights are offered within seven key components of focus group research:

1. **Time frame.** Whereas many companies are accustomed to developing a project on Monday and having it completed by the end of the following week, this is almost impossible to do in foreign countries. Lead times tend to be much longer, with the Far East being particularly troublesome. If it takes two weeks to set up groups in the United States, figure almost double that in most of Europe and even more than that in Asia.

2. **Structure.** Eight to 10 people in a group is a large number for most foreign groups, which often consist of 4 to 6 people, our minigroup. Further, the length of sessions outside the United States can be up to four hours. Be very specific when arranging for international focus groups. Most foreign research organizations seem to adapt well to our format if properly informed and supervised.

3. **Recruiting and rescreening.** In general, the United States is much more rigid in adhering to specifications both in recruiting and screening. These processes must be monitored very carefully.

4. **Approach.** Foreign moderators tend to be much less structured and authoritative, which can result in a great deal of downtime during the sessions. Also they tend to use fewer writing exercises and external stimuli such as concept boards and photos. This must be considered when planning foreign sessions.

5. **Project length.** Projects can take much longer to execute. In the United States, we are accustomed to doing two, sometimes three or four, groups a day, but in many overseas markets, one group is the limit because of the time they are scheduled, the length of the sessions, or demands of the moderators. Also, some moderators have a break in the middle of the group, which would be very unusual in U.S. sessions.

6. **Facilities.** The facility environment outside the United States and Canada is much like the setup here 20 years ago. For example, it is more common than not to watch a group in a residential setting on a television which is connected to the group room by cable. Many of the facilities with one-way mirror capabilities simply do not have the amenities we are accustomed to in the United States.

7. **Costs.** Finally, the cost of conducting focus group research varies considerably by region and country. It would not be unusual to pay almost twice as much per group for sessions conducted in Europe and almost three times as much for many areas in Asia.

In light of these differences, it is important that companies take action to ensure that they get the results needed from foreign research. Greenbaum suggests having the international research managed by the same people who run the U.S. studies or use a U.S.-based foreign research company that can be a central point of contact and will handle the details abroad. So if you are going to conduct qualitative research outside the United States, spend the extra time and money, and do it right. It will be a small investment over the long term.

Source: Thomas L. Greenbaum, "Understanding Focus Group Research Aboard," *Marketing News* 30, no. 12 (June 3, 1996), pp. H16, H36.

A CLOSER LOOK AT RESEARCH   Using Technology

Advances in Technology Move Focus Groups into the 21st Century

Few would argue that the future of focus group interviewing will remain very bright. Recent technological advances in the telecommunication and computer industries offer new trends in conducting focus group interviews that will keep this particular qualitative data collection method popular into the 21st century. Rapid advancements in interactive marketing technologies (IMT) are opening new avenues for conducting telephone and video focus group interviews through such formats as teleconference networks, TeleSessions, and FocusVision Networks, which expand telephone capabilities into videoconferencing systems.[*] In addition, Market Opinion Research (MOR) offers its interactive group research system that allows customization of any business's needs, whether these involve testing new TV ads, testing product or advertising concepts, or observing consumers' reactions to words, phrases, or visuals.[†] In

the near future, these innovative technologies will play a more prominent role in how, what, when, and where qualitative data are collected and analyzed and information is disseminated to researchers and decision makers. These new approaches will make it easier to reach today's hard-to-reach subjects and shorten the time cycle in completing focus group research projects.[‡] In turn, costs of conducting focus group sessions will most certainly increase. The planning phase associated with focus groups will become more important as critical planning activities increase in complexity.

[*]"Feedback on the Phone," *Business Marketing*, March 1991, p. 46; also Michael Silverstein, "Two-Way Focus Groups Can Provide Startling Information," *Marketing News*, January 4, 1988, p. 31.

[†]Rebecca Piirto Heather, "Future Focus Groups," *American Demographics*, January 1, 1994, p. 6; also Tibbert Speer, "Nickelodeon Puts Kids Online," *American Demographics*, January 1, 1994, p. 16.

[‡]Thomas L. Greenbaum, "Focus Group Spurt Predicted for the '90's," *Marketing News*, January 8, 1990, pp. 21–22; also Cyndee Miller, "Anybody Ever Hear of Global Focus Groups," *Marketing News*, May 27, 1991, p. 14.

Summary on Focus Groups

As advances in telecommunications and computers continue, focus group interviewing will take on new directions. The Using Technology box discusses these new directions. Furthermore, to investigate motivational research problems, there is a family of projective techniques that includes such qualitative methods as word association tests, sentence completion tests, picture tests, cartoon or balloon tests, and role-playing activities. Discussions of these qualitative research methods will be provided in Chapter 10.

SUMMARY OF LEARNING OBJECTIVES

Identify the fundamental differences between qualitative and quantitative research designs and explain their appropriateness in creating useful managerial information.

In business problem or opportunity situations where secondary information alone cannot answer management's questions, attention must turn to collecting primary data and transforming them into usable information. Researchers can choose between two types of data collection methods: qualitative or quantitative. There are many differences between these two approaches with respect to their research objectives and goals, type of research,

type of questions, time of execution, representativeness of (or generalizability to) large target populations, type of analysis, and researcher skill requirements.

Moreover, qualitative methods focus on generating exploratory, preliminary insights into decision problems and opportunities. Qualitative methods focus on collecting detailed amounts of data from relatively small samples by questioning or observing what people do and say. These methods require the use of researchers well trained in interpersonal communication, observation, and interpretation. The data are normally collected using open-ended or nonstructured questioning formats that allow for either depth probing of hidden attitudes, feelings, or behavior patterns or human/mechanical observation techniques for current behaviors or events. While the data can be collected in short periods of time, they are difficult to analyze and transform into generalized inferences about the larger defined target group.

In contrast, quantitative (or survey) research methods place heavy emphasis on using formalized, standard, structured questioning practices where the response options have been predetermined by the researcher. These questions tend to be administered to significantly large numbers of respondents. Quantitative methods are directly related to descriptive and conclusive (or causal) types of research projects where the objectives or goals are either to make more accurate predictions about relationships between market factors and behaviors or to verify (or validate) the existence of relationships. Quantitative researchers are well trained in construct development, scale measurements, questionnaire designs, sampling, and statistical data analyses.

Describe and explain two popular qualitative techniques used in gathering raw primary data.

While there are many qualitative methods available for collecting data, this chapter focuses on in-depth interviews and focus group interviews. An in-depth interview is a formalized process of asking a subject a set of semistructured, probing questions in a face-to-face setting. Focus group interviews involve bringing a small group of people together for an interactive and spontaneous discussion of one particular topic or concept. While the success of in-depth interviewing depends heavily on the interpersonal communication and probing skills of the interviewer, success in focus group interviewing relies more on the group dynamics of the members, the willingness of members to engage in an interactive dialogue, and the moderator's abilities to keep the discussion on track.

Both types of questioning approaches are guided by similar research objectives: (1) to provide data for defining and redefining marketing problem or opportunity situations; (2) to identify specific hidden information requirements; (3) to provide data for better understanding the results from other quantitative survey studies; (4) to reveal and understand consumers hidden needs, wants, attitudes, feelings, behaviors, perceptions, and motives regarding services, products, or practices; (5) to generate new ideas about products, services, or delivery methods; (6) to discover new constructs and measurement methods; and (7) to better understand changing consumer preferences.

Explain the basic pros and cons of using qualitative methods of developing data structures.

The general advantages of qualitative research methods include the economy and timeliness of data collection; richness of the data; accuracy of recording marketplace behaviors; and preliminary insights into building models and scale measurements. The potential disadvantages include the lack of generalizability of the data to larger target groups; inability of the data to distinguish small differences; lack of data reliability; and difficulty of finding well-trained investigators, interviewers, and observers.

Explain what focus groups are, the importance of a moderator, and how the resulting data are transformed into information.

A focus group is a small group of people (6 to 12) brought together for an interactive, spontaneous discussion. The three phases of a focus group study are planning the study, conducting the actual focus group discussions, and analyzing and reporting the results. In planning a focus group, critical decisions have to be made regarding who should participate, how to select and recruit the appropriate participants, what size the group should be, what incentives to offer to encourage and reinforce participants' willingness and commitment to participate, and where the group sessions should be held. Exhibit 8.10 lists important traits of the focus group moderator, and Exhibit 8.11 illustrates a moderator's guide. There are different analysis techniques appropriate for creating data structures and interpreting the results, and the results can be written up in a professional report format.

KEY TERMS AND CONCEPTS

Content analysis 236

Debriefing analysis 236

Focus group moderator 231

Focus group research 222

In-depth interview 219

Interpersonal communication skills 221

Listening skills 221

Moderator's guide 233

Probing questions 219

Qualitative research 216

Quantitative research 216

REVIEW QUESTIONS

1. What are the major differences between quantitative and qualitative research methods? What skills must a researcher have to develop and implement each type of design?

2. Compare and contrast the unique characteristics, main research objectives, and advantages/disadvantages of the in-depth and focus group interviewing techniques.

3. Explain the pros and cons of using qualitative research methods as the means of developing raw data structures for each of the following situations:
   a. Adding carbonation to Gatorade and selling it as a true soft drink.
   b. Finding new consumption usages for Arm & Hammer baking soda.
   c. Inducing customers who have stopped shopping at Sears to return to Sears.
   d. Advising a travel agency that wants to enter the cruise ship vacation market.

4. What are the characteristics of a good focus group moderator? What is the purpose of a moderator's guide?

5. Why is it important to have 6 to 12 participants in a focus group? What difficulties might exist in meeting that objective?

6. Why are the screening activities so important in the selection of focus group participants? Develop a screening form that would allow you to select participants for a focus group on the benefits and costs of leasing new automobiles.

DISCUSSION QUESTIONS

1. What type of exploratory research design (observation, in-depth interview, focus group) would you suggest for each of the following situations and why?
   a. The research and development director at Calvin Klein suggests a new type of cologne for men that could be promoted by a sports celebrity like Michael Jordan.
   b. The director of on-campus housing at your university proposes some significant changes to the physical configuration of the current on-campus dorm rooms for freshmen and new transfer students.
   c. The vice president of marketing in charge of new-store locations for Home Depot must decide on the best location for a new store in your hometown.
   d. The senior design engineer for the Ford Motor Company wishes to identify meaningful design changes to be integrated on the 2000 Ford Taurus.
   e. The general manager at Clyde's Restaurant in Washington, D.C., wishes to offer customers two "new and exciting" dinner items that would be a blend of spicy herbs, chicken, and lemon.
   f. A retail supermarket manager would like to know the popularity of a new brand of cereal produced by General Mills.

2. Develop a moderator's guide that could be used in a focus group interview to investigate the following question: Why do 30 percent of Time Warner cable subscribers disconnect their cable services after the initial three-month special package offer?

3. Thinking about how most participants are recruited for focus groups, identify and discuss three ethical issues that the researcher and decision maker must consider when using a focus group research design to collect primary data and information.

Planning the Focus Group Interviews

In designing the necessary focus group sessions, the researcher's focus was on defining, selecting, and recruiting prospective participants for the six sessions. BBPC's records showed that there were approximately 26,000 current senior bank customers living within BBPC's service market area. Records also indicated that about 4,000 senior customers had closed their accounts with BBPC within the past 12 months. A random probability sampling procedure was used to select the needed 20 current senior customers along with 40 alternates and 40 ex-customers with 100 alternates. A multiphase process was used to contact and recruit the focus group participants. Selected prospective participants were first contacted and screened for eligibility by telephone using the "screening" instrument displayed in Exhibit 1. Next, each selected individual who agreed to participate in the focus

---

EXHIBIT 1   **Telephone Screening Questionnaire Used to Recruit Focus Group Participants for Barnett Bank of Pasco County Study**

Respondent's Name: _____   Date: _____

Mailing Address: _____   Phone #: _____

_____   Fax #: _____
(City)   (State)   (Zip Code)

Hello, my name is _____, and I'm calling for the Marketing Resources Group in Tampa, Florida. We are conducting a short interesting survey in your area and would like to include your opinions. The Marketing Resources Group is conducting a study on retail banking practices in your metropolitan area and I would like to ask you a few questions. The questions will take less than two minutes. Let me begin by asking . . .

1. Do you or any member of your immediate household work for a retail bank, for a research firm, or for an advertising agency that produces or markets banking products or services?
   (____) Yes **[THANK THE PERSON AND TERMINATE AND TALLY.]**
   (____) No **[CONTINUE.]**

2. Do you conduct some of your banking transactions at a retail commercial bank?
   (____) Yes **[CONTINUE.]**
   (____) No **[THANK THE PERSON AND TERMINATE AND TALLY.]**

3. Please stop me when I come to the age category to which you belong.
   (____) Under 20 **[THANK THE PERSON AND TERMINATE AND TALLY.]**
   (____) 21 to 35 **[THANK THE PERSON AND TERMINATE AND TALLY.]**
   (____) 36 to 54 **[THANK THE PERSON AND TERMINATE AND TALLY.]**
   (____) 54 to 65 **[RECRUIT AT LEAST 40.]**
   (____) Over 65 **[RECRUIT AT LEAST 20.]**

[PARTICIPANT RECRUITMENT PART—READ BY INTERVIEWER]

(Mr., Mrs., Ms.) **(Person's Last Name Here),** the Marketing Resources Group (MRG) is sponsoring a meeting with people, like yourself, to discuss retail banking practices. We understand that many people are busy yet have opinions about different topics concerning retail banking practices. We would like you to join a group of people, like yourself, to discuss and get your opinions about some banking topics. This is not a sales meeting, but strictly a research project. The group will meet on Tuesday, June 16, at the Youth and Family Service Center, in New Port Richey. We would like you to be our guest. The session will start promptly at 5:00 P.M., there will be refreshments and the session will be over by 7:00 P.M. Those people who participate will receive $100 as our token of appreciation for participating in this important discussion session. Will you be able to attend?

   (____) Yes **[CONFIRM NAME, ADDRESS, PHONE, AND FAX NUMBERS.]**
   (____) No **[THANK THE PERSON AND TERMINATE AND TALLY.]**

[If YES], I will be sending you a letter and information packet in a few days confirming the meeting and your participation. If you have any questions or need to cancel, please telephone our office at **[GIVE OFFICE PHONE NUMBER].** On behalf of MRG, thank you and have a pleasant (day or evening).

EXHIBIT 2   **Thank You/Confirmation Letter**

June 8, 1998

Mr. Henry C. Aniello
2305 Windsor Oaks Avenue
New Port Richey, FL 34655

Dear Mr. Aniello:

Thank you for agreeing to participate in the retail banking focus group study being held on Tuesday, June 16, at 5:00 P.M. I look forward to meeting you and hearing your comments and suggestions about the retail banking industry.

This letter is to confirm the date, time, and location that the focus group will meet. There is a map enclosed for your convenience. I have arranged to have sandwiches and beverages provided for you. As discussed via telephone, I will be videotaping our session to assist me with the study.

Please bring the enclosed videotaping consent form to the focus group meeting on Tuesday.

There is no particular "dress code" for the meeting. I would suggest you wear something comfortable and casual. Please try to be at the meeting location (The Youth and Family Service Center) at about **4:45 P.M.** so that I can begin the focus group as close to 5:00 P.M. as possible.

DATE: TUESDAY, JUNE 16, 1998

TIME: 5:00 P.M. TO 7:00 P.M.

PLACE: THE YOUTH AND FAMILY SERVICE CENTER

Thank you in advance for your willingness and cooperation in participating in this focus group. The success of this stage of the research project depends heavily on the opinions of all the participants of the focus group.

If you have any questions, please call me at our MRG offices (813) 974-2313.

Sincerely,

Thomas G. Smith
MRG Moderator

EXHIBIT 3   **Videotaping Consent Form**

VIDEOTAPE CONSENT FORM

Retail Banking Study Focus Group 06/16/98

I have given my consent to Thomas G. Smith and Market Resources Group, Inc., to videotape my comments during the retail banking customer focus group to be held on Tuesday, June 16, 1998. I fully understand this tape will not be used for commercial purposes or monetary gains.

_____

(Participant's Signature and Date)

group study was mailed a thank-you/confirmation letter, displayed in Exhibit 2, that provided the specific date, time, location, and other information pertinent to his or her scheduled focus group session. Since the sessions were going to be videotaped, each participant was also mailed a consent form (Exhibit 3) to sign and bring to the session.

As prospective participants were being recruited, the researcher also developed the scripted moderator's guide that would be used to actually conduct the focus group sessions. As discussed in the chapter, the main function of a moderator's guide is to provide the framework and necessary guidance of *what* and *how* topics are to be covered in the session. The guide is really nothing more than a specific outline that helps ensure that the required informational topics are covered. Exhibit 4 displays the moderator's guide used in the BBPC study.

EXHIBIT 4	**Moderator's Guide Used in the BBPC Study**

I. INTRODUCTION AND WARMUP
   A. Welcome the participants! As a warmup, have each participant introduce and say one or two things about himself or herself; create the comfort zone.
   B. Explain the rules of the session.
   C. Ask if anyone has any questions; clearly address each question.

II. INTRODUCE FIRST TOPIC—GENERAL DISCUSSION ABOUT CHANGING TRENDS IN BANKING
   A. Consumers' viewpoints of changing trends

   "FROM YOUR VIEWPOINT, HOW HAS RETAIL BANKING CHANGED OVER THE PAST FIVE YEARS?"

   (Probe for clear, meaningful, and specific changes.)

   B. Banks' ability to handle or manage those changes

   "HOW (OR WHAT) HAVE RETAIL BANKS DONE TO MANAGE THOSE CHANGES, MAKING THEM UNDERSTANDABLE TO US CONSUMERS?"

   (Probe for detail and clarification; if necessary, use ATM technology example.)

   C. Today's retail banks' operating motives and/or missions

   (Set up following scenario: Some people believe that today's retail banks are "BIG BUSINESSES" like the General Motors Corp. with their primary goal being one of "making large profits at all cost," but other consumers view retail banks more like an extension of the government—federal, state, local— with the goal of "serving people at the lowest possible cost.")

   "WHAT ARE YOUR FEELINGS ABOUT RETAIL BANKS OPERATING SOLELY FOR THE PURPOSE OF MAKING A PROFIT? HOW MUCH IS TOO MUCH PROFIT?"

   (Where appropriate, probe for specifics.)

III. RETAIL BANK SELECTION CRITERIA
   A. Consumers' perceptions of **important** banking factors used to select a bank to do business with

   "IN DECIDING WHERE TO BANK, WHAT BANKING CHARACTERISTICS OR FACTORS DO PEOPLE USE IN THEIR SELECTION PROCESS?"

   (Use the factors below to help guide the discussion.)

   B. **"WHAT ARE SOME IMPORTANT AND NOT SO IMPORTANT BANKING FEATURES TO YOU?"**

   (Probe for features and reasons of importance.)

   Bank's Product and Service Offerings

__ Checking	__ Regular savings	__ CDs
__ Money markets	__ Credit lines	__ IRAs
__ Visa/MC cards	__ Installment loans	__ Trusts
__ Senior partner	__ Brokerage services	__ Safety deposit
__ Ease of statement	__ Accuracy of statements	__ Mortgages
__ Community support	__ Interest rates on deposits	__ On loans

   Bank's Facilities and Parking Availability

__ Inside the bank comfortability	__ Has 24-hour ATMs	__ Banking hours
__ Easy-to-get-to location	__ Clean facilities	__ Easy to reach by phone
__ Parking availability	__ Has many service outlets	__ Has online banking services
__ Lobby hours	(branches)	*(continued)*

EXHIBIT 4   *(concluded)*

Banking Methods
__ Inside the bank   __ 24-hour ATMs   __ Drive-up windows
__ Bank by phone   __ Bank by mail   __ Online banking

Bank's Personnel and Staff
__ Courteous/friendly people   __ Using your name
__ Availability to answer questions   __ Speed of handling transaction
__ Explains things clearly and correctly __ Ability to resolve problems
__ Responsive to customer's needs/wants   __ Knowledgeable staff personnel
__ Accuracy in completing transaction   __ Professional in appearance

IV. RETAIL BANK SERVICE QUALITY

A. Consumers' view of what retail bank service quality means

   "WHAT DOES RETAIL BANK SERVICE QUALITY MEAN?"

   (Probe for clarity and details.)

B. **"WHAT CAN (SHOULD) RETAIL BANKS DO TO ENSURE OR IMPROVE SERVICE QUALITY TO THEIR CUSTOMERS?"**

   (Probe for details and clarity.)

C. **"WHAT DO YOU FEEL RETAIL BANKS DO WRONG RESULTING IN A LOWER SERVICE QUALITY TO CUSTOMERS?"**

   (Probe for clarity and specifics.)

V. RETAIL BANK CUSTOMER SERVICE SATISFACTION

A. Consumers' view of what customer service satisfaction means

   "WHAT DOES BANK CUSTOMER SERVICE SATISFACTION MEAN?"

   (Probe for clarification of thoughts.)

B. **"WHAT DO YOU FEEL RETAIL BANKS CAN (OR SHOULD) DO TO ENSURE OR IMPROVE THEIR CUSTOMERS' SERVICE SATISFACTION?"**

   (Probe for specific ways and clarity.)

C. **"WHERE DO RETAIL BANKS GO WRONG IN THEIR EFFORT TO CREATE CUSTOMER SATISFACTION?"**

   (Probe for specifics and clarity.)

VI. CLOSING SESSION WITH SUGGESTIONS AND FINAL THOUGHTS

A. Overall, what specific action(s) would you suggest or recommend to improve customer service quality and satisfaction in today's retail banking industry?

   (Make sure every participant has an opportunity to answer.)

B. Introduce the fact that everyone is (or used to be) a customer of BBPC.

   If session is with current customers, ask:

   "WHAT COULD BARNETT BANK DO (IF ANYTHING) TO IMPROVE YOUR BANKING RELATIONSHIP WITH THEM?"

   If session is with ex-customers, ask:

   "PLEASE SUMMARIZE YOUR SPECIFIC REASON(S) FOR ENDING YOUR BANKING RELATIONSHIP WITH BBPC."

   (Probe for specific answers.)

   "WHAT COULD BARNETT BANK HAVE DONE (IF ANYTHING) TO HAVE KEPT YOU FROM ENDING YOUR RELATIONSHIP WITH THEM?"

   (Probe for specific ideas.)

C. End the focus group session.

   Debrief the participants.
   Thank them for their cooperation and input.
   Give each participant his or her gift of appreciation.
   Extend a warm wish to drive home carefully.

Conducting the Focus Group Discussions

Given the fact that senior consumers tend not to like to drive at night, the two focus group sessions that had participants age 65 or older were held from 5:00 to 7:00 P.M.; all the other sessions were scheduled for 6:30 to 8:30 P.M. The times were deemed appropriate in that the two sessions were conducted during June and July, when there was sufficient daylight to allow the participants to drive back home before dark. For each session, participants were contacted by telephone the night before their scheduled session to reconfirm their attendance and were asked to arrive about 15 minutes prior to the start of their session. This time was used to check in participants and allow some informal socializing to get to know the moderator and other participants. Another critical objective of this presession time frame was to give the participants, initially strangers, an opportunity to relax and become familiar with the setting.

Each two-hour focus session was segmented into three parts: beginning, main, and closing. The beginning part of the session included introductions and warmup activities. Here, participants were formally welcomed and thanked again for their willingness to participate; the moderator highlighted and explained the guidelines for the session and made every effort to quickly establish a comfort zone for the participants. In addition, it was important for the subjects to get comfortable about being videotaped and forget about the individual who was operating the camera. As part of this process, the moderator began the actual discussion by focusing on general changing trends in banking. For example, the first question placed out on the table for participants' discussion was, "From your viewpoint, how has retail banking changed over the past five years?" The main function of this first question was to relax the participants rather than to obtain their opinions about a critical item to bank management's problem situation. The topical questions presented to the participants took on a general-to-specific order.

The main section of the session focused on topics relevant to retail bank selection criteria, bank service quality, and bank customer service satisfaction (see Exhibit 4 for the actual questions used for each topic area). The moderator kept control over the flow, direction, and depth of the discussions. Using listening and interpersonal communication skills, the moderator would guide, if necessary, the discussions by asking probing questions. While presentation of the complete transcripts of the actual dialogues between the focus group participants is beyond the scope of this application, the following example illustrates the questioning procedure used by the moderator.

Focus Group 4 held Tuesday, June 16, 1998: Ex-customer group (subjects 65 and older):

Moderator: "To bring closure to our session today, I would like for you to discuss and respond to this question: 'What were some of the specific reasons for ending your banking relationship with Barnett Bank of Pasco County?'"

Sally P: "For me it was that I got tired of being treated like a 'stupid' person when asking the loan officer questions about my house mortgage. That loan officer made me feel like I was not important and wasting his time."

Henry A: "Yep, I had the same problem with several of the tellers when asking specific questions about my saving account balance."

Moderator: "Sally, what did that loan officer say or do to make you feel stupid and not very important?"

Sally P: "I remember two specific things; first, his facial expressions when I asked a question. And second, his phone rang three times and each time he would answer it and carry on a conversation with that person and just left me sitting there."

Moderator: "What kinds of facial expressions did that loan officer exhibit when you were asking your questions?"

Sally P: "He would wrinkle up his forehead and nose as though he was saying 'So what do you want me to do about that?' or that he could not understand what I was asking."

Moderator: "Henry was your experience with the tellers similar in nature?"

Henry A: "Yes and no! My problem was somewhat different. One time, the teller came across as though I was asking the wrong person my questions about my saving account, but could not direct me to the right individual. I guess it was similar in that the teller just had a bad attitude toward helping me. She made it appear that saving accounts were not her area of interest or responsibility."

Mary F: "I just got tired of all the errors on my monthly statements. With one error, the bank said I had $300 less in my checking account than what my records showed, it took the bank three months to correct their mistake and then they wanted to charge me a $21 service charge! That's when I decided to close out all my accounts with Barnett and go to Nationsbank."

Although analyzing and reporting the results of the focus group research is beyond the scope of this application, a couple of comments are worth mentioning. After completing the focus group interviews, the researcher would take the raw responses from the six separate sessions and perform a content analysis to identify the overall themes of what the subjects, collectively, were expressing. Working with BBPC's management team, the results could be presented a number of ways. One approach might be a comparison of identified themes between current and ex-customer groups or between BBPC's 55-to-64 and over-65 senior market segments.

MARKETING RESEARCH CASE EXERCISE

OREGON PUBLIC BROADCASTING

This Exercise Corresponds to the Video Oregon Public Broadcasting: Evaluations of Communications

This video presents a lively discussion on reasons and reactions to programming on Oregon Public Broadcasting. In the video, participants of a focus group interview discuss many of their attitudes, motivations, and behaviors regarding programming on public broadcasting networks. While watching this video, try to record some of the participants' responses. See if you can categorize their motivations for watching public broadcasting programming. After viewing the video, prepare a brief report on the focus group interview. Specifically analyze the responses of the participants and use your analysis to draw some conclusions as to the outcome of the focus group interview.

Using what you learned from reading this chapter and viewing the video, develop your own focus group interview on the topic of why students chose to attend the university in which they are enrolled. Questions may concern why they selected their particular university, degree program, or major area of study. Select five to seven of your fellow classmates to serve as focus group participants. Choose a moderator or take this role yourself. Analyze the discussion and prepare a brief summary of your findings.

Learning Objectives

After reading this chapter, you will be able to

1. Explain the advantages and disadvantages of using quantitative, descriptive survey research designs to collect primary raw data.

2. Discuss the many types of survey methods available to researchers. Identify and discuss the factors that drive the choice of survey methods.

3. Explain how the electronic revolution is affecting the administration of survey research designs.

4. Identify and describe the strengths and weaknesses of each type of survey method.

5. Identify and explain the types of errors that occur in survey research.

Descriptive Research Designs: Survey Methods and Errors

❝ The basic techniques of market research—interview, focus groups, surveys, observation—are used in all corners of the globe. ❞

MICHAEL R. CZINKOTA AND ILKKA A. RONKAINEN[1]

Realty One's Use of Survey Research to Redirect Its Marketing Strategies[2]

It has been called the $500 million difference. Realty One, a national chain of realtors based in Independence, Ohio, has launched a new marketing strategy designed to increase sales to $3 billion in the year 2000 from the current $2.5 billion. The sales figures represent the gross value of homes sold by Realty One in the Cleveland-Akron, Canton, Sandusky, and Ashtabula, Ohio, areas. The new strategy is an integrated, multimedia marketing program. The program is viewed as the key to Realty One's success in the years leading up to the new millennium. Realty One will not disclose the cost of the new marketing strategy, but the company has described it as a "multimillion-dollar" effort.

The new marketing strategy shifts the focus of Realty One's advertising. In the past, Realty One, like most real estate sales firms, relied heavily on daily newspapers. The new strategy uses a much broader approach to disseminate as much information to potential home buyers as possible, according to Joseph Aveni, Chairman and Chief Executive of Realty One. The old method of newspaper advertising made the firm's information seem stingy. Realty One intends to achieve market differentiation by becoming information-generous.

The new marketing strategy incorporates several methods of information dissemination. A biweekly publication called *Realty One Home Book* will be produced in three geographic editions. Each edition will feature about 4,000 pictures of homes. A second information-dissemination vehicle will be a weekly half-hour television show to be called *Fine Homes*. The show will be broadcast on a local station and will incorporate video walk-throughs of various houses. The homes featured will be in the $400,000-plus range in upscale East Cleveland suburbs as well as in lower price ranges in other areas. Realty One will also use the Internet through the National Association of Realtors'

Realtor Information Network. The final major change in advertising focus is an advanced, $250,000 telephone hot-line system developed by Realty One. Home buyers can receive information about particular homes through the automated telephone system. Realty One will not abandon the daily newspaper advertising by any means. However, the advertisements will change from merely listing homes to listing open houses and promoting other marketing elements.

Realty One's new marketing strategy is the result of extensive quantitative survey research in Cleveland's real estate market. Costing over $100,000, the research consisted of numerous one-on-one interviews, hundreds of telephone interviews, and other methods of communicating with customers. Anthony Ciepiel, Realty One's chief financial officer, summarized the research results by saying, "Research shows that by sharing information early on we will be the company they (home buyers) need to meet their needs." The company consciously borrowed research techniques from consumer-products firms such as Procter & Gamble and applied them to the home buying/selling process.

Some marketing experts outside of Realty One hold strong expectations of success for the new research-based marketing strategy. The integrated marketing approach is probably an attempt to control advertising costs, according to Robert Redmond, President of the Cleveland Area Board of Realtors. Susan Rotman, President of ad firm Winning Strategies, calls the new strategy "great marketing." Rotman notes that no realtors can afford to make their entire inventory of homes available in the *Cleveland Plain Dealer*, the major newspaper. Rotman said, "If it's successful, it's going to change things and will be followed by others."

Value of Descriptive Survey Research Designs

This chapter opener points to the fact that sometimes the decision problem situation facing management requires primary data that can only be gathered by questioning a large number of respondents who are representative of the defined target population. Survey research can play an important role in providing the necessary information for guiding a firm's development of new marketing strategies.

This chapter is the second of three chapters devoted to methods for collecting primary data. Whereas discussions in Chapter 8 were limited to qualitative methods used in exploratory research, this chapter will focus on survey designs used in descriptive research. Experimental research designs and observation practices will be treated fully in Chapter 10.

We begin this chapter with an overview of survey research methods and their main objectives. The next section examines the various types of survey methods in more detail. This is followed by a discussion of factors in survey method selection. The remainder of the chapter deals with types of errors common in survey research.

Overview of Survey Research Methods

Survey research methods
Research procedures for collecting large amounts of raw data using question-and-answer formats.

As noted in Chapter 8, marketing researchers can observe behaviors, survey respondents, or conduct experiments. **Survey research methods** tend to be the mainstay of marketing research in general and are normally associated with descriptive and causal research situations. One of the distinguishing factors of survey research methods is the dominant need to collect raw data from large groups of people (e.g., 200 or more people). This size factor necessitates the use of "bidirectional communication practices," which means that selected individuals are asked questions and their responses are recorded in a structured, precise manner. By far the majority of marketing or information research is conducted through one or more of the various survey methods. In most cases, the research problems or opportunities are very well defined and there is agreement on the precise data requirements.

Success in collecting raw data is more of a function of correctly designing and administering a survey instrument, such as a questionnaire, than of relying on the communication and interpretive skills of an interviewer or observer. The main goal of quantitative survey research methods is to provide specific facts and estimates—from a large, representative sample of respondents—that decision makers can use to (1) make accurate predictions about relationships between market factors and consumer behaviors; (2) understand the relationships and differences; and (3) verify and validate the existing relationships.

Survey research tends to focus on collecting "standardized" raw data that allow the researcher to create information for precisely answering the how, who, what, where, and when questions concerning market factors and conditions. Occasionally, survey research might be appropriately employed to address simple types of why questions. As discussed in earlier chapters, survey research designs have a number of advantages over other means of collecting raw data, as well as some disadvantages. These are listed in brief in Exhibit 9.1 and discussed more fully in the following sections.

Advantages of Survey Methods

One major advantage of surveys, briefly noted above, is their ability to accommodate large sample sizes at relatively low costs. Using a large sample increases the geographic flexibility of the research. When implemented correctly, the data structures created from survey methods can increase the researcher's ability to make generalized inferences about the defined target population as a whole. The raw data can be analyzed in many different ways according to the diversity of the variables. For example, the data can be analyzed according to gender, income, occupational classifications, or any other variable incorporated into the survey. The analysis can also be based on multiple variables. For example, an analysis of product purchasing behaviors among households headed by female single parents in the

EXHIBIT 9.1	Advantages and Disadvantages of Quantitative Survey Research Designs

Advantages of Survey Methods

Ability to accommodate large sample sizes; increases generalizability of results

Ability to distinguish small differences

Ease of administering and recording questions and answers

Capabilities of using advanced statistical analysis

Abilities of tapping into factors and relationships not directly measurable

Disadvantages of Survey Methods

Difficulty of developing accurate survey instruments (questionnaire designs)

Limits to the in-depth detail of data structures

Lack of control over timeliness, and potentially low response rates

Difficulties in determining whether respondents are responding truthfully

Misinterpretations of data results and inappropriate use of data analysis procedures

---

Northeast can be compared to purchasing behaviors among households headed by female single parents in the Southeast to reveal small differences in regional preferences that may not be apparent in more aggregated data analysis.

Another major advantage of surveys is their ease of administration. Most surveys are fairly easy to implement because there is no need for sophisticated devices to record actions and reactions, as with observations or experiments. Even personal interviews can be routinized. As an offshoot of the ease of implementation, surveys allow for the collection of standardized common data. All respondents give answers to the same questions and have the same set of responses available to them. This allows for direct comparisons between respondents.

Another factor in favor of surveys is that they collect quantitative data ripe for advanced statistical analysis. Patterns and trends within the data can be determined by using mathematical analysis to identify large and small differences within the data structures. As discussed in Chapter 8, qualitative data suffer from problems of subjectivity; interpretations may be speculative or anecdotal.

A final advantage of surveys is their ability to tap into factors or concepts that are not directly observable (e.g., attitudes, feelings, preferences, personality traits). Through both direct and indirect questioning techniques, people can be asked why they prefer, say, one package over another. Predetermined questions can concern what thought process a consumer used to select a particular brand or how many brands he or she considered. Observation, for example, would only show that a particular individual selected a particularly packaged brand. Most survey research methods allow the researcher to collect all types of data (see Chapter 12 for descriptions of four data categories) and all potential time frames (i.e., the past, the present, and the future).

Disadvantages of Survey Methods

While quantitative research holds distinct advantages over qualitative research, survey methods are not without problems. Implementation is fairly easy, but developing the appropriate survey method can be very difficult. To ensure precision, the researcher must contend with a variety of issues associated with construct development, scale measurements, and questionnaire designs. Inappropriate treatment of these issues will create inaccuracies in construct development and measurement, opening the floodgates to systematic errors. As the possibility of systematic error increases, so does the likelihood of collecting irrelevant or poor-quality data. The critical development, measurement, and design issues associated with surveys are discussed in detail in Chapters 12, 13, and 14.

A second potential disadvantage of survey designs relates to their limited use of probing questions. In general, survey designs limit the use of extensive probing by the interviewer and rarely use unstructured or open-ended questions. Consequently, the data might easily lack the detail or depth that the researcher desires for addressing the initial research problems. A third disadvantage of surveys is the lack of control researchers have over their timeliness. Depending on the administration techniques, surveys can take significantly longer to complete than other methods. In direct mail surveys, for example, the researcher must carefully develop a questionnaire packet, disseminate the packets, and wait for them to be returned via the postal service. The researcher can only estimate how long it will take the postal service to actually get the questionnaire packet to each selected respondent, how long the respondents will take to complete the survey, and how long it will take the postal service to return the packets. In reality, the researcher loses control of the process as soon as the questionnaire packets are given to the postal service. While the researcher might estimate that the process will take 14 days to complete, direct mail designs can take up to 45 days. Getting the surveys out and back within a reasonable amount of time remains a great challenge for researchers using direct mail surveys. Associated with the problem of response time is the problem of guaranteeing a high response rate (or return rate of completed surveys).

A fourth disadvantage of some survey designs is that it can be difficult to know whether the selected respondents are being truthful. This difficulty varies in degree, depending on the actual method employed by the researcher. For example, in those designs that incorporate a trained interviewer in a face-to-face communication process (e.g., personal in-home or mall-intercept interviews) this problem is minimal due to the fact that the interviewer can either observe facial movements and other body language of the respondent or use probing techniques for more clarity. In contrast, in self-administered surveys (e.g., direct mail or fully automatic computer-assisted surveys) truthfulness becomes a greater concern. Finally, although surveys are designed to collect quantitative raw data, the statistical techniques selected may introduce very subtle and insidious levels of subjectivity to the derivation or interpretation of data structures. Such subjectivity, or bias, may not be as apparent in survey research as it is in qualitative research. Critical issues associated with appropriate analysis of data are given detailed treatment in Chapters 16, 17, and 18.

Types of Survey Methods

There are probably as many ways of gathering primary raw data as there are types of communication and researchers. The continual advances in communication, telecommunication, and personal computer technologies, along with their creative uses by today's researchers, have created an almost limitless number of survey methods. Nevertheless, almost all survey methods can be classified as either *person-administered, self-administered,* or *telephone-administered.* More recently, emerging computer technologies have had a significant effect on what are known as *automatic* or *computer-assisted* survey techniques. It is expected that advances in telecommunication technologies will continue to affect survey research designs far into the future. Exhibit 9.2 lists and briefly describes a variety of survey methods available for collecting raw data; each of these is discussed in detail in the following sections.

EXHIBIT 9.2	Types of Survey Research Methods

Type of Survey Research	Description
Person-Administered	
In-home interview	An interview takes place in the respondent's home or, in special situations, within the respondent's work environment (in-office).
Executive interview	A business executive is interviewed in person.
Mall-intercept interview	Shopping patrons are stopped and asked for feedback during their visit to a shopping mall.
Purchase-intercept interview	The respondent is stopped and asked for feedback at the point of purchase.
Telephone-Administered	
Telephone interview	An interview takes place over the telephone. Interviews may be conducted from a central telephone location or the interviewer's home.
Computer-assisted telephone interview (CATI)	A computer is ued to conduct a telephone interview; respondents give answers by pushing buttons on their phone.
Self-Administered	
Mail panel survey	Surveys are mailed to a representative sample of individuals who have agreed in advance to participate.
Drop-off survey	Questionnaires are left with the respondent to be completed at a later time. The surveys may be picked up by the researcher or returned via mail.
Mail survey	Questionnaires are distributed to and returned from respondents via the postal service.
Computer-Assisted	
Fax survey	Surveys are distributed to and returned from respondents via fax machines.
E-mail survey	Surveys are distributed to and returned from respondents via electronic mail.
Internet survey	The Internet is used to ask questions and record responses from respondents.

Person-Administered Surveys

Person-administered surveys Data collection techniques that require the presence of a trained human interviewer who asks questions and records the subject's answers.

Person-administered survey methods are distinguished by the presence of a trained interviewer who asks questions and records the subject's answers. Depending on the defined information problem and data requirements, there are different types of person-administered methodologies that offer unique strengths and weaknesses to the researcher.

In-Home Interviews

In-home interview A structured question-and-answer exchange conducted in the respondent's home.

As the term implies, an **in-home interview** is a structured question-and-answer exchange conducted in the respondent's home. (Sometimes the interviewer/respondent exchange occurs in the respondent's work environment rather than in the home, in which case the term becomes *in-office interview*.) The trained interviewer communicates face-to-face with the respondent. This survey method offers several advantages. The interviewer can explain confusing or complex questions, use visual aids or other stimuli to elicit responses, and assess contextual conditions. This helps generate large amounts of feedback from the respondent. In addition, the respondent is in a comfortable, familiar environment where he or she feels safe and secure, thus increasing the likelihood of the respondent's willingness to respond to the survey's questions.

Frequently, in-home interviewing is accomplished through door-to-door canvassing of geographic sections. This canvassing process is associated with one of the disadvantages of in-home interviewing. Interviewers who are not under constant supervision may skip homes they find threatening or may simply fabricate interviews. To ensure the safety of the interviewer, researchers may have to provide training on how to avoid potentially threatening situations. In addition, in-home or in-office interviews are expensive and time-consuming.

Executive Interviews

Executive interview A personal exchange with a business executive conducted in his or her office.

An **executive interview** is a personal exchange with a business executive that frequently takes place in the executive's office. In general, executive interviews focus on collecting primary data concerning industrial product or service offerings because few executives are willing to share business hours for discussing their nonbusiness or personal consumer preferences.

Conducting executive interviews is very expensive, in terms of not only interviewer compensation but also travel expenses. In addition, securing an appointment with an executive can be a time-consuming process, and even then his or her agreement or commitment to be interviewed can be problematic. Finally, executive interviews require the use of well-trained and experienced interviewers because the topics may be highly technical.

Mall-Intercept Interviews

Mall-intercept interview A face-to-face personal interview that takes place in a shopping mall.

The expense of in-home and executive interviews has forced many researchers to conduct their surveys in central locations, frequently within regional shopping centers.[3] A **mall-intercept interview** is a face-to-face personal interview that takes place in a shopping mall. Mall shoppers are stopped and asked for feedback on one or more products or services. The survey may take place in a common area of the mall or in the researcher's on-site offices.

Mall-intercept interviews share the advantages of in-home and in-office interviews except for the familiarity of the environment for the respondent. However, the mall-intercept is less expensive and more convenient for the researcher. A researcher does not spend much time or effort in securing a person's willingness to participate in the interview because both are already at a common location. In addition, the researcher benefits from reduced screening costs and time because interviewers can easily identify potential members of the target population by using their observation skills on location.

The disadvantages of mall-intercept interviews are similar to those of in-home or in-office interviews in terms of time, but as respondents are easy to recruit and travel time is nil, the total time investment is lower. However, mall patrons may not be representative of the general population. In addition, individuals representative of the general population may shop at different stores or at different times during the day. Normally, mall-intercept interviews incorporate only nonprobability sampling plans to select the prospective respondents. (See Chapter 11 for descriptions of different types of sampling plans.) Such sampling techniques can have adverse effects on being able to generalize the data results. Marketing researchers using mall-intercept interviews need to be sensitive to these issues.

Purchase-Intercept Interviews

Purchase-intercept interview A face-to-face interview that takes place immediately after the purchase of a product or service.

As in a mall-intercept, in a **purchase-intercept interview,** potential respondents are stopped and asked for feedback while on a shopping trip. However, purchase-intercept is different in that the intercept takes place after the interviewer has observed a prespecified behavior, usually the selection or purchase of a particular product. An advantage of this type of interview is that the recency of the behavior aids the respondent's recall capabilities.

There are two major disadvantages to purchase-intercept interviews in addition to those of mall-intercepts. First, many stores are reluctant to allow their customers to be intercepted and their shopping interrupted in the store. Second, purchase-intercepts involve only those individuals who demonstrate some observable behavior. Thus, consumers who are only considering a purchase are excluded from this type of data collection technique.

Telephone-Administered Surveys

Telephone Interviews

Telephone interviews
Question-and-answer exchanges that are conducted via telephone technology.

Telephone interviews have become a major source of market information, supplanting many personal interviewing methods. Compared to face-to-face interviews, telephone interviews are cheaper, faster, and more suitable for gathering data from large numbers of respondents. On a basic level, telephone surveys are simply personal interviews conducted via telephone technology. Individuals working from their homes or from central locations use telephones as the medium for asking questions and recording responses. However, telephone surveys have several unique aspects that need to be addressed.

As mentioned above, telephone survey methods have a number of advantages over face-to-face survey methods. One advantage is that interviewers can be closely supervised if they work out of a central location. Supervisors can record calls and review them later, and they can listen in on calls. These management practices can spotlight training needs, uncover employee innovations, and identify employees in need of another job. Trained interviewers who work out of their own home can set hours that are convenient for them, within limits prescribed by the employer and the law.

Telephone interviews are less expensive than face-to-face interviews in a number of ways. They allow individual interviewers to do more surveys in a given time period, and they reduce travel time and time spent on searching for respondents. Although there is the added cost of the telephone call and related equipment, wide area telephone service (WATS) has made telephone calling a cost-efficient survey medium. Telephone interviews also increase the geographical flexibility of the overall survey design.

Another advantage of telephone surveys is that they allow interviewers to call back respondents who did not answer the telephone or respondents who found it inconvenient to grant interviews when first called. The callbacks are very cheap compared to personal survey costs. A third advantage is that respondents perceive telephone surveys to be more anonymous and may feel less threatened and therefore be more candid. (However, although one would expect that responses of a personal nature would be more candid, research on that topic is mixed.)[4] Anonymity also reduces the opportunity for interviewer bias. Finally, telephone survey designs may well be the best hope for conducting executive interviews. While executives may not grant time for a personal interview, they will frequently take time for a telephone call. The same is true for many busy, hard-to-reach people. Using the telephone at a time convenient to the respondent has garnered information from many individuals who would be almost impossible to personally interview.[5]

While some researchers believe the above advantages will help telephone survey designs become the dominant form of collecting primary data, the telephone method, like any other data survey method, has several drawbacks. One disadvantage is that pictures or other nonaudio stimuli cannot be presented over the telephone. A second disadvantage is that it is difficult for telephone respondents to perform complex tasks. For example, imagine the confusion in the mind of a respondent asked to remember seven brands of a product, each with multiple variations, throughout an entire interview. Third is that telephone surveys tend to be shorter than personal interviews because people hang up on long telephone calls. Telephone surveys are also generally limited, at least in practice, by national borders—seldom is the telephone used in international research. Probably the greatest dis-

ETHICS

Sugging Is a Federal Offense

Sugging is the term used for the illegal telemarketing practice of selling under the guise of research. Sugging has been described as the bane of teleresearch and especially the researcher. Researchers are frequently forced to deal with respondents who challenge them to prove the call is a legitimate research effort and not a disguised sales solicitation.

Consumer outrage at the practice of sugging prompted the U.S. Congress to pass the Telemarketing Sales Act (TSA) which went into effect, under Federal Trade Commission implementation rules, at the end of 1995. The final rules state:

The legislative history of the Telemarketing Act noted the problem of deceptive telemarketers contacting potential victims under the guise of conducting a poll, survey, or other such type of market research. To address these problems, the Commission believes that in any multiple purpose call where the seller or telemarketer plans, at least in some of the calls, to sell goods or services, the disclosures required by this Section of Rule should be made "promptly," in the first part of the call, before the non-sales portion of the call takes place.

The TSA follows the 1991 Telephone Consumer Protection Act (TCPA), which prescribed the hours of 8:00 A.M. to 9:00 P.M. local time as the only hours during which telephone solicitations can be made. Under the provisions of both the TCPA and the TSA, the teleresearch industry is clearly exempted. The new laws apply to telemarketers, those persons making calls to or receiving calls from a customer in connection with a sales transaction. A "telephone solicitation" is defined as "the initiation of a telephone call or message for the purpose of encouraging the purchase or rental of, or the investment in, property, goods, or services, which is transmitted to any person." Telemarketing and marketing research using the telephone are different.

The Direct Marketing Association, the National Association of Attorneys General, and the Council for Marketing and Opinion Research combined to support the outlawing of sugging. The intent of the law is to ensure that the recipient is informed about a call from someone he or she doesn't know. The call recipient can choose whether or not to participate in legitimate telephone survey research or make a purchase from a telemarketer.

Source: Diane K. Bowers, "Sugging Banned, At Last," *Marketing Research* 7, no. 4 (Fall 1995), p. 40.

advantage, though, lies in the the restrictions on the types of data that can be collected over the phone. Researchers find it quite difficult to collect detailed state-of-mind data (attitudes, beliefs, and feelings) from respondents over the phone when structured scale responses are of five or more points.[6] Researchers are not able to use multiple levels of agreement/disagreement, likes/dislikes, and so on. For example, it is all but impossible to accurately ask a brand-image question that would require the respondent to answer using a semantic differential scale (see Chapter 13).

Another disadvantage is the poor perception of teleresearch in some people's minds, due in part to the increased use of telemarketing practices and the misperception that teleresearch is the same as telemarketing.[7] The Ethics box describes the illegal and unethical act of "sugging," or *s*elling *u*nder the *g*uise of research, which no doubt contributes to this poor perception. The public has been vocal enough regarding sugging that it is against federal law. Even so, some people are annoyed by teleresearch because it interrupts their privacy, their dinner, or their relaxation time. The federal government has responded with legislation limiting the hours of teleresearch and telemarketing. Generally, the most productive hours from the researcher's standpoint are during the day, to reach homemakers. Evening hours during the week and midmorning to early evening on weekends are good times to reach people who normally work during the week.

A difficult but critical task in being able to conduct telephone interviewing is selecting the telephone number to be called. Using a telephone directory does not produce a complete random sample because many people choose to have unlisted numbers. In some cases, the client will supply the researcher with a customer list or another prescribed list, but most marketing research studies need a random sample. Three techniques—plus-one dialing, systematic random digit dialing, and random digit dialing—have been developed to overcome the telephone-number selection problem.

PLUS-ONE DIALING. In plus-one dialing, the researcher generates telephone numbers to be called by choosing numbers randomly from a telephone directory and adding 1. For example, suppose the telephone number 727-7119 is selected from the directory. Adding 1, we would dial 727-7120. This method is easy and allows for the possibility of unlisted telephone numbers to be included in the sample. But researchers should remember any telephone directory provides an initial weak sampling frame in most situations.

SYSTEMATIC RANDOM DIGIT DIALING. Systematic random digit dialing is a technique in which researchers randomly dial telephone numbers, but only numbers that meet specific criteria. For example, numbers that are not within a specified area code would be ignored. Assuming the researcher is interested in consumer responses, exchanges that are devoted to government or business organizations would also be ignored. In this method, the marketing researcher randomly selects a telephone number as a starting point and uses a constant, or "skip," pattern in the selection process. The starting point, or seed number, is based on the sample interval. Specifically, the skip interval is added to the seed based on the number of telephone numbers available divided by the number to be interviewed. For example, say that there are 10,000 telephone numbers in the 727 exchange. Assuming the researcher wants to interview 500 households within that exchange, the skip interval would be 10,000/500 = 20. The researcher would randomly choose a telephone number between 727-0000 and 727-0020, say 727-0009. Then, to generate additional numbers, the researcher would add the interval. Thus, the second number dialed in this example would be 727-0029, the third 727-0049, and so on.

The advantages of this method are that each number within an exchange has a known but not equal chance of being called. Thus, within an area, the selection of respondents is random. If the same number of calls are made in several exchanges, the sample will tend to share the attributes of the area and have the same geographic dispersion. Finally, the method is fairly simple to set up and administer.

RANDOM DIGIT DIALING. Random digit dialing, in its purest form, refers to a random selection of area code, exchange, and suffix numbers. The advantage is that all numbers have an equal chance of being called—the unlisted numbers are just as likely to be called as listed numbers. However, the random digit dialing is very costly because many numbers either are not in service or are in use by people or organizations not included in the scope of the researcher's survey design. These techniques are discussed in more depth later in Chapter 11.

Computer-Assisted Telephone Interviews (CATI)

The computer revolution has had a huge impact on telephone surveys. Until the mid-1970s, telephone and mall-intercept interviews were primarily paper-and-pencil processes.[8] However, the widespread use of microcomputers has enabled teleresearchers to alleviate most of the problems associated with manual systems of callbacks, complex quotas, skip logic, rotations, and randomization. Today, computer and telephone survey techniques run the gamut from simple computerized telephone-number selection systems to fully automated systems where the respondent listens to an electronic voice and responds by pushing keys on the Touch-Tone telephone keypad.

Computer-assisted telephone interview (CATI) A fully automated system in which the respondent listens to an electronic voice and responds by pushing keys on the Touch-Tone telephone keypad.

While many of the advantages of **computer-assisted telephone interviews (CATI)** are based on lower costs per call, there are other advantages as well. In sophisticated systems, it is possible to switch from one questionnaire to another during the interview. Switching allows for interviewing family members other than the head of household, for example. The advantage is that common information is shared between all the questionnaires, saving the need for multiple calls. Another advantage is ownership of the call. Sometimes people need to stop in the middle of an interview but are willing to finish at another time. Computer technology has the capability of routing inbound calls to a particular interviewer who "owns" the interview. Not only is there greater efficiency in terms of labor per call, but there can also be cost savings as well. A cost advantage, perhaps not so obvious, is the ability of computer systems to select the least expensive routing for a particular call.

A disadvantage of CATI is its high initial investment and operating costs. The investment in computers, especially for large and sophisticated systems, is still very high. Software to control the hardware, monitor calls, and record responses is also expensive and, especially if customized, very time-consuming to develop and debug. Another disadvantage is that, in addition to having traditional skills, interviewers must have various computer skills in order to effectively administer this type of survey. However, the advantages of CATI are so apparent that most significant teleresearch operations now incorporate it to some degree.

Self-Administered Surveys

Self-administered survey A data collection technique in which the respondent reads the survey questions and records his or her own answers without the presence of a trained interviewer.

The third generic type of interviewing exchange is the self-administered survey. A **self-administered survey** is a data collection technique in which the respondent reads the survey questions and records his or her own responses without the presence of a trained interviewer. The advantages are low cost per survey and less interviewer bias—but the latter comes at a price. There is no interviewer to probe for a deeper response. For example, on a self-administered survey a particular respondent can indicate that he or she did not purchase a certain product, but that respondent can also fail to answer "Why not?"

Although the emergence of telecommunications technology has allowed delivery systems for self-administered surveys to expand, the most common type of self-administered survey is still the direct mail survey. Below we will discuss three types of self-administered surveys: direct mail, mail panel, and drop-off.

Direct Mail Surveys

Direct mail survey A self-administered questionnaire that is delivered to selected respondents and returned to the researcher by mail.

In situations where the researcher decides that a **direct mail survey** is the prudent method, a questionnaire is developed and mailed to a list of people who return the completed surveys by mail. The researcher must be careful to select a list that accurately reflects the target population of interest. Sometimes obtaining the required mailing addresses is an easy task, but in other cases it might prove to be time-consuming and difficult. In addition, there are production considerations. For example, the envelope needs to be designed to pique the potential respondent's interest enough that the questionnaire is not simply thrown out. The questionnaire itself needs to be carefully designed to garner as much information as possible and still be short enough for people to complete in a reasonable length of time.

This type of survey has the advantage of being cheap to implement. There are no interviewer-related costs such as compensation, training, travel, or search costs. Plus, most of the production expenses are one-time costs which can be amortized over many surveys. The variable costs are primarily postage, printing, and the cost of the incentive. Another advantage is that direct mail surveys can reach even hard-to-interview people.

However, direct mail surveys have their drawbacks. One major drawback is that response rates tend to be much lower than with face-to-face or telephone interviews. The risk of nonresponse bias is very real with mail surveys—the researcher gives up control over who responds and who actually supplies the answers. The researcher is never exactly sure who filled out the questionnaire, leaving the question of whether someone else provided the answers instead of the intended person. For example, in sending a mail survey to Mr. Jones in Dallas, Texas, on Network Television Programming, the researcher cannot determine precisely whether Mr. Jones or some other member of his household answered the survey.

Another problem is that of misunderstood or skipped questions. Direct mail surveys make it difficult to handle problems of both vagueness and potential misinterpretation in question-and-answer setups. People who simply do not understand a question may record a response the researcher did not intend or expect. Or the respondent may skip one or more questions entirely. These are all problems associated with not having a trained interviewer available to assist the respondent. Finally, mail surveys are also slow; there can be a significant time lag between when the survey is mailed and when the survey is returned.

Mail Panel Surveys

Mail panel survey   A questinnaire sent to a group of individuals who have agreed in advance to participate.

To aviod some of the drawbacks of the direct mail survey technique discussed above, a researcher may choose a mail panel survey method. A **mail panel survey** is a questionnaire sent to a group of individuals who have agreed in advance to participate. The panel can be tested prior to the survey so that the researcher knows that the panel is representative; the prior agreement usually produces high response rates. In addition, the mail panel survey method allows for longitudinal research; that is, the same people can be tested multiple times over an extended period. This allows the researcher to observe changes in the panel members' responses over time.

The major drawback to mail panels is that the qualified members are very likely not to be representative of the target population at large. For example, individuals who agree to be on a panel may have a special interest in the topic or may simply have a lot of time available. At this time, it is unclear how much, if any, these aspects of mail panels bias the results of the research. Still, researchers should be cautious regarding the degree of generalizability of the resulting data. It is important to remember that the different survey methods are not necessarily mutually exclusive. It is quite common for several methods to be employed in the same project. For example, the researcher may contact potential in-home respondents via the mail to help improve the response rate or as a part of the screening process. Telephone calls may be used to inform people of impending mail surveys. Sending multiple copies of a mail survey to nonrespondents is frequently a useful way to increase response rates.

Drop-Off Surveys

Drop-off survey   A self-administered questionnaire that a representative of the researcher hand-delivers to selected respondents; the completed surveys are returned by mail or picked up by the representative.

One common combination technique is termed the **drop-off survey.** In this method, a representative of the researcher hand-delivers survey forms to respondents; the completed surveys are returned by mail or picked up by the representative. The advantages of drop-off surveys include the availability of a person who can answer general questions, screen potential respondents, and spur interest in completing the questionnaire. The disadvantage to drop-offs is that they are fairly expensive in comparison to direct mail surveys.

Computer-Assisted Surveys

As marketing research and data collection practices enter the 21st century, it is expected that many companies will simply continue to use current practices and methodologies. But there is little doubt that computers, telecommunications, and other technological advances will have a substantial impact on the future delivery systems used in collecting primary data. Numerous new high-tech, high-speed mechanisms are already available to researchers. Some research experts think that computers are just too good to pass up when collecting marketing research data.[9] Exhibit 9.3 summarizes eight new computer-assisted data collection techniques that can replace or augment manual methods.

Using the computer to collect data has many advantages. "Branching" can be incorporated so that respondents do not have to deal with questions that are clearly not applicable to them. Response time can be measured and recorded. Graphics can be incorporated into questions. Encoding errors and other errors associated with manual labor are reduced if not eliminated entirely. Finally, data collection may be much faster with electronic media.[10] The following discussions focus on three new types of survey designs—fax, e-mail, and Internet surveys—that researchers are increasingly using to collect data.

Fax Surveys

Fax survey A self-administered question-naire that is sent to the selected subject via fax.

A **fax survey** is essentially a mail survey sent by fax. The fax survey allows researchers to collect responses to visual cues, as in a mail survey, as well as semantic differential or constant sum scales (see Chapter 13), which are difficult to use in telephone interviews. The potential benefit of fax surveys is that the flexibility of mail can be combined, to an extent, with the speed of the telephone.[11]

EXHIBIT 9.3   **Computer Technology Integrates with Survey Data Collection Methods**

Computer-assisted personal interviewing	The interviewer reads respondents the questions from a computer screen and directly keys in the responses.
Computer-assisted self-interviewing	Respondents are directed to a computer where they read questions from the computer screen and directly enter their responses.
Fully automated self-interviewing	Respondents independently approach a central computer station or kiosk, read the questions, and respond, all without researcher intervention.
Computer-assisted telephone interviewing	The interviewer telephones respondents, reads questions from a computer screen, and directly enters the responses into the computer system.
Fully automated telephone interviewing	The computer calls respondents and asks questions. The respondents use the keypad of their Touch-Tone telephone to enter responses.
Computer disks by mail	Computer disks are mailed to respondents; the respondents complete the survey on their own computer and return the disk to the researcher via the mail.
Electronic-mail survey	The batch feature available on many e-mail systems is used to send a "mass mailing" to potential respondents. They complete the survey and return it via e-mail.
Computer-generated fax surveys	A computer is used to dial and send a survey to potential respondents via fax. The respondents return the survey via fax or mail.

Collecting a fax survey.

In comparison to mail surveys, the fax technology delivery system allows for faster delivery and response speed and may even be less expensive. Administrative and clerical functions can also be reduced, because there is no need to fold surveys and stuff envelopes. Finally, a fax survey implies urgency and is not perceived as being junk mail by many recipients. Even in a normal mail survey, merely offering the option to respond by fax can increase the response rate.[12]

One disadvantage of fax surveys is that many consumers and small businesses have yet to incorporate fax technology into their communication practices and therefore would be out of reach. In addition, respondents may have to pay to fax back their responses, which could reduce the response rate. Sending a prepaid mailing label would increase response time, and offering a toll-free fax response line would increase the cost. In addition, fax surveys can be delayed or not delivered because of operator error, equipment malfunctions, or busy signals. These problems may be particularly acute in high-volume operations. The relative lack of privacy may cause response problems as well. Finally, fax surveys may lack the clarity of image of a printed mail survey, and a color scheme fax may be too expensive.

Nevertheless, fax surveys offer an attractive alternative to direct mail surveys under proper conditions. Fax surveys can provide relatively faster responses, higher response rates, and similar data quality. In addition, fax surveys can be cheaper due to low transmission and paper-handling costs. Still, the image-quality and limited-reach problems are not likely to be resolved in the foreseeable future.

E-mail Surveys

E-mail survey A self-administered data collection technique in which the survey is delivered to and returned from the respondent by e-mail.

E-mail surveys represent a technology that is still emerging. Proponents of e-mail predict a glowing future in which data can and will be collected at lightning speeds in large numbers at a very low cost. It may happen—the evolution of the information superhighway makes such thinking within the realm of possibilities. However, at this time, e-mail is not sufficiently diffused to be of much value to general marketing research. E-mail does, however, offer a fast and inexpensive way to accomplish international research if the target market has access to the Internet.

Virtual Reality in Marketing Research

Tom Allison, president of Allison Hollander in Atlanta, Georgia, thinks that a computer program can do a better job of tabulating what customers will actually do rather than what the customers think they will do. The problem, according to Allison, is that people communicate in words but do not think or feel in words. People think and feel in pictures. Computer technology has the added bonus of reducing interviewer and consumer bias as well.

To illustrate the problem of consumer bias as a result of thinking in pictures and communicating in words, Allison asks audiences to think of the following sentence: "You are standing by the water's edge." Then, he produces four images: an ocean scene, a lake scene, a river scene, and a stream. Each image elicits different feelings, according to Allison. In practice, this consumer bias is the reason that people react differently to a can of Coca-Cola than they do to an old-style bottle of Coca-Cola.

The prescription, according to Allision, is to take the consumer to the McDonald's restaurant instead of simply talking about a McDonald's. In this way, the researcher can get a truer picture of the consumer's reactions than time-lagged thoughts and feelings allow. The way to take the consumer to McDonald's is by computer simulation.

By using full-scale electronic simulations, the consumer can be exposed to menus, store shelves, coolers, and vending machines. The realism of the simulations allows for accurate communications with respondents and also for meaningful data collection. Allison suggests that the simulation should be engaging and short enough to hold the respondent's attention. Letting the respondent do, observe, and question elicits the entire selection process. And the computer can track and record the mental process step by step.

Allison says that consumer companies can use simulations in many different ways. For example, a consumer might be asked to build a stereo system, spending only a given amount of money. The researcher using the computer simulation could see what the respondent would buy. Another example could be a sunglasses boutique. The consumer could have his or her face scanned into a computer and then electronically "try on" sunglasses by clicking a mouse.

Other researchers think that virtual reality may offer an exciting way of testing. The consumer could "shop" the store, picking up items from shelves as they would in an ordinary store. The computer could track the respondent's actions and reactions. This virtual reality testing would allow companies to very accurately pretest pricing changes, packaging, promotions, shelf layout, new-product interest, and substitution behaviors.

Proponents of the computer simulation research say the tests are becoming faster and the cost is decreasing as technology advances. Other benefits include a realistic context for the respondent; a controlled, low-risk environment; and no need for back data or norms.

Source: Chad Rubel, "Researcher Praises On-Line Methodology," *Marketing News* 30, no. 12 (June 3, 1996), p. H18.

Internet Surveys

Internet survey A self-administered questionnaire that is placed on a World Wide Web site for prospective subjects to read and complete.

By using the World Wide Web, researchers can prepare an **Internet survey** with the speed and accuracy of electronics, the graphics of paper, and the help of an individual interviewer. The Using Technology box illustrates an example of using computer simulations as a creative method of integrating computer technology with survey research. However, the general populace's limited access to the World Wide Web puts Internet survey research at risk to nonresponse bias. In addition, response bias may be a problem because Internet surveys are available to everyone without being targeted to anyone. In the current state of the art, Internet surveys are passive—the respondent must seek out the Web site. Therefore, only those who have a prior interest are likely to even find the survey, let alone complete it. However, the potential for Internet survey research is such that this technology bears watching closely. Exhibit 9.4 summarizes the different benefits of using computer-assisted survey methods for collecting primary raw data in marketing research.

EXHIBIT 9.4   Computer-Assisted Data Collection Methods

Benefits	Personal Computer-Assisted Personal Interview	On-Site Computer-Assisted Self-Interview	On-Site Fully Automated Self-Interview	Telephone Computer-Assisted Telephone Interview	Telephone Fully Automated Telephone Interview	Mail Computer Disks by Mail	E-mail Electronic-Mail Survey	Fax Computer-Generated Fax Survey
No need for respondents to have computer-related skills	X			X	X			X
Allows respondents to choose own schedule for completing survey		X	X			X	X	X
Can incorporate complex branching questions into survey	X	X	X	X	X	X	X*	
Can incorporate respondent-generated words in questions	X	X	X	X	X	X	X*	
Can accurately measure response times to questions	X	X	X	X	X	X	X*	
Can display graphics and directly relate them to questions	X	X	X	X		X	X*	
Eliminates the need to encode data from paper survey forms	X	X	X	X	X	X	X	
Errors in data less likely compared to manual methods	X	X	X	X	X	X	X	
Speedier data collection and encoding compared to manual methods	X	X	X	X	X	X	X	X

*Assumes interactive e-mail population specification.

Source: Scott Dacko, "Data Collection Should Not Be Manual Labor," *Marketing News* 29, no. 18 (August 28, 1995), p. 31.

Factors for Selecting the Appropriate Survey Method

Researchers must consider several factors when choosing a survey method. As the preceding discussions may suggest, researchers are limited only by their own imagination. Yet merely selecting any method of communication that the researcher finds interesting or convenient may not produce usable, cost-efficient raw data or patterns. For example, in determining the appropriate communication method, the researcher must consider a number of important factors and characteristics, such as those listed in Exhibit 9.5. The

---

EXHIBIT 9.5   **Important Factors to Consider in Selecting a Survey Method**

Factors and Characteristics	Important Issues and Questions
Situational Characteristics	
Budget of available resources	What degree of appropriate resources can be committed to the project? What are the total dollars and man-hours available for committing to the research project's activities of gathering raw data, developing data structures, and creating/presenting information? What is the cost of collecting the required data?
Completion time frame	How much time is needed for completing the research project? How quickly do data-gathering, analysis, and information-generation activities have to be completed?
Quality requirement of the data	How accurate and representative is the derived information to the research problem? *Completeness:* How much information and what degree of detail are needed for the defined research problem? *Generalizability:* At what level of confidence does the researcher want to make inferences about the defined target population from the data results? *Precision:* What is the acceptable level of error that the data results may have in representing true population parameters?
Task Characteristics	
Difficulty of the task	How much effort is required by the respondent to answer the questions? How hard does the subject have to work to answer the questions? How much preparation is required to create a desired environment for the respondents?
Stimuli needed to elicit a response	How much physical stimulus does a respondent need? Do specific stimuli have to be used to elicit a response? How complex do the stimuli have to be?
Amount of information needed	How detailed do the respondent's answers have to be? Will probing activities be needed? How many questions should there be? How long should the respondent expect to take?
Research topic sensitivity	To what degree are the survey's questions socially, politically, and/or personally sensitive?
Respondent Characteristics	
Diversity	What commonalities exist among the prospective respondents? How many and which common characteristics have to exist?
Incidence rate	What percentage of the defined target population has the key characteristics to qualify for being included in the survey?
Degree of survey participation	Are the selected respondents able to completely interact in the question-and-answer process? What is the person's ability to participate? What is the person's degree of willingness to participate? What is the knowledge-level requirement for a person to participate in the survey process?

following sections describe these situational, task, and respondent characteristics in more detail.

Situational Characteristics

In an ideal situation, the researcher's sole focus would be on the collection of accurate and complete data. However, we live in an imperfect world and researchers must reckon with the competing and frequently contradictory objectives of budget, time, and data quality. In most survey research methods, the goal is to produce usable raw data and structures in as short a time as possible at the lowest cost. Finding the optimal balance between these three factors is frequently a ticklish task. It is easy to generate large amounts of data in a short time if quality is ignored, and excellent data quality can be achieved through expensive and time-consuming methods. In selecting the survey methodology, the researcher commonly considers all the situational characteristics in combination.

Budget of Available Resources

The budget factor refers to the amount of resources available to the researcher. While budgets are commonly thought of in terms of dollar spending, other resources such as man-hours can have similar constraining effects. All researchers face budget constraints. The resources available for a study can greatly affect choice of the method. For example, if only 500 man-hours are available in the research department, it would be impossible to conduct more than 1,000 personal interviews of 30 minutes each. The researcher might select a direct mail survey method because developing the survey form, mailing it, and collecting the responses would take much less time than personal interviews. In a similar manner, a $20,000 budget for a 1,000-person study limits the researcher to spending $20 per person. Given this constraint, the researcher might elect to use a telephone survey because the cost per response can be much lower than in a personal interview. It should be noted that the researcher is not required to spend all the budgeted money or personnel resources in conducting any type of quantitative survey, but most researchers will try to keep the research design and activities cost-effective if at all possible.

In truth, budget determinations are frequently much more arbitrary than researchers would prefer. However, it is rare that the budget is the sole determinant of the survey method. Much more commonly, the budget is considered along with the data quality and time factors.

Completion Time Frame

For marketing and management decisions to be effective, they must be made within a specified time period, called a time frame. The time frame commonly has a direct bearing on the data-gathering method. Long time frames allow the researcher the luxury of selecting the method that will produce the very best data. In many problem situations, however, the affordable time frame is much shorter than desired, forcing the researcher to choose a method that may not be the researcher's ideal one. Some primary data survey methods, such as direct mail or personal interview surveys, require relatively long time frames. Other methods, such as telephone surveys or mall-intercepts, can be done more quickly.

Quality Requirement of the Data

Data quality is a very complex issue that encompasses issues of scale measurement, questionnaire design, sample design, and data analysis. As such, data quality is far too complex to fully discuss in this short section, but a brief overview of three key issues will help explain the impact of data quality on the selection of survey methods. A more detailed treatment of data quality is provided in Chapters 12, 13, and 14.

The first key data quality issue is the completeness of the data. *Completeness* refers to the depth and breadth of the data. Having complete data allows the researcher to paint a total picture, fully describing the information from each respondent. Incomplete data will lack some amount of detail, resulting in a picture that is somewhat vague or unclear. Personal interviews can be very complete, while mail surveys may not be. In some cases, the depth of information needed to make an informed decision will dictate that an in-depth personal survey is the appropriate method. In other cases, a telephone interview that allows for short calls and brief response times may be the appropriate choice.

The second data quality issue is generalizability. As discussed in earlier chapters, *generalizability* refers to the data being an accurate portrait of the defined target population. Data that are generalizable reliably and accurately describe the population being studied. In contrast, data that are not generalizable cannot accurately reflect the total population. In this situation, the data can only lead to estimates about the total population and may truly reflect only the respondents who supplied it. For example, primary data from mail surveys are frequently thought of as being relatively less generalizable due to low response rates or small samples.

The third data quality issue is precision. Precision is related to, but still distinct from, completeness. *Precision* refers to the degree of exactness of the raw data in relation to some other possible response at the population level. For example, a car company may want to know what colors will be "hot" for their new models. Respondents may indicate their preference for a bright color for automobiles. The completeness issue refers to the respondents' preference for red, for example. Precision refers to the preference of red over blue by a two-to-one margin. If all we need to know is that bright colors are preferred, then fairly incomplete and imprecise data will suffice. If we need to know that red is preferred by a two-to-one margin, then both complete and precise data are needed. Mail surveys can frequently deliver precise results, but may not always produce the most generalizable results. Telephone surveys may be generalizable but may lack precision due to short questions and short interview times.

Task Characteristics

The characteristics of the task requirements placed on respondents will also influence the survey method used to collect raw data. The respondent's task characteristics can be categorized into four major areas: (1) the difficulty of the task; (2) the stimuli needed to elicit a response from the respondent; (3) the amount of information the respondent is asked to give; and (4) the sensitivity of the research topic.

Difficulty of the Task

Task difficulty How hard a survey respondent needs to work and how much preparation the researcher needs to do.

Task difficulty refers to how hard a survey respondent needs to work. Some marketing research questions involve very difficult tasks. For example, taste tests require respondents to sample foods prepared under very controlled conditions. In this example, the task difficulty is primarily in creating the exact same stimulus for each respondent. In other cases, the respondent may have to work very hard to answer the questions. Sometimes product or brand preference testing involves many similar products and therefore can be laborious for the respondents. Generally speaking, the more complex the survey environment, the greater the need for a trained individual to administer the interview or conduct the questioning process. Regardless of the difficulty of the survey task, the researcher should try to make it easy for the respondent to fully answer the questions.

Stimuli Needed to Elicit the Response

Frequently, researchers need to expose respondents to some type of stimulus in order to elicit a response. The stimuli may consist of products (as in taste tests), promotional visuals (as in advertising research), or some physical entity used to elicit the respondent's opinion. As a general rule, some sort of personal intervention is needed in situations where respondents have to touch, see, or taste something. It is very difficult for the researcher to maintain control over such situations without a trained human interviewer. In product concept research, for example, respondents frequently need to see and touch the product in order to form an opinion.

The actual form of the personal interview may vary. It is not always necessary to design a one-on-one interview. For example, people may come in groups to a central location for taste testing, or people in mall-intercepts can be shown videotapes to elicit their opinions on advertising.

Amount of Information Needed from the Respondent

Researchers are always looking for ways to get more data or responses from respondents. But respondents have limits in time, knowledge, and patience, among other things. Generally speaking, if a great amount of detailed information is required from respondents, the need for personal interaction with a trained interviewer increases. Conversely, if very simple information is needed in small amounts, very little interviewer interaction may be needed.

While some people tend to be resistant to long mail surveys, this might not cause a dramatic drop in response rates. Although some people will terminate long interviews at shopping malls, some may not even stand for short interviews. People hang up on long telephone calls, too. The survey researcher's task is to achieve the best match between the survey method and the amount of information needed. Consequently, a researcher has to assess the trade-off between getting more information and risking respondent fatigue.

Research Topic Sensitivity

Topic sensitivity The degree to which a survey question leads the respondent to give a socially acceptable response.

In some cases, the defined information problem might require researchers to ask some socially or personally sensitive questions. **Topic sensitivity** is the degree to which a specific survey question leads the respondent to give a socially acceptable response. In general, topic sensitivity relates to questions about income, but from time to time sensitive questions may be asked about racial issues, environmental issues, politics, religion, and personal hygiene. In these areas, and perhaps a few others, the researcher should be careful. When asked about a sensitive issue, some respondents will feel they should give a socially acceptable response even if they actually feel or behave otherwise. In addition, some respondents simply refuse to answer questions they consider to be too personal or sensitive; others may even terminate the interview. Normally, the less sensitive research topics are those that relate to brand preference, shopping behaviors, and satisfaction levels. Such questions are usually viewed by respondents as being nonintrusive or otherwise not problematic. Another sensitivity issue is competitor confidentiality—sometimes the sponsoring client of the survey just does not want written surveys to get into the wrong hands (i.e., a competitor's possession).

Respondent Characteristics

Since most marketing research projects target prespecified types of people, the third major factor in selecting the appropriate survey method is the respondents' characteristics. The extent to which members of the target group of respondents share common characteristics will have some influence on the survey method selected. The following discussions will center on three facets of respondent characteristics: diversity, incidence, and participation.

Diversity

Diversity The degree to which the respondents share characteristics.

Diversity of respondents refers to the degree to which respondents share characteristics. The more diverse the respondents, or the more heterogeneous, the fewer similarities they share. The less diverse the respondents, or the more homogeneous, the more similitarities. For example, if the defined target population is specified as people who own or have access to a fax machine, then diversity is low and a fax survey can be an effective and cost-efficient method. However, if the defined target population does not have convenient access to a fax machine (high diversity), the fax survey is very likely to fail in collecting the necessary primary raw data.

There are cases where the researcher may assume that a particular personal characteristic or behavior is shared by many people in the defined target population when in fact very few share that characteristic. For example, there are very significant differences in the rates of unlisted telephone numbers. In some areas (e.g., small rural towns in Illinois), the rate of unlisted numbers is very low, while in others (e.g., large cities like New York or Los Angeles), the rate is very high.[13] If researchers used telephone survey methods that merely selected prospective respondents from published numbers, there could be significant problems with the accuracy of the data results. People who do not have listed numbers may be different from people with listed telephone numbers in some meaningful way. In general, the more diverse the defined target population, the greater the need for trained interviewer intervention. For example, public opinion polls on welfare reform, government spending, and education are commonly conducted via telephone surveys because most people have opinions on these issues. Compare that to a situation in which Mazda Motor Corporation wants to ask Millenia automobile owners about their satisfaction with the service provided with that car; with this less diverse target population a mail survey would most likely be the method chosen.

Incidence Rate

Incidence rate The percentage of the general population that is the subject of the market research.

The term **incidence rate** refers to the percentage of the general population that is the subject of the market research. Sometimes the researcher is interested in a large portion of the general population. In those cases, the incidence rate is high. For example, the incidence rate of auto drivers is very high in the general population. In contrast, if the defined target group is small in relation to the total general population, then the incidence rate is low. The incidence rate of airplane pilots in the general population is much lower than that of car drivers. Normally, the incidence rate is expressed as a percentage. Thus, an incidence rate of 5 percent means that 5 out of 100 members of the general population have the qualifying characteristics sought in a given study.

Complicating the incidence factor is the persistent problem of contacting prospective respondents. For example, a researcher may have taken great care in generating a list of prospective respondents for a telephone survey, but may then discover that a significant number of them have either moved, changed their telephone number, or simply been disconnected (with no further information). In this case, the incidence rate will be lower than initially anticipated.

As you may imagine, the incidence rate can have an impact on the cost of conducting survey research. When the incidence rate is very low, the researcher will spend considerably more time and money in locating and gaining the cooperation of enough respondents. In low-incidence situations, personal interview surveys would be used very sparingly—it costs too much to find that rare individual who qualifies. In cases where the defined target group is geographically scattered, a direct mail survey may be the best choice. In other cases, telephone surveys can be very effective as a method of screening. Individuals who pass the telephone screen, for example, could receive a mail survey. In doing survey research, the goal for the researcher is to reduce the search time and cost of qualifying prospective respondents while increasing the amount of actual, usable raw data.

Degree of Survey Participation

Respondent participation breaks down into three basic forms: the respondent's ability to participate, the respondent's willingness to participate, and the respondent's knowledge level of the topic or object.

Ability to participate refers to the ability of both the interviewer and the respondent to get together in a question-and-answer interchange. The ability for a respondent to share his or her thoughts with the researcher or interviewer is an important method-selection consideration. It is very frustrating to the researcher to find a qualified respondent who is willing to respond but for some reason is unable to participate in the study. For example, personal interviews require uninterrupted time. Finding an hour to personally interview a busy executive can present real problems for both the researcher and the executive. Although they might like to participate in a mall-intercept survey, some shoppers may be in a hurry to pick up children from day care or school. An optometrist may have only five minutes until the next patient. The list of distractions is endless. A method such as a direct mail survey, in which the time needed to complete the questions does not need to be continuous, may be an attractive alternative in such cases.

As the above examples illustrate, the inability-to-participate problem is very common. To get around it, most telephone surveys, for example, allow for the respondent to be called back at a more convenient time. This illustrates the general rule that marketing researchers make every possible effort to respect the respondent's time constraints.

A second component of survey participation is the prospective respondent's **willingness to participate.** This is, simply, the respondent's inclination or disposition to share his or her thoughts. Some people will respond simply because they have some interest in the subject. Some people will not respond because they are either not interested, wish to preserve their privacy, or find the topic objectionable for some reason. In either case, a self-selection process is in effect. The type of survey selected to collect data does have an effect on the self-selection process. People find it much easier to ignore a mail survey or hang up on a telephone call than to refuse a person in a mall-intercept or personal in-home interview.

Knowledge level refers to the degree to which the selected respondents feel they have knowledge of or experience with the survey topic. The respondents' knowledge level will play a critical role in whether or not they engage in the question-and-answer process that underpins all survey methods. This knowledge-level component also has a direct impact on the quality of the data collected through survey research practices. For example, a large manufacturer of computer software wanted to identify the key factors that small wholesalers use to decide what electronic inventory tracking system (EITS) they would need for improving their just-in-time delivery services to retailers. The manufacturer decided to conduct a telephone survey among a selected group of 100 small wholesalers who do not currently use any type of EITS. In the process of trying to establish the initial interviewer/respondent encounter for administering the survey, the trained telephone interviewers were noticing about an 80 percent "not interested" response. In probing that response, they discovered that most of the respondents could not clearly identify with the information requests being made by the interviewers. These wholesalers felt they were not familiar enough with the details of EITS to be able to discuss the requested decision factors. As a general rule, the more detailed the information needed in survey research is, the higher the knowledge level of the prospective respondents must be. The degree to which prospective respondents have knowledge or experience with the topics being investigated will directly influence both their ability and willingness to participate in the survey.

Ability to participate The ability of both the interviewer and the respondent to get together in a question-and-answer interchange.

Willingness to participate The respondent's inclination or disposition to share his or her thoughts.

Knowledge level The degree to which the selected respondents feel they have knowledge of or experience with the survey's topics.

A CLOSER LOOK AT RESEARCH　　　Small Business Implications

Farmers Speak Their Mind

"Farmers as a group, when compared to the general population, show relatively high levels of cooperation in telephone surveys," says Tony Blum, vice president of Kansas City–based Market Directions, Inc. However, that high response rate may not last. In a recent study of Midwest farmers who had more than 250 acres and had participated in prior research studies, Blum found that farmers have a generally negative and skeptical attitude toward marketing research.

In the study, Blum found that 78 percent of farmers had some level of disagreement to the statement that marketing research serves a useful purpose, and that 44 percent thought answering public opinion polls was a waste of time. A whopping 92 percent said they do not entirely believe that surveys give people the opportunity to provide feedback to manufacturers.

Still, the response rate from farmers is quite high. In the study by Blum, 70 percent of those called participated in the study, which did not include an incentive. The response from farmers is approximately double the nonfarm response rate experienced by Market Directions. Incentives can help the response rate even for farmers. Cenex/Land O' Lakes Ag Services, of St. Paul, Minnesota, finds that farmers consider $5 to $10 for a 30-minute interview to be fair compensation. Growthmark, of Bloomington, Illinois, finds that for its usual four-page survey, $2 seems to work well. Blum says that the $5 incentive is the best amount to offer farmers. According to him, 86 percent of farmers participate in his studies with a $5 incentive. The response rate is virtually identical for a $2 and $10 incentive, at 80 percent and 81 percent respectively. No incentive reduces the response rate to 70 percent.

Maintaining the high response rate from farmers is important to agricultural researchers. Researchers suggest that changing farmers' attitudes regarding the value of marketing research over the long term is the key to maintaining high participation levels. The researchers think that sharing results with farmers, even in a summarized form, may help show the value of research. Companies are urged to follow up with farmers and tell them that the company is making changes based on what they learned in the research. The problem with providing research results to farmers, at least according to one marketing researcher, is that farmers want some meaty results. The research sponsor may not be willing to share the meat.

Source: Debby Hartke, "What Farmers Think of Market Research," *Agri Research* 34, no. 3 (March 1996), pp. 54–58.

Over the years, researchers have tried very hard to develop and implement various strategies to increase levels of participation from the pool of potential respondents. One frequently used strategy is that of offering some type of incentive. Incentives can include both monetary "gifts" such as a dollar bill and nonmonetary items such as a pen, a coupon to be redeemed for a food product, or entry into a drawing. For example, let's assume the researcher decides to collect raw data by executing a personal interview design. A strategy to increase the overall response rate might be to offer the respondents money, product samples, or T-shirts. Another strategy might be to personally deliver the questionnaire to potential respondents. In survey designs that involve group situations, researchers can use social influences to increase participation. It is important to note that incentive strategies should not be promoted as a "reward" for respondent participation. Rewards can serve as the wrong motivator for people deciding to participate in a survey. In general, the researcher tries to get as much participation as possible to avoid the problems associated with nonresponse bias. Read the Small Business Implications box for a specific case involving farmers' participation in surveys.

Overview of the Types of Errors in Survey Research Methods

Errors can quickly reduce the accuracy and quality of the raw data that the marketing researcher collects for resolving business problem situations. To make the best decision possible, business managers must be able to make some determination of the overall accuracy of the raw data and resulting information being provided by the researcher. In any research design, whether qualitative or quantitative, there are numerous opportunities for careless researchers to let in errors. This is particularly true with survey research designs. All potential survey research errors can be classified as either *random sampling errors* or *nonsampling errors*. Exhibit 9.6 outlines and describes the major errors in survey research methods. Researchers must be aware of these and must attempt to either eliminate or at least control them. As the exhibit shows, there are numerous types of systematic errors that can compromise the success of any survey method. Also, errors can occur in any phase of the information research process.

Random Sampling Error

Any survey research design that involves collecting raw data from a sample of the defined target population will have a certain amount of error associated with the sampled data results simply due to some form of natural random chance of occurrences or random fluctuations in the data estimates. In simple terms, random sample error is the statistically measured difference between the actual sampled results and the estimated true population results. Random sampling error is discussed in detail in Chapter 11 and in later chapters on data analysis.

Nonsampling Errors

In survey research, the counterpart to random sampling error is nonsampling error or systematic error. Nonsampling error simply represents all errors that can enter the survey research design that are not related to the sampling method or sample size. Most types of nonsampling errors can be traced back to four major source groups: respondent error, researcher's measurement/design error, faulty problem definition, and researcher's administration error.

Regardless of the survey research method used to collect raw data from respondents, there are several common characteristics among all nonsampling errors. First, they tend to create some form of "systematic variation" in the raw data that is not considered a natural occurrence or fluctuation on the part of the surveyed respondents. Systematic variations usually result from imperfections in the survey design or from mistakes in the execution of the research process. Second, nonsampling errors are controllable. They stem from some type of human mishap in either the designing or executing of a survey design. Consequently, the responsibility for reducing or eliminating nonsampling errors falls squarely on the shoulders of the researcher and requires that a set of controls (or rules) be imposed during the design and execution processes of any type of survey research project.[14] Third, unlike random sampling errors, which can be statistically measured, nonsampling errors cannot be directly measured by a statistical formula. Finally, nonsampling errors are interactive; one type of error can potentially induce other types of errors to enter the data collection process. When the researcher designs a poor survey instrument, for example, the errors (e.g., poor questions) can potentially cause respondent errors such as auspices errors, extremity errors, or social desirability errors. (These will be discussed in later chapters.) Overall, nonsampling errors can only lower the quality level of the data being collected and the information being provided to the decision maker.

| EXHIBIT 9.6 | Types of Errors in Survey Research Methods (Description and Sources of Bias) |

Respondent Error Sources

Nonresponse error: Occurs when a sufficient number of the initial prospective respondents are not included in the final sample of a study. Results in a portion of the population not being represented or being underrepresented when the response pool is systematically and significantly different from those respondents who did respond.

Main biases:

Refusal: when a prospective respondent is simply unwilling to participate in the question-and-answer exchange.

Not at home: when reasonable attempts to initially reach the prospective respondent fail to produce an interviewer/respondent encounter.

Wrong mailing address: when prospective respondent's address is outdated or no longer active.

Wrong telephone number: when the prospective respondent's telephone number either is no longer in service or is incorrect on the sample list.

Response error: Occurs when a significant number of respondents either unconsciously misrepresent or deliberately falsify their responses.

Main biases:

Hostility: responses that arise from feelings of anger or resentment engendered by the response task.

Social desirability: response based on what is perceived as being socially acceptable or respectable.

Prestige: response intended to enhance the image of the respondent in the eyes of others.

Auspices error: response dictated by the image or opinion of the sponsor, rather than the actual question.

Yea- and nay-saying: response influenced by the global tendency toward positive or negative answers.

Mental set error: cognitions or perceptions based on the influence of previous responses over later ones.

Extremity error: responses influenced by clarity of extreme scale points and ambiguity of midrange options.

Acquiescence error: response based on respondent's perception of what would be desirable to the sponsor.

Measurement and Design Error Sources

Construct development error: Occurs when the researcher does not accurately or completely identify the important subdimensions of the various topics or constructs being included in the survey research. The necessary data is misdefined, or mistakes are made of what the overall composite should be of the critical concepts and constructs being investigated.

Main biases:

Incomplete constructs: only partial data requirements are met; creates inappropriate guidelines for scale measurement and question-naire design activities.

Low reliability/validity: construct validity is not maintained, which increases the likelihood of collecting either irrelevant or low-quality data.

Scaling measurement error: Occurs when inaccuracies are designed into the various scale measures used to collect the primary raw data. Errors could come from inappropriate questions or setups, scale attributes, or actual scale points used to represent respondents' answers.

Main biases:

Lack of precision: decreases reliability of data quality.

Lack of discriminatory power: respondents encounter difficulties in accurate expression of sensitivity between possible answers; data cannot be used to detect small differences.

Ambiguity of questions or setups: misleads or confuses the respondent.

Inappropriate scale descriptors: wrong or incomplete data is collected; severely reduces the researcher's ability to create meaningful information.

(continued)

EXHIBIT 9.6   *(concluded)*

Survey instrument design error: Represents a "family" of design or format errors that produces a questionnaire that does not accurately collect the appropriate raw data. These nonsampling errors severely limit the generalizability, reliability, and validity features of the collected data.

Main biases:

Improper sequence of questions: taints the data and lowers data quality.

Lack of instructions: increases the likelihood of response bias and misinterpretation bias; decreases data quality.

Questionnaire length: could increase forms of nonresponse error; reduces the generalizability of the data and information.

Data analysis error: Represents a group of errors that relate to subjecting the raw data to inappropriate analysis procedures.

Main biases:

Inappropriate analysis: creates the wrong data structure results and can lead to misinterpretation errors.

Predictive bias: wrong statistical facts and estimates invalidate the researcher's ability to predict and test relationships between important factors.

Misinterpretation error: Inaccurate transformations of data structures and analysis results into usable bits of information for the decision maker.

Main biases:

Interpretive bias: when the wrong inference about the real world or defined target population is made by the researcher or decision maker due to some extraneous factor.

Selective perception: situations where the researcher or decision maker uses only a selected portion of the survey results to paint a partial picture of reality.

Administrative Error Sources

Data processing error: Occurs when researchers are not accurate or complete in transferring the raw data from respondents to computer data files.

Main biases:

Data coding errors: the incorrect assignment of computer codes to the raw responses from the respondents.

Data entry errors: the incorrect assignment of computer codes to their predesignated location on the computer data file.

Data editing errors: careless verifying procedures of raw data to computer data files.

Interviewer Error: Occurs when interviewers distort information, in a systematic way, from respondents during or after the interviewer/respondent encounter. Errors could come from misrecording, unconscious misrepresentation, or cheating.

Main biases:

Unconscious misrepresentation: occurs when the interviewer unconsciously induces a pattern of responses that is not indicative of the defined target population.

Recording errors: when interviewers inadvertently check or record the wrong response from a respondent.

Cheating: represents the deliberate falsification of respondents' answers.

Sample design error: Represents systematic inaccuracies created by using a faulty sampling design to identify and reach the selected "right" respondents who make up a representative cross-section of the defined target population. These nonsampling errors will severely limit the generalizability, reliability, and validity features of the collected data.

Main biases:

Population specification error: represents an incorrect definition of the true target population to the research question.

Sample selection error: occurs when an inappropriate sample is drawn from the target population because of incomplete or faulty sampling procedures or by not following the correct procedures.

Sampling frame error: occurs when a sample is drawn from an incomplete list of potential or prospective respondents.

SUMMARY OF LEARNING OBJECTIVES

Explain the advantages and disadvantages of using quantitative, descriptive survey research designs to collect primary raw data.

Some of the main advantages of using survey designs to collect primary raw data from respondents are ability to accommodate large sample sizes; generalizability of results; ability to distinguish small differences between diverse sampled groups; ease of administering and recording questions and answers; increased capabilities of using advanced statistical analysis; and abilities of tapping into latent factors and relationships. In contrast, the main disadvantages of survey research designs tend to focus on potential difficulties of developing accurate survey instruments; inaccuracies in construct and scale measurements of factors; and limits to the depth of the data structures. In addition, researchers can lack control over long time frames and potentially low response rates, among other problems.

Discuss the many types of survey methods available to researchers. Identify and discuss the factors that drive the choice of survey methods.

Survey methods are generally divided into three generic types. One is the *person-administered survey,* in which there is significant face-to-face interaction between the interviewer and the respondent. Second is the *telephone-administered survey.* In these surveys the telephone is used to conduct the question-and-answer exchanges. Computers are now used in many ways in telephone interviews, especially in management functions, data recording, and telephone-number selection. Third is the *self-administered survey.* In these surveys, there is little, if any, actual face-to-face contact between the researcher and prospective respondent. The respondent reads the questions and records his or her answers. Most of the emerging technology survey methods are self-administrated, although some, such as virtual reality, will require human intervention.

There are three major factors affecting the choice of survey method: *situational characteristics, task characteristics,* and *respondent characteristics.* With situational factors, consideration must be given to such elements as available resources, completion time frame, and data quality requirements. Also, the researcher must consider the overall task requirements and ask questions like, "How difficult are the tasks?," "What stimuli will be needed to evoke responses?," "How much informa-

tion is needed from the respondent?," and "To what extent do the questions deal with sensitive topics?" Finally, researchers must be concerned about the diversity of the prospective respondents, the likely incidence rate, and the degree of survey participation. Maximizing the quantity and quality of data collected while minimizing the cost and time of the survey generally requires the researcher to make trade-offs.

Explain how the electronic revolution is affecting the administration of survey research designs.

With the increasing advances in telecommunication and computer technologies, numerous new, fast techniques are available to researchers for collecting primary raw data from people. The range of new techniques continues to grow and includes such methods as computer-assisted telephone interviewing methods; fully automated self-administered techniques; and electronic mail, fax, and Internet surveys. There is little doubt that the time requirements of collecting data will significantly decrease with these new methods.

Identify and describe the strengths and weaknesses of each type of survey method.

It is important to remember that all methods have strengths as well as weaknesses. No single method is the best choice under all circumstances. Nor is the information researcher limited to a single method. Innovative combinations of survey methods can produce excellent results, as the strengths of one method can be used to overcome the weakness of another.

Identify and explain the types of errors that occur in survey research.

The researcher needs to evaluate the errors in the research results. All errors are either *random sampling errors* or *nonsampling errors.* By far the greatest amount of error that can reduce data quality comes from nonsampling (or systematic) error sources. Three major sources of error are *respondent error* (i.e., nonresponse errors and response biases); *measurement and design error* (i.e., construct development, scale measurement, and survey instrument design errors); and *administrative errors* (i.e., data processing, interviewer, and sample design errors). In survey research, systematic errors decrease the quality level of the data being collected.

KEY TERMS AND CONCEPTS

Ability to participate 272

Computer-assisted telephone interview (CATI) 261

Direct mail survey 261

Diversity 270

Drop-off survey 262

E-mail survey 264

Executive interview 257

Fax survey 263

Incidence rate 271

In-home interview 256

Internet survey 265

Knowledge level 272

Mail panel survey 262

Mall-intercept interview 257

Person-administered survey 256

Purchase-intercept interview 257

Self-administered survey 261

Survey research methods 253

Task difficulty 269

Telephone interviews 258

Topic sensitivity 270

Willingness to participate 272

REVIEW QUESTIONS

1. Identify and discuss the advantages and disadvantages of using quantitative survey research methods to collect primary raw data in marketing research.

2. What are the three critical components for determining data quality? How does achieving data quality differ in person-administered surveys and self-administered surveys?

3. Explain why survey designs that include a trained interviewer are more appropriate than computer-assisted survey designs in situations where the task difficulty and stimuli requirement factors are extensive.

4. Explain the major differences between in-home interviews and mall-intercept interviews; make sure you include their advantages and disadvantages.

5. How might measurement and design errors affect respondent errors? Develop three recommendations to help researchers increase the response rates in direct mail and telephone-administered surveys.

6. What possible issues associated with consumer behaviors and consumption patterns might be extremely sensitive ones to directly question respondents about? How might researchers overcome the difficulties of collecting sensitive data?

DISCUSSION QUESTIONS

1. Develop a cross-table of the factors used to select from person-administered, telephone-administered, self-administered, and computer-assisted survey designs. Then discuss the appropriateness of those selection factors across each type of survey design.

2. What impact, if any, will advances in telecommunication and computer technologies have on survey research practices? Support your thoughts.

3. Situation: The regional sales manager for Procter & Gamble interviews its sales representatives in the Midwest and asks them questions about the percentage of

their time they spent making presentations to new potential customers, talking on the telephone with current customers, working on the computer, and engaging in on-the-job activities. What potential sources of error might be associated with the manager's line of questioning?

4. Revisiting Exhibit 9.6, which decribes the different types of sampling and nonsampling errors found in survey research designs, identify five potential sources of error that have direct ethical implications. Write a short report that discusses the ethical issues associated with each type of error source and the strategies that a researcher should implement to resolve each issue.

5. **EXPERIENCE THE INTERNET.** Go to the latest Gallup Poll survey (www.gallup.com) and evaluate the survey design being used. Write a two-page report that points out the design's strengths and weaknesses.

ENDNOTES

1. Michael R. Czinkota and Ilkka A. Ronkainen, "Conducting Primary Market Research: Market Research for Your Export Operations, Part 2," *International Trade Forum* (January 1995), p. 18.

2. Stan Bullard, "Realty One Alters Marketing Strategy," *Crain's Cleveland Business, Real Estate* (October 9, 1995), pp. 3+.

3. Alan J. Bush and Joseph F. Hair, Jr., "An Assessment of the Mall Intercept as a Data Collect Method," *Journal of Marketing Research* 22 (May 1985), pp. 158–67.

4. J. Colombotos, "Personal vs. Telephone Interviews Effect Responses," *Public Health Reports* (September 1969), pp. 773–820; also see F. Kelly Shuptrine, "Survey Research: Respondent Attitudes Response and Bias," in *Marketing Perspectives for the 1990s,* ed. R. L. King, Southern Marketing Association Proceedings (November 1992), pp. 197–200.

5. William A. Lucus and William C. Adams, "An Assessment of Telephone Survey Methods," *Rand Report R-2135-NSF* (October 1997); also see T. F. Rogers, "Interviewing by Telephone and In-Person Quality of Response and Field Performance," *Public Opinion Quarterly* (Spring 1976), pp. 51–65.

6. Donald E. Stem, Jr., and Charles W. Lamb, Jr., "The Marble-Drop Technique: A Procedure for Gathering Sensitive Information," *Decision Sciences* (October 1981), pp. 702–8.

7. Todd D. Remington, "Telemarketing and Declining Survey Response Rates," *Journal of Advertising Research* 33, no. 1 (1993), pp. RC-6, RC-7; also see T. Remington, "Rising Refusal Rates: The Impact of Telemarketing," *QUIRKS Marketing Research Review* (May 1992), pp. 8–15.

8. Leif Gjestland, "Net? Not Yet: CATI Is Still Superior to Internet Interviewing but Enhancements Are on the Way," *Marketing Research: A Magazine of Management & Applications* 8, no. 1 (1996), pp. 26+.

9. Scott Dacko, "Data Collection Should Not Be Manual Labor," *Marketing News* 29, no. 18 (August 28, 1995), p. 31.

10. John P. Dickson and Douglas L. MacLachlan, "Fax Surveys?," *Marketing Research: A Magazine of Management & Applications* 4, no. 3 (September 1992), pp. 26–30; also see Aileen Crowley, "E-mail Surveys Elicit Fast Response, Cut Costs," *PC Week,* January 30, 1995.

11. John P. Dickson and Douglas L. MacLachlan, "Fax Surveys: Return Patterns and Comparison with Mail Survey," *Journal of Marketing Research* 33 (February 1996), pp. 108–13.

12. Paul R. Murphy and James M. Daley, "Mail Surveys: To Fax or Not to Fax," *Proceedings of the Association of Marketing Theory and Practice Annual Meetings* (Chicago, IL: American Marketing Association, 1995), pp. 152–57.

13. Patricia E. Moberg, "Biases in Unlisted Phone Numbers," *Journal of Advertising Research* (August–September 1982), p. 55.

14. Robert M. Groves, Robert B. Cialdini, and Mick P. Couper, "Understanding the Decision to Participate in a Survey," *Public Opinion Quarterly* 56 (1992), pp. 475–95; also see Henry Assael and John Keon, "Nonsampling vs. Sampling Errors in Survey Research," *Journal of Marketing* 46 (Spring 1982), pp. 114–23; and Gary Lilien, Rex Brown, and Kate Searls, "Cut Errors, Improve Estimates to Bridge Biz-to-Biz Info Gap," *Marketing News* 25, no. 1 (January 7, 1991), pp. 20–22.

MARKETING RESEARCH ILLUSTRATION

DETERMINING AND PLANNING THE APPROPRIATE SURVEY METHOD

The JP Hotel Preferred Guest Card Study

This illustration is designed to integrate the chapter's information on survey research methods with the ongoing example of JP Hotels. The objective here is specifically limited to illustrating the activities and decisions a researcher undertakes in deciding which communication mode is appropriate when using survey research methods to collect primary data. These activities normally begin Phase II of the information research process (Development of the Appropriate Research Design). To enhance understanding of this illustration, it will be helpful to review the information on the JP Hotel Preferred Guest Card study presented in earlier end-of-chapter illustrations.

Selecting and Planning the Appropriate Survey Method

Initially, the information research objectives and data requirements identified in Phase I of the research process play a key role in determining whether an observation, a survey, or an experiment should be used to collect the needed primary data. Previously the researcher, Alex Smith, described the five information research objectives of the JP Hotel study as follows:

1. To determine the card usage patterns among known JP Hotel Preferred Guest Card holders.

2. To identify and evaluate the privileges associated with the card program and how important the card is as a factor in selecting a hotel for business purposes.

3. To determine business travelers' total awareness of the card program.

4. To determine whether or not JP Hotel should charge an annual fee for card membership.

5. To identify profile differences between heavy users, moderate users, rare users, and nonusers of the card.

An assessment of these objectives shows that some type of descriptive research study should be conducted among known JP Hotel Preferred Guest Card holders. The corresponding data requirements suggest the need for attitudinal, behavioral, and demographic data from the prospective respondents. These research objectives and data requirements led Smith to decide that a survey design would be the most effective approach to collect the needed data. Now a decision had to be made regarding the most feasible communication mode for asking the questions and recording responses. In other words, should the survey approach use a person-administered, telephone-administered, or self-administered framework.

While there are many factors to consider, Smith conducted a comparison analysis of the three basic communication approaches using some of the situational, task, and respondent characteristics displayed in Exhibit 9.5 (see p. 267). Smith created an evaluation matrix (see Exhibit 1). Using his knowledge of the three alternative communication approaches and their strengths and weaknesses, he cross-evaluated the survey methods by ranking how well each method would handle or achieve each of the listed factors. His ranking scheme consisted of using 1 to represent "excellent," 2 for "good," 3 for "weak,"

EXHIBIT 1   Survey Design Selection Factors

Factors	Personal Interviews	Telephone Interviews	Self-Reporting Surveys
Resource budgets			
Need for available dollars	3	2	1
Need for available manpower	3	2	1
Total completion time	3	1	2
Data quality			
Completeness	1	3	2
Generalizability	1	2	2
Precision	1	2	2
Difficulty of task			
Amount of thought	3	2	1
Preparation time	3	2	1
Information requirements			
Amount of information	1	3	2
Depth of information	1	3	2
Type of data	1	3	1
Length of survey/interview	1	3	1
Topic sensitivity	3	2	1
Diversity of respondents	1	1	2
Geographic dispersion	3	1	1
Incidence rate	1	1	1
Search/contacting time	3	2	1
Survey participation			
Ability to participate	3	2	2
Willingness to participate	3	2	2
Knowledge level of topics	1	1	1
Overall cost per respondent	3	2	1
Likely response rate	1	2	2
Control of potential errors			
Interviewer errors	3	2	[N/A]
Response errors	2	2	2
Nonresponse errors	1	2	2

and N/A for "not applicable." In doing the actual evaluations, his rankings were influenced by such factors as cost and time considerations, the need to use multiattribute scales with multisensitivity scale descriptors (see Chapter 13), the difficulty of the question/response process, and the geographic diversity of the defined target population.

The Survey Design Decision

After reviewing the results, Smith determined that the appropriate communication mode for conducting the survey would be a self-reporting one where the selected respondents would read and respond to the survey's questions without the aid of any trained interviewer. How did he arrive at that decision? Initial interpretation of the cross-evaluation results suggested that any of the three alternative modes for administering a descriptive survey could be appropriate. There is no one method that stands out as being the best. They all have their own benefits and weaknesses.

In this situation, the final decision was influenced by the fact that the defined target population was 17,000 business travelers spread across the country. Therefore, using a person-administered design would require either hiring and training a significant number of interviewers or hiring and training a few interviewers but significantly increasing the search/contact time required to meet face-to-face with the selected respondents. Either way, the increased costs and time requirements for collecting the necessary data outweighed the potential quality factor. Given the attitudinal, behavioral, and demographic data requirements associated with the five research objectives, the survey would have to include a significant number of question scales. In addition, some of the question scales would have to use sets of multisensitive scale descriptors in order to capture and meet the study's information requirements. Consequently, employment of a telephone-administered survey would not be desirable for two reasons. First, administering questions that use multisensitive scale descriptors creates a difficult task for respondents to complete over the phone because they cannot easily visualize the different scale point alternatives. Second, the respondents are businesspeople who generally will not answer a survey that takes more than 7 to 10 minutes to complete. Given the stated research objectives and information requirements, any designed survey would be too long.

In this particular research situation, a self-administered survey would not run into the same problems associated with either person- or telephone-administered methods. Overall, self-administered surveys are cheaper than the alternatives. Major concerns focus on potentially low response rates, control over possible nonresponse errors, overall time frame for completing data collection activities, and data quality. Alex Smith was concerned about these weaknesses, but felt that good planning and execution of the processes underlying the self-administered survey method would minimize the weaknesses while still meeting the study's information requirements.

MARKETING RESEARCH CASE EXERCISE

KNOW SAN DIEGO

This Exercise Corresponds with the Video Know San Diego

In the video *Know San Diego,* the importance of collecting information on consumers was discussed. This discussion centered on the collection of demographic, lifestyle, and value-oriented information. The value of this information ranges across such industries as consumer product firms, advertising agencies, banks, retailers, and other market-oriented organizations. The main message of the video was that companies must use information to know their market.

After viewing this video in its entirety, answer the following questions:

1. How important is demographic, lifestyle, and value information for companies that want to know more about their market? How do companies use such information in their marketing decisions?

2. Is there ever a situation in which the information discussed in the video would have no impact on marketing decisions?

3. Get to know the city where you live. Develop a list of questions that would help businesses in your area better know their market. More specifically, develop 10 demographic, 10 lifestyle, and 15 value-oriented questions that would provide critical market information to local businesses in your community. Explain why you chose those particular questions.

Learning Objectives

After reading this chapter, you will be able to

1. Describe and explain the importance of and differences between the variables used in experimental research designs.

2. Explain the theoretical importance and impact of internal, external, and construct validity measures in experiments and interpreting functional relationships.

3. Discuss the three major types of experimental designs used in marketing research. Explain the pros and cons of using causal designs as a means of assessing relationship outcomes.

4. Explain what test markets are, the importance and difficulties of executing this type of research design, and how the resulting data structures are used by researchers and marketing practitioners.

5. Discuss the characteristics, benefits, and weaknesses of observational techniques, and explain how these techniques are used to collect primary data.

Causal Research: Experiments, Test Markets, and Observation Methods

❝ Experimental investigations are the linemen in the game of scientific research. They don't gain much publicity, but scientific research cannot advance without them. ❞ [1]

GREGORY SCHADABERG
Senior Research Analyst
EMI Corporation

R. J. Reynolds Tobacco: Using Test Marketing to Gauge New-Product Acceptance

Still reeling from the effects of its $2 billion mistake with Premier cigarettes, R. J. Reynolds Tobacco (RJR) is at it again, testing and evaluating a new smokeless cigarette product called Eclipse. With knowledge gained by the failure of the smokeless product Premier, RJR is conducting a series of extensive market tests on Eclipse. Testing of the product is currently being conducted in five major market areas throughout the United States. The overall objective of these tests is to gain greater insights into customer use, acceptance, and repeat purchase behavior for the new smokeless cigarette. Company officials are determined to test and evaluate the entire marketing program for Eclipse before any decision is made regarding a national launch of the product. In several test cities, package and product sizes are being manipulated. Longer cigarettes, with flatter and wider packages are being monitored and evaluated based on customer sales. Even the color of the product—brown versus traditional white—is being tested for customer reaction. In one particular test city, the cigarette comes with lighting instructions. Smokeless cigarettes do not burn like traditional cigarettes, so many initial users of Premier destroyed the product by lighting it in a normal fashion. Product instructions enclosed with Eclipse are being used as a way to avoid possible customer confusion.

Direct mail and product samples are being used to evaluate communication vehicles for the new product. Point-of-sale coupons and price discounts are being varied across different retail stores as a way to monitor price sensitivity. Operating in conjunction with a battalion of data-collection personnel, RJR is attempting to determine customer reaction to a variety of different marketing programs for the new smokeless product.

Based on initial responses, company officials are hopeful that the test marketing for Eclipse will be highly successful. In addition to positive customer reaction indicated by early test results, RJR hopes to gather critical information that will allow the company to avoid past marketing mistakes.[2]

Value of Experimentation and Test Marketing

Test marketing Using controlled field experiments to gain information on specified market performance indicators.

As the chapter opener suggests, one growing area in marketing research is that of test marketing using causal research designs. **Test marketing** consists of controlled field experiments usually conducted in limited market areas on specified market performance indicators. Its main objective is either to predict sales, uncover valuable market information, or anticipate adverse consequences of a marketing program for a particular product. With growing popularity, experimental procedures are employed to investigate and collect important cause–effect relationship data regarding new products or improvements of existing products. As explained in more detail later in this chapter, many practitioners use test marketing to determine customer attitudes toward new-product ideas, service delivery alternatives, or marketing communication strategies. While exploratory and descriptive studies are extremely effective for collecting primary raw data in certain situations, they do not necessarily establish causal links between various factors and events. As mentioned in Chapter 2, causal research designs are powerful methods that can provide researchers and decision makers with the appropriate data from which to develop clear insights into why certain events occur and why they happen under some conditions and not others. This chapter focuses on the popular experimental and test marketing designs used in marketing research. Along with these, we will discuss important reliability and validity issues concerning causal research methods in general. The chapter concludes with discussions on how observational methods are integrated with research design practices. We begin with an overview of experimentation in marketing research.

The Nature of Experimentation

Variable Any observable and measurable element (or attribute) of an item or event.

All marketing research practices require either the manipulation or the measurement of **variables.** Variables are the observable and measurable elements (or attributes) of an item or an event. They are the qualities the researcher specifies, studies, and draws conclusions about. They can differ in different situations and at different times. To illustrate this concept, let's take the vehicle you are currently driving. Your automobile or truck is really a composite of many different attributes. The color, the make and model, the number of cylinders, the miles per gallon, and the price are all variables. Furthermore, different automobiles and trucks possess different variables, and any one vehicle has one given set of variables at any given time. Whenever an object, idea, or event is described, every element by which it could be observed and measured can be considered a variable, including where it is, how it is used, and what surrounds it.

When conducting an experiment, the researcher attempts to identify the relationships among different variables. Let's consider, for example, the following research question: "How long does it take a customer to place and receive an order from the drive-through at a Wendy's fast-food restaurant?" The time it takes to receive a food order is a variable that can be measured quantitatively. That is to say, the different values of the time variable are determined by some method of measurement. But how long it takes a particular customer to receive a food order is complicated by a number of other variables. For instance, what if there were 10 cars waiting in line, or it was 12:00 noon, or it was raining? Additionally, such factors as the number of drive-up windows, the training level of order takers, and the number of patrons waiting are all variables. Consequently, all of these variables probably have some effect on the time variable.

In turn, the make of the car the person is driving, the number of brothers he has, and the quantity of food he orders are also variables. But the first two variables are unlikely to have much effect on order time. However, there is a relationship between the quantity of the order and the waiting time, because the more items in the order, the longer it takes to prepare.

Functional relationship An observable and measurable systematic change in one variable as another variable changes.

If it is true that the quantity of food ordered increases one's wait at a drive-through, the researcher can say that there is a **functional relationship** between food quantity ordered and waiting time. As such, it can be stated that waiting time at a fast-food drive-through is a function of the amount of food being ordered. In causal research designs that use experimental procedures, the researcher desires to investigate the functional relationships between variables. The focus is on investigating the systematic change in one variable as another variable changes. The Using Technology box illustrates a version of this, called BehaviorScan.

Types of Variables Used in Experimental Designs

In using experimental designs, researchers must be especially careful to confirm that the relationships they find between the variables being investigated actually do exist. Attempts must be made to hold constant the influence of extraneous variables so that accurate measures can be made of those variables under investigation. When designing causal research experiments, researchers must have an understanding of the four types of variables that are critical in the design process: independent, dependent, control, and extraneous (see Exhibit 10.1).

A CLOSER LOOK AT RESEARCH   Using Technology

BehaviorScan:
A Device Used for Testing New Products and Marketing Programs

BehaviorScan is a one-of-a-kind, in-market laboratory for testing new products and marketing programs under tightly controlled yet real-world conditions. The impact of the test program can be measured in terms of both total store sales as well as household-level purchasing behavior. BehaviorScan offers the only targetable TV service in the nation, capable of delivering different ad copy and/or media weight to two or three selected groups of households within a market.

In seven markets around the United States, Information Resources Inc. (IRI), the company providing BehaviorScan, maintains an infrastructure optimally designed for test marketing. IRI handles everything from retail sell-in to product stocking and promotion execution to data collection and analysis. IRI can con-

trol the distribution, price, shelf placement, trade, consumer promotion, and TV advertising for each product in a test. This ability to control all the variables enables highly accurate evaluation of the test variable.

In each BehaviorScan market, a large, ongoing household panel is maintained, making it possible to track household purchasing behaviors on an item-by-item level over time. Panel data collection is passive: members need only present their "Shopper's Hotline ID" card at checkout in participating retailers. Scanner sales data are collected on an ongoing basis from groceries, drugstores, and mass merchandisers. In-store promotion activity in most categories is monitored as well as documented pricing, displays, and features by item. Data from other outlets, such as convenience stores or hardware stores, can be collected on a custom basis. More details on BehaviorScan can be obtained at www.infores.com.

Independent variables

Variables whose value are directly manipulated by the researcher.

Independent variables are those whose values are directly manipulated by the researcher. The researcher is interested in establishing functional relationships between independent and dependent variables. In many market research experiments, marketing mix variables such as price levels, product/package designs, distribution channel systems, and advertising themes are treated as independent variables. Let's say, for example, that Procter & Gamble (P&G) is interested in determining the relationship between several

---

EXHIBIT 10.1   Types of Variables Used in Experimental Research Designs

Type of Variable	Comments
Independent variable	Also called *predictor* or *treatment variable* (X). An attribute or element of an object, idea, or event whose measurement values are directly manipulated by the researcher. The independent variable is assumed to be the causal factor of a functional relationship with a dependent variable.
Dependent variable	Also called *criterion variable* (Y). A singular observable attribute or element that is the measured outcome or effect change on specified test subjects that is derived from manipulating the independent variable(s).
Control variables	Variables that the researcher controls so that they do not affect the functional relationship between the independent and dependent variables included in the experiment.
Extraneous variables	Uncontrollable variables that should average out over a series of experiments. If not accounted for, they can have a confounding impact on the dependent variable measures that could weaken or invalidate the results of an experiment.

A consumer examines Tide brand of laundry detergent.

new package designs for its Tide brand of laundry detergent and Tide's unit sales. Using experimental design procedures, the researchers could observe customers' purchasing of the product on four different occasions. On each occasion, the researchers can change the package design from, say, round to square, to rectangular, to oval. Every time the package design is changed, a unit sales measure can be recorded. Since the researchers directly manipulated it, package design serves as the independent variable.

Dependent variables are measures of effect or outcome that occur during the experiment, or measures of change in the conditions that exist after the experiment is completed. These variables may include such market performance factors as unit sales, profit levels, and market shares. While values of independent variables are assigned before the experiment begins, this procedural control activity is not possible with dependent variables. Dependent variables are attributes or elements that are affected by the process of the experiment. Their specific outcome values cannot be measured before the experiment begins. In the P&G package design example, the dependent variable is Tide's unit sales. This variable is measured under each manipulation of the package design. If the researchers want to state the results in terms of a functional relationship, they would say that Tide's unit sales total (the dependent variable) is a function of package design (the independent variable).

Control variables are the conditions or elements that make the research design a true experiment. These are variables the researcher controls, or does not allow to vary freely or systematically with independent variables. Thus, the average value of a control variable or its impact should not change as the independent variable is manipulated. Researchers must design the experiment so that control variables cannot freely or systematically affect the relationship between the independent and dependent variables. Control variables can present a major problem in using experimental designs to investigate hypothesized functional relationships. For example, if P&G wants to investigate the true relationship between Tide's unit sales and package design alternatives, the researchers do not want any other variables to influence the measure of unit sales. They would want to make sure that the conditions surrounding Tide's unit sales (the dependent variable) are as similar as possible for each of the package design manipulations (the independent variable). For example, the

Dependent variables
Measures of effect or outcome that occur during the experiment, or measures of change in the conditions that exist after the experiment is completed.

Control variables Variables that the researcher does not allow to vary freely or systematically with independent variables; control variables should not change as the independent variable is manipulated.

customers should (1) shop at the same store during each package design manipulation; (2) shop at the same time of day with the same amount of store crowding; and (3) shop on successive days without being exposed to any advertised message for Tide. In addition, the price and shelf location of Tide should remain the same on all successive package design manipulations. This points to the problem that there are so many possible influences on Tide's unit sales that the researchers cannot possibly control all of them. The researchers must, however, control as many as they can.

Extraneous variables

Variables that cannot be controlled by researchers but that should average out over different trials and thus not systematically affect the results of the experiment.

Extraneous variables such as changes in temperature, mood, health, or even physical conditions of the store, to name a few, cannot be controlled by the researchers. These types of variables may average out over the different manipulations of the independent variables, and thus not have systematic influences on the dependent variable, but they also may weaken the results of the experiment.

One method the P&G researchers could use to reduce the effects of extraneous variables is to randomize the same manipulation condition of the package design across a number of customers and then measure unit sales. This procedure would have to be accomplished across all of the package design manipulations until a significant number of customers were measured for Tide unit sales under each manipulation. This procedure is referred to as **randomization** of subjects; the desired outcome is that the influence of the extraneous variables will average out over all manipulations of the independent variable. While the measured results under these conditions might not be very precise for any individual test subject, they may be precise enough to show a fairly accurate relationship between the independent and dependent variables.

Randomization   The procedure whereby many subjects are assigned to different experimental treatment conditions, resulting in each group averaging out any systematic effect on the investigated functional relationship between the independent and dependent variables.

The Role of Theory in Experimental Designs

From an experimental design perspective, **theory** is a large body of interconnected propositions about how some portion of a certain phenomenon operates. Theory underpins the development of hypotheses about relationships. As such, hypotheses are smaller versions of theories. Experimental research is primarily a hypothesis-testing method and can therefore be referred to as *deductive* research. Researchers derive a hypothesis from a theory, design an experiment, and gather data to test the hypothesis. There are situations when researchers will use causal design procedures to generate hypotheses in order to create new theories or extend existing theories about a phenomenon; these are referred to as *inductive* research. In practice, researchers often use both deductive and inductive design methods. A researcher may begin an investigation using causal research procedures to test some hypotheses that focus on the cause–effect relationships between variables, but then develop new hypotheses when he sees the data results. Existing theoretical insights can help a researcher in identifying the critical independent variables that might bring about changes in dependent variables. It is important to understand that experimental and other causal research designs are most appropriate when the researcher wants to find out why certain events occur, and why they happen under certain conditions and not others. Identifying and being able to explain cause–effect relationships allow marketing researchers and business practitioners alike to be in a position to make reasonable predictions about marketing phenomena under certain conditions.

Theory   A large body of interconnected propositions about how some portion of a certain phenomenon operates.

Validity and Reliability Concerns with Experimental Research Designs

Before learning about the specific types of causal research designs and procedures available to marketing researchers, it is critically important to be aware of the general validity issues that directly affect causal designs. As we discussed earlier, extraneous variables are numerous and are difficult to control when using causal designs for testing hypothesized relationships. Their presence may result in the contamination of the functional relationship. This contamination clouds the researcher's ability to conclusively determine whether

Validity The extent to which the conclusions drawn from the experiment are true.

or not the results of the experiment are valid. **Validity,** in its simplest form, refers to the extent to which the conclusions drawn from the experiment are true. In other words, do the differences in the dependent variable found through experimental manipulations of the independent variables really reflect a cause–effect relationship? While there are many ways to classify the validity of causal research designs, we will discuss three: internal validity, external validity, and construct validity.

Internal Validity

Internal validity The extent to which the research design accurately identifies causal relationships.

Internal validity refers to the extent to which the research design accurately identifies causal relationships. In other words, internal validity exists when the researcher can rule out rival explanations for the observed results and conclusions about the functional relationship. For example, in an experiment on the effects of electricity, if you shock someone (experimental treatment) and he jumps (observed effect), and he jumps only because of the shock and for no other reason, then internal validity exists.

Why is establishing internal validity of causal research designs important to researchers? The following example illustrates the answer. Let's say a small bakery in White Water, Wisconsin, wanted to know whether or not putting additional frosting on its new cakes would cause customers to like the cakes better. Using an experimental design, it tested the hypothesis that its customers liked additional frosting on their cakes. As the amount of frosting was being manipulated, the bakery discovered that the additional frosting allowed the cakes to stay more moist. Consequently, it might have been the moistness and not the frosting that caused the customers' positive reaction to the new cakes. In an attempt to assess internal validity, control groups were established consisting of customers who were not exposed to the treatment (extra frosting, original moistness), but all other conditions (original moistness) were kept the same.[3] Adding the control group to the experimental design reduced the possibility that the observed effect of the new cakes was caused by something other than the treatment. In this case, if it was the frosting, then the treated group should like the new cake more than the control group. But if it was the moistness, then both groups would like the new cake equally.

Exhibit 10.2 displays the types of threats that can negatively affect internal, external, and construct validities associated with causal research designs. The latter two will be discussed in the next sections; here we will discuss the threats to internal validity. History threats would involve events that occur between the first manipulation of the independent variable and the second manipulation. Where the objective of the manipulation was to measure changes in a person's attitude about political integrity resulting from a political history course, the results could be strongly affected if a major political scandal, like the recent savings and loan debacle, occurred between the two manipulation treatments.

Without a doubt, our attitudes and behaviors change as we grow older (and hopefully wiser), and these changes can also represent a maturation threat to internal validity. The threat of testing refers to the second administration of the treatment where the experience with the first administration may well affect scores on the second administration. Changes in observers' attitudes, reduced accuracy of scorers, or changed administration techniques are all examples of the instrumentation threat to internal validity.

When strict random assignment to treatment and control groups is not followed, then selection bias resulting in noncomparable groups could occur, threatening internal validity. Mortality involves the loss of subjects from groups from natural causes, thereby creating groups of subjects that are no longer comparable. Primarily a factor in correlational, non-experimental studies, ambiguity of causal direction may also constitute a threat. For instance, do higher family incomes result from higher education levels, or do higher income levels allow higher education levels? Such ambiguities reduce the researcher's ability to differentiate between cause and effect.

EXHIBIT 10.2   Validity Types and Threats to Validity

Threats to Internal Validity

History	When extraneous factors that enter the experiment process between the first and later manipulations affect measures of the dependent variable.
Maturation	Changes in the dependent variable based on the natural function of time and not attributed to any specific event.
Testing	When learned understanding gained from the first treatment and measures of the dependent variable distort future treatments and measurement activities.
Instrumentation	Contamination from changes in measurement processes, observation techniques, and/or measuring instruments.
Selection bias	Contamination created by inappropriate selection and/or assignment processes of test subjects to experimental treatment groups.
Statistical regression	Contamination created when experimental groups are selected on the basis of their extreme responses or scores.
Mortality	Contamination due to changing the composition of the test subjects in the experiment.
Ambiguity	Contamination from unclear determination of cause–effect relationship.

Threats to External Validity

Treatment vs. treatment	When test subjects in different treatment groups are exposed to different amounts of manipulations.
Treatment vs. testing	When the premeasurement process sensitizes test subjects to respond in an abnormal manner to treatment manipulations.
Treatment vs. selection	Generalizing the results to other categories of people beyond those types used in the experiment.
Treatment vs. setting	Generalizing the results to other environments beyond the one used in the experiment.
Treatment vs. history	Using the existing functional relationship to predict future phenomenon outcomes.

Threats to Construct Validity

Inadequate preoperationalization of variables	Contamination due to inadequate understanding of the complete makeup of the independent and dependent variables included in the experimental design.
Mono-operation bias	Contamination created by using only one method to measure the outcomes of the dependent variable.
Monomethod bias	Contamination due to assessing multiattribute treatment manipulations (independent variables) using single-item measuring instruments.
Hypothesis-guessing	Contamination by test subjects believing they know the desired functional relationship prior to the manipulation treatment.
Evaluation apprehension	Contamination caused by test subjects being fearful that their actions or responses will become known to others.
Demand characteristics	Contamination created by test subjects trying to guess the true purpose behind the experiment, thus giving abnormal socially acceptable responses or behaviors.
Diffusion of treatment	Contamination due to test subjects discussing the treatment and measurement activities to individuals yet to receive the treatment.

Source: Edward G. Carmines and Richard A. Zeller, *Reliability and Validity Assessment* (Newbury Park, CA: Sage, 1979), pp. 9–48; also see Donald T. Campbell and Julian C. Stanley, *Experimental Designs for Research* (Skokie, IL: Rand-McNally, 1966).

The threat of statistical regression is a manifestation of the phenomenon whereby human beings tend to score differently on each trial in an experiment, with the recorded scores regressing toward the true population mean. In other words, the errors balance out. In those cases where subjects are selected for particular groups based on extreme pretreatment responses, the observed posttreatment measures will be even more biased. As mentioned earlier, the primary and most powerful weapon against threats to internal validity is random selection of subjects from a heterogeneous target population and then random assignment to treatment groups. This is considered standard practice in reputable research studies.

External Validity

External validity The extent to which a causal relationship found in a study can be expected to be true for the entire target population.

External validity refers to the extent to which a causal relationship found in a study can be expected to be true for the entire target population. For example, let's say that a food company wanted to find out if its new dessert would appeal to a commercially viable percentage of U.S. citizens between the ages of 18 and 35. It would be prohibitively costly to ask each 18- to 35-year-old in the United States to taste the product. Therefore, using sound experimental design procedures, the company would randomly select test subjects of the defined target market population (18–35) and assign them to different treatment groups, varying one component of the dessert for each group. The subjects then taste the new dessert. If 60 percent indicated that they would purchase the product, and if in fact 60 percent of the entire population did purchase the new product when it was marketed, then the results of the study would be considered externally valid.

Threats to external validity include interactions of treatment with history, setting, selection, testing, and treatment exposures. Interactions with history that might lessen external validity could include testing on a special day such as Christmas or Halloween. If the researcher were interested in charitable behavior, then a treatment manipulation and effect measures administered on Christmas Day might give quite different results than one given at some other less notable time. After watching several movies emphasizing charity and love for our fellow man, the average subject might react significantly differently on this day than on some other. By the same token, polls on gun control might very likely be affected if taken immediately after the assassination of a major public figure. Generalizability to other time frames would therefore be considerably reduced.

Similar reductions in external validity might occur if the location or setting of the experiment influenced the observed results. Surely, a fear-of-heights scale administered on top of a mountain would have different results than one administered in a classroom. The final threat of selection bias occurs when the sample is not truly representative of the target population. Asking subjects to participate in a survey or experiment requiring several hours will limit the actual sample to only those who have the spare time and may not generate a truly representative sample.

Another possible threat to external validity can occur when some of the test subjects experience more than one treatment in the experimental setting. The conclusions drawn could not be generalized to situations where individuals received fewer or more treatments. For example, if an experiment was designed to study the effects of a price reduction on product sales in which the product was displayed in two separate locations, the results could not be generalized to situations where only one display was used. Here, the extra display competes with price reduction as an explanation for sales.

Construct Validity

Critical to all causal research designs is the ability to accurately identify, define, and understand the key independent and dependent variables included in the study. In addition, researchers must be able to accurately measure or observe those variables in order to

Construct validity

The extent to which the variables under investigation are completely and accurately identified prior to hypothesizing any functional relationships.

assess their true functional or cause–effect relationships. Consequently, researchers must attempt to assess the **construct validity** of both independent and dependent variables prior to executing their experimental or causal research design. Construct validity can simply be viewed as the extent to which the variables under investigation are completely and accurately identified prior to hypothesizing any functional relationships. Establishing construct validity for the variables included can be an elusive, even if essential, goal. Of the many approaches to establishing construct validity, one that is used widely consists of three steps.[4]

First, the relationship between the constructs (or variables) of interest must be accurately identified. To illustrate, let's assume a researcher wanted to use a construct called *motivation to succeed (MTS)* as an independent variable in predicting the likelihood of individuals' life success. Those who measure the highest on the MTS construct would be those most likely to have succeeded in life. The fundamental question that must be addressed is, "What are the observable, real-life indicants of such success?" Using a process referred to as *specifying the domain of observable subcomponents related to the construct,*[5] let's assume that peer respect, academic achievement, and personal financial security represent success in the particular society being investigated. The precise nature of this specification is necessary so that the hypothesized relationship can be empirically tested with real data. Otherwise, the details collected will be insufficient to either support or refute the hypothesis.

Second, the researcher executes an experimental design that manipulates MTS and measures the outcome "life success." If it is determined that the data are both positive and substantial in support of the hypothesized functional relationship, then evidence of construct validity exists. As discussed earlier, researchers would also attempt to determine what other constructs these observables might be related to, such as social position, inherited wealth, or athletic prowess. To the extent that the observable subcomponents are not related to MTS, but rather to other alternative constructs, then the evidence in support of construct validity would be weakened. For example, peer respect and personal financial security might be the result of inherited wealth and have little to do with motivation to succeed. As a result, it would be necessary to find other observable subcomponents that are more closely related to MTS and that could not generally be caused by other constructs.

Third, prior to executing the experiment, a diligent researcher will attempt to assess the proposed measurement methods of the independent and dependent variables to those of other methods. When existing measures of the same construct are highly correlated with the researcher's measures, then we have evidence of *convergent validity* in support of the construct validity that we seek. Additional evidence, of what is called *discriminant validity,* may come from a negative correlation between the experiment's measuring methods and those designed to measure completely different constructs.[6] Construct validity is discussed further in later chapters.

As described in Exhibit 10.2, construct validity can be threatened in many ways, including (1) inadequate preoperationalization of constructs; (2) mono-operation bias; (3) monomethod bias; (4) hypothesis-guessing; (5) demand characteristics; (6) evaluation apprehension; and (7) diffusion of treatment. To avoid inadequate preoperationalization, the researcher should carefully and completely define the construct as exactly as possible. Fear of heights cannot simply be defined as a fear of high places, since some people are afraid of being on high mountain roads but not in an office in a high building or on an airplane. As a researcher, it is essential that you know *exactly* what form of fear you are trying to measure. Then, once the definition has been refined in light of the purpose of the study and existing literature, you can more precisely select the measurable, observable manifestations of the construct.

Mono-operation and monomethod bias can threaten construct validity through contamination created by using only one method or single-item measuring instruments. Where possible, researchers should use more than one measuring method (pen and pencil, interview, or physical reactions) and more than a single measure in each method to collect data.[7]

Interestingly, researchers have found that many subjects try to guess the purpose of the research and respond as they feel the researcher wants them to respond. Called the *demand characteristic* by some scholars, this threat can be reduced by limiting the reactivity of the researchers to the subjects and by making the hypothesis difficult to guess. For example, one clever psychologist invited people to participate in an experiment, had them wait in an outer office, and then took them into a room where they were asked several questions. In actuality, the experiment involved interpersonal conversational patterns and took place in the waiting room with the help of confederates posing as subjects (without the knowledge of the real subjects).[8]

Most of us have exhibited evaluation apprehension before a college entrance exam, sports physical, or even our first school dance. Because such apprehension can seriously bias the results of many studies, researchers will attempt to reduce it as much as possible. One ethical technique frequently used in marketing research involves ensuring the anonymity of subjects or respondents. Careful briefing of each subject by the research team can also go far in reducing this threat.

The final threat to construct validity discussed here involves the diffusion of treatment. Since it is rarely possible to completely isolate subjects, the control group may exchange information with the treatment group, or those who previously completed a questionnaire may discuss it with those who have yet to participate. Although the researcher may caution the subjects not to discuss the research, such efforts are usually unsuccessful. Taking several samples from the target population at various locations and under different conditions will usually reduce this threat. As a matter of fact, this process of using widely different samples from the population of interest is a powerful tool in combating many threats to construct and other forms of validity.

Reliability of Causal Research Designs

Experimental design reliability The degree to which the design and its procedures can be replicated and achieve similar conclusions about hypothesized relationships.

Although reliability tends to be a bigger concern in scaling measurement development, and is therefore discussed in later chapters, a couple of comments can be made here regarding reliability of the causal research design. **Experimental design reliability** can be indirectly assessed through the notion that reliable research findings are repeatable and that the conclusions drawn can be generalized beyond the particular conditions in the initial experiment (i.e., external validity). For design reliability to exist, researchers must be able to demonstrate that their experiment can be repeated or replicated and that similar conclusions would be reached. While there tends to be little reward in replicating the experiments of other researchers or scientists, marketing research practitioners might find significant benefits in replicating the procedures associated with causal research designs. For example, a company such as AT&T, which has many different types of telecommunication products, might standardize its design and testing procedures for investigating new-product acceptance relationships. Such standardization of procedural activities could lead to significant cost reductions within AT&T's research and development activities.

Improving the Internal and External Validity of Experimental Designs

As mentioned earlier, the ultimate goal of experimental research is determining the true causal or functional relationship between the independent and dependent variables. Researchers must worry about the extent to which extraneous variables can confound experimental results and induce invalid conclusions about the investigated relationships. As a way to counter the threats to internal and external validity, researchers can implement several techniques unique to experimental designs.

Inclusion of Control Groups

When designing an experiment, the researcher must determine who will be assigned to the groups that will be exposed to the manipulation and who will be assigned to the control group that does not receive the manipulation. Control groups represent the greatest strength of the experiment and the best way to ensure internal validity.

Time Order of the Manipulation Exposure

The researcher also must determine which variables, independent or dependent, will occur first. This can be accomplished by using pre-experimental measures of the variables prior to manipulation or by establishing experimental treatment and control groups that do not differ in terms of influencing the dependent variable before the manipulation takes place.

Exclusion of Nonsimilar Test Subjects

To increase internal validity, the researcher can select only those test subjects who have similar and controllable characteristics. Let's say, for example, that the researcher is interested in certain product-purchasing behaviors among a highly defined targeted group of consumers. This study's results might be confounded by differences in age and occupational status of the test subjects. To counter this possibility, the researcher would select only those test subjects with age and occupational status characteristics similar to the target market. By doing so, the researcher is eliminating extraneous variation due to age and occupation.

Matching Extraneous Variables

Through the process of matching, the researcher measures certain extraneous variables on an individual-by-individual basis. Those who respond similarly to the variables are then allocated to the experimental and control groups. Again, this process can control for both selection and statistical regression threats and enhance internal validity.

Randomization of Test Subjects to Treatment Groups

As described earlier, randomization of the assignment of test subjects to the experimental and control groups can help make the groups equivalent. The key to true randomization of test subjects is that the randomness must be secured in a carefully controlled manner. To enhance external validity, the researcher should also randomly select settings and times for the experiment based on the population or events under investigation.

By ensuring that the above procedures are integrated into the experimental design, the researcher increases the experiment's ability to accurately identify true causal or functional relationships. Moreover, these procedures help the researcher control contamination of the relationships between the independent and dependent variables.

Types of Causal Research Designs

Experimental research designs can be classified into three groups: (1) pre-experiments, (2) true experiments, and (3) quasi-experiments (see Exhibit 10.3). The main difference among these groups is the degree of control that the researcher can exercise in the design and execution. To facilitate discussion and understanding of the different types of experi-

EXHIBIT 10.3	Types of Causal Research Designs in Marketing Research

Pre-experimental Designs

One-shot study	A single group of test subjects is exposed to the independent variable treatment *X*, and then a single measurement on the dependent variable is taken (O_1).
One-group, pretest-posttest	First a pretreatment measure of the dependent variable is taken (O_1), then the test subjects are exposed to the independent treatment *X*, and then a posttreatment measure of the dependent variable is taken (O_2).
Static group comparison	There are two groups of test subjects: one group is the experimental group (EG) and is exposed to the independent treatment, and the second group is the control group (CG) and is not given the treatment. The dependent variable is measured in both groups after the treatment.

True Experimental Designs

Pretest-posttest, control group	Test subjects are randomly assigned to either the experimental or control group, and each group receives a pretreatment measure of the dependent variable. Then the independent treatment is exposed to the experimental group, after which both groups receive a posttreatment measure of the dependent variable.
Posttest-only, control group	Test subjects are randomly assigned to either the experimental or the control group. The experimental group is then exposed to the independent treatment, after which both groups receive a posttreatment measure of the dependent variable.
Solomon Four Group	This design combines the "pretest-posttest, control group" and "posttest-only, control group" designs and provides both direct and reactive effects of testing. Not used in marketing research practices because of complexity and lengthy time requirements.

Quasi-experimental Designs

Nonequivalent control group	This design is a combination of the "static group comparison" and the "one-group, pretest-posttest" pre-experimental designs.
Separate-sample, pretest-posttest	Two different groups of test subjects are drawn; neither group is directly exposed to the independent treatment variable. One group receives a pretest measure of the dependent variable. Then after the insignificant independent treatment occurs, the second group of test subjects receives a posttest measure of the dependent variable.
Field experiment	This is a causal design that manipulates the independent variables in order to measure the dependent variable in the natural setting of the event or test.

mental designs used to collect data for making inferences about causal relationships, we define a set of symbols commonly used in marketing research:[9]

X = The exposure of an independent variable (treatment manipulation) to a group of test subjects for which the effects are to be determined

O = The process of observation or measurement of the dependent variable (effect outcome) on the test subjects

$[R]$ = The random assignment of test subjects to separate treatment groups

EG = The experimental group of test subjects

CG = The control group of test subjects

$Æ$ = A movement through time, normally displayed as left-to-right movement

Note also that vertical alignment of symbols implies that those symbols refer to activities that occur simultaneously at a prescribed point in time, and that horizontal alignment of symbols implies that all those symbols refer to a specific treatment group of test subjects.

Pre-experimental Designs

There are three specific pre-experimental designs available to marketing researchers: the one-shot study; the one-group, pretest-posttest; and the static group comparison. These designs are commonly referred to as crude experiments and should only be undertaken when a stronger experimental design is not possible. These designs are characterized by an absence of randomization of test subjects. Their major weakness is the inability to meet internal validity criteria due to a lack of equivalent group comparisons.[10]

One-Shot Study

The one-shot case study can be illustrated as follows:

$$\text{(EG):} \quad X \; \text{æ} \; \text{Æ} \, O_1$$

An example of this design would be when a researcher wishes to observe or measure all customer reactions to a product display in a single store. A design of this nature obviously fails to provide any control over extraneous variables. It ignores the process of group comparisons that is fundamental in the experimental process. In one-shot designs, the only comparisons made are those based on common knowledge, past experiences, or general impressions of what the condition would have been had the manipulation not occurred. In this instance, even careful development of accurate measures will not compensate for the inadequate design.

One-Group, Pretest-Posttest

The only value of the "one-group, pretest-posttest" design is its ability to provide the researcher with a comparison measure. It is diagrammed as follows:

$$\text{(EG):} \quad O_1 \; \text{æ} \; \text{Æ} \, X_1 \; \text{æ} \; \text{Æ} \, O_2$$

The design is subject to the same extraneous confounding factors discussed earlier. In addition, history contamination is a major weakness, given the events that may occur between O_1 and O_2. Even environmental noise (sirens, thunder, phones) can affect results. The only way to control for the occurrence is to isolate the experiment in a controlled environment. Unfortunately, this is a widely used design in marketing research, often to measure advertising effects among consumers. Many advertisers will take a pretest criterion measure of either ad recall, product involvement, media habits, or purchase history. Then an experimental independent treatment manipulation is delivered (e.g., exposure to an ad during a TV program), followed by a posttest measure of the dependent variable, usually ad recall. Experimental designs such as these are further affected by maturation and instrumentation problems. The effect of the pretest measure also introduces problems with the testing factor.

One advantage of the "one-group, pretest-posttest" design is its lack of selection bias. Since only one group exists, it automatically eliminates the problem of differential selection. Overall, this design has imperfect safeguards to internal validity and should be used only when nothing better is available.

Static Group Comparison

Static group comparison is a two-group experimental design consisting of an experimental group (EG) and a control group (CG) of test subjects, but it lacks any randomization. The experimental group receives the independent treatment manipulation, with the second operating as the control. It can be illustrated as follows:

$$\text{(EG):} \quad X \; \text{æ} \; \text{Æ} \, O_1$$
$$\text{(CG):} \qquad\qquad O_2$$

Selection bias is the major defect of this design mainly because the groups are formed on a nonrandom basis. For example, many studies look at two store settings or heavy users versus light users when comparing new-product trials or sales. While the groups are selected to be random, in theory there is no assurance that the two groups are equivalent. Yet in comparison to the other pre-experimental designs, the static group comparison is substantially less susceptible to history, maturation, instrumentation, and testing contaminations.

True Experimental Designs

There are only three forms of true experimental designs: (1) pretest-posttest, control group; (2) posttest-only, control group; and (3) Solomon Four Group. The common denominator is that all three designs ensure equivalence between experimental and control groups by random assignment to the groups.[11]

Pretest-Posttest, Control Group

The "pretest-posttest, control group" design consists of one experimental group and one control group of test subjects, who are assigned to either group by the process of randomization. It can be illustrated as follows:

$$\text{(EG):} \quad [R] \quad O_1 \text{ æ Æ } X \text{ æ Æ } O_2$$
$$\text{(CG):} \quad [R] \quad O_3 \qquad\qquad O_4$$

With the treatment effect (TE) of the experimental manipulation being

$$TE = (O_2 - O_1) - (O_4 - O_3)$$

This experimental design controls for extraneous factors contributing to the contamination of internal validity, but does not necessarily ensure true internal validity. For example, if extraneous history events produce a difference between O_2 and O_1, and a difference between O_4 and O_3, it can be assumed that the researcher has control for history contamination in the resulting relationship. Yet the researcher cannot directly determine whether the same exact history events occurred in both groups. Certain events may have taken place in the experimental group and not the other, even if the results suggest that there is still internal validity. This can occur due to some disturbance, diversion, or environmental factor influencing the test subjects in the control group. To prevent this problem, the researcher would first randomly assign individuals into experimental and control groups, then have each individual tested for any such disturbance.

Regression, testing, and maturation threats are controlled since differences should be measured equally in experimental and control groups. An instrumentation problem might arise from the researcher knowingly modifying the measuring instrument between the pretest and posttest measures of the dependent variable. Differences in dropout rates among group members can also develop into a mortality issue. Selection is adequately handled through the process of randomization, with match techniques being employed to improve equivalency. Matching should only be used as a supplement to randomization.

Procedural operations of this design are quite simple. To illustrate this point, let's consider testing the impact of a direct mail promotional message regarding customers' knowledge of automobiles. To begin, a sample of individuals would be selected at random. Half would be randomly assigned to the control group, the other half to the experimental group (i.e., the group that receives direct mail on automobiles). Everyone selected would be measured on automobile knowledge. The experimental group would then receive the promotional message and, after an acceptable period of time, the "automobile knowledge" measure would again be administered to all subjects.

Sources of extraneous variation would be realized if differences occurred between the measures of O_4 less O_3 (e.g., an actual product recall occurred during the experiment). However, if this type of extraneous effect did occur, it would be measured equally on those individuals in the experimental group. While the design produces adequate control for internal validity, it does not necessarily do so for external validity. Two factors serve as threats to the external validity of this design: testing and selection contaminations. Pretests run the risk of introducing bias into the design based on the mere topic area being pretested. This can cause unusual attitudes to develop among experimental group subjects that can ultimately bias the posttest measures. In addition, a high mortality rate of subjects can destroy the intentions of sound randomization procedures. If this were a factor, replication of the experiment over time among different groups would be necessary to ensure external validity.

Posttest-Only, Control Group

This experimental design is identical to the previous design except that the pretest measures of the dependent variable are absent. This type of causal design is well practiced if the process of randomization is totally assured. The design is illustrated as follows:

$$\text{(EG):} \quad [R] \quad X \to O_1$$
$$\text{(CG):} \quad [R] \qquad\quad O_2$$

Solomon Four Group

Although a highly complex design, the Solomon Four Group enables the researcher to learn more about internal and external validity than any other experimental design does. But being so complex, marketing researchers do not use it as widely as the other design alternatives. It is illustrated as follows:

Design 1

$$\text{(EG):} \quad [R] \quad O_1 \to X \to O_2$$
$$\text{(CG):} \quad [R] \quad O_3 \qquad\qquad O_4$$

Design 2

$$\text{(EG):} \quad [R] \qquad\qquad X \to O_5$$
$$\text{(CG):} \quad [R] \qquad\qquad\quad O_6$$

The design is a combination of the "pretest-posttest, control group" and the "posttest only, control group" experimental designs. It provides both direct and reactive effects of testing, based on $O_1 \to X \to O_2$ and $X \to O_5$, respectively. External validity is enhanced, along with true experimental effect assurance by comparing $[O_2$ less $O_1]$, $[O_2$ less $O_4]$, $[O_5$ less $O_6]$, and $[O_5$ less $O_3]$. When these four comparisons agree, the researcher's ability to infer that the resulting functional relationship between the dependent and independent variables is being caused by the experimental independent variable treatment dramatically increases.

Quasi-experimental Designs

Between the extremes of pre-experimental designs (which have little or no control) and true experimental designs (based on randomization), we have the quasi-experimental designs. These designs are appropriate when the researcher can control some variables (e.g., price level, media vehicle, package design) but cannot establish equal experimental and control groups based on randomization (e.g., store types or customer groups). While there are many different types of quasi-experimental designs available to marketing researchers, as illustrated in Exhibit 10.4, we will focus only on the two more widely used ones: (1) nonequivalent control group and (2) separate-sample, pretest-posttest.[12]

EXHIBIT 10.4	Summary of Other Quasi-Experimental Designs Used in Marketing Research Practices
Nonequivalent dependent variable design	Single group of test subjects and pretest measures on two scales, one that is expected to change due to treatment manipulation and one that is not. This design is restricted to theoretical contexts where differential change is predicted. The design must be powerful enough to determine that the nontreated variable is reliably measured. These results are interpretable only when the two outcome measures are conceptually similar and both would be affected by the same nontreatment effect.
Removed treatment design with pretest and posttest	There could be an ethical problem in the removing of the treatment manipulation in the second scenario. There needs to be a noticeable discontinuity after the removal of the second treatment; otherwise, it could be that the initial treatment had no long-term effects.
Repeated treatment design	This design is most interpretable when the results of the first experiment occur in the same direction as the second experiment and the initial pretest measure differs from any of the following test measures. This design is best when there are unobservable treatments and long periods between a treatment and its reintroduction.
Reversed-treatment, non-equivalent control group design	This design requires both pretest and posttest measures and directional hypotheses. There is potential for high construct validity, but it depends on the research revealing the existence of an inverse relationship.
Cohort designs with cyclical turnover	*Cohorts* are test subjects who follow each other through a formal institutional environment such as school or work. In this type of design, the researcher pretests a group of test subjects, then gives the treatment manipulation to the next group and collects posttest measures from the second group. The major underlying premise to this type of quasi-experimental design is that the samples are drawn from the same population. This design can eliminate the threats of history and testing by stratifying the treatment groups.
Regression discontinuity design	This causal design is used when the experimental groups are given rewards or those in special need are given extra assistance. The regressed lines for the treatment and nontreatment groups should be different due to the effect of the treatment. Interpretation of the results becomes difficult with the possibility of curvilinear relationships. The knowledge of the reward could lead to extra actions in order to receive it.

Nonequivalent Control Group

Commonly used in marketing research, the "nonequivalent control group" design differs from the true experimental designs in that the experimental and control groups are not equivalent. It can be illustrated as follows:

$$\text{Group 1} \quad \text{(EG):} \quad O_1 \ æ \ Æ X æ \ Æ \ O_2$$
$$\text{Group 2} \quad \text{(CG):} \quad O_3 \qquad\qquad O_4$$

This quasi-experimental design can operate at two levels. The intact equivalent design allows experimental and control groups to be formed in natural settings. For example, many marketing research quasi experiments recruit test subjects from established organizations such as church clubs or civic groups; they also use customers from similar stores. Ideally, the groups should be as similar as possible. In this self-selected experimental group design, group membership is based on the subject's interest or desire to participate. Many times, this is accomplished by selecting test subjects from a shopping mall, whereas control subjects are selected based on availability.

The difference between O_1 and O_3 becomes an indication of equivalency between the experimental and control groups. If pretest measures are significantly different, group compatibility must be seriously questioned. However, if the measures appear similar, then there is an increased certainty of internal validity. While this design may conform to sound validity practices, it is highly dependent on the circumstances that lead to the selection of test subjects.

Separate-Sample, Pretest-Posttest

When it is virtually impossible to determine who is to receive the independent treatment manipulation, but when measures of the dependent variable can be determined, a "separate-sample, pretest-posttest" design is an appropriate choice. This design can be illustrated as follows:

$$
\begin{array}{ll}
\text{Sample 1} & O_1 \ \text{æ} \ \text{Æ} \ (X) \\
\text{Sample 2} & \phantom{O_1 \ \text{æ} \ \text{Æ}} \ X \ \text{æ} \ \text{Æ} \ O_2
\end{array}
$$

When the experimental treatment manipulation (X) is insignificant to the research, it simply indicates that the experimental group of test subjects cannot be controlled for treatment. Although this is a weak design, it is not an uncommon situation in marketing research practices. This type of quasi design is most often used when the population is large, a pretest measure will not produce any meaningful information, and there is no way to control for application of the experimental manipulation. This quasi-experimental framework is commonly used in advertising research. Let's say, for example, that the advertising agency for Home Depot, the "do-it-yourself" building supply chain, may be launching a major image campaign. First, it draws two samples of test subjects. One sample is interviewed about their perception of Home Depot's image (dependent variable) prior to the image campaign. After the campaign ends, test subjects in the second group are interviewed about their perception of Home Depot.

Obviously, this design must deal with a number of threats to internal validity. History and morality are the greatest concerns. Repetition of the experiment over several settings can reduce these effects somewhat. Yet this quasi-experimental design is considered superior to true experiments with regard to external validity. This occurs from its natural setting and the use of large samples of test subjects who are representative of the target group. Overall, the reason why quasi-experimental designs are practiced in marketing research is that they conform to a natural setting. Thus, they are a type of field experiment. Field experiments, to which we devote the next section of this chapter, provide valuable information to the researcher because they allow both functional and causal relationships to be generalized to the target population.

Field Experiments

Field experiments
Causal research designs that manipulate the independent variables in order to measure the dependent variable in a natural setting of the test.

Field experiments are causal research designs that manipulate the independent variables in order to measure the dependent variable in the natural setting of the test. Field experiments are often conducted in retail environments such as malls, supermarkets, or other retail stores. These settings tend to create a high level of realism. However, high levels of realism contribute to a lack of control of the independent variables and increase extraneous variation. Problems with control can occur in several ways. For example, conducting a field experiment of a new product in a supermarket requires the retailer's commitment to authorize the product in the store. Today, retailers are becoming more hesitant about adding new products, given the large number of new-product introductions each year. Even if the product is authorized, proper display and retailer support are needed to appropriately conduct the experiment. Competition can also negatively influence a field experiment. In some field experiments of new products, competitors have negatively affected sales of the experimental product by using heavy price discounts and promotions to increase sales of their own products at the time of the test.

Considerations for Using Field Experiments

Besides realism and control, there are at least three other issues to consider when deciding whether or not to use a field experiment: time frames, costs, and competitive reactions. Field experiments take longer to complete than laboratory experiments. The planning stage—which can include determining which test market cities to use and which retailers to approach with product experiments, securing advertising time, and coordinating the distribution of the experimental product—adds to the length of time needed to conduct field experiments. Field experiments are more expensive to conduct than laboratory experiments because of the high number of independent variables that must be manipulated. For example, the cost of an advertising campaign alone can increase the cost of the experiment. Other items adding to the cost of field experiments are coupons, product packaging development, trade promotions, and product sampling. Because field experiments are conducted in a natural setting, competitors can learn about the new product almost as soon as it is introduced, and can respond by using heavy promotional activity or by rushing similar products to market. If secrecy is desired, then laboratory experiments are generally more effective.

Validity Concerns

In deciding whether to use field experiments, researchers should consider the proposed experiment's internal validity and external validity. Although the ideal experiment would be high in both internal and external validity, this is difficult to achieve in a field setting; usually a trade-off must be made. Researchers who want to be able to generalize an experiment's results to other settings or markets might select field experiments. If the lack of control over the independent variables associated with field experiments is a concern, then laboratory experiments are more appropriate for assessing the true functional relationship.[13] Researchers opting for field experiments can choose from several types depending on the objectives of the experiment and the considerations mentioned above. The next section discusses the most common type of field experiment—test marketing—and includes overviews of five different methods for conducting market tests.

Test Marketing

We defined *test marketing* at the beginning of this chapter as the use of controlled field experiments to gain information on specified market performance indicators. Companies have several options available when choosing a test marketing method. Regardless of the method used, test marketing measures the sales potential of a product and evaluates variables in the product's marketing mix. The cost of conducting test marketing experiments can be high. However, with the failure rate of new consumer products estimated to be between 80 and 90 percent, many companies believe the expense of conducting a test market experiment can help them avoid the more expensive mistake of an unsuccessful product rollout. Exhibit 10.5 presents the five types of test marketing methods most popular in marketing practices: traditional, controlled, electronic, simulated, and virtual.[14]

Traditional Test Markets

The most frequently used form of test marketing is a *traditional test market*. This method tests a product's marketing mix variables through existing distribution channels. Companies select specific cities, or test markets, which have demographic and market characteristics similar to those of the targeted users of the product or service being tested. The most

EXHIBIT 10.5	Different Types of Test Marketing Used in Marketing Research

Types of Test Marketing	Comments
Traditional test markets	Also referred to as "standard" tests; these use experimental design procedures to test a product and/or a product's marketing mix variables through existing distribution channels.
Controlled test markets	Tests that are performed by an outside research firm that guarantees distribution of the test product through prespecified outlets in selected cities.
Electronic test markets	Tests that integrate the use of select panels of consumers who use a special identification card in recording their product-purchasing data.
Simulated test markets	Also referred to as "laboratory tests" or "test market simulations." These are quasi experiments where test subjects are preselected, then interviewed and observed on their purchases and attitudes toward the test product.
Virtual test markets	Tests that are completely computerized, allowing the test subjects to observe and interact with the product as though they were actually in the test store's environment.

common use of a traditional test is to evaluate consumer acceptance of a new product or variation of an existing product. For example, Procter & Gamble test-marketed Sunny Delight Smoothies, a blend of Sunny Delight fruit beverage and milk, in Mobile, Alabama, and New Orleans, Louisiana.[15] In addition, test marketing is used to evaluate the potential of new marketing concepts. Spalding, a major sporting goods manufacturer, test-marketed a women's theme shop in 58 stores of four national sporting goods retailers in an effort to reach female consumers.[16]

Advantages and Disadvantages of Traditional Test Markets

The primary advantage of a traditional test is that the test is conducted in actual distribution channels. Other test marketing methods attempt to simulate distribution channels, while traditional test markets place products in actual distribution outlets, typically retail outlets. In addition to measuring consumer acceptance of a product, standard test markets can determine the level of trade support for the tested item. If retailers are reluctant to give a company additional shelf space or displays for the new product, then plans for the product rollout may need to be reevaluated. Even products that have a high level of consumer appeal will have difficulty succeeding if certain levels of distribution cannot be attained.

The limitations of traditional test markets are cost, time, and exposure to competition. First, traditional test markets are much more expensive compared to laboratory experiments. Expenses incurred during a traditional test market include product development, packaging, distribution, and advertising and promotion. Second, traditional test markets require more time to conduct than other forms of test marketing. Most standard test markets take between 12 and 18 months to complete. Third, because traditional test marketing uses actual distribution channels, other companies are able to observe a competitor's activity and can take action to hurt a test market. Competitors can respond with heavy promotional activity such as increased advertising, more coupons, and deep price discounts to combat the test product.

Also, a lengthy test market allows competitors to rush competing products into the market, thus taking away the testing company's advantage of being first to market. The combination of time and competitive pressures has changed the ways in which many companies introduce new products. The need to introduce products more quickly than competitors is leading to large-scale rollouts of new products. The traditional approach of beginning with a test market and then increasing distribution region by region is being replaced, in many cases, by introducing a product in multiple regions simultaneously. In addition, test marketing does not always mean success, as illustrated in Exhibit 10.6, which describes the problems experienced by Coors.

Controlled Test Markets

A second type of test market is a *controlled test market.* A controlled test market is performed by an outside firm that guarantees distribution of the test product through outlets in selected cities. ACNielsen and Audits & Surveys are two firms that offer controlled test marketing services. These companies offer financial incentives to distributors to allow the test product to be added to the product line. The outside firm handles all distribution functions for its client during the test market, including inventory, stocking, pricing, and billing. Sales data are gathered by the research firm. UPC scanner data and consumer surveys are used to compile information on trial and repeat rates, market penetration, and consumer demographics.

Advantages and Disadvantages of Controlled Test Markets

Controlled test markets overcome many of the disadvantages of traditional test markets. First, distribution of the test product is assured by the outside firm handling the test market. Second, the cost of a controlled test market is less than that of a traditional test market. Third, competitive monitoring of a controlled test market is somewhat difficult compared with traditional test markets, given the level of control that can be implemented.

EXHIBIT 10.6　　Good Test Market Results Do Not Guarantee New-Product Success

---

Coors Gives the Cold Shoulder to Wine Coolers

Adolph Coors Company, manufacturer of Coors beer, suffered through a series of new-product disasters in the early 1980s, so when the company made a second attempt to enter the wine cooler market it relied on simulated test marketing to determine consumer acceptance for its new offering.

The company's test marketing woes began in 1978 when it introduced Coors Light. By the time the Coors product reached the market, Miller Lite was firmly entrenched as the number one light beer. The slow rollout did not seem to bother the company. In fact, it was consistent with their philosophy. Pete Coors remarked that his company let other companies do the pioneering work, referring to product development. "Then we'll take what they've done, and do it better," he added. Another product failure, Killian's Irish Red Ale, was introduced in 1982 using traditional test markets. The product stalled in the test marketing phase before national rollout could happen. Perhaps the worst experience was with Herman Josephs, a new beer positioned as a premium-priced beer that was supposed to compete with Michelob and Löwenbräu. Once again, Coors relied on traditional test marketing, planning to iron out bugs in the product and marketing mix before introducing the product in all markets. The test marketing for Herman Josephs began in 1981. Coors abandoned the product in 1989 after years of remaining in the test market phase.

Coors had made a previous attempt to enter the wine cooler market with its Colorado Chiller coolers. The failure of Colorado Chiller was attributed in part to failure to get input from consumers about the product. Coors sought to correct this mistake when another cooler product, Crystal Springs Cooler, was tested in 1986. The company used simulated test marketing (STM) to find out how consumers would respond to the new product. Results of the STM were encouraging. Approximately 63 percent of cooler drinkers surveyed were interested in purchasing Crystal Springs Cooler, and 74 percent said they would buy the product after sampling it. Sales projections for Crystal Springs exceeded 300,000 barrels per year, which would have been Coors's third largest product. In 1987, the company decided to discontinue its plans for Crystal Springs Cooler. Undoubtedly, its past new-product failures left Coors with little confidence about rolling out a new product like Crystal Springs Cooler despite strong test marketing results.

Source: Robert Burgess, "Coors Chiller Fiasco Cost Brewer Dearly," *The Denver Business Journal* 44, no. 32 (April 23, 1993), p. 1A.

Controlled test markets are not without limits. First, the limited number of markets used makes accurate projections of sales and market penetration difficult. Second, the amount of actual trade support for a test product may be unclear if the research firm offered incentives to retailers to obtain shelf space. Will trade acceptance of the new product be the same without incentives? Third, the effect of a proposed advertising program is difficult to evaluate.

Despite these limitations, controlled test markets can be beneficial for marketers. Many companies use controlled test markets to determine whether a product warrants a full-scale standard test market. Also, controlled test markets are used to test such pricing and promotional variables as coupons and displays.

Electronic Test Markets

An *electronic test market* gathers data from consumers who agree to carry an identification card that they present when buying goods or services at participating retailers in selected cities. The test is performed by an outside firm such as ACNielsen or Information Resources Inc. The advantage of this method is the identification card allows the researcher to collect demographic data on consumers who purchase the test product. A primary disadvantage of this method is that the card-carrying consumers probably are not representative of the entire market because they are not chosen at random. In addition, there is a high cost associated with the use of advanced technologies. As a result, small businesses normally cannot afford electronic test marketing.

Simulated Test Markets

Another type of test market that uses computer models to estimate consumer response to a new marketing program is a *simulated test market (STM)*. STMs are used to project sales volume and to evaluate the planned marketing mix. Some common STM services are Assessor, Bases II, ESP, and Litmus. While each of these methods uses its own approach to sampling, questionnaires, and modeling, the overall process normally includes the following steps:

1. Potential participants are screened to satisfy certain demographic and product usage criteria.

2. Participants are shown commercials or print advertisements for the test product, as well as commercials or print advertisements for other products. These products may be competitive or noncompetitive.

3. Participants are then allowed to purchase items in a simulated retail store. Regardless of whether the test item is selected, the participants receive a free sample.

4. After a usage period, participants are contacted to gather information on the product as well as their repurchase intentions.[17]

Advantages and Disadvantages of Simulated Test Markets

STMs offer several advantages. First, STMs can offer substantial cost and time savings. STMs can be conducted in four to six months, compared with a year or more for traditional test markets, and they cost approximately 5 to 10 percent of what a traditional test market costs. Second, a simulation can predict product trial rate, repurchase rate, and purchase cycle length with a great deal of accuracy. Third, computer modeling allows several alternative marketing mix plans to be tested for their effect on sales volume. Finally, exposure to competition is minimized because the test market is not conducted in normal channels of distribution.[18]

The isolation of STMs from the real-world environment leads to some weaknesses with this method. Trade acceptance of a new product cannot be measured using STMs—it must be assumed. A traditional test market would be more desirable if a company believes agreement for distribution with the trade will be difficult to secure. For example, Ore-Ida once conducted an STM for a new product in which it assumed a 90 percent distribution rate in the normal channels. However, the actual distribution rate was only 10 percent, making the sales volume projections from the STM impossible to attain. Second, broad-based consumer reaction to a new product is difficult to measure using STMs. A traditional test market allows a larger number of consumers the opportunity to try a new product. In addition, STMs are more effective in estimating trial rates than repurchase rates. However, a good estimate of repurchase intentions is needed to determine a new product's potential for success. Third, although STMs cost less than traditional test markets, they are still expensive, at a cost of $75,000 to $150,000. Only the largest of companies have the option of using STMs.[19]

STMs are a very effective method for testing new products, especially variations of an existing brand or category of consumer package goods. For example, when Reynolds Metal Company introduced Reynolds Crystal Color plastic wrap, a variation of the traditional Reynolds clear plastic wrap, it used an STM to evaluate the potential of the new product. In the STM, 40 percent of the participants indicated they would definitely try it, which is double the average predicted trial rate for new products.[20]

STMs serve two important purposes. First, they can be used as either a substitute or a supplement to traditional test markets. STMs can be used as a substitute when the risk of product failure or cost is less than that for a traditional test market. They can be used as a supplement to test combinations of marketing mix variables prior to a traditional test market introduction, when making changes would be too costly, if not impossible. Second, STMs can serve as a pilot test to determine whether a particular concept or product has the potential for success. If not, the idea can be dropped before further testing increases the cost of the mistake.

Virtual Test Markets

The idea of using computer simulation to test product acceptance is taken to a different level in a *virtual test market*. In virtual test markets, not only can different marketing mixes be evaluated using computer modeling, but even the simulated store itself appears on a computer screen. Using this method, participants can view store shelves stocked with many different kinds of products. The shoppers can pick up an item by touching its image on the monitor, and they can examine the product by moving a tracking ball device that rotates the image. Items are purchased by placing them in a shopping cart which appears on the screen. Information collected during this process includes the amount of time the consumer spends shopping in each product category, the time the consumer spends examining each side of a package, the quantity of product purchased, and the order of items purchased.[21]

Advantages and Disadvantages of Virtual Test Markets

Although virtual test markets are similar to simulated test markets, they do offer some unique advantages. First, the "stores" that appear in virtual test markets more closely resemble actual stores than the ones created in simulated test markets. Second, researchers can make changes in the stores rather quickly. Different arrays of brands, pricing, packaging, promotions, and shelf space allocations can appear in a matter of minutes. Third, virtual test markets can be used for different purposes. They can be used to test entirely new concepts or products as well as to test for changes in existing products. Finally, as with simulated test markets, virtual test markets allow for these tests to be conducted without exposure to competition.

A CLOSER LOOK AT RESEARCH   In the Field

Goodyear Steps Out of Its Own Stores

Goodyear Tire and Rubber Company used virtual test marketing to evaluate a major change in distribution strategy. For many years, the company sold its tires through its own retail outlets. The new strategy was to sell Goodyear tires through general merchandise stores and still maintain the current system of Goodyear stores. While such a move would no doubt allow Goodyear to reach more consumers, the new strategy would place Goodyear tires in direct competition with other brands in the general merchandise stores. Goodyear questioned whether this increased competition would dictate a change in marketing strategy. Specifically, the company needed to determine what the level of brand equity was for its products. Was it strong enough to be able to charge a premium over other brands, or would it be forced to reduce prices and/or extend warranties to be competitive with other brands?

Goodyear turned to virtual test marketing to find answers to its questions. The company conducted a study of 1,000 consumers who had recently bought or planned to purchase passenger tires, high-performance tires, or light-truck tires. Participants shopped several different virtual tire stores, each store offering a different assortment of products, pricing, and warranties. Goodyear believed it achieved brand equity if a consumer purchased a Goodyear product at a higher price than competitors' products, if it captured sales from competitors when Goodyear products were reduced in price, and if it maintained sales levels despite competitors' price cuts.

The results of the study assisted Goodyear in several ways. First, the company determined how shoppers in different product-market segments valued the Goodyear brand compared with competing brands. Second, the virtual market test allowed the company to test many different pricing strategies. This feature allowed Goodyear to evaluate how different prices, both its own and competitors' prices, affected consumer tendencies to switch brands. Third, major competitors were identified. Goodyear is aware of the companies it should consider its major competitors in general merchandise stores.

Source: Raymond R. Burke, "Virtual Shopping: Breakthrough in Marketing Research," *Harvard Business Review*, March/April 1996, p. 120.

The disadvantages of virtual test markets are similar to those of simulated test markets. The primary concern for many companies is whether consumers will shop in virtual stores using the same patterns they use in actual stores. However, research into this concern suggests that there is a high degree of correlation between virtual store and actual store sales. A study in which 300 consumers took six trips through a virtual store and an actual store to purchase cleaning and health-and-beauty-aid products revealed similar market shares. Correlations were .94 for the cleaning product and .90 for the health-and-beauty-aid product. Another concern is the cost of the computer hardware and software needed to conduct virtual test markets. While the cost is still prohibitive for many companies, improvements in technology should lower it in the future. Finally, in a virtual store, consumers cannot feel, smell, or touch a product. Items that involve special handling from consumers might not be suited for virtual test marketing. Virtual test markets can be used to study such questions as the following:

1. What is our brand equity in a new retail channel?

2. Do we offer a sufficient variety of products?

3. How should products be displayed?[22]

The In the Field box provides an example of how one company used virtual test markets for a purpose other than new-product evaluation.

Other Issues in Test Marketing

Consumer versus Industrial Test Marketing

Our discussion of test marketing has centered on the evaluation of consumer products. However, test marketing is used by manufacturers of industrial products as well, though with different methods. Rather than develop a product for trial in the market, industrial manufacturers seek input from customers to determine the features and technologies needed for new products. Manufacturers develop prototypes based on customers' input. These prototypes are then evaluated by selected customers. The manufacturers receive feedback from customers involved in the product test and use the feedback to make further changes to the product before introducing it to the entire market. As with consumer test markets, industrial test markets can be lengthy. The longer a test market runs, the more likely it is that a competitor will learn of the new product and respond by rushing a similar product to market or by becoming more competitive with existing products.

Matching Experimental Method with Objectives

When selecting a test marketing method, researchers should consider the objectives of the experiment. For example, if a company is test-marketing an extension of its present product line, maybe a new color or flavor, it would be interested in the consumer acceptance of this new product. Therefore, it will want experiment results that can be generalized to all markets, not just the test markets (high external validity). Also, it would want to observe how the new product performs in the market relative to the competition or how the trade accepts the new product. The decision for the company would be whether to use a standard test market or use a simulated or virtual test market. This decision is based on factors mentioned earlier (time, cost, exposure to competition). Regardless of the method chosen, the objective is to project the potential of the new product for the entire market.

Other field experiments may require more control over the real-world variables. Consider a company that wants to evaluate the effectiveness of an advertising campaign for a new product. While the ability to generalize the results of the experiment to the entire market is important, the company must try to determine whether a relationship is present between the advertising campaign and consumers' acceptance of the new product. In other words, did the promotional campaign influence sales, or did the influence come from other variables, such as pricing, display position, or competition? This objective requires that the experiment have high internal validity. An experimental design for this objective might be an electronic test market that can record information about the consumers' television viewing (did they view the advertisement?), and purchase and repurchase behaviors (did they buy the advertised product and, if so, how many times?), and determine whether a relationship exists between the advertising campaign and product sales. Such an experiment might not be generalizable, but the company can determine whether the advertising campaign has the intended effect on a small sample of consumers. If the results are positive, the company might roll out the advertising campaign to other areas or even nationwide. If the results are not positive, the company can make changes to the advertising campaign or drop it completely.

Each test marketing approach possesses certain strengths and weaknesses. The researcher must weigh these strengths and weaknesses with the objectives of the field experiment. Once the researcher identifies the objective of the experiment, he or she can select the method that offers the greatest amount of the desired validity, internal or external.

Some of the difficulties associated with standard test markets are leading to two developing trends in new-product testing. First, companies that do not want to undertake the time and expense of standard test markets could turn to simulated and virtual test markets. Also, the growing resistance of retailers to add thousands of new products to product authorization lists may lead more companies to use test marketing methods other than standard test markets. Second, companies that find the standard test market process difficult, but that are not willing to try other methods, might begin to roll out more products without any test marketing, especially if the risk of product failure is low.

Overview of Observational Techniques

Observation   The systematic process of witnessing and recording the behavioral patterns of objects, people, and events without directly communicating with them.

Now that we have discussed the different research designs (exploratory, descriptive, causal) available to marketing researchers, we will close this chapter with an overview of the *observational techniques* used by researchers. While most research texts portray observation methods as a separate type of research design, isolating them to their own chapter, we treat observational techniques as *tools* for collecting primary data in all types of research designs (exploratory, descriptive, causal). Characteristic of all observational techniques is the notion that researchers must rely heavily on their powers of observing rather than actually communicating with people to collect primary data. Basically, the researcher depends on watching and recording what people do. In marketing research, **observation** refers to the systematic process of witnessing and recording the behavioral patterns of objects, people, and events without directly communicating with them. One of the main reasons for using observation methods is to generate primary data structures as events occur or to compile evidence of behaviors from records of past events. Normally, employment of observational techniques requires a behavior or event to be observed and a system of recording it. Recording can be achieved by using such devices as videotapes, movie cameras, audiotapes, handwritten notes and logs, or some other tangible recording mechanism.

Appropriate Conditions for Using Observational Techniques

Several conditions are required for the successful use of observation as an information research tool. The information research objectives must clearly indicate that some type of event or behavior is to be witnessed. For the most part, the event or behavior must be repetitive, frequent, and relatively predictable. Finally, the behavior normally should take place in some type of public setting that allows the researcher to observe the behavior directly. Exhibit 10.7 summarizes these important conditions.

Information Condition

If current behavior patterns are important to the success of the study, then the researcher must give consideration to using an observational data collection technique. Trying to collect current-behavior data using any other method might lessen the data's accuracy and meaningfulness due to faulty recall on the part of the subjects. For example, people might not accurately recall the number of times they zap commercials while watching their favorite one-hour TV program on Monday nights.

Type-of-Data Condition

If the researcher wants to know why an individual purchased one brand of cereal over the other brands available, observational techniques alone will not provide the answers. Observation methods do not allow for accurately collecting the motivations, beliefs, attitudes, or feelings that may underlie the observable behavior. Only in those cases when a respondent's feelings are relatively unimportant to the research objective or believed to be readily inferable from the behavior might it be appropriate to use solely observational techniques. For example, in studying children playing with toys, it is possible to use facial

EXHIBIT 10.7	Conditions for Using Observational Techniques

Condition	Brief Description
Information	Current behavior patterns must be part of the data requirements.
Type of data	Necessary data must be observable.
Time frame	Data patterns must meet repetitiveness, frequency, and predictability factors in a prespecified time frame.
Setting	Behavior must be observable in some type of public or laboratory setting.

expressions as an indicator of a child's attitudes or preferences toward the toys because children often react with conspicuous physical expressions. However, this type of observation places extreme pressures on the investigator's interpretive skills.

Time-Frame Condition

For observational techniques to be feasible, the investigated behaviors or events need to be completed within a relatively short time span. That means they also must be repetitive and frequent. For example, attempting to observe all the activities involved during the process of buying a new home or automobile would be infeasible in terms of data collection costs and time.

Setting Condition

Activities are limited to those that the investigator can readily observe firsthand or through a mechanical device such as a video camera. Normally, activities such as private worshiping or using in-home products (e.g., products used when cooking, turning up and down air conditioning controls, or washing clothes) are not readily observable.

It is important to recognize that all four conditions for using observational techniques apply to those situations involving *current* events. They do not really hold for situations in which researchers are interested in collecting data on *past* events, since it is impossible to observe those events firsthand. Some experts suggest that indirect observational techniques can be used to accurately infer past behaviors or events. What researchers normally observe in those situations is some type of artifact (e.g., a video- or audiotape, a written transcript).[23] These artifacts are often like secondary data. The main emphasis would be on interpreting the reported outcomes and making preliminary inductive statements about the actual behavior.

Unique Characteristics of Observational Techniques

There are four long-acknowledged general characteristics of observational techniques for collecting primary data (see Exhibit 10.8). Depending on the researcher's need for (1) directness, (2) subjects' awareness, (3) structuredness, and (4) a certain type of observing/recording mechanism, he or she can choose from a number of ways to observe events and record primary data. The main thing to remember about these characteristics is that they directly influence the framework for conducting the observations. It is critically important that the observation methods are designed to allow for the gathering of consistent and generalizable primary data. With good designs, researchers can eliminate, or at least control for, possible methodological differences or other problems that could confound the findings.

EXHIBIT 10.8	Unique Characteristics of Observation Research Methods

Characteristic	Description
Directness of observation	The degree to which the researcher or trained observer actually observes the behavior/event as it occurs. Researchers can use either *direct* or *indirect* observation techniques.
Subjects' awareness of being observed	The degree to which subjects consciously know their behavior is being observed and recorded. Researchers may use either *disguised* or *undisguised* observation techniques.
Structuredness of observation	The degree to which the behavior activities or events to be observed are specifically known to the researcher prior to doing the observations. *Structured* and *unstructured* techniques are available to collect primary behavioral data.
Type of observing mechanism	How the behavior activities or events will be observed and recorded. Basically researchers have the option either of using a *trained human observer* or some type of *mechanical device*.

Directness of Observation

Direct observation The process of observing actual behaviors or events and recording them as they occur.

Simply put, **direct observation** is the process of observing actual behavioral activities or events and recording them as they occur. Direct observation uses a human being, rather than a mechanical device, for observing and recording actual behaviors. For example, if researchers were interested in conducting a field experiment to find out how often people read tabloid magazines while waiting to check out at a supermarket, they could use any of several different direct observation techniques. In contrast, some experts believe that indirect observation techniques can be used to capture subjects' past behaviors in special situations.[24] As discussed earlier, **indirect observation** focuses on directly observing the artifacts that, at best, represent specific behaviors from some earlier time. It can be easily argued that this direct observing of artifacts of past human behavior is really nothing more than a trained investigator interpreting a form of secondary data. While indirect observation might allow a researcher some preliminary insights into past behaviors, those insights should be viewed as tenuous, at best. For example, management of Tech Data, a company that sells computer systems nationwide, can review and interpret the company's telephone logs to find out how many long-distance telephone calls its sales department made during the previous month. After interpreting the logs, management might make general inferences concerning the impact of cold-calling behaviors of highly productive salespeople compared to less productive salespeople. Secondary sources that record past behavior tend to be referred to as *archives, physical audits,* or *traces.*[25] These types of artifacts simply represent tangible evidence of some past event. For example, a retail chain looking to expand its operations to new locations might directly observe the amount of graffiti on existing buildings around proposed site locations to estimate the potential crime factor in those areas.

Indirect observation The process of directly observing the recorded artifacts of past behaviors.

Subjects' Awareness of Being Observed

This characteristic refers to the degree to which subjects consciously know their behavior is being observed and recorded. When the subjects are completely unaware that they are being observed, the observation method is termed *disguised observation*. A popular and easy-to-understand example of disguised observation is the "mystery-shopper" technique used by many retailers. A retailer such as Wal-Mart hires a research firm to send in well-trained observers disguised as ordinary shoppers to observe how well the stores' employees and staff interact with customers. The observers might look for interpersonal behavior that would demonstrate attributes like friendliness, courtesy, helpfulness, and store/product knowledge. The resulting data can aid Wal-Mart's management in determining how its employees' interpersonal skills can enhance the customers' overall shopping experience. Wal-Mart's management can use other methods (e.g., one-way mirrors and hidden cameras) to prevent its employees from knowing or becoming aware that they are being observed. Disguised observations are used because, if people know they are being watched, they naturally tend to modify their normal behavior. The resulting behavior would therefore be atypical. For example, if you were a salesclerk for Wal-Mart, how would you act if the store manager told you that she would be watching you for the next several hours? Most likely you would be on your best behavior for that time period.

Researchers may, however, face situations in which it is impossible to keep the subjects from knowing that they are being observed. Take, for example, observing such activities as the interpersonal behavior of a new waiter or waitress with customers at a restaurant like T.G.I.F. in Washington, D.C., or textbook sales representatives' behavior with faculty members on sales calls. Nielsen Media Research would find it difficult to use its audiometers on in-home TV sets without the subjects' knowledge or awareness. Whenever the subjects are aware that they are being watched, the process is termed *undisguised observation.* As a general practice, the presence of the observer should be minimized to avoid the possibility of atypical behavior by subjects.

Structuredness of Observation

This characteristic refers to the degree to which the behaviors or events are specifically known to the researcher prior to the observation. When a researcher knows specifically which behaviors or events are to be recorded, a *structured observation* technique is most appropriate. In these situations, all other behaviors are ignored by the trained observer. Some type of checklist or standardized recording form is used to help the observer restrict his or her attention to just those prespecified behaviors or events.

In contrast, *unstructured observation* formats place no restrictions on the observer regarding what should be recorded. Ideally, all events would be observed and recorded. In employing an unstructured technique, what usually happens is that the trained observers are briefed on the research objectives and information requirements and then allowed to use their own discretion (based on interest and relevancy) in determining what behaviors are actually recorded. For example, let's say that the director of parks and recreation in your town or city wanted to develop a proposal for renovating several of the city's aging parks. Not sure what type of equipment should be included in the renovations, he sends out two park supervisors to observe people using the facilities at several of the city's most popular parks. The primary data collected could prove to be useful in not only redesigning the aging parks but also in providing ideas about how to make the parks more safe for people.

Type of Observing Mechanism

This characteristic relates to how the behaviors or events will be observed. The researcher can choose between human and mechanical observers. With *human observation,* the observer is either a person hired and trained by the researcher or part of the researcher team itself. To be effective, the observer must have strong observation skills and a good understanding of the research objectives. There are many situations where it might be more desirable to use a *mechanical device,* instead of a person, to collect the primary data. Such devices may reduce the cost and improve the flexibility, accuracy, or other functions of the research. An example would be a traffic-flow study. In this case, air pressure lines could be laid across the road and connected to a mechanical counter box that would be activated every time a car's tires rolled over the lines. While the data collected would be limited to the number of vehicles passing by within a specified time span, this method would be less costly and more accurate than using human observers to record traffic flows. Other examples of appropriate mechanical observation include using security cameras at ATM locations, using scanning devices to count the number and types of products purchased at a retail establishment, and taking turnstile counts of fans at major sporting or entertainment events. With advances in high technology, telecommunications, and computer hardware and software, mechanical observation techniques are rapidly becoming very useful and cost-effective for collecting certain types of primary data.[26]

Selecting the Appropriate Observation Method

To determine the most appropriate type of observation method for collecting primary data, researchers must integrate their knowledge and understanding of the defined research objective, specific information requirements, conditions for using observations, and characteristics of observation methods.

The first step in determining the right observation method is for the researcher to understand the specific information requirements and give consideration to how that information will be used later on. Without this understanding, the task of deciding a technique's appropriateness becomes significantly more difficult. The researcher must answer the following questions prior to method selection: (1) What types of behavior are pertinent to the defined research problem?; (2) How simple or complex are the behaviors?; (3) How much detail of the behavior needs to be recorded?; and (4) What is the most appropriate setting (natural or contrived) for the behavior? Only after the researcher gains at least a basic understanding of the information needs can he or she undertake the second step.

The second step involves integrating the researcher's knowledge of the conditions for observing behavior and the characteristics of observation methods in order to develop an objective method of observing and recording the specified behavior. The issues that must be addressed include the following: (1) How complex is the required public setting? Is it available for observing the specified behaviors or events?; (2) To what extent are the desired behaviors or events repetitious and frequently exhibited?; (3) What degrees of directness and structuredness should be associated with observing the behaviors or events?; (4) How aware should the subjects be that they and their behaviors are being observed?; and (5) Are the observable behaviors or events complex enough to require the use of a mechanical device for observing the behavior? If so, which specific method would be most appropriate?

The last step focuses on the cost, flexibility, accuracy, efficiency, and objectivity factors associated with observational techniques, as well as the ethical issues. Prior to implementing any observation method, the researcher must assess the proposed method's ability to accurately observe and record the specified behavior. The costs—time, money, manpower—involved must be determined and compared to the expected efficiency of collecting the data based, in part, on the number of subjects needed in the investigation. In addition, the researcher must consider the possible ethical issues that might exist with the proposed observation method. The Ethics box discusses ethical issues associated with observation methods.

Highlights of the Benefits and Limitations of Observational Techniques

Observational data collection techniques have several specific strengths and weaknesses worthy of discussion (see Exhibit 10.9). Probably the most obvious benefit is that observational techniques allow for very accurate gathering of consumers' actual behavior patterns or marketing events rather than reported activities. This is especially true in those situations

ETHICS

The *subjects' awareness* characteristic of observation methods raises some ethical questions worth noting. When using observations to collect primary behavior data, should the subjects be informed that they are being observed? If so, what changes in their natural behavior might occur? Remember, the researcher wants to capture the subjects' natural behavior as it *actually occurs* and *relates* to the specified situation. Subjects being observed might feel uncomfortable about their true behavior or actions and try to behave in a more socially acceptable manner. For example, a marketing professor at a certain university is told by his department chair that as part of his annual performance review, on Thursday an outside observer will be in class to observe the professor's teaching style. How likely will the professor be to modify his "normal" classroom behavior for that

Thursday's class session to make double sure that his effectiveness meets or exceeds the standards? Would you behave in a more socially acceptable manner if you knew someone was going to be observing you? In disguised observations, the researcher resorts to using some degree of deceit in order to capture behavior without the subjects' knowledge. In this situation, the ethical questions focus on the subjects' right to privacy. Are there certain public or private behaviors that are protected by U.S. law? Is spying on people an acceptable norm of our society? These are tough but pertinent questions that a researcher must address prior to conducting research with observational techniques, and there are no easy, clear-cut answers. In part, ethical issues surrounding the use of disguised techniques might be related to whether or not the investigated behaviors are legal versus illegal.

EXHIBIT 10.9	Benefits and Limitations of Observation Data

Major Benefits of Observation Data	Limitations of Observation Data
Accuracy of actual behavior	Lack of generalizability of data
Reduction of confounding factors	Inability of explaining behaviors or events
Detail of the behavioral data	Complexity of setting and recording of behavior(s) or events

where the subjects are observed in a natural public setting using a disguised technique. In situations where the behaviors or events are complex and unstructured, mechanical observation techniques are particularly useful. In addition, observational techniques can help in reducing potential subject recall error, response bias, and refusal to participate, as well as in reducing potential observer errors. In many situations, observational techniques, especially mechanical devices, afford the researcher the opportunity to gather and record in-depth details about current behavior or events. Usually, the data can be collected in less time and at a lower cost than through other types of collection procedures.

Observational techniques do have several limitations. One of the ongoing shortcomings of observational techniques is that they produce data and information that are difficult to generalize. It is difficult to make accurate inferences about larger groups of subjects beyond those test subjects who were actually observed. Typically, observation methods are integrated in research projects that focus on a small number of subjects (between 5 and 60) under unique or special circumstances, thus reducing the representativeness of larger groups of people. Given the nature of observation methods, it is extremely difficult for the researcher to logically explain why the observed behaviors or events took place. This inability to interrogate the subjects on their attitudes, motives, feelings, and other nonobservable factors means that any resulting insights into the behavior should be considered preliminary and subjective. Complete understanding of the observed behavior is severely limited to "intellectual guesses."

In those situations where the natural public setting includes a large number of subjects, it is very difficult even for trained observers to note all the activities occurring at the same time. While an observer is focused on the behavior of one particular subject, she or he is likely to completely miss that of the other subjects in the setting during that same time frame. Disguised observation situations pose an additional limitation in that the human observers cannot instantaneously or automatically record the behavior activities as they occur. There is some amount of lag time between observing the behavior or event and recording what was observed. With this natural lag time, there is the potential for faulty recall on the part of the observer. One way to overcome these potential limitations is that the observations should be made with the appropriate mechanical device whenever possible.

SUMMARY OF LEARNING OBJECTIVES

Describe and explain the importance of and differences between the variables used in experimental research designs.
In order to conduct causal research, the researcher must understand the four key types of variables involving experimental designs (independent, dependent, extraneous, control) as well as randomization of test subjects and the role that theory plays in creating experiments. The most important goal of any experiment is to determine what, if any, relationships exist among different variables (independent, dependent). Functional, or cause–effect, relationships require systematic change in one variable as another variable changes.

Explain the theoretical importance and impact of internal, external, and construct validity measures in experiments and interpreting functional relationships.
Experimental designs are developed to control for contamination, which may serve to confuse the true relationship being studied. While a variety of issues exist regarding the concept of contamination, internal validity, external validity, and construct validity are at the center of the discussion. Internal validity refers to the level of exact conclusions the researcher draws about a demonstrated functional relationship. The question is, Are the experimental results truly due to the experimental variables? External validity is concerned with the interaction of experimental manipulations with extraneous factors causing a researcher to suspect the generalizability of the results to other settings. Construct validity is important in the process of correctly identifying and

understanding both the independent and dependent variables included in an experimental design.

Several techniques unique to the experimental design are used to control for problems of internal and external validity. These techniques center on the use of control groups, pre-experimental measures, exclusion of subjects, matching subjects into groups, and randomization of group members. These dimensions, built into the experimental design, provide true power for controlling contamination.

Discuss the three major types of experimental designs used in marketing research. Explain the pros and cons of using causal designs as a means of assessing relationship outcomes.
Pre-experimental designs fail to meet internal validity criteria due to a lack of group comparisons. Despite this weakness, three designs are still used quite frequently in marketing research: the one-shot study; the one-group, pretest-posttest design; and the static group comparison.

True experimental designs ensure equivalence between experimental and control groups by random assignment of subjects into groups. Three forms of true experimental designs exist: pretest-posttest, control group; posttest-only, control group; and the Solomon Four Group.

Quasi-experimental designs are appropriate when the researcher can control some of the variables but cannot establish true randomization of groups. While a multitude of these designs exist, two of the most common forms are the nonequivalent control group and the separate-sample, pretest-posttest.

Explain what test markets are, the importance and difficulties of executing this type of research design, and how the resulting data structures are used by researchers and marketing practitioners.

Test markets are a specific type of field experiment and are commonly conducted in natural field settings. Most common in the marketing research field are traditional test markets, controlled test markets, electronic test markets, simulated test markets, and virtual test markets. Data gathered from test markets provide both researchers and practitioners with invaluable information concerning customers' attitudes, preferences, purchasing habits/patterns, and demographic profiles. This information is very useful in predicting new product/service acceptance levels and advertising and image effectiveness, as well as in evaluating current marketing mix strategies.

Discuss the characteristics, benefits, and weaknesses of observational techniques, and explain how these techniques are used to collect primary data.

Observational techniques are used by researchers in all types of research designs (exploratory, descriptive, causal). In addition to the general advantages of observation, major benefits are the accuracy of collecting data on actual behavior as it unfolds, reduction of confounding factors, and the amount of detailed behavioral data that can be recorded. The unique limitations of using observation methods are lack of generalizability of the data, inability of explaining current behaviors or events, and the complexity of setting and recording the behavior.

KEY TERMS AND CONCEPTS

Construct validity 294	**Extraneous variables** 290	**Observation** 310
Control variables 289	**Field experiments** 302	**Randomization** 290
Dependent variables 289	**Functional relationship** 287	**Test marketing** 286
Direct observation 312	**Independent variables** 288	**Theory** 290
Experimental design reliability 295	**Indirect observation** 312	**Validity** 291
External validity 293	**Internal validity** 291	**Variable** 287

REVIEW QUESTIONS

1. List the three types of experimental design variables and provide an explanation of each.

2. Identify the significant variables that a consumer would take into consideration when purchasing a computer.

3. Using college students as subjects for experimental studies is a common occurrence in marketing research. What possible problems could arise from this practice?

4. Identify the specific tests used for (*a*) pre-experimental testing and (*b*) true experimental testing. What advantages and disadvantages are associated with each?

5. Explain the difference between internal validity and external validity. In your explanation, discuss the common causes of each type of validity.

6. When using field experiments, what factors are detrimental to the observational techniques that could be used as a control aspect?

DISCUSSION QUESTIONS

1. Which of the five types of test marketing are gaining acceptance with America's top advertisers? Why is this taking place?

2. Why do you feel that Adolph Coors Company has encountered so many problems in the past two decades concerning new-product introductions? What would you recommend that Coors do to solve these problems?

3. What type of observational technique and experimental design would you suggest for each of the following situations and why?
   a. The research and development director at Calvin Klein suggests a new type of cologne for men that could be promoted by a sports celebrity like Michael Jordan.
   b. The director of on-campus housing at your university proposes some significant style changes to the physical configuration of the current on-campus dorm rooms for freshmen and new transfer students.
   c. The vice president of marketing in charge of new store locations for Home Depot must decide on the best location for a new store in your hometown.
   d. The senior design engineer for the Ford Motor Company wishes to identify meaningful design changes to be integrated on the 2000 Ford Taurus.
   e. A retail supermarket manager would like to know the popularity of a new brand of cereal that is produced by General Mills.

4. **EXPERIENCE THE INTERNET.** Go to the home page for the ACNielsen research company, at www.acnielsen.com. Examine the tools, procedures, and techniques the company uses for conducting test markets. Provide a brief explanation of the goals and objectives the company provides for its clients regarding test marketing.

ENDNOTES

1. Betsy Peterson, "Trends Turn Around," *Marketing Research* 7, no. 3 (Summer 1995).

2. R.J. Reynolds Tobacco, 1997 annual report; and Caravan, *Quarterly Report of the R.J. Reynolds Tobacco Company* (Summer 1997).

3. Thomas D. Cook and Donald T. Campbell, *Quasi-Experimentation: Design & Analysis Issues for Field Settings* (Boston, MA: Houghton Mifflin, 1979), pp. 39–41, 51, 59, 64, 70–73.

4. Gilbert A. Churchill, Jr., "A Paradigm for the Development of Better Measures of Marketing Constructs," *Journal of Marketing Research* 16 (February 1979), pp. 64–73.

5. William D. Crano and Marilyn B. Brewer, *Principles and Methods of Social Research* (Boston: Allyn and Bacon, 1986), pp. 23–38.

6. Churchill, "A Paradigm for the Development of Better Measures of Marketing Constructs."

7. Carmines and Zeller, *Reliability and Validity Assessment;* also Fred N. Kerlinger, *Foundations of Behavioral Research* (New York: Holt, Reinhart and Winston, 1986), pp. 324–26, 461–63.

8. Martin Fishbein, "Attitude and the Prediction of Behavior," in *Readings in Attitude Theory and Behavior,* M. Fishbein, ed. (New York: John Wiley and Sons, 1967), pp. 477–92.

9. S. Banks, *Experimentation in Marketing* (New York: McGraw-Hill, 1965), pp. 168–79.

10. Kerlinger, *Foundations of Behavioral Research.*

11. Ibid.

12. Ibid.

13. Cook and Campbell, *Quasi-Experimentation.*

14. Peterson, "Trends Turn Around."

15. Mark Gleason, "P&G Tests Smoothie," *Advertising Age* 66 (October 30, 1995).

16. Andrew Bernstein, "Spalding and Four Major Chains Launch Women's Theme Shops," *Sporting Goods Business* 28 (November 1985).

17. Melvin Prince, "Choosing Simulated Test Marketing Systems," *Marketing Research* 4 (September 1992).

18. Ibid.

19. Raymond Burke, "Virtual Shopping: Breakthrough in Marketing Research," *Harvard Business Review* (March/April 1996).

20. Ibid.

21. Ibid.

22. Ibid.

23. William Rathje and Cullen Murphy, "Garbage Demographics," *American Demographics* (May 1992), pp. 50–53; also see Eugene J. Webb, Donald T. Campbell, Richard D. Schwartz, and Lee Sechrest, *Unobtrusive Measures: Nonreaction Research in the Social Sciences* (Chicago, IL: Rand-McNally, 1971), pp. 113–14; and Joseph A. Cote, James McCullough, and Michael Reilly, "Effects of Unexpected Situations on Behavior-Intention Differences: A Garbology Analysis," *Journal of Consumer Research* (September 1985), pp. 188–94.

24. See Bernie Whalen, "Marketing Detective Reveals Competitive-Intelligence Secrets," *Marketing News* (September 16, 1983), p. 1; also Witold Rybcznski, "We Are What We Throw Away," *New York Times Book Review* (July 5, 1992), pp. 5–6.

25. Webb et al., *Unobtrusive Measures,* chapter 2.

26. James M. Sinkula, "Status of Company Usage of Scanner Based Research," *Journal of the Academy of Marketing Science* (Spring 1986), pp. 63–71; and "Some Factors Affecting the Adoption of Scanner-Based Research in Organizations," *Journal of Advertising Research* (April/May 1991), pp. 50–55.

MARKETING RESEARCH ILLUSTRATION

RIDERS FITS NEW DATABASE INTO BRAND LAUNCH

This illustration was designed by the Acxiom Corporation in Conway, Arkansas. It illustrates using market test data from a field experiment to build a customer database and help successfully launch a new brand of jeans by the Lee Apparel Company.

In 1993, the Lee Apparel Company decided to market a new apparel line of jeans under the name Riders. The brand's management team seized the opportunity to begin building a customer database. Unlike the normal process of building a customer database around promotions, merchandising, and advertising efforts that directly benefited retailers, their goal was to make marketing dollars build both the brand and the database simultaneously. In 1994, the launch of the Riders apparel line went well with rollouts in the company's Midwest and Northeast regional markets. The initial positioning strategy called for the products to be priced slightly higher than competitive brands, and marketed premium mass-channel retailers like Ames, Bradlee's, Caldor, Target, and Venture. The 1994 communication program emphasized the line's "comfortable fit" and in 1996 the rollouts went national, using major retail channels like superstore marketer Wal-Mart. Initially, Riders used a spring promotion called "Easy Money" to generate product trial and to gather name, address, and demographic information about the line's first customers. These data were collected using a rebate card and certificate from the retailer. Upon completing and mailing the rebate card to Riders, the customer was rewarded with a check in the mail. This initial market test provided valuable data elements on each customer, such as the exact type of product purchased, how much was spent, who they bought for, where they heard of the Riders brand, and information about their lifestyle interests. As part of the test market, Riders supported the effort with point-of-purchase (POP) displays and promotions in Sunday newspaper circulations. In addition, the Riders management team funded the promotion and handled all development, redemption, and fulfillment in-house. The results of the first test market were as follows: a total of $1.5 million in certificates were printed, yielding a 2.1 percent response, or just over 31,000 customer names. About 20 percent of the buyers bought more than one item.

Another part of the test market design was the follow-up phone survey among the new customers, three months after the initial promotion. Of the customers surveyed, 62 percent had purchased Riders products. This survey allowed Riders to provide detailed information back to salespeople and consumers. In 1995, Riders repeated the test market design adding a postcard mailing to the existing database names. The promotional effort netted over 40,000 new customer names and information for the growing database. It also proved the responsiveness of database customers—3.8 percent of the database customers who received the postcard promotion came into the store to make a purchase, compared to a 2.8 percent response to the POP and circular ads.

To build a successful customer database from test market designs, the critical first step is figuring out the most efficient way to gather the names you want. Then comes the question of how you want to use the information with customers, prospects, and retailers. Finally, you begin the process of testing and evaluating the relationships, and applying what you have learned to build customer loyalty.

Focus on Retail Partnerships

The main goal of all the test marketing was to create valuable information that could be used to build relationships with Riders consumers and those retail accounts that Riders depended on for distribution. The growing philosophy within the Riders brand management team was "The more we know about our customers, the better the decisions we'll be able to make in dealing both with them and with our retailers." Moreover, the detailed information created from the database—such as hard dollar results of each promotion as well as the demographic profiles—is shared with retailers, as is the research showing the consumer behavior benefits. For example, a recent tracking study found that purchase intent of database customers was twice that of nondatabase customers in a given trade area. Unaided brand awareness was likewise high (100 percent, compared to 16 percent of the general population), and awareness of Riders advertising was 53 percent compared to 27 percent.

The Riders team believed so strongly in tying database information with promotion efforts that they insisted that a database component be part of any chain-specific promotions. Riders management hoped to convince the retailers who build their own database capabilities to share their information. For example, retail account information can identify more product and promotion opportunities. Riders believed that the real payoff comes when both manufacturer and retailer can use data, from either source, to do a better job of attracting and keeping the key assets for both channel members—the customer. Riders must continue convincing retailers that putting Riders merchandise on their shelves is bringing people into their stores.

From test marketing to creating complete customer databases, the Riders team has begun to put a major part of its marketing investment into image-building advertising strategies focused on print and television media. For instance, they say,

> The more we know about our customers and their preferences, the better we'll be able to hone our advertising messages and media buys, pinpoint what kind of promotions work best, and understand what new products we ought to be developing. As competitive pressures continue to mount, Riders expects detailed customer information to become more valuable in helping define the brand position clearly. Defining ourselves and what's different about Riders products is going to be an increasingly important element in drawing customers who have a great many choices to stores where Riders products are on the shelves. Although it initially began with test markets guiding the development of a complete customer database program, it's now the databases that are guiding the inclusion of key elements in our test market research. Riders' ultimate goal is creating a tool (database research) that is going to make its products more attractive to retailers and to consumers.

MARKETING RESEARCH CASE EXERCISE

SEGA ENTERPRISES

With new corporate leadership, Sega announced it would launch a new high-powered "superconsole" in Japan during the spring of 1998 and in Europe and America in the spring of 1999. Sega reportedly spent $500 million in development of this console, branded as Dreamcast. To help ensure its success and produce the world's first game console with Internet access, Sega chose several major companies with which to unite efforts. Hitachi, NEC, and Yahama were involved in joint ventures with Sega to produce a game system designed to speed up access time and allow for bigger games and larger playing fields.

Unveiled at the Electronics Entertainment Expo in 1999, Dreamcast was positioned to outperform all in home gaming platforms and most commercial arcade systems. According to Sega executives, Dreamcast's success would be based on three key benefits: (1) advanced technical capability of a superconsole, (2) increased retailer support, and (3) the interactive nature of playing the games. In March of 1999, Sega announced that Dreamcast would be supported with a $100 million marketing budget that included an extensive test marketing program. Consult the Web page for Sega at www.sega.com for complete background on the Dreamcast system.

1. Given the high-tech nature of this new product, what are some of the pressing issues that Sega must address before developing the test market for Dreamcast? For example, who should be considered as the subjects for this test market, consumers or retailers? Where should the test marketing take place, in a retail setting or on the Internet?

2. Develop your own plan for developing a test market for Dreamcast. How should the test be implemented, and what critical marketing variables would you manipulate and measure?

PART III

Gathering and Collecting Accurate Data

Learning Objectives

After reading this chapter, you will be able to

1. Discuss the concept of sampling and list reasons for sampling.

2. Identify and explain the different roles that sampling plays in the overall information research process.

3. Identify the fundamental differences between probability and non-probability sampling methods, and point out their strengths and weaknesses.

4. Discuss and calculate sampling distributions, standard errors, and confidence intervals and how they are used in assessing the accuracy of a sample.

5. Identify the criteria involved in determining the appropriate sample design for a given research project.

6. Discuss the factors that must be considered when determining sample size.

7. Discuss the methods of calculating appropriate sample sizes.

8. Identify and explain the steps involved in developing a sampling plan, and design a variety of different sampling plans.

Sampling: Theory, Designs, and Issues in Marketing Research

❝ I am convinced that we need to conduct some type of a nationwide survey to determine consumers' attitudes, feelings, and general consumption patterns toward air travel prior to forecasting our flight route loads. But how many people do we need to include in the study to guarantee the collection of quality data and information? And what should be the sampling plan and process in selecting those people? **❞**

RONALD P. BRENSINGER, PH.D.
Manager, Capacity Planning
American Airlines

Sampling Design Decisions: American Airlines

Recently, the executive vice president of marketing for American Airlines (AA) received an end-of-quarter cost report from the accounting department that suggested the costs of operating the airline's routes from California to New York and Washington, D.C., were increasing and the company was again losing money. In an attempt to better understand the situation, the vice president called in Ron Brensinger, manager of capacity planning, to discuss alternative plans of action. During the discussions, Brensinger mentioned that one of the problems that AA was experiencing was that the models used to estimate the number of passengers on AA flights did not include passengers' attitudes or intentions. Brensinger explained that while the price of airline tickets and past passenger load records were important factors in predicting future route loads, the models did not currently incorporate the possible effects of consumers' attitudes toward flying as a mode of transportation. He further explained that customers' feelings of satisfaction toward in-flight services as well as their beliefs about American Airlines' ability to provide high-quality passenger services also played important roles in their airline selection process and future purchase intentions. The discussion made it clear that AA needed to collect some primary data from its known customer markets as well as from the general flying public.

Because of his academic training, Brensinger was asked to write up a research proposal outlining the processes needed to capture the necessary primary data. A week later, he presented his proposal to AA's vice president of marketing for final approval. In the presentation, Brensinger discussed the information problems and research objectives, then turned to the proposed methods for collecting the data. After explaining that a self-administered survey would be the most cost-efficient way to go, he proceeded to discuss a multistaged sampling plan. It was at this point that the vice president of marketing became confused and asked, "What is the real purpose behind such a complex-sounding sampling plan?" Brensinger said that just the act of collecting data from people would not guarantee the quality of the data. Given that AA had flown over 39.7 million people in the past 12 months, it would be impossible to contact and interview each of those customers. Therefore, a sample of those people would have to be taken and it would be critically important to ensure that the sample represented the company's total customer base. In addition, Brensinger pointed out that AA's total customer base flew with the same frequency. For example, some of the people who fly American Airlines choose the airline carrier significantly more often than others, and some fly first class and others business class or economy class, and some are business travelers and others nonbusiness travelers. These groups of customers would have to be appropriately represented in any survey to ensure that the collected data portrayed a true picture of customers' attitudes and feelings toward flying AA. These pictures then could be used to generalize about the attitudes and behavior intentions of AA's total customer base. Brensinger further explained that deciding who should be included in the study would affect the constructs and dimensions to be investigated, development of the appropriate question/scale measurements, and the design of the questionnaire and support materials.

Because the airline's total customer population divided into different groups of air travelers, Brensinger proposed the use of a multistage stratified sampling plan. In such a plan it would be necessary not only to define each stratum very carefully but also to determine the appropriate sample size for each. Sample sizes become critical in determining the overall cost of collecting the required primary data, the accuracy or representativeness of the data, and the insights that should be included in the company's current forecasting models. At this point, Brensinger could only "ballpark" the costs of collecting the data, because the actual sample sizes were not calculated as part of the proposal. Given the nature of management's immediate concerns with certain routes, Brensinger suggested that the proposed research be a "pilot study"; depending on the results, the research could be expanded over time to include all AA routes. As a pilot study, the costs of data collection would be significantly less.

At the end of Brensinger's presentation, tentative approval was given for budgeting $50,000 for the pilot study. One condition attached was that more specific cost figures would be offered prior to management's final approval. At this point, Brensinger knew he would have to develop the complete sampling plan. Developing the plan would require seven basic stages: (1) specifically define the target population, (2) select the data collection method (e.g., self-administered survey or interview), (3) identify the sampling frame(s) needed, (4) determine the most appropriate sampling method (i.e., probabilistic or nonprobabilistic), (5) determine necessary sample sizes, (6) create an operational plan for selecting sample units, and (7) execute the operational plan. The Marketing Research Illustration at the end of this chapter tells how Brensinger developed the sampling plan.

Value of Sampling in Information Research

Sampling is an important concept that we practice in our everyday activities. Take, for example, going on a job interview. We have been taught that making a good first impression in a job interview is extremely important, because after that initial exposure (i.e., sample) many times people will make judgments about the type of person we are. People sit in front of their cable TV with a remote control in their hand and rapidly flip through a number of different channels (channel-surf), stopping a few seconds to take a sample of the program on each channel until they find a program worth watching. Next time you have a free moment, go to a bookstore like Barnes and Noble and observe sampling at its best. People at a bookstore generally pick up a book or magazine, look at its cover, and then read a few pages to get a feeling for the author's writing style and the content before deciding whether to buy the book. When people go automobile shopping, they have the desire to test-drive a particular car for a few miles to see how that car feels and performs before deciding whether to buy it. One commonality in all these situations is that a decision is based on the assumption that the smaller portion, or sample, is representative of the larger population. From a very general perspective, **sampling** involves selecting a relatively small number of elements from a larger defined group of elements and expecting that the information gathered from the small group will allow judgments to be made about the larger group.

Sampling The selection of a small number of elements from a larger defined target group of elements and expecting that the information gathered from the small group will allow judgments to be made about the larger group.

Sampling as a Part of the Research Process

Sampling is often used when it is impossible or unreasonable to conduct a census. When using a **census,** the researcher is interested in collecting primary data about or from every member of a defined target population. Intuitively, it is easy to see that sampling, versus conducting a census, can save both time and money. For example, it would be much less expensive and time-consuming to gather data about 2,000 people than about 2 million. In most research projects, time and money are usually critical to a decision maker. For researchers, shorter projects are more likely to fit into the decision maker's time frames.

Census A research study that includes data about every member of the defined target population.

The concept of sampling plays an important role in the process of identifying, developing, and understanding new marketing constructs (or objects) that need to be investigated by researchers. Take, for example, a researcher who is interested in understanding the concept of service quality in medical delivery practices. She or he must identify the various dimensions that might make up service quality. Through the use of different qualitative methods, the researcher can establish a manageable set of dimensions and attributes representative of the whole concept of service quality.

Another area in which sampling plays a significant role is the process of developing the scale measurements used to actually collect raw primary data about objects or people. When the researcher creates a scale measurement, she or he must be able to determine the scale's reliability and validity levels. These activities require the researcher to administer the proposed scale measurement to a representative subset of the proposed target population.

Samples also play an important, if indirect, role in the process of designing questionnaires. Depending on the defined information problem and the selected needed population, sampling decisions will affect the decisions regarding the type of survey instrument (e.g., interview or self-administered survey) and the actual questionnaire's structural design attributes. Finally, in cases where the process of measurement in a study results in the destruction of the element studied, sampling may be the only alternative. For example, if every Ruffles potato chip that came off Frito-Lay's production line were tested for salt, oil, color, and so on, there would be none left to package and sell. While this reason for sampling is usually thought of in terms of quality control, it can be applied to many business or marketing problem situations that require primary research data in the testing of new products or ideas. As these examples illustrate, there are different reasons for the inclusion of sampling procedures in information research. The main objective is that of allowing researchers to make informed judgments or decisions on the basis of limited information, or in the absence of perfect knowledge, about the total population. The concept of sampling involves two basic issues: (1) making the right decisions in the selection of items (people, products, or services), and (2) feeling confident that the data generated by the sample can be transformed into accurate information about the overall population.

Overview: The Basics of Sampling Theory

Basic Sampling Terminology

Population

Population The identifiable total set of elements of interest being investigated by a researcher.

A **population** is an identifiable total group or aggregation of elements (e.g., people, products, organizations, physical entities) that are of interest to the researcher and pertinent to the specified information problem. For example, let's say that the Mazda Motor Corporation hired J. D. Power and Associates to measure "customer satisfaction among automobile owners." This wording would suggest that the population of interest would be all people who own automobiles. It is very unlikely, however, that J. D. Power and Associates could draw a sample that would be truly representative of such a broad, heterogeneous population—any data collected would probably not allow for generalizations about customer satisfaction that would be of use to Mazda (or that would be accurate or meaningful at all). Such specification (or lack of it) is unfortunately very common in marketing research. Most businesses that require the collection of raw data are not really concerned with total populations, but rather with a prescribed segment of the total. For purposes of discussion and practicality of understanding the important sampling issues in research, we will use a modified version of *population:* **defined target population.** A defined target population consists of the complete group of elements (people or objects) that are specifically identified for investigation according to the objectives of the research project. A precise definition of the target population is essential and is usually done in terms of elements, sampling units, and time frames.

Defined target population The complete set of elements identified for investigation.

Element

Element A person or object from the defined target population from which data and information are sought.

An **element** is a person or object from which data and information are sought. Often in research, the element is a particular product or group of individuals. Elements must be unique, be countable, and, when added together, comprise the whole of the target population. You can view elements collectively as the target population frame for which some type of sample will be drawn. Target population elements might include a particular consumer product (e.g., Mazda automobiles); specific groups of people (e.g., females aged 18 to 34, or households with checking accounts); or specific organizations (e.g., Fortune 500 companies). When the initial definition of the target population misdefines the elements, it creates a bias referred to as *target population frame error.*

Sampling units

Sampling units The target population elements available for selection during the sampling process.

Sampling units are the target population elements available for selection during the sampling process. In a simple, single-stage sample, the sampling units and the population elements may be the same. However, many studies involve complex problems that require the use of a multistage sampling process. Using the Mazda example as a case in point, owners of Mazda cars might be the population elements of interest, but J. D. Power and Associates might only be concerned with the owners who have purchased new Mazdas rather than used ones. Therefore, the defined target population would be redefined. Refining the set of population elements with a second factor creates population segments from which to draw a representative sample.

Target population elements might also be identified using a specified time frame (e.g., the year 2000, the month of August 2000, or the period from April 15 to April 30, 2000). For instance, the Mazda Corporation might specify its interest in understanding customer satisfaction among only Mazda automobile owners who have purchased new cars in 1999. Consequently, J. D. Power and Associates would have to further refine its definition of the target population, thus reducing the eligible sampling units. Exhibit 11.1 illustrates some hypothetical examples that summarize the impact of element, sampling-unit, and time-frame factors on target populations.

EXHIBIT 11.1 | **Hypothetical Examples of the Impact of Elements, Sampling Units, and Time Frames**

Mazda Automobiles

Elements	Adult purchasers of automobiles
Sampling unit	New Mazda automobiles
Time frame	January 1, 1999, to September 30, 1999

Nail Polish

Elements	Females between the ages of 18 and 34 who purchased at least one brand of nail polish during the past 30 days
Sampling units	U.S. cities with populations between 100,000 and 1 million people
Time frame	June 1 to June 15, 1999

Retail Banking Services

Elements	Households with checking accounts
Sampling units	Households located within a 10-mile radius of NationsBank's central location in Charlotte, North Carolina
Time frame	January 1 to April 30, 1999

Sampling Frame

Sampling frame
The list of all eligible sampling units.

After defining the target population, the researcher must assemble a list of all eligible sampling units, referred to as a **sampling frame.** Some common sources of sampling frames are lists of registered voters and customer lists from magazine publishers, credit card companies, or even maps. Today, there are also specialized commercial companies (e.g., Survey Sampling, Inc.; American Business Lists, Inc.; Scientific Telephone Samples) that are in the business of developing data bases that contain names, addresses, and telephone numbers of potential population elements. These companies can also generate and sell needed sampling frames. Although the costs of obtaining such sampling frame mailing lists will vary, a list can normally be purchased for between $50 and $200 per 1,000 names.[1]

Regardless of the source, it is usually very difficult and expensive for a researcher to gain access to truly accurate, or representative, current sampling frames.[2] It is doubtful, for example, that a list of individuals who have eaten a taco from a fast-food chain in a particular city in the past six months will be readily available. In this instance, a researcher would have to employ an alternative method such as random-digit dialing (if conducting telephone interviews) or a location survey (e.g., a mall-intercept interview) in order to generate a sample of prospective respondents. Exhibit 11.2 describes how telephone numbers can be randomly generated using several different approaches. The sampling frame contains the operational population (or working population) from which the sample will be drawn. In an ideal situation, the operational population, the defined target population frame, and the sampling frame are identical. In those situations where a sampling frame contains all of the eligible sampling units of the defined target population plus additional ones, we say that it has *overregistration.* For example, let's say we were interested in collecting opinions from people who regularly use their MasterCard credit cards for purchasing gasoline. To conduct the survey, we might purchase a current mailing list from MasterCard International. In essence, this list becomes our sampling frame. Most likely it will suffer from overregistration because it will include people who do not regularly use their MasterCard for purchasing gasoline.

In contrast, when eligible sampling units are accidentally left out of the sampling frame, then the frame has an *underregistration* condition. A classic example that illustrates this condition is when a local telephone book is used as the sampling frame for conducting a telephone survey. Telephone books do not include people who have unlisted numbers, people whose telephone numbers were activated after the publishing date of the telephone book, and people who do not have a phone or are not directly recorded in a listing. Today, a telephone directory should never be used as the primary source for developing a sample frame used in marketing research projects. In underregistration situations, there will be a **sampling gap.**

Sampling gap The representation difference between the population elements and sampling units in the sampling frame.

While both overregistration and underregistration factors create sampling gaps, the latter creates more serious representativeness problems. A sampling gap can also be viewed as sampling frame error, and occurs when certain sample units are not necessarily excluded or complete segments of the defined target population are not accurately represented in the sampling frame. The larger the sampling frame error, the greater the chance for misleading and inaccurate data results. The following classic example illustrates the impact of sampling frame error on data accuracy. In 1936, a telephone survey poll was conducted by *Literary Digest* predicting the winner of that year's U.S. presidential election. The poll was conducted using a sampling frame that was compiled from telephone directories and automobile registration records. The prediction, based on *Literary Digest*'s telephone poll results, was that Herbert Hoover would win the presidency by a margin of 20 percent. In reality, Franklin D. Roosevelt actually won the election by a 20 percent margin.[3] Where did the pollsters go wrong? The sampling frame used in the study included

EXHIBIT 11.2	Random-Digit Dialing Approaches to Generating Telephone Sampling Frame Lists

The only solution to the problem of unlisted telephone numbers is to generate phone numbers by some random process. This practice, referred to as random-digit dialing (RDD), is simple in theory—phone numbers are generated at random. However, practical considerations complicate the picture greatly. The first and foremost of these is the relatively small proportion of working numbers among all possible 10-digit telephone numbers. Only about 1 in 170 of all possible telephone numbers (9,999,999,999 possible) is actually in use (60,000,000 residential numbers). The proportion of working residential numbers in RDD samples can be increased dramatically by selecting from only the 103 working area codes (first three digits). This approach yields approximately 1 working residential number for every 17 randomly generated. From a cost standpoint, this rate is still too low, entailing too many unproductive dialings. The question at this point is, What type of RDD system will simultaneously cut the proportion of unproductive dialings while including a proportionate number of unlisted phone homes in the sample? There are three alternative approaches built around the use of a telephone book.

Four-Digit Approach

Taking the four-digit approach the researchers must, in addition to restricting the sample to the 103 working area codes, select numbers only from working central offices or exchanges. The last four digits of the number are generated via some process that approaches randomness. There are approximately 30,000 working exchanges in the continental United States or about 300 million possible numbers. This approach will, therefore, yield approximately one working number for every five generated randomly. Problems with this approach relate to the fact that all exchanges have an equal probability of being selected, while some have a high proportion of all possible numbers in service and others have only a small proportion in service.

Three-Digit Approach

The next logical progression in RDD technology is the three-digit approach. The three-digit method increases the proportion of working numbers to better than one in three. This is possible because the phone company does not assign numbers from a particular exchange at random but from within working banks of 1,000 numbers. Consulting the section of a criss-cross directory where phone numbers are listed numerically will show that within a particular exchange certain sequences of 1,000 numbers (000–999) are totally unused while other groups of 1,000 are, for example, 70 percent in use. Employing the three-digit option, the user must specify area codes, exchanges, and "working banks" (fourth digit) of numbers within exchanges. Working banks may be identified from a criss-cross directory or selected via a probability sample from the telephone book. A bank with no working listed numbers has no chance of being selected, while a bank with 60 percent of its numbers listed has twice as much chance of being selected as one with only 30 percent listed. The final step of the three-digit approach is to generate the last three digits of each working area code/exchange/bank by means of some random process.

The three-digit method is more efficient in eliminating nonworking numbers, but increases bias due to missing (from the directory) new working banks that have been activated. The four-digit method is safer from the standpoint of avoiding bias, but more expensive due to the greater number of calls that must be made. It is suggested that the three-digit method is most appropriate when the directory or directories for the area of interest are relatively current or when there has been little growth in the area since the publication of the recent directory. In other cases, the four-digit method should be given serious consideration.

Using Telephone Books

RDD samples can also be generated from the telephone book. In general, this is accomplished by selecting numbers at random from the book and adding a random number as the sixth or seventh digit. Somewhere between one in two and one in three of the numbers generated will be working residential numbers. This is a viable approach because all exchanges and banks are proportionately represented in the book. Generally, the phone book is recommended as an RDD sample source only in those cases where the appropriate computer hardware and software are not available. There are two major reasons for making this recommendation. First, the construction of a sample by this approach is fairly time-consuming and expensive whether it is done for or by the interviewers. Second, if the interviewers are given directions and left to generate the numbers themselves, the researcher loses all control over the validity of the sample.

Computer programs can incorporate three- or four-digit approaches and generate RDD samples at a very low cost. In addition, the printout can be set up to capture additional data and to help the researcher control field costs and proper execution of the sampling plan.

Source: Roger Gates and Bob Brobst, "RANDIAL: A Program for Generating Random Telephone Numbers," *Journal of Marketing Research* 14 (May 1977), p. 240.

A voter takes an exit poll conducted by an NBC pollster.

only those registered voters who owned a telephone or automobile, both considered luxury items in 1936. Consequently, the sampling frame omitted a significantly large proportion of eligible voters and generated inaccurate results.

The Main Factors Underlying Sampling Theory

To understand sampling theory, it will be important for you to acquaint yourself with its related concepts and symbols. Exhibit 11.3 displays a summary of the basic concepts and their symbols. Descriptions and discussions of these concepts are provided in this chapter and revisited in later chapters.

In many statistics texts, sampling concepts and approaches are discussed for situations where the key population parameters of interest are either known or unknown by the researcher prior to conducting the research project. Here, the sampling discussions are purposely limited to those situations where the researcher primarily does not know the true population parameters of interest. The logic behind this perspective is twofold. First, today's business environments are so complex and so rapidly changing that it is highly unlikely that business decision makers actually know the true parameters of their target populations. One of the major goals of researching small, yet representative, samples of assumed members of a defined target population is that of using sample results to either predict or estimate what the true population parameters are within a certain degree of confidence.

Second, if business decision makers had complete knowledge about their defined target populations, they would have perfect information about the realities of those populations, thus eliminating the need to conduct primary research activities. Moreover, we believe that

EXHIBIT 11.3 Concepts and Symbols Used in Sampling Theory

Population Parameters	Symbol	Sample Notations	Symbol
Size	N	Size	n
Mean value	μ	Mean value	$\bar{x}$
Percentage value (population proportion)	P	Percentage value (sample proportion)	$\bar{p}$
	Q or $[1-P]$		$\bar{q}$ or $[1-\bar{p}]$
Standard deviation	σ	Estimated standard deviation	$\bar{s}$
Variance	σ^2	Estimated sample	$\bar{s}^2$
Standard error (population parameter)	SE_μ or SE_P	Estimated standard error (sample statistics)	$SE_{\bar{x}}$ or $SE_{\bar{p}}$
Other Sampling Concepts			
Confidence intervals	$CI_{\bar{x}}$ or $CI_{\bar{p}}$		
Tolerance level of error	α		
Critical z-value	Z_B		
Confidence levels	CL		
Finite correction factor (the overall square root of $[N-n/N-1]$ (also referred to as "finite multiplier" or "finite population correction")	fcf		

better than 95 percent of today's business or marketing problem situations exist primarily because decision makers lack both perfect information about their problem situations and understanding of who their customers are, as well as those people's attitudes, preferences, feelings, and marketplace behavior patterns.

One important assumption that underlies sampling theory is that the population elements are randomly distributed. That is to say, if a researcher were able to do a census of the entire target population elements, then the probability distribution of the population, or the relative frequencies of a population's parameters (e.g., actual dollar sales revenue per Home Depot store), would depict a normal bell-shaped distribution pattern. Theoretically, this assumption allows the researcher to believe that if she or he were to take repeated random, representative samples of the known sampling units (or population elements), then the resulting **sampling distribution** of a specified sample statistic would approximately emulate a normal bell-shaped distribution pattern similar to that of the probability distribution of the population.[4]

Let's say, for example, that researchers were interested in determining the average household income in the state of Florida. Let's also say that there are 4.73 million households in Florida, and the researchers were able to take 1,000 separate random samples, each the size of 500 households. Let's further assume that state records indicated the average household income (μ) of these 4.73 million households was reported as being $28,000 and the sampling distribution of average household income ($\bar{x}$) from the 1,000 random

Sampling distribution The frequency distribution of a specific sample statistic (e.g., sample mean or sample proportion) from repeated random samples of the same size.

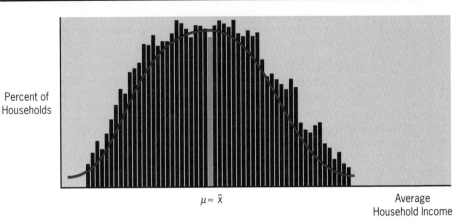

EXHIBIT 11.4   **Example of the Sampling Distribution of Average Household Incomes Among 1,000 Random Samples**

samples was found to range from \$15,500 to \$41,000. The frequency distribution of the means ($\bar{x}$), or averages of those samples, would take the shape of a normal, bell-shaped curve with the population mean (μ) as the mean of the distribution, as shown in Exhibit 11.4. In reality, it would not be practical to take 1,000 different samples. The idea of a sampling distribution is a theoretical concept. However, it is a fundamental concept in statistics and sampling. To deal with the reality of this sampling factor, most researchers will rely on the basic theoretical underpinnings of the central limit theorem (also referred to as the normal approximation rule) in drawing one representative random sample from a defined target population rather than many repeated samples.

Central Limit Theorem

Central limit theorem (CLT) Theorem that states that for almost all target populations, the sampling distribution of the means ($\bar{x}$) or the percentage ($\bar{p}$) value derived from a simple random sample will be approximately normally distributed provided that the sample size is sufficiently large.

The **central limit theorem (CLT)** becomes the theoretical backbone for doing survey research and data collection through experimental designs. The CLT plays an important role in understanding the concepts of sampling error, statistical significance, and determination of sample sizes. In brief, the theorem states that for almost all defined target populations (virtually with disregard to the actual shape of the original population), the sampling distribution of the mean ($\bar{x}$) or the percentage ($\bar{p}$) value derived from a simple random sample will be approximately normally distributed, provided that the sample size is sufficiently large (i.e., when n is greater than or equal to 30). In turn, the sample mean value ($\bar{x}$) of that random sample with an estimated sampling error ($SE_{\bar{x}}$) fluctuates around the true population mean value (μ) with a standard error of $\sigma/\sqrt{n}$ and has an approximately normal sampling distribution, regardless of the shape of the probability frequency distribution curve of the overall target population.[5] In other words, there is a high probability that the mean of any sample ($\bar{x}$) taken from the target population would be a close approximation of the actual or true target population mean (μ), as one increases the size of the drawn sample (n). With an understanding of the basics of the central limit theorem, the researcher can

1. Draw representative samples from any target population regardless of the true shape of the population's probability distribution.

2. Obtain sample statistics from one large randomly drawn sample that can serve as accurate estimates of the target population's parameters, reducing the need to draw multiple samples from the same target population frame.

3. Draw one random sample, instead of many, reducing the costs of raw data collection activities.

4. Test more accurately the reliability and validity of constructs and scale measurements.

5. Statistically analyze data structures and transform them into meaningful information about the target population.

Theoretical Tools Used to Assess the Quality of Samples

As discussed in earlier chapters, there are numerous opportunities for researchers to make mistakes, or errors in judgment, that result in creating some type of bias in any research study. All types of errors can be logically classified as either sampling or nonsampling errors. Random sampling errors can be detected by observing the difference between the sample results and the results of a census conducted using identical procedures. Two of the difficulties associated with the detection of sampling error are (1) the fact that very seldom is a census conducted in survey research and (2) sampling error can be determined only after the sample is drawn and data collection has been completed.

Sampling error Any type of bias that is attributable to mistakes in either drawing a sample or determining the sample size.

From a theoretical perspective, **sampling error** is any type of bias that is attributable to mistakes made in either the selection process of prospective sampling units or determining the sample size. Moreover, random sampling error tends to occur because of chance variations in the scientific selection of the needed sampling units. Even if the sampling units were properly selected according to the stringent guidelines of sampling theory, those units still might not be a perfect representation of the defined target population, but they generally are reliable estimates. When there is a discrepancy between the statistic calculated or estimated from the sample and the actual value from the population, a sampling error has occurred.

Based on the principles of the central limit theorem, the size of sampling error and its impact can be reduced by increasing the size of the sample. Exhibit 11.5 illustrates an example of the relationship between sample sizes and the projected sizes of sampling error.

The results demonstrate that doubling the size of the sample does not automatically reduce the relative magnitude of the sampling error by the same factor. In fact, the possible sampling error can become so small that it raises questions concerning the overall costs involved with data collection—increasing the sample size primarily for purposes of statistically reducing the magnitude of the estimated standard error may not be worth the cost.

Nonsampling error A bias that occurs in a research study regardless of whether a sample or census is used.

Nonsampling errors are those types of bias that occur in a research study regardless of whether a sample or a census is used. These errors may occur at any stage of the research process. For example, the target population may be inaccurately defined, causing population frame error; inappropriate question/scale measurements can result in measurement error (see Chapters 12 and 13); a questionnaire may be poorly designed, causing forms of response error (see Chapter 14); or there may be other errors in gathering and recording data or when raw data are coded and entered for analysis (see Chapter 15). In general, the more extensive a study, the greater the potential for nonsampling errors. Unlike sampling error, there are no clear statistical models available to approximate the true relative magnitude of the impact of nonsampling errors on the quality of the raw data collected. Researchers do not know exactly the limiting effects, because there are no accurate direct measures of the error's impact. Nonsampling errors are normally related in some form to accuracy of the data (or the data quality) used by researchers and practitioners, whereas sampling errors relate to the representativeness of the sample to the defined target population.

EXHIBIT 11.5	Theoretical Example of the Relationship of Sample Sizes to Estimates of Sampling Error

In this example, the researcher is interested in better understanding the impact of sample size on predicted estimates of sampling error. Using the estimated standard error for a sample percentage where $(SE_{\bar{p}})$ equals the overall square root of $(\bar{p})(\bar{q})/n$ and $\bar{p}$ is held constant at 50%, the researcher calculates the predicted estimated standard error as the sample is doubled holding all other factors constant. The results would be as follows:

Sample Results ($\bar{p}$)	Sample Size	Estimated Standard Error ($SE_{\bar{p}}$)	Change in $SE_{\bar{p}}$
50%	10	±15.8%	—
50	20	±11.2	4.6%
50	40	±7.9	3.3
50	80	±5.6	2.3
50	160	±4.0	1.6
50	320	±2.8	1.2
50	640	±2.0	0.8

Graphically displaying the results:

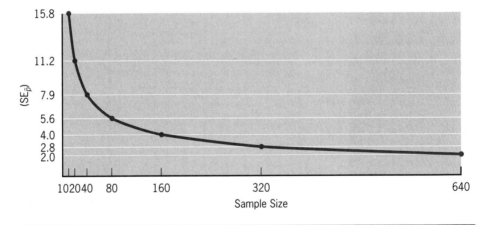

Determining Statistical Precision

As discussed earlier, knowing the sampling distributions and their shapes allows the researcher to make estimates or inferential judgments regarding the true position of the target population. Using several statistical methods, the researcher is able to specify the critical tolerance level of error (i.e., allowable margin of error) prior to undertaking a research study. This critical tolerance level of error, also referred to as the *alpha factor* (α), represents general precision (SE) with no specific confidence level or precise precision $[(SE)(Z_{B,CL})]$ when a specific level of confidence is required. In simple terms, the **critical tolerance level of error** is the amount of observed difference between a sample statistical value (e.g., $\bar{x}$ or $\bar{p}$) and the true or hypothesized target population parameter value that is deemed acceptable by the researcher prior to data collection activities.

General precision can be viewed as the amount of general sampling error associated with the given sample of raw data that was generated through some type of data collection activity. **Precise precision** represents the amount of measured sampling error associated

Critical tolerance level of error   The observed difference between a sample statistical value and the corresponding true or hypothesized population parameter.

General precision   The amount of general sampling error associated with raw data.

Precise precision   The amount of sampling error at a specified level of confidence.

with the raw data at a specified level of confidence. When attempting to measure the precision of raw data, researchers must incorporate the theoretical understanding of the concepts of sampling distributions, the central limit theorem, and estimated standard error in order to calculate the necessary confidence intervals.

Estimated Standard Error

Estimated standard error, also referred to as general precision, gives the researcher a measurement of the sampling error and an indication of how far the sample result lies from the actual target population parameter value estimate. The formula to compute the estimated standard error of a sample mean value ($SE_{\bar{x}}$) is

$$SE_{\bar{x}} = \bar{s}/\sqrt{n}$$

where: $\bar{s}$ = Estimated standard deviation of the sample mean

n = Sample size

For example, let's suppose that Burger King conducts a survey among the general population to determine how many hamburgers the average household in America purchases and consumes in a typical 30-day period. The researcher randomly draws a sample of 950 telephone numbers from the corporation's newly purchased telephone-number database, which consists of over 95 million residential telephone numbers. The survey results indicate that the average number of hamburgers purchased and consumed per household in the given period is 36 (i.e., $\bar{x} = 36$), and the estimated sample standard deviation is 12.5 hamburgers. Using the above formula, the researcher calculates the estimated standard error of the sample to be ±.406 hamburgers. Now assume that the researcher had randomly sampled only 400 households and the average number of hamburgers and estimated standard deviation values were found to be the same as before; in this case, the calculated general sampling error associated with the study increases to ±.625 hamburgers. Without concern for any confidence factor, the results suggest that there is a greater chance of sampling error when the actual sample size is reduced. This further illustrates the inherent inverse relationship between sample size (n) and the estimated standard error of a sample mean ($SE_{\bar{x}}$).

We can also find the estimated standard error of a sample percentage value ($SE_{\bar{p}}$) by using the following formula:

$$SE_{\bar{p}} = \sqrt{\frac{[(\bar{p})(\bar{q})]}{n}}$$

where:

$\bar{p}$ = The percentage of the sample possessing a specific characteristic

$\bar{q}$ = The percentage of the sample *not* possessing the characteristic or $(1 - \bar{p})$

n = Sample size

Let's suppose, for example, that NationsBank conducted a survey of customers with checking accounts and found that 65 percent of those sampled maintain a savings account in addition to a checking account (i.e., $\bar{p} = 65\%$). The result was from randomly sampling 489 currently known NationsBank customers. Using the above $SE_{\bar{p}}$ formula for sample percentages, the estimated standard error associated with the sample percentage would be ±2.16 percentage points. Again, the relative magnitude of the sampling error associated with the results is in lieu of any consideration for confidence by the researcher.

The estimated standard error is a measure of variability since it measures the range in which the actual value for the target population can be expected to fall. The more spread out or dissimilar the data, the greater the variability and the larger the estimated standard error. The more similar the survey results, the less the variability. The estimated standard error now can be used to construct a confidence interval in which the actual target population's parameter is expected to fall.

Confidence Interval

Confidence interval

The statistical range of values within which the true value of the defined target population parameter is expected to lie.

A **confidence interval** represents a statistical range of values within which the true value of the target population parameter is expected to lie. The endpoints of a confidence interval (upper and lower values) are determined on the basis of the sample's results. The following formulas may be used to establish a confidence interval for a population's mean value (μ) and a population's proportion value (P). The confidence interval formula for a population mean parameter is:

$$CI_\mu = \bar{x} \pm (SE_{\bar{x}})(Z_{B,CL})$$

where:

CI_μ = Confidence interval for a target population mean parameter

$\bar{x}$ = Sample mean value

$SE_{\bar{x}}$ = Estimated standard error of the sample mean

$Z_{B,CL}$ = Level of confidence expressed in standardized z-values

The confidence interval formula for a population proportion parameter is:

$$CI_P = \bar{p} \pm (SE_{\bar{p}})(Z_{B,CL})$$

where:

CI_P = Confidence interval for a target population proportion parameter

$\bar{p}$ = Sample proportion value

$SE_{\bar{p}}$ = Estimated standard error of the sample proportion

$Z_{B,CL}$ = Level of confidence expressed in standardized z-values

While in theory, there are an infinite number of confidence levels, ranging from almost 0 percent to almost 100 percent, the most commonly used confidence levels in information research are the 90, 95, and 99 percent levels. Since the central limit theorem allows researchers to assume normal sampling distribution curves, researchers can apply their knowledge of basic statistics regarding normal distribution curves and use a standardized critical z-value of 1.65 for a 90 percent level of confidence, a z-value of 1.96 for a 95 percent level of confidence, and a z-value of 2.58 for a 99 percent level of confidence. Since these are the standardized z-values, their values are the only ones represented from their respective confidence levels and will never change when used in calculating confidence intervals. Critical z-values are discussed in more detail in later chapters.

Using the above NationsBank example, if the researcher wished to construct a 95 percent confidence interval for the bank survey results, she or he could do so by using the above formula for a population proportion confidence interval and incorporating the estimated standard error previously calculated:

$$CI_P = 65\% \pm (2.16)(1.96)$$

$$= 65\% \pm 4.23\%$$

$$= (65\% - 4.23\%), (65\% + 4.23\%)$$

$$= 60.77\% \leq P \leq 69.23\%$$

In interpreting the constructed confidence interval, we are 95 percent confident that the actual percentage of NationsBank customers who have a checking account and a savings account with the bank will fall between 60.77 and 69.23 percent. Stated another way, if the researcher would have drawn repeated random samples of NationsBank's checking account customers, then 95 percent of the time (19 out of 20 times, or 95 out of 100 times), the true percentage of customers holding both checking and savings accounts with NationsBank would be somewhere between 60.77 and 69.23 percent.

It should be clear to see that the derived value generated by multiplying the estimated standard error associated with the given sample statistic by the critical z-value associated with the desired level of confidence determines the precise amount of random sampling error that may occur due to the sampling process. This, of course, is the definition of precise precision at a given level of confidence. As you read this chapter and the remaining chapters of the book, you should be able to see the strong importance of sampling error measurements and a researcher's ability to construct confidence intervals.

Determining Appropriate Sample Sizes

Determining the appropriate sample size is not an easy task. The researcher must consider how precise the estimates must be and how much time and money are available to collect the required data, since data collection is generally one of the most expensive components of a study. Three factors play an important role in determining appropriate sample sizes:

1. **The variability of the population characteristic under investigation (σ_μ or σ_P).** The greater the variability of the characteristic, the larger the size of the sample necessary.

2. **The level of confidence desired in the estimate (CL).** The higher the level of confidence desired, the larger the sample size needed.

3. **The degree of precision desired in estimating the population characteristic (α).** The more precise the required sample results, the larger the necessary sample size.

As with confidence intervals, there are separate yet similar formulas for determining sample size based on a predicted population mean (μ) and a population proportion (P). These formulas are fundamental in estimating the appropriate sample size for a simple random sample. When the situation involves information that relates to projected estimates of a population mean, the appropriate standardized formula for calculating the necessary sample size would be:

$$n = (Z^2_{B,CL}) \left(\frac{\sigma^2}{\alpha^2} \right)$$

where:

$Z_{B,CL}$ = The standardized z-value associated with the level of confidence

σ_μ = Estimate of the population standard deviation (σ) based on some type of prior information

α = Acceptable tolerance level of error (stated in percentage points)

In those situations where estimates of a population proportion are of concern, the standardized formula for calculating the needed sample size would be:

$$n = (Z^2_{B,CL}) \left(\frac{[P \times Q]}{\alpha^2} \right)$$

where:

$Z_{B,CL}$ = The standardized z-value associated with the level of confidence

P = Estimate of expected population proportion having a desired characteristic based on intuition or prior information

Q = $[1 - P]$, or the estimate of expected population proportion not holding the characteristic of interest

α = Acceptable tolerance level of error (stated in percentage points)

The formulas for determining the necessary sample size for a given situation are really nothing more than a manipulation of the standard formula for calculating the standard error of the population parameter, either SE_μ or SE_P, at a particular desired confidence level. Interpretation of the above sample-size models illustrates the existence of several general relationships between the models' components and the needed size of a sample. For example, when using the population mean formula, as the measurement of the variability (σ_μ) of the probability distribution of the population mean (μ) increases, holding the other factors constant, the larger the required sample size. Fundamentally, this relationship holds because σ_μ is part of the numerator of the equation. In contrast, when the situation requires the use of a population proportion (P) value, any population proportion value other than 50 percent (e.g., P = 70% or P = 30%), holding the other factors constant, will result in a decrease in the required sample size.

With regard to the confidence level, there is a direct relationship between the desired level of confidence (e.g., 90 percent, 95 percent, 99 percent) and the required sample size. As discussed earlier in the chapter, confidence levels are directly associated with corresponding standardized critical z-values (i.e., 90% CL $\approx$ 1.65; 95% CL $\approx$ 1.96; 99% CL $\approx$ 2.58). Since the confidence level component is part of the numerator, the higher the level of confidence required, the larger the required number in the sample.

The last key component in the formulas is the acceptable tolerance level of error (α); this represents the amount of statistical precision desired by the researcher. This value is normally stated as a percentage in either whole percentage points or decimal format (e.g., 2% [.02], 5% [.05], or 10% [.10]). The lower the percentage, the more precise the estimate and therefore the larger the required sample size. Normally, the degree of statistical precision is prespecified by the research user. This inverse relationship exists because this component is the denominator in each of the sample-size models.

The following example is offered to illustrate how researchers would calculate the required sample size in a situation where they use population parameter estimates from a pilot study. Assume you are the research analyst for LDS Technologies, a new long-distance telephone service provider located in Chicago, Illinois. Three months ago, LDS conducted a small pilot study in San Diego, California, among 200 households that used a variety of long-distance telephone services. The results suggested that 50 percent of the households studied could be classified as regular users of long-distance telephone services. Now, LDS has decided to do a larger study that would allow it to predict potential long-distance telephone usage patterns and understand people's criteria for choosing long-distance telephone services within its total proposed West Coast market. Management wants data precision to be ±3 percent with a 99 percent confidence level. To determine the necessary sample size, you would use the standard formula for a population proportion:

$$n = (Z^2_{B,CL})\left(\frac{[P \ \times \ Q]}{\alpha^2}\right)$$

where:

$Z_{B,CL}$ = 2.58, the standardized *z*-value associated with the 99% confidence level

P = 50%, the estimate proportion of LDS's potential customer base who are regular users of long-distance telephone services

Q = 50%, $[1 - P]$ or the estimate proportion of LDS's potential customer base who are not regular users of long-distance telephone services

α = ±3.0%, the acceptable tolerance level of error (stated in percentage points)

Thus,

$$n = 2.58^2 \frac{(50 \times 50)}{3.0^2}$$

$$= 6.6564 \frac{(2,500)}{9.0}$$

$$= 6.6564 \, (277.8) = 1,849.15, \text{ or } 1,850 \text{ households}$$

As a result, LDS's management will have to randomly select and survey a sample of 1,850 households in LDS's West Coast market in order to feel comfortable that the research results would be within the desired ±3.0 percent acceptable tolerance level of error range at a 99 percent confidence level.

Sample Size and Small Finite Populations

In most marketing research situations, the actual size of a population does not have a major impact on the sample-size estimates. When considering sampling there is often a misconception that a larger population requires that a larger sample be taken to generate an accurate result. In the formulas discussed, the size of the population is not a direct factor in determining sample size. This is always true when the population is large. However, if a population is small relative to the calculated sample size, a **finite correction factor (fcf)**, also referred to as the finite population factor, should be used to determine the required sample size. Research industry standards suggest that a population is considered small if the calculated sample size is more than 5 percent of the population. The formula for the finite correction factor is:

Finite correction factor (fcf) An adjustment factor to the sample size that is made in those situations where the drawn sample is expected to be equal to 5% or more of the defined target population. Fcf is equal to the overall square root of $[N – n/N – 1]$.

$$\sqrt{\frac{N - n}{N - 1}}$$

where:

N = Known (or given) defined target population size

n = Calculated sample size using the original sample size formula

Using the finite correction factor is a two-step process. First, we determine whether the sample size is more than 5 percent of the population by taking the calculated sample size and dividing it by the target population size. Second, if it is more than 5 percent, we calculate the appropriate finite correction factor and multiply the originally calculated sample size by it to adjust the required sample size. To illustrate how the finite correction factor affects estimates of sample sizes, let's use the above LDS Technologies example.

Initially not knowing how many households actually made up LDS's West Coast market, the researcher estimated that 1,850 randomly selected households would have to be

A CLOSER LOOK AT RESEARCH   In the Field

Dannon Yogurt Eliminates the Need for Costly Customized Random Sampling Designs

During the 1980s, the Dannon Yogurt Company established itself as the market leader of yogurt in the United States. Increased competition in the early 1990s forced Dannon to decide it needed a better understanding of the attributes and benefits that differentiated Dannon's brand of yogurt from the competition in the eyes of consumers. For this needed information, Dannon turned to its advertising firm, Grey Advertising, Inc., which in partnership with Marketplace Measurement Worldwide and Ambrosino Research created the Dannon Consumer Awareness, Attitude and Usage Tracking System. As an ongoing system to monitor the yogurt market, it allowed Dannon to quickly build a 300-member yogurt consumer profile database. Rather than having to periodically develop expensive random sampling designs of yogurt users to collect data, the profile database allowed Grey Advertising to conduct quarterly telephone interviews among all 300 database members to assess consumers' category, brand, and advertising awareness; brand usage; and attitudes toward Dannon and competitors' brands.

Using the latest three waves of interviews (900 altogether), the data were analyzed using Competitive Leverage Analysis, a customized statistical tool created by Grey Advertising, Inc. Some of the findings indicated that consumers valued Dannon Yogurt because of the company's commitment to quality and purity in its ingredients, its manufacturing, and its packaging efforts. "Consumers felt a strong emotional attachment to buying Dannon, a sense of nurturing self and family." From the findings, Grey Advertising developed a new ad campaign slogan—"Taste Why It's Dannon"—to emphasize the care Dannon takes to use high-quality ingredients and suggest that this care is evident in the yogurt's taste. Measurement of the campaign's impact on Dannon's sales was partially achieved by having sales tracked by Information Resources Inc. (IRI) using supermarket scanner data. Analysis results indicated that Dannon's yogurt sales were growing at a faster pace than the yogurt category itself was growing. An interesting side effect of this type of sampling and research approach was that not only did the new ad campaign help stimulate Dannon sales to new heights, but in 1995, Grey Advertising, Dannon, Ambrosino Research, and Marketplace Measurement Worldwide were the recipients of the prestigious Advertising Research Foundation (ARF) David Ogilvy Award in recognition of the effective use of research in developing powerful advertising.

A key notion from this case is that creating accurate consumer profile databases can provide researchers with effective alternative sampling frameworks from which to collect needed data rather than the traditionally more costly random sampling designs.

Source: Paula Kephart, "The Leader of the Pack: How Dannon Yogurt Put Research to Work—and Came Out a Winner," *Marketing Tools* (September 1995), pp. 16, 18, 19.

---

included in the study, with data precision of ±3 percent and a 99 percent confidence level. Now let's assume that LDS's management learns that the initial target population size of the West Coast market is expected to be about 15,000 households. To determine whether the initial sample size needs to be adjusted, the researcher would first determine if the initial sample size was greater than 5 percent of the total defined target population size. This is achieved simply by dividing the estimated sample size [n] (1,850 households) by the target population size [N] (15,000 households). The results of this first step suggest that the initial estimated sample size represents about 12.33 percent of the defined target population; therefore, the finite correction factor should be calculated and applied to adjust the needed sample-size estimate. Using the above standard formula, the needed correction factor is .93634. Now multiplying the initial sample-size estimate (1,850 households) by the correction factor, LDS's management realizes that the number of households needed in the larger study is only 1,733, a reduction of 117 households. When appropriately used, the single biggest benefit of the finite correction factor is that it reduces the overall costs of collecting primary raw data.

In those cases where it is determined that the defined target population size is 500 elements or less, we strongly advocate that the researcher do a census of the population elements rather than worry about estimating correct sample sizes. The logic behind this suggestion relates to the theoretical notion that at least 384 sampling units would need to be included in most studies for the researcher to operate at a 95 percent confidence level with a tolerance in sampling error of ±5 percentage points.

Nonprobability Sampling and Sample Size

Since sample-size formulas cannot be appropriately used for nonprobability samples, the determination of the necessary sample size is usually a subjective, intuitive judgment made by the researcher based on either past studies (to be used for comparison), industry standards, or the amount of resources available. Regardless of the method used, the sampling results cannot be used to make statistical inferences about the true population parameters of interest. The best that can be offered are preliminary insights into the defined target population parameters.

Sample Sizes versus Usable Observations for Data Analysis

One issue of concern in estimating required sample sizes that is rarely discussed but that researchers must consider has to do with which observations are actually usable. Using the principles of sampling theory, researchers are able to estimate the number of sampling units that must be surveyed in order to ensure that the sample statistics represent the parameters of the defined target population. In theory, all the selected sampling units' responses need to be included in the data analysis. In reality, however, not all the initial sampling units are actually usable. Reasons for this include inactive mailing addresses, telephone numbers no longer in service, and incomplete responses.

A question can be raised concerning the sample-size value that is incorporated into many of the statistical models used to estimate the defined target population's parameter values from a survey's sample statistics. For example, if in the sampling process researchers estimate that one sample size—say, 1,850—is needed but fewer sampled units—say, 1,500—are entered into data analysis, then what sample size value should be used in the statistical models to calculate and test estimates of the target population, 1,850 or 1,500? This difference of 350 sampling units can have a significant impact on the relative magnitudes of the sample statistics. More detailed discussions on this issue are provided in later chapters, with the topic of nonresponse bias.

How specifically the target population is defined (i.e., the number of qualifying factors) will affect the researcher's ability to obtain a representative list of all the sampling units that can be effective in locating the drawn sampling units. While there are a number of factors that can come into play, making any list less than 100 percent usable, the list's *reachable rate* and *overall incidence rate,* combined with the study's *expected completion rate* and the estimated sample size, are key in determining the actual number of contacts (e.g., telephone calls, initial mall-intercepts, or mailings) that will be necessary to obtain the required raw data from a drawn sample. The total number of necessary contacts will directly affect the overall cost of data collection. The reachable rate (RR) will reflect the quality of the overall derived sampling frame. For example, in a direct mail survey, the mailing list that serves as the sampling frame may be dated, with some of the listed addresses no longer active. Normally, the percentage of active addresses on a mailing list serves as the reachable rate.

The overall incidence rate (OIR) is the percentage of the defined target population elements who actually qualify for inclusion into the survey. For example, let's assume researchers are doing a telephone survey for Time Warner Cable on people's TV viewing habits. Assume the needed sample size was estimated to be 1,500 people. In addition, Time Warner decides that to qualify for the survey, individuals must meet the following set of requirements:

- Are between the ages of 20 and 60.

- Have (or have access to) a cable TV set.

- Do not work for a telecommunication company, marketing research firm, or TV station, or have anyone in their immediate household who does.

- Have not participated in a marketing research study in the past six months.

The more qualifying factor requirements placed on prospective respondents, the greater the chance that the individual will not qualify. A rule of thumb is that as more qualifying (or screening) factors are activated in the process of locating prospective respondents, the overall incidence rate significantly decreases.

In the research industry, the expected completion rate (ECR) reflects the percentage of prospective respondents who will follow through and complete the survey. This factor is also referred to as the *anticipated response rate*. In the Time Warner example, let's say that the reachable rate was determined to be 90 percent, the overall incidence rate was estimated to be 55 percent, and the expected completion rate for telephone interviews of this nature was 85 percent. Using the following formula,

$$\text{Number of contacts} = \frac{n}{(\text{RR}) \times (\text{OIR}) \times (\text{ECR})}$$

$$= \frac{1,500}{.90 \times .55 \times .85}$$

$$= \frac{1,500}{.421} = 3,562.95, \text{ or } 3,563 \text{ people}$$

To ensure that the estimated sample size of 1,500 will be obtained, this number must be adjusted by the reachable, overall incidence, and expected completion rates. Consequently, this means that Time Warner Cable must contact about 3,563 people in order to ensure that the needed sample size of 1,500 people is obtained. Prior to conducting the study, Time Warner's management group will have to consider the cost of contacting an extra 2,063 people in order to base the data results on the needed 1,500 respondents.

Overview: Probability and Nonprobability Sampling

Probability sampling
A technique of drawing a sample in which each sampling unit has a known, nonzero probability of being included in the sample.

How to obtain a sample is a very important issue when designing a study that uses interviewing or surveys for raw data collection. Overall, there are two basic sampling designs: probability and nonprobability (see Exhibit 11.6).

In **probability sampling,** each sampling unit in the defined target population has a known, nonzero probability of being selected for the sample.[6] The actual probability of selection for each sampling unit may or may not be equal depending on the type of probability sampling design used. Specific rules for selecting members from the operational population for inclusion in the sample are set forth at the beginning of a study and are

EXHIBIT 11.6	Types of Probability and Nonprobability Sampling Methods

Probability Sampling Methods	**Nonprobability Sampling Methods**
Simple Random Sampling	Convenience Sampling
Systematic Random Sampling	Judgment Sampling
Stratified Random Sampling • Proportionate • Disproportionate	Quota Sampling
	Snowball Sampling
Cluster Sampling • Area Sample	

made to ensure (1) unbiased selection of the sampling units and (2) proper sample representation of the defined target population. Probability sampling allows the researcher to judge the reliability and validity of raw data collected by calculating the probability to which the findings based on the sample would differ from the defined target population.[7] As discussed earlier, this observed difference can be partially attributed to the existence of sampling error. The results obtained by using probability sampling designs can be generalized to the target population within a specified margin of error through the use of statistical methods. In **nonprobability sampling,** the probability of selection of each sampling unit is not known. Therefore, potential sampling error cannot be accurately known either. The selection of sampling units is based on some type of intuitive judgment, desire, or knowledge of the researcher. The degree to which the sample may or may not be representative of the defined target population depends on the sampling approach and how well the researcher executes and controls the selection activities.[8] Although there is always a temptation to generalize nonprobability sample data results to the defined target population, in reality those results are limited to just those people who provided the raw data in the survey. A researcher should not even attempt to generalize the survey's data results or make inferences about those people in a nonprobability sample who for some reason demonstrated an unwillingness to participate. Exhibit 11.7 provides a comparison of probability and nonprobability sampling methods based on several sampling factors.

Nonprobability sampling The sampling process where the probability of selection of each sampling unit is unknown.

Types of Probability Sampling Designs

Simple Random Sampling

Simple random sampling (SRS) A probability sampling procedure that ensures that every sampling unit in the target population has a known, equal, nonzero chance of being selected.

Simple random sampling (SRS) is a probability sampling procedure that ensures that every sampling unit making up the defined target population has a known, equal, nonzero chance of being selected. For example, let's say an instructor decided to draw a sample of 10 students ($n = 10$) from among all the students in a marketing research class that consisted of 30 students ($N = 30$). The instructor could write each student's name on a separate, identical piece of paper and place all of the names in a jar. Each student would have an equal, known probability of selection for a sample of a given size that could be expressed by the following formula:

$$\text{Probability of selection} = \frac{\text{Size of sample}}{\text{Size of population}}$$

Here, each student in the marketing research class would have a 10/30 (or .333) chance of being randomly selected in the drawn sample.

EXHIBIT 11.7   Summary of Comparative Differences of Probability and Nonprobability Sampling Methods

Comparison Factors	Probability Sampling	Nonprobability Sampling
List of the Population Elements	Complete List Necessary	None Necessary
Information about the Sampling Units	Each Unit Identified	Need Detail on Habits, Activities, Traits, etc.
Sampling Skill Required	Skill Required	Little Skill Required
Time Requirement	Time-Consuming	Low Time Consumption
Cost per Unit Sampled	Moderate to High	Low
Estimates of Population Parameters	Unbiased	Biased
Sample Representativeness	Good, Assured	Suspect, Undeterminable
Accuracy and Reliability	Computed with Confidence Intervals	Unknown
Measurement of Sampling Error	Statistical Measures	No True Measure Available

When the defined target population consists of a larger number of sampling units, a more sophisticated method would be used to randomly draw the necessary sample. One of the procedures commonly used in marketing research is to incorporate a printed or computer-generated table of random numbers to select the sampling units. A table of random numbers is just what its name implies, a table that lists randomly generated numbers (see Exhibit 11.8). Many of today's computers have the ability to generate a table of random numbers.

Using the same marketing research students defined above as the target population, a random sample could be generated (1) by using the last two digits of the students' social security numbers or (2) by assigning each student a unique two-digit code ranging from 01 to 30. Using the first procedure, we would have to make sure that no two students have the same last two digits in their social security number; the range of acceptable numbers would

EXHIBIT 11.8   A Partial Table of Random Numbers

31	25	81	44	54	34	67	03
14	96	99	80	14	54	30	74
49	05	49	56	35	51	68	36
99	67	57	65	14	46	92	88
54	14	95	34	93	18	78	27
57	50	34	89	99	14	57	37
98	67	78	25	06	90	39	90
40	99	00	87	90	42	88	18
20	82	09	18	84	91	64	80
78	84	39	91	16	08	14	89

Source: M. G. Kendall and B. Babington Smith, "Table of Random Sampling Numbers," *Tracts for Computers, 24* (Cambridge, England: Cambridge University Press, 1946), p. 33.

be from 00 to 99. Then we could go to the table of random numbers and select a starting point, which can be anywhere on the table. Using Exhibit 11.8, let's say we select the upper left-hand corner of the table (31) as our starting point. We would then begin to read down the first column (or across the first row) and select those two-digit numbers that matched the numbers within the acceptable range until 10 students had been selected. Reading down the first column, we would start with 31, then go to 14, 49, 99, 54, and so on.

If we had elected to assign a unique descriptor (01 to 30) to each student in class, we would follow the same selection procedure from the random number table, but use only those random numbers that matched the numbers within the acceptable range of 01 to 30. Numbers that fell outside the acceptable range would be disregarded. Thus, we would begin and select students with numbers 14, 20, 25, 05, 09, 18, 06, 16, 08, and 30. If the overall research objectives call for telephone interviews, drawing the necessary sample can be achieved using the random-digit dialing (RDD) technique (refer back to Exhibit 11.2).

ADVANTAGES AND DISADVANTAGES. The simple random sampling technique has several noteworthy advantages. The technique is easily understood and the survey's data results can be generalized to the defined target population with a prespecified margin of error α. Another advantage is that simple random samples allow the researcher to gain unbiased estimates of the population's characteristics. This method basically guarantees that every sampling unit of the population has a known and equal chance of being selected, no matter the actual size of the sample, resulting in a valid representation of the defined target population. The primary disadvantage of simple random sampling is the difficulty of obtaining a complete, current, and accurate listing of the target population elements. Simple random sampling requires that all sampling units be identified. For this reason, simple random sampling often works best for small populations or those where computer-derived lists are available.

Systematic Random Sampling

Systematic random sampling (SYMRS)
A probability sampling technique that requires the defined target population to be ordered in some way.

Systematic random sampling (SYMRS) is similar to simple random sampling but requires that the defined target population be ordered in some way, usually in the form of a customer list, taxpayer roll, or membership roster. In research practices, SYMRS has become a very popular alternative probability method of drawing samples. Compared to simple random sampling, systematic random sampling is potentially less costly because it can be done relatively quickly.[9] When executed properly, SYMRS can create a sample of objects or prospective respondents that is very similar in quality to a sample drawn using SRS.

To employ SYMRS, the researcher must be able to secure a complete listing of the potential sampling units that make up the defined target population. But unlike SRS, there is no direct need to transcribe the sampling units or give them any special code prior to drawing the sample. Instead, individual sampling units are selected according to their position using a skip interval. The skip interval is determined by dividing the number of potential sampling units in the defined target population by the number of units desired in the sample. The required skip interval is calculated using the following standardized formula:

$$\text{Skip interval} = \frac{\text{Defined target population list size}}{\text{Desired sample size}}$$

For instance, if the researcher wants a sample of 100 to be drawn from a defined target population of 1,000, the skip interval would be 10 (1,000/100). Once the skip interval is determined, the researcher would then randomly select a starting point and take every 10th unit until he or she had proceeded through the entire target population list. Exhibit 11.9 displays the steps that a researcher would take in drawing a systematic random sample.

EXHIBIT 11.9	**Steps in Drawing a Systematic Random Sample**

Step 1 → **Obtain a List of Potential Sampling Units that Contains an Acceptable Frame of the Target Population Elements.**
Example: Current list of students (names, addresses, telephone numbers) enrolled at your university or college from the registrar's office.

Step 2 → **Determine the Total Number of Sampling Units Comprising the List of the Defined Target Population's Elements and the Desired Sample Size.**
Example: 30,000 current student names on the list. Desired sample size is 1,200 students, for a confidence level of 95%, *P* value equal to 50%, and tolerance sampling error of ± 2.83 percentage points.

Step 3 → **Compute the Needed Skip Interval by Dividing the Number of Potential Sampling Units on the List by the Desired Sample Size.**
Example: 30,000 current student names on the list, desired sample of 1,200, so the skip interval would be every 25th name.

Step 4 → **Using a Random Number-Generation System, Randomly Determine a Starting Point to Sample the List of Names.**
Example: Select: Random number for starting page of the multiple-page listing (e.g., 8th page).
Select: Random number for name position on that starting page (e.g., Carol V. Clark).

Step 5 → **With Carol V. Clark as the First Sample Unit, Apply the Skip Interval to Determine the Remaining Names That Should Be Included in the Sample of 1,200.**
Example: Clark, Carol V. (Skip 25 names.)
Cobert, James W. (Skip 25 names.)
Damon, Victoria J. (Skip 25 names; repeat process until all 1,200 names are drawn.)

Note: The researcher must visualize the population list as being continuous or "circular"; that is, the drawing process must continue past those names that represent the Z's and include names representing the A's and B's so that the 1,200th name drawn will basically be the 25th name prior to the first drawn name (i.e., Carol V. Clark).

There are two important considerations when using systematic random sampling. First, it is important that the natural order of the defined target population list be unrelated to the characteristic being studied. Second, the skip interval must not correspond to a systematic change in the target population. For example, if a skip interval of 7 were used in sampling daily sales or invoices from a retail store like Bloomingdale's and Tuesday was randomly selected as the starting point, we would end up with data from the same day every week. We would not want to draw conclusions regarding overall sales performance based on what has happened every Tuesday.

ADVANTAGES AND DISADVANTAGES. Systematic sampling is frequently used because, done correctly, it is a relatively easy way to draw a sample while ensuring randomness. The availability of lists and the shorter time required to draw a sample versus simple random sampling makes systematic sampling an attractive, economical method for researchers. The greatest weakness of systematic random sampling is the potential for there to be hidden patterns in the data that are not found by the researcher. This could result in a sample that is not truly representative of the defined target population. Nonetheless, the potential small loss in overall representativeness of the target population is normally countered by significantly larger economic savings in time, effort, and cost. Another difficulty is that the researcher must know exactly how many sampling units make up the defined target population. In research situations in which the size of the target population is extremely large or unknown, identifying the true number of units is difficult, and even estimates may not be accurate.

Stratified Random Sampling

Stratified random sampling (STRS) requires the separation of the defined target population into different groups, called *strata,* and the selecting of samples from each stratum. Stratified random sampling is very useful when the divisions of the target population are skewed or when extremes are present in the probability distribution of the target population elements of interest. The goal in stratifying is to minimize the variability (or skewness) within each stratum and maximize the differences between strata. In some ways, STRS can be compared to segmentation of the defined target population into smaller, more homogeneous sets of elements. Depending on the problem situation, there are cases in which the defined target population does not portray a normal symmetric distribution of its elements.

To ensure that the sample maintains the required precision of the total population, representative samples must be drawn from each of the smaller population groups (i.e., each stratum). Drawing a stratified random sample involves three basic steps:

1. Dividing the target population into homogeneous subgroups or strata.

2. Drawing random samples from each stratum.

3. Combining the samples from each stratum into a single sample of the target population.

Let's say, for example, that the researchers were interested in the market potential for home security systems in a specific geographic area. They may wish to divide the homeowners into several different strata. The subdivisions could be based on such factors as assessed value of the homes, household income, population density, or location (e.g., sections designated as high and low crime areas).

There are two common methods for deriving samples from the strata: proportionate and disproportionate. In **proportionate stratified sampling,** the sample size from each stratum is dependent on that stratum's size relative to the defined target population. Therefore, the larger strata are sampled more heavily using proportionate stratified sampling because they comprise a larger percentage of the target population. In **disproportionate stratified sampling,** the sample size selected from each stratum is independent of that stratum's proportion of the total defined target population. This approach is used when stratification of the target population produces sample sizes for subgroups that contradict their relative importance to the study. For example, stratification of manufacturers based on the factor *number of employees* will usually result in a large segment of manufacturers with less than 10 employees and a very small proportion with, say, 500 or more employees. The obvious economic importance of those firms with 500 or more employees would dictate taking a larger sample from this stratum and a smaller sample from the subgroup with less than 10 employees than indicated by the proportionality method.

An alternative type of disproportionate stratified method is *optimal allocation.* In this method, consideration is given to both the relative size of the stratum as well as the variability within the stratum to determine the necessary sample size of each stratum. The basic logic underlying optimal allocation is that the greater the homogeneity of the prospective sampling units within a particular stratum, all else the same, the fewer the units that would have to be selected to estimate the true population parameter (μ or P) accurately for that subgroup. In contrast, the opposite would hold true for any stratum that

---

Stratified random sampling (STRS) A probability sampling method in which the defined target population is divided into groups, called strata, and samples are selected from each stratum.

Proportionate stratified sampling A stratified sampling method in which each stratum is dependent on its size relative to the population.

Disproportionate stratified sampling A stratified sampling method in which the size of each stratum is independent of its relative size to the population.

had considerable variance among its sampling units or that was perceived as heterogeneous. Exhibit 11.10 displays the basic steps that a researcher would take in drawing a proportionate stratified random sample.

ADVANTAGES AND DISADVANTAGES. Dividing the defined target population into homogeneous strata provides several advantages, including: (1) the assurance of representativeness in the sample; (2) the opportunity to study each stratum and make relative comparisons between strata; and (3) the ability to make estimates for the target population with the

---

EXHIBIT 11.10   Steps in Drawing a Stratified Random Sample

Step 1: ➤ **Obtain a List of Potential Sampling Units That Contains an Acceptable Frame of the Defined Target Population Elements.**
Example: List of known performance arts patrons (names, addresses, telephone numbers) living in a three-county area from the current database of the Asolo Performing Arts Centre. Total number of known patrons on the current database is 10,500.

Step 2: ➤ **Using Some Type of Secondary Information or Past Experience with the Defined Target Population, Select a Stratification Factor for Which the Population's Distribution Is Skewed (Not Bell-Shaped) and Can Be Used to Determine That the Total Defined Target Population Consists of Separate Subpopulations of Elements.**
Example: Using attendance records and county location, identify strata by county and number of events attended per season (i.e., regular, occasional, or rare). Total: 10,500 patrons with 5,900 "regular" (56.2%); 3,055 "occasional" (29.1%); and 1,545 "rare" (14.7%) patrons.

Step 3: ➤ **Using the Selected Stratification Factor (or Some Other Surrogate Variable), Segment the Defined Target Population into Strata Consistent with Each of the Identified Separate Subpopulations. That is, use the stratification factor to regroup the prospective sampling units into their mutually exclusive subgroups. Then determine both the actual number of sampling units and their percentage equivalents for each stratum.**
Example: County A: 5,000 patrons with 2,500 "regular" (50%); 1,875 "occasional" (37.5%); and 625 "rare" (12.5%) patrons.

County B: 3,000 patrons with 1,800 "regular" (60%); 580 "occasional" (19.3%); and 620 "rare" (20.7%) patrons.

County C: 2,500 patrons with 1,600 "regular" (64%); 600 "occasional" (24%); and 300 "rare" (12%) patrons.

Step 4: ➤ **Determine Whether There Is a Need to Apply a Disproportionate or Optimal Allocation Method to the Stratification Process; Otherwise, Use the Proportionate Method and Then Estimate the Desired Sample Sizes.**
Example: Compare individual county strata percentage values to overall target population strata values. Let's assume a proportionate method and a confidence level of 95% and a tolerance for sampling error of ±2.5 percentage points. Estimate the sample size for total target population with no strata needed and assuming $P = 50\%$. The desired sample size would equal 1,537 people. Then proportion that size by the total patron percentage values for each of the three counties determined in step 2 (e.g., County A = 5,000/10,500 [47.6%]; County B = 3,000/10,500 [28.6%]; County C = 2,500/10,500 [23.8%]. New sample sizes for each county would be: County A = 732; County B = 439; County C = 366. Now for each county sample size, proportion the sample sizes by the respective within-county estimates for "regular," "occasional," and "rare" strata percentages determined in step 3.

Step 5: ➤ **Select a Probability Sample from Each Stratum, Using either the SRS or SYMRS Procedure.**
Example: Use the procedures discussed earlier for drawing SRS or SYMRS samples.

ETHICS

The U.S. government is interested in gaining public support for its idea of investing budget surpluses in the stock market as the approach to ensure the stability of the country's ailing Social Security Program for years to come. The administration's thought is that the members of the U.S. Congress respond in a predictable manner when they have American public opinion results in front of them. Government officials decide on using a quick telephone survey to ask the American people their opinions about three possible approaches: (1) invest a significant portion of government budget surpluses in the stock market; (2) use the surpluses to reduce overall income taxes of all Americans; or (3) use the surpluses to pay down the national debt. To conduct this study, the administration requests that U.S. Census Bureau researchers develop a sampling plan for the telephone survey to be administered to 5,000 randomly selected Americans that ensures representation across four age-groupings described as (a) 20 to 35, (b) 36 to 50, (c) 51 to 65, and (d) 66 and older. Reminded of the importance of the study's main objective, the researchers choose to develop a disproportionate stratified random sampling plan that would place heavier emphasis on those Americans in the 36 to 50 and

51 to 61 age groupings than on those people in the other two groupings. To help ensure the desired outcome, interviewers would be encouraged to "work hard" on getting responses from respondents between ages 36 and 65. It was further determined that no matter the actual within age-grouping response rates, only the study's overall response rate and normal error factor would be released to Congress, the media, and the general public.

- Is it ethical to conduct a study that knowingly misrepresents the true defined population for purposes of seeking a predetermined outcome?
- Is it ethical to encourage the interviewers to make disproportionate efforts to obtain completed interviews from less than all the defined sampled strata?
- Is it ethical to report only the overall response rate and error factor when a disproportionate stratified random sampling method is used to collect the data?
- Is it ethical not to report these facts to Congress, the media, and the general public, thereby causing these groups to misinterpret the results?
- Would it be more ethical to use a proportionate stratified random sampling approach?

expectation of greater precision or less error in the overall sample. The primary difficulty encountered with stratified sampling is determining the basis for stratifying. It is imperative that the basis for stratifying be directly associated with the target population's characteristics of interest. Secondary information relevant to the required stratification factors might not be readily available, therefore forcing the researcher to use less than desirable surrogate variables as the factors for stratifying the target population. Normally, the larger the number of relevant strata, the more precise the results. However, the inclusion of excess or irrelevant strata will only waste time and money without providing meaningful results.

Cluster Sampling

Cluster sampling

A probability sampling method in which the sampling units are divided into mutually exclusive and collectively exhaustive subpopulations, called clusters.

While **cluster sampling** is similar to stratified random sampling, it is different in that the sampling units are divided into mutually exclusive and collectively exhaustive subpopulations, called clusters, rather than individually.[10] Each cluster is assumed to be representative of the heterogeneity of the target population. Examples of possible divisions for cluster sampling include the customers who patronize a store on a given day, the audience for a movie shown at a particular time (e.g., the matinee), or the invoices processed during a specific week. Once the cluster has been identified, the prospective sampling units (or population elements) are drawn into the sample by either using a simple random sampling method or canvassing all the elements (i.e., doing a census) within the defined cluster.

Area sampling A form of cluster sampling in which the clusters are formed by geographic designations.

In information and marketing research, a popular form of cluster sampling is **area sampling.** In area sampling, the clusters are formed by geographic designations. Examples include metropolitan statistical areas (MSAs), cities, subdivisions, and blocks. Any geographical unit with identifiable boundaries can be used. When using area sampling, the researcher has two additional options: the one-step approach or the two-step approach. When deciding on using a one-step approach, the researcher must have enough prior information about the various geographic clusters to believe that all the geographic clusters are basically identical with regard to the specific cluster designation factors that were used to initially identify the clusters. By assuming that all the clusters are identical, the researcher can focus his or her attention on surveying the sampling units within one designated cluster group and then generalize the data results to the full target population. The probability aspect of this particular sampling method is executed by randomly selecting one geographic cluster and performing a census on all the sampling units located within that selected cluster.

Let's say, for example, that the corporate vice president of merchandising for Dillard's Department Stores is interested in learning about a variety of shopping behaviors among people who shop at the 36 Dillard's stores located throughout Florida. Given budget constraints and a review of customer profile information available on the database kept at corporate headquarters, the vice president assumes that the same types of customers shop at Dillard's regardless of the store's geographic location or day of the week. Consequently, the new Dillard's store located in University Mall in Tampa, Florida, is randomly selected as the store site for conducting random in-store personal interviews. Although conducting a census of all shoppers in the store would be preferred, it is deemed impossible to accomplish. Alternatively, 300 interviews are scheduled to be conducted on Wednesday, February 17, 2000.

Weaknesses exist with the vice president's logic of using a one-step cluster sampling method to collect data on customers' shopping behaviors. First, his assumption that customers at the University Mall store are similar to customers who shop at the other 35 stores in Florida might well be unfounded. Second, to assume that geographic differences in stores and consumers do not exist is basically a leap of faith. Limiting the sampling to only Wednesday can create problems as well. To assume that heterogeneity of consumers' attitudes and shopping behaviors (i.e., traffic flow patterns) toward Dillard's Department Stores are the same on a weekday as they are on the weekend might prove to be very misleading.

Alternatively, the researcher may execute a two-step cluster sampling approach. First, the researcher would randomly sample a set of clusters and then would decide on the most appropriate probability method to sample individuals within each of the selected clusters. Usually, the two-step approach is preferable over the one-step approach, because there is a strong possibility that a single cluster will not be as representative of all other clusters as the researcher thinks. To illustrate the basics of the two-step cluster sampling approach, let's go back and use the above Dillard's Department Store example. In reviewing Dillard's database on customer profiles, let's assume that the 36 stores can be clustered, based on annual gross sales revenue, into three groups: (1) store type A (stores with gross sales under $2 million), (2) store type B (stores having gross sales of between $2 million and $5 million), and (3) store type C (stores with over $5 million in gross sales). As a result, the vice president of merchandising identifies that among the 36 stores operating in the Florida market, 6 stores can be grouped as being type A, another 18 stores as type B, and 12 stores as type C. In addition, it was determined that sales were significantly heavier on weekends (i.e., Friday, Saturday, and Sunday) than during the week (i.e., Monday through Thursday). Exhibit 11.11 displays the basic steps that the researcher would take in drawing a cluster sample for the Dillard's situation.

EXHIBIT 11.11 Steps in Drawing a Two-Step Cluster Sample

Step 1 → **Fully Understand the Information Problem Situation and Characteristics That Are Used to Define the Target Population. Then Determine the Clustering Factors to Be Used to Identify the Clusters of Sampling Units.**

Example: Initial sampling units would be the 36 known Dillard's stores located throughout Florida. Using secondary data of stores' annual gross sales revenue, establish the cluster categories (i.e., store type A, B, and C) and weekday versus weekend dollar sales figures.

Step 2 → **Determine the Number of Sampling Units That Make Up Each Cluster, Obtain a List of Potential Sampling Units for Each Cluster, and Assign Them with a Unique Designation Code.**

Example: 6 type A stores—(01) Jacksonville; (5) Fort Lauderdale; (3) Gainesville; etc. 18 type B stores—(01) Tampa; (16) Sarasota; (07) Vero Beach; etc.
12 type C stores—(10) Miami; (02) West Palm Beach; (07) Orlando; etc.
Weekday sales—(01) through (52).
Weekend sales—(01) through (52).

Step 3 → **Determine Whether to Use a One-Step or Two-Step Cluster Sampling Method.**

Example: Given that both *store type* and *weekday/weekend sales* factors are being used to designate the clusters, a two-step clustering approach will be used to draw the sampling units.

Step 4 → **Determine How Many Sampling Units in Each Cluster Need to Be Sampled to Be Representative of That Cluster.**

Example: Given the perceived homogeneity within each cluster group of stores and cost considerations, let's assume that the researcher feels comfortable in sampling only one store in each store type over two weekday periods and four weekend periods.

Step 5 → **Using Random Numbers, Select the Sampling Unit (i.e., Store) within Each Cluster and the Weekday and Weekend Time Frames to be Sampled.**

Example: For store type A: (1) Jacksonville; weekday periods for weeks (10) and (34); weekend periods for weeks (03), (14), (26), and (41).
For store type B: (12) Lakeland; weekday periods for weeks (33) and (45); weekend periods for weeks (09), (24), (29), and (36).
For store type C: (10) Miami; weekday periods for weeks (22) and (46); weekend periods for weeks (04), (18), (32), and (37).

Step 6 → **Determine the Needed Sample Sizes for Each Cluster by Weekday/Weekend Time Frames.**

Example: Let's assume a desired confidence level of 95% and a tolerance for sampling error of ±2.5 percentage points. Estimate the desired sample size for total target population with no cluster grouping needed and assuming $P = 50\%$. The desired sample size would equal 1,537 people. Then proportion that size by the percentage values for each type of store to total number of stores making up the defined target population frame (i.e., store type A = 6/36 [16.7%]; store type B = 18/36 [50.0%]; store type C = 12/36 [33.3%]). New sample sizes for each store type would be: store type A = 257; store type B = 769; store type C = 512. Now for each store type sample size, proportion the sample sizes by the respected within weekday and weekend estimates, determined in step 4. As a result, the required sample sizes by store type by weekday/weekend time frames would be:

Store type A: Weekday periods 43 people in week (10), 43 people in week (34); Weekend periods 43 people in week (03) and the same number for weeks (14), (26), and (41).
Store type B: Weekday periods 43 people in week (33), 43 people in week (45); Weekend periods 43 people in week (09) and the same number for weeks (24), (29), and (46).
Store type C: Weekday periods 43 people in week (22), 43 people in week (46); Weekend periods 43 people in week (04) and the same number for weeks (18), (32), and (37).

Step 7 → **Select a Probability Sampling Method for Selecting Customers for In-Store Interviews.**

Example: Randomize the weekday interviews (i.e., Monday, Tuesday, Wednesday, and Thursday) as well as the weekend interviews (i.e., Friday, Saturday, and Sunday) so that the data are represented across shopping days and store operating hours.

ADVANTAGES AND DISADVANTAGES. For the most part, the cluster sampling method is widely used in marketing research due to its overall cost-effectiveness and feasibility of implementation, especially in area sampling situations.[11] In many cases, the only reliable sampling unit frame available to researchers, that is representative of the defined target population, is one that describes and lists clusters (e.g., states, counties, MSAs, census tracts). These lists of geographic regions, telephone exchanges, or blocks of residential dwellings can normally be easily compiled, thus avoiding the need of accurately compiling lists of all the individual sampling units (i.e., objects or people) comprising the target population. Clustering methods tend to be a cost-efficient way of sampling and collecting raw data from a defined target population.

In turn, cluster sampling methods are not without their disadvantages. One primary disadvantage related to cluster sampling is the tendency for clusters to be homogeneous. The more homogeneous the cluster, the less precise the derived sample estimates in representing the defined target population's parameters. Ideally, the actual objects or people within a cluster should be as heterogeneous as those in the target population itself. When the researcher believes that there are several sets of homogeneous clusters that are uniquely different on the basis of the designated clustering factor (i.e., Dillard's store type A, B, and C), this problem may be lessened by randomly selecting and sampling a unit from each of the cluster groups. Exhibit 11.11 illustrates how a researcher can overcome this problem of different homogeneous clusters within a defined target population.

Another concern with cluster sampling methods—one that is rarely addressed—is the appropriateness of the designated cluster factor used to identify the sampling units within clusters. Again let's use the Dillard's example to illustrate this potential weakness. Dillard's vice president of merchandising used a single geographic cluster designation factor (i.e., state of Florida) to derive one cluster consisting of 36 stores. By assuming that there was equal heterogeneity among all Dillard's shoppers, regardless of the store location, he randomly sampled one store to conduct the necessary in-store interviews. Then by changing the designation cluster factor to "annual gross sales revenue," he determined that there were three different sets of store clusters (i.e., store type A, B, and C) among the same 36 Dillard's stores located within Florida. This clustering method required a more complex sampling technique to ensure that the sample data collected would be representative of the defined target population of all Dillard's customers. The point here is that while the defined target population remains constant, the subdivision of sampling units can be modified depending on the selection of the designation factor used to identify the clusters.[12] This raises concerns about the most appropriate designation factor for determining the clusters in area sampling situations.

Types of Nonprobability Sampling Designs

Convenience Sampling

Convenience sampling
A nonprobability sampling method in which samples are drawn at the convenience of the researcher.

As the name implies, **convenience sampling** (or accidental sampling) is a method in which samples are drawn at the convenience of the researcher or interviewer, often as the study is being conducted. For example, mall-intercept interviewing of individuals at shopping malls or other high-traffic areas is a common method of generating a convenience sample. The assumptions are that the target population is homogeneous and the individuals interviewed at the shopping mall are similar to the overall defined target population with regard to the characteristic being studied. In reality, there is no way to accurately assess the representativeness of the sample. Given the self-selection and the voluntary nature of participating in the data collection process associated with convenience sampling, researchers should, but rarely do, give serious consideration to the extremely important issue of nonresponse error.

ADVANTAGES AND DISADVANTAGES. Convenience sampling allows a large number of respondents (e.g., 150–200) to be interviewed in a relatively short time. For this reason, it is commonly used in the early stages of research (i.e., construct and scale measurement development as well as pretesting activities of questionnaire designs). In turn, the use of convenience samples in the development phases of constructs and scale measurements can have a seriously negative impact on the overall reliability and validity of those measures and instruments used to collect raw data. Let's take, for example, a situation in which the researcher is developing a more accurate measurement of service quality and in the preliminary testing stages uses a convenience sample of 300 undergraduate business students to test his or her service-quality instrument. While college students are consumers of services, serious questions should be raised about whether these people are truly representative of either the general population or a more specific defined target population that might be investigated at a later time (i.e., patients at a hospital emergency room). By developing and refining constructs and scale measurements from data obtained from a convenience sample of college students, the construct's measurement instrument might later prove to be unreliable when used in investigations of other defined target populations. Another major disadvantage of convenience samples is that the raw data and results are not generalizable to the defined target population with any measure of precision. It is not possible to measure the representativeness of the sample, because sampling error estimates cannot be accurately determined.

Judgment Sampling

Judgment sampling
A nonprobability sampling method in which participants are selected according to an experienced individual's belief that they will meet the requirements of the study.

In **judgment sampling,** also referred to as purposive sampling, participants are selected according to an experienced individual's belief that they will meet the requirements of the study. In many industrial sales studies, the regional sales manager will often sample and survey the company's sales representatives rather than its actual customers to determine whether customers' wants and needs are changing or to assess the firm's product or service performance. Many consumer packaging manufacturers (e.g., Procter & Gamble) regularly select a sample of key accounts believed to be capable of providing insightful information about consumption patterns and possible changes in demand for selected products (e.g., Crest toothpaste, Cheer laundry detergent). The underlying assumption in these examples is the researcher's belief that the opinions of a group of perceived experts on the topic of interest are representative of the entire target population.

ADVANTAGES AND DISADVANTAGES. If the judgment of the researcher or expert is correct, then the sample generated from judgment sampling will be much better than one generated by convenience sampling, as far as providing information about the characteristic of interest. However, as is the case with all nonprobability sampling procedures, it is not possible to measure the representativeness of the sample. At best, the raw data and information collected from sampling units generated through the judgment sampling method should be interpreted as nothing more than preliminary insights.

Quota Sampling

Quota sampling A
nonprobability sampling method in which participants are selected according to prespecified quotas regarding demographics, attitudes, or behaviors.

The **quota sampling** method involves the selection of prospective participants according to prespecified quotas regarding either demographic characteristics (e.g., age, race, gender, income), specific attitudes (e.g., satisfied/dissatisfied, liking/disliking, great/marginal/no quality), or specific behaviors (e.g., regular/occasional/rare customer, product user/nonuser). The underlying purpose of quota sampling is to provide an assurance that prespecified subgroups of the defined target population are represented on pertinent sampling factors that are determined by the researcher or client. Moreover, surveys frequently use quotas that have been determined by the specific nature of the research objectives. For example, if an information research study were being conducted about fast-food restaurants, the researcher may establish quotas regarding an age factor and specific patronage behaviors of prospective respondents as follows

Age	Patronage Behavior
[1] Under 25	[1] Patronize a fast-food establishment an average of once a month or more
[2] 25 to 54	[2] Patronize fast-food establishments less frequently than once a month
[3] 55 and over	

Using these demographic and patronage behavior factors, the researcher identifies six different subgroups of people to be included in the study. Determining the quota size for each of the subgroups is somewhat of a subjective process on the part of the researcher. Here, the researcher might use secondary company sales information to determine the percentage size of each subgroup of respondents by the proportion that each subgroup has contributed to the firm's total sales. This ensures that the sample will contain the desired number in each subgroup. Once the individual percentage sizes for each quota category are established, the researcher would simply segment the total estimated sample size by those percentage values to determine the actual number of prospective respondents to include in each of the prespecified quota groups. Let's say, for example, that a fast-food restaurant wanted to interview 1,000 people and, using both industry-supplied sales reports and company sales records, determined that individuals aged 25 to 54 who patronize fast-food restaurants at least once a month make up 50 percent of its total sales. Here, the researcher would probably want that subgroup to make up 50 percent of the total sample. Let's further assume that company records indicated that individuals aged 25 to 54 who frequent fast-food restaurants less than once a month make up only 6 percent of sales. This particular subgroup should consist of only 6 percent of the total sample size.

ADVANTAGES AND DISADVANTAGES. The greatest advantage of quota sampling is that the sample generated contains specific subgroups in the proportions desired by researchers. In those research projects that require interviews, the use of quotas ensures that the appropriate subgroups are identified and included in the survey. The quota sampling method may eliminate or reduce selection bias on the part of the field workers. An inherent limitation of quota sampling is that the success of the study will again be dependent on subjective decisions made by the researchers. As a nonprobability sampling method, it is not possible to measure the true representativeness of the sample or accuracy of the estimate obtained. Therefore, attempts to generalize the data results beyond those respondents who were sampled and interviewed become very questionable and may misrepresent the given defined target population.

Snowball Sampling

Snowball sampling

A nonprobability sampling method in which a set of respondents is chosen and then helps the researcher identify additional people to be included in the study.

Snowball sampling involves the practice of identifying and qualifying a set of initial prospective respondents who can, in turn, help the researcher identify additional people to be included in the study. This method of sampling is also called *referral sampling,* because one respondent refers other potential respondents. Snowball sampling is typically used in research situations where (1) the defined target population is very small and unique, and (2) compiling a complete list of sampling units is a nearly impossible task.[13] Take, for example, the problem situation of researching the attitudes and behaviors of people who volunteer significant amounts of their time and energy to charitable organizations like the

Children's Wish Foundation. While the traditional probability and most other nonprobability sampling methods would normally require an extreme search effort (both in time and cost) to qualify a sufficient number of prospective respondents, the snowball method would yield better results at a much lower cost. Here the researcher would identify and interview one qualified respondent, then solicit his or her help in identifying other people with similar characteristics. While membership to these types of social circles might not be publicly well known, intracircle knowledge is very accurate. The main underlying logic of this method is that rare groups of people tend to form their own unique social circles.

ADVANTAGES AND DISADVANTAGES. Snowball sampling is a reasonable method of identifying and selecting prospective respondents who are members of small, hard-to-reach, uniquely defined target populations. As a nonprobability sampling method, it is most useful in qualitative research practices, like focus group interviews. Reduced sample sizes and costs are primary advantages to this sampling method. In turn, snowball sampling definitely allows bias to enter the overall research study. If there are significant differences between those people who are known within certain social circles and those who are not, there may be some problems with this sampling technique. Like all other nonprobability sampling approaches, data structures are limited in any attempts to generalize the results to members of the larger defined target population.

Determining the Appropriate Sampling Design

While keeping in mind the theoretical components, sampling issues, and advantages and disadvantages of the different sampling techniques, selection of the most appropriate sampling design should incorporate the seven factors displayed in Exhibit 11.12.

Research Objectives

A full understanding of the overall information problem situation and the research objectives provides the initial guidelines for determining the appropriate sampling design. If the research objectives include the desire to generalize the sample data results to the

EXHIBIT 11.12	**Critical Factors in Selecting the Appropriate Sampling Design**
Selection Factors	**Questions**
Research objectives	Do the research objectives call for the use of qualitative or quantitative research designs?
Degree of accuracy	Does the research call for making predictions or inferences about the defined target population or only preliminary insights?
Availability of resources	Are there tight budget constraints with respect to both dollars and manpower that can be allocated to the research project?
Time frame	How quickly does the research project have to be completed?
Advanced knowledge of the target population	Are there complete lists of the defined target population elements? How easy or difficult is it to generate the required sampling frame of prospective respondents?
Scope of the research	Is the research going be international, national, regional, or local?
Perceived statistical analysis needs	To what extent are accurate statistical projections required and/or testing of hypothesized differences in the data structures?

defined target population, then the researcher must seriously consider using some type of probability sampling method rather than a nonprobability sampling method. In addition, the stage of the research project (i.e., exploratory or conclusive) and type of research (i.e., qualitative versus quantitative) will influence the researcher's selection of sampling method.

Degree of Accuracy

The degree of accuracy required or the researcher's tolerance for error may vary from project to project, especially when cost savings or other considerations may be traded off for a reduction in accuracy. If the researcher wants to be able to make predictions or inferences about the "true" position of all members of the defined target population, then he or she must choose some type of probability sampling method. In contrast, if the researcher is solely trying to identify and obtain preliminary insights into the defined target population, nonprobability methods might prove to be more appropriate.

Availability of Resources

If the researcher's financial and human resources are restricted, these limitations will most certainly eliminate some of the more time-consuming, complex probability sampling methods. Marketing practitioners who are influenced by the cost concerns versus the value of the information will often opt for a nonprobability sampling method rather than conduct no research at all.

Time Frame

Researchers who need to meet a short deadline will be more likely to select a simple, less time-consuming sampling method rather than a more complex and accurate method. For example, researchers tend to opt for using some form of convenience sampling to gather data necessary to test the reliability of a newly developed construct or scale measurement. While data from this type of sampling method might appear to provide the researcher with preliminary insights about the defined target population, there is no accurate means of truly assessing the representativeness of the data or test results.

Advanced Knowledge of the Target Population

In many cases, a complete list of the population elements will not be available to the researcher. A lack of adequate lists may automatically rule out systematic random sampling, stratified random sampling, or any other type of probability sampling method. It may dictate that a preliminary study (e.g., a short telephone survey using random-digit dialing) be conducted to generate information to build a sampling frame for the study. Overall, the researcher must gain a strong understanding of the key descriptor factors that make up the true members of any target population. Review the following Using Technology box for insights on using the Internet to gain valuable intelligence information by sampling within databases.

Scope of the Research

Whether the scope of the research project is to be international, national, regional, or local will influence the choice of the sampling method. The projected geographic proximity of the defined target population elements will influence not only the researcher's ability to compile needed lists of sampling units, but also the selection design. When the target population elements are known or viewed to be unequally distributed geographically, a cluster sampling method may become much more attractive than other available methods. Generally speaking, the broader the geographical scope of the research project, the more exten-

A CLOSER LOOK AT RESEARCH | Using Technology

Sampling within Database Marketing Can Provide Invaluable Intelligence Information

As more businesses turn to online and database marketing research practices for solving marketing problems, sampling issues and procedures will play an increasing role in the success of obtaining the right information in a timely fashion. Advanced technologies used in creating and maintaining company-owned customer profile databases afford many businesses the opportunity to improve their capability to identify, understand, target, reach, and monitor customers. Increased availability of information from various online databases has enhanced the value of geodemographic segmentation and mapping practices. U.S.-based business owners seeking to expand their markets internationally can easily turn to the World Wide Web and locate businesses like Business

Geographic Online (www.geoweb.com) to gain access to geodemographic information. For example, a business could use this information to determine whether expansion in the United Kingdom would be economically and financially feasible. Population size, demographic composite and lifestyle characteristics, competitive situation, media coverage and efficiency, media isolation, overused test markets, self-contained trading areas, and availability of scanner data all could be used to sample a number of prospective target markets. The resulting information would prove to be invaluable in assessing the feasibility of expansion as well as determining the appropriate marketing strategy for expansion. In addition, online geodemographic information provides opportunities for digital mapping, store location planning, demographic customer profiling, and gravity modeling activities.

sive and complex the sampling method becomes to ensure proper representation of the target population.

Perceived Statistical Analysis Needs

The need for statistical projections (i.e., estimates) based on the sample results is often a criterion. Only probability sampling techniques allow the researcher to appropriately use statistical analysis for estimates beyond the immediate set of sampled respondents. While statistical analysis methods can be performed on data structures obtained from nonprobability samples of people and objects, the researcher's ability to accurately generalize the results and findings to the larger defined target population is very suspect and technically inappropriate. More detailed discussions concerning data analysis will be presented in later chapters. As discussed earlier, another important topic to most researchers in deciding on the appropriateness of any proposed sample design is that of determining the appropriate sample size for which to collect the necessary primary data for a given research project. Sample size has a direct impact on assessments of data quality, statistical precision, and generalizability of findings.

After understanding the key components of sampling theory, the methods of determining sample sizes, and the various designs available, the researcher is ready to integrate them into a workable sampling plan. A **sampling plan** is the blueprint or framework needed to ensure that the raw data collected are representative of the defined target population. A good sampling plan will include, at least, the following steps: (1) define the target population, (2) select the data collection method, (3) identify the sampling frames needed, (4) select the appropriate sampling method, (5) determine necessary sample sizes and overall contact rates, (6) create an operating plan for selecting sampling units, and (7) execute

Sampling plan The blueprint or framework needed to ensure that the raw data collected are representative of the defined target population.

the operational plan. For more information on these steps in developing a sampling plan, go to the Appendix at the end of this chapter.

Your understanding of the material covered in this chapter will set the tone for understanding the topics presented in the remainder of the text: construct and scale measurement development, questionnaire designs, coding and fieldwork, and data analysis techniques. Chapter 12 focuses on the process for collecting primary raw data and information by introducing construct development and scale measurement in marketing research practices.

SUMMARY OF LEARNING OBJECTIVES

Discuss the concept of sampling and list reasons for sampling.

Sampling can be thought of as taking a portion of the whole and studying that portion to make estimates about the whole. We use the fundamentals of sampling in many of our everyday activities (e.g., selecting a TV program to watch, test-driving a car before deciding whether to purchase it, determining if our food is too hot or if it needs some additional seasoning). The term *target population* is used to identify the complete group of elements (e.g., people or objects) that are specifically identified for investigation and determined by the specific objectives of the research project. The researcher is able to select sampling units from the target population and use the results obtained from the sample to make conclusions about the target population. It is essential that the sample be representative of the target population if it is to provide accurate estimates of population parameters.

Sampling is frequently used in marketing research projects as opposed to conducting a census because sampling can significantly reduce the amount of time and money required in data collection activities. In instances where the process of measurement in a study destroys or contaminates the elements being studied, sampling may be the only alternative.

Identify and explain the different roles that sampling plays in the overall information research process.

Sampling plays an important role when there are short time frames for gathering the needed information. These time frames are more likely to fit into the decision time frames of the users of the new information. Sampling plays a significant role in the process of identifying, developing, and understanding new marketing/business constructs as well as in developing the scale measurements used to actually collect raw primary data

about people or objects. Decisions concerning the use of samples indirectly affect the process of designing questionnaires. Finally, sampling plays a significant role in decisions concerning the type of data analysis procedures that can be employed to statistically investigate the sample data statistics.

Identify the fundamental differences between probability and nonprobability sampling methods, and point out their strengths and weaknesses.

We discussed probability and nonprobability sampling methods. Probability sampling methods require that each element in the target population be identified and have a known, nonzero probability of being selected for the sample, so that statistical methods can be used to project sample results to the target population within a specified margin of error. Probability sampling methods produce unbiased estimates of the defined target population characteristic of interest and ensure the representativeness of the sample. However, probability sampling designs can be time-consuming and expensive compared to nonprobability sampling methods.

Nonprobability sampling does not allow for the use of statistical methods to determine the degree of representativeness to the defined target population. Rather, sampling units are selected based on the subjective judgment or intuitive knowledge of the researcher. The success of the research project will depend on the decisions made by the researcher because it is all but impossible to accurately generalize the sample data derived from a nonprobability-based method to all the elements making up the target population.

Types of probability sampling designs include simple random sampling (SRS), systematic random sampling (SYMRS), stratified random sampling (STRS), and cluster sampling. Four types of nonprobability sampling designs are convenience (or accidental) sampling, judgment (or purposive) sampling, quota sampling, and snowball sampling.

Discuss and calculate sampling distributions, standard errors, and confidence intervals and how they are used in assessing the accuracy of a sample.

A sampling distribution is the frequency distribution of a specific sample statistic (e.g., sample mean [$\bar{x}$] or sample proportion [$\bar{p}$]) that would result if we took repeated random samples of the same size. The central limit theorem from statistics tells us that there is a high probability that the mean of any random sample taken from a target population will closely approximate the actual population mean as the sample size increases. Formulas are used to compute the estimated standard error of a sample mean ($\bar{x}$) and the estimated standard error of a sample percentage ($\bar{p}$). The estimated standard error $SE_{\bar{x}}$ or $SE_{\bar{p}}$ gives us an indication of how far the sample data results lie from their respective actual population parameters.

Confidence intervals are based on the researcher's desired level of confidence and within a calculated degree of sampling error for which estimates of the true value of the population parameter could be expected to fall.

Identify the criteria involved in determining the appropriate sample design for a given research project.

The sampling design for a given research project is chosen after considering several factors: (1) the research objectives, (2) degree of accuracy required, (3) availability of resources, (4) time frames, (5) advanced knowledge of the target population; (6) geographic scope of the project (e.g., local or national), and (7) perceived data analysis needs.

Discuss the factors that must be considered when determining sample size.

The researcher must consider several factors when determining the appropriate sample size to use for a given study. The amount of time and money available often affect this decision. In general, the larger the sample, the greater the amount of resources required to collect raw data. Three factors that are of primary importance in the determination of sample size are (1) the variability of the population characteristic under consideration (σ_μ or σ_P), (2) the level of confidence desired in the estimate (CL), and (3) the degree of precision desired in estimating the population characteristic (α). The greater the variability of the characteristic under investigation, the higher the level of confidence required; and the more precise the required sample results, the larger the necessary sample size.

Discuss the methods of calculating appropriate sample sizes.

Statistical formulas are used to determine the required sample size in probability sampling. Sample sizes for nonprobability sampling designs are determined using subjective methods such as industry standards, past studies, or the intuitive judgments on the part of the researcher. The size of the defined target population does not affect the size of the required sample unless the population is small relative to the sample size. Sample sizes are not the same as usable observations for data analysis. Having fewer observations than desired will affect the accuracy of the data. Researchers must therefore consider reachable rates, overall incidence rates, and expected completions rates on the number of prospective respondent contacts necessary to ensure sample accuracy.

Identify and explain the steps involved in developing a sampling plan, and design a variety of different sampling plans.

In the appendix to this chapter, we will briefly summarize the seven steps that should be included in the development of a sampling plan: (1) define the target population, (2) select the data collection method, (3) identify the sampling frames needed, (4) select the appropriate sampling method, (5) determine the necessary sample sizes and overall contact rates, (6) create an operating plan for selecting sampling units, and (7) execute the operational plan.

KEY TERMS AND CONCEPTS

REVIEW QUESTIONS

1. Why do many of today's research situations place heavy emphasis on correctly defining a target population rather than a total population?

2. What are the main difficulties associated with a sampling frame that has an overregistration condition? For an underregistration condition?

3. Why is so much importance placed on the central limit theorem in survey research designs?

4. Identify, graph, and explain the relationship between sample sizes and estimated standard error measures. What does the estimated standard error really measure in survey research?

5. Describe the major differences between probability and nonprobability sampling designs. What are the advantages and disadvantages of each?

6. The vice president of operations at Busch Gardens knows that 70 percent of the patrons like roller-coaster rides. He wishes to have an acceptable margin of error of no more than ±2 percent and wants to be 95 percent confident about the attitudes toward the "Gwazi" roller coaster. What sample size would be required for a personal interview study among on-site patrons?

DISCUSSION QUESTIONS

1. Critically discuss why a current telephone directory is not a good source from which to develop a sampling frame for most research studies.

2. Why do researchers find it necessary to calculate confidence intervals? In a telephone survey of 700 people, 45 percent responded positively to liking cats. Calculate a confidence interval, at the 95 percent confidence level, that will reveal the interval estimate for the proportion of people who like cats within a target population of 60,000 people. How would you interpret the results?

3. You work for the tourist commission in Fort Lauderdale, Florida. You are doing a survey on beer consumption and beer prices during spring break at Fort Lauderdale

Beach. Last year, the average price per six-pack of beer was $3.75, with a standard deviation of $.30, and average daily consumption of beer was 12 cans per person, with a deviation of 3.5 cans. Your survey requires a 90 percent confidence level and allowable errors of $.10 on the price of six-packs and 1.5 cans on beer consumption. Calculate the needed sample size for doing this year's survey among college students at Fort Lauderdale Beach during spring break.

4. Microsoft, Inc., contracts with an independent researcher to conduct a nationwide survey on in-home computer usage of Windows 98. The research proposal called for a confidence level of 95 percent, an acceptable error of ±2.0 percent, and a random sample of 2,500 respondents. The researcher is having difficulties getting qualified respondents. The deadline for completing the data collection activities is four days away, and only 1,000 surveys have been completed. To meet his sampling requirements, he goes to a local university and administers the survey to 1,500 college students within selected classroom environments. What are some of the ethical considerations of this situation?

5. **EXPERIENCE THE INTERNET.** Log on to the Internet and go to NYNEX Interactive Yellow Pages at www.niyp.com. The Interactive Yellow Pages consist of over 16 million businesses. After getting to the above Web site, select the Business Type option; then select the state of Colorado and *snow skiing equipment.* How many snow skiing equipment dealers are there in Colorado? Using a systematic random sampling design, draw a representative sample of those snow skiing equipment companies.

ENDNOTES

1. The actual prices of these types of lists will vary based on the complexity of the characteristics needed to define and qualify a population element.

2. Susan Garland, "Money, Power and Numbers: A Firestorm Over the Census," *Business Week,* September 19, 1990, p. 45.

3. Richard M. Jaeger, *Sampling in Education and the Social Sciences* (New York: Longman, 1984), p. 30; also see William G. Cochman, *Sampling Techniques,* 2nd ed. (New York: John Wiley and Sons, 1963).

4. William L. Hayes, *Statistics* (New York: Holt, Rinehart and Winston, 1963), p. 193.

5. T. H. Wonnacott and R. Wonnacott, *Introductory Statistics,* 2nd ed. (New York: John Wiley and Sons, 1972), p. 125.

6. James McGlove and P. George Benson, *Statistics for Business and Economics* (San Francisco: Dellen, 1988), pp. 184–85; also see "Probability Sampling in the Real World," *CATI NEWS* (Summer 1993), pp. 1, 4–6.

7. Jaeger, *Sampling in Education and the Social Sciences,* pp. 31–37.

8. Seymour Sudman, *Applied Sampling* (San Francisco: Academic Press, 1976); also see Morris H. Hansen, William N. Hurwitz, and William G. Madow, *Sample Survey Methods and Theory* (New York: John Wiley and Sons, Inc., 1953).

9. Richard L. Schaeffer, William Mendenhall, and Lyman Ott, *Elementary Survey Sampling,* 4th ed. (Boston: PNS-Kent, 1980).

10. Earl R. Babbie, *The Practice of Social Research,* 2nd ed. (Belmont, CA: Wadsworth, 1979), p. 167.

11. Fred N. Kerlinger, *Foundations of Behavioral Research,* 2nd ed. (New York: Holt, Rinehart and Winston, 1973), pp. 129–30.

12. Seymour Sudman, "Efficient Screening Methods for the Sampling of Geographically Clustered Special Populations," *Journal of Marketing Research* 22 (February 1985), pp. 20–29.

13. Leo A. Goodman, "Snowball Sampling," *Annals of Mathematical Statistics* 32 (1961), pp. 148–70.

APPENDIX: STEPS IN DEVELOPING A SAMPLING PLAN

Sampling is much more than just finding some people to participate in a research study. This chapter discusses a number of different concepts, procedures, and decisions that a researcher must consider in order to successfully achieve gathering raw data from a relatively small group of people that can, in turn, be used to generalize or make inferential predictions about all the elements in a larger target population. Armed with an understanding of these individually discussed aspects, the researcher can integrate them into a workable sampling plan. A sampling plan can be thought of as the blueprint or framework needed to ensure that the raw data collected are representative of the target population.

This appendix presents the logical steps that make up a sampling plan, as well as some of the key activities involved in each step (see Exhibit 1). You are encouraged to review the chapter for more detailed discussions of these activities. In addition, you will find that the sampling information provided there will be very useful in understanding the topics discussed in the remainder of the text.

Step 1: Define the Target Population

In any sampling plan, the first task of the researcher is to determine and identify the complete group of people or objects that should be investigated in the project. Using both the defined information problem statement and the established research objectives as guidelines, the target population should be given its identity by using descriptors that represent the characteristics of elements that make the target population's frame. These elements become the prospective sampling units from which a sample will be drawn. Clear understanding of the target population will help the researcher successfully draw a representative sample.

Step 2: Select the Data Collection Method

Using the information problem definition, the data requirements, and the established research objectives, the researcher must choose a method for collecting the required raw data from the target population elements. Choices include some type of interviewing approach (e.g., personal or telephone) or a self-administered survey. The method of data

---

EXHIBIT 1   **Steps Involved in Developing a Sampling Plan**

Step 1	→ Define the Target Population
Step 2	→ Select the Data Collection Method
Step 3	→ Identify the Sampling Frame(s) Needed
Step 4	→ Select the Appropriate Sampling Method
Step 5	→ Determine Necessary Sample Sizes and Overall Contact Rates
Step 6	→ Create an Operating Plan for Selecting Sampling Units
Step 7	→ Execute the Operational Plan

collection guides the researcher in identifying and securing the necessary sampling frame(s) for conducting the research.

Step 3: Identify the Sampling Frame(s) Needed

After gaining an understanding of who or what should be investigated, the researcher must assemble a list of eligible sampling units. This list needs to contain enough information about each prospective sampling unit so that the researcher can successfully contact them. Having an incomplete sampling frame decreases the likelihood of drawing a representative sample. Sampling frame lists can be created from a number of different sources (e.g., customer lists from a company's internal database, random-digit dialing, an organization's membership roster). In creating the necessary sampling frames, the researcher must be aware of possible conditions of overregistration and underregistration of the prospective sampling units. These conditions will create "sampling gaps" or sampling frame errors that decrease the likelihood of being able to draw a representative sample.

Step 4: Select the Appropriate Sampling Method

The researcher must choose between two types of sampling orientations: probability and nonprobability. Depending on the extent to which the raw data will be used to form estimates about the target population, using a probability sampling method will always yield better and more accurate information about the target population's parameters than will any of the available nonprobability sampling methods. In determining the appropriateness of the sampling method, the researcher must seriously consider seven factors: (1) research objectives, (2) degree of desired accuracy, (3) availability of resources, (4) time frame, (5) advanced knowledge of the target population, (6) scope of the research, and (7) perceived statistical analysis needs. These factors were discussed in detail in the chapter; you are encouraged to review those discussions.

Step 5: Determine Necessary Sample Sizes and Overall Contact Rates

In this step of a sampling plan, the researcher must consider how precise the sample estimates must be and how much time and money are available to collect the required raw data. To determine the appropriate sample size, decisions have to be made concerning (1) the variability of the population characteristic under investigation, (2) the level of confidence desired in the estimates, and (3) the degree of precision desired in estimating the population characteristic. Also in this step of the plan, the researcher must decide how many completed surveys will need to enter the data analysis activities of the overall research project, understanding that sample size normally is not equal to the usable observations.

At this point the researcher must consider what impact having fewer surveys than initially desired would have on the accuracy of the sample statistics. An important question is, How many prospective sampling units will have to be contacted to ensure that the estimated sample size is obtained, and at what additional costs? To answer this, the researcher must be able to calculate the reachable rates, overall incidence rates, and expected completion rates associated with the sampling situation.

Step 6: Create an Operating Plan for Selecting Sampling Units

In this step, the researcher wants to clearly lay out, in detail, the actual procedures to use in contacting each of the prospective respondents who were drawn into the sample. All instructions should be clearly written so that interviewers know exactly what to do and how to handle any problems in the process of contacting prospective respondents. For example, if the raw data for a study is to be collected using mall-intercept interviews, then clear detailed instructions on how to select respondents and conduct the interviews must be made available to the interviewer.

Step 7: Execute the Operational Plan

In some research projects, this step is similar to actually conducting the data collection activities (e.g., actual calling of a prospective respondent to do a telephone interview). The important thing in this stage is to maintain consistency and control. For more information related to this step, see the discussions on fieldwork provided in Chapter 15.

MARKETING RESEARCH ILLUSTRATION

SAMPLING DESIGN DECISIONS AND PROVIDING MEANINGFUL PRIMARY DATA

This illustration is a continuation of the American Airlines research and sampling problem in the chapter opener. You should review that situation before continuing here.

Using both AA's existing marketing research and route load databases, Ron Brensinger researched the average total number of passengers who flew on American Airlines routes from California to New York and Washington, D.C., over the past three years. The route load records indicated that, on average, 2.73 million people (i.e., 30 daily flights × 7 days × 52 weeks × 250 passengers [83.3 percent average load factor]) boarded flights having a final destination of New York and another 1.92 million people (i.e., 22 daily flights × 7 days × 52 weeks × 240 passengers [80.0 percent average load factor]) boarded flights with their final destination being Washington, D.C. On average, 18 of the daily flights to New York (60 percent) were direct flights, and AA averaged 11 daily direct flights (50 percent) to Washington, D.C. Based on total passengers to the two destinations, total passenger population was estimated to be about 4.85 million people per year, with a little over 60 percent going to New York airports and about 40 percent to airports in Washington, D.C. A complicating factor in determining the appropriate sample sizes was with those "indirect" flights for which passengers might not have New York or Washington, D.C., as their final destination or new passengers that might have boarded the flight at one of the intermediate stops. Consequently, Brensinger used the known percentage values of direct flights to each final destination to initially calculate the needed sample sizes for the segment of passengers flying to New York ($P = 60\%$) and those to Washington, D.C. ($P = 50\%$). Furthermore, he wanted to operate at a 99 percent confidence level and a sampling error tolerance level of ±2.5 percentage points because the data would be used as input factors for his route load forecasting models.

Using the standard statistical model for calculating sample size from known population parameter values [$n = (Z^2_{CI})(P*Q)/\alpha^2$], Brensinger estimated that the sample sizes should be 2,556 passengers flying to New York and 2,663 people going to Washington, D.C. Now the question became one of how to select the actual people from each of the respective target populations. Thoughts of using direct mail surveys, personal interviews, or telephone interviews were eliminated based on a combination of time factors, high interviewing costs, low response rates, and survey design costs. Instead, he selected an "in-flight" self-administered surveying approach. Armed with the information that AA flew 126 direct routes (averaging 31,500 passengers) to New York and 77 (averaging 18,480 passengers) to Washington, D.C., per week, he could randomly select specific flights over either the entire year, month, week, or day and obtain the needed number of surveys. He obtained information from AA's marketing research department that the usual response rate for in-flight surveys was about 50 percent. This rate accounted for the possibility that not all passengers are willing to participate in surveys and that some passengers are children. Using this response factor, Brensinger determined that passengers on 21 direct flights to New York and 23 direct flights to Washington, D.C., would be needed for the study.

Since the project was being viewed as a pilot study, he decided to cut the overall time frame for collecting the data to one week. His new sampling frame from which he would randomly select the flights for the study was reduced to 126 flights for the New York passengers and 77 flights for those traveling to Washington, D.C. For each of the flights selected, Brensinger knew that there was a possibility that more passengers than expected might fill out the survey. This would create the possibility of oversampling for each segment of prospective respondents. He explained that oversampling does not affect the representativeness of the sample to the target population, but undersampling does. Using his flight route load database, he wanted to select a week that route loads were predicted to be consistent across each day of the week. In addition, he had to consider the time requirements needed to develop the survey and get everything ready for administering the surveys. Brensinger selected the third week in August as the target date for data collection. That gave him a month to get everything in place.

By knowing the required sample sizes for the project, he was now able to accurately estimate the costs for collecting the data. Taking into consideration the cost of questionnaire development, reproduction of 10,800 surveys, cover letters, and other required materials as well as a 50 percent response rate, cost per completed survey would be $5.15, or $26,878 in total. This cost and the other research costs in the initial proposal brought the total cost for the project to $42,550. As it turned out, total cost estimates were within management's tentative budget allocation of $50,000. Consequently, the project was given final approval and Brensinger began the research project the following day.

The above American Airlines situation brings up several interesting points. First, a good sampling plan and techniques are required to ensure that quality primary data are collected that can be used to represent true pictures about the target population. Second, decisions about sampling and sample sizes must be made early in the overall research process, for they will affect the development of constructs, scale measurements, and questionnaires. Third, development of a sample plan can vary widely from one technique to a complex structure involving multiple stages and steps. Finally, information needed for a sample plan can be used to help determine the overall cost of conducting a research project that requires primary data collection.

MARKETING RESEARCH CASE EXERCISE

AMERICA ONLINE: SAMPLING ISSUES ASSOCIATED WITH INTERNET USERS

America Online (AOL) serves over 12 million households, capturing over 47 percent of the Internet market. The audience that AOL targets consists of less technically sophisticated people, ethnically diverse people, women, and families. AOL is planning to design its content to appeal specifically to these groups, as well as to people using high-speed modems and low-end computers (cost of less than $1,000).

The percentage of time AOL members spend online grew from 56.9 percent in July 1998 to 58.3 percent in December of that same year. This is almost three-fifths of all time spent in cyberspace from home. However, as new competitors enter the market, online usage will most certainly change.

Currently AOL estimates that its membership exceeds 11 million. In addition, when the company acquired CompuServe, the membership increased by an additional 2 million subscribers. While in the past AOL has targeted households and small businesses, the acquisition of CompuServe now has AOL moving into the big-corporation segment of the market. With competition increasing, and AOL moving into segments different from its traditional markets, the company is planning to launch a research project to assess the changing needs and desires of its current users. More specifically, AOL wishes to determine if its customers are satisfied with its current product offerings, and what changes in these offerings are necessary in order to maintain its current level of subscribers. See the Web page for AOL at www.aol.com for a complete listing of the offerings provided to AOL subscribers.

In developing this research project, AOL is faced with some unique sampling issues. Specifically, how does AOL determine and develop a sample for this research project? Assess the following issues:

1. What should be the universe and sampling frame used by AOL when selecting participants for this upcoming research project?

2. What type of sampling design should AOL employ (random, stratified, etc.), and why?

3. Given the unique composition of its membership, what problems, pitfalls, and biases should AOL expect to encounter in its sampling plan? How can it overcome these sampling problems?

Learning Objectives

After reading this chapter, you will be able to

1. Explain what constructs are, how they are developed, and why they are important to measurement and scale designs.

2. Discuss the integrated validity and reliability concerns underlying construct development and scale measurement.

3. Explain what scale measurement is, and describe how to correctly apply it in collecting raw data from respondents.

4. Identify and explain the four basic types of scales, and discuss the amount of information they can provide a researcher or decision maker.

5. Discuss the ordinally-interval hybrid scale design and the types of information it can provide researchers.

6. Discuss three components of the scale development and explain why they are critical to gathering primary data.

Overview of Measurement: Construct Development and Scale Measurement

❝ Success in predicting consumer sales for new Burger King stores came about after we understood how to better measure location site criteria using information research practices. ❞

C. MICHAEL POWELL
Former Director of Financial Analysis
Burger King Corporation

Fast Food, Side by Side: A Prediction of Store Location Success

During the early days of the Burger King Corporation, one of the most critical problems was to select sites for new restaurants that would attract sufficient customers for the new store to be profitable. Since the company was not as well known as its major competitor, McDonald's, Burger King decided to locate its stores no closer than about three miles to a McDonald's, on streets with high traffic, in neighborhoods with schools, and in areas of predominantly middle-income families. This decision was based on management's belief that these locations would produce the greatest probability of success.

Unfortunately, the decision-making process did not include any organized marketing research data and was based primarily on the experience and knowledge of the Burger King senior management team. After some years of following this site location model, it became increasingly difficult to meet these criteria and new stores' sales forecasts were often inaccurate. At this point management began to seek a new formula for site location. Because a Burger King marketing research department did not exist at the time, the task of developing the new model was assigned to the financial analysis department. Using sales and geographic data from existing Burger King stores as well as estimates of McDonald's sales, the financial analysts then added interview and survey data from customers of both chains.

The objectives of the study were to measure the strength of the relationship between the site-location criteria and sales, and then to seek any other criteria that would predict sales more accurately. In those years the success of each restaurant was of critical importance to

the fledgling company and if several new stores failed, then the entire organization might have been at risk. The research findings showed that while traffic density was a significant indicator of sales, neither the proximity of schools nor income levels of the surrounding area were good indicators. Moreover, customers seemed to desire places where several fast-food establishments were clustered together so that more choice was available. Another important bit of information provided to management was the discovery that the sales of new Burger King restaurants located close to a McDonald's could accurately and consistently be estimated as a percentage of that nearby McDonald's sales.

During the next several years, the company opened stores next door to McDonald's, in shopping malls, and in very low income areas. At one time the highest-grossing units were in low-income areas of Detroit, an area that the company had avoided studiously in the past. Today when you find several fast-food establishments clustered together, and all doing well, that location is partially due to the marketing studies performed by the Burger King financial analysis department.

Several insights about the importance of construct and measurement developments can be gained from the Burger King Corporation experience. First, not knowing exactly the critical construct criteria for locating a business can lead to intuitive guesswork and counterproductive results. Second, making accurate location decisions requires identifying and precisely defining the patronage constructs (e.g., attitudes, emotions, behavioral factors) that consumers deem important.

Value of Measurement within Information Research

Measurement is an integral part of the modern world, yet the beginnings of measurement lie in the distant past. Before a farmer could sell his crop of corn, potatoes, or apples, both he and the buyer had to decide on units of measurement. Over time this particular measurement became known as a bushel or four pecks or, more precisely, 2,150.42 cubic inches. In the early days, measurement was simply achieved by using a basket or container of standard size that everyone agreed was a bushel.

From such simple everyday devices as the standard bushel basket, we have progressed in the physical sciences to such an extent that we are now able to measure the rotation of a distant star, the altitude of a satellite in micro-inches, or time in pico-seconds (1 trillionth of a second). Today, such precise physical measurement is critical to the airline pilot flying through a dense fog or a physician controlling a surgical laser.

In many marketing situations, however, the majority of the measurements are applied to things that are much more abstract than altitude or time. For example, most decision makers would agree that information about whether or not a firm's customers are going to like a new product or not is critically important prior to introducing that product. In many cases, such information has made the difference between business success and failure. Yet, unlike time or altitude, people's preferences can be very difficult to measure accurately. As we described in the opener of Chapter 3, the Coca-Cola company introduced New Coke after inadequately measuring consumers' preferences, and thereby suffered substantial losses. In a similar fashion, such inadequate measurements of consumer attitudes quite often lead to the early cancelation of many television series, the withdrawal of new products, and the failure of entire companies.

Since accurate measurement of constructs is essential to effective decision making, the purpose of this chapter is to provide you with a basic understanding of the importance of measuring customers' attitudes and behaviors, and other marketplace phenomena. We describe the measurement process and the central decision rules needed for developing sound scale measurements. The focus here is on basic measurement issues, construct development, and scale measurements. We want you to understand that construct development is not exactly the same as construct measurement. For true construct measurement to take place, the researcher needs to understand scale measurements as well as the interrelationships between what is being measured and how to measure it. Chapter 13 continues the topic of measurement and discusses several popular advanced attitudinal, emotional, and behavioral intention scales used in marketing research.

Overview of the Measurement Process

Measurement An integrative process of determining the intensity (or amount) of information about constructs, concepts, or objects.

In marketing research, **measurement** is viewed as the integrative process of determining the intensity (or amount) of information about constructs, concepts, or objects of interest and their relationship to a defined business problem or opportunity. Critical to the process of collecting primary data is the development of well-constructed measurement procedures. It is important to realize that the measurement process consists of two distinctly different development processes: construct development and scale measurement. To achieve the overall goal of obtaining high-quality primary data, researchers must first understand what they are attempting to measure prior to developing the measurements. The goal of construct development is to precisely identify and define *what is to be measured,* including any dimensionality traits. In turn, the goal of scale measurement is to determine *how to precisely measure* the constructs.

Construct Development

As discussed in earlier chapters, the necessity for precise definitions in marketing research may appear to be obvious, but it is frequently the area where the entire program begins to go wrong. Precise definition of marketing constructs fundamentally begins with defining the purpose of the study and providing clear expressions of the research problem. Without a clear initial understanding of the research problem before the study begins, the researcher can end up collecting irrelevant or low-quality data, thereby wasting a great deal of time, effort, and money. Misguided research endeavors have contributed to many mistakes being made in such industries as music, fashion, and food. Take the U.S. auto industry as a case in point; even after the first Volkswagens were introduced into the United States, most U.S. manufacturers continued to invest in factories designed to produce large, inefficient automobiles. They ignored studies that suggested that increasing fuel prices, highway congestion, and pollution controls favored more modest vehicles. As a result, hundreds of millions of dollars in auto sales were lost to foreign competitors. Such cases show that a very careful definition of the purpose of the study is essential.

Construct development An integrative process in which researchers determine what specific data should be collected for solving the defined research problem.

Construct development can be viewed as an integrative process in which researchers determine what specific data should be collected for solving the defined research problem. In this process, accurate identification of what should be investigated requires knowledge and understanding of constructs and their dimensionality, validity, and operationalization.

Abstractness of the Construct

At the heart of construct development is the need to determine exactly what is to be measured. If something is abstract, rather than concrete, we call it a construct. Normally constructs are not directly observable; therefore, their measurement becomes indirect. Exhibit 12.1 offers some examples of abstract constructs and concrete objects.

For instance, a hammer is very concrete. Researchers can directly measure its weight and length; the hardness of its head; and the composition of the handle. In marketing, however, decision makers and researchers are concerned with such things as attitudes, emotions, beliefs, advertising effectiveness, customer satisfaction, service quality, and employee performance, to name a few. There are no physical instruments that can directly measure these constructs. They are much more abstract than the hammer. A simple rule of thumb is that if you can measure it directly using physical instruments, then it is not a construct.

Determining Dimensionality of the Construct

In determining exactly what is to be measured, researchers must keep in mind the need to acquire relevant, high-quality data, data structures, and information to support management's decisions. For example, if the purpose is to assess the service quality of an automobile dealership, then what exactly should be measured? Since dealership service quality is

EXHIBIT 12.1 | Examples of Concrete Objects and Abstract Constructs

Concrete Objects	Abstract Constructs
Hammer	Advertising effectiveness
Airplane	Service quality
Person's age, height	Intelligence
Roller coaster	Brand loyalty
Market share	Employee performance
Profitability	Consumers' emotions (fear, love, anxiety)
Computer	Retail store image
Automobile	Customer satisfaction

an abstract construct, perhaps the most appropriate way to begin to answer this question is to indirectly identify those dealership attributes that are important to customers.

As discussed in earlier chapters, the researchers in this case can use a variety of qualitative data collection methods (e.g., focus groups or in-depth interviews) among a few customers to develop preliminary insights into service quality and its **domain of observables,** which is the set of identifiable and measurable components associated with an abstract construct.[1] In turn, this preliminary information would then be used as a guideline for collecting data from a more representative sample of customers about important service quality attributes. During the discovery process, the researcher must be careful to include in the qualitative procedures people who are representative of the defined target population. It is also necessary to evaluate the extent to which the actions taken as a result of the preliminary insights fit the organization's goals and objectives. For instance, most customers usually desire lower service prices. Yet, if the dealership is price-competitive in the marketplace, then it may not be in the best interests of the dealership to reduce its prices.

Domain of observables

The set of identifiable and measurable components associated with an abstract construct.

Assessing Construct Validity

Another important activity at this point of the construct development process is that of assessing the validity of the construct, especially if the construct is believed to be multidimensional. As discussed in Chapter 10, the researcher needs to perform statistical analyses to test for content validity, convergent validity, and discriminant validity.[2] *Content validity* (sometimes referred to as *face validity*) is the subjective yet systematic assessment of how well a construct's measurable components represent that construct. *Convergent validity* focuses on how well the construct's measurement positively correlates with different measurements of the same construct. For researchers to be able to evaluate convergent validity, they must use several different measurement techniques to determine the existence of the construct. For *discriminant validity* to exist, researchers must be able to establish the fact that the construct being investigated does not significantly correlate with other constructs that are operationalized as being different. Finally, in some specific cases, such as theory building situations, *nomological validity* allows researchers to evaluate how well one particular construct theoretically networks with other established constructs that are related yet different. Usually one of two approaches is used to collect data for assessing construct validity. If there are enough resources, researchers will conduct a pilot study among 50 or so people who are believed to be representative of the defined target population. In situations where resources are not available for a pilot study, researchers will attempt to approximate content validity at least by having a panel of experts independently judge the dimensionality of the construct. Then construct validity is actually assessed after the fact, using the data gathered from the ensuing survey. While these approaches have become common measurement practices, they contain several weaknesses worth noting.

Inappropriate Scale Measurement Formats

When after-the-fact data are used to assess construct validity, there are risks of inaccurate results due to the set of actual scale point descriptors used in collecting the data.[3] This is to say that the use of untested or inappropriate scale measurement indicators to measure the construct creates a measurement artifact that could lead to misinterpretations of the true components as well as the true dimensionality traits making up the investigated construct. This situation represents the case where raw data is driving the researcher's theoretical framework instead of theory driving the measurement process. A procedure that can be used to overcome this type of weakness is *direct cognitive structural analysis,* in which respondents are simply asked to determine whether an attribute is part of the construct and, if so, how important it is to that construct.[4]

A CLOSER LOOK AT RESEARCH   In the Field

Recently, a marketing researcher wanted to identify the source areas that people might use in their process of judging banking service quality. The researcher conducted several focus groups among both undergraduate students in a basic marketing course and graduate students in a marketing management course in order to identify the service activities and offerings that might represent service quality. The researcher's rationale for using these groups was that they did have experience in conducting bank transactions, they were consumers, and the researcher had easy access to them for their opinions. The preliminary results of the focus group interviews revealed that the students used four dimensions for judging a bank's service quality: (1) interpersonal social skills of bank staff, (2) reliability of bank statements, (3) convenience of ATM delivery systems, and (4) diagnostic competence of bank tellers.

A month later, the researcher conducted a series of four focus groups among known customers of one of the large banks in Charlotte, North Carolina. The preliminary results clearly suggested that those customers used seven dimensions for judging a bank's service quality. Those dimensions were identified as the bank's ability to: (1) communicate with and listen to consumers; (2) demonstrate diagnostic compe-

tence in understanding the customer's banking needs and wants; (3) elicit sincere empathy by showing concern for how consumers interpret their requirements; (4) be tactful in responding to customers' questions, objections, or problems; (5) create an impression of reliability and credibility inherent in a bank service encounter; (6) demonstrate sufficient technological competence in handling the critical aspects of bank transactions; and (7) exhibit strong positive interpersonal social skills in conducting bank transactions.

The researcher had placed himself in a tentative position of not knowing for sure whether people perceive bank service quality as having four or seven critical components. Which qualitative source of information should be used to better understand the construct of bank service quality? Which preliminary information should the researcher rely on to conduct the empirical survey on bank service quality? These issues would directly affect the operationalization of construct development.

Source:These studies were conducted by the author in 1991 and 1992. Part of the results were reported in David J. Ortinau and Ronald P. Brensinger, "An Empirical Investigation of Perceived Quality's Intangible Dimensionality Through Direct Cognitive Structural (DCS) Analysis," In *Marketing: Perspectives for the 1990s*, ed. Robert L. King (New Orleans, LA: Southern Marketing Association, 1992), pp. 214–19.

Inappropriate Set of Respondents

In academic research settings, for example, researchers too often rely heavily on college students' input in their process of determining the components of the construct being investigated. Although college students are consumers and may have some knowledge and experience with certain products and services, in most cases their attitudes, feelings, and buying behaviors are not representative of the general population or of many specifically defined target populations. A second problem that relates to using college students in the preliminary stage of construct development is that student samples are normally drawn using a nonprobability convenience sampling approach. As discussed in Chapter 11, the use of convenience sampling does not guarantee true representation of a college student population, let alone a larger defined target population. As a consequence, the components originally thought to make up the construct often prove not to be stable when scale measures are attached to them and the study is extended to a larger sample of subjects from the target population. The In the Field box offers an example of this problem as it occurred in a banking study.

Operationalization

Explaining a construct's meaning in measurement terms by specifying the activities or operations necessary to measure it.

Construct Operationalization

Operationalization is a process wherein the researcher explains a construct's meaning in measurement terms by specifying the activities or operations necessary to measure it. The process focuses on the design and use of questions and scale measurements to gather the needed data structures. Since many constructs, such as customer satisfaction, preferences, emotions, quality images, and brand loyalty, to name a few, cannot be directly observed or measured, the researcher attempts to indirectly measure them through operationalization of their components.

Recently, for example, a researcher developed a questionnaire of 100 questions seeking to determine if customers were satisfied with their recent automobile purchase and the dealer's service.[5] Using a variety of different question scale measurement formats, customers were asked to rate a number of component items, including the salesperson's listening skills; the reliability of the service; the appearance of the service facilities; and the serviceperson's interpersonal skills. They were also asked about attributes of the vehicle purchased, including road-holding ability, overall comfort, cost of routine maintenance, overall durability, overall exterior styling, visibility, steering precision, security features, fuel economy, and overall power. Exhibit 12.2 illustrates two different measurement approaches used to capture data about the construct of service satisfaction provided by automobile dealerships.

EXHIBIT 12.2   **Selected Question/Scales Used to Measure Service Satisfaction with Auto Dealerships**

Example 1:

Now combining all your knowledge, opinions, feelings, and personal experiences that you have acquired as a customer with your *primary* automobile service provider (ASP), I would like to know how satisfied or dissatisfied you are concerning several service features.

Using the scale described below, where

6 = Completely satisfied	4 = Somewhat satisfied	2 = Definitely dissatisfied
5 = Definitely satisfied	3 = Somewhat dissatisfied	1 = Completely dissatisfied

please write a number from 1 to 6 in the space provided that best expresses how satisfied or dissatisfied you are with **each listed** service feature.

____ Convenience of ASP's location	____ ASP's communication skills
____ Flexibility in ASP's operating hours	____ Availability of quality service offerings
____ Service provider's personal social skills	____ Overall reputation of your primary ASP
____ Personnel's understanding of customer needs	____ ASP's concern of putting its customers "first"
____ Reliability/credibility of ASP's service providers	____ ASP's listening skills
____ Service provider's technical knowledge/competence	____ Quality of the ASP's products (or services)

Example 2:

Using the educational letter grading system of "A+," "A," "B," "C," "D," and "F," please **circle** the one "letter grade" that best expresses the overall grade that you would give each of the following service factors at your primary ASP.

a. The communication skills of the service people at my primary ASP are . . .	A+	A	B	C	D	F
b. The listening capabilities of the service people at my primary ASP are . . .	A+	A	B	C	D	F
c. The ability of the service staff to understand my various repair/maintenance service needs are . . .	A+	A	B	C	D	F
d. The ability of service employees to demonstrate understanding of my auto service needs (or requirements) from my point of view are . . .	A+	A	B	C	D	F
e. The service personnel's ability to respond quickly to my objections (or problems, questions) are . . .	A+	A	B	C	D	F
f. The reliability (or credibility) demonstrated by the service representatives are . . .	A+	A	B	C	D	F
g. The technical knowledge (or understanding) demonstrated by the service personnel are . . .	A+	A	B	C	D	F
h. The personal social skills used by the employees in dealing with me are . . .	A+	A	B	C	D	F
i. The facilities/equipment/personnel all demonstrate that it is a "professional" organization to deal with . . .	A+	A	B	C	D	F

These examples suggest that assessing what appears to be a simple construct of service satisfaction can be more involved than it might seem at first. Here, the researcher was trying to fully capture data and information on all dimensions that may affect a customer's service satisfaction. Certainly this approach will give dealerships a more accurate basis for evaluating how successful they have been in satisfying customers. Moreover, this type of in-depth analysis provides a business with better opportunities to pinpoint areas of concern and take corrective actions. With only a single-question approach, corrective action would be very difficult if not impossible since the researcher would not be able to determine the exact problem area. After constructs and their possible dimensionality traits have been adequately identified and understood, the researcher then needs to turn attention to the processes involved with creating appropriate scale measurements. The remainder of this chapter focuses on basic issues associated with the development of scale measurements used to collect primary raw survey data.

Basic Concepts of Scale Measurement

Types of Data Collected in Research Practices

Regardless of whether the researcher is attempting to collect secondary or primary data to address a stated information problem, all data and their structures can be logically classified as being one of four basic types: state-of-being, state-of-mind, state-of-behavior, or state-of-intentions.

State-of-Being Data

When the information problem requires the researcher to collect responses that are pertinent to the physical, demographic, or socioeconomic characteristics of individuals, objects, or organizations, the resulting raw data are considered **state-of-being data.** State-of-being data represent factual characteristics that can be verified through several sources other than the person providing the responses. For example, a researcher can directly ask respondents their sex, age, income level, education level, marital status, number of children, occupation, height, weight, color of eyes, and telephone number—or the researcher could obtain these data through secondary sources such as birth certificates, loan applications, income tax returns, driver's licenses, public documents at a county courthouse, the telephone company, and so on. For organizations, raw data total dollar/unit sales, computer capacity, number of employees, total assets, number and types of stores, and so on can be obtained through secondary sources, eliminating the need to ask someone direct questions about them. The same holds true for the physical characteristics of many objects. The main point to remember about state-of-being data is that the researcher is not limited to collecting the raw data by only asking questions.

State-of-Mind Data

State-of-mind data represent the mental attributes of individuals that are not directly observable or available through some type of external source. State-of-mind data exist only within the minds of people. To collect such data, the researcher has to directly ask a person to respond to stated questions or directives. Verification through secondary or external sources is all but impossible. Some examples of state-of-mind data would be a person's personality traits, attitudes, feelings, perceptions, beliefs, cognitive decision processes, product/service preferences, awareness levels, and images. Therefore, data quality and accuracy are limited to the degree of honesty of the person providing the responses to the researcher's questions.

State-of-being data
The physical and/or demographic or socioeconomic characteristics of people, objects and organizations.

State-of-mind data
The mental attributes of people.

A shopper inspects a frozen-food entrée.

State-of-Behavior Data

State-of-behavior data
A person's or organization's current observable or recorded actions or reactions.

State-of-behavior data represent an individual's or organization's current observable actions or reactions or their recorded past actions/reactions. The researcher has several options available in his or her quest to obtain state-of-behavior data. A person can be asked carefully designed questions about current or past behavior. For example, a person could be asked to respond to such questions as "In the past six months, how many times have you purchased dry cereal for your household?" or "In a typical week, how often do you go shopping at a mall?" To obtain current behavior, a person could be asked to respond to such questions as "Are you currently enrolled in college?" or "How many courses are you currently taking in marketing?" As we discussed in Chapter 10, another option for the researcher is to use either a trained observer or some type of mechanical device to directly observe and record the person's current behavior. For example, a disguised observer or hidden camera can be used to selectively observe and record customers' frozen-food selections at the local Winn-Dixie supermarket. Such behavioral data might include length of time in the frozen-food section of the store, the specific brands or types of frozen food inspected or selected, or the number of units of a product that were placed in the shopping cart.

A third option pertinent to collecting data from past behavior would be for the researcher to find records of previously conducted behavior. For example, a researcher could examine a restaurant's charge-card receipts over a specified period to determine how often a selected individual came in and ate at that particular restaurant. There are definitely some limitations to the quality and accuracy of the raw data using this option. In general, verification of an individual's past behaviors through any type of external, secondary source is a difficult process in terms of time, effort, and accuracy. This method places heavy emphasis on the existence of well-documented behaviors.

State-of-Intention Data

State-of-intention data
A person's or organization's expressed plans of future behavior.

State-of-intention data represent an individual's or organization's expressed plans of future behavior. State-of-intention data can only be collected by asking a person to respond to carefully designed questions about behaviors that are yet to take place. For instance, a researcher can ask such questions as "How likely are you to purchase a new Mazda in the next six months?" or "Do you plan to come and visit the Museum of Science and Industry next time you are in Chicago?" or "To what extent would you buy Tide next time you need laundry detergent?" Like state-of-behavior data, state-of-intention data are very difficult to verify through external, secondary sources, but verification is possible.

The Nature of Scale Measurement

As we have stressed throughout this book, to be successful in generating useful primary information for addressing business information problems, the researcher must be able to gather the appropriate raw data. The quantity and quality of the responses associated with any question or observation technique depend directly on the scale measurements used by the researcher. **Scale measurement** can be defined as the process of assigning a set of descriptors to represent the range of possible responses to a question about a particular object or construct.[6]

Within this process, the focus is on measuring the existence of various properties or characteristics of a person's response. Scale measurement directly determines the amount of raw data that can be ascertained from a given questioning or observation method. Scale measurement attempts to assign designated degrees of intensity to the responses. These designated degrees of intensity are commonly referred to as **scale points.** For example, a retailer might want to know how important a preselected set of store or service features is to consumers in deciding where to shop. The level of importance attached to each store or service feature would be determined by the researcher's assignment of a range of intensity descriptors (scale points) to represent the possible degrees of importance (e.g., definitely, generally, only slightly, not at all important) associated with each feature.

Properties of Scale Measurements

The researcher can control the amount of raw data that can be obtained from asking questions by incorporating scaling properties or assumptions into the scale points. Drawing from mathematical theory, there are four scaling properties that a researcher can use in developing scales: assignment, order, distance, and origin (see Exhibit 12.3).

Assignment

The **assignment property,** also referred to as *description* or *category property,* is the researcher's employment of unique descriptors to identify each object within a set.[7] When activated, this property allows a researcher to take the responses and categorize them into mutually exclusive groups each with its own identity. Any descriptor can be used for a response. Some examples are the use of numbers (12, 34, 45, 8, 58, etc.) to identify the players on a basketball team so that the scorekeeper can correctly record points scored or fouls committed; *yes* and *no* responses to the question "Are you going to purchase a new automobile within the next six months?"; the use of colors (red, green, blue, pink, etc.) to identify the types of cars, clothes, or bathroom towels that consumers buy for personal consumption; and the use of size indicators (large, medium, small, etc.) to identify the quantity of soft drinks, or fitting of clothes, or amount of pizza that people might order from a retail store.

Order

The **order property** refers to the relative magnitude between the descriptors used as scale points (or raw responses).[8] In any situation where multiple descriptors are used to identify the possible raw responses to stated questions, order (also known as rank) is established when the researcher or respondent knows the relative magnitude of the descriptors. Relative magnitude between descriptors is based on the existence of three pure mathematical relationships between two or more descriptors or objects. For example, there are only three pure mathematical relationships that could exist between objects A and B or responses from person A and person B: A can be *greater than* B; A can be *less than* B; or A can be

---

Scale measurement The process of assigning descriptors to represent the range of possible responses to a question about a particular object or construct.

Scale points Designated degrees of intensity assigned to the responses in a given questioning or observation method.

Assignment property The employment of unique descriptors to identify each object in a set.

Order property The relative magnitude assigned to each scale point descriptor.

EXHIBIT 12.3	Four Scaling Properties: Description and Examples

Scaling Properties	Description and Examples
Assignment property	The employment of unique descriptors to identify an object in a set.
	Some examples: the use of numbers (10, 38, 44, 18, 23, etc.); the use of colors (red, blue, green, pink, etc.); yes and no responses to questions that identify objects into mutually exclusive groups.
Order property	Establishes "relative magnitudes" between the descriptors, creating hierarchical rank-order relationships among objects.
	Some examples: 1st place is better than a 4th-place finish; a 5-foot person is shorter than a 7-foot person; a regular customer purchases more often than a rare customer.
Distance property	Allows the researcher and respondent to identify, understand, and accurately express absolute differences between objects.
	Some examples: family A with six children living at home, compared to family B with three children at home, has three more children than family B; differences in income ranges or age categories.
Origin property	A unique scale descriptor that is designated as being a "true zero" or "true state of nothing."
	Some examples: asking a respondent his or her weight or current age; the number of times one shops at a supermarket; or the market share of a specific brand of hand soap.

equal to B. In those situations where the researcher or the respondent can identify and understand the existence of a "greater than" or a "less than" relationship between two or more objects or responses, then the order scaling property is activated and some type of meaningful rank order can be established among the reported raw responses. Some examples of the order property include the following: 1 is less than 5; "Extremely satisfied" is more intense than "somewhat satisfied"; "most important" has greater importance than "only slightly important"; "somewhat disagree" has less disagreement than "definitely disagree"; and a person holding a master of business administration (MBA) degree has more formal years of education than a person holding an associate of arts (AA) degree. When the order scaling property is incorporated into a set of scale points, it allows the researcher to establish either a "highest to lowest" or a "lowest to highest" rank order among the raw responses. It is important to remember that the order scaling property, by itself, identifies only the relative differences between raw responses and not the absolute differences.

Distance

Distance property The measurement scheme that expresses the exact (or absolute) difference between each of the descriptors, scale points, or raw responses.

The **distance property** is the measurement scheme that expresses the exact (or absolute) difference between each of the descriptors, scale points, or raw responses.[9] In other words, the distance property establishes the fact that the researcher knows the absolute (or precise) magnitude that exists between each raw response to a stated question or directive. For example, family A drives two cars, and family B drives four cars; family A has two fewer cars than family B. A student who has to travel 20 miles to go to school drives twice as many miles as a student who drives only 10 miles to the same school. Normally, the distance scaling property is restricted to those situations where the raw responses represent some type of numerical answer.

In a lot of cases researchers try to imply that many of the scales associated with collecting state-of-mind data activate the distance property. This is a growing myth that causes misunderstanding of particular types of raw data and their structures. For example, some experts believe that "extremely spicy" is one unit of spiciness away from "very spicy," or that "strongly agree" is two units of agreement away from "somewhat agree," or that "extremely important" is four units of importance away from "only slightly important." In all these examples, there is no way a researcher could statistically verify that the assumed absolute relationship between those scale descriptors exists. This measurement problem will be discussed in more detail later in this chapter.

Origin

Origin property Having a unique starting point in a set of scale point descriptors that is designated as a true zero.

The last scaling property, the **origin property,** refers to the use of a unique starting (or beginning) point in a set of scale points that is designated as being a "true zero" or true state of nothing. For the most part, the origin property relates to a numbering system where zero is the displayed or referenced starting point in the set of possible raw responses. It is a possible response that has a special interpretive meaning. Normally, this scaling property is activated when the researcher asks a specific question that requires a numerical response. In turn, a person's response of "don't know," "no opinion," "neither agree nor disagree," "don't care," "not at all important," or "no response," and so on to a phrased question does not represent the origin property.[10] However, responses that would prompt this scaling property are current age; income level; number of dependent children living at home; the number of miles one travels to go shopping at a supermarket; and the number of times a person purchases a specific product or service in a week.

When developing scale measurements, it is important to understand and remember that the more scaling properties that can be simultaneously activated in a scale design, the more sophisticated the raw data. As a scale design includes more scaling properties, it increases the amount of raw data that can be collected by the researcher. Finally, you should notice that each scaling property builds on the previous one. This means that any scale will have the assignment property. A scale that includes the order property automatically possesses the assignment property. If the researcher designs a scale with the distance property, the scale also activates assignment and order. Scales that are built with the origin property also have assignment, order, and distance properties.

Four Basic Types of Scales

While scaling properties determine the amount of raw data that can be obtained from any scale design, all questions and scale measurements can be logically and accurately classified as one of four basic scale types: nominal, ordinal, interval, or ratio. There are specific relationships between the type of scale and which scaling properties are activated within the scale (see Exhibit 12.4).

EXHIBIT 12.4 **Relationships between Types of Scales and Scaling Properties**

Type of Scale	Scaling Properties			
	Assignment	**Order**	**Distance**	**Origin**
Nominal	Yes	No	No	No
Ordinal	Yes	Yes	No	No
Interval	Yes	Yes	Yes	No
Ratio	Yes	Yes	Yes	Yes

Nominal Scales

Nominal scale The type of scale in which the questions require respondents to provide only some type of descriptor as the raw response.

A **nominal scale** is the most basic of the four types of scale designs. In this type of scale, the questions require respondents to provide only some type of descriptor as the raw response. The response does not contain any level of intensity; therefore, it is impossible to establish any form of rank order among the set of given responses. That is, nominal scales provide data that cannot be arranged in a "greater than/less than" or "bigger than/smaller than" hierarchical pattern. Nominal scales allow the researcher only to categorize the raw responses into mutually exclusive subsets that do not illustrate relative magnitudes between them.[11] Some examples of nominal scale structures are given in Exhibit 12.5.

Ordinal Scales

Ordinal scale A scale that allows a respondent to express relative magnitude between the answers to a question.

The structure of an **ordinal scale** activates both the assignment and order scaling properties. This type of scale allows respondents to express relative magnitude between the answers to a question. The researcher can rank-order the raw responses into a hierarchical pattern.[12] As such, it is easy to determine "greater than/less than," "higher than/lower than," "more often/less often," "more important/less important," or "less agreement/more agreement" types of relationships between the responses. It is important to remember that ordinal scale designs do not allow the researcher to determine the absolute difference in any of the ordinal relationships. In reality, almost all state-of-mind data responses

---

EXHIBIT 12.5   **Examples of Nominal Scale Structures**

Example 1:
Please indicate your current marital status.

___ Married   ___ Single   ___ Single, never married   ___ Widowed

Example 2:
How do you classify yourself?

___ Asian   ___ Black   ___ Hispanic   ___ White   ___ Other (Please specify: _____)

Example 3:
Please check those information and HCP service areas in which you have had a face-to-face or telephone conversation with a representative of your main HCP in the past six months. (Check as many as apply).

___ Appointments   ___ Treatment at home   ___ Referral to other HCP
___ Prescriptions   ___ Medical test results   ___ Hospital stay

Some other service area(s); Please specify _____

Example 4:
Please indicate your gender:

___ Female   ___ Male

Example 5:
Which of the following supermarkets have you shopped at in the last 30 days? (Please check all that apply)

___ Albertson   ___ Winn-Dixie   ___ Publix   ___ Safeway   ___ Kash&Karry

EXHIBIT 12.6	Examples of Ordinal Scale Structures

Example 1:

Which one category best describes your knowledge about the assortment of services offered by your main HCP?

(Please check just one category.)

___ Complete knowledge of services
___ Good knowledge of services
___ Basic knowledge of services
___ Little knowledge of services
___ No knowledge of services

Example 2:

To what extent were each of the following bank items an important consideration to you in selecting "your" bank?

(Please be sure to check only one response for each bank item.)

Bank Items	Definitely an Important Consideration	Somewhat of an Important Consideration	Not at All an Important Consideration
Convenience/location	___	___	___
Banking hours	___	___	___
Good service charges	___	___	___
The interest rates on loans	___	___	___
The bank's reputation	___	___	___
The interest rates on savings	___	___	___
Bank's promotional advertising	___	___	___

Example 3:

We would like to know your preferences for actually using different banking methods. Among the methods listed below, please indicate your top three preferences using a "1" to represent your "first" choice, a "2" for your second preference, and a "3" for your third choice of methods.

(Please write the numbers on the lines next to your selected methods.)

_____ Inside the bank   _____ Bank by mail
_____ Drive-in (Drive-up) windows   _____ Bank by telephone
_____ 24-hour ATM   _____ Bank by Internet

are collected using ordinal scales. Exhibit 12.6 provides several examples of ordinal scale structures.

Interval Scales

Interval scale   A scale that demonstrates absolute differences between each scale point.

The structure of a true **interval scale** activates not only the assignment and order scaling properties but also the distance property. By activating the distance property, the researcher can build scale responses that demonstrate absolute differences between each scale point. Here the researcher and respondent alike can identify and understand what the exact difference is among the possible raw responses. In reality, an interval scale is nothing more than a collapsed set of ratio-based responses. Normally, numerical descriptors are used to represent the set of interval ranges that make up the raw response categories. When the researcher employs the distance property, it allows for more powerful statistical techniques to be used to analyze the raw data into meaningful data structures.[13] With interval scale structures, researchers can identify not only some type of hierarchical order among the raw data but also the specific differences between the data. In true interval scales, the distance between each scale point or response does not have to be equal. The research can employ disproportional scale descriptors when developing an interval scale. Interval scales are most appropriate when the researcher wants to collect either state-of-behavior, state-of-intentions, or certain types of state-of-being data.

There are many situations where state-of-mind data are of interest to the researcher and the desire to apply more powerful statistical analysis forces the researcher to, after the fact, transform ordinal scale data into what many consider interval scale data. The transformation is achieved by assuming that the original scale point descriptors activated the distance scaling property.[14] However, this transformation is a researcher artifact that violates the fundamental mathematical principles that underpin the four scaling properties. We will discuss the "assumed interval" scale format later in this chapter. Exhibit 12.7 illustrates some examples of interval scale formats.

Ratio Scales

Ratio scale A scale that allows the researcher not only to identify the absolute differences between each scale point but also to make comparisons between the raw responses.

A **ratio scale** is the only type of scale that simultaneously activates all four scaling properties. A ratio scale tends to be the most sophisticated scale in the sense that it allows the researcher not only to identify the absolute differences between each scale point (or raw response) but also to make absolute comparisons between the raw responses.[15] For instance, in collecting data about how many cars are driven by households in Atlanta,

---

EXHIBIT 12.7   **Examples of Interval Scale Structures**

Example 1:

Approximately how many charges for overdrawn checks (NSF checks) has "your" bank imposed on you in the past year?

____ None   ____ 1–2   ____ 3–7   ____ 8–15   ____ 16–25   ____ More than 25

Example 2:

Approximately how long have you lived at your current address?

____ Less than 1 year   ____ 4 to 6 years   ____ 11 to 20 years
____ 1 to 3 years   ____ 7 to 10 years   ____ Over 20 years

Example 3:

In which one of the following categories does your current age fall?

____ Under 18   ____ 26 to 35   ____ 46 to 55   ____ Over 65
____ 18 to 25   ____ 36 to 45   ____ 56 to 65

Example 4:

Into which of the following categories does your total (approximate) current family income, before taxes, fall?

____ Under $10,000   ____ $25,000 to $29,999
____ $10,000 to $14,999   ____ $30,000 to $50,000
____ $15,000 to $19,999   ____ Over $50,000
____ $20,000 to $24,999

Georgia, a researcher knows that the difference between driving one car and that of driving three cars is always going to be two. Furthermore, when comparing a one-car family to a three-car family, the researcher can assume that the three-car family will have significantly higher total car insurance and maintenance costs than the one-car family.

It is necessary to remember that ratio scale structures are designed to allow a "zero" or "true state of nothing" response to be a valid raw response to the question. Normally, the ratio scale requests that respondents give a specific singular numerical value as their response, regardless of whether or not a set of scale points is used. Exhibit 12.8 displays several examples of ratio scale structures.

Ordinally-Interval Hybrid Scales

There are many situations in marketing research where the information problem, defined construct, and data requirements call for the collection of certain types of state-of-mind, state-of-behavior, and state-of-intention data that are truly ordinal but that have an assumed distance scaling property artificially imposed on them so that the researcher can perform some type of advanced statistical analysis.[16] For example, the researcher might be interested in knowing not only an individual's attitudes or feelings toward a given product or service, but also the combined overall attitudes or feelings of a group of individuals at one time. To achieve this, the researcher must be able to add together many separate raw responses and perform some type of basic mathematical procedure, like establishing the "mean" response of the group. Thus, the researcher must temporarily violate the distance

---

EXHIBIT 12.8   **Examples of Ratio Scale Structures**

Example 1:

Please circle the number of children under 18 years of age currently living in your household.

        0   1   2   3   4   5   6   7   (If more than 7, please specify: _____.)

Example 2:

In the past seven days, how many times did you go shopping at a retail shopping mall?

_____ # of times

Example 3:

In whole years, what is your current age?

_____ # of years old

Example 4:

When buying soft drinks for your household, approximately how many 12-ounce six-packs do you normally buy of each of the following listed brands?

____ Regular Pepsi	____ Regular Coke	____ Orange Crush
____ Diet Pepsi	____ Diet Coke	____ Sprite
____ A&W Root Beer	____ Mountain Dew	____ 7UP

Example 5:

In a typical 12-month period, how many miles do you drive your automobile and/or truck for personal activities?

     ____ # of miles driven in your car   ____ # of miles driven in your truck

and origin properties and artificially assume that they can exist in a scale that normally cannot activate those two properties.[17] When a researcher incorporates artificial distance and/or origin properties into an ordinal scale design, we call this type of scale an **ordinally-interval scale.** The term refers to the taking of an ordinal scale and artificially transforming it into an interval scale.

Ordinally-interval scale

An ordinal scale that is artificially transformed into an internal scale by the researcher.

To create an ordinally-interval scale, the researcher uses two sets of scale point descriptors. The first set consists of narratively expressed indicators, referred to as the *primary scale point descriptors.* The second set consists of whole integer numbers that are arbitrarily assigned to the primary set of descriptors and are denoted as the *secondary scale descriptors.* Let's take, for example, a situation in which the researcher originally develops an ordinal scale to collect general opinions from respondents. The original set of scale points ranged from "definitely agree" to "definitely disagree" (i.e., "definitely agree," "generally agree," "slightly agree," "slightly disagree," "generally disagree," and "definitely disagree"). These scale point indicators would be considered the primary descriptors and the complete scale measurement might look as follows:

For each of the following statements, please check the response that best expresses the extent to which you either agree or disagree with that statement.

Statements	Definitely Agree	Generally Agree	Slightly Agree	Slightly Disagree	Generally Disagree	Definitely Disagree
It is good to have charge accounts.	___	___	___	___	___	___
I buy many things with a bank (or credit) card.	___	___	___	___	___	___
I like to pay cash for everything. I buy at department stores.	___	___	___	___	___	___
I wish my family had a lot more money.	___	___	___	___	___	___

One option that a researcher has is to artificially redefine those scale points to include the distance property by arbitrarily assigning a secondary set of number descriptors to specifically represent each of the original primary scale descriptors. Usually the researcher will use a set of cardinal numbers as the secondary set of descriptors. In the simplest form, cardinal numbers are any set of consecutive whole integers (1, 2, 3, 4, 5, 6, 7, etc.). Because numerical descriptors are elements of a ratio-based numbering system, the distance and origin scaling properties are automatically activated on the scale. By combining the primary and secondary sets of descriptors, the researcher creates a false relationship between the original scale descriptors by now thinking that "definitely agree" = "6," "generally agree" = "5," "slightly agree" = "4," "slightly disagree" = "3," "generally disagree" = "2," and "definitely disagree" = "1." By using these secondary numerical values to represent the original scale points, the researcher can now apply higher levels of data analysis techniques to the raw data.

Another option used quite frequently by some researchers focuses on using primary descriptors to identify only the extreme end points of a set of secondary cardinal numbers that make up the range of raw scale descriptors. This approach leaves the interpretation of what the in-between numerical scale descriptors truly represent up to the imagination of the respondent. Again, such a method forces the researcher and respondent to assume that there is a known distance property between each of the scale point descriptors.[18] Using the above example, this second approach would make the scale measurement appear something like the following:

For each of the following statements, please circle the number that best expresses the extent to which you either agree or disagree with that statement.

Statements	Definitely Agree					Definitely Disagree
It is good to have charge accounts.	6	5	4	3	2	1
I buy many things with a bank (or credit) card.	6	5	4	3	2	1
I like to pay cash for everything. I buy at department stores.	6	5	4	3	2	1
I wish my family had a lot more money.	6	5	4	3	2	1

In the above example, for researchers to believe that the absolute difference between a respondent's response of "definitely agree" and that of "generally agree" is one unit of agreement is really nothing more than a leap of faith. There is no way of ever proving that relationship to be true. The researcher has to be very careful in how she or he interprets the data structures that are generated from data created by this hybrid scale design. (Additional examples of ordinally-interval-type scale structures are provided in Exhibit 12.9.) Problems caused by ordinally-interval scale designs will be further discussed in the data analysis chapters.

Development and Refinement of Scaling Measurements

The keys to designing solid, high-quality scale measurements are (1) understanding the defined information problem, (2) establishing detailed data requirements, (3) identifying and developing the critical constructs, and (4) understanding that a complete measurement scale consists of three critical components (the question, the dimensions and attributes, and the scale point descriptors). After the information problem and data requirements are understood, the researcher must develop constructs, as discussed earlier in this chapter, in order to know what types of data to collect. The researcher must carefully select the appropriate type of scale format (e.g., nominal, ordinal, interval, ratio, or ordinally-interval) to use in collecting raw data. For example, if the information problem situation is determined to require interval data patterns, but the researcher asks the questions using a nominal scale, the wrong level of data will be collected and the final information that can be generated will not be helpful in resolving the initial problem. To illustrate this point, Exhibit 12.10 offers examples of the different levels of data that are obtained on the basis of how the question is phrased to a respondent. It is important to note that the researcher can logically expect to obtain different levels of raw responses applicable to the initial information requirement. Therefore, how the questions included on a complete scale are phrased will directly affect the amount of raw data that can be collected. It should be clear that nominal scale questions provide the least amount of raw data and ratio scale questions provide the most specific data.

Some Criteria for Scale Development

By understanding the importance of question phrasing, the researcher can now focus his or her attention on developing the most appropriate scale descriptors to be used as the primary scale point elements. While there is no one agreed-on set of criteria for establishing the actual scale point descriptors, we offer several criteria.

EXHIBIT 12.9	Examples of Ordinally-Interval Scale Structures

Example 1:

For each of the brands of soft drinks listed below, please circle the number that best expresses your overall performance judgment of that brand.

Soft Drink Brands	Very Poor						Outstanding
Coke	1	2	3	4	5	6	7
Pepsi	1	2	3	4	5	6	7

Example 2:

Using the scale provided below, select the number that best describes how important each of the listed attributes were in your deciding which restaurant to eat at. Please place your response on the line provided next to each attribute.

Importance Scale

1 = Not at all important   3 = Somewhat important   5 = Definitely important
2 = Only slightly important   4 = Important   6 = Extremely important

Restaurant Attributes

____ Quality of the food	____ Dining atmosphere	____ Convenience of location
____ Wide variety in selection	____ Speed of service	____ Has a no-smoking section
____ Allows reservations	____ Reasonable-priced entrees	

Example 3:

Thinking about the different banking methods which you may or may not use, we would like to know your feelings toward these methods. Next to each of the listed banking methods, please circle the number that best describes the degree to which you like or dislike using that method.

Banking Methods	Very Much Dislike Using					Very Much Like Using
Inside the bank	1	2	3	4	5	6
Drive-up window	1	2	3	4	5	6
24-hour ATM	1	2	3	4	5	6
Bank by mail	1	2	3	4	5	6
Bank by phone	1	2	3	4	5	6
Bank by Internet	1	2	3	4	5	6

Intelligibility of the Questions

The researcher must give thought to the intellectual capacity and language ability of those to whom the scale will be administered. The researcher should assume that the prospective respondents are unaware of the research project's information requirements. This is to say, researchers should not automatically assume that respondents understand the questions being asked or the response choices. The **intelligibility** criterion for scale design relates to the degree to which the questions are understood by the respondents. The researcher must use appropriate language in both the questions and the answer choices.

Intelligibility The degree to which the questions on a scale are understood by the respondents.

The researcher should try to eliminate all guessing on the part of the respondent. Respondents should be able to understand what types of data are being asked for and how to respond. Refer back to scale example 3 in Exhibit 12.9; suppose that in the setup portion of that scale the research had used only the first sentence ("Thinking about the different banking methods which you may or may not use, we would like to know your feelings toward these methods"). This would suggest that the researcher assumed that respondents

EXHIBIT 12.10	Example of the Four Basic Types of Question Phrasings

Information requirement: To determine how often customers use their primary automobile service provider's facilities/services.

NOMINAL QUESTION PHRASING:

When your vehicle requires maintenance service or you have problems, do you usually take the vehicle to your primary automobile service provider?

The logical raw response to this question would be a simple *Yes* or *No.*

ORDINAL QUESTION PHRASING:

When your vehicle requires maintenance service or you have problems, how often do you take it to your primary automobile service provider? **(Check only one response.)**

The logical raw responses might be as follows:

___ Never   ___ Seldom   ___ Occasionally   ___ Usually   ___ Every time

INTERVAL QUESTION PHRASING:

Since purchasing your automobile, approximately how often have you used the services at your primary automobile service provider? **(Check the one appropriate response.)**

The logical raw responses might be as follows:

___ Less than 3 times   ___ 9 to 12 times   ___ Over 16 times
___ 4 to 8 times   ___ 13 to 16 times

RATIO QUESTION PHRASING:

In the past twelve (12) months, how many times did you take your vehicle for service or repairs to your primary automobile service provider? **(Write the # of times on the line provided.)**

_____ # of times

---

would automatically understand how to complete the scale question. Without the second sentence (the exact instructions), respondents may not know what to do. Such assumptions on the part of the researcher could easily increase the likelihood of incomplete data responses. The intelligibility factor thus promotes the use of "respondent instructions" in scale measurement designs, especially in self-administered surveys. For in-person or telephone interviews, it is quite possible that "interviewer instructions" will also have to be included in the question/setup portion of the scale measurements. More discussions on instruction requirements will be provided in Chapters 14 and 15.

Appropriateness of Primary Scale Descriptors

Appropriateness of descriptors The extent to which the scale point elements match the data being sought.

Researchers must make sure the scale descriptors match the type of raw data they are seeking. Therefore, another criterion is that the researcher must consider the **appropriateness of the descriptors.** That is, the adjectives or adverbs used to distinguish the relative magnitudes must be related to the primary scale descriptors. Let's say, for example, that the researcher wants to find out respondents' opinions about whether or not the Winn-Dixie supermarket has "competitive meat prices." The critical task becomes one of determining which primary scale descriptors most appropriately represent the notion of "competitive prices." There are several creative ways of achieving this task. First, if the researcher designs the question/setup to ask the respondents to agree or disagree that "Winn Dixie has competitive meat prices," then the appropriate set of scale descriptors would be levels of agreement/disagreement (e.g., "strongly agree," "agree," "neither agree nor disagree," "disagree," "strongly disagree"). Stating the question in terms of competitiveness would require an ordinal set of descriptors such as "extremely competitive," "definitely competitive," "generally competitive," "only slightly competitive," and "not at all competitive." In contrast, it would be inappropriate to try to represent respondents' opinions about "competitive prices" using a performance-oriented set of descriptors like "excellent," "very good," "good," "average," "fair," and "poor."

Discriminatory Power of the Scale Descriptors

This scale criterion relates to those situations when either (1) the information problem requires the inclusion of relative magnitudes to the set of possible raw responses or (2) the researcher arbitrarily elects to establish the existence of magnitudes (relative or absolute) of differences between the scale points. The **discriminatory power** of a scale is the scale's ability to significantly differentiate between the categorical scale responses.[19] Moreover, the researcher must decide how many scale points are necessary to make up the relative magnitudes of a desired response scale. Remember, it is the number of scale points that directly relates to the depth of information that can be obtained from asking respondents questions.

Discriminatory power
The scale's ability to significantly differentiate between the categorical scale responses.

While there is no clear rule about the number of scale points that should be used in creating a scale, many researchers acknowledge that most scales that include the order and distance scaling properties should be between three and seven points.[20] In most cases, respondents find it difficult to make a choice when there are more than seven levels of relative or absolute magnitudes. To illustrate this point, suppose Marriott International is interested in determining which hotel features business patrons consider important in their process of choosing a hotel for a business trip. In developing an "importance" scale to capture the relative magnitude of importance attributed to each hotel feature, the researcher must subjectively decide how many recognizable levels of importance exist in the minds of business travelers. The researcher must first understand that the basic dichotomous scale descriptors are simply "important" and "not important." Second, the researcher must decide how detailed or how varied the raw importance data responses have to be to address the initial information problem.[21] Typically, a complete importance scale consists of five different levels of importance *and* a "not at all important" category (giving the respondent six actual choices). The five differential degrees are normally expressed as "extremely," "definitely," "generally," "somewhat," and "only slightly" important.

By understanding the makeup of the complete importance scale, the researcher can correctly incorporate variations that may better fit the specific information requirements in different situations. When developing an importance scale, remember that the root scale descriptors are not simply "important" and "unimportant." In reality, most human beings do not think or express their "not at all important" feelings in degrees of "unimportant" (e.g., "extremely unimportant," "definitely unimportant," "generally unimportant"). In addition, there are times when attempting to incorporate too many degrees of relative magnitude to the scale results in decreasing its discriminatory power. Suppose in the above Marriott hotel example the researcher designs an importance scale that consists of 15 scale descriptors and presents the scale as follows:

IMPORTANCE SCALE

Not at All Important: 1 2 3 4 5 6 7 8 9 10 11 12 13 14 15 :Extremely Important

While this scale denotes "not at all important" as being a 1 and "extremely important" as being a 15, it is very unlikely that either the researcher or the respondent can attach any meaningful, differential descriptor interpretations to the scale points of 2 through 14. This potential discriminatory power problem can exist in any type of scale design.

Reliability of the Scale

Scale reliability The
extent to which a scale
can produce the same
measurement results in
repeated trials.

Scale reliability refers to the extent to which a scale can reproduce the same measurement results in repeated trials. As discussed in earlier chapters, random error produces inconsistency in scale measurements that leads to lower scale reliability. Two of the techniques that can help a researcher assess the reliability of scales are test-retest and equivalent form.

Test-retest A technique
of measuring scale relia-
bility by administering
the same scale to the
same respondents at two
different times or to two
different samples of
respondents under similar
conditions.

First, the **test-retest** technique involves repeating the administration of the scale measurement to either the same sample of respondents at two different times or two different samples of respondents from the same defined target population under as nearly the same conditions as possible. The idea behind this approach is simply that if random variations are presented, they will be revealed by variations in the scores between the two sampled measurements.[22] If there are very few differences between the first and second administrations of the scale, the measuring scale is viewed as being stable and therefore reliable. For example, assume that determining the teaching effectiveness associated with your marketing research course involved the use of a 28-item scale designed to measure the degree to which respondents agree or disagree with each item. To gather the necessary raw data on teaching effectiveness, your professor administers this scale to the class after the 7th week of the semester and again after the 12th week. Using a mean analysis procedure to create data structures on the items for each measurement period, the professor then runs correlation analysis on those mean values. If the correlations between the mean value measurements from the two assessment periods were high, the professor would conclude that the reliability of the 28-item scale was high.

There are several potential problems with the test-retest approach. First, some of the students who completed the scale the first time might be absent for the second administration of the scale. Second, students might become sensitive to the scale measurement and therefore alter their responses in the second measurement. Third, environmental or personal factors may change between the two administrations, thus causing changes in student responses in the second measurement.

Equivalent form
A technique to establish
scale reliability by mea-
suring and correlating the
measures of two equiva-
lent scaling instruments.

Some researchers believe that the problems associated with the test-retest reliability technique can be avoided by using the **equivalent form** technique. In this technique, the researcher creates two similar yet different (e.g., equivalent) scale measurements for the given construct (e.g., teaching effectiveness) and administers both forms to either the same sample of respondents or two samples of respondents from the same defined target population.[23] In the marketing research course "teaching effectiveness" example, the professor would construct two 28-item scales whose main difference would lie in the wording of the item statements, not the agreement/disagreement scaling points. Although the specific wording of the statements would be changed, their meaning would remain constant. After administering each of the scale measurements, the professor calculates the mean values for each item and then runs correlation analysis. Equivalent form reliability would be assessed by measuring the correlations of the item-mean value scores on the two scale measurements. High correlation values would be interpreted as meaning high scale measurement reliability.

There are two potential drawbacks associated with the equivalent form reliability technique. First, if the testing process suggests that equivalence can be achieved, it might not be worth the time, effort, and expense of determining that two similar yet different scales can be used to measure the same construct. Second, it is very difficult and perhaps impossible to create two totally equivalent scale measurements. Questions may be raised as to which scale measurement is the most appropriate to use in measuring teaching effectiveness.

Internal consistency
The degree to which the
various dimensions of a
multidimensional
construct correlate with
the scale.

When investigating multidimensional constructs, summated scale measurements tend to be the most appropriate scales. In this type of scale, each dimension represents some aspect of the construct. Thus, the construct is measured by the entire scale, not just one component. **Internal consistency** refers to the degree to which the various dimensions of a multidimensional construct correlate with the scale. In other words, the set of attribute items that make up the scale must be internally consistent. There are two popular techniques used to assess internal consistency: split-half tests and coefficient alpha, also referred to as Cronbach's alpha. In a **split-half test,** the items in the scale are divided into two halves (odd versus even attributes, or randomly) and the resulting halves' summated scores are correlated against one another. High correlations between the halves indicate good (or acceptable) internal consistency. A **coefficient alpha** takes the average of all possible split-half measures that result from different ways of splitting the scale items.[24] The coefficient value can range from 0 to 1 and, in most cases, a value of less than 0.6 would typically indicate marginal to low (or unsatisfactory) internal consistency. These reliability tests will be revisited in later chapters. Researchers need to remember that just because their scale measurement designs prove to be reliable, the data collected are not necessarily valid. Separate validity assessments must be made on the constructs being measured.

Split-half test A technique used to evaluate the internal consistency of scale measurements that have multiple dimensions.

Coefficient alpha A technique of taking the average of all possible split-half coefficients to measure the internal consistency of multidimensional scales.

Balancing Positive/Negative Scale Descriptors

This scale development criterion relates to the researcher's decision to maintain objectivity in a scale that is designed to capture both positive and negative raw responses. To maintain scale objectivity, the researcher must design a balance of positive and negative descriptors as scale points. For example, let's assume that J. D. Power and Associates wants to add to its "New Vehicle Survey" a global, single-item scale measurement that would measure a purchaser's satisfaction with his or her new vehicle's overall performance. Since most people would consider the feeling of satisfaction to be positive and the feeling of dissatisfaction to be negative, J. D. Power and Associates would need to decide whether or not the scale measurement should be "objective" and not bias the respondent's feelings one way or the other. By having equal relative magnitudes of satisfaction (positive) and dissatisfaction (negative), the global scale measure would maintain a level of objectivity. Such a balanced scale measurement design might look like the following:

Based on your experiences with your new vehicle since owning and driving it, to what extent are you presently satisfied or dissatisfied with the overall performance of the vehicle?

(PLEASE CHECK THE ONE APPROPRIATE RESPONSE)

____ Completely satisfied (no dissatisfaction)   ____ Slightly dissatisfied (some satisfaction)

____ Definitely satisfied   ____ Generally dissatisfied

____ Generally satisfied   ____ Definitely dissatisfied

____ Slightly satisfied (some dissatisfaction)   ____ Completely dissatisfied (no satisfaction)

With a balanced scale measurement, objectivity is maintained in both the question/setup portion of the scale and the descriptors.[25]

Now let's assume that J. D. Power and Associates is primarily interested in assessing new-vehicle purchasers' satisfaction with their vehicle's overall performance and that dissatisfaction data are not that important. This type of data requirement might be better met by using an unbalanced global scale measurement[26] that placed heavier emphasis on the positive (satisfaction) scale descriptors than on the negative (dissatisfaction) ones. The unbalanced scale measurement design might look like the following:

Based on your experiences with your new vehicle since owning and driving it, to what extent are you presently satisfied with the overall performance of the vehicle?

(PLEASE CHECK THE ONE APPROPRIATE RESPONSE)

____ Completely satisfied   ____ Generally satisfied   ____ Dissatisfied

____ Definitely satisfied   ____ Slightly satisfied

It is important to remember that with an unbalanced scale measurement, objectivity is lost in both the question/setup portion of the scale and the descriptors.

Inclusion of a Neutral Response Choice

In scale measurement design, the number of scale point descriptors becomes an important criterion only if the raw data requirements call for capturing either state-of-mind data or specific types of state-of-intention data that focus on positive/negative continuum ranges. The fundamental issue here is one of offering the respondent the opportunity to express a neutral response.[27] Having an even number of positive/negative scale descriptors tends to force the respondent to select either a positive or a negative answer only.

A scale that does not have a neutral descriptor to divide the positive and negative domains is referred to as a *forced-choice* scale measurement. In contrast, a scale that includes a center neutral response is referred to as a *free-choice* scale measurement. Exhibit 12.11 presents several different examples of both "even-point, forced-choice" and "odd-point, free-choice" descriptors.

Some experts believe that scales used to collect state-of-mind data should be designed as "odd-point, free-choice" scale measurements[28] since not all respondents will have enough knowledge or experience with the given topic to be able to accurately assess their thoughts or feelings. If those respondents are forced to choose, the scale may produce lower-quality data than the researcher desires. In free-choice scale designs, however, the so-called neutral scale point offers respondents a very easy way out of having to think or express their feelings about the given topic. The raw data from a neutral scale response becomes diagnostically useless to both the researcher and the business decision maker.

From an interpretation perspective, there is no such thing as a neutral attitude or feeling; these mental aspects almost always have some degree of a positive or negative orientation attached to them. A person either has an attitude or does not have an attitude about a given object; likewise, a person will either have a feeling or not have a feeling. An alternative approach to handling situations in which respondents may feel uncomfortable about expressing their thoughts or feelings about a given object, because they have no knowledge of or experience with it, would be to incorporate a "not applicable" response choice that would not be part of the actual scale measurement. The following example illustrates the *not applicable* (NA) response:

> Based on your experiences with your new vehicle since owning and driving it, to what extent are you presently satisfied or dissatisfied with the overall performance of the vehicle? If you feel that you lack enough experience with your vehicle or that the statement is not pertinent to you, please check the "NA" (Not Applicable) response. **(PLEASE CHECK THE ONE APPROPRIATE RESPONSE.)**
>
> ____ Completely satisfied (no dissatisfaction)   ____ Slightly dissatisfied (some satisfaction)
>
> ____ Definitely satisfied   ____ Generally dissatisfied
>
> ____ Generally satisfied   ____ Definitely dissatisfied
>
> ____ Slightly satisfied (some dissatisfaction)   ____ Completely dissatisfied (no satisfaction)
>
> ____ NA (Not Applicable)

This approach allows the researcher to sort all the "NA" responses out of the raw data and ensures that only quality raw data will be included in the data analysis procedures.

Desired Measures of Central Tendency and Dispersion

In determining what types of scale measurements should be developed, the researcher must consider the data analysis that will be used after the raw data is collected from

EXHIBIT 12.11	Examples of "Even-Point, Forced-Choice" and "Odd-Point, Free-Choice" Scale Descriptors

---

"Even-Point, Forced-Choice" Itemized Rating Scale Descriptors

PURCHASE INTENTION (BUY/NOT BUY)

___ Definitely will buy   ___ Probably will buy   ___ Probably will not buy   ___ Definitely will not buy

PERSONAL BELIEFS/OPINIONS (AGREEMENT/DISAGREEMENT)

Definitely agree	Generally agree	Slightly agree	Slightly disagree	Generally disagree	Definitely disagree
____	____	____	____	____	____

MODERNITY (MODERN/OLD-FASHIONED)

___ Very modern   ___ Somewhat modern   ___ Somewhat old-fashioned   ___ Very old-fashioned

COST (EXPENSIVE/INEXPENSIVE)

Extremely expensive	Definitely expensive	Somewhat expensive	Somewhat inexpensive	Definitely inexpensive	Extremely inexpensive
____	____	____	____	____	____

"Odd-Point, Free-Choice" Itemized Rating Scales

PURCHASE INTENTION (BUY/NOT BUY)

Definitely will buy	Probably will buy	Neither will nor will not buy	Probably will not buy	Definitely will not buy
____	____	____	____	____

PERSONAL BELIEFS/OPINIONS (AGREEMENT/DISAGREEMENT)

Definitely agree	Generally agree	Slightly agree	Neither agree nor disagree	Slightly disagree	Generally disagree	Definitely disagree
____	____	____	____	____	____	____

MODERNITY (MODERN/OLD-FASHIONED)

Very modern	Somewhat modern	Neither modern nor old-fashioned	Somewhat old-fashioned	Very old-fashioned
____	____	____	____	____

COST (EXPENSIVE/INEXPENSIVE)

Definitely expensive	Somewhat expensive	Neither expensive nor inexpensive	Somewhat inexpensive	Definitely inexpensive
____	____	____	____	____

Measures of central tendency The basic sample statistics that are generated through analyzing raw data; these are the mode, the median, and the mean.

respondents. The researcher must therefore have an understanding of the measures of central tendency and the measures of dispersion associated with different types of scale measurement designs. **Measures of central tendency** refer to the basic sample statistics that are generated through analyzing the collected raw data; these are the mode, the median, and the mean. The *mode* is the raw response that is the most frequently given among all of the respondents. The *median* represents the sample statistic that splits the raw data into a hierarchical pattern where half the raw data is above the statistic value and half is below. The *mean* is nothing more than the arithmetic average of all the raw data responses.

Measures of dispersion
The sample statistics that allow a researcher to report the diversity of the raw data collected from scale measurements; they are the frequency distribution, the range, and the estimated sample standard deviation.

Measures of dispersion relate to how all the raw data are actually dispersed around a given central tendency value. These sample statistics allow the researcher to report the diversity of the raw responses to a particular scale measurement; they are the frequency distribution, the range, and the estimated sample standard deviation. A *frequency distribution* is a summary of how many times each possible raw response to a scale question/setup was recorded by the total group of respondents. This distribution can be easily converted into percentages or histograms for ease of comparison between raw data responses. The *range* represents the grouping of raw data responses into mutually exclusive subgroups, each with an identifiable lower and upper boundary. The *estimated sample standard deviations* is the statistical value that specifies the degree of variation in the raw data responses in such a way that allows the researcher to translate the variations into normal curve interpretations (e.g., 99 percent of the raw responses fall between the mean value plus or minus 3 standard deviations).

Given the important role that these six basic sample statistics play in data analysis procedures, understanding how different types of scales activate these statistics becomes critical in scale measurement design. Exhibit 12.12 displays these relationships. It is important to remember that data collected through a nominal scale can be analyzed only by using modes and frequency distributions. It would be inappropriate in such cases to attempt analyses that require medians, means, ranges, or estimated standard deviations. For ordinal scales, it would be more appropriate to analyze the raw data using medians and ranges, but these data could also be analyzed with modes and frequency distributions. It is inappropriate in these cases to use means and estimated standard deviations.

For interval or ratio scale measurements, the most appropriate analysis procedures would be those that require the use of sample means and estimated standard deviations as the sample statistics. In addition, interval and ratio raw data can also be appropriately analyzed using modes, medians, frequency distributions, or ranges. These sample statistics and measures are discussed in more detail in later chapters.

EXHIBIT 12.12	**Relationships between Scale Types and Measures of Central Tendency and Dispersion**

Measurements	Four Basic Types of Scales			
	Nominal	**Ordinal**	**Interval**	**Ratio**
Central Tendency				
Mode	**Appropriate**	Appropriate	Appropriate	Appropriate
Median	Inappropriate	**More Appropriate**	Appropriate	Appropriate
Mean	Inappropriate	Inappropriate	**Most Appropriate**	**Most Appropriate**
Dispersion				
Frequency distribution	Appropriate	Appropriate	Appropriate	Appropriate
Range	Inappropriate	**More Appropriate**	Appropriate	Appropriate
Estimated standard deviation	Inappropriate	Inappropriate	**Most Appropriate**	**Most Appropriate**

A CLOSER LOOK AT RESEARCH   Using Technology

Deciding on a market segmentation strategy can be a very difficult task for any manager or business owner. For small-business owners, the choice can be especially daunting. Macro Consulting, Inc., realizes that small-business owners and managers are forced to make most decisions with very little input or outside help. To provide guidance in this area, Macro Consulting publishes articles on its World Wide Web page (www.macroinc.com/articles/imageq.htm) that promote, among other options, innovative market segmentation strategies. Below is an excerpt from Macro Consulting's Internet page that describes ImageQ, a unique approach to measuring customer segmentation. By using Macro Consulting's Web site, small-business owners and managers have access to many innovative marketing ideas.

For example, ImageQ offers several advantages over other methods: (1) consumers are grouped together based not on how each of them perceive various brands but rather on which brand imagery attributes are most important to their individual purchase decisions; (2) the most important brand perceptions (as well as the least important) are clearly identified for each consumer segment; (3) brand imagery importance data do not need to be collected; and (4) virtually any existing brand imagery data can serve as the basis for this segmentation approach, making expensive data collection unnecessary.

These technical advantages of ImageQ provide marketers, advertisers, and anyone else needing to communicate to his or her customers several key benefits: (1) a completely new insight into the target market's motivations; (2) a customer-focused foundation for developing communications strategies; (3) a fresh perspective on how to best define the primary and secondary market segments; and (4) a new and deeper understanding of how brand imagery affects sales to specific market segments. The approach involves a unique and proprietary analytic protocol. It is an ideal tool for secondary analysis of existing data sets.

ImageQ uses McCullough's correlation measures (MCM), a family of nonparametric correlations that measure the relationships between a battery of brand imagery attributes and purchase interest at the individual respondent level. For virtually any data set that contains brand imagery data and some purchase interest or preference measure, one of these correlations can be calculated. MCMs reflect the importance of each brand imagery attribute to the purchase interest of all brands tested for each respondent in the sample. Cluster analysis is then conducted, using an MCM as its basis. Typically, several cluster solutions are examined and evaluated. The solution that offers the most interpretable and actionable results is selected for profiling and further analysis. The resulting segmentation provides a unique look at brand imagery-based market dynamics, on a segment-by-segment basis.

This is the only method that we are aware of that can segment the marketplace based on the relevance of various brand imagery attributes to individual consumers. In a dynamic marketplace it is essential to gather information and make decisions as quickly as possible. Getting the right message to the right consumer quickly is critical to success. This approach gleans additional and powerful information from existing data sets, saving time and money, while providing insights unattainable with other approaches or measures.

Source: Macro Consulting, Inc. 1998, www.macroinc.com/articles/imageq.htm.

Now that we have presented the basics of construct development as well as the elements and rules surrounding the development of scale measurements, we are ready to move forward to the popular attitudinal, emotional, and behavior scales used by marketing researchers. Chapter 13 focuses on these more advanced scales. First, however, read the Using Technology box, about how a consulting firm integrates advanced technologies to create high-quality segmentation measures.

SUMMARY OF LEARNING OBJECTIVES

Explain what constructs are, how they are developed, and why they are important to measurement and scale designs.

Within the overall process of creating meaningful information for resolving today's and future business/marketing problems, researchers must be able to develop appropriate questions and record the raw responses to those questions. Next to correctly defining the information problem, determining what type of data should be collected is the second most critical aspect in information research. Gaining access to raw data responses is achieved by the scale measurement incorporated into the questioning process. A construct can be viewed as any object that cannot be directly observed and measured by physical devices. Within the development process, researchers must consider the abstractness of the construct, its dimensionality, assessments of validity, and its operationalization. Not knowing exactly what it is that one needs to measure makes it difficult to design the appropriate scale measurements.

Discuss the integrated validity and reliability concerns underlying construct development and scale measurement.

Regardless of the method used for data collection, researchers must strive to collect the most accurate data and information possible. Data accuracy depends heavily on the validity of the constructs and the reliability of the measurements applied to those constructs. Constructs can be assessed for content, convergent, discriminant, and nomological validity. Testing for reliability of constructs is indirectly achieved by testing the reliability of the scale measurements used in data collection. Scale reliability test methods available to researchers include test-retest, equivalent form, and internal consistency. Although scale measurements may prove to be reliable, reliability alone does not guarantee construct validity.

Explain what scale measurement is, and describe how to correctly apply it in collecting raw data from respondents.

Scale measurement is the process of assigning a set of descriptors to represent the range of possible responses that a person gives in answering a question about a particular object, construct, or factor. This process aids in determining the amount of raw data that can be obtained

from asking questions, and therefore indirectly impacts the amount of primary information that can be derived from the data. Central to the amount of data issue is understanding that there are four basic scaling properties (i.e., assignment, order, distance, and origin) that can be activated through scale measurements. The rule-of-thumb is that as a researcher simultaneously activates more properties within the question/answering process, the greater the amount of raw data that can be gathered from people's responses. All raw data can be classified into one of four mutually exclusive types: state-of-being, state-of-mind, state-of-behavior, and state-of-intention. Understanding the categorical types of data that can be produced by individuals' responses to questions improves the researcher's ability in determining not only *what* questions should be asked, but also *how* to ask those questions.

Identify and explain the four basic types of scales, and discuss the amount of information they can provide a researcher or decision maker.

The four basic types of scales are nominal, ordinal, interval, and ratio. Nominal scales are the most basic and provide the least amount of data. They activate only the "assignment" scaling property; the raw data do not exhibit relative magnitudes between the categorical subsets of responses. The main data structures (or patterns) that can be derived from nominal raw data are in the form of modes and frequency distributions. Nominal scales would ask respondents about their religious affiliation, gender, type of dwelling, occupation, or last brand of cereal purchased, and so on. The questions require yes/no, like/dislike, or agree/disagree responses.

Ordinal scales require respondents to express their feelings of relative magnitude about the given topic. Ordinal scales activate both the assignment and order scaling properties and allow researchers to create a hierarchical pattern among the possible raw data responses (or scale points) that determine "greater than/less than" relationships. Data structures that can be derived from ordinal scale measurements are in the forms of medians and ranges as well as modes and frequency distributions. An example of a set of ordinal scale descriptors would be "complete knowledge," "good knowledge," "basic knowledge," "little knowledge," and "no knowledge." While the ordinal scale measurement is an excellent design for capturing the relative magnitudes in respondents' raw responses, it cannot capture absolute magnitudes.

An interval scale activates not only the assignment and order scaling properties but also the distance property. This scale measurement allows the researcher to build into the scale elements that demonstrate the existence of absolute differences between each scale point. Normally, the raw scale descriptors will represent a distinct set of numerical ranges as the possible responses to a given question (e.g., "less than a mile," "1 to 5 miles," "6 to 10 miles," "11 to 20 miles," "over 20 miles"). With interval scaling designs, the distance between each scale point or response does not have to be equal. Disproportional scale descriptors (e.g., different-sized numerical ranges) can be used. With interval raw data, researchers can develop a number of more meaningful data structures that are based on means and standard deviations, or create data structures based on mode, median, frequency distribution, and range.

Ratio scales are the only scale measurements that simultaneously activate all four scaling properties (i.e., assignment, order, distance, and origin). Considered the most sophisticated scale design, they allow researchers to identify absolute differences between each scale point and to make absolute comparisons between the respondents' raw responses. Ratio question/scale structures are designed to allow "zero" or "true state of nothing" responses. Normally, though, the respondent is requested to choose a specific singular numerical value. The data structures that can be derived from ratio scale measurements are basically the same as those for interval scale measurements. It is important to remember that the more scaling properties simultaneously activated, the greater the opportunity to derive more detailed and sophisticated data structures and therefore more information. Interval and ratio scale designs are most appropriate to use when researchers want to collect either state-of-behavior, or state-of-intentions, or certain types of state-of-being data.

Discuss the ordinally-interval hybrid scale design and the types of information it can provide researchers.

Some researchers misidentify certain types of ordinal scales as being interval scales. They take an ordinal scale design and artificially assume that the scale has activated the distance (and the origin) scaling properties. This assumption comes about when the researcher arbitrarily assigns a secondary set of numerical scale descriptors (e.g., consecutive whole integers) to the original primary set of ordinal descriptors. What drives a researcher to misrepresent the ordinal scale format is the need to know not only an individual's attitudes or feelings but also the combined overall attitude or feeling of a group of individuals. To achieve this overall response outcome, the researcher must be able to add together many separate raw responses and perform some type of basic mathematical procedure, like establishing the mean response of the group. There are two main approaches to developing an ordinally-interval scale measurement: (1) using a secondary set of cardinal number descriptors and redefining the complete set of primary scale descriptors (1 = definitely agree, 2 = generally agree, 3 = slightly agree, 4 = slightly disagree, 5 = generally disagree, and 6 = definitely disagree); or (2) using primary descriptors to identify only the extreme end points of a set of secondary cardinal numbers that make up the range of raw scale descriptors or scale points (definitely agree 1 2 3 4 5 6 definitely disagree). Regardless of the method used, for the researcher to believe that the absolute difference between a respondent's response of "definitely agree" and that of another respondent's "generally agree" is one unit of agreement is really nothing more than a leap of faith. Researchers are cautioned to be very careful how they interpret the data structures generated from this hybrid scale design.

Discuss the three components of scale development and explain why they are critical to gathering primary data.

In developing high-quality scale measurements, the researcher must understand that there are three critical components to any complete scale measurement: question/setup; dimensions of the object, construct, or behavior; and the scale point descriptors. Some of the criteria for scale development are the intelligibility of the questions, the appropriateness of the primary descriptors, the discriminatory power of the scale descriptors, the reliability of the scale, the balancing of positive/negative scale descriptors, the inclusion of a neutral response choice, and desired measures of central tendency (mode, median, and mean) and dispersion (frequency distribution, range, estimated standard deviation). If the highest-quality raw data is to be collected to transform into useful primary information, researchers and practitioners alike must have an integrated understanding of construct development and scale measurement.

KEY TERMS AND CONCEPTS

Appropriateness of descriptors 388

Assignment property 378

Coefficient alpha 391

Construct development 372

Discriminatory power 389

Distance property 379

Domain of observables 373

Equivalent form 390

Intelligibility 387

Internal consistency 390

Interval scale 382

Measurement 371

Measures of central tendency 393

Measures of dispersion 394

Nominal scale 381

Operationalization 374

Order property 378

Ordinally-interval scale 385

Ordinal scale 381

Origin property 380

Ratio scale 383

Scale measurement 378

Scale points 378

Scale reliability 390

Split-half test 391

State-of-behavior data 377

State-of-being data 376

State-of-intention data 377

State-of-mind data 376

Test-retest 390

REVIEW QUESTIONS

1. How does activating scaling properties determine the amount of data and information that can be derived from scale measurement designs?

2. Among the four basic types of scale measurements, which one provides the researcher with the most data and information? Why is this particular scale type the least used in research practices? Explain the main differences between interval and ratio scale measurements.

3. What are ordinally-interval scale measurements? Why do researchers insist on creating them to measure or gather state-of-mind data from respondents? Make sure you discuss their strengths and weaknesses in your answer.

4. Identify and explain the three components that make up any type of scale measurement. What are the interrelationships between these components?

5. When developing the scale point descriptors for a scale measurement, what rules of thumb should the researcher follow?

6. Why should researchers complete construct development activities prior to actually designing a complete scale measurement?

DISCUSSION QUESTIONS

1. What are some of the weaknesses of using college students as respondents when developing constructs like "retail store loyalty," "telecommunication service quality," or "attitudes toward kids' advertisements"?

2. For each of the listed scale measurements, answer the following questions:
   a. What type of raw data are being collected?
   b. What type of scale measurement is being used?

c. What scaling properties are being activated in the scale?

d. What is the most appropriate measure of central tendency?

e. What is the most appropriate measure of variation (or dispersion)?

f. What weakness, if any, exists with the scale?

A. How often do you travel for business or pleasure purposes?

___ 0–1 times per month	___ 0–1 times per year
___ 2–3 times per month	___ 2–3 times per year
___ 4–5 times per month	___ 4–5 times per year
___ 6 or more times per month	___ 6 or more times per year

B. How do you pay for your travel expenses?

___ Cash	___ Company charge
___ Check	___ Personal charge
___ Credit card	___ Other _____

C. Please check the one category that best approximates your total family annual income, before taxes. (Please check only one category.)

___ Under $10,000	___ $30,001–$40,000	___ $60,001–$70,000
___ $10,000–$20,000	___ $40,001–$50,000	___ $70,001–$100,000
___ $20,001–$30,000	___ $50,001–$60,000	___ Over $100,000

3. For each of the listed concepts or objects, design a scale measurement that would allow you to collect data on that concept/object.

a. An excellent long-distance runner.

b. A person's favorite Mexican restaurant.

c. Size of the listening audience for a popular country and western radio station.

d. Consumers' attitudes toward the Colorado Rockies professional baseball team.

e. The satisfaction a person has toward his or her automobile.

f. Purchase intentions for a new tennis racket.

4. **EXPERIENCE THE INTERNET.** Using a browser of your choice, log on to the Internet and go to American Demographics' home page at www.demographics.com. Now surf the "hot spots" until you come across one of their segmentation questionnaires. Take the first five question/scales that appear on the questionnaire and evaluate each of them for the following five questions:

a. What type of data are being sought?

b. What type of scale measurement is being employed?

c. What scaling properties are being activated?

d. What would be the most appropriate measure of central tendency for analyzing the data?

e. What would be the most appropriate measure of dispersion?

ENDNOTES

1. William D. Crano and Marilyn B. Brewer, *Principles and Methods of Social Research* (Boston: Allyn and Bacon, 1986), pp. 23–38; also see Edward G. Carmines and Richard A. Zeller, *Reliability and Validity Assessment* (Newbury Park, CA: Sage Publications, 1979), pp. 9–48; and Paul E. Spector, *Summated Rating Scale Construction: An Introduction* (Newbury Park, CA: Sage Publications, 1992), pp. 12–17, 46–65.

2. Gilbert A. Churchill, Jr., "A Paradigm for the Development of Better Measures of Marketing Constructs," *Journal of Marketing Research* 16 (February 1979), pp. 64–73.

3. Jum C. Nunnally, *Psychometric Theory,* 2nd ed. (New York: McGraw-Hill, 1978), p. 102.

4. David J. Ortinau and Ronald P. Brensinger, "An Empirical Investigation of Perceived Quality's Intangible Dimensionality Through Direct Cognitive Structural (DCS) Analysis," in *Marketing: Perspectives for the 1990s,* ed. Robert L. King (New Orleans, LA: Southern Marketing Association, 1992), pp. 214–19.

5. Ronald P. Brensinger, "An Empirical Investigation of Consumer Perceptions of Combined Product and Service Quality: The Automobile," unpublished doctoral dissertation (Tampa, FL: The University of South Florida, 1993) pp. 54–60.

6. Nunnally, *Psychometric Theory,* p. 3.

7. Stanley S. Stevens, "Mathematics, Measurement and Psychophysics," in *Handbook of Experimental Psychology,* ed. S.S. Stevens (New York: John Wiley and Sons, Inc., 1951).

8. Fred N. Kerlinger, *Foundations of Behavioral Research,* 3rd ed. (New York: Holt, Rinehart and Winston, 1986), p. 403; also see Stanley S. Stevens, "On the Theory of Scales of Measurement," *Science* 103 (June 7, 1946), pp. 677–80.

9. Melvin R. Crask and Richard J. Fox, "An Exploration of the Interval Properties of Three Commonly Used Marketing Research Studies: A Magnitude Estimation Approach," *Journal of the Marketing Research Society* 29, no. 3 (1987), pp. 317–39.

10. Wendell R. Garner and C. D. Creelman, "Problems and Methods of Psychological Scaling," in *Contemporary Approaches to Psychology,* ed. Helson and William Bevan (New York: Van Nostrand, 1967), p. 4.

11. Stevens, "On the Theory of Scales of Measurement," pp. 677–80.

12. Kerlinger, *Foundations of Behavioral Research,* p. 405.

13. Ibid., p. 411.

14. Crask and Fox, "An Exploration of the Interval Properties," p. 326.

15. Wendell R. Garner and C. D. Creelman, "Problems and Methods of Psychological Scaling," in *Contemporary Approaches to Psychology,* ed. Helson and William Bevan (New York: Van Nostrand, 1967), p. 7; also see E. T. Goetz, P. A. Alexander, and M. J. Ash, *Educational Psychology* (New York: Macmillan, 1992), pp. 670–74.

16. William D. Perreault, Jr., and Forrest W. Young, "Alternating Least Squares Optimal Scaling: Analysis of Nonmetric Data in Marketing Research," *Journal of Marketing Research* 17 (February 1980), pp. 1–13; also see

Neil R. Barnard and Andrew S. C. Ehrenberg, "Robust Measures of Consumer Brand Beliefs," *Journal of Marketing Research* 27 (November 1990), pp. 477–484.

17. Mark Taylor, "Ordinal and Interval Scaling," *Journal of the Marketing Research Society* 25, no. 4 (November 1977), pp. 297–303; also see Gerald Albaum, Robert Best, and Del I. Hawkins, "Measurement Properties of Semantic Scales Data," *Journal of the Marketing Research Society* 25, no. 1 (January 1977), pp. 21–28; and Norbert Schwarz et al., "Rating Scales: Numeric Values May Change the Meanings of Scale Labels," *Public Opinion Quarterly* 55 (Winter 1991), pp. 570–82.

18. John Gaito, "Measurement Scales and Statistics: Resurgence of an Old Misconception," *Psychological Bulletin* 87 (1980), pp. 564–67.

19. Nunnally, *Psychometric Theory,* pp. 3–30, 86–90, 102, 225–40.

20. Albert R. Wildt and Michael B. Mazis, "Determinants of Scale Response: Labels Versus Position," *Journal of Marketing Research* 15 (May 1978), pp. 261–67; also see Jacob Jacoby and Michael S. Matell, "Three Point Likert Scales Are Good Enough," *Journal of Marketing Research* 8 (November 1971), pp. 495–506.

21. "Measuring the Importance of Attributes," *Research on Research* 28 (Chicago: Market Facts, Inc., undated).

22. Gilbert A. Churchill and J. Paul Peter, "Research Design Effects on the Reliability of Rating Scales: A Meta-Analysis," *Journal of Marketing Research* 21 (February 1984), pp. 360-75.

23. M. N. Segal, "Alternate Form Conjoint Reliability," *Journal of Advertising Research* 4 (1984), pp. 31–38.

24. L. J. Cronbach, "Coefficient Alpha and Internal Structure of Tests," *Psychometrika* 16 (1951), pp. 297–334.

25. H. Schuman and S. Pesser, *Questions and Answers in Attitude Survey* (New York: Academic Press, 1981), pp. 179–201.

26. Ibid., p. 192.

27. G. J. Spagna, "Questionnaire: Which Approach Do You Use?" *Journal of Advertising Research* (February–March 1984), pp. 67–70; also see E. A. Holdaway, "Different Response Categories and Questionnaire Response Patterns," *Journal of Experimental Education* (Winter 1971), p. 59.

28. K. C. Schneider, "Uninformed Response Rate in Survey Research," *Journal of Business Research* (April 1985), pp 153–62; also see Del I. Hawkins and K. A. Coney, "Uninformed Response Error in Survey Research," *Journal of Marketing Research* 18 (August 1981), pp. 370–74.

MARKETING RESEARCH ILLUSTRATION

WHAT YOU CAN LEARN FROM A CUSTOMER LOYALTY INDEX

This illustration is presented in a two-part format. Here in part one, you will read how researchers at Burke Customer Satisfaction Associates, a commercial research firm that specializes in customer satisfaction measurement and management programs, define *customer loyalty* and how this construct is operationalized into a measurable index called the *secure customer index*. The second part is presented in the Marketing Research Illustration at the end of Chapter 13 and will focus on how this construct is actually measured by Burke Customer Satisfaction Associates.

The idea that loyal customers are especially valuable is not new to today's business managers. Loyal customers repeatedly purchase products or services. They recommend a company to others. And they stick with a business over time. Loyal customers are worth the special effort it may take to keep them. But how can you provide that special treatment if you don't know your customers and how their loyalty is won and lost?

Understanding loyalty—what makes your customers loyal and how to measure and understand loyal customers—enables your company to improve customer-driven quality. A customer loyalty index provides management with an easily understood tool that helps focus the organization toward improving satisfaction and retention, for a positive impact on the bottom line.

What Customer Loyalty Is and Isn't

To better understand the *concept* of customer loyalty, let's first define what customer loyalty is *not*. Customer loyalty is *not* customer satisfaction. Satisfaction is a necessary component of loyal or secure customers. However, the mere aspect of being satisfied with a company does not necessarily make customers loyal. Just because customers are satisfied with your company today does not mean they will continue to do business with you in the future.

Customer loyalty is *not* a response to trial offers or incentives. If customers suddenly begin buying your product or service, it may be the result of a special offer or incentive and not necessarily a reflection of customer loyalty. These same customers may be just as quick to respond to your competitors' incentives.

Customer loyalty is *not* strong market share. Many businesses mistakenly look at their sales numbers and market share and think, "Those numbers are surrogates for direct measures of customer loyalty. After all, we wouldn't be enjoying high levels of market share if our customers didn't love us." However, this may not be true. Many other factors can drive up market share, including poor performance by competitors or pricing issues. And high share doesn't mean low churn (the rate at which existing customers leave you—possibly to patronize your competition—and are replaced by new customers).

Customer loyalty is *not* repeat buying or habitual buying. Many repeat customers may be choosing your products or services because of convenience or habit. However, if they learn about a competitive product that they think may be less expensive or better quality, they may quickly switch to that product. Habitual buyers can defect; loyal customers usually don't.

Now that we know what does *not* constitute customer loyalty, we can talk about what does. Customer loyalty is a composite of a number of qualities. It is driven by customer satisfaction, yet it also involves a commitment on the part of the customer to make a sustained investment in an ongoing relationship with a brand or company.

| EXHIBIT 1 | The Secure Customer Index (i.e.,Customer Loyalty Index) |

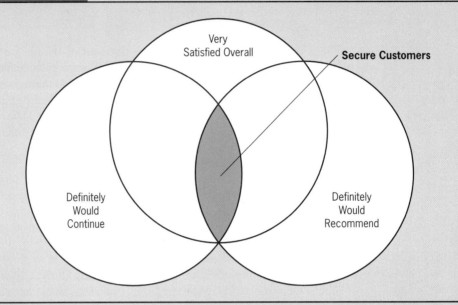

Finally, customer loyalty is reflected by a combination of *attitudes* and *behaviors*. These attitudes include:

- The intention to buy again and/or buy additional products or services from the same company.

- A willingness to recommend the company to others.

- A commitment to the company demonstrated by a resistance to switching to a competitor.

Customer behaviors that reflect loyalty include:

- Repeat purchasing of products or services.

- Purchasing more and different products or services from the same company.

- Recommending the company to others.

Any one of these attitudes or behaviors in isolation does not necessarily indicate loyal customers. However, by recognizing how these indicators work together in a measurement system, we can derive an index of customer loyalty, or in a broader sense, customer *security*. At Burke Customer Satisfaction Associates, we have developed a *Secure Customer Index* (SCI) using three major components to measure customer loyalty: overall customer satisfaction, likelihood of repeat business, and likelihood to recommend the company to others. Other elements may be included in the index depending upon the industry. However, in our experience, these three components are the core of a meaningful customer loyalty index.

Source: Amanda Prus and D. Randall Brandt, "Understanding Your Customers—What You Can Learn from a Customer Loyalty Index," *Marketing Tools* (July/August 1995), pp. 10–14.

MARKETING RESEARCH CASE EXERCISE

TRYING TO REFORMULATE A MARKETING STRATEGY

The personal computer (PC) industry consists of consumer, business, education, and government markets. Those in the consumer market basically seek products that allow them to use the Internet, shop, perform office work at home, and play video games. These customers are also seeking computers that are reliable and compatible in regard to software usage. If problems arise with their computers, customers want access to the manufacturer via online help centers, and they want it 24 hours a day. Business market customers not only care about company technical support, aftersale service, and software compatibility, but they also require PCs that will give them the necessary networking capability for both Internet and intranet usage.

Apple believes the consumer market holds vast potential for new users. As of 1998, the computer industry sold only 40 million PCs, and Apple estimates that there are over 100 million households remaining to be penetrated.

The education market, always a stronghold for Apple, is estimated to grow 30 percent by the year 2001. Apple's current level of penetration in this area is 27.2 percent of the market. The business market, which accounts for nearly 70 percent of all PC sales, is the largest market for computer manufacturers. Apple's products are especially popular with those companies in the multimedia and publishing businesses. Yet Apple occupies only 1.4 percent of this group. A breakdown of each market by competitor is illustrated below:

	Percent of Sales for		
Company	Consumer Market	Education Market	Business Market
Apple	5.0	27.2	1.4
Compaq	18.0	13.0	15.0
Dell	23.0	10.0	12.0
Gateway	11.0	7.0	9.0

Apple is currently developing a marketing research study to assess computer usage habits for the above three markets. In this study, Apple wishes to assess issues on purchase decision criteria, product attribute and evaluative criteria, usage patterns, and where and how customers buy the product.

For each market (consumer, education, and business) develop a list of issues that Apple needs to measure in order to obtain accurate representation of that market. Remember, your list should focus on purchase decision criteria, product attribute and evaluative criteria, usage patterns, and how and where customers buy computers.

Learning Objectives

After reading this chapter, you will be able to

1. Discuss the importance of attitude measurement, and describe two different approaches to measuring people's attitudes toward a given object.

2. Tell how to correctly design and test Likert, semantic differential, and behavior intention scales, and explain their strengths and weaknesses.

3. Discuss the differences between noncomparative and comparative scale designs as well as the appropriateness of rating and ranking scale measurements.

4. Identify and discuss the critical aspects of consumer attitudes and other marketplace phenomena that require measurement to allow us to make better decisions.

5. Discuss the overall rules of measurement and explain the differences between single versus multiple measures of a construct as well as direct versus indirect measures.

Attitude Scale Measurements Used in Survey Research

" What specific types of scale measurements should be used to capture my customers' evaluative judgments toward the service quality of my firm's delivery system? **"**

KAREN ZWERLING
Former Owner
Aca Joe, Inc.

Attitude Measurements and Meaningful Diagnostic Marketing Research Information

Aca Joe, Inc., had been operating for three years in the Tampa Bay metropolitan area. Prior to opening the business, the owner decided to present the image of Aca Joe as being a specialty men's casual-wear store that was conveniently located, with a good reputation of offering a wide selection of high-quality, fashionable/stylish men's casual apparel at competitive prices. In addition, the owner wanted Aca Joe to be known as having very knowledgeable sales associates and store staff who were committed to providing outstanding customer service and satisfaction.

The owner created and implemented various marketing strategies to ensure that this image was communicated to potential and actual customers. Three years later, however, the sales and financial bottom-line figures were lower than expected, causing the owner to question the effectiveness of the store's current marketing strategies. The owner was not sure how consumers viewed the store.

Realizing that help was needed, Aca Joe's owner consulted a marketing research expert. After several preliminary discussions, it was decided that a store image study should be conducted to gain insights into how Aca Joe's image compared to several direct competitors. The ensuing information research process combined both qualitative and quantitative research methods in a two-phase study. First, using qualitative research practices, the researcher completed several in-depth interviews with Aca Joe's owner and sales associates as well as a review of the retail literature; and four focus group sessions among known customers were conducted to identify the dimensions and store-service features that were most closely related to the store's desired image. The results from the qualitative stage suggested that customers viewed seven dimensions (quality, assortment, style/fashion, and prices of the merchandise; store's location; store's overall reputation; and knowledge of sales staff) with 18 store-service

features as being relevant to Aca Joe's image. Once the critical store image dimensions and features were identified, the researcher had to determine the appropriate scale measurements needed to collect data on those factors. Guided by the information research problem, the established list of information needs, and the understanding of the different types of scale measurements that could be used, the researcher developed a seven-point semantic differential scale to measure the seven recognized dimensions and a modified four-point, self-rating importance scale for the store-service features. These scale measurements were included in an eight-page store image questionnaire.

Using quantitative information research practices to collect the necessary data, the scales were developed, tested, and administered to a randomly selected sample of 300 known Aca Joe customers using a direct mail survey. Interpretation of the findings from the semantic differential data structures revealed that customers perceived Aca Joe as having a good reputation as a retail men's specialty store that offered high-quality, stylish/fashionable merchandise but had only an average assortment of items that were somewhat high priced. In addition, customers viewed the store as being only somewhat conveniently located, but the sales staff as generally knowledgeable and very helpful.

When cross-matched to the owner's desired store image, the image information created from the quantitative data structures identified several areas of concern. The results suggested that Aca Joe's overall desired store image was being somewhat compromised by the store's current merchandising and pricing strategies. The owner needed to further evaluate these particular strategies with the willingness to modify them in order to change the current image held by customers toward the store's merchandise selection and prices.

Value of Attitude Measurement in Information Research

In today's business world, more and more marketers are making attempts to better understand their customers' attitudes and feelings toward their products, services, and delivery systems, as well as those of their direct competitors. This chapter continues the discussion of scale measurement begun in Chapter 12. It also builds on the concepts discussed in earlier chapters, especially Chapters 2, 8, 9, 10, and 11. Therefore, you are encouraged to review the information in those chapters. After the scientific elements and considerations that must be employed in the process of developing solid scale measurements, we are ready to explore some specific types of scales commonly used in marketing research. This chapter focuses on scales used to collect attitudinal, emotional, and intentional responses from people. These scales have a common link in that they are normally used to collect state-of-mind and state-of-intention data from respondents. They include noncomparative rating and comparative ranking scales.

In addition, there are several fundamental principles from earlier chapters that you need to think about as you read this chapter: (1) Raw data, data structures, and information are not the same things; they are unique concepts with different origins and uses (Chapter 2); (2) Raw data are nothing more than a given set of responses to a stated question and/or directive (Chapters 2, 3, 9, 11); and (3) A complete scale measurement consists of three components: the question/setup, the scale dimensions and attributes, and the scale point descriptors (Chapter 12). The importance of the last principle cannot be overstated. If they want to collect high-quality data to transform into useful primary information, researchers and practitioners alike must have an integrated understanding of the relationships that exist among the three components making up scale measurements.

The Nature of Attitudes and Marketplace Behaviors

As they move into the 21st century, many businesses are attaching more and more importance to identifying their customers' attitudes and feelings as a way to diagnose their strengths and weaknesses in the marketplace. Attitudinal structures are useful in understanding consumers' and industrial buyers' observable marketplace behaviors. Yet measuring attitudes and their components is a difficult process that uses less precise scales than what are found in the physical sciences. Although complete treatment of the theory of attitudes goes well beyond the scope of this chapter, we believe that by having a fundamental understanding of what an attitude is, you will be in a better position to develop good scale measurements of that construct. For complete exposure to the theory of attitude, we suggest that you go to any current consumer behavior textbook or to the *Handbook of Consumer Behavior* by T. S. Robertson and H. H. Kassarjian[1] or *Attitude Theory and Measurement* by Martin Fishbein.[2]

Attitude A learned predisposition to react in some consistent positive or negative way to a given object, idea, or set of information.

For our purposes here, an **attitude** is defined as a learned predisposition to react in some consistent positive or negative way to a given object, idea, or set of information.[3] Attitudes are state-of-mind constructs that are not directly observable. The true structure of an attitude lies in the mind of the individual holding that attitude. To have a chance at accurately capturing customers' attitudes, the researcher must be able to understand the dimensions of the construct. Today, there are two prevailing schools of thought regarding the structure of an attitude: the trilogy approach and the affect global approach. The following discussions illustrate how different attitude scaling formats will yield different results about the same attitude construct.

The Trilogy Approach

Trilogy approach   The theoretical viewpoint that a person's overall attitude consists of the interaction between three specific components: (1) their beliefs (cognitive), (2) their feelings (affect), and (3) their outcome behavior (conative).

First, the **trilogy approach** recognizes that a person's complete attitude toward an object consists of three components: the cognitive, affective and conative factors. The **cognitive component** of an attitude represents the person's beliefs, perceptions, and knowledge about a specified object. These aspects are the key elements and outcomes of learning. For example, think back to the impeachment proceedings against President Bill Clinton. Many people held a variety of different beliefs on the matter, which they developed as they learned more about it. Moreover, people have hundreds of beliefs about many different items or objects that make up their everyday environment. An attitude's **affective component** represents the person's emotional feelings toward the given object. Many times, this is the component that is normally expressed when a person is asked to verbalize his or her attitude toward the object. The affective component can also be viewed as the amount of feeling attached to a given belief; thus, it serves as a mechanism that allows a person to create some type of hierarchical order among a set of beliefs about an object or behavior. For example, a person considering the purchase of a new Mazda Millenia might deem several factors about cars in general to be important in the selection process. The affective component of that person's attitude toward the Millenia allows him or her to decide which of those factors are important (or less important or unimportant) with regard to that specific car.

Cognitive component   The part of an attitude that represents a subject's beliefs, perceptions, and knowledge about a specified object.

Affective component   The part of an attitude that represents the person's emotional feelings held toward the given object.

Conative component   The part of an attitude that represents a person's intended or actual behavioral response to the given object.

The **conative component** of an attitude represents the person's intended or actual behavioral response to the given object. This part of an attitude tends to be an observable outcome driven by the interaction of a person's cognitive and affective components toward a given object. In the Millenia purchase example, the actual decision (i.e., conative component) to buy a gold-colored 1999 Mazda Millenia with leather/wood interior, an antilock braking system, cruise control, automatic seat and side mirror adjustment, a high-performance six-cylinder engine, dual air bags, and a high-tech CD sound system would be directly influenced by the set of beliefs (i.e., cognitive components) and the feelings (i.e., affective components) attached to those beliefs concerning each of the listed options.

The trilogy approach suggests that the complete measurement of attitudes cannot be achieved using a single-item or multiple-item global scale design but rather requires the development of some type of multiplicative-additive model. In other words, to measure attitudes, the researcher must collect several types of attitudinal data and then, through a modeling process, derive a composite attitude score. While there are several types of multiplicative-additive models that have been developed within the trilogy framework, we are going to limit discussions to two of the most commonly used ones: attitude-toward-object and attitude-toward-behavior.

Attitude-toward-Object Model

Attitude-toward-object model   A multiplicative-additive model that attempts to capture a person's attitude about a specific object, where the attitude is a separate indirectly derived composite measure of a person's combined thoughts and feelings for or against a given object.

One popular attitudinal model is Fishbein's **attitude-toward-object model,** which is normally presented in the form of the following equation:[4]

$$\text{Attitude}_O = \sum_{i=1}^{k} b_i e_i$$

where Attitude_O is a separate, indirectly derived composite measure (sometimes considered an overall or global measure) of a person's combined thoughts and feelings for or against the given object (i.e., product, service, brand, manufacturer, retail establishment); b_i is the strength of the belief that the person holds toward the ith attribute of the object (e.g., the 1999 Millenia has a satisfactory mileage rating); e_i is the person's affect evaluation (expressed feeling or importance) of the belief toward that ith attribute of the object (e.g., it is *very important* that my car has an excellent mileage rating); and Σ indicates that there are k salient attributes making up the object over which the multiplicative combinations of b_i and e_i for those attributes are summated. The In the Field box illustrates the

These customers leaving a Mazda dealership represent an example of the cognitive component.

development processes, activities, and examples of the scales that might be used in an attitude-toward-object model to capture a person's overall attitude toward a 1999 Mazda Millenia. It is important to remember that in this measurement approach, equal emphasis is given to measuring both a person's beliefs (cognitive) and feelings (affective) toward the attributes of the object under investigation.

This modeling approach can provide the researcher and decision maker with a lot of diagnostic insights into the components that make up the consumer's attitude. For example, the decision maker can learn how and what the customer used to evaluate either the potential or actual performance of the given object.

Attitude-toward-Behavior Model

Another popular multiplicative-additive attitude model is Fishbein's **attitude-toward-behavior model**.[5] In this approach, the interest is in capturing a person's attitude toward his or her behavior with a given object rather than the attitude toward the object itself. One benefit of this approach is that it gives researchers a picture that more closely demonstrates the actual behavior of individuals than does the attitude-toward-object model. Normally, the attitude-toward-behavior model is presented by the following equation:

$$\text{Attitude}_{(\text{beh})} = \sum_{i=1}^{n} b_i \, a_i$$

where Attitude$_{(\text{beh})}$ is a separate, indirectly derived composite measure (sometimes considered an overall or global measure) of a person's combined thoughts and feelings for or against carrying out a specific action or behavior (e.g., the purchasing and driving of a 1999 Mazda Millenia); b_i is the strength of the person's belief that the ith specific action will lead

Attitude-toward-behavior model A multiplicative-additive model that attempts to capture a person's attitude toward behaving or acting toward a given object rather than their attitude of the object itself; where the attitude is a separate, indirectly derived composite measure of a person's combined thoughts and feelings for or against carrying out a specific action or behavior.

A CLOSER LOOK AT RESEARCH   **In the Field**

Scale Measurements Used in Determining the Attitude toward the Performance of a 1999 Mazda Millenia

In this example, both qualitative and quantitative research activities were employed to create the different scale measurements needed to collect both the cognitive components (b_i) and the affective components (e_i) that relate to assessing the respondents' attitude toward the performance of automobiles (attitude-toward-object).

I. Qualitative research activities

A. Several general focus group interviews were conducted among a cross-section of people who were known to have purchased a new automobile in the past 12 months. One of the topics of those interviews was focused on the elements people use to judge the performance of automobiles. The study discovered and identified the following seven attributes.

1. The car being viewed as a *trouble free (or practically defect free)* automobile.
2. The actual *miles per gallon (MPG) rating* of the automobile.
3. The *comfort (or smoothness) of the ride* provided by the car.
4. The *craftsmanship (or workmanship)* built into the automobile.
5. The *overall quality* of the automobile.
6. The *dependability (or reliability)* of the automobile.
7. The *responsiveness* of the car in different weather conditions.

B. To validate the seven attributes as the meaningful subfactors that people use to assess their attitudes toward the performance of automobiles, 300 randomly selected respondents were given a survey that included those seven attributes and were asked to judge them using the following four-point scale: (4) "definitely a factor of performance"; (3) "generally a factor of performance"; (2) "only somewhat a factor of performance"; (1) "not at all a factor of performance." Using direct cognitive structural (DCS) analysis, the results demonstrated that all seven attributes were considered factors people used in assessing the performance of automobiles, all having mean values of 3.8 or higher.

II. Quantitative research activities

A. To capture respondents' emotional importances (e_i) associated with each of the seven performance factors, the following scale measurement was developed and tested for internal consistency.

Using the scale below, please write a number from 1 to 6 in the space provided that best expresses how emotionally important you feel each listed factor is to you in assessing the performance of an automobile.   *(continued)*

Not at All Important	Only Slightly Important	Somewhat Important	Generally Important	Definitely Important	Extremely Important
(1)	(2)	(3)	(4)	(5)	(6)

____ The car being viewed as a *trouble free (or practically defect free)* automobile.

____ The actual *miles per gallon (MPG) rating* of the automobile.

____ The *comfort (or smoothness) of the ride* provided by the car.

____ The *craftsmanship (or workmanship)* built into the automobile.

____ The *overall quality* of the automobile.

____ The *dependability (or reliability)* of the automobile.

____ The *responsiveness* of the car in different weather conditions.

(concluded)

B. To capture respondents' evaluative performance beliefs (b_i) about the 1999 Mazda Millenia, the following scale measurement was developed and tested for internal consistency.

Thinking about all experiences with driving your 1999 Mazda Millenia, we would like to know your opinion about each of the following factors. For each factor, please circle the number that best expresses how you believe your 1999 Mazda Millenia has performed on that factor. For any factor(s) that are not relevant to your assessment, please circle the "zero" (0), which means "not applicable" (NA).

1999 Mazda Millenia	Truly Terrible	Fair	Average	Good	Excellent	Truly Exceptional	(NA)
Trouble (or practically defect) free	1	2	3	4	5	6	0
Miles per gallon (MPG) rating	1	2	3	4	5	6	0
Comfort (smoothness) of the ride	1	2	3	4	5	6	0
Craftsmanship (or workmanship)	1	2	3	4	5	6	0
Overall quality	1	2	3	4	5	6	0
Dependability (or reliability)	1	2	3	4	5	6	0
Responsiveness (or handling)	1	2	3	4	5	6	0

to a specific outcome (e.g., that driving a 1999 Millenia will increase the person's social standing in the community); a_i is the person's expressed feeling (affect) toward the ith action outcome (e.g., the "favorableness feeling" of knowing friends admire the 1999 Millenia); and Σ indicates that there are n salient action outcomes making up the behavior over which the multiplicative combinations of the b_i and a_i for those outcomes are summated. To illustrate the scales that might be used in an attitude-toward-behavior model to capture a person's overall attitude toward purchasing a 1999 Mazda Millenia, we added a second In the Field box. The key things to remember here are that behavior-oriented beliefs are used and that greater emphasis is placed on measuring the person's affective evaluation of the behavioral outcome. This approach can help the researcher or decision maker understand why customers might behave as they do toward a given object. For example, collecting this type of attitudinal data offers the researcher insights into how and why customers judge the "service quality" construct associated with purchasing a new automobile.

From a scale measurement perspective, deciding which affective or cognitive scale point descriptors to use for an attitudinal scale measurement can be difficult. To help make that decision a little easier, we advocate the following rules:

1. If the measurement objective is one of collecting data that enable you to describe how the respondent is thinking, then the focus should be on using scale descriptors that emphasize the cognitive component.

2. If the measurement objective is one of collecting data that enable you to identify how the respondent is feeling, then the focus should be on using scale descriptors that reflect the affective component.

Scale Measurements Used in Determining the Attitude toward Purchasing a 1999 Mazda Millenia

In this example, both qualitative and quantitative research activities were employed to create the different scale measurements needed to collect both the cognitive components (b_i) and the affective components (a_i) that relate to assessing respondents' attitude toward the purchasing of automobiles (attitude-toward-behavior).

I. Qualitative research activities

A. Several general focus group interviews were conducted among a cross-section of people who were known to be considering the purchasing of a new automobile within the next six months. One of the topics of those interviews was focused on the elements people deemed as factors in purchasing a new automobile. The study discovered and identified the following 15 factors.

1. The car is viewed as being a *trouble free (or practically defect free)* automobile.
2. The car's *miles per gallon (MPG) rating.*
3. The *comfort (or smoothness)* in the car's ride.
4. The *craftsmanship (or workmanship)* built into the car.
5. The *overall quality* of the car.
6. The *dependability (or reliability)* of the car.
7. The car will have the *responsiveness* in different weather conditions.
8. The car's potential *resale value.*
9. The *warranty guarantee program* associated with the car.
10. The car must have the *styling features (or options)* I want.
11. The car's price is *affordable.*
12. *Overall reputation* of the dealership.
13. *Reputation* of the dealer's service department.
14. The car's *safety features.*
15. The *quality reputation* of the manufacturer.

B. To validate the 15 factors as the meaningful items that people consider in their purchasing of a new automobile, 250 randomly selected respondents were given a survey that included those 15 factors and were asked to express the degree to which each one was a factor of consideration they would use in purchasing a new automobile, using the following five-point scale: (5) "a critical factor"; (4) "definitely a factor"; (3) "generally a factor"; (2) "only somewhat of a factor"; (1) "not at all a factor." Using direct cognitive structural (DCS) analysis, the results demonstrated that all 15 factors were reasonable elements of consideration that people used in their process of purchasing a new automobile, all having mean values of 3.1 or higher. *(continued)*

Not at all Important	Only Slightly Important	Somewhat Important	Generally Important	Definitely Important	Extremely Important
(1)	(2)	(3)	(4)	(5)	(6)

Buying a car . . .

____ that is *trouble (or practically defect) free.*

____ with an acceptable *miles per gallon (MPG) rating.*

____ that provides a *comfortable (or smooth) ride.*

____ that has the *craftsmanship (or workmanship)* built into it.

____ that is built with *overall quality.*

____ that is *dependable (or reliable).*

____ that will have the *responsiveness* in different weather conditions.

____ that keeps its *resale value.*

____ that is backed by a solid *warranty (or guarantee) program.*

____ that has the *styling features (or options)* I want.

____ that has a *price that is affordable.*

____ from a dealership having *overall reputation excellence.*

____ from a dealership whose service department is *reputable.*

____ that has the *safety features* I want.

____ that is made by a manufacturer with a *quality reputation.*

(concluded)

II. Quantitative research activities

A. To capture respondents' emotional importances (a_i) associated with each of the 15 purchasing attributes, the following scale measurement was developed and tested for internal consistency.

Using the scale on page 412, please write a number from 1 to 6 in the space provided that best expresses how emotionally important you feel each listed factor is to you in purchasing an new automobile.

B. To capture respondents' evaluative expectation beliefs (b_i) about the 1999 Mazda Millenia being able to satisfy the individual's needs/wants, the following scale measurement was developed and tested for internal consistency.

Thinking about all your expectations about a new car, we would know your opinions about each of the following factors as they relate to the 1999 Mazda Millenia. For each factor please circle the number that best expresses the extent to which you agree or disagree that buying a 1999 Mazda Millenia will meet that factor. For any factor(s) that are not relevant to your assessment, please circle "zero" (0), which means "not applicable" (NA).

Buying a 1999 Mazda Millenia Will . . .	Definitely Agree	Generally Agree	Slightly Agree	Slightly Disagree	Generally Disagree	Definitely Disagree	(NA)
Give me a *trouble free (or practically defect free)* mode of transportation	(6)	(5)	(4)	(3)	(2)	(1)	(0)
Give me a car with acceptable *miles per gallon (MPG)* rating	(6)	(5)	(4)	(3)	(2)	(1)	(0)
Allow me a *comfortable (smooth) ride*	(6)	(5)	(4)	(3)	(2)	(1)	(0)
Give me a car with great *craftsmanship*	(6)	(5)	(4)	(3)	(2)	(1)	(0)
Give me a car with the *overall quality* I was looking for	(6)	(5)	(4)	(3)	(2)	(1)	(0)
Give me a car that is *dependable (or reliable)*	(6)	(5)	(4)	(3)	(2)	(1)	(0)
Give me a car that has *responsiveness* in different weather conditions	(6)	(5)	(4)	(3)	(2)	(1)	(0)
Give me a car that keeps its *resale value*	(6)	(5)	(4)	(3)	(2)	(1)	(0)
Give me a solid *warranty (guarantee) program*	(6)	(5)	(4)	(3)	(2)	(1)	(0)
Give me a car that has the *styling features (or options)* I want	(6)	(5)	(4)	(3)	(2)	(1)	(0)
Give me a car I can *afford*	(6)	(5)	(4)	(3)	(2)	(1)	(0)
Give me a car from a dealership with an *overall reputation of excellence*	(6)	(5)	(4)	(3)	(2)	(1)	(0)
Give me a car from a dealership whose service department is *reputable*	(6)	(5)	(4)	(3)	(2)	(1)	(0)
Give me a car that has the safety *features* I want	(6)	(5)	(4)	(3)	(2)	(1)	(0)
Be a car made by a manufacturer with a quality reputation	(6)	(5)	(4)	(3)	(2)	(1)	(0)

The Affect Global Approach

Affect global approach
The theoretical approach of viewing the structure of a person's attitude as nothing more than the person's overall (global) expression of his or her evaluative favorable or unfavorable feelings toward a given object or behavior.

In contrast to the trilogy approach to attitude measurement, the **affect global approach** maintains that an attitude is nothing more than a person's global (or overall) expression of favorable or unfavorable feelings toward a given object. The idea here is that a person's feelings can have dominant influence on his or her overall judgment of a given object. In other words, affect equals attitude. Within this approach, heavy emphasis is placed on capturing a person's global evaluative feeling of an object as being either positive or negative (i.e., liking/disliking, good/bad, satisfied/dissatisfied). Rating scale formats use a set of affective scale descriptors to capture the necessary responses. A limitation to the affect global approach is that it does not give the researcher insights into what beliefs contribute to the formation of the overall attitude. At best, the researcher can only speculate about the beliefs underlying the expressed emotional ratings. Exhibit 13.1 displays several affect-based attitude scale formats.

EXHIBIT 13.1   **Examples of Affect Scale Formats for Measuring Attitudes**

Example 1:
For each of the following listed items, please *fill in* the box that best expresses the extent to which you were satisfied or dissatisfied with that item at the time you purchased or leased your vehicle.

	Very Satisfied	Somewhat Satisfied	Somewhat Dissatisfied	Very Dissatisfied
Availability of parts and service	❑	❑	❑	❑
Trouble-free operation	❑	❑	❑	❑
Quality of workmanship	❑	❑	❑	❑
Reputation of manufacturer	❑	❑	❑	❑
Low purchase price	❑	❑	❑	❑
High resale value	❑	❑	❑	❑

Example 2:
Now we would like for you to think about your driving experiences, then read each of the following statements and *fill in* the box that best expresses your feelings about that statement.

	Like Very Much	Like Somewhat	Neither Like nor Dislike	Dislike Somewhat	Dislike Very Much
Selecting option for my car	❑	❑	❑	❑	❑
Changing the oil myself	❑	❑	❑	❑	❑
Driving on an extended trip	❑	❑	❑	❑	❑
Letting someone else do the driving	❑	❑	❑	❑	❑
Observing the speed limit at all times	❑	❑	❑	❑	❑

Example 3:
Overall, how angry or happy were you with the outcome of the impeachment trial of President Clinton? **(Please check only one response.)**

Very Angry	Somewhat Angry	Neither Angry nor Happy	Somewhat Happy	Very Happy
❑	❑	❑	❑	❑

Overview of the Links between Measurements of Cognitive, Affective, and Actual or Intended Behavior

Researchers tend to have mixed feelings about the strength of the relationships between the cognitive and affective components as they are used to explain or predict marketplace behaviors. Some researchers have found that when people's beliefs toward an object (e.g., the 1999 Mazda Millenia) coincide with their associated feelings, then attitude consistency exists and behavior is more likely to be predictable.[6] Yet others have found only limited relationships among the three components.[7] Today's marketers should be aware of several factors that can operate to reduce the consistency between measures of beliefs, feelings, and observations of marketplace behavior:[8]

1. A favorable attitude requires a need or motive before it can be translated into action.

2. Translating favorable beliefs and feelings into ownership requires ability.

3. Some attitude scales measure only one concept, construct, or object at a time.

4. If the cognitive and affective components are weakly held, when the consumer obtains additional information within the shopping process, then the initial attitudes may give way to new ones.

5. Researchers typically measure attitudes of an isolated member of the family; the other members may affect the purchase behavior.

6. Researchers generally measure brand attitudes independent of the purchase action.

7. In reality, it is difficult to measure all of the relevant aspects of an attitude.

Special Types of Attitude and Behavior Scales

Although the specifically defined information problem and research objectives dictate which type of scale measurement a researcher should use, there are several specific types of attitudinal scaling formats that have proved to be very reliable across many different situations. The following section discusses three attitude scale formats: Likert scales, semantic differential scales, and behavior intention scales. As discussed in Chapter 12, the development of any itemized rating scale measurement begins with understanding the constructs to be measured. Exhibit 13.2 lists the general steps in the construct development/ scale measurement process.

Likert Scale

Likert scale An ordinal scale format that asks respondents to indicate the extent to which they agree or disagree with a series of mental belief or behavioral belief statements about a given object.

The **Likert scale** asks respondents to indicate the extent to which they either agree or disagree with a series of mental belief or behavioral belief statements about a given object. Normally, the scale format is balanced between agreement and disagreement scale descriptors. Named after its original developer, Rensis Likert, this scale consists of a set of five scale descriptors: "strongly agree," "agree," "neither agree nor disagree," "disagree," "strongly disagree."[9] In developing a Likert scale, the researcher identifies a set of belief statements that is representative of the object, idea, or set of information being investigated and then simply asks respondents to use the five scale descriptors to indicate the extent to which they agree or disagree with each of the statements. Over the years, the Likert scale has been so extensively modified and adapted by marketing researchers that its current definition varies from researcher to researcher. Today, the modified Likert scale expands the original five-point format to either a six-point forced-choice format with such scale

EXHIBIT 13.2	A General Construct Development/Scale Measurement Process

Process Steps	Key Activities
1. Theoretically Identify and Define the Construct	Determine Dimensionality of Construct
2. Create Initial Pool of Attribute Items	Determine Theory, Secondary Data, Qualitative Research
3. Assess and Select a Reduced Set of Items	Perform Structural Analysis and Qualitative Judgments
4. Construct Initial Measurements and Pretest	Conduct Pilot Study, Collect Data from Pretest Sample
5. Do Appropriate Statistical Data Analysis	Conduct Construct Validity and Scale Reliability Tests
6. Refine and Purify Scale Measurements	Eliminate irrelevant attribute items
7. Collect More Data on Purified Scale	Select New Sample of Subjects from Defined Target Population
8. Statistically Evaluate Scale Measurements	Conduct Reliability, Validity, Generalizability Tests
9. Perform Final Scale Measurement	Include Scale Measurement in Final Questionnaire

descriptors as "definitely agree," "generally agree," "slightly agree," "slightly disagree," "generally disagree," "definitely disagree" or a seven-point free-choice format with these same descriptors plus "neither agree nor disagree" in the middle. In addition, many researchers have treated the Likert scale format as an ordinally-interval scale.

Regardless of the actual number of scale descriptors that are used in creating them, Likert scales have several other characteristics worth pointing out. First, the Likert scale is the only summated rating scale that uses a set of agreement/disagreement scale descriptors. A Likert scale collects only cognitive-based or specific behavioral beliefs. Despite the popular notion that Likert scales can be used to measure a person's complete attitude, they can capture only the cognitive components of a person's attitude and are therefore only partial measures. They also do not capture the different possible intensity levels of expressed affective or conative components of a person's attitude. This misunderstanding of a Likert scale's capability might account for the scale's weak interpretive results in situations where identifying and measuring respondents' attitudes are critical to solving the information problem.

As another point of interest, a Likert scale is best suited to research designs that use either self-administered surveys or personal interviewers to collect the data. It becomes somewhat difficult to administer a Likert scale over the telephone because respondents have trouble visualizing and remembering the relative magnitudes of agreement and disagreement that make up the scale descriptors. Exhibit 13.3 illustrates an example of a modified Likert scale in a self-administered survey.

To point out the interpretive difficulties associated with the Likert scale, we have used boldface in each of the statements in Exhibit 13.3 for the words that indicate a single level of intensity. For example, in the first statement (I buy many things with a credit card), the main belief focuses on **many things.** If the respondent checks the "generally disagree" response, it would be a leap of faith for the researcher to interpret that response to mean that the respondent buys only a few things with a credit card. In addition, it would be a speculative guess on the part of the researcher to assume that the respondent's attitude

EXHIBIT 13.3	Example of a Modified Likert Scale

For each of the listed statements, please check the one response that best expresses the extent to which you agree or disagree with that statement.

Statements	Definitely Agree	Generally Agree	Slightly Agree	Slightly Disagree	Generally Disagree	Definitely Disagree
I buy **many things** with a credit card.	____	____	____	____	____	____
I wish we had **a lot more** money.	____	____	____	____	____	____
My friends **often come** to me for advice.	____	____	____	____	____	____
I am **never influenced** by advertisements.	____	____	____	____	____	____

toward purchasing products or services with a credit card is unfavorable. The intensity level assigned to the agree/disagree scale point descriptors do not truly represent the respondent's feelings associated with the belief response. The intensity levels used in a Likert scale identify only the extent to which the respondent thinks the statement represents his or her own belief about credit card purchases.

Let's take the last statement in Exhibit 13.3 (I am never influenced by advertisements) as another example. The key words in this statement are **never influenced.** If the respondent checks "definitely disagree," it would again be the researcher's subjective guess that the response means that the respondent is very much influenced by advertisements. In reality, all that the "definitely disagree" response indicates is that the statement is not one that the respondent would make; no measure of feeling can be attached to the statement.

Likert scales can also be used to identify and assess personal or psychographic (lifestyle) traits of individuals. The Global Insights box illustrates how international marketing research companies, like the Gallup Organization, use attitude and psychographic scale measurements to profile consumers across Latin American countries.

Semantic Differential Scale

Semantic differential scale A unique bipolar ordinal scale format that captures a person's attitudes or feelings about a given object.

Another ordinal rating scale used quite often in information and marketing research endeavors is the **semantic differential scale.** This rating scale was initially developed by Charles Osgood, George Suci, and Percy Tannenbaum.[10] This type of scale is unique in its use of bipolar adjectives and adverbs (good/bad, like/dislike, competitive/noncompetitive, helpful/unhelpful, high quality/low quality, dependable/undependable, etc.) as the endpoints of an apparently symmetrical continuum.[11] Normally, there will be one object and a related set of factors, each with its own set of bipoles to measure either a cognitive or an affective element. Because the individual scale descriptors are not identified, each bipolar scale appears to be a continuum. In most cases, semantic differential scales will use between five and seven scale descriptors, though only the endpoints are identified.[12] The respondent is asked to select the point on the continuum that expresses his or her thoughts or feelings about the given object.

In most cases a semantic differential scale will use an odd number of scale points, thus creating a so-called neutral response that symmetrically divides the positive and negative poles into two equal parts.[13] One interpretive problem that arises with an odd-number (or free-choice) scale point format comes from the natural neutral response in the middle of the scale. As we noted in Chapter 12, in many cases a neutral response has little to no diagnostic

GLOBAL INSIGHTS · BEYOND NATIONAL BOUNDARIES

The Gallup Organization recently completed a regional multinational segmentation study among the metropolitan areas within five Latin American countries: Argentina, Brazil, Chile, Colombia, and Mexico. The results suggest the existence of the following eight consumer segments: emerging professional elite; traditional elite; progressive upper middle class; self-made middle class; skilled middle class; self-skilled lower middle class; industrial working class; and the struggling working class. Some of the key characteristics are as follows:

Emerging Professional Elite

14% of the total; occupies top professional, executive positions; 51% graduated from university or technical college; 55% are married; 98% have color TV; 96% have VCR; 97% have at least one car; 98% have credit cards; and 90% have vacuum cleaner.

Traditional Elite

11%; almost half in top professional, executive positions; 53% finished secondary education; 54% are married; all have color TV; 91% VCR; 89% cars; 60% credit cards; 60% vacuum cleaner.

Progressive Upper Middle Class

13%; 36% in top or middle management; 75% studied beyond primary education; 25% studied beyond secondary school; 48% are married; 99% have color TV; 77% VCR; 74% cars; 31% credit card; 30% vacuum cleaner.

Self-Made Middle Class

11%; skills gained through entrepreneurship; most ended education with primary school, "virtually none"

went beyond secondary school; 50% are married; 98% have color TV; 72% VCR; 81% a car; 46% credit card; 51% vacuum cleaner.

Skilled Middle Class

9%; 45% have top operational jobs and 14% own small business; 60% completed secondary education, 18% completed university or technical college; 50% are married; 96% have color TV; 60% VCR; 28% a car; 29% credit card; 32% vacuum cleaner.

Self-Skilled Lower Middle Class

13%; 58% employed in operational jobs; 42% went beyond primary school, 11% went beyond secondary education; 50% are married; 97% have color TV; 50% VCR; 4% a car; 8% credit card; 15% vacuum cleaner.

Industrial Working Class

14%; a third are in skilled worker positions and another third in average operational jobs; 16% went beyond secondary school, 26% completed secondary school, and 35% completed primary; 57% are married; 92% have color TV; 13% VCR; 5% credit card; 15% vacuum cleaner.

Struggling Working Class

15%; most in operational, skilled, and unskilled jobs; 29% completed primary school, 24% completed secondary school; 53% are married; 63% have color TV; no more than 10% have VCR, car, credit card, or vacuum cleaner.

Source: Jeffrey D. Zbar, "Gallup Offers New Take on Latin America," *Advertising Age,* November 13, 1995, p. 21.

value to the researcher or decision maker. Sometimes it is interpreted as meaning "no opinion," "don't know," "neither/nor," or "average." None of these interpretations gives much information to the researcher.[14] To overcome this problem, the researcher can use an even-point (or forced-choice) format and incorporate a "not applicable" response out to the side of the bipolar scale.[15]

A semantic differential scale is one of the few attitudinal scale formats that allows the researcher to collect both cognitive and affective data for any given factor. However, it does not allow for collecting both types of data at the same time. For a given factor, a bipolar scale can be designed to capture either a person's feelings **or** his or her cognitive beliefs. Although some researchers believe that a semantic differential scale can be used to measure a person's complete attitude about an object or behavior, this scale type is best for identifying a "perceptual image profile" about the object or behavior of concern.[16]

The actual design of a semantic differential scale can vary from situation to situation. To help you gain an understanding of the benefits and weaknesses associated with design differences, we present three different formats and discuss the pros and cons of each. In the first situation, the researcher is interested in developing a credibility scale that can be used to assess the credibility of people in TV or print advertisements for brands of personal grooming products. The researcher determines that the credibility construct consists of three factors—(1) expertise, (2) trustworthiness, and (3) attractiveness—with each factor measured using a specific set of five bipolar scales (see Exhibit 13.4).

RANDOMIZE THE POSITIVE AND NEGATIVE POLE DESCRIPTORS. While the semantic differential scale format in Exhibit 13.4 appears to be correctly designed, there are several technical problems that might unnecessarily create response bias. First, notice that all

EXHIBIT 13.4	**Example of a Semantic Differential Scale Format for Spokesperson's Credibility**

Now thinking about Tiger Woods as the spokesperson for Nike golf apparel, we would like to know your opinions about the expertise, trustworthiness, and attractiveness that you believe he brings to the advertisement. Each dimension has five factors that may or may not represent your opinion. For each listed factor, **please check the line that best expresses your opinion about that factor.**

Expertise:

Knowledgeable	___ ___ ___ ___ ___ ___ ___	Unknowledgeable
Expert	___ ___ ___ ___ ___ ___ ___	Not an Expert
Skilled	___ ___ ___ ___ ___ ___ ___	Unskilled
Qualified	___ ___ ___ ___ ___ ___ ___	Unqualified
Experienced	___ ___ ___ ___ ___ ___ ___	Unexperienced

Trustworthiness:

Reliable	___ ___ ___ ___ ___ ___ ___	Unreliable
Sincere	___ ___ ___ ___ ___ ___ ___	Insincere
Trustworthy	___ ___ ___ ___ ___ ___ ___	Untrustworthy
Dependable	___ ___ ___ ___ ___ ___ ___	Undependable
Honest	___ ___ ___ ___ ___ ___ ___	Dishonest

Attractiveness:

Sexy	___ ___ ___ ___ ___ ___ ___	Not Sexy
Beautiful	___ ___ ___ ___ ___ ___ ___	Ugly
Attractive	___ ___ ___ ___ ___ ___ ___	Unattractive
Classy	___ ___ ___ ___ ___ ___ ___	Not Classy
Elegant	___ ___ ___ ___ ___ ___ ___	Plain

Source: Roobina Ohanian, "Construction and Validation of a Scale to Measure Celebrity Endorsers' Perceived Expertise, Trustworthiness, and Attractiveness," *Journal of Advertising* 19, no. 3 (1990), pp. 39–52.

the positive pole descriptors are arranged on the left side of each scale and the negative pole descriptors are all on the right side. Past research has demonstrated that such a design characteristic has a tendency to cause a *halo effect* bias.[17] That is, it tends to lead the respondent to react more favorably to the positive poles on the left side than to the negative poles on the right side. To prevent this problem, the researcher should randomly mix the positions of the positive and negative pole descriptors.[18]

LACK OF EXTREME MAGNITUDE EXPRESSED IN THE POLE DESCRIPTORS. A second response problem with the scale format displayed in Exhibit 13.4 is that the descriptors used to express the ends of each scale lack expression of extreme intensity associated with those end poles. The respondent is asked to check one of seven possible lines to express his or her opinion, but only the two end lines are given narrative meaning. The researcher can only guess how the respondent is interpreting the other lines of intensity between the two endpoints. Let's take, for example, the "dependable/undependable" scale within the trustworthiness dimension. Notice that the extreme left scale line represents "dependable" and the extreme right scale line represents "undependable." Because dependable and undependable are natural dichotomous phrase descriptors, the scale design does not allow for any significant magnitudes to exist between them. This raises the logical question of what the other five scale lines really represent, which in turn raises the question of whether or not the scale truly represents a continuum ranging from dependable to undependable. This problem can easily be corrected by attaching a narratively expressed extreme magnitude to the bipolar descriptors (i.e., "extremely" or "quite" dependable, and "extremely" or "quite" undependable).

USE OF NON-BIPOLAR DESCRIPTORS TO REPRESENT THE POLES. A third response problem that occurs in designing semantic differential scales relates to the inappropriate narrative expressions of the scale descriptors. In a good semantic differential scale design, the individual scales should be truly bipolar so that a symmetrical scale can be designed. Sometimes the researcher will express the negative pole in such a way that the positive one is not really its opposite. Such a decision creates a skewed scale design that is difficult for the respondent to interpret correctly.

Take, for example, the "expert/not an expert" scale in the "expertise" dimension in Exhibit 13.4. While the scale is dichotomous, the words "not an expert" do not allow the respondent to interpret any of the other scale points as being relative magnitudes of that phrase. Other than that one endpoint described as "not an expert," all the other scale points would have to represent some intensity of "expert," thus creating a skewed scale toward the positive pole. In other words, interpreting "not an expert" as really meaning "extremely" or "quite" not an expert makes little to no diagnostic sense. The researcher must be careful when creating the bipolar descriptors to make sure the words or phrases are truly extreme bipolar in nature and they allow for creating symmetrical scale designs. For example, the researcher could use pole descriptors such as "complete expert" and "complete novice" to correct the above-described scale point descriptor problems.

MATCHING STANDARDIZED INTENSITY DESCRIPTORS TO POLE DESCRIPTORS. The scale design in Exhibit 13.5 eliminates the three problems we discussed regarding the example in Exhibit 13.4, as well as a fourth—it gives narrative expression to the intensity level of each scale point. Notice that all the separate poles and scale points in between them are anchored by the same set of intensity descriptors (i.e., "very," "moderately," "slightly," "neither one nor the other," "slightly," "moderately," "very"). In using standardized intensity descriptors, however, the researcher must be extra careful in determining the specific phrases for each pole—each phrase must fit the set of intensity descriptors in order for the

EXHIBIT 13.5	Example of a Semantic Differential Scale That Expresses Each Scale Descriptor

For each of the following banking traits/features, please check the one line that best expresses your impression of that feature as it relates to NationsBank. **Make sure you give only one response for each listed feature.**

	Very	Moderately	Slightly	Neither One nor the Other	Slightly	Moderately	Very	
Courteous Employees	____	____	____	____	____	____	____	Discourteous Employees
Helpful Staff	____	____	____	____	____	____	____	Unhelpful Staff
Unattractive Exterior	____	____	____	____	____	____	____	Attractive Exterior
Competitive Rates	____	____	____	____	____	____	____	Noncompetitive Rates
Limited Service Offerings	____	____	____	____	____	____	____	Wide Variety of Service Offerings
Good Operating Hours	____	____	____	____	____	____	____	Bad Operating Hours
High-Quality Service	____	____	____	____	____	____	____	Low-Quality Service
Unreliable	____	____	____	____	____	____	____	Reliable
Successful Bank	____	____	____	____	____	____	____	Unsuccessful Bank
Makes You Feel at Home	____	____	____	____	____	____	____	Makes You Feel Uneasy

scale points to make complete sense to the respondent. Take, for example, the "makes you feel at home/makes you feel uneasy" scale in Exhibit 13.5; here, the intensity descriptor of "very" does not make much sense when applied to that scale (i.e., "very makes you feel at home" or "very makes you feel uneasy"). As such, including standardized intensity descriptors in a semantic differential scale design might force the researcher to limit the types of bipolar phrases used to describe or evaluate the object or behavior of concern. This can only raise questions about the appropriateness of the raw data collected using this type of scale design.

The fundamentals discussed in Chapter 12 can help the researcher learn how to correctly develop customized scales to collect the most appropriate raw attitudinal or behavioral data for the given information problem. To illustrate this point, Exhibit 13.6 presents a customized semantic differential scale format used to collect attitudinal data about the performance of the respondent's primary automobile service provider. Notice that each of the 15 different features that make up the automobile service provider's profile has its own bipolar scale communicating clearly what intensity level is attached to the positive and negative poles. This reduces the possibility that the respondent will misunderstand the scale's continuum range. This example also illustrates the use of an "NA"—not applicable—response as a replacement for the more traditional midscale neutral response. After the raw data are collected from this scale format, the researcher could artificially calculate aggregate mean values for each of the 15 features, plot those mean values on each of their respective scale lines, and graphically display the results using "profile" lines. The result is an overall profile that depicts the automobile service provider's performance patterns (see Exhibit 13.7). In addition, the researcher could use the same scale and collect raw data on several competing

EXHIBIT 13.6 **Example of a Semantic Differential Scale for Automobile Service Providers**

From your personal experiences with your primary automobile service provider's (ASP) service representatives, please rate the performance of your ASP on the basis of the following listed ASP features. Each feature has its own scale ranging from "one" (1) to "six" (6). **Please circle the response number that best describes how your ASP has performed on that feature.** For any feature(s) that you feel is (are) not relevant to your evaluation, please circle the (NA)—Not applicable—response code.

Cost of Repair/Maintenance Work	(NA)	Extremely High	6	5	4	3	2	1	Very Low, Almost Free
Appearance of Facilities	(NA)	Very Professional	6	5	4	3	2	1	Very Unprofessional
Customer Satisfaction	(NA)	Totally Dissatisfied	6	5	4	3	2	1	Truly Satisfied
Promptness in Delivering Service	(NA)	Unacceptably Slow	6	5	4	3	2	1	Impressively Quick
Quality of Service Offerings	(NA)	Truly Terrible	6	5	4	3	2	1	Truly Exceptional
Understands Customer's Needs	(NA)	Really Understands	6	5	4	3	2	1	Doesn't Have a Clue
Credibility of ASP	(NA)	Extremely Credible	6	5	4	3	2	1	Extremely Unreliable
ASP's Keeping of Promises	(NA)	Very Trustworthy	6	5	4	3	2	1	Very Deceitful
ASP Services Assortment	(NA)	Truly Full Service	6	5	4	3	2	1	Only Basic Services
Prices/Rates/Charges of Services	(NA)	Much Too High	6	5	4	3	2	1	Great Rates
Service Personnel's Competence	(NA)	Very Competent	6	5	4	3	2	1	Totally Incompetent
Employee's Personal Social Skills	(NA)	Very Rude	6	5	4	3	2	1	Very Friendly
ASP's Operating Hours	(NA)	Extremely Flexible	6	5	4	3	2	1	Extremely Limited
Convenience of ASP's Locations	(NA)	Very Easy to Get to	6	5	4	3	2	1	Too Difficult to Get to

EXHIBIT 13.7 **Example of an Automobile Service Provider's Performance Profile**

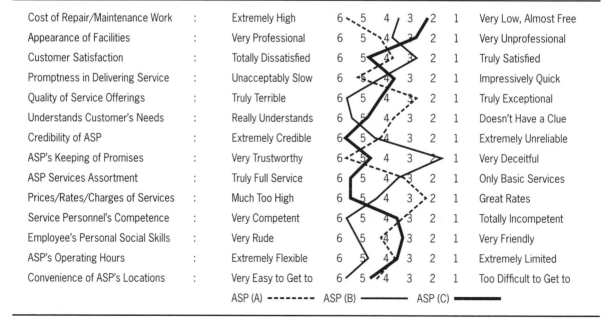

Cost of Repair/Maintenance Work	:	Extremely High	6	5	4	3	2	1	Very Low, Almost Free
Appearance of Facilities	:	Very Professional	6	5	4	3	2	1	Very Unprofessional
Customer Satisfaction	:	Totally Dissatisfied	6	5	4	3	2	1	Truly Satisfied
Promptness in Delivering Service	:	Unacceptably Slow	6	5	4	3	2	1	Impressively Quick
Quality of Service Offerings	:	Truly Terrible	6	5	4	3	2	1	Truly Exceptional
Understands Customer's Needs	:	Really Understands	6	5	4	3	2	1	Doesn't Have a Clue
Credibility of ASP	:	Extremely Credible	6	5	4	3	2	1	Extremely Unreliable
ASP's Keeping of Promises	:	Very Trustworthy	6	5	4	3	2	1	Very Deceitful
ASP Services Assortment	:	Truly Full Service	6	5	4	3	2	1	Only Basic Services
Prices/Rates/Charges of Services	:	Much Too High	6	5	4	3	2	1	Great Rates
Service Personnel's Competence	:	Very Competent	6	5	4	3	2	1	Totally Incompetent
Employee's Personal Social Skills	:	Very Rude	6	5	4	3	2	1	Very Friendly
ASP's Operating Hours	:	Extremely Flexible	6	5	4	3	2	1	Extremely Limited
Convenience of ASP's Locations	:	Very Easy to Get to	6	5	4	3	2	1	Too Difficult to Get to

ASP (A) -------- ASP (B) ———— ASP (C) ▬▬▬▬

A CLOSER LOOK AT RESEARCH   **Small Business
Implications**

Instant On-Site
Customer Satisfaction Feedback

Most small-business owners are constantly in search of different methods to evaluate customer satisfaction. An integral component of any small business, positive customer satisfaction is vital in building long-term relationships with valuable customers. Below is an excerpt taken from Direct Network Access, Inc.'s Web site (www.opinionmeter.com) that describes a tool small business owners can use to quickly and efficiently evaluate customer satisfaction. We recommend browsing through some of the "hot links" to reveal other technologically advanced products that will improve small business operations.

The Opinionmeter is a flexible, easy-to-use interactive survey system designed to collect customer satisfaction feedback at point-of-service. No more paper surveys or data entry—the Opinionmeter instantly tabulates responses and provides immediate on-site access to survey results. When placed in a business lobby, cus-

tomers interact with the freestanding battery-operated Opinionmeter to self-administer their own surveys, anonymously. Opinionmeter takes advantage of customers' waiting time and captures feedback while opinions are still fresh. In addition, on-site surveying sends a powerful message about a company's commitment to customer satisfaction.

Easy to use. Now you can have the questionnaire customized, the machine programmed, the data collected and the formal report completed in a single day. Opinionmeter's unique questionnaire display system permits questions & answers printed in any language to be displayed in the easy-to-read Questionnaire Holder. Reprogramming for a new questionnaire takes only 2–3 minutes.

Quick results. Respondent answers are screened and tallied, and results made instantly available after any survey. Results can be called up on the screen, hardcopied by a handheld infrared printer or transmitted via serial cable to your PC for in-depth analysis using Opinionmeter's Opinion Analyzer statistical software package. Full cross-tabulations are available, including date and time bracketing of data.

automobile service providers, then show each of the semantic differential profiles on one display.

Behavior Intention Scale

Behavior intention scale
A special type of rating scale designed to capture the likelihood that people will demonstrate some type of predictable behavior intent toward purchasing an object or service in a future time frame.

One of the most widely used scale formats in commercial marketing research is the **behavior intention scale**.[19] In using this format, the decision maker is attempting to obtain some idea of the likelihood that people will demonstrate some type of predictable behavior regarding the purchase of an object or service. In general, behavior intent scales have been found to be good predictors of consumers' choices of frequently purchased and durable consumer products.[20]

Behavior intention scales (i.e., purchase intent, attendance intent, shopping intent, usage intent) are very easy to construct. Consumers are simply asked to make a subjective judgment on their likelihood of buying a product or service, or taking a specified action. The scale descriptors normally included in a behavior intention scale format are "definitely would," "probably would," "not sure," "probably would not," and "definitely would not." Let's take, for example, Vail Valley Foundation's interest in identifying how likely it is that people will attend a variety of performing arts events at its new outdoor Ford Amphitheater in Vail, Colorado. Exhibit 13.8 illustrates the behavior intention scale the Vail Valley Foundation Management Team used to collect the raw intention data. Note that this scale uses a forced-choice design by not including the middle logical scale point

| EXHIBIT 13.8 | Example of Behavior Intention Scale for Determining Attendance to Performing Arts Events In Vail, Colorado |

Now thinking about the next six months, we would like to know the extent to which you would consider attending various types of entertainment/performing arts events if they were held in the Vail Valley area.

Next to each type of event, please check the one box that best expresses the extent to which you would consider attending within the next six months.

(PLEASE CHECK ONLY ONE BOX FOR EACH EVENT)

Type of Event	Definitely Would Consider Attending	Probably Would Consider Attending	Probably Would Not Consider Attending	Definitely Would Not Consider Attending
I. Music Concerts				
Popular Music	❑	❑	❑	❑
Jazz Music	❑	❑	❑	❑
Country Music	❑	❑	❑	❑
Bluegrass Music	❑	❑	❑	❑
Classical Music	❑	❑	❑	❑
Chamber Music	❑	❑	❑	❑
II. Theatrical Productions				
Drama	❑	❑	❑	❑
Comedy	❑	❑	❑	❑
Melodrama	❑	❑	❑	❑
Musical	❑	❑	❑	❑
III. Dance Productions				
Classical Dance	❑	❑	❑	❑
Modern Dance	❑	❑	❑	❑
Jazz	❑	❑	❑	❑
Folk Dance	❑	❑	❑	❑

of "not sure." It is important to remember that when designing a behavior intention scale, you should include a specific time frame (e.g., "would consider attending in the next *six months*") in the question/setup portion of the scale. Without an expressed time frame, you increase the possibility that the respondents will bias their response toward the "definitely would" or "probably would" scale categories.

To increase the clarity of the scale point descriptors, the researcher can attach a percentage equivalent expression to each one. To illustrate this concept, let's assume that Sears is interested in knowing how likely it is that consumers will shop at certain types of retail stores for men's casual clothing. The following set of scale points could be used to obtain the necessary raw intention data: "definitely would shop at (90% to 100% chance)"; "probably would shop at (50% to 89% chance)"; "probably would not shop at (10% to 49% chance)"; and "definitely would not shop at (less than 10% chance)." Exhibit 13.9 shows what the complete shopping intention scale might look like.

| EXHIBIT 13.9 | Retail Store: Shopping Intention Scale for Men's Casual Clothes |

When shopping for men's casual wear for yourself or someone else, how likely are you to shop at each of the following types of retail stores? (**Please check one response for each store type.**)

Type of Retail Store	Definitely Would Shop At (90–100% chance)	Probably Would Shop At (50–89% chance)	Probably Would Not Shop At (10–49% chance)	Definitely Would Not Shop At (less than 10% chance)
Giant Retail Stores (e.g., Sears, JCPenney, Montgomery Ward)	❑	❑	❑	❑
Department Stores (e.g., Burdine's, Dillard's Marshall Field)	❑	❑	❑	❑
Discount Department Stores (e.g., Marshall's, TG&Y, Kmart, Target)	❑	❑	❑	❑
Retail Mall Outlets (e.g., Orlando Mall Outlet)	❑	❑	❑	❑
Men's Clothing Specialty Shops (e.g., Wolf Brothers, Surrey's George Ltd.)	❑	❑	❑	❑
Men's Casual Wear Specialty Stores (e.g., The Gap, Banana Republic, Aca Joe's)	❑	❑	❑	❑

Strengths and Weaknesses of Attitude and Behavior Intention Scale Measurements

Information researchers and marketing practitioners alike must understand that no matter what types of scale measurements are developed and employed to capture people's attitudes and behaviors, there is no one best or guaranteed approach. While there are solid and proven scale measurements for capturing the components that make up people's attitudes as well as their behavioral intentions, the data provided from these scale measurements should not be interpreted as being true facts about a given object or behavior. Instead, the raw data and any derived structures should be viewed as stable *insights* into what might be reality. For example, if the defined information problem is one of predicting some type of shopping, purchase, or consumption behavior, then developing and administering behavioral intention scales might well be the best approach. The strongest direct predictor of actual behavior is that of understanding behavioral intentions.[21]

In contrast, if the information problem is that of better understanding why consumers or customers behave or respond as they do in the marketplace, the researcher needs something other than a basic measurement of their buying intentions. Behavior can be explained, directly or indirectly, by measuring both the cognitive and affective elements of the consumers' attitudes. Read the Small Business Implications box on page 423 to see how small business owners might use the Internet and Opinionmeters to measure their customers' satisfaction.

Other Types of Comparative and Noncomparative Scale Formats

Graphic rating scales
A scale measure that uses a scale point format that presents the respondent with some type of graphic continuum as the set of possible raw responses to a given question.

Performance rating scales   A scale measure that uses an evaluative scale point format that allows the respondent to express some type of postdecision or behavior evaluative judgment about an object.

Besides the specific noncomparative rating scale formats discussed earlier, there are several variations, both noncomparative and comparative, that remain popular among commercial marketing research firms. The noncomparative scales include graphic scales, performance scales, and staple scales, and the tried-and-true comparative scales include rank-order scales, paired comparisons, and constant sums scales.

Exhibit 13.10 offers some examples of the scale point descriptors used in graphic scales, performance scales, and staple scales.

Graphic rating scales (also referred to as continuous rating scales) use a scaling format that presents a respondent with some type of graphic continuum as the set of possible raw responses to a given question. These scales are most appropriate in self-administered surveys or personal interviews and are obviously difficult to use in telephone interviews. This type of scaling format can be used in either single-item or multi-item scale measurements.

Performance rating scales use a scale point format that allows the respondents to express some type of postdecision or evaluative judgment about an object. These are great for use in self-administered questionnaires or personal interviews, and poor for telephone interviews, unless the number of scale point descriptors is kept to three or four. The letter-grade scale descriptors (see Exhibit 13.10) are fairly easy to administer in a telephone interview.

EXHIBIT 13.10 **Different Forms of Noncomparative Rating Scales Used in Marketing Research**

A. Graphic Rating Scales

Usage (Quantity) Descriptors:

Never Use										Use all the Time
0	10	20	30	40	50	60	70	80	90	100

Smiling Face Descriptors:

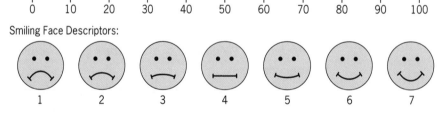

B. Performance Rating Scales

Performance Level Descriptors:

Truly Terrible	Poor	Fair	Average	Good	Excellent	Truly Exceptional
1	2	3	4	5	6	7

Letter Grade Descriptors:

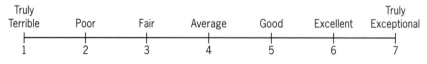

C. Staple Scales

−5	−4	−3	−2	−1	Good MPG Rating	+1	+2	+3	+4	+5
−5	−4	−3	−2	−1	Understands Service Needs	+1	+2	+3	+4	+5
−5	−4	−3	−2	−1	Competitively Priced	+1	+2	+3	+4	+5

Staple scales A modified version of the semantic differential scale that takes a single narratively expressed descriptor and centers it within a numeric set of plus and minus descriptors.

Staple scales are considered a modified version of the semantic differential scale. The scale design takes a single narratively expressed descriptor and centers it within a numeric set of plus (+) and minus (−) descriptors. The numerical descriptors can range anywhere from +5 to −5, which normally gives either a 6-, 8-, or 10-point scale. Staple scale formats are used to simultaneously measure the direction and intensity of a single dimensional attitude; they eliminate the need for creating pairs of bipolar descriptors. However, they are not very popular in marketing research today.[22] Staple scales need a carefully crafted question/setup so not to confuse the respondent. They are most appropriate to use in self-administered surveys and personal interviews.

Exhibit 13.11 illustrates the scale point descriptors associated with rank-order rating scales, paired comparisons, and constant sums scales.

EXHIBIT 13.11 | **Different Forms of Comparative Rating Scales Used in Marketing Research**

A. Rank-Order Rating Scales

Thinking about the different types of music, please rank your top three preferences of types of music you enjoy listening to by writing in your first choice, second choice, and third choice on the lines provided below.

First Preference: _____

Second Preference: _____

Third Preference: _____

B. Paired-Comparison Rating Scales

We are going to present you with several pairs of traits associated with a salesperson's on-the-job activities. For each pair, please indicate which trait you feel is more important for being a salesperson.

a. trust	b. competence
a. trust	b. communication skills
a. trust	b. personal social skills
a. competence	b. communication skills
a. competence	b. personal social skills
a. communication skills	b. personal social skills

Note: the researcher would want to scramble and reverse the order of these paired comparisons to avoid possible order bias.

C. Constant Sums Rating Scales

Below is a list of seven banking features. Please allocate 100 points among those features such that the allocation represents the importance each feature was to you in your selecting "your" bank. The more points you assign to a feature, the more important that feature was to your selection process. If the feature was "not at all important" in your process, you should not assign it any points. When you have finished, please double-check to make sure your total adds to 100.

Banking Features	Number of Points
Convenience/location	_____
Banking hours	_____
Good service charges	_____
The interest rates on loans	_____
The bank's reputation	_____
The interest rates on savings	_____
Bank's promotional advertising	_____
	100 points

Rank-order rating scales   These allow respondents to compare their own responses by indicating their first, second, third, and fourth preferences and so forth until all the desired responses are placed in a rank order.

Paired-comparison rating scales   This format creates a preselected group of traits, product characteristics, or features that are paired against one another into two groups; respondents are asked to select which in each pair is more important to them.

Constant sums rating scales   Requires the respondent to allocate a given number of points, usually 100, amolng several attributes or features based on their importance to the individual; this format requires a person to evaluate each separate attribute or feature relative to all the other listed ones.

Rank-order rating scales incorporate a scale point format that allows respondents to compare their own responses by indicating their first preference, second preference, third preference, and so forth until all the desired responses are placed in either a "highest to lowest" or a "lowest to highest" rank order. This format allows for easy comparison of each possible raw response. These scales are easy to use in personal interviews and all types of self-administered surveys. Although it can be difficult, it is possible to use them in telephone interviews as well.

Paired-comparison rating scales create a preselected group of traits, product characteristics, or features that are paired against one another into two groups. The respondents are asked to select which trait, characteristic, or feature in each pair is more important to them. Consequently, the respondents make a series of paired judgments between the features. It is important to remember that the number of paired comparisons increases geometrically as a function of the number of features being evaluated. This scale design can be administered in all types of data collection methods. Comparison items should be kept to one word or short phrases.

Constant sums rating scales require the respondent to allocate a given number of points, usually 100, among several attributes or features based on their importance to him or her. Thus, this format requires the respondent to value each separate feature relative to all the other listed features. The resulting value assignments indicate the relative magnitude of importance each feature has to the respondent. The individual values should add up to 100. This type of comparative scale format is most appropriate for use in self-administered surveys, especially since it requires a lot of mental energy on the part of the respondent.

Recap of Key Measurement Design Issues

Before moving forward to Chapter 14, on developing questionnaires, we will briefly recap the main design issues related to both construct development and scale measurement.

Construct Development Issues

Researchers should clearly define and operationalize constructs before they attempt to develop the necessary scale measurements. For each construct being investigated, the researcher must determine its dimensionality traits (i.e., single versus multidimensional) before developing appropriate scale measurements. In a multidimensional construct, all relevant dimensions must be identified as well as their related attributes.

Avoid creating double-barreled dimensions; that is, avoid presenting two different dimensions of a construct as though they are one. For example, when investigating consumers' perceptions of service quality, do not attempt to combine the service provider's technological competence and diagnostic competence as one dimension. Within a singular dimension, avoid using double-barreled attributes. For example, avoid asking a respondent to rate two attributes simultaneously (e.g., Indicate to what extent you agree or disagree that President Clinton *perjured himself* and *should be impeached*). For a multidimensional construct, use scale designs in which multiple attribute items are used separately to measure each dimension independently from the other dimensions (see the Tiger Woods example in Exhibit 13.4). For a unidimensional construct, use scale designs to measure a different component of the construct (refer back to the Mazda example in the In the Field box on pp. 410–11). Construct validity assessments should always be performed prior to creating the final scale measurement.

Scale Measurement Issues

When phrasing the question/setup element of a scale, avoid asking two or more questions in one setting (i.e., double-barreled questions). Use clear wording and avoid ambiguity.

ETHICS

Any set of scale point descriptors used to frame a noncomparative rating scale can be manipulated incorrectly to bias the results in any direction. Inappropriate scale descriptors to collect brand-image data can be used to incorrectly create a positive view of one brand or a negative view of a competitor's brand, which might not paint a true picture of the situation. To illustrate this point, let's revisit the Aca Joe situation from the chapter opener. Let's assume that in creating the seven-point semantic differential scale used to col-

lect the image data for the seven noted dimensions of Aca Joe's store image (i.e., quality, assortment, style/fashion, prices of merchandise, store's location, overall reputation, and knowledgeability of sales staff), the researcher decided not to follow many of the process guidelines or principles in developing accurate scale measurements, including no pretesting of the scales. Instead, he just used his intuitive judgment of what he thought the owner of Aca Joe's was hoping for. Consequently, the following semantic differential scale measurement was developed:

For each of the following attributes, please circle the number that best expresses how you would rate that attribute for the Aca Joe retail store.

Quality of Merchandise	Truly Terrible	1	2	3	4	5	6	7	Good
Merchandise Assortment	Limited	1	2	3	4	5	6	7	Extremely Wide
Style of Merchandise	Very Stylish	1	2	3	4	5	6	7	Not Stylish
Merchandise Prices	Extremely High	1	2	3	4	5	6	7	Reasonable
Overall Store Reputation	Good	1	2	3	4	5	6	7	Extremely Poor
Store's Location	Very Inconvenient	1	2	3	4	5	6	7	Convenient
Sales Staff	Professional	1	2	3	4	5	6	7	Very Unprofessional

Now, select a retail store of your choice, assume it to be Aca Joe's, and rate that store using the above scale. Interpret the image profile that you create and compare it to Aca Joe's desired and actual images described in the chapter opener. What differences do you detect? How objective were your ratings? Did you find yourself rating your store positively like Aca Joe? What problems did you encounter on each dimension? Using the above scale, a researcher can negatively bias evaluations of competitors' image by providing mildly negative descriptors against strong descriptors or vice versa. Ethically, you see how

important it is to correctly use balanced scales with comparable positive and negative descriptors. In addition, when a researcher does not follow scale development guidelines, responses can be biased and interpreted accordingly. This example also points out the need to pretest and establish scale measurements that have adequate reliability, validity, and generalizability factors. Remember that scales that either are unreliable, are invalid, or lack generalizability to the defined target population will provide flawed results and misleading findings (garbage in, garbage out) and will create unwanted ethical problems.

Unless absolutely necessary, avoid using "leading" words or phrases in any scale measurement's question/setup.

Regardless of the data collection method (e.g., personal, telephone, or computer-assisted interviews, or any type of self-administered survey), all necessary instructions for both respondent and interviewer should be part of the scale measurement's question/setup. All instructions should be kept simple and clear. When using multiattribute items, make sure the items are phrased unidimensionally (i.e., avoid double-barreled item phrases). When determining the appropriate set of scale point descriptors, make sure the descriptors are relevant to the type of data being sought. Use only scale descriptors and formats that have been pretested and evaluated for scale reliability and validity. Scale descriptors should have adequate discriminatory power, be mutually exclusive, and make sense to the respondent.

Screening Questions

Screening questions (also referred to as "screeners" or "filter questions") should always be used in any type of interview. Their purpose is to identify qualified prospective respondents and prevent unqualified respondents from being included in the study. It is very difficult to implement screening questions in most self-administered questionnaires, except for computer-assisted surveys. Screening questions need to be administered at the very beginning of the interview or survey.

Skip Question

Skip questions (also referred to as "conditional" or "branching" questions) should be avoided if at all possible. If they are needed, the instructions must be clearly communicated to the respondent or interviewer. Skip questions can appear anywhere within the questionnaire and are used if the next question (or set of questions) should be responded to only by a respondent who meets a previous condition. A simple expression of a skip command might be: "If you answered *yes* to Q.5, skip to Q.9." Skip questions help ensure that only specifically qualified respondents answer certain items.

Ethical Responsibility of the Researcher

When developing scale measurements to be used in marketing research, it is the ethical responsibility of the researcher to develop and use the most appropriate scales possible. Intentionally using scale measurements to produce biased information raises questions about the professional ethics of the researcher. For a discussion of some potential ethical problems associated with scale measurement development, see the Ethics box.

SUMMARY OF LEARNING OBJECTIVES

Discuss the importance of attitude measurement, and describe two different approaches to measuring people's attitudes toward a given object.

There is a growing need among today's marketers to better understand their customers' attitudes and feelings toward the company's products, services, and delivery systems. Some researchers view "attitude" as a derived composite outcome of the interaction between a person's beliefs (i.e., cognitive thoughts) and expressed emotions (i.e., affective feelings) regarding those beliefs. Knowing these interactions can be helpful in predicting a person's behavior (i.e., conative action). Not all researchers accept this trilogy approach to measuring attitudes; some simply see attitudes as a global indicator of a person's feelings (i.e., affect = attitude) toward an object or behavior. No matter the approach, there is significant diagnostic value to both researchers and practitioners in understanding the different scale measurements used to capture people's belief structures versus emotional feelings versus behavior tendencies.

Tell how to correctly design and test Likert, semantic differential, and behavior intention scales, and explain their strengths and weaknesses.

Likert scale designs uniquely use a set of agreement/disagreement scale descriptors to capture a person's attitude toward a given object or behavior. Contrary to popular belief, a Likert scale format does not measure a person's complete attitude, only the cognitive structure. Semantic differential scale formats are exceptional in capturing a person's perceptual image profile about a given object or behavior. This scale format is unique in that it uses a set of bipolar scales to measure several different yet interrelated factors (both cognitive and affective) of a given object or behavior.

Multiattribute affect scales use scale point descriptors that consist of relative magnitudes of an attitude (e.g., "very important," "somewhat important," "not too important," "not at all important," or "like very much," "like somewhat," "neither like nor dislike," "dislike somewhat," "dislike very much"). With respect to behavior intention scale formats, the practitioner is interested in obtaining some idea of the likelihood that people (i.e., actual or potential consumers, customers, buyers) will demonstrate some type of predictable behavior toward purchasing an object or service. The scale point descriptors like "definitely would," "probably would," "probably would not," and "definitely would not," are normally used in an intentions scale format. If the information objective is that of collecting raw data that can directly predict some type of marketplace behavior, then behavior intention scales should be used in the study. In turn, if the objective is understanding the reasons why certain types of marketplace behavior take place, then it is necessary to incorporate scale measurement formats that capture both the person's cognitive belief structures and feelings.

Discuss the differences between noncomparative and comparative scale designs as well as the appropriateness of rating and ranking scale measurements.

The main difference is that comparative scale measurements require the respondent to do some type of direct comparison between the attributes of the scale from the same known reference point whereas noncomparative scales rate each attribute independently of the other attributes making up the scale measurement. The data from comparative scales must be interpreted in relative terms and only activate the assignment and order scaling properties. Noncomparative scale data are treated as interval or ratio, and more advanced statistical procedures can be employed in analyzing the data structures. One benefit of comparative scales is that they allow for identifying small differences between the attributes, constructs, or objects. In addition, their comparative scale designs require fewer theoretical assumptions and are easier for respondents to understand and respond to than are many of the noncompara-

tive scale designs. However, noncomparative scales provide opportunity for greater insights into the constructs and their components.

Identify and discuss the critical aspects of consumer attitudes and other marketplace phenomena that require measurement to allow us to make better decisions.

In order for organizations to make informed decisions regarding their suppliers, customers, competitors, employees, or organizational members, they must gather detailed, accurate information. The selection of a supplier may rest partially on their history of on-time delivery, reputation for quality, and experience within the industry. Information concerning the preferences, purchase behavior, shopping patterns, demographics, and attitudes of consumers can be vital to the success or failure of an organization.

Similarly, in-depth profiles of competitors may reveal opportunities or challenges facing the company and can lead to coherent plans designed to create a significant competitive advantage. If consumers prefer a competitor's product, then it would be quite valuable to understand through the use of proper measurement techniques why such preferences exist.

Discuss the overall rules of measurement and explain the differences between single versus multiple measures of a construct as well as direct versus indirect measures.

No single set of rules exists for all measurements; however, certain standards can be applied to the measurement process. For example, the rules for correctly using a thermometer to measure the temperature of water would be quite different from the rules for the use of a telescope to measure the distance to a star. Even so, the rules must be explicit and detailed so as to allow consistent application of the instrument.

KEY TERMS AND CONCEPTS

Affective component 408	**Behavior intention scale** 423	**Paired-comparison rating scales** 428
Affect global approach 414	**Cognitive component** 408	**Performance rating scales** 426
Attitude 407	**Conative component** 408	**Rank-order rating scale** 428
Attitude-toward-behavior model 409	**Constant sums rating scales** 428	**Semantic differential scale** 417
Attitude-toward-object model 408	**Graphic rating scales** 426	**Staple scales** 427
	Likert scale 415	**Trilogy approach** 408

REVIEW QUESTIONS

1. Conceptually, what is an attitude? Is there one best method of measuring a person's attitude? Why or why not?

2. Explain the major differences between "rating" and "ranking" scales. Which is a better scale measurement technique for collecting attitudinal data on salesforce performance of people who sell commercial laser printers? Why?

3. When collecting importance data about the features business travelers use to select a hotel, should a researcher use a balanced or an unbalanced scale measurement? Why?

4. Explain the main differences between using "even-point" and "odd-point" scale measurement designs for collecting purchase intention data. Is one approach better than the other? Why?

5. If a semantic differential has eight attribute dimensions, should all the positive pole descriptors be on the left side and all the negative pole descriptors be on the right side of the scale continuum? Why or why not?

6. What are the benefits and limitations of comparative scale measurements? Design a paired comparison scale that will allow you to determine brand preference between Bud Light, Miller Light, Coors Light, and Old Milwaukee Light beers.

DISCUSSION QUESTIONS

1. Develop an ordinally-interval semantic differential scale that can identify the perceptual profile differences between Outback Steakhouse and Longhorn Steakhouse restaurants.

2. Explain the differences between a Likert summated scale format and a numeric rating scale format. Should a Likert scale ever be considered an interval scale? Why or why not? Now develop a forced-choice Likert scale measurement that can be used to measure consumers' perceptions about the movie *Titanic*.

3. Design a behavior intention scale with the capability of addressing the following research question: "To what extent are college students likely to purchase a new automobile within six months after graduating from college?" Discuss the potential shortcomings of your scale design.

 4. **EXPERIENCE THE INTERNET.** One company that relies heavily on asking Americans about their attitudes and values is SRI International. It has developed a unique segmentation technique that uses VALS-type data to classify people into different lifestyle categories. Get on the Internet and go to SRI's Web site at www.future.sri.com:/valshome.html. Take their short survey to determine your VALS type. While you are taking the survey, evaluate what scale measurements are being used. What type of possible design bias might exist?

ENDNOTES

1. Thomas S. Robertson and Harold H. Kassarjian, *Handbook of Consumer Behavior* (Englewood Cliffs, NJ: Prentice Hall, 1991).

2. Martin Fishbein, *Readings in Attitude Theory* (New York: John Wiley and Sons, 1967).

3. Gordon W. Allport, "The Composition of Political Attitudes," *American Journal of Sociology* 35 (1929), pp. 220–38.

4. Martin Fishbein, "Attitude and the Prediction of Behavior," in *Readings in Attitude Theory and Behavior,* ed. M. Fishbein (New York: Wiley, 1967); also see Martin Fishbein, "An Investigation of the Relationships Between Beliefs About an Object and the Attitude Toward That Object," *Human Relations* 16 (1983), pp. 233–40.

5. Icek Ajzen and Martin Fishbein, *Understanding Attitudes and Predicting Social Behavior* (Englewood Cliffs, NJ: Prentice Hall, 1980), pp. 53–89; and Icek Ajzen and Martin Fishbein, "Attitude-Behavior Relations: A Theoretical Analysis and Review of Empirical Research," *Psychological Bulletin* 84 (September 1977), pp. 888–948.

6. Y. Tsai, "On the Relationship Between Cognitive and Affective Processes," *Journal of Consumer Research* 12, no. 3 (December 1985), pp. 358–62; also see P. A. Dabholkar, "Incorporating Choice into an Attitudinal Framework," *Journal of Consumer Research* 21, no. 1 (June 1994), pp. 100–18.

7. Sharon E. Beatty and Lynn R. Kahle, "Alternative Hierarchies of the Attitude-Behavior Relationship," *Journal of Academy of Marketing Science* (Summer 1988), pp. 1–10; A. Sahni, "Incorporating Perceptions of Financial Control in Purchase Prediction," in *Advances in Consumer Research XXI,* eds. Chris T. Allen and Debbie R. John (Provo, UT: Association for Consumer Research, 1994), pp. 442–48; and J. A. Cote, J. McCullough, and M. Reilly, "Effects of Unexpected Situations on Behavior-Intention Differences," *Journal of Consumer Research* 12, no. 3 (September 1985), pp. 188–95.

8. These factors were adopted from the discussion in Del I. Hawkins, Roger J. Best, and Kenneth A. Coney, *Consumer Behavior: Building Marketing Strategy,* 7th ed. (Burr Ridge, IL: Irwin/McGraw-Hill, 1998), pp. 401–3.

9. Rensis A. Likert, "A Technique for the Measurement of Attitudes," *Archives of Psychology* 140 (1932).

10. Charles E. Osgood, George J. Suci, and Percy H. Tannenbaum, *The Measurement of Meaning* (Urbana, IL: University of Illinois Press, 1957).

11. Ibid.; also see John Dickson and Gerald Albaum, "A Method for Developing Tailor-Made Semantic Differentials for Specific Marketing Content Areas," *Journal of Marketing Research* 14 (February 1977), pp. 87–91.

12. Seymour Sudman and Norman Bradburn, *Asking Questions* (San Francisco: Jossey-Bass, 1982), pp. 219–21.

13. Osgood, Suci, and Tannenbaum, *The Measurement of Meaning,* pp. 140–53; and William D. Barclay, "The Semantic Differential as an Index of Brand Attitude," *Journal of Advertising Research* 4 (March 1964), pp. 30–33.

14. Dudley Duncan and Magnus Stenbeck, "No Opinion or Not Sure," *Public Opinion Quarterly* 52 (Winter 1988), pp. 513–25.

15. Seymour Sudman and Norman Bradburn, *Asking Questions* (San Francisco, CA: Jossey-Bass, 1982), p. 220.

16. R. H. Evans, "The Upgraded Semantic Differential: A Further Test," *Journal of the Marketing Research Society* 2 (1980), pp. 143–47; also see John E. Swann and Charles M. Futrell, "Increasing the Efficiency of the Retailer's Image Study," *Journal of the Academy of Marketing Science* (Winter 1980), pp. 51–57.

17. Robert T. W. Wu and Susan M. Petroshius, "The Halo Effect in Store Image Management," *Journal of the Academy of Marketing Science* 15 (1987), pp. 44–51.

18. Rajendar K. Garg, "The Influence of Positive and Negative Wording and Issues Involvement on Response to Likert Scales in Marketing Research," *Journal of Marketing Research Society* 38, no. 3 (July 1996), pp. 235–46.

19. M. V. Kalwani and A. J. Silk, "On the Reliability and Prediction Validity of Purchase Intention Measures," *Marketing Science* 1 (Summer 1982), pp. 243–87; also see Tony Siciliano, "Purchase Intent: Facts from Fiction," *Marketing Research* 21 (Spring 1993), p. 56.

20. Siciliano, "Purchase Intent," p. 56.

21. J. Paul Peter and Jerry C. Olson, *Consumer Behavior and Marketing Strategy,* 3rd ed. (Homewood, IL: Richard D. Irwin, 1993), pp. 175–217.

22. Michael J. Etzel, Terrell G. Williams, John C. Rogers, and Douglas J. Lincoln, "The Comparability of Three Staple Forms in a Marketing Setting," in R. Bush and S. Hunt, eds., *Marketing Theory: Philosophy of Science Perspectives* (Chicago, IL: American Marketing Association, 1982), pp. 303–6.

MARKETING RESEARCH ILLUSTRATION

SCALE MEASUREMENTS USED IN CREATING A CUSTOMER LOYALTY INDEX

This illustration presents the second part of the Marketing Research Illustration at the end of Chapter 12. Recall that researchers at Burke Customer Satisfaction Associates measured the three main components (i.e., overall customer satisfaction, likelihood of repeat business, and likelihood to recommend the company) making up their derived construct of Secure Customer Index (SCI).

Measuring Customer Loyalty

At Burke Customer Satisfaction Associates, we measure these three components (i.e., overall customer satisfaction, likelihood of repeat business, and likelihood to recommend the company) by looking at the combined scores of three survey questions. For example, in examining the overall or global satisfaction of restaurant customers, we may ask, "Overall, how satisfied were you with your visit to this restaurant?" To examine their likelihood to recommend: "How likely would you be to recommend this restaurant to a friend or associate?" And finally, to examine the likelihood of repeat purchases, we'd ask, "How likely are you to choose to visit this restaurant again?"

Using these three components, with the appropriate scales for each, secure customers would be defined as those giving the most positive responses across *all three components*. All other customers would be considered vulnerable or at risk of defecting to a competitor. The degrees of vulnerability or risk also can be determined from responses to these questions.

When we interpret a company's SCI, we typically compare it to other relevant SCI scores, such as the company's SCI score in past years, the SCI scores of competitors, and the SCI scores of "best-in-class" companies. While a company should always strive for higher scores, understanding how "good" or "bad" a given score might be is best done in comparative terms.

Customer Loyalty and Market Performance

Increasingly, we are able to link customer satisfaction and customer loyalty to bottom-line benefits. By examining customer behaviors over time and comparing them to SCI scores, we see a strong connection between secure customers and repeat purchasing of products or services. For example, we examined the relationship between customer satisfaction survey data and repeat purchasing levels in the computer industry. Secure customers in this industry were *twice* as likely to renew contracts than were vulnerable customers. Secure customers also were *twice* as likely as vulnerable customers to expand their business with their primary vendor.

As we've continued to look at cases across customer and industry types, we've found other compelling illustrations that show a connection between the index scores and financial or market performance. These findings demonstrate the value of examining index scores not only across an industry but also over time within the same company to determine changes within the proportion of secure customers.

Competition, Customers, and Surveys

As with any measurement, a customer loyalty index may be influenced by additional factors depending on the industry, market characteristics, or research methods. These factors should be considered when interpreting the meaning of any loyalty index.

Industries with more than one provider of services tend to produce higher customer satisfaction scores than industries with limited choices. For example, the cable industry, which in many markets still tends to be monopolistic, generally has lower customer satisfaction scores in comparison to other industries. The notion that competition breeds more opportunities clearly affects customer satisfaction as well.

A second factor that may contribute indirectly to a customer loyalty index score is the type of market being examined. In specialty markets where the product is tailored or customized for the customer, loyalty index scores tend to be higher than general or noncustomized markets. For example, index scores for customers of a specialized software or network configuration would likely be higher than scores for customers of an airline.

The type of customer being measured also may influence the index scores. For example, business-to-business customers may score differently than general consumers. Again, the type of industry involved also will influence the type of customers being examined.

Finally, the data collection method may influence the customer's response. Researchers have long recognized that the different methods used to collect information, such as live interviews, mail surveys, and telephone interviews, may produce varying results.

Recognizing these factors is important not only in collecting information but also in interpreting an index. Learning how to minimize or correct these influences will enhance the validity or true "reading" of a customer loyalty index.

Using Data to Evaluate Your Own Efforts

Businesses committed to customer-driven quality must integrate the voice of the customer into their business operations. A customer loyalty index provides actionable information by demonstrating the ratio of secure customers to vulnerable customers. An index acts as a baseline or yardstick for management to create goals for the organization, and helps to focus efforts for continuous improvement over time. And as changes and initiatives are implemented in the organization, the index's score may be monitored as a way of evaluating initiatives.

Using a customer loyalty index helps companies better understand their customers. By listening to customers, implementing change, and continuously monitoring the results, companies can focus their improvement efforts with the goal of winning and keeping customers.

Source: Amanda Prus and D. Randall Brandt, "Understanding Your Customers—What You Can Learn from a Customer Loyalty Index," *Marketing Tools* (July/August 1995), pp. 10–14.

MARKETING RESEARCH CASE EXERCISE

JOHN McCAIN COMPANY

The John McCain Company is a regional printer, distributor, and warehouser of office supply products. The company has been in business for only two years, yet during that time the company has grown to accumulate almost $2 million in sales. John McCain, founder and president of the company, is concerned, however, about increased competition and more sophisticated buyers of office supply products. McCain believes that the secret of the company's success lies in its ability to serve small to medium retail businesses—businesses that larger office suppliers don't cater to because of the small volume of orders these businesses request. McCain wants to maintain his company's firm hold in this market segment, and has requested a marketing research study to profile the various small to medium retail businesses.

Currently, McCain feels that three types of retail customers exist. One is the traditional retailer that sells both hard and soft goods; such customers seek office suppliers for invoice forms, sales forms, and general office products. Second is the service retailer such as dry cleaners, law firms, and accountants; these customers use letterhead, special business forms, and customized office supplies. Third are the entertainment retailers, radio stations, and TV stations; these customers use office suppliers for script and programming documents.

McCain believes that by understanding the motivations and decisions behind the purchases of office supplies, he can determine the ability of his company to successfully compete for each segment's business.

1. From the standpoint of a market researcher, how would you go about developing items and proper measurements to address the motivations and purchase behavior for each of the three segments?

2. What would be the implications if the researcher used Likert scales as opposed to semantic differential scales?

3. Should each segment receive the same type of scales or different scale measures? Explain your response.

Learning Objectives

Questionnaire Design and Issues

> **Having recently completed our test trial of Time Warner's Interactive Cable System, we now need an accurate tool to collect the participants' attitudes, feelings, and behaviors toward this new system. Predicting future acceptance rates and usage patterns of such an interactive cable system is the next critical step in determining its long-term success as well as the development and marketing of potential product offerings.**

KEVIN NOLAN
Vice President, Marketing and Customer Operations
Time Warner Cable–FSN

The Value of a Survey Instrument in Creating Meaningful Diagnostic Information

A major university in the Southeast decided that it needed to develop a marketing plan for a comprehensive on-campus housing program that would directly influence the quality of the students' living experiences at the university over the next 15 years. Administrators developed a "Residence Life" program to identify, investigate, and gain insights into the factors on-campus students needed to enrich their academic and social experiences while attending the institution.

Some of their short-term goals evolved around the idea that high-quality on-campus living facilities and programs could help attract new students to the university. Other concerns focused on developing solid marketing strategies that could (1) aid the university in increasing the occupancy rate of its current housing facilities to 100 percent; (2) improve retention levels of students, thus increasing the likelihood that students would renew their on-campus housing contracts for multiple years; and (3) predict renovation, redevelopment, and new construction needs of on-campus housing facilities regarding style of structures, lifestyle configurations, rent prices, amenities, and integrative learning programs.

Upon understanding the basic objectives of the Residence Life program, the director of the project realized that new primary information was needed to address the objectives. Consequently, the MPC Consulting Group, Inc., a firm that specializes in the assessment of on-campus housing programs, was retained to advise and oversee the project. This firm was not known for its capability of conducting primary information marketing research. After several consultations with university administrators, MPC's representatives determined that the appropriate method for collecting the needed information would require the development of a self-administered survey instrument. It was decided that the survey would be administered through the existing student e-mail system at the university. Behind the e-mail approach was the consultants' belief that all 28,000 university students had access to and used e-mail, and this method would save time and costs.

Given the project's multiple objectives, the consulting team brainstormed a list of 59 questions to be asked of both on-campus and off-campus students currently enrolled at the university. A variety of questions focused on housing attitudes and preferences (state-of-mind data); importance of different housing structures, lifestyle configurations, rent prices, amenities, and integrative learning programs (state-of-mind data); likelihood of selecting on-campus housing or off-campus housing based on amenities, prices, and availability (state-of-intention data); and approximately 17 demographic/socioeconomic characteristics (state-of-being data). Efforts were made to create 59 different scale formats that were reasonably representative of the initial list of questions.

Now the task at hand for the consultants was to take the 59 scales and create a questionnaire that could be sent to students via e-mail. Not having strong understanding of scientific survey instruments, the consulting firm established the initial questionnaire, which began by asking about personal demographic characteristics, followed by some questions concerning students' current housing situations, then assessments of those conditions. Then the survey asked questions about the importance of a list of preselected housing characteristics followed by questions designed to capture the student's intention of living in on-campus versus off-campus housing facilities and the reasons for those intentions. After a few more questions concerning marital status and number of young children, questions were presented on the types of housing structures and amenities most desired by students. The survey ended with personal thoughts about the need for child care services.

When placed on the computer for access by e-mail, the questionnaire was 12 pages long with six different "screener" questions having the respondents skipping back and forth between computer screens depending on how they responded to the screening questions. After three weeks of having the survey out on the computer, only 17 students had responded, and 8 of those surveys were incomplete. University officials asked three simple but critical questions: (1) Why such a low response rate? (2) Was the survey a good or bad instrument for collecting the needed primary information?, and (3) Is there any diagnostic value of the data for addressing the given objectives?

Based on your knowledge and understanding of good information research practices to this point, can you give some answers to these three questions? Take a few moments to write down the potential problems that were created by the consulting firm's process described above. Then, after reading this chapter, return here and see if you would answer these questions any differently.

Value of Questionnaires in Information Research

The chapter opener shows that designing a single question/scale for collecting a specific type of raw data is different from taking a set of scale measurements and creating a good scientific questionnaire. A researcher's ability to design a good scale measurement is, by itself, not enough to guarantee that the appropriate primary raw data will automatically be collected.

This chapter focuses on developing a clear understanding of the importance of questionnaire designs and the process that should be undertaken in the development of survey instruments. Understanding questionnaire designs will require that you integrate many of the concepts discussed in earlier chapters, particularly Chapters 3, 8, 9, 10, 11, 12, and 13. As discussed in Chapters 12 and 13, scale measurements consist of three different components: (1) the question/setup; (2) the dimensions and attributes of the object, construct, or concept being investigated; and (3) the actual scale points or descriptors that represent the set of possible raw responses. Detailed discussions concerning the second component were presented in Chapter 12. Chapter 13 discussed in detail the third component and aspects of the first.

As a future marketing or business decision maker, you might not have to ever personally design a questionnaire for collecting primary data, but most certainly you will be in a client's position of determining whether or not a survey designed for you is good or bad. Therefore, you should know about the considerations, preliminary activities, and processes that are undertaken in designing scientific questionnaires.

As discussed in earlier chapters, much of the primary data necessary to create new information for resolving business and marketing information problems requires the researcher to ask people questions and record their responses in some recognizable fashion. If business information problems were simple and required only one bit of raw data, questionnaires would not be necessary. A researcher could develop a single question measurement and administer it to a sample of respondents, collect the raw data, analyze it, and derive a meaningful bit of information from the data structure. For example, let's say a retailer like Sears wanted to know if having a "50 percent off" sale on Saturday, January 9, 2000, would increase sales revenues that day. A researcher could develop the following question: "If Sears had a storewide 50 percent off sale on all merchandise Saturday, January 9, 2000, would you come to Sears and buy at least one item? ___YES ___NO" and administer it to 1,000 consumers representative of the general population. Let's assume that 650 people say yes (65 percent) and 350 people say no (35 percent) to the above question and the researcher interprets the results as being "the majority (65 percent) of shoppers would come to Sears and buy merchandise." By having this one bit of information, does Sears have enough information to decide whether or not to hold the sale?

In reality, it is highly unlikely that this one bit of information would be a good predictor of actual shopping behavior. Some of the other factors that also directly affect a person's decision to shop at Sears might be: (1) their attitude toward Sears and its merchandise, (2) other obligations or activities the day of the sale, (3) lack of a mode of transportation on that particular day, or (4) limited financial resources. The point is that many business situations or problems are not unidimensional, and therefore one bit of information about a defined problem situation is normally not sufficient to resolve it.

Questionnaire A formalized framework consisting of a set of questions and scales designed to generate primary raw data.

A **questionnaire** (also called a *survey instrument*) is a formalized framework consisting of a set of questions and scales designed to generate primary raw data. Questionnaire construction involves taking established sets of scale measurements and formatting them into a complete instrument for communicating with and collecting raw data from respondents.

Theoretical Principles of Questionnaire Design

One of the great weaknesses of questionnaire design today is that many researchers still do not understand the theory behind questionnaire development. Many researchers believe that designing questionnaires is an art rather than a science, where *art* relates to the researcher's creative use of words in asking the right questions and developing the related scale points. While there is some level of creativity involved in designing a questionnaire, the process itself should be a scientific one that integrates established rules of logic, objectivity, discriminatory powers, and systematic procedures.[1] Everyone understands that words go into questions and that questions go into questionnaires, but not everyone understands that writing questions does *not* give you a questionnaire.

Four Theoretical Components of a Questionnaire

Theoretically, a questionnaire consists of several components—words, questions, formats and hypotheses—that are integrated into a recognizable, hierarchical layer system.[2]

Words

The most obvious component is words. The researcher must carefully consider which words to use in creating the questions and scales for collecting raw data from respondents. A few examples of wording problems include ambiguity, abstraction, and connotation. The words selected by the researcher can definitely influence a respondent's answer to a given question. The following examples are used to illustrate this point:

1. Do you think anything *could* be done to make it more convenient for people to conduct their financial transactions at Citicorp Bank?

2. Do you think anything *should* be done to make it more convenient for people to conduct their financial transactions at Citicorp Bank?

3. Do you think anything *might* be done to make it more convenient for people to conduct their financial transactions at Citicorp Bank?

The different answers each of these questions would generate show how word phrasing variations can become significant in questionnaire designs. Slight changes in wording can introduce different concepts or emotional levels into the questionnaire.

Questions/Setups

The next component is the question/setup used in a particular scale measurement to collect raw data from the respondent. Question reliability, question validity, and question bias should have already been addressed during the scale measurement design activities and are therefore not part of questionnaire design itself. Two important issues relating to question phrasing that have a direct impact on survey designs are (1) the type of question format (unstructured or structured) and (2) the quality of the question (good or bad).[3]

Unstructured questions

Open-ended questions formatted to allow respondents to reply in their own words.

Unstructured questions are open-ended questions formatted to allow respondents to reply in their own words. There is no predetermined list of responses available to aid or limit the respondents' answers. This type of question requires more thinking and effort on the part of respondents. In most cases, an interviewer is required for purposes of asking follow-up probing questions. If administered correctly, unstructured questions can provide the researcher with a rich array of information. (Review Chapter 8's discussions on open-ended question formats.) The actual format of open-ended questions might vary depending on the data collection method (e.g., personal interview, telephone interview, or self-administered survey). Exhibit 14.1 provides several examples to illustrate these format differences.

Structured questions

Closed-ended questions that require the respondent to choose from a predetermined set of responses or scale points.

Structured questions are closed-ended questions that require the respondent to choose from a predetermined set of responses or scale points. This question format reduces the amount of thinking and effort required by respondents. In general, structured questions are more popular than unstructured ones in self-administered questionnaires. Interviewer bias is eliminated because either (1) the interviewer simply checks a box or line, circles a category,

---

EXHIBIT 14.1 **Examples of Unstructured Question Setup Designs**

Personal or Telephone Interviews

What toppings, if any, do you usually add to a pizza other than cheese when ordering a pizza for yourself from Pizza Hut? **(Interviewer: Record all mentioned toppings in the space provided below. Make sure you probe for specifics and clarity of responses.)**

_____

_____

_____

or

What toppings, if any, do you usually add to a pizza other than cheese when ordering a pizza for yourself from Pizza Hut? **(Interviewer: DO NOT read the listed toppings; just record the toppings by checking the box next to the mentioned toppings below. Make sure you probe for specifics and clarity of responses.)**

❑ anchovies	❑ bacon	❑ barbecue beef
❑ black olives	❑ extra cheese	❑ green olives
❑ green peppers	❑ ground beef	❑ ham
❑ hot peppers	❑ mushrooms	❑ onions
❑ pepperoni	❑ sausage	❑ some other topping. _____

Self-Administered Survey

In the space provided below, please write the types of toppings, if any, that you usually add to a pizza other than cheese when ordering a pizza for yourself from Pizza Hut. **(Please indicate as many toppings as apply.)**

_____

_____

_____

| **EXHIBIT 14.2** | **Examples of Structured Question/Setup Designs** |

Personal Interview

(HAND RESPONDENT CARD.) Please look at this card and tell me the letters that indicate what toppings, if any, you usually add to a pizza other than cheese when ordering a pizza for yourself from Pizza Hut. **(Interviewer: Record all mentioned toppings by circling the letters below,** and **make sure you probe for any other toppings.)**

[a] anchovies	[b] bacon	[c] barbecue beef
[d] black olives	[e] extra cheese	[f] green olives
[h] green peppers	[i] ground beef	[j] ham
[k] hot peppers	[l] mushrooms	[m] onions
[n] pepperoni	[o] sausage	[p] some other topping: _____

Telephone Interview

I'm going to read you a list of pizza toppings. As I read each one, please tell me whether or not that topping is one that you usually add to a pizza when ordering a pizza for yourself from Pizza Hut. **(Interviewer: Read each topping category slowly and record all mentioned toppings by circling their corresponding letter below, and make sure you probe for any other toppings.)**

[a] anchovies	[b] bacon	[c] barbecue beef
[d] black olives	[e] extra cheese	[f] green olives
[h] green peppers	[i] ground beef	[j] ham
[k] hot peppers	[l] mushrooms	[m] onions
[n] pepperoni	[o] sausage	[p] some other topping: _____

Self-Administered Survey

Among the pizza toppings listed below, what toppings, if any, do you usually add to a pizza other than cheese when ordering a pizza for yourself from Pizza Hut?

(Please check as many boxes as apply.)

❑ anchovies	❑ bacon	❑ barbecue beef
❑ black olives	❑ extra cheese	❑ green olives
❑ green peppers	❑ ground beef	❑ ham
❑ hot peppers	❑ mushrooms	❑ onions
❑ pepperoni	❑ sausage	❑ some other topping: _____

---

or records a number or (2) the respondents themselves check a box or line, circle a category, or record a number that best represents their response to the question.[4] In many ways, structured formats give the researcher greater opportunities to control the thinking that respondents must do in order to answer a question. Exhibit 14.2 shows some examples.

Bad questions are any questions that prevent or distort the fundamental communication between the researcher and the respondent. A researcher may think she or he has written an excellent question because it accurately conveys her or his point of view or interest to the respondent, but if the respondent cannot answer it in a meaningful way, it is a bad question. Some examples of bad questions are those that are

Bad questions Any questions that prevent or distort the fundamental communication between the researcher and the respondents.

1. **Incomprehensible to the respondent** because either the wording, the concept, or both cannot be understood. An example would be: "What is your attitude about the linkage between the 1998 war on Iraq and the Democrats decrying of sexual McCarthyism toward improving the environment in Arizona?"

2. **Unanswerable** either because the respondent does not have access to the information needed or because none of the answer choices apply to the respondent. An example would be: "What was your parents' exact annual income two years ago?"

3. **Leading (or loaded)** in that the respondent is forced or directed into a response that she or he would not ordinarily give if all possible response categories or concepts were provided, or if all the facts of the situation were provided. An example of this would be: "Do you believe that Democrats who loved William Jefferson Clinton agreed he did a good job as president of the United States?"

4. **Double-barreled** in that they ask the respondent to address more than one issue at a time. An example would be: "To what extent do you agree or disagree that Monica Lewinsky and Representative Henry Hyde, R-Ill., were responsible for the impeachment vote against President Clinton?"

Questionnaire Format

This component does not directly relate to the process of developing the individual questions but rather the integrated layout of sets of questions or scale measurements into a systematic instrument. The questionnaire's format should allow for clear communication. Later in the chapter, we will discuss in detail the flowerpot approach to designing scientific questionnaires that improves the researcher's ability to collect quality primary raw data.

Hypothesis Development

Hypothesis A formalized statement of a testable relationship between two or more constructs or variables.

This final component focuses on the notion that questionnaires are designed for collecting meaningful raw data to test a **hypothesis** rather than merely to gather facts about objects under investigation. Theoretically, each of the questions and scale measurements used within a questionnaire design should either directly or indirectly relate to a recognizable research hypothesis that is pertinent to the overall research objectives. Hypotheses can relate to

1. The nature of the respondent.

2. The relationship between the expressed attitudes and behavior of the respondent (e.g., motivation).

3. The sociological structures and their influence on the respondent.

4. The meaning of words and the respondent's grasp of language and/or concepts.

5. The relationships among a respondent's knowledge, attitudes, and marketplace behaviors.

6. The descriptive and predictive capabilities of attributes and dimensions with regard to the investigated constructs and concepts (e.g., customer satisfaction, product or service quality, and behavioral intentions).[5]

By taking the time to identify the hypothesis associated with each of the questions or scale measurements to be included in a questionnaire design, researchers can enhance their ability to determine which measurements are necessary for collecting primary raw data and which ones are nice but not necessary. Collecting "nice but not necessary" data only increases the length of the questionnaire and the likelihood of nonresponse bias.

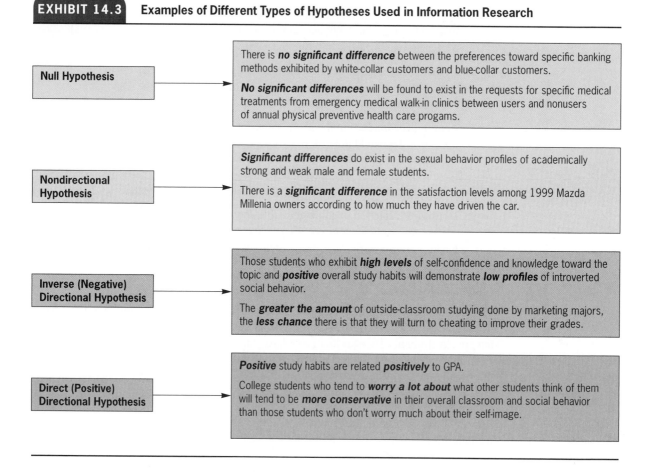

EXHIBIT 14.3   **Examples of Different Types of Hypotheses Used in Information Research**

Null Hypothesis

> There is **no significant difference** between the preferences toward specific banking methods exhibited by white-collar customers and blue-collar customers.
>
> **No significant differences** will be found to exist in the requests for specific medical treatments from emergency medical walk-in clinics between users and nonusers of annual physical preventive health care progams.

Nondirectional Hypothesis

> **Significant differences** do exist in the sexual behavior profiles of academically strong and weak male and female students.
>
> There is a **significant difference** in the satisfaction levels among 1999 Mazda Millenia owners according to how much they have driven the car.

Inverse (Negative) Directional Hypothesis

> Those students who exhibit **high levels** of self-confidence and knowledge toward the topic and **positive** overall study habits will demonstrate **low profiles** of introverted social behavior.
>
> The **greater the amount** of outside-classroom studying done by marketing majors, the **less chance** there is that they will turn to cheating to improve their grades.

Direct (Positive) Directional Hypothesis

> **Positive** study habits are related **positively** to GPA.
>
> College students who tend to **worry a lot about** what other students think of them will tend to be **more conservative** in their overall classroom and social behavior than those students who don't worry much about their self-image.

Exhibit 14.3 displays some examples of different types of hypotheses that a researcher can establish about the questions or scale measurements included in a questionnaire. Hypothesis development will be revisited in later chapters.

Description versus Prediction

While all good questionnaires are systematically structured, most surveys are designed to be descriptive or predictive.[6] A descriptive design allows the researcher to collect raw data that can be turned into facts about a person or object. For example, the U.S. Census Bureau uses questionnaire designs that collect primarily state-of-being or state-of-behavior data that can be translated into facts about the U.S. population (e.g., income levels, marital status, age, occupation, family size, usage rates, quantities of consumption). In contrast, predictive questionnaires force the researcher to collect a wider range of state-of-mind and state-of-intention data that can be used in predicting changes in attitudes and behaviors as well as in testing hypotheses.

Accuracy versus Precision

Another theoretical principle that should guide the design of questionnaires is that of accuracy. This quality can be viewed as obtaining a true report of the respondent's attitudes, preferences, beliefs, feelings, behavioral intentions, and actions/reactions. Questions and

A CLOSER LOOK AT RESEARCH   **Using Technology**

Computerized Questionnaires

A very important development in marketing research has been the use of "smart" questionnaires provided by personal computers. These questionnaires are structured with a mathematical logic capability that allows the computer to customize them for each respondent as the interview progresses. Through the use of interactive software, the computer constantly evaluates new information and presents the respondent with a new decision to make. In this type of survey, different respondents taking the same questionnaire would answer different sets of questions, each custom-designed to provide the most relevant data.

For global corporations with diverse product lines, computerized questionnaires could provide important information related to each product line. Before computerized questionnaires, corporations would be forced to rely on survey data that used scripted questions that often did not provide relevant data. However, with computerized questionnaires, the information obtained is pertinent to the needs of the organization.

Important advantages of computerized questionnaires over pen-and-paper surveys include increased ease of participation, decreased time requirements, and a reduction in resources needed to conduct the survey, thereby reducing the overall cost of survey administration. For corporations with constantly increasing time demands, computerized questionnaires would seem to be a natural choice for their marketing research needs.

scale measurements must be incorporated that allow the researcher to gain an overall total picture rather than just a fragment.[7] *Accuracy* refers to the degree to which the data provide the researcher with a description of the true state of affairs. In contrast, *precision* in questionnaire designs focuses on the reproducibility of the results over repeated usages (i.e., similar to reliability of scale measurements).

The Value of a Good Survey Instrument

The value of a well-constructed questionnaire cannot be overestimated by researchers and marketing practitioners. How a survey instrument is developed becomes a critical component in the overall process of creating new information that can be used to solve business problems. The main function of a questionnaire is to capture people's true thoughts and feelings about different issues or objects. The raw data collected through a survey instrument can be viewed as the critical keys for unlocking understanding and truth about predetermined elements of a defined problem situation.[8]

In contrast, a bad questionnaire can be very costly in terms of time, effort, and money. It produces nothing more than "garbage" data that, if used by decision makers, result in inappropriate or incorrect marketing actions.[9] Advanced computer technologies are providing new alternatives for designing good questionnaires. Read the Using Technology box for a discussion of computerized questionnaire designs.

The Flowerpot Approach to Questionnaire Designs

The process that researchers use to develop a questionnaire tends to be very systematic. While the specific steps may vary, most researchers follow established rules. Exhibit 14.4 displays a set of steps for developing survey instruments. Note that some of the activities in each step are critically necessary but not part of the actual layout. For example, some

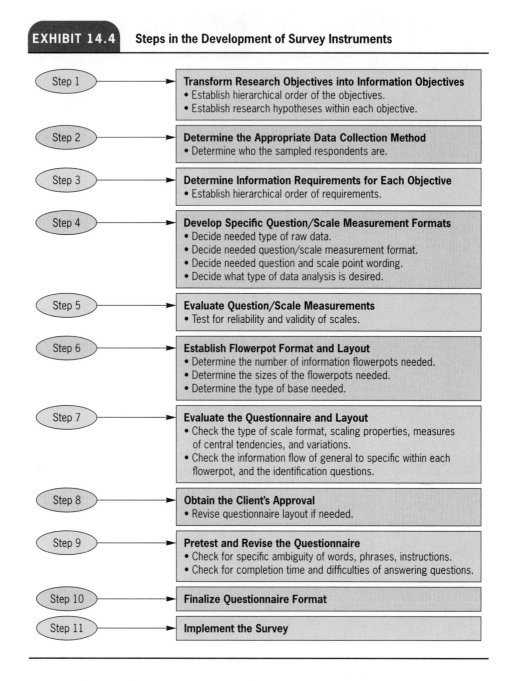

EXHIBIT 14.4   **Steps in the Development of Survey Instruments**

Step 1 → **Transform Research Objectives into Information Objectives**
• Establish hierarchical order of the objectives.
• Establish research hypotheses within each objective.

Step 2 → **Determine the Appropriate Data Collection Method**
• Determine who the sampled respondents are.

Step 3 → **Determine Information Requirements for Each Objective**
• Establish hierarchical order of requirements.

Step 4 → **Develop Specific Question/Scale Measurement Formats**
• Decide needed type of raw data.
• Decide needed question/scale measurement format.
• Decide needed question and scale point wording.
• Decide what type of data analysis is desired.

Step 5 → **Evaluate Question/Scale Measurements**
• Test for reliability and validity of scales.

Step 6 → **Establish Flowerpot Format and Layout**
• Determine the number of information flowerpots needed.
• Determine the sizes of the flowerpots needed.
• Determine the type of base needed.

Step 7 → **Evaluate the Questionnaire and Layout**
• Check the type of scale format, scaling properties, measures of central tendencies, and variations.
• Check the information flow of general to specific within each flowerpot, and the identification questions.

Step 8 → **Obtain the Client's Approval**
• Revise questionnaire layout if needed.

Step 9 → **Pretest and Revise the Questionnaire**
• Check for specific ambiguity of words, phrases, instructions.
• Check for completion time and difficulties of answering questions.

Step 10 → **Finalize Questionnaire Format**

Step 11 → **Implement the Survey**

questionnaires call for the development of separate screening questions that are used to qualify the prospective respondents. Other activities are pertinent to the actual design task.

With all these steps and particulars to understand, the development process can seem overwhelming at first. To simplify the questionnaire development process, we present the **flowerpot approach.** This scientific approach involves a series of activities that have a logical, hierarchical order.[10] The Flowerpot notion is symbolically derived from the natural shape associated with a clay pot used for planting and growing flowers. The shape is wide at the top and tapered (or narrower) at the bottom—symbolizing a natural flow of data from general to specific. Although this approach is primarily used to create a solid questionnaire structure, it has direct impact on steps 1 and 3 of the development process out-

Flowerpot approach   A specific framework for integrating sets of question/scale measurements into a logical, smooth-flowing questionnaire.

lined in Exhibit 14.4. The flowerpot approach helps the researcher make decisions regarding (1) construct development, (2) dimensions and attributes of objects, (3) various question/scale measurement formats, (4) wording of actual questions, and (5) scale points. In situations where there are multiple research objectives, each objective will have its own pot of data. To reduce the likelihood of creating biased data, the size and width of the data requirements must be determined for each objective, with the most general data requirements going into the biggest flowerpot and the next most general set of data going into a smaller pot. As illustrated in Exhibit 14.5, when stacking multiple pots the larger pot is

---

EXHIBIT 14.5   **Illustrative Diagram of the Flowerpot Approach**

This diagram illustrates the overall flowerpot design of a questionnaire that fits a research survey that has two defined information objectives and calls for an identification base that contains both psychographic and demographic-socioeconomic traits about the respondent.

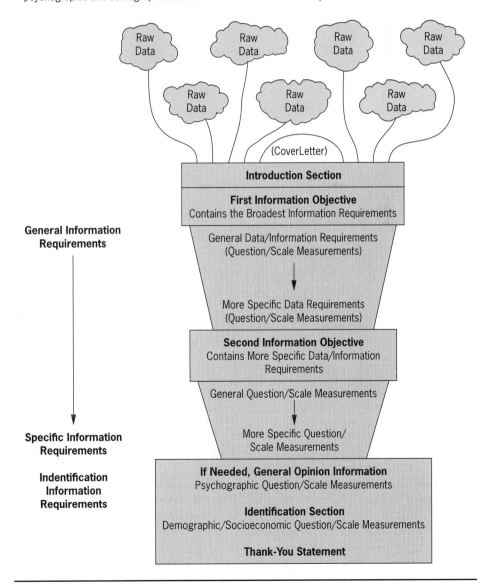

always placed on top of a smaller pot to ensure that the overall general to specific flow of data is maintained in a questionnaire design.

According to the flowerpot concept, in a good questionnaire design, the data will flow from a general information level, down to a more specific information level, and end with identification data. A questionnaire should begin with an introductory section that gives the respondent a basic idea of the main topic of the research. This section should also include general instructions for filling out the survey. The introduction's appearance will vary based on the desired data collection method (e.g., self-administered or interview). For example, the introduction needed for a self-administered questionnaire in a banking study might look as follows:

> Thank you for your participation in this study. Your participation will aid us in determining what people in our community think about the present products and services offered by banks. The results of the study will provide the banking industry with insights into how to better serve the needs of people in the Baton Rouge community.
>
> Your attitudes, preferences, and opinions are important to this study; they will be kept strictly confidential.
>
> **DIRECTIONS: Please read each question carefully. Answer the question by checking the appropriate box(es) that represent your response or responses.**

In contrast, an introduction for a county housing survey using telephone interviews might look as follows:

Hillsborough County Housing Study

Verified
By: _____
Date: _____

Phone # _____
Call Back Date: _____ Time: _____
Time Started: _____ (a.m.) (p.m.)
Serial # _____

MARKETS: [1] NW Hillsborough   [2] NE Hillsborough   [3] Brandon

INTERVIEWER: Ask to speak with the man of the house. If not available or none, ask for the lady of the house.

Hello, I'm (Your Name) representing the Marketing Resources Group here in Tampa. Today, we are conducting an interesting study on housing in Hillsborough County and would like to include your opinions in it.

As it was explained in the letter mailed to your residence about a week ago, we are not interested in selling you anything. We are only interested in your honest opinions about housing structures in the Hillsborough area.

Notice how the two introductions differ. The telephone interview requires specific interviewer instructions.

Next, the researcher must determine how many different information objectives there are (i.e., the number of flowerpots needed to construct the questionnaire) and the true breadth and depth of the information requirements (i.e., the different pot sizes).

First working with the largest flowerpot (i.e., most general information objective), the researcher must identify the specific information requirements and arrange them from general to more specific. Then, going to the next largest flowerpot, the researcher again arranges the information requirements from general to specific. Because stacking the larger pots on top of smaller pots tends to create an unstable, top-heavy structure, a good questionnaire design will also end with demographic and socioeconomic questions about the respondent to form a solid identification base. All questionnaires produced by the flowerpot approach will end with a thank-you statement.

The Flowerpot Approach's Impact on Questionnaire Development

Although the flowerpot approach is primarily used to determine the appropriate sequential order of the questions and scale measurements used to collect the raw data, it has a direct impact on several of the other development steps.

Determining the Information Objectives (Step 1)

After transforming the research objectives into information objectives, the researcher must evaluate each information objective based on its broadness. This activity achieves two things for the researcher. First, it helps the researcher decide which information objectives truly represent a flowerpot of information. Second, it helps the researcher to determine how many flowerpots, and in what sizes, will need to be stacked up in the questionnaire design.

Determining the Information Requirements (Step 3)

Rather than using general brainstorming techniques to develop all the data requirements for the entire set of information objectives, the researcher using the flowerpot approach can focus on one information topic at a time. This decreases the likelihood of generating irrelevant or "nice but not necessary" data requirements. This approach also enhances the researcher's ability to determine the necessary order (e.g., general to specific) among the data requirements within a given pot.

Development of a Flowerpot-Designed Questionnaire

This section describes how the flowerpot approach influences the 11 steps in the survey instrument development process described in Exhibit 14.4. A detailed example concerning a study conducted for the American Bank and Trust Company located in Baton Rouge, Louisiana, will be integrated into the discussion.

The Situation

The research project was conducted on behalf of the American Bank and Trust Company, a local bank serving the greater metropolitan area of Baton Rouge, Louisiana. The primary goal of the survey and subsequent analysis was to provide the American Bank's marketing management team with pertinent information regarding banking habits and patterns, as well as demographic and lifestyle characteristics of the bank's current customers.

Step 1: Transform Research Objectives into Information Objectives

In step 1 of the development process, the flowerpot approach guides the researcher not only in transforming the research objectives into information objectives but also in determining how many information objectives to include (i.e., the number of pots), along with parts of the base stand and those objectives which represent testable hypotheses. The researcher then determines the order of the information objectives (i.e., the size of the pots). In the American Bank study, the initial research objectives (in bold) were rewritten into information objectives (in italics) as follows:

1. **To obtain a demographic profile of American Bank's current customers.**
   (To collect data on selected demographic characteristics that can be used to create a descriptive profile identifying people who are current American Bank customers.)

2. **To obtain a partial lifestyle profile of the people who currently bank with American Bank, with particular emphasis on financial dimensions.**
   (To collect data on selected financial-oriented lifestyle dimensions that can be used to create a descriptive profile that further identifies people who currently bank at American Bank.)

3. **To determine banking habits and patterns of these customers.**
   (To collect data pertinent to identifying and describing desired and actual banking habits and patterns exhibited by customers, as well as their selected attitudes and feelings toward those banking practices.)

4. **To investigate the existence of possible differences between the psychological and demographic dimensions associated with customers' perception of being either a blue-collar or white-collar person.**
   (To collect data that will allow the researcher to (1) classify customers as being socially either "blue collar" or "white collar" and (2) test for significant demographic and lifestyle profile differences between these two social class based customer groups.)

5. **To determine the various geographic markets presently being served by American Bank on the basis of customers' length of residence in the area.**
   (To collect selected state-of-being data that will allow the researcher to identify and describe existing strong geographic service markets.)

After transforming the research objectives into information objectives, the researcher determined that objectives 1 and 2 directly related to data that would be part of the questionnaire's base structure. Objective 3 represents an information flowerpot. In contrast, objectives 4 and 5 do not represent information flowerpots but rather hypotheses about data structures that will be derived from raw data obtained within either the base or the identified information flowerpot. Although there were five initial information objectives in this example, the actual structure consists of only one information flowerpot and its base.

Step 2: Determine the Appropriate Data Collection Method

On the basis of the information objectives and target population (i.e., American Bank's own current customers), bank management and the researcher jointly decided that a direct mail survey approach would be the most efficient method of reaching the randomly selected respondents and collecting raw data. This step has a direct influence on creating the individual questions and scale measurements, although these are designed only after the specific information items are determined for each objective.

Step 3: Determine Information Requirements for Each Objective

The flowerpot approach has a significant impact on this predesign step of the development process. In this step, the researcher interacts with bank management to determine what specific data requirements are needed to achieve each of the stated information objectives as well as the classification factors that will make up the questionnaire's base. The researcher must establish the general-to-specific order among the identified data requirements. The study's data requirements and flow are detailed as follows:

1. **Flowerpot 1** (i.e., the third objective): To collect data that are pertinent to identifying and describing desired and actual banking habits and patterns exhibited by customers as well as their selected attitudes and feelings toward those banking practices.

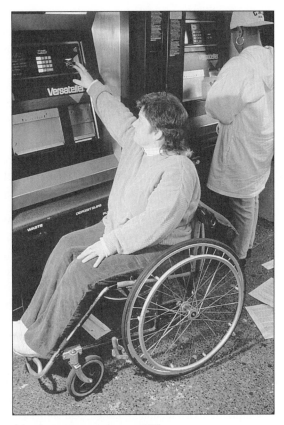

A bank customer using an ATM.

   a. Consideration toward the bank patronized most often.
   b. Bank items (characteristics) deemed important in selecting a bank (i.e., convenience/location, banking hours, good service charges, interest rates on savings accounts, knew a person at the bank, bank's reputation, bank's promotional advertisements, interest rates on loans).
   c. Considerations toward having personal savings accounts at various types of financial institutions.
   d. Preference considerations toward selected banking methods (i.e., inside the bank, drive-up window, 24-hour ATM, electronic banking, bank by mail, bank by phone, some other person).
   e. Actual usage considerations toward various banking methods (i.e., inside the bank, drive-up window, 24-hour ATM, electronic banking, bank by mail, bank by phone, some other person).
   f. Frequency of balancing a checkbook as well as the number of not-sufficient-funds (NSF) charges.

  2. **Flowerpot base—lifestyle dimensions** (i.e., the second objective): To collect data on selected financial-oriented lifestyle dimensions that can be used to create a descriptive profile that further identifies people who currently bank at American Bank.

    Belief statements that will measure the existence of a customer's lifestyle as being financial optimist, financially dissatisfied, information exchanger, credit card user, advertising viewer, family oriented, price conscious, blue/white-collar oriented.

3. **Flowerpot base—demographic characteristics** (i.e., the first objective): To col-
    lect data on selected demographic characteristics that can be used to create a
    descriptive profile identifying people who are current American Bank customers.

    Include characteristics of gender, years in area, years at current residence, present
    employment status, present marital status, spouse's current employment status,
    number of dependent children, education level, age, occupation, nature of work,
    union membership, income level, zip code.

Notice that the fourth and fifth information objectives have no direct bearing on determining the data requirements because they incorporate data factors that are covered either
in the information flowerpot or its base. Therefore, the researcher does not have to integrate them into this particular step of the development process.

Step 4: Develop Specific Question/Scale Measurement Formats

The flowerpot approach does not have any real impact on the activities that take place in this
development process step. Nevertheless, this step remains a critical part of questionnaire
design. The researcher must use his or her construct and scale measurement knowledge in
developing complete scale measurements (i.e., question/setup, dimension/attributes, scale
points/responses) for each individual data factor identified in step 3. The researcher must
make three key decisions for each factor: (1) the type of data (i.e., state of being, mind,
behavior, intention); (2) question/scale format (i.e., open-ended or closed-ended format and
nominal, ordinal, interval or ratio structure) and (3) the question and specific scale point
wording.

The flowerpot approach advocates that when designing the specific question/scale
measurements, researchers should split their mind as if they were two different people, one
thinking like a technical, logical researcher and the other like a respondent. (Revisit chapters 12 and 13 for details.) The results of this step can be seen in the final questionnaire displayed in the Marketing Research Illustration at the end of this chapter.

Step 5: Evaluate Question/Scale Measurements

Again, the flowerpot approach does not have any real impact on the activities that take
place in this step of the development process. The researcher must individually assess each
question and scale measurement for reliability and validity. He or she would also evaluate
the instructions and revise where necessary. See Exhibit 14.6 for a summary of the guidelines for evaluating the adequacy of questions.

Step 6: Establish Flowerpot Format and Layout

This step is at the center of the flowerpot approach to questionnaire designs. Taking all the
individual questions and scales developed in step 4, the researcher must present them in a
specific yet logical order. After creating a title for the questionnaire, the researcher must
include a brief introductory section and communicate any general instructions prior to asking the first question. The questions that make up the first (in this example, the only) information flowerpot must be asked in a natural general-to-specific order, to reduce the
potential for sequence bias.

In a self-administered questionnaire, all instructions should be included within each
question or scale, where appropriate. After completing the information flowerpot, the
researcher must stabilize the structure by building a base. In the American Bank example,
there is a two-part base structure. The lifestyle belief (i.e., general opinions) section is presented first, and then the more standardized classification section (i.e., demographic
descriptors). The final part of any base is the thank-you statement.

EXHIBIT 14.6	Guidelines for Evaluating the Adequacy of Questions

1. Questions should be simple and straightforward whenever possible.

2. Questions should be expressed clearly whenever possible.

3. Questions should avoid qualifying phrases or extraneous references, unless they are being used as a type of qualifying (screening) factor.

4. Descriptive words should be avoided, unless absolutely necessary.

5. The question/setups, attribute statements, and data response categories should be unidimensional, except when there is a need for a multiple-response question.

6. Raw data response categories (scale points) should be mutually exclusive.

7. The question/setups and the response categories should be meaningful to the respondent.

8. Question/scale measurement formats should avoid arrangement of response categories that might bias the respondent's answer.

9. Unless called for, question/setups should avoid undue stress of particular words.

10. Question/setups should avoid double negatives.

11. Question/scale measurements should avoid technical or sophisticated language, unless necessary.

12. Where possible, question/setups should be phrased in a realistic setting.

13. Question/scale measurements should be designed to read logically.

14. Question/scale measurements should always avoid the use of double-barreled items.

At the beginning of the classification section is this statement to the respondent: Now just a few more questions so that we can combine your answers with those of the other people taking part in this study. This is a "transition phrase," which serves three basic purposes. First, it communicates to the respondents that a change in their thinking process is about to take place. No longer do they have to think about their specific belief structures; they can clear their mind before thinking about their personal data. Second, it hints that the task of completing the survey is almost over. Third, it assures the respondent that the information she or he gives will be used only in aggregate combinations—that is, it will be blended with information from other respondents participating in the survey.

Step 7: Evaluate the Questionnaire and Layout

After drafting the questionnaire, but before submitting it to the marketing management team for approval, the researcher should review the layout to make sure the questionnaire meets all the stated information objectives. Normally, this step would focus on determining whether each question is necessary and whether the overall length is acceptable. In contrast, the flowerpot approach would give more attention to (1) checking whether the instrument meets the overall objectives; (2) checking the scale format, scaling properties, and measures of central tendencies and variations; and (3) checking general-to-specific order.

An easy method of evaluating questionnaires is to answer the following five questions for each question or scale measurement included in the design:

1. What specific types of raw data (state of being, mind, behavior, or intention) are being sought in the question, and to what purpose?

2. What types of questions or scale measurements (nominal, ordinal, interval, ratio, ordinally-interval) are being used?

3. What scaling properties (assignment, order, distance, origin) are being activated in the scale measurement?

4. What is the most appropriate measure of central tendency (mode, median, mean)?

5. What is the most appropriate measure of dispersion (frequency distribution, range, standard deviation)?

Step 8: Obtain the Client's Approval

The flowerpot concept does not have any unique impact in this step of the overall development process other than providing the researcher with a solid framework for explaining why the particular questions or scale measurements were chosen and the resulting layout of the survey instrument. Copies of the questionnaire draft should be made and distributed to all parties that have authority over and interest in the project. Realistically, the client may step in at any time in the design process to express a need for some type of modification.

Nevertheless, it is important to get final approval of the questionnaire prior to pretesting it. The logic behind client approval is that it commits the management team to the body of data and eventually to the information that will result from the specific questionnaire design. This step helps reduce unnecessary surprises and saves time and money. If fundamental changes (major or minor) are deemed necessary, this is where they should occur. The researcher must make sure that any changes adhere to the design requirements.

Step 9: Pretest and Revise the Questionnaire

While fine-tuning of the questionnaire can take place via discussions between the researcher and client, the final evaluation should come from people representing the individuals who will be asked to actually fill out the survey. Remember, pretesting the questionnaire does not mean that one researcher administers the questionnaire to another researcher, or to the client's management or staff. Furthermore, it does not mean that the pretest is done with college students unless they are representative of the study's target population.

An appropriate pretest involves a simulated administration of the survey to a small, representative group of respondents. How many respondents should be included in a pretest is open to debate. Some researchers will use as few as 5 respondents, while others might use as many as 50 depending on the purpose of the pretest, the method of administering the survey, and how the survey was developed. For example, if the questions were not properly tested for reliability and validity in step 5, then the pretest should include at least 50 respondents so that the researcher can run the proper statistical testing procedures on the data structures to address reliability and validity issues.[11] In contrast, if the main purpose of the pretest is to check for specific wording problems, then only about 10 respondents are needed in the pretest.[12] Normally in a pretest, the respondents are asked to pay attention to such elements as words, phrases, instructions, question flow patterns and point out anything they feel is confusing, difficult to understand, or otherwise a problem.

When using the flowerpot approach, the researcher should find no reliability/validity or wording issues at this point, since those issues would have been addressed back in steps 4 and 5. Rather, the pretest should help the researcher determine how much time respondents will need to complete the survey, whether to add any instructions, and what to say in the cover letter. If any problems or concerns arise in the pretest, modifications must be made and approved by the client prior to moving to the next step. In the American Bank study, the pretest, administered to 25 randomly selected bank customers, revealed no surprises.

Step 10: Finalize the Questionnaire Format

In this step, the questionnaire is placed in final format. Decisions are made about typing instructions, spacing, numbers for questions and pages, folding, and stapling—all of which relate to the professional appearance of the questionnaire. Quality in appearance is more important in self-administered surveys than in personal or telephone interview documents. Duplication considerations would also come in this step. Any support materials—such as interviewer instructions, cover letters, rating cards, mailing and return envelopes—are finalized and reproduced for distribution. Support materials are discussed in Chapter 15.

Another set of decisions relates to the precoding of the response categories used to represent the scaling points. Precoding is discussed in Chapter 15. In the American Bank study, the questionnaire was formatted as a four-page booklet with a separate cover letter and a self-addressed, stamped return envelope. (See Exhibit 1 in the Marketing Research Illustration at the end of this chapter for the cover letter used by American Bank.)

Step 11: Implement the Survey

This last step really has nothing to do with the actual design process of the questionnaire. Its purpose is to bring closure to the development process. This step indicates the processes that must be followed to begin the collection of the required raw data. These will vary according to the data collection method. Review Chapter 9 for the different activities associated with personal and telephone interviews and self-administered surveys; additional discussions on administering surveys are provided in Chapter 15.

Although the American Bank example does illustrate how the flowerpot approach plays an important and useful role in the development process of survey instruments, no one study can exemplify all of the numerous factors researchers and practitioners must consider when designing a scientific questionnaire. We offer a general summary of the major considerations in questionnaire designs in Exhibit 14.7. Today's firms are also faced

---

EXHIBIT 14.7   **Summary of Important Considerations in Questionnaire Designs**

1. Determine the information objectives and the number of information flowerpots required to meet those objectives.

2. Determine the specific data requirements (i.e., the size) for each information flowerpot, and stack the pots from largest to smallest.

3. Introduction section should include a general description of what the study is pertaining to; this may well be in a disguised format.

4. All types of instructions, if necessary, should be given clear expression.

5. Perhaps most important, the question/scale measurements have to follow some logical order—that is, an order that appears logical to the respondent rather than to the researcher or practitioner.

6. Begin an interview or questionnaire with simple questions that are easy to respond to, and then gradually lead up to the more difficult questions. Create a general-to-specific data flow.

7. Postpone highly personal questions (state-of-being data) until late in the interview or survey (i.e., place in the base after the last information flowerpot).

8. Place questions that involve psychological tests (i.e., lifestyle beliefs) toward the end of the interview or survey, but before the identification base.

9. Do not ask too many questions of the same measurement format (i.e., nominal, ordinal, interval, ratio scale formats) in sequence.

10. Taper off an interview or survey with a few relatively simple questions that do not require extensive thoughts or expressions of feelings (i.e., the demographic data questions are very appropriate here).

11. Always end the interview or survey with the appropriate thank-you statement.

GLOBAL INSIGHTS · VOTRE OPINION EN 30 SECONDES (30 SECONDS FOR YOUR OPINION)

Mark X in the appropriate oval. (X) Cochez d'une croix la résponse appropriée.

Sexe/Gender: Masculin/Male ( )   Féminin/Female ( )

Motif du séjour/Purpose of Visit:

Affaires/Business ( )   Loisir/Pleasure ( )   Séminaires/Conference ( )   Voyage de groupe/Group ( )

Durée du séjour/Length of Stay:

1 nuit/1 night ( )   de 2 à 4 nuits/2 to 4 nights ( )   5 nuits ou plus/5 or more nights ( )

Combien de nuits avez-vous passé à l'hôtel au cours de l'année passée?
How many nights have you spent in a hotel over the past year?

1–10 ( )   11–25 ( )   26–50 ( )   50+ ( )

Niveau de Satisfaction/Level of Satisfaction	Faible Low		Moyen Average		Élevé High
Fonctionnement du chauffage/de la climatisation Operation of heating/air conditioning	( )	( )	( )	( )	( )
État général de l'hôtel Overall physical condition of this hotel	( )	( )	( )	( )	( )
Qualité du service au moment du départ (gentillesse) Service received at check-out (friendly)	( )	( )	( )	( )	( )
Qualité du service détage Quality of room service	( )	( )	( )	( )	( )
Rapport qualité/prix Value received for price paid	( )	( )	( )	( )	( )
Niveau de satisfaction gén'rate de l'hôtel Overall satisfaction with this hotel	( )	( )	( )	( )	( )

Veuillez nous faire part de tout autre commentaire/Please share any additional comments:

_____
_____
_____

Date/Date:_____   **Numéro de chambre/Room number:**_____

with new challenges as they expand into global markets. One question they must address is whether the research techniques they used in their own country can be directly applied in foreign countries. See the Global Insights box, which provides an example of a customer survey the Holiday Inn Resort Saint Laurent-du-Var in France's Côte d'Azur uses to gain customer satisfaction information from its international and local guests. Beyond the obvious bilingual characteristic of the survey, evaluate the survey's design. Is this a good or bad questionnaire? Why or Why not? What potential information problems (if any) might this questionnaire design create for the Holiday Inn Resort's management team? How would you design the survey instrument? Conclude your assessment by discussing the environmental (or country-of-origin) factors that might affect this instrument for collecting data from American, French, and German hotel guests.

Development of Cover Letters

The Role of a Cover Letter

Cover letter A separate written communication to a prospective respondent designed to enhance that person's willingness to complete and return the survey in a timely manner.

A critical aspect associated with good questionnaire design is the development of an appropriate cover letter. Many marketing research textbooks tend to offer little to no discussion of cover letter development. Normally, a **cover letter,** or letter of introduction, is restrictively viewed as a letter accompanying a self-administered questionnaire (e.g., direct mail survey) that serves to explain the nature of the survey. With personal or telephone interviews, researchers might not think to use a cover letter. However, cover letters play several important roles in the successful collection of primary raw data, regardless of the data collection method. A cover letter is not the same as the introductory section on the actual questionnaire, nor is it the same as a screener.

The main role of the cover letter should be that of winning over the respondent's cooperation and willingness to participate in the research project. In other words, the cover letter should help persuade a prospective respondent either to fill out the questionnaire and return it in a timely fashion or to participate in the current interview. With self-administered surveys, many times a research project falls short of its goal because the response rate (i.e., the number of completed surveys compared to the number of surveys administered) ends up very low (e.g., 25 percent). Usually when the response rate is low, the researcher can only guess at why. When either telephone or personal interviewing, similar problems occur when large numbers of prospective respondents decline to participate.

Secondary roles of a cover letter include (*a*) introducing the respondent to the research project and the researcher, (*b*) informing the respondent of the importance of the study, and (*c*) communicating the study's legitimacy and other particulars such as the deadline for returning the completed survey, and where to return it.[13]

Having a standardized cover letter that will fit all survey or interviewing situations is highly unlikely, but there are several factors that should be included in any cover letter, as well as an appropriate order of inclusion. Exhibit 14.8 presents guidelines for developing cover letters; each of these is discussed in the next section.

Guidelines for Developing Cover Letters

Regardless of a research project's chosen method of data collection, the researcher should include a well-developed cover letter that directly pertains to the survey instrument. For self-administered questionnaires, a separate cover letter should be sent with the questionnaire. For most telephone surveys and some types of personal interviews, a cover letter should be mailed to each prospective respondent prior to the initial contact by the interviewer.

Although the prior mailing of cover letters in interviewing situations is not a common practice among researchers, this procedure can definitely help increase the prospective respondent's willingness to participate.[14] The reason for this comes from an understanding of human behavior. For example, the prospective respondent and interviewer are normally strangers to one another. People are more hesitant to express their opinions or feelings about a topic to a stranger than to someone they know, even to a limited extent. Mailing a cover letter to prospective respondents enables the researcher to break the ice prior to the actual interview.

The cover letter should introduce the potential respondent to the research project, stress its legitimacy, encourage participation, and let the respondent know that a representative (i.e., interviewer) will be contacting him or her in the near future. Using a cover letter in interviewing situations does increase the initial cost of data collection, but the resulting increase in the response rate can reduce the overall cost of the project.

EXHIBIT 14.8	Guidelines for Developing Cover Letters

Factors	Description
1. Personalization	Cover letter should be addressed to the specific prospective respondent; use researching firm's professional letterhead stationery.
2. Identification of the organization doing the study	Clear identification of the name of the research firm conducting the survey or interview; decide on disguised or undisguised approach of revealing the actual client (or sponsor) of the study.
3. Clear statement of the study's purpose and importance	Describe the general topic of the research and emphasize its importance to the prospective respondent.
4. Anonymity and confidentiality	Give assurances that the prospective respondent's name will not be revealed. Explain how the respondent was chosen, and stress that his or her meaningful input is important to the study's success.
5. General time frame of doing the study	Communicate the overall time frame of the survey or interview.
6. Reinforcement of the importance of the respondent's participation	Where appropriate, communicate the importance of prospective respondents' participation.
7. Acknowledgment of reasons for nonparticipation in survey or interview	Point out "lack of leisure time," "surveys classified as junk mail," and "forgetting about survey" reasons for not participating, and defuse them.
8. Time requirements and compensations	Clearly communicate the approximate time required to complete the survey; discuss incentive program, if any.
9. Completion date and where and how to return the survey	Communicate to the prospective respondent all instructions for returning the completed questionnaire.
10. Advance thank-you statement for willingness to participate	Thank the prospective respondent for his or her cooperation.

While the exact wording of a cover letter will vary from researcher to researcher and from situation to situation, any cover letter should include as many of the factors displayed in Exhibit 14.8 as possible.

Factor 1: Personalization

Whenever possible, the cover letter should be addressed to the particular person who was randomly selected as a prospective respondent. The cover letter should be typed on professional letterhead that represents the researching organization's affiliation, not the client's.

Factor 2: Identification of the Organization Doing the Study

The first comments should identify the research company that is conducting the survey but not necessarily the sponsor or client. If the sponsor wants or needs to be identified, then the researcher can choose one of two options: an undisguised or a disguised approach. With an undisguised approach, the actual sponsor's name will appear as part of the introduction statement. For example, the opening statement might read as follows:

We at the Nationwide Opinion Research Company here in New York are conducting an interesting study on people's banking practices for Citibank.

In contrast, a disguised approach would not divulge the sponsor's identity to the respondent and would appear like this:

> We at the Nationwide Opinion Company here in New York are conducting an interesting study on people's banking habits and would like to include your opinions.

Which sponsorship approach to use will be determined by the overall research objectives or a mutual agreement between the researcher and client regarding the possible benefits and drawbacks of revealing the sponsor's name to the respondent. One reason for going with a disguised approach is that it prevents competitors from finding out about the survey.[15]

Factor 3: Clear Statement of the Study's Purpose and Importance

One or two statements must be included in any cover letter to describe the general nature or topic of the survey and emphasize its importance. In the American Bank survey example discussed earlier, the researcher might use the following statements:

> Consumer banking practices are rapidly changing in the 1990s. With more bank locations, many new bank services, new technologies, the growth of credit unions and savings and loans, and the increased complexity of people's financial needs and wants, financial institutions are indeed changing. These changes are having important effects on you and your family. We would like to gain insights into these changes and their impact from the consumer's perspective by better understanding your opinions about different banking services, habits, and patterns.
>
> We think you will find the survey interesting.

When stating the purpose of the survey, it is important that you introduce the general topic of the survey in an interesting manner using words that are familiar to most members of the target audience. The purpose statement should be followed by a statement that conveys the importance of the respondent's opinions on the topic. Some researchers like to follow up the purpose by adding a disclaimer that strongly emphasizes that (1) the company is not trying to sell anything and (2) the respondent's name will not be added to any type of mailing list.

Factor 4: Anonymity and Confidentiality

After describing the purpose of the survey, the researcher must let the respondent know how and why people were selected for the study. The researcher can use a statement like this:

> Your name was one of only 2,000 names randomly selected from a representative list of people living in the Baton Rouge community. Because the success of the survey depends upon the cooperation of all people who were selected, we would especially appreciate your willingness to help.

The phrasing should emphasize the importance of the respondent's participation to the success of the study and indirectly suggest that the respondent is special.

Anonymity The assurance that survey respondents will in no way be matched to their responses.

If the researcher and client decide that assurances about anonymity and confidentiality are necessary, those factors should be incorporated at this point. **Anonymity** simply relates to the assurance that the prospective respondent's name or any identifiable designation will not be associated with his or her responses. Among the different data collection methods, anonymity statements are most appropriately associated with self-administered questionnaires. The researcher might use the following as an anonymity statement:

> The information obtained from the survey will in no way reflect the identities of the people participating in the study.

When using an interview to collect raw data, an anonymity statement can appear in the letter of introduction that is mailed prior to the interviewer's initial contact with a prospective respondent.

Confidentiality The assurance that the respondent's identity will not be divulged to a third party, including the client of the research.

A statement of **confidentiality** assures to the prospective respondent that his or her name, while known to the researcher, will not be divulged to a third party, especially the client. Regardless of the data collection method, a confidentiality statement should always be included in a cover letter. A confidentiality statement might be phrased as follows:

> Your cooperation, attitudes, and opinions are very important to the success of the study and will be kept strictly confidential. Your opinions and responses will only be used when grouped with those of the other people participating in the survey.

Once the prospective respondent is promised confidentiality, it is the researcher's responsibility to keep that promise.

Factor 5: Time Frame

The cover letter should identify the general time frame for the survey. To encourage a prospective respondent to participate, it should state the actual completion time requirements and any compensation that might be offered. When using an interview, for example, the researcher would include a statement or phrase like the following:

> In the next couple of days, one of our trained representatives will be contacting you by phone . . . The survey will only take a few moments of your time.

The key consideration with this factor is not to use a question format that requires a simple yes or no response. For example, "May I have one of our trained representatives contact you in the next couple of days?" or "May we have a few moments of your time?" If the researcher allows the prospective respondent to answer no to a question asked in the cover letter, he or she is not likely to participate in the study.

Factor 6: Reinforcement of the Importance of the Respondent's Participation

The researcher can incorporate simple phrases into any part of the cover letter to reinforce the point that the respondent's participation is critical to the success of the study. Such phrases should be worded positively, not negatively.

Factor 7: Acknowledgment of Reasons for Not Participating in the Study

There are numerous reasons people use when declining the role of being a respondent in a survey. Numerous focus group interviews over a 10-year period among a variety of different groups of people show that three of the most common reasons for not participating in a survey are (1) not having enough time, (2) seeing surveys as junk mail, and (3) forgetting about the survey.

First, people treasure their leisure time and feel they do not have enough of it. Therefore, when they receive a survey or telephone call or are asked on the spot to answer a few questions, potential respondents tend to use "do not have the time" as a reason not to participate. Since, as we mentioned before, people are more likely to take the time to answer questions from someone they know, or are at least aware of, than from a stranger, the researcher has to acknowledge the time factor in the cover letter. To do this, a researcher should use a statement like this:

> We realize that to most of us in the community our leisure time is scarce and important and that we do not like to spend it filling out a questionnaire for some unknown person's or organization's study. Please remember that you are among a few being asked to participate in this study and your opinions are very important to the success of it.

This type of statement can easily be combined with statements about time requirements and compensation to effectively negate the time objection.

Second, many people have the tendency to classify surveys received through the mail as "junk mail" or a telephone interviewer's call as an attempt to sell them something they do not need nor want. To acknowledge this, something like the following statement could be used:

> We realize that many of us in the community receive a lot of things through the mail for which we classify as "junk mail" and not important to respond to, but please do not consider the attached survey as being "junk mail." Your opinions, attitudes, and viewpoints toward each question are very important to us and the success of this study.

And for interviews, the researcher should incorporate a statement like the following:

> We realize that many of us in the community receive a lot of phone calls from strangers trying to sell us some product or service that we neither need nor want. Let me assure you that I am not trying to sell you anything. I would just like to get your honest opinions on several questions pertaining to your banking habits and preferences; they are important to the success of this study.

Third, the issue of forgetting the survey primarily relates to direct mail surveys. To help eliminate this problem, the researcher should incorporate a statement in the cover letter something like this:

> Past research has suggested that many questionnaires received through the mail, if not completed and returned within the first 36 hours, have a tendency to get misplaced or forgotten about. Upon receiving this survey, please take the time to complete it. Your opinions are very important to us.

By taking away these three main reasons for not participating in a research study, the researcher significantly improves the likelihood that the prospective respondent will complete and return the direct mail survey or cooperate in a telephone interview.

Factor 8: Time Requirements and Compensation

In an effort to win over a prospective respondent, the researcher might emphasize in the cover letter that the survey will not take much time or effort. For a self-administered survey, the researcher can incorporate statements like the following:

> We have designed the questionnaire to include all the directions and instructions necessary to complete the survey without the assistance of an interviewer. The survey will take approximately 15 minutes to complete. Please take your time in responding to each question. Your honest responses are very important to the success of the study.

For interviews, the researcher could incorporate the following statement into the letter of introduction: "The interview will take approximately 15 minutes to complete." These types of statements reinforce the notion that the survey will not take up much of the person's leisure time.

As we discussed in earlier chapters, the researcher and client might decide that some form of compensation is needed to encourage the respondent's participation. The type of compensation will depend on the study's topic and the data collection method. A token dollar amount (e.g., $1 or $5) can be offered to each prospective respondent and included in the questionnaire packet. The idea is that giving respondents a reward up front for participating will make them feel obligated to complete the survey and return it as requested.[16] Experience with this method, however, suggests that people tend to assign a higher price than $1 or even $5 to their leisure time. In other situations, nonmonetary incentives (e.g., a

Lottery approach The pooling of individual incentive offerings into a significantly larger offering for which those people who participate have an equal chance of receiving the incentive.

sample product, tickets to a movie, a certificate redeemable for specific products or services) might be used to encourage a respondent's participation.

An alternative to the individual reward system is the **lottery approach,** in which the incentive money forms a significantly larger dollar amount and everyone who completes and returns the survey has an equal chance of receiving the incentive. A significant reward is most likely to increase the response rate. The lottery approach is not, however, restricted to direct monetary rewards. Alternative rewards might be the chance to win an expense-paid trip somewhere. For example, the JP Hotel Corporation has used a "three-day, two-night all-expenses-paid weekend stay for two people" at one of its luxury hotel complexes as the incentive for respondents who completed and returned their questionnaire by the specified date.

Among the different incentive programs available to the researcher, the lottery incentive system is advocated whenever possible. When a lottery is used, extra effort is required by the researcher to develop and include a **separate** identification form in the questionnaire packet that can be filled out and returned with a respondent's completed questionnaire. This incentive system tends to be most appropriate for self-administered surveys. Comments concerning incentives in a cover letter might be phrased, for example, as follows:

> To show, in part, our appreciation for your taking the time to participate in this study, we are going to hold a drawing for $500 among those of you who donate some of your leisure time to help us in completing this survey. The drawing procedure has been designed in such a way that everyone who completes and returns the questionnaire will have an equal opportunity to receive the appreciation gift of $500.

Factor 9: Completion Date and Where and How to Return the Survey

At the end of the cover letter, the researcher must give the respondent instructions for how, where, and when to return their completed survey. The *how* and *where* instructions can be simply expressed through the following type of statement:

> After completing all the questions in the survey, please use the enclosed stamped, addressed envelope to return your completed survey and appreciation gift card.

To deal with the return deadline date, the researcher should include a statement like this:

> To help us complete the study in a timely fashion, we need your cooperation in returning the completed questionnaire and incentive drawing card by **no later than Friday, June 25, 1999.**

Factor 10: Advance Thanks

Prior to closing the cover letter with a thank-you statement, the researcher might want to include a final reassurance that she or he is not trying to sell the prospective respondent anything. In addition, legitimacy can be reinforced by supplying a name and telephone number if there are any concerns or questions, as follows:

> Again, let me give you my personal guarantee that we are not trying to sell you something. If you have any doubts, concerns, or questions about this survey, please give me a call at (504) 974-6236. Thank you in advance; we deeply appreciate your cooperation in taking part in our study.

The researcher should sign the cover letter and include his or her title.

As you can see, a good cover letter or letter of introduction entails as much thought, care, and effort as the questionnaire itself. While the actual factors will vary from researcher to researcher, these 10 are standard elements of any good cover letter. The specific examples given above should not be viewed as standardized phrases that must be included in all cover letters, but they do show how a researcher might increase a prospective respondent's will-

A CLOSER LOOK AT RESEARCH   **In the Field**

MARKETING RESOURCES GROUP
2305 Windsor Oaks Drive, Suite 1105
Baton Rouge, Louisiana 70814

CONSUMER BANKING OPINION STUDY
BATON ROUGE, LOUISIANA

If you have a bank account—

We need your opinion.

With more bank locations, new banking services, and the growth of credit unions and savings and loans, financial institutions are indeed changing. These changes will have an effect on you and your family, and that's why your opinion is important.

Your name has been selected in a sample of Baton Rouge residents to determine what people in our community think about the present products and services offered by banks. Your individual opinions in this survey can never be traced back to you, and all results will be held strictly confidential. The results of the study will provide the banking industry with insight into how to better serve the needs of its customers.

The brand-new quarter enclosed with this letter is not enough to compensate you for your time, but it may brighten the day of a youngster you know.

Thank you for your assistance.

Sincerely,

Thomas L. Kirk
MRG Project Director

P.S. Please return no later than June, 25, 1999. A postage-paid envelope is enclosed.

ingness to participate in a given study. To see how these factors fit together in a cover letter, see Exhibit 1 of the Marketing Research Illustration at the end of this chapter.

A rarely discussed design question that directly affects the development of cover letters is, How long should the cover letter be? There is no simple answer that is correct in all situations, and in fact there are two opposing views. First, many researchers believe that the cover letter should be simple, direct to the point, and no longer than one page. The In the Field box illustrates a hypothetical cover letter for the American Bank and Trust survey that follows the direct, one-page approach.

While the one-page cover letter includes some of the factors we have discussed for influencing a prospective respondent's willingness to participate, it tends to lack the intensity level and clarity needed to win over a stranger. Still, many researchers tend to go with a one-page design because of cost factor and because they believe that people do not like to read correspondence from unknown commercial organizations like a research company. It is true that it costs less to develop, reproduce and mail a one-page cover letter than a multiple-page letter, but if the one-page cover letter does not produce an adequate response rate, the study will cost more in the long run. The notion that people do not like to

ETHICS

Telephone Survey Goes Sour

In the spring of 1999, the Quality A-1 Rainbow Rug Cleaners, a new franchised carpet cleaning business, began operations in San Diego, California. This company was a member of San Diego's chamber of commerce. The owners of this franchised carpet cleaning business were struggling to get customers. They turned to a telemarketing firm for help. After several conversations with the telemarketing experts, a joint decision was made to use a disguised approach to solicit prospective customers by phone. The telemarketing firm developed what it called a telephone survey that would capture the necessary information to identify people in need of carpet cleaning services. Upon determining the need, the survey was designed for the telephone interviewer to activate the customized sales pitch for Quality A-1 Rainbow Rug Cleaners' services. The survey started out by informing prospective respondents that they were randomly selected to participate in a short survey about cleaning products. Once it was determined that the individual qualified, the survey transformed into a sales pitch, telling the qualified prospective customers that Quality A-1 Rainbow Rug Cleaners would be in their neighborhood that week and asking when would they like to schedule an appointment. Those unsuspecting respondents who agreed were scheduled on the spot by the telemarketing interviewer. The telemarketing firm convinced the owners that the survey process should run for one month at a cost of $4,000. Two weeks into the project, Quality A-1 Rainbow's owners received a call from San Diego's chamber of commerce notifying them that it had received about 100 calls from residents complaining about unwanted sales solicitations for Quality A-1 Rainbow's carpet cleaning services. Identify the ethical problems Quality A-1 Rainbow Rugs created for itself through their research program. How might the cleaning company have avoided those problems?

read correspondence from unknown commercial senders is basically true and, as we discussed earlier, is one of the reasons people use to justify not participating in a survey.

The contrasting view focuses on the need to deliver an emotion-laden story that compels the prospective respondent to cooperate. If a cover letter is well crafted and interesting, the prospective respondent will not only read the first page but the complete cover letter and move on to the questionnaire.

As always, the researcher should keep in mind the importance of ethical behavior. The Ethics box discusses a carpet cleaning company's misuse of a telephone survey to gain new sales.

SUMMARY OF LEARNING OBJECTIVES

Identify and discuss the critical factors that can contribute to directly improving the accuracy of surveys, and explain why questionnaire development is not a simple process.

Questionnaire development is much more than just writing a set of questions and asking people to answer them. Designing good surveys goes beyond just developing reliable and valid scale measurements. There are a number of design factors, systematic procedural steps, and rules of logic that must be considered in the development process. In addition, the process requires knowledge of sampling plans, construct development, scale measurement, and types of data. It is important to remember that a questionnaire is a set of questions/scales designed to generate enough raw data to allow the researcher and decision maker to generate information to solve the business problem.

Discuss the theoretical principles of questionnaire design, and explain why a questionnaire is more than just asking a respondent some questions.

Many researchers, unaware of the underlying theory, still believe that questionnaire designing is an art rather than a science. Questionnaires are, however, hierarchical structures consisting of four different components: words, questions, formats, and hypotheses. Most surveys are descriptive instruments that rely heavily on the collection of state-of-being or state-of-behavior data; others are predictive instruments that focus on collecting state-of-mind and state-of-intention data that allow for predicting changes in people's attitudes and behaviors as well as testing hypotheses.

Identify and explain the communication roles of questionnaires in the data collection process.

Good questionnaires allow researchers to gain a true report of the respondent's attitudes, preferences, beliefs, feelings, behavioral intentions, and actions/reactions in a holistic manner, not just a fragment. Through carefully worded questions and clear instructions, a researcher has the ability to control a respondent's thoughts and ensure objectivity. By understanding good communication principles, researchers can avoid bad questioning procedures that might result in either incomprehensible information requests, unanswerable questions, or leading questions that obscure, prohibit, or distort the meaning of a person's responses.

Explain why the type of information needed to address a decision maker's questions and problems will substantially influence the structure and content of questionnaires.

Once research objectives are transformed into information objectives, determining the specific information requirements plays a critical role in the development of questionnaires. For each information objective, the researcher must be able to determine the types of raw data (state of being, mind, behavior, or intentions); types of question/scale measurement formats (nominal, ordinal, interval, or ratio); types of question structures (open-ended and closed-ended); and the appropriate selection of scale point descriptors. Researchers must be aware of the impact that different data collection methods (personal, telephone, self-administered, computer-assisted, etc.) have on the wording of both questions and response choices.

List and discuss the 11 steps in the questionnaire development process, and tell how to eliminate some common mistakes in questionnaire designs.

Using their knowledge of construct development and scale measurement development (Chapter 12) and attitude measurement (Chapter 13), researchers can follow an 11-step process to develop scientific survey instruments. Refer back to Exhibit 14.4 (on p. 446), which lists these steps.

Discuss and employ the flowerpot approach in developing scientific questionnaires.

The flowerpot approach serves as a unique framework or blueprint for integrating different sets of questions and scale measurements into a scientific structure for collecting high-quality raw data. This ordered approach helps researchers make critical decisions regarding (1) construct development, (2) the appropriate dimensions and attributes of objects, (3) question/scale measurement formats, (4) wording of actual questions and directives, and (5) scale points and descriptors. Following the flowerpot approach assures that the data flow will correctly go from a general information level down to a more specific level.

Discuss the importance of cover letters, and explain the guidelines to help eliminate common mistakes in cover letter designs.

While the main role of any cover letter should be that of winning over a prospective respondent, a set of secondary roles ranges from initial introduction with a person to communicating the legitimacy and other important factors about the study. There are 10 critical factors that should be included in most, if not all, cover letters. Including these will help the researcher counteract the three major reasons that prospective respondents use to avoid participating in self-administered survey and personal interviews. A lottery-based incentive or compensation system can significantly improve a prospective respondent's willingness to participate.

KEY TERMS AND CONCEPTS

Anonymity 459

Bad questions 442

Confidentiality 460

Cover letter 457

Flowerpot approach 446

Hypothesis 443

Lottery approach 462

Questionnaire 440

Structured questions 441

Unstructured questions 441

REVIEW QUESTIONS

1. Discuss the advantages and disadvantages of using unstructured (open-ended) and structured (closed-ended) questions in developing a direct mail survey instrument.

2. Explain the role of a questionnaire in the information research process. What should be the role of the client during the questionnaire development process?

3. Identify and discuss the guidelines available for deciding the form and layout of a questionnaire. Discuss the advantages and disadvantages of using the flowerpot approach in developing survey instruments.

4. What are the factors that constitute bad questions in questionnaire design? Develop three examples of bad questions. Then, using the information in Exhibit 14.6, rewrite your examples so they could be judged as good questions.

5. Discuss the value of a good questionnaire design. Discuss the main benefits of including a brief introductory section in questionnaires. Unless needed for screening purposes, why shouldn't classification questions be presented up front in most questionnaire designs?

6. Discuss the critical issues involved in pretesting a questionnaire.

DISCUSSION QUESTIONS

1. Identify and discuss the guidelines for developing cover letters for a survey research instrument. What are some of the advantages of developing good cover letters? What are some of the costs of a bad cover letter?

2. Using the five specific questions that should be asked in evaluating any questionnaire design (see p. 453–54), evaluate the American Bank and Trust questionnaire at the end of this chapter. Write a one-page assessment report.

3. **EXPERIENCE THE INTERNET.** Using any browser of your choice, go to www.open text.com and type in the search phrase *questionnaire design*. Browse the various listings until you find a questionnaire of your liking. Evaluate the extent to which your selected questionnaire follows the flowerpot approach and write a two-page summary of your findings. (Make sure you include in your report the exact Web site address used for reaching your selected questionnaire.)

4. **EXPERIENCE THE INTERNET.** Get on the Net and go to Visual Research's Web site at www.vrcinc.com. Browse through the site and evaluate the various new technologies being offered for conducting surveys via the Internet. Write a one-page summary that focuses on the advantages and disadvantages associated with collecting survey data through the Internet.

ENDNOTES

1. These characteristics are known as the cornerstones for conducting scientific inquiries into many different types of marketing phenomena. An excellent overview can be obtained by reading Stanley L. Payne's classic book *The Art of Asking Questions* (Princeton, NJ: Princeton University Press, 1951). Also see Patricia J. Labaw, *Advanced Questionnaire Design,* 2nd ed. (Cambridge, MA: Abt Books, 1982).

2. Payne, *The Art of Asking Questions,* pp. 8–9.

3. Labaw, *Advanced Questionnaire Design,* pp. 5–6; also see Seymour Sudman and Norman Bradburn, *Asking Questions* (San Francisco: Jossey-Bass, 1983); and Maria Elena Sanchez, "Effects of Questionnaire Design on the Quality of Survey Data," *Public Opinion Quarterly* 56 (1992), pp. 206–17.

4. Pamela L. Alreck and Robert B. Settle, *The Survey Research Handbook* (Burr Ridge, IL: Irwin/McGraw-Hill, 1985), pp. 120–22.

5. Labaw, *Advanced Questionnaire Design,* p. 9.

6. Ibid., p. 17.

7. James H. Barns and Michael J. Dotson, "The Effects of Mixed Grammar Chains on Response to Survey Questions," *Journal of Marketing Research* 26, no. 4 (November 1989), pp. 468–72; and Labaw, *Advanced Questionnaire Design,* p. 18; also see Sanchez, "Effects of Questionnaire Design on the Quality of Survey Data."

8. Alreck and Settle, *The Survey Research Handbook,* pp. 97–100; and Labaw, *Advanced Questionnaire Design,* p. 34.

9. Susan Carroll, "Questionnaire's Design Affects Response Rate," *Marketing News* 28 (January 3, 1994), pp. 14, 23; and Paul Hayne, "Good and Bad in Questionnaire Design," *Industrial Marketing Digest* 12 (3rd Quarter 1987), pp. 161–70.

10. The flowerpot design approach is a symbolic model developed in 1974 by David J. Ortinau while teaching at Illinois State University.

11. Shelby D. Hunt, Richard D. Sparkman, Jr., and James Wilcox, "The Pretest in Survey Research: Issues and Preliminary Findings," *Journal of Marketing Research* 19, no. 2 (May 1982), pp. 269–73.

12. A. Diamantopoula, B. B. Schlegelmilch, and N. Reynolds, "Pretesting in Questionnaire Design: The Impact of Respondent Characteristics on Error Detection," *Journal of Marketing Research Society* 35 (April 1994), pp. 295–314.

13. Michael J. Houston and John R. Nevin, "The Effects of Source and Appeal on Mail Survey Response Patterns," *Journal of Marketing Research* 14, no. 3 (August 1977), pp. 374–78.

14. Ibid., p. 376.

15. Jim L. Finlay and Fazal J. Seyyed, "The Impact of Sponsorship and Respondent Attitudes on Response Rate to Telephone Surveys: An Exploratory Investigation," in *Proceedings of the Atlantic Marketing Association,* ed. D. L. Moore (1988), pp. 715–21.

16. H. H. Friedman, "The Effects of a Monetary Incentive and the Ethnicity of the Sponsor's Signature on the Rate and Quality of Response to a Mall Survey," *Journal of the Academy of Marketing Science* (1979), pp. 95–100; also see Raymond Hubbard and Eldon L. Little, "Cash Prizes and Mail Response Rates: A Threshold Analysis," *Journal of the Academy of Marketing Science* (Fall 1988), pp. 42–44.

MARKETING RESEARCH ILLUSTRATION

DESIGNING A QUESTIONNAIRE TO ASSESS CONSUMERS' BANKING HABITS

This illustration extends the chapter discussions on questionnaire development via the flowerpot approach. Using the American Bank and Trust example from the chapter, the cover letter (Exhibit 1) and questionnaire (Exhibit 2) represent the actual instruments developed for the American Bank and Trust marketing management team to collect the primary raw data needed to address its initial research problems. The numbers in the letter refer to the guidelines listed in Exhibit 14.8 in the chapter. The questionnaire was designed so that data entry could be achieved through the use of optical scanning techniques.

| EXHIBIT 1 | Cover Letter Used with the American Bank Survey |

MARKETING RESOURCES GROUP
2305 Windsor Oaks Drive, Suite 1105
Baton Rouge, Louisiana 70814

June 10, 1999

[1]
Ms. Caroline V. Livingstone
873 Patterson Drive
Baton Rouge LA 70801

Dear Ms. Livingstone:

[2]We at Marketing Resources Group here in Baton Rouge are conducting an interesting study this month on people's banking habits and services **[5]**this month and would like to include your opinions.

[3]As you know, consumer banking practices are rapidly changing in the 1990s. With more bank locations, many new bank services, new technologies, the growth of credit unions and savings and loans, and the increased complexity of people's financial needs and wants, financial institutions are indeed changing. These changes are having important effects on you and your family. We would like to gain insights into these changes and their impact from the consumer's perspective by better understanding your opinions about different banking services, habits, and patterns.

We think you will find the survey interesting.

[4]Your name was one of only 600 names randomly selected from a representative list of people currently living in the Baton Rouge community. **[6]**Because the success of the survey depends upon the cooperation of all the people who were selected, we would especially appreciate your willingness to help us in this study.

[4]The information obtained from the survey will in no way reflect the identities of the people participating. Your cooperation, attitudes, and opinions are very important to the success of the study and will be kept strictly confidential. Your response will only be used when grouped with those of the other people taking part in the study.

[7]We realize that many of us in the community receive a lot of things through the mail for which we classify as "junk mail" and not important to respond to, but please do not consider the attached survey as being "junk mail." **[6]**Your opinions, attitudes and viewpoints toward each question are very important to us.

[7]To most of us in the community our leisure time is scarce and important, and we do not like to spend it filling out a questionnaire for some unknown organization's survey. Please remember that you are among a few being asked to participate in this study and **[6]**your opinions are very important to the success of it. **[8]**We have designed the questionnaire to include all the directions and instructions necessary to complete the survey without the assistance of an interviewer. You will find that the survey will only take about 15 minutes of your time. Please take your time in responding to each question. **[6]**Your honest responses are what we are looking for in the study.

[8]To show, in part, our appreciation for your taking the time to participate in this important study, we are going to hold a drawing for $500 among those of you who donate some of your leisure time to help us in completing this survey. The drawing procedure has been designed in such a way that everyone who completes and returns the questionnaire will have an equal opportunity to receive the appreciation gift of $500.

[7]Past research has suggested that many questionnaires that are received through the mail, if not completed and returned within the first 36 hours, have a tendency to get misplaced or forgotten about. Upon receiving this survey, please take the time to complete it. **[6]**Your opinions are very important to us.

(continued)

EXHIBIT 1 *(concluded)*

[9]After completing all the questions in this survey, please use the enclosed stamped and addressed envelope to return your completed survey and appreciation gift card. To help us complete the study in a timely fashion, we need your cooperation in returning the survey and gift card by **no later** than **Friday, June 25, 1999.**

Again, let me give you my personal guarantee that we are not trying to sell you something. If you have any doubts, concerns, or questions about this survey, please give me a call at (504) 974-6236.

[10]Thank you in advance, we deeply appreciate your cooperation in taking part in our study.

Sincerely,

Thomas L. Kirk

Thomas L. Kirk
MRG Project Director

EXHIBIT 2 **Consumer Banking Opinion Survey: Baton Rouge, Louisiana**

THANK YOU for your participation in this interesting study. Your participation will aid us in determining what people in our community think about the present products and services offered by banks. The results will provide the banking industry with additional insights on how to better serve the needs of people in the Baton Rouge community. Your attitudes, preferences, and opinions are important to this study; they will be kept strictly confidential.

DIRECTIONS: PLEASE READ EACH QUESTION CAREFULLY. ANSWER THE QUESTION BY FILLING IN THE APPROPRIATE BOX(ES) THAT REPRESENT YOUR RESPONSE OR RESPONSES.

I. GENERAL BANKING HABITS SECTION

1. Which one of the following banks would you consider the one that you use most often in conducting banking or financial transactions? **(PLEASE FILL IN THE ONE APPROPRIATE BOX)**

   ❑ American Bank   ❑ Capital Bank   ❑ Fidelity National Bank
   ❑ Baton Rouge Bank   ❑ City National Bank   ❑ Louisiana National Bank
   ❑ Some other bank; please specify: _____

2a. To what extent were each of the following bank items an important consideration to you in selecting your bank mentioned in Q.1 above? **(PLEASE BE SURE TO FILL IN ONLY ONE RESPONSE FOR EACH BANK ITEM.)**

Bank Items	Definitely an Important Consideration	Somewhat of an Important Consideration	Not at All an Important Consideration
Convenience of location	❑	❑	❑
Banking hours	❑	❑	❑
Good service charges	❑	❑	❑
Interest rates on savings	❑	❑	❑
Personally knew someone at the bank	❑	❑	❑
Bank's reputation	❑	❑	❑
Bank's promotional advertising	❑	❑	❑
Interest rate on loans	❑	❑	❑

(continued)

EXHIBIT 2 *(continued)*

2b. If there was some other reason (or bank item) you deemed important in selecting your bank mentioned in Q.1, please write it in the space below.

3. At which of the following financial institutions do you or some member of your immediate household have a personal savings account? **(PLEASE FILL IN AS MANY OR AS FEW AS ARE NECESSARY.)**

Financial Institutions	Yourself	Some Other Member	Both You and Some Other Member
A credit union	❑	❑	❑
Savings & loan	❑	❑	❑
American Bank	❑	❑	❑
Baton Rouge Bank	❑	❑	❑
Capital Bank	❑	❑	❑
City National Bank	❑	❑	❑
Fidelity National Bank	❑	❑	❑
Louisiana National Bank	❑	❑	❑
Another institution: _____	❑	❑	❑
(Please Specify)			

4. Thinking about the different banking methods which you may or may not use, we would like to know your feeling toward these methods. For each listed banking method, please fill in the appropriate response that best describes your desire for using that method.

Banking Methods	Definitely Like Using (Strong Desire)	Somewhat Like Using (Moderate Desire)	Somewhat Dislike Using (Weak Desire)	Definitely Dislike Using (No Desire)
Inside the bank	❑	❑	❑	❑
Drive-in (Drive-up)	❑	❑	❑	❑
24-hour machine	❑	❑	❑	❑
Bank by phone	❑	❑	❑	❑
Bank by mail	❑	❑	❑	❑
Electronic banking	❑	❑	❑	❑
Third-person banking	❑	❑	❑	❑

5. Now we would like to know to what extent you actually use each of the following banking methods. **(PLEASE FILL IN THE APPROPRIATE RESPONSE FOR EACH LISTED BANKING METHOD.)**

Banking Methods	Usually	Occasionally	Rarely	Never
Inside the bank	❑	❑	❑	❑
Drive-in (Drive-up)	❑	❑	❑	❑
24-hour machine	❑	❑	❑	❑
Bank by phone	❑	❑	❑	❑
Bank by mail	❑	❑	❑	❑
Electronic banking	❑	❑	❑	❑
Third-person banking	❑	❑	❑	❑

6. Thinking about your monthly bank statement, approximately how often do you balance your checkbook with the aid of your statement?

❑ Always (every statement)   ❑ Rarely (once or twice a year)
❑ Occasionally (every 2 or 3 months)   ❑ Never

EXHIBIT 2 *(continued)*

7. Approximately, how many overdrawn charges on your checking account (NSF checks) has your bank imposed on your account in the past year?

❑ None ❑ 1–2 ❑ 3–7 ❑ 8–15 ❑ 16–25 ❑ More than 25

II. GENERAL OPINION SECTION

In this section, there is a list of general opinion statements for which there are no right or wrong answers. As such, the statements may or may not describe you or your feelings.

8. Next to each statement, please fill in the one response box that best expresses the extent to which you agree or disagree with the statement. Remember, there are no right or wrong answers—we just want your opinions.

Statements	Definitely Agree	Generally Agree	Somewhat Agree	Somewhat Disagree	Generally Disagree	Definitely Disagree
I often seek out the advice of my friends regarding a lot of different things.	❑	❑	❑	❑	❑	❑
I buy many things with credit cards.	❑	❑	❑	❑	❑	❑
I wish we had a lot more money.	❑	❑	❑	❑	❑	❑
Security for my family is most important to me.	❑	❑	❑	❑	❑	❑
I am definitely influenced by advertising.	❑	❑	❑	❑	❑	❑
I like to pay cash for everything I buy.	❑	❑	❑	❑	❑	❑
My neighbors or friends often come to me for advice on many different matters.	❑	❑	❑	❑	❑	❑
It is good to have charge accounts.	❑	❑	❑	❑	❑	❑
I will probably have more money to spend next year than I have now.	❑	❑	❑	❑	❑	❑
A person can save a lot of money by shopping around for bargains.	❑	❑	❑	❑	❑	❑
For most products or services, I try the ones that are most popular.	❑	❑	❑	❑	❑	❑
Unexpected situations often catch me without enough money in my pocket.	❑	❑	❑	❑	❑	❑

(continued)

EXHIBIT 2   **(continued)**

Statements	Definitely Agree	Generally Agree	Somewhat Agree	Somewhat Disagree	Generally Disagree	Definitely Disagree
Five years from now, the family income will probably be a lot higher than it is now.	❑	❑	❑	❑	❑	❑
Socially, I see myself more as a blue-collar person rather than a white-collar one.	❑	❑	❑	❑	❑	❑

III. CLASSIFICATION DATA SECTION

Now just a few more questions so that we can combine your responses with those of the other people taking part in this study.

9. Please indicate your gender.   ❑ Female   ❑ Male

10. Please fill in the one response that best approximates how long you have lived in the Baton Rouge area.

    ❑ Less than 1 year   ❑ 4 to 6 years   ❑ 11 to 20 years
    ❑ 1 to 3 years   ❑ 7 to 10 years   ❑ Over 20 years

11. Approximately, how long have you lived at your current address?

    ❑ Less than 1 year   ❑ 4 to 6 years   ❑ 11 to 20 years
    ❑ 1 to 3 years   ❑ 7 to 10 years   ❑ Over 20 years

12. Please indicate your current employment status.

    ❑ Employed full-time   ❑ Employed part-time   ❑ Not currently employed   ❑ Retired

13. Please indicate your current marital status.

    ❑ Married   ❑ Single (widowed, divorced, or separated) ⟶ **PLEASE SKIP TO Q.15**
                     ❑ Single -(never married) ⟶ **PLEASE SKIP TO Q.15**

14. **IF MARRIED**, please indicate your spouse's current employment status.

    ❑ Employed full-time   ❑ Employed part-time   ❑ Not currently employed   ❑ Retired

15. **IF YOU HAVE CHILDREN**, please indicate the number of children under 18 years of age in your household.

    1   2   3   4   5   6   7   8   More than 8; please specify: _____
    ❑   ❑   ❑   ❑   ❑   ❑   ❑   ❑

16. Which one of the following categories best corresponds with your last completed year in school?

    ❑ Some grammar school (1–8 grade)   ❑ Some college or technical school
    ❑ Completed grammar school   ❑ Completed college (4-year degree)
    ❑ Some high school (9–12 grade)   ❑ Graduate studies or degree
    ❑ Completed high school   ❑ Post-graduate studies or advanced degree

17. In which one of the following categories does your current age fall?

    ❑ Under 18   ❑ 26 to 35   ❑ 46 to 55   ❑ 66 to 70
    ❑ 18 to 25   ❑ 36 to 45   ❑ 56 to 65   ❑ Over 70

EXHIBIT 2   *(concluded)*

---

18. What is your occupation; that is, in what kind of work do you spend the major portion of your time?

_____

19. Which one of the following categories best describes the nature of your work?

   ❑ Government (Fed., State, City) ❑ Legal   ❑ Financial   ❑ Insurance
   ❑ Petrochemical   ❑ Manufacturing ❑ Transportation ❑ Consulting
   ❑ Educational   ❑ Medical   ❑ Retailing   ❑ Wholesaling

   ❑ Some other area, please specify: _____

20. Do you consider yourself a non-union or union worker? ❑ Non-union worker ❑ Union worker

21. Into which of the following categories does your total (approximate) family income, before taxes, fall?

   ❑ Under $10,000   ❑ $30,001 to $50,000
   ❑ $10,000 to $15,000   ❑ $75,001 to $100,000
   ❑ $15,001 to $20,000   ❑ $50,001 to $75,000
   ❑ $20,001 to $30,000   ❑ Over $100,000

22. What is your residence address five-digit zip code? ❑ ❑ ❑ ❑ ❑

THANK YOU VERY MUCH FOR PARTICIPATION IN THIS STUDY!
YOUR TIME AND OPINIONS ARE GREATLY AND DEEPLY APPRECIATED.

MARKETING RESEARCH CASE EXERCISE

BUD VERSUS MILLER

Level of Market Penetration among Major Brewers

Among the top three U.S. brewers, market shares are generally in equilibrium. The highly competitive nature of the beer industry, however, means that vendors are continually fighting for market share.

U.S. Beer Market Share by Supplier

Brewer	1997 Market Share	1993 Market Share
Anheuser-Busch	47%	46.9%
Miller	22	23.7
Coors	11	10.7
Others	20	18.7
Total domestic sales:	190.6 million barrels	180.7 million barrels

With regard to beer segments, the light category continues to experience the most growth for domestic beer, while microbrews and craft beers stabilize, and imports gain ground. Data from Information Resources Inc. show that in 1997, four of the top five brands of beer in supermarkets are light. Budweiser was the number one brand, with

$762.2 million in sales, up 1.2 percent, for a 13.6 percent share of the market. Bud Light was number two, with $621.4 million in sales, up 15.2 percent, for an 11 percent share. Miller Lite was number three, with $419 million in sales, up 4.9 percent, for a 7.4 percent share.

Market Segments Served

The segment analysis focuses on the premium and light categories.

Segment Profiles	Premium	Light
Consumer age	21–30	21–30
Sex	Male and some female	More female
Education	At least high school	College educated
Income	Medium	Medium to high
Desired attributes	Taste	Low calories
Degree of knowledge of product	Very high	Low

It is well known that the strongest demographic for beer is males, aged 21 to 34. In fact, in 1997 48 percent of supermarket beer shoppers were between the ages of 21 and 34. This was an increase of 15 percent over 1996.

Customers purchase microbrew and craft beers because they are looking for good quality. If they sample a few different brands and don't feel as though they are getting their money's worth, they are going to turn to another brand that they know will provide them with the quality they are seeking. It would appear the import category provides that comfort for them.

Strengths and Weaknesses of Anheuser-Busch

Strengths

1. **Brand-name recognition.** A strong brand is the key to staking a competitive advantage. Strong brand fosters consumer loyalty. Loyalty creates the opportunity for market share growth and above-average pricing flexibility and profitability. A strong brand also opens the possibility of extending product lines.

2. **Market leader.** Anheuser-Busch has the number one position by a wide margin, selling 70 percent more beer than its nearest rival in 1996. Their success is due to their raw materials procurement, manufacturing efficiency, and marketing.

3. **Solid management team.** They were slow to react (to the Miller price initiatives), but they certainly know the business. A noteworthy factor contributing to the success of Anheuser-Busch has been competent management. Since the time of Adolphus Busch the company has had the good fortune to retain capable men of enterprise.

4. **The industry's strongest wholesaler system.** Approximately 900 independently owned beer wholesalers and 13 company-owned wholesale operations provide Anheuser-Busch with the most extensive and effective beer distribution system in the brewing industry.

5. **Effective marketing campaigns.** Anheuser-Busch has the most effective marketing programs in the industry. In 1998, the company will increase its marketing

spending, especially for the media. Its intent is to continue to build brand equity and generate renewed market share gains.

Weaknesses

1. **Market share was down.** The Miller-created discount environment forced Anheuser-Busch to respond. Anheuser-Busch volumes were affected and, most significantly, in the third quarter of 1997 its market share was down.

2. **Net revenue per barrel in negative.** Beer industry analysts predict that the year 1998 would be a very complicated year, and that major brewer Anheuser-Busch would start off with net revenue per barrel in the negative.

3. **Losing volume.** Budweiser has spent the past decade losing about a quarter of its volume. More alarming for Anheuser-Busch is that the combination of Bud and Bud Light barrelage was less in 1997 than it was in 1990. Most nondemographic growth in the beer industry in the next few years will come from brands stealing share from brands.

Given the data provided, address the following issues:

1. Design a questionnaire that would assess the current level of beer consumption in the United States. Construct this questionnaire as if you were preparing it for Anheuser-Busch.

2. In your questionnaire, be sure to provide questions about the level of competition that may exist for beer products, as well as questions that could assess the true state of strengths and weaknesses facing Anheuser-Busch.

PART IV

Data Preparation
and Analysis

Learning Objectives

After reading this chapter, you will be able to

1. Illustrate the process of preparing data for preliminary analysis.

2. Demonstrate the procedure for assuring data validation.

3. Illustrate the process of editing and coding data obtained through survey methods.

4. Acquaint the user with data entry procedures.

5. Illustrate a process for detecting errors in data entry.

6. Discuss techniques used for data tabulation and data analysis.

Coding, Editing, and Preparing Data for Analysis

" The rapid proliferation of computer technology has made the procedure for raw data entry appear almost second nature for many data analysts. Yet everyone in this field understands the fundamental concept behind this task—GIGO: garbage in, garbage out. "[1]

ROBERT W. KNEEN
Senior Systems Analysis
Union Bancorporation

Wal-Mart and Scanner Technology

Every item you purchase in a retail store is scanned into a computer. The bar code permits each store to know exactly what is selling and when. It also enables store managers to keep very accurate control of inventory, so that they can easily order more of the necessary items when they run low. Probably the ultimate example of scanning use is Wal-Mart, for which the scanner has been vital. Wal-Mart does not own the products on its shelves; they remain there on consignment by the manufacturers. With its scanning system, however, Wal-Mart always knows what is there, what is selling, and what needs replenishment. The scanner has pushed back the law of diminishing returns and made it possible to build and manage larger inventories than would have been possible a short time ago.

The same equipment that scans product codes can also scan a bar-coded customer card so that the customer is associated with his or her purchase in a central computer. This process takes only a second or two per transaction, and requires only that the customer produce the card at purchase time.

Scanner technology is widely used in the marketing research industry. Questionnaires can be prepared through any of a number of word processing software packages and printed on a laser printer. Respondents can complete the questionnaire with any type of writing instrument. With the appropriate software and scanning device, the researcher can scan the completed questionnaires and the data are checked for errors, categorized, and stored within a matter of seconds. When a researcher expects to receive 400 to 500 completed surveys, scanner technology can be worth its weight in gold.[2]

Value of Preparing Data for Analysis

The process of converting information from a questionnaire so it can be read by a computer is referred to as *data preparation*. This process normally follows a five-step approach, beginning with data validation, then editing and coding of the data, followed by data entry, error detection, and data tabulation. The purpose of the data preparation process is to take data in its raw form and convert it so as to establish meaning and create value for the user. This chapter discusses in detail each of these five steps in the data preparation process.

Data Validation

Data validation The process of determining, to the extent possible, whether a survey's interviews or observations were conducted correctly and are free of fraud or bias.

Curbstoning Cheating or falsification in the data collection process.

Data validation is concerned with determining, to the extent possible, if surveys, interviews, or observations were conducted correctly and free of fraud or bias. It should appear quite obvious that in many data collection approaches (personal interview, mall-intercept, etc.) it is not always convenient to monitor the data collection process. As an attempt to control for the accurate collection of response data, each respondent's name, address, and phone number may be recorded. While this information is not used for analysis, it does allow the validation process to develop.

Curbstoning is a term used in the marketing research industry to imply cheating or falsification of data. As the name implies, curbstoning is when interviewers find an out-of-the-way location, such as a curbstone, and fill out the survey/interview form themselves rather than follow the procedure with an actual respondent. Because of the potential for such falsification, data validation becomes a necessary step in the data acquisition process.

Most marketing research professionals will target between 10 and 30 percent of completed interviews for "callbacks." Specifically for telephone, mail, and door-to-door interviews, a certain percentage of respondents from the total pool of returned interviewers will be recontacted by the research firm to make sure the interview was conducted correctly. Normally through telephone recontact, respondents will be asked several short questions as a way of validating the returned interview.

Generally, the process of validation attempts to cover five areas:

1. **Fraud.** Was the person actually interviewed, or was the interview falsified? Did the interviewer contact the respondent simply to get a name and address, and then proceeded to fabricate responses? Did the interviewer use a friend or confederate to obtain the necessary information?

2. **Screening.** Many times an interview must be conducted only with qualified respondents. To ensure accuracy of the data collected, many respondents will be screened according to some preselected criteria, such as household income level, a recent purchase of a specific product or brand, or even sex or age. For example, the interview procedure may require that only female heads of households with a family income of $25,000 or more be interviewed. In this case, a validation callback would verify each of these separate factors.

3. **Procedure.** In many marketing research projects it is critical that the data be collected according to a specific procedure. For example, many customer exit interviews must occur in a designated place as the respondent leaves a certain retail establishment. In this particular example a validation callback may be necessary to ensure the interview took place at the proper setting, not some social gathering area like a restaurant or park.

4. **Completeness.** In order to speed through the data collection process, an interviewer may ask the respondent only a few of the requisite questions. Normally in such cases, the interviewer will ask the respondent a few questions from the beginning of the interview form and then skip to the end, omitting questions from other sections. The interviewer may then make up answers to the remaining questions. To determine if the interview is valid, the researcher could recontact a sample of respondents and ask about questions from different parts of the interview form.

5. **Courtesy.** A normal assumption is that a respondent is treated with courtesy and respect during the interviewing process. However, situations can occur where the interviewer may, unconsciously or not, inject a tone of negativity into the interviewing process. For the simple fact of establishing a positive image with respondents, respondent callbacks are common to determine whether the interviewer was courteous. Other aspects of the interviewer checked during callbacks include appearance, pleasantness, and proper personality.

Data Editing and Coding

Editing   The process whereby the raw data are checked for mistakes made by either the interviewer or the respondent.

After being validated, the data must be edited for the possibility of mistakes. **Editing** is the process whereby the raw data are checked for mistakes made by either the interviewer or the respondent. Through a manual scanning of each completed interview, the researcher can check several areas of concern: (1) proper asking of questions, (2) proper recording of answers, (3) proper screening of respondents, and (4) proper recording of open-ended questions.

Asking the Proper Questions

One aspect of the editing process especially important to interview methods is to make certain that the proper questions were asked of the respondent. As illustrated in Exhibit 15.1, question 2 should have been asked of all respondents, yet the responses show that this question was not asked in this instance. The normal procedure would be to recontact this respondent in order to obtain a response to this question.

Proper Recording of Answers

It is also evident in Exhibit 15.1 that two key pieces of information were not recorded properly. In this interview the gender of the respondent was not recorded and the last digit of the respondent's telephone number was omitted. If not for a careful edit of this questionnaire, two vital responses would have been missing. Fortunately, the ability to recontact this respondent was established and the recording of the omitted responses was accomplished.

Proper Screening Questions

Inspection of the questionnaire in Exhibit 15.1 shows that the first three items are actually screening questions that determine whether the respondent is eligible to complete the interview. During the editing phase, the researcher will make certain that only qualified respondents were included.

It is also critical in the editing process to establish that the questions were asked and (for self-administered surveys) answered in the proper sequence. For example, in Exhibit 15.1, if a "no" response was recorded to question 6A, the interviewer should have skipped to question 7A. In this instance the proper pattern was followed and question 6B was passed over. Had this not been the case, the respondent would have most likely been recontacted.

Responses to Open-Ended Questions

Highly meaningful data resulting from survey instruments are responses to open-ended questions. These types of questions, when properly answered, can provide greater insight into the research project than forced-choice questions or rating scales. A major part of editing the answers to open-ended questions is interpretation. Exhibit 15.2 shows some typical responses and thus points to problems associated with interpreting open-ended questions. For example, one response to the question "Why has your use of [this restaurant's] Burgers increased?" is simply "They have good service." This answer by itself is not sufficient to determine what the respondent means by "good service." The interviewer needed to probe for a deeper response. For example, are the employees friendly, helpful, courteous? Do they appear neat and clean? Do they smile when taking an order? Probes such as these would allow the researcher to interpret the "good service" answer more narrowly. In cases such as these, the individual doing the editing must use judgment in classifying responses. At some point he or she must standardize the responses; those that are incomplete may simply be categorized as useless. The Marketing Research Illustration at the end of this chapter focuses on assessing data completeness.

The Coding Process

Coding Grouping and assigning value to various responses from the survey instrument.

Coding involves grouping and assigning value to various responses from the survey instrument. Both parts of the coding process usually entail labeling the responses with some numeric meaning—a number from 0 to 9, for example. Like editing, coding can be very tedious if certain issues are not addressed prior to disseminating the survey instrument. A

| EXHIBIT 15.1 | **Questionnaire for Data Editing and Coding** |

RESPONDENT NAME B Bells   TELEPHONE # 236-277

INTERVIEWER 1127   DATE 3-30

TIME BEGAN 7:05pm   TIME ENDED 7:20pm   LENGTH_____

```
1[ ] [ ] [ ]
2[ ] [ ] [ ]
3[ ] [ ] [ ]
4[ ] [ ] [ ]
5[ ] [ ] [ ]
6[ ] [ ] [ ]
7[ ] [ ] [ ]
8[ ] [ ] [ ]
9[ ] [ ] [ ]
0[ ] [ ] [ ]
```

COMMUNICATION BARRIER _____

Male.......[ ]
Female.....[ ]

Good evening, my name is _____ from _____. We are a professional
marketing research firm. We don't sell anything, we just conduct
various types of studies for our clients.

INTRO REFUSAL_____

1. Does any member of your family work for: (READ LIST.)
                                                    Yes
      A department store................................[ ]
      A hospital..[ ]

      An advertising agency or marketing research firm...[ ]   -> TERMINATE &
      A fast service restaurant..........................[ ]   TALLY _____

2. Has any family member 18 or older, <u>presently at home</u>, eaten at or from a fast
   service restaurant in your neighborhood in the <u>past month</u>?

      No.......[ ] -> TERMINATE & TALLY_____
      Yes......[ ] -> REPEAT INTRO IF NEW RESPONDENT. TERMINATE & TALLY IF:

                  NO MEMBER OF HOUSEHOLD QUALIFIES_____
                  QUALIFIED PERSON UNAVAILABLE_____

3a. Which of the following items have you consumed at or from a fast service restaurant
    in your neighborhood in the past month? (READ LIST. MARK ALL THAT APPLY IN 3a.)

3b. ASK FOR EACH NOT MARKED IN 3a: Would you like to eat/drink (_____), if available?
    (MARK IN 3b.)

	3a Past Month	3b Would Like
Hand dipped, real ice cream milkshake....	[ ]	[ ]
Homemade fresh squeezed lemonade.........	[ ]	[ ] -> IF NONE MARKED,
Large (1/3 or 1/2 pound) hamburger.......	[✓]	[ ] TERMINATE & TALLY
Charbroiled chicken sandwich.............	[✓]	[ ] _____

QUALIFIED REFUSAL_____

4a. When you think of fast service <u>hamburger</u> restaurants in your neighborhood, which
    ones come to mind? (DO NOT READ LIST. MARK ALL THAT APPLY IN 4a.) PROBE: Any
    others?

4b. (ASK FOR EACH NOT MARKED IN 4a:) Have you heard of _____? (MARK IN 4b.)

	4a Unaided	4b Aided
@ Back Yard Burgers.........................[ ]	[ ]
@ Burger King..............................[✓]	[ ]
@ McDonald's...............................[✓]	[ ]
@ Rally's..................................[ ]	[ ]
@ Wendy's..................................[✓]	[ ]
Other_____......[ ]	

EXHIBIT 15.1   *continued*

5a. When you think of fast service hamburger restaurants which sell large (1/3 or 1/2 pound) hamburgers, which ones come to mind? (MARK ALL THAT APPLY IN 5a.)

5b. When you think of fast service hamburger restaurants which sell charbroiled chicken sandwiches, which ones come to mind? (MARK ALL THAT APPLY IN 5b.)

5c. When you think of fast service hamburger restaurants which sell homemade fresh squeezed lemonade, which ones come to mind? (MARK ALL THAT APPLY IN 5c.)

5d. When you think of fast service hamburger restaurants which sell hand dipped, real ice cream milkshakes, which ones come to mind? (MARK ALL THAT APPLY IN 5d.)

	5a Burgers	5b Chicken Sandwich	5c Lemonade	5d Shakes
Back Yard Burgers	[ ]	[ ]	[ ]	[ ]
Burger King	[✓]	[✓]		
McDonald's	[✓]	[✓]		
Rally's	[ ]	[ ]		
Wendy's	[✓]	[ ]		
Other _____	[ ]	[ ]	[ ]	

6a. Have you seen, read or heard any advertising recently for fast service hamburger restaurants?

No.....[✓] -> SKIP TO QUESTION 7.

Yes....[ ] -> 6b.   Which fast service hamburger restaurants did you recently see, read or hear advertising for? (DO NOT READ LIST. MARK ALL THAT APPLY.)

	6b Unaided Advertising Awareness
Back Yard Burgers	[ ]
Burger King	[ ]
McDonald's	[ ]
Rally's	[ ]
Wendy's	[ ]
Other _____	[ ]

7a. At or from which of the following fast service hamburger restaurants would you consider eating? (READ LIST IN INDICATED ORDER. MARK ALL THAT APPLY IN 7a.)

7b. At or from which one of those fast service hamburger restaurants would you most prefer to eat? (MARK ONE ONLY IN 7b.)

7c. At or from which of those fast service hamburger restaurants would you just as soon not eat? (MARK ALL THAT APPLY IN 7c.)

	7a Would Consider	7b One Most Prefer	7c Not Prefer
@ Back Yard Burgers	[✓]	[✓]	[ ]
@ Burger King	[✓]	[✓]	[ ]
@ McDonald's	[✓]	[ ]	[ ]
@ Rally's	[✓]	[ ]	[ ]
@ Wendy's	[✓]	[ ]	[ ]
Other _____	[ ]	[ ]	[ ]

8a. Approximately how many times in the past month have you eaten at or from: (READ LIST IN INDICATED ORDER. RECORD NUMBERS IN 8a.)

8b. Approximately how many of those (NUMBER) times at or from (EACH RESTAURANT) were for lunch, that is 11:00 a.m. to 4 p.m.? An evening meal, that is 4 p.m. to 9 p.m.? (RECORD IN 8b.)

8c. Approximately how many of those (NUMBER) times at or from (EACH RESTAURANT) were work-related? Home-related? (RECORD IN 8c.)

	8a Total	8b Lunch	8b Evening	8c Work	8c Home
@ Back Yard Burgers	____	____	____	____	____
@ Burger King	____	____	____	____	____
@ McDonald's	____	____	____	____	____
@ Rally's	____	____	____	____	____
@ Wendy's	____	____	____	____	____
Other _____	____	____	____	____	____

EXHIBIT 15.1   *continued*

9. Which <u>two</u> of the following fast service hamburger restaurants are you most familiar
    with? (READ LIST IN INDICATED ORDER. MARK <u>ONE</u> IN BOX A AND <u>ONE</u> IN BOX B.)

                              MARK <u>ONE ONLY</u> IN A-> | A | | B | <-MARK <u>ONE ONLY</u> IN B

    @ Back Yard Burgers......................... [✓]   [ ]
    @ Burger King.............................. [✓]   [ ]
    @ McDonald's............................... [✓]   [ ]
    @ Rally's.................................. [✓]   [ ]
    @ Wendy's.................................. [✓]   [ ]
      Other_____ .. [ ]   [ ]

10. Now, I'd like you to compare (<u>READ THOSE MARKED IN Q9</u>) on several characteristics.
    For each characteristic I read you, please tell me whether you think:

                -- <u>One</u> of the fast service hamburger restaurants <u>is better</u>, or
                -- <u>Both</u> are <u>about the same</u>

    For example, would you say (<u>READ RESTAURANT MARKED IN BOX A IN Q.9</u>) is better,
    (<u>READ RESTAURANT MARKED IN BOX B IN Q.9</u>) is better, or both are about the same in
    terms of (<u>READ ATTRIBUTE WITH * IN LIST BELOW</u>)? (MARK APPROPRIATE RESPONSE BELOW,
    THEN CONTINUE IN DIRECTION OF * UNTIL ALL ARE ASKED.)

	"A" Is Better	"B" Is Better	Both About The Same
@ 1. Attention getting signs	[ ]	[ ]	[✓]
@ 2. Convenient location	[ ]	[ ]	[✓]
@ 3. Drink prices	[ ]	[ ]	[✓]
@ 4. Easy to understand menu	[ ]	[ ]	[✓]
@ 5. Each order prepared fresh	[ ]	[ ]	[✓]
@ 6. Healthy food	[ ]	[ ]	[✓]
@ 7. Portion size	[ ]	[ ]	[✓]
@ 8. Prices of food items	[ ]	[ ]	[✓]
@ 9. Employees can answer questions and solve problems	[ ]	[ ]	[✓]
@ 10. Specials and promotions	[ ]	[ ]	[✓]
@ 11. Speed of service	[ ]	[ ]	[✓]
@ 12. Offers children's menu	[ ]	[ ]	[✓]
@ 13. Variety of food	[ ]	[ ]	[✓]
@ 14. Cleanliness	[ ]	[ ]	[✓]
@ 15. Uses extra lean ground beef	[ ]	[ ]	[✓]
@ 16. Gets orders correct	[ ]	[ ]	[✓]
@ 17. Good tasting food	[ ]	[ ]	[✓]
@ 18. Fun place to go	[ ]	[ ]	[✓]
@ 19. Consistent quality every visit	[ ]	[ ]	[✓]
@ 20. Food hot when served	[ ]	[ ]	[✓]
@ 21. Large hamburger	[ ]	[ ]	[✓]
@ 22. Quality of ingredients	[ ]	[ ]	[✓]
@ 23. Food well prepared	[ ]	[ ]	[✓]
@ 24. Unique menu items	[ ]	[ ]	[✓]
@ 25. Quality of food	[ ]	[ ]	[✓]
@ 26. Selection of types of french fries	[ ]	[ ]	[✓]
@ 27. Method of cooking hamburgers	[ ]	[ ]	[✓]
@ 28. Friendly employees	[ ]	[ ]	[✓]
@ 29. Value for the money	[ ]	[ ]	[✓]
@ 30. Prepares food to customer's special request	[ ]	[ ]	[✓]
@ 31. Selection of desserts	[ ]	[ ]	[✓]

EXHIBIT 15.1   *concluded*

11a.   REFER TO Q8a.   IF BACK YARD BURGERS IS MENTIONED, SKIP TO Q11b.   OTHERWISE ASK:

       Have you ever eaten at/from Back Yard Burgers?

              Yes.........[ ] -> ASK Q11b
              No.........[ ] -> SKIP TO Q12

11b.   Would you eat food at/from Back Yard Burgers more often if: (<u>READ LIST IN INDICATED</u>
       <u>ORDER</u>).   Would you say <u>definitely</u>, <u>probably</u>, <u>probably not</u>, or <u>definitely not</u>?

                                        <u>Definitely</u>   <u>Probably</u>   <u>Probably Not</u>   <u>Definitely Not</u>

       @ They delivered to your home.....[ ]   [4]   [ ]   [ ]
       @ They had a carry-out window.....[ ]   [4]   [ ]   [ ]
       @ They had faster drive
          through service................[ ]   [4]   [ ]   [ ]
       @ They had inside seating.........[ ]   [4]   [ ]   [ ]

12.   Which of the following categories best describes your age?   (READ LIST. <u>MARK ONE</u>
       <u>ONLY</u>.)

              19 or younger......[ ]
              20-29..............[ ]
              30-34..............[4]
              35-44..............[ ]
              45-54..............[ ]
              55 or older........[ ]

              REFUSED...........[ ]

13a. Are you currently employed?

              Yes.....[ ] -> ASK Q. 13b

              No......[4] -> Are you: Retired.........[ ]
                                       Unemployed......[4]
                                       Housewife.......[ ]

13b.   Which one of the following categories best describes your occupation?   (READ LIST.
       MARK <u>ONE ONLY</u>.)

              Executive/professional...............[ ]
              Manager/owner/proprietor.............[ ]
              White collar.........................[ ]
              Service..............................[ ]
              Blue collar..........................[ ]

              REFUSED..............................[ ]

14.   Which of the following categories best describes the approximate total income of
       your household last year?

              Less than $15,000.......[ ]
              $15,000-$24,999.........[T]
              $25,000-$34,999.........[ ]
              $35,000-$49,999.........[ ]
              $50,000-$74,999.........[ ]
              $75,000 or more.........[ ]

              REFUSED.................[ ]

Thank you for your help!

I hereby attest that this is a true and honest interview and complete to the best of my
knowledge. I guarantee that all information relating to this interview shall be kept
strictly confidential.

              _____
                       INTERVIEWER'S SIGNATURE

| EXHIBIT 15.2 | **Responses and Problems with Interpreting Open-Ended Questions** |

10a. Why has your use of _____ Burgers increased?

_____

72032

- Found out how good the food is.
- I enjoy the food.
- We just moved up here and where we were there was no _____ .
- That part of town is building up so fast. It is right by Wal-Mart.
- They have a couple of offers in the newspaper.
- It is right beside where my husband works.

72076

- Tastes better—grilled.
- They started giving better value packages.
- They have good service.
- We really like their chicken sandwiches, so we go more often now.
- The good food.
- Only because they only put one in within the last year.
- Just opened lately.

72113

- I love chicken sandwiches, but not the fries.
- Just moved into area. They have good food, but are not local to Maumelle.
- There is one in the area where I work.

---

well-planned and constructed questionnaire can reduce the amount of time spent on coding while increasing the accuracy of the process. Best practices suggest that coding should be incorporated into the design of the questionnaire. Exhibit 15.3 shows a questionnaire with built-in coded responses.

In questionnaires that do not use such simple coded responses, the researcher will establish a master code on which the assigned numeric values are shown for each response. Exhibit 15.4 provides an example of such a form. In this case, if the respondent checked "$4.01–$6.00" in question 3, the coder would assign the value of 3 to that response. If a respondent checked "more than $12," the coder would assign a value of 7 to the category. Such closed-ended questions as these are normally precoded at the time of questionnaire design. The use of a master code is an additional safeguard to ensure that the coding sequence is followed correctly.

EXHIBIT 15.3	Using Scales as an Application of Coding Procedures

6. Below are several statements concerning Environmental Compliance. On a scale of 1 to 5, 1 being "strongly disagree" and 5 being "strongly agree," how would you respond to the following issues?

	Strongly disagree				Strongly agree
A. My company is very aware of all documentation that must be submitted regarding Environmental Compliance.	1	2	3	4	5
B. Improving resistance to RCRA penalties requires more attention on my company's part to physical management of waste.	1	2	3	4	5
C. We would improve our resistance to RCRA penalties if we submitted required documents in a timely and accurate manner.	1	2	3	4	5
D. It is very important that our company test the knowledge and understanding of our employees regarding hazardous communications as mandated by OSHA.	1	2	3	4	5
E. Gaining access to current and proposed HAZMAT regulations is not a major concern of this company.	1	2	3	4	5
F. This company makes every attempt to train employees on the response procedures concerning hazardous materials.	1	2	3	4	5
G. In my opinion, Training Employees, as required by the EPA, should be a formal, ongoing process within this company.	1	2	3	4	5
H. The implementation of a formal Auditing System would be highly beneficial for this company regarding EPA and other Regulatory Compliance Issues.	1	2	3	4	5
I. Being cited as noncompliant by OSHA is something this company vigorously tries to avoid.	1	2	3	4	5
J. Being cited as noncompliant by the EPA is a small issue in our business.	1	2	3	4	5
K. Being cited as noncompliant by the DOT is a very serious consequence for this business.	1	2	3	4	5

In contrast, open-ended questions pose unique problems to the coding process. Open-ended questions do not allow for an exact list of potential responses; therefore the data they provide are not easy to prepare. Yet in most cases, the value of the information obtained from open-ended questions far outweighs the problems of coding the responses.

The researcher can use a four-step process to develop codes for the anticipated responses. This procedure begins by generating a list of as many potential responses as possible. These responses can then be assigned values within a range determined by the actual number of separate responses identified. As the researcher begins to edit the responses to the open-ended questions, he or she can simply attach a value from the developed response list. For responses that do not appear on the list, the researcher can simply add a new response and corresponding value to the list or consolidate the response into one of the existing categories.

EXHIBIT 15.4   **An Illustration of a Master Code Form**

Master Code Form   **Questionnaire Identification**
                                                    Number 000 (1–3)

FAST-FOOD OPINION SURVEY

This questionnaire pertains to a project being conducted by a marketing research class at The University of Memphis. The purpose of this project is to better understand the attitudes and opinions of consumers toward fast-food restaurants. The questionnaire will take only 10–15 minutes to complete, and all responses will remain strictly confidential. Thank you for your help on this project.

1. Below is a listing of various fast-food restaurants. How many of these restaurants would you say you visited in the past two months? Check as many as may apply.

(4–5)	Taco Bell	01	(18–19)	Church's Fried Chicken	08
(6–7)	Hardee's	02	(20–21)	McDonald's	09
(8–9)	Kentucky Fried Chicken	03	(22–23)	Burger King	10
(10–11)	Wendy's	04	(24–25)	Back Yard Burgers	11✓
(12–13)	Rally's	05	(26–27)	Arby's	12
(14–15)	Popeye's Chicken	06	(28–29)	Sonic	13
(16–17)	Krystal's	07	(30–31)	Other, please specify → see code sheet	
			(32–33)	Have not visited any of these establishments	20

(34) **2. In a typical month, how many times would you say you visit a fast-food restaurant, such as the ones indicated above? (X ONE BOX)**

One ☐   Two ☐   Three ☑   Four ☐   Five ☐   Six ☐   Seven or more ☐
     1   2   3   4   5   6   7

(35) **3. On your last visit to a fast-food restaurant, what was the dollar amount you spent on food and beverages?**

Under $2	☐ 1		$8.01–$10.00	☐ 5
$2.01–$4.00	☐ 2		$10.01–$12.00	☐ 6
$4.01–$6.00	☑ 3		More than $12	☐ 7
$6.01–$8.00	☐ 4		Don't remember	☐ 8

Consolidation of responses is actually the second phase of the four-step process. Exhibit 15.5 illustrates several actual responses to the question "Why has your use of [this restaurant] decreased [in the past six months]?" Four of these—related to not liking the food—can be consolidated into a single response category because they all have the same shared meaning. The establishment of consolidated categories is, of course, a subjective decision that should be made only by an experienced research analyst with input from the project's client or sponsor.

The third step of the process is to assign a numerical value as a code. While at first this may appear to be a simple task, the structure of the questionnaire and the number of responses per question need to be taken into consideration. For example, if a question has more than 10 responses, then double-digit codes need to be used, such as "01," "02," . . . "12." Another good practice is to assign higher-value codes to positive responses than to negative responses. For example, "no" responses are coded 1 and "yes" responses coded 2; dislike responses are coded as 1 and like responses coded as 5. Coding of this

---

EXHIBIT 15.5   **Illustration of Response Consolidation Using Open-ended Questions**

Q10a. Why has your use of _____ *decreased?*

_____

72113

- (I'm a) state employee. I look for bargains. (Need) more specials.
- Because I'm no longer close to a _____ .

72114

- I do not like their food.

72116

- They never get my order right.
- I got tired of the hamburgers. I don't like the spices.
- Prices (are) too high. Family doesn't like it. My husband didn't like the way the burgers tasted. They should give more with their combos than they do. More fries.
- Because they always got our orders wrong and they are rude.
- The order is never right.
- Health reasons.
- I work longer hours, and don't think about food.
- Cannot eat the food.
- We started using _____ .
- The location of my work moved so I am not near a _____ .

nature makes subsequent analysis easier. For example, the researcher will find it easier to interpret means or averages if higher values occur as the average moves from "dislike" to "like."

More important, assigning a coded value to missing data is very critical. If, for example, a respondent completes an entire questionnaire except for the very last question and a recontact is not possible, how do you code the response to the unanswered question? A good practice in this situation is to first consider how the response (or lack thereof) is going to be used in the analysis phase.[3] In certain types of analysis, if the response is left blank and has no numerical value, the entire questionnaire (not just the individual question) will be deleted. The best way to handle the coding of omitted responses is first to check on how your data analysis software will handle data or code omissions. Allow this to be the guide for determining whether omissions should be coded or left blank.

The fourth step of the coding process is to assign a coded value to each response. This is probably the most tedious process because it is done manually. Unless an optical scanning approach is being used to enter the data, however, this task is almost always necessary to guard against problems in the data entry phase.

First, each questionnaire needs to be assigned a numerical value. This is normally a three-digit code if there are fewer than 1,000 questionnaires to code, and a four-digit code if there are 1,000 or more. For example, if 452 completed questionnaires were returned, the first would be coded 001, the second 002, and so on, finishing with 452. Questionnaire coding will be referred to again in our discussion on data entry.

Immediately following each questionnaire code, a numbered reference should be included in parentheses next to the code. This informs the data entry operator to place the questionnaire code in the corresponding data fields of the data record. It is important to realize that throughout the questionnaire the numbers in parentheses indicate the data field where each coded response will be added on the data record.

The researcher should proceed through the entire questionnaire, assigning the appropriate numerical codes to each response. Exhibit 15.6 illustrates a fully coded questionnaire. The individual physically applied the appropriate code as dictated by the master code sheet. Responses to open-ended questions (question 8) were also coded as expressed in the master code sheet. Keep in mind that each question is also assigned a data field number; question 3, for example, is marked (35) to ensure that data entry personnel will enter the code into the proper fields of the data record.

Data Entry

Data entry Those tasks involved with the direct input of the coded data into some specified software package that ultimately allows the research analyst to manipulate and transform the raw data into useful information.

Following validation, editing, and coding comes the procedure for entering the data into the computer for subsequent data analysis. **Data entry** includes those tasks involved with the direct input of the coded data into some specified software package that will ultimately allow the research analyst to manipulate and transform the raw data into useful information.

There are four principal ways of entering coded data into a computer. The most popular options are the keyboard terminal and the personal computer (PC) keyboard. Both are key-driven devices connected directly to a computer processor. The PC keyboard is connected directly to the computer, whereas the keyboard terminal is connected to the computer by a data communications link such as a phone line or satellite that may span thousands of miles.

Other labor-saving devices are also available for data entry. Some terminals have touch-screen capabilities that allow the analyst to simply touch an area of the terminal

EXHIBIT 15.6 | **Illustration of a Completed Questionnaire in a Fully Coded Format**

FAST-FOOD OPINION SURVEY

This questionnaire pertains to a project being conducted by a marketing research class at The University of Memphis. The purpose of this project is to better understand the attitudes and opinions of consumers toward fast-food restaurants. The questionnaire will take only 10–15 minutes to complete, and all responses will remain strictly confidential. Thank you for your help on this project.

1. Below is a listing of various fast-food restaurants. How many of these restaurants would you say you visited in the past two months? Check as many as may apply.

(4–5)	Taco Bell	✓ 01		Church's Fried Chicken	_____
	Hardee's	_____	(20–21)	McDonald's	✓ 09
(8–9)	Kentucky Fried Chicken	✓ 03		Burger King	_____
(10–11)	Wendy's	✓ 04	(24–25)	Back Yard Burgers	✓ 11
	Rally's	_____	(26–27)	Arby's	✓ 12
	Popeye's Chicken	_____		Sonic	_____
(16–17)	Krystal's	✓ 07		Other, please specify →	_____
				Have not visited any of these establishments	_____

(34) **2. In a typical month, how many times would you say you visit a fast-food restaurant, such as the ones indicated above? (X ONE BOX)**

One ☐   Two ☐   Three ☐   Four ☐   Five ☐   Six ☒   Seven or more ☐
                                                    6

(35) **3. On your last visit to a fast-food restaurant, what was the dollar amount you spent on food and beverages?**

Under $2	☐	$8.01–$10.00	☒ 5
$2.01–$4.00	☐	$10.01–$12.00	☐
$4.01–$6.00	☐	More than $12	☐
$6.01–$8.00	☐	Don't remember	☐

4. Within the past two weeks, which fast-food restaurant(s) have you visited most frequently? Check as many as apply:

(36–37)	Taco Bell	✓ 01		Church's Fried Chicken	_____
	Hardee's	_____	(52–53)	McDonald's	✓ 09
	Kentucky Fried Chicken	_____		Burger King	_____
	Wendy's	_____		Back Yard Burgers	_____
	Rally's	_____	(58–59)	Arby's	✓ 12
	Popeye's Chicken	_____		Sonic	_____
	Krystal's	_____		Other, please specify →	_____

EXHIBIT 15.6 *continued*

5. **Listed below are a set of attributes (reasons) many people use when selecting a fast-food restaurant to visit. Regarding your most recent selection of a fast-food restaurant, please rank each attribute from 1 to 7, with 1 being the most important attribute for selecting the fast-food restaurant and 7 being the least important attribute.**

	Attribute	Rank	
(64)	a) Prices of food items	6	6
(65)	b) Speed of service	2	2
(66)	c) Convenient location	4	4
(67)	d) Consistent quality of food	1	1
(68)	e) Variety of menu items	3	3
(69)	f) Friendly employees	5	5
(70)	g) Large size portions	7	7

6. **On a scale from 1 to 6, 1 being Very Dissatisfied to 6 being Very Satisfied, please rate the fast-food restaurant that you visited most recently on the following dimensions:**

		Very Dissatisfied				Very Satisfied		
(71)	Reasonable prices of food items	1	2	3	4	⑤	6	5
(72)	Friendliness of employees	1	2	3	4	⑤	6	5
(73)	Variety of menu items	1	2	3	4	⑤	6	5
(74)	Speed of service	1	2	3	④	5	6	4
(75)	Conveniently located	1	2	3	④	5	6	4
(76)	Quality of food	1	2	3	4	⑤	6	5
(77)	Large size portions	1	2	3	④	5	6	4

7. **The following questions refer to your perceptions on the quality, value, and offerings of a fast-food restaurant. On a scale of 1 to 6, with 1 being Strongly Agree, and 6 being Strongly Disagree, how would you rate fast-food restaurants on the following dimensions:**

		Strongly Agree				Strongly Disagree		
(1)	I only visit those fast-food establishments that are conveniently located to my home or work	1	2	3	4	⑤	6	5
(2)	I prefer to visit fast-food restaurants that serve healthy/nutritious food	1	②	3	4	5	6	2
(3)	The price of food items is not important when visiting a fast-food restaurant	1	2	3	④	5	6	4
(4)	In my opinion, fast-food restaurants are all the same	1	2	3	4	5	⑥	6

continued

EXHIBIT 15.6   *continued*

		Strongly Agree					Strongly Disagree	

(5) All fast-food restaurants should offer some type of child's menu or kid's meal 1   2   3   ④   5   6   4

(6) I tend to visit those fast-food restaurants that offer coupons or special price promotions...................1   2   3   4   5   ⑥   6

(7) Home delivery would be a great service for fast-food restaurants to offer customers 1   2   3   ④   5   6   4

(8) When visiting a fast-food restaurant, I normally use the drive-thru window service................................1   2   3   ④   5   6   4

(9) Variety of menu items is important in my selection of a fast-food restaurant........................1   ②   3   4   5   6   2

(10) In my opinion, the quality of ingredients a fast-food restaurant uses is more important than price ....①   2   3   4   5   6   1

(11) Getting my food order correct is a major problem with many fast-food restaurants 1   2   ③   4   5   6   3

(12) Friendly employees are important in my selection of a fast-food restaurant.......................................1   ②   3   4   5   6   2

(13) I prefer to visit fast-food restaurants that offer salads or salad bars.....................................1   2   ③   4   5   6   3

(14) I go to fast-food restaurants mainly at lunchtime...................1   2   3   4   ⑤   6   5

(15) I rarely visit a fast-food restaurant for breakfast.....................1   2   3   ④   5   6   4

(16) I prefer to buy combination meals having all items at one price as opposed to ordering single items from the menu 1   2   3   ④   5   6   4

(17) Cooking with extra-lean ground beef is very important in my selection of a fast-food restaurant 1   ②   3   4   5   6   2

(18) The advertisements I see for fast-food restaurants influence my decision to visit the establishment.....................1   2   ③   4   5   6   3

(19) I normally eat inside fast-food restaurants 1   2   3   ④   5   6   4

(20) A major problem with many fast-food restaurants is the inconsistency of quality in food preparation 1   2   3   ④   5   6   4

(21) I tend to order large size portions or servings at fast-food restaurants.......................................1   2   3   4   5   ⑥   6

8. Please respond by filling in the blank to the statement below:

If I had to recommend my favorite fast-food restaurant to a friend, it would probably be

(22-23)   ARBY's   12

EXHIBIT 15.6 *continued*

9. **In this section, we have listed a number of statements about interests and opinions. For each statement listed, we would like to know whether you personally agree or disagree with this statement.**

After each statement, there are six numbers from 1 to 6. The higher the number, the more you tend to <u>agree</u> with the statement. The lower the number, the more you tend to <u>disagree</u> with the statement. The numbers from 1 to 6 may be described as follows:

1. I <u>definitely</u> disagree with the statement.
2. I <u>generally</u> disagree with the statement.
3. I <u>moderately</u> disagree with the statement.
4. I <u>moderately</u> agree with the statement.
5. I <u>generally</u> agree with the statement.
6. I <u>definitely</u> agree with the statement.

For each statement, please circle the number that best describes your feelings about that statement. You may think many items are similar. Actually, no two items are exactly alike, so be sure to circle **ONE NUMBER FOR EACH STATEMENT.**

CIRCLE ONLY ONE NUMBER FOR EACH STATEMENT

		Disagree				Definitely Agree		
(24)	I am careful about what I eat in order to keep my weight under control	1	2	3	4	⑤	6	5
(25)	I would rather spend a quiet evening at home than go out to a party	1	2	3	4	5	⑥	6
(26)	I am concerned about getting enough calcium in my diet	①	2	3	4	5	6	1
(27)	At noontime, I often skip lunch or just have a light snack	1	2	③	4	5	6	3
(28)	I am a homebody	1	2	3	4	⑤	6	5
(29)	I like to be considered a leader	1	2	3	4	5	⑥	6
(30)	It seems as though everyone in our family is always on the run	1	2	3	4	⑤	6	5
(31)	I try to avoid foods that are high in cholesterol	1	2	3	4	⑤	6	5
(32)	There is too much violence on prime-time television	1	2	3	4	5	⑥	6
(33)	I dread the future	①	2	3	4	5	6	1
(34)	I am not satisfied until my family's clothes look perfectly clean	1	2	③	4	5	6	3
(35)	When I buy gasoline, I look for one particular brand	1	②	3	4	5	6	2
(36)	I try to avoid foods with a high salt content	1	2	3	4	⑤	6	5

continued

EXHIBIT 15.6   *continued*

		Disagree					Definitely Agree	
(37)	When I get a free sample of a product I usually buy that product later	1	2	3	④	5	6	4
(38)	I would be willing to pay more for a product with all-natural ingredients	1	2	3	4	⑤	6	5
(39)	A nationally advertised brand is usually a better buy than a generic brand	1	②	3	4	5	6	2
(40)	My friends and neighbors often come to me for advice about products and brands	1	2	③	4	5	6	3
(41)	I am influential in my neighborhood	1	2	3	4	⑤	6	5
(42)	Children are the most important thing in a marriage	1	2	3	4	⑤	6	5
(43)	I have somewhat old-fashioned tastes and habits	1	2	3	4	⑤	6	5
(44)	I like to buy new and different things	1	2	3	4	⑤	6	5
(45)	My days seem to follow a definite routine—eating meals at the same time each day, etc.	1	2	3	4	⑤	6	5
(46)	I usually eat balanced, nutritious meals	1	2	3	④	5	6	4
(47)	I spend a lot of time visiting friends	1	②	3	4	5	6	2
(48)	I shop a lot for specials	1	②	3	4	5	6	2
(49)	A store's own brand is usually a better buy than a nationally advertised brand	1	2	3	4	⑤	6	5
(50)	When I watch television, I usually change the station during the commercials	1	2	3	④	5	6	4
(51)	I refuse to buy a brand whose advertising I dislike	1	2	3	④	5	6	4
(52)	I will probably have more money to spend next year than I have now	1	2	3	4	⑤	6	5
(53)	I often seek out the advice of my friends regarding brands and products	①	2	3	4	5	6	1
(54)	I am more concerned about nutrition than most of my friends	1	2	③	4	5	6	3
(55)	I would like to be able to buy more food products in single-serving packages	1	②	3	4	5	6	2
(56)	We usually have a large family breakfast on weekends	1	2	3	4	⑤	6	5
(57)	Meal preparation should take as little time as possible	1	2	3	④	5	6	4
(58)	Shopping is no fun anymore	1	②	3	4	5	6	2
(59)	I like to cook	1	2	3	4	⑤	6	5
(60)	I enjoy looking through fashion magazines	1	②	3	4	5	6	2
(61)	I am the kind of person who would try anything once	①	2	3	4	5	6	1
(62)	The kitchen is my favorite room	1	②	3	4	5	6	2
(63)	I try to avoid fried foods	1	2	3	4	⑤	6	5

EXHIBIT 15.6 *continued*

---

10. On a scale of 0% to 100%, what percentage of your weekly television viewing
(64–65) time is devoted to cable TV networks such as TBS, ESPN, CNN, HBO, etc.?

(Circle the appropriate %.)

0%   10%   20%   30%   40%   50%   ⬭60%   70%   80%   90%   100%   06

11. On a scale of 0% to 100%, what percentage of your weekly viewing time is
(66–67) devoted to traditional TV networks such as ABC, CBS, Fox, NBC, etc.?

(Circle the appropriate %.)

0%   10%   20%   30%   ⬭40%   50%   60%   70%   80%   90%   100%   04

12. Within the past week, would you say you devoted most of your television viewing
(68) time to:

Morning programming (7 A.M. to noon) ...._____

Afternoon programming (noon to 6 P.M.) ...._____

Evening programming (6:01 P.M. to 11 P.M.) ...._√_ 3

Late-night programming (11:01 P.M. and later) ...._____

Did not watch television ...._____

13. Within the past week, do you recall seeing any television advertisements for fast-
(69–70) food restaurants?

No _____   Yes _√_, if so, what restaurant? 02

(71–72)   McDonald's 09

14. Here is a list of different types of music. Would you please read down the list and
check each type of music that you listen to <u>fairly often</u>?

(Check as many as apply.)

(1) Country/western	√	(6) Soft rock	√ 1	Popular vocalists	
Country rock		New wave		Urban contemporary	
Classic rock		Rhythm & blues		(13) East listening	√ 1
Classical		New age		Gospel	
Hard rock		Jazz		None of these	

15. We need some information for classification purposes. Please tell us a little
about yourself.

(16)   **Do you have any children? (X <u>ONE</u> box.)**

Yes ☒ (1)   No ☐

(IF YES) How many children do you have living at home? (X <u>ONE</u> box.)

(17)   None ☐   (SKIP THE NEXT QUESTION)

(18)   One ☒   Two ☐   Three ☐   Four ☐   Five ☐   Five or more ☐
           1

continued

EXHIBIT 15.6   *concluded*

What are the ages of each of those children living at home with you? (X all age ranges that apply.)

Under 1 year ☐	3–5 years ☐	12 years ☐	25–34 years ☐
1 year ☐	6–9 years ☐	13–17 years ☐	35 or over ☐
2 years ☐	10–11 years ☐	(27) 18–24 years ☒ 1	

(30) **How many people are there in your household? Include yourself, your spouse, any children living at home with you, and any other living with you. (X ONE box.)**

One ☐	Three ☒ 3	Five ☐	Seven ☐
Two ☐	Four ☐	Six ☐	Eight or more ☐

(31) **Which of the following best describes your marital status? (X ONE box.)**

Married ☒   Widowed ☐   Separated ☐   Divorced ☐   Never married ☐
     1

(32–33) **Into which category does your total annual household income fall? (X ONE box.)**

Under $10,000 ☐	$30,000–$34,999 ☐	$60,000–$69,999 ☐
$10,000–$14,999 ☐	$35,000–$39,999 ☐	$70,000–$79,999 ☐
$15,000–$19,999 ☐	$40,000–$44,999 ☐	$80,000–$89,999 ☐
$20,000–$24,999 ☐	$45,000–$49,999 ☐	$90,000–$99,999 ☐
$25,000–$29,999 ☐	$50,999–$59,999 ☐	$100,000 or more ☒ 15

(34–35) **Which of the following best describes your occupation? (X ONE box.)**

01   Managerial ☒   Professional ☐   Sales ☐   Clerical ☐   Craftsman ☐

Factory worker ☐   Self-employed ☐   Homemaker ☐   Retired ☐   Student ☐

Other _____ (please specify)

(36) **What is the highest level of education you have attained? (X ONE box.)**

Some high school ☐	High school graduate ☐	Some college ☐
4 College graduate ☒	Post graduate ☐	

(37) **What is your race? (X ONE box.)**

Black ☐   Hispanic ☐   3 White ☒   Other _____ (please specify)

(38) **What is your gender? (X ONE box.)**

Female ☐   (2) Male ☒

(39-43) **What is your zip code?**

| 37922 | 37922 |

THANK YOU FOR SHARING YOUR FAST-FOOD OPINIONS WITH OUR MARKETING RESEARCH CLASS.

A computer storage room containing reels of data.

screen to enter a data element. A similar technique employs the use of a light pen, which is a handheld electronic pointer used to enter data through the terminal screen.

Recent changes in scanning technology and the proliferation of personal computers have created a new approach to data entry.[4] Questionnaires prepared on any form of Microsoft Windows software packages and printed on laser printers can be readily scanned through an optical scanning procedure. Exhibit 15.7 shows a questionnaire that has been designed for optical character recognition. This approach allows the computer to read alphabetic, numeric, and special character codes through a scanning device. On the questionnaire in Exhibit 15.7, the respondent would use a number two pencil to fill in his or her responses, which would then be scanned directly into a computer.

One critical task of data entry personnel is to ensure that the data entered are correct and error free. Customized software can prevent errors by making it impossible for data entry personnel to make certain types of mistakes. Due to the cost of development, however, such software is too expensive for many projects. Therefore, error detection is still a separate procedure that takes place as the output of the data entry process is analyzed.

Error Detection

The first step in error detection is to determine whether the software used for data entry and tabulation will allow the researcher to perform "error edit routines." These routines can identify the wrong type of data. For example, say that for a particular field on a given data record, only the codes of 1 or 2 should appear. An error edit routine can display an error message on the data output if any number other than 1 or 2 has been entered. Such routines can be quite thorough. For example, a particular coded value can be rejected if it is too large or too small for a particular scaled item on the questionnaire. In some instances, given the proper software, a separate error edit routine can be established for every item on the questionnaire.

EXHIBIT 15.7 **Example of Optical Character Recognition Questionnaire**

WELLNESS ASSESSMENT QUESTIONNAIRE

Risk Assessment Systems, Inc.
5846 Distribution Drive
Memphis, Tennessee 38141

INSTRUCTIONS

To ensure an accurate Personal Wellness Assessment, please answer all of the following questions as accurately and completely as possible.

USE A NO. 2 PENCIL ONLY   Example: ▢ ▢ ▆ ▢ ▢   Erase *completely* to change

Name _____

Street address _____

City _____

State _____

Phone # (_____) _____

Zip Code

Social Security Number

PHYSICAL DATA/CURRENT HEALTH STATUS

Sex
Date of Birth
Month — Day — Year
Height   ft.   in.
Weight   lbs.
Blood Pressure
If you know your Blood Pressure, enter it here ------>

Systolic (High)
Diastolic (Low)

If not, which best describes it?
▢ High
▢ Normal or Low
▢ Don't Know

▢ Male
▢ Female

1. In general, would you say your current state of health is:
▢ Excellent   ▢ Very Good   ▢ Good   ▢ Fair   ▢ Poor

2. During the past 12 months, how many days of work have you missed due to your own injury or sickness?
▢ None   ▢ 1 to 3   ▢ 4 to 6   ▢ 7 or more   ▢ Does not apply

PERSONAL/FAMILY MEDICAL HISTORY

3. How often are you given a routine physical examination by a physician?
▢ More than once a year   ▢ Once a year   ▢ Once every 2 years   ▢ Every 3 years or longer   ▢ Never had one

4. How long has it been since your last electrocardiogram (EKG)?
▢ Less than 1 year ago   ▢ 1 to 2 years ago   ▢ 2 to 3 years ago   ▢ 3 or more years ago   ▢ Never had one

5. Have you or has anyone in your family (parents, grandparents, brother or sister) had any of the following health problems? If so, please mark the corresponding box. *(Please mark all that apply.)*

	Self	Brother	Sister	Father	Mother	Father's side Grandfather	Father's side Grandmother	Mother's side Grandfather	Mother's side Grandmother
Heart disease before age 55	▢	▢	▢	▢	▢	▢	▢	▢	▢
Heart disease age 55 to 64	▢	▢	▢	▢	▢	▢	▢	▢	▢
Heart disease age 65 or later	▢	▢	▢	▢	▢	▢	▢	▢	▢
High blood pressure	▢	▢	▢	▢	▢	▢	▢	▢	▢
Stroke	▢	▢	▢	▢	▢	▢	▢	▢	▢
Diabetes	▢	▢	▢	▢	▢	▢	▢	▢	▢
Breast cancer	▢	▢	▢	▢	▢	▢	▢	▢	▢
Colon cancer	▢	▢	▢	▢	▢	▢	▢	▢	▢
Cancer (except breast/colon)	▢	▢	▢	▢	▢	▢	▢	▢	▢
Kidney disease	▢	▢	▢	▢	▢	▢	▢	▢	▢
Tuberculosis	▢	▢	▢	▢	▢	▢	▢	▢	▢
Mental illness	▢	▢	▢	▢	▢	▢	▢	▢	▢
Suicide	▢	▢	▢	▢	▢	▢	▢	▢	▢
Drug/alcohol addiction	▢	▢	▢	▢	▢	▢	▢	▢	▢

Continued on Page 2

© 1992 Risk Assessment Systems, Inc. 11/92

1

SCANTRON FORM NO. F-5414-RAS

P4 3593-C C1520- 5 4 3 2

Another approach to error detection is for the researcher to review a printed representation of the entered data. Exhibit 15.8, for example, illustrates the coded values for 23 observations that were collected from the questionnaire in Exhibit 15.6. In this example the very top row indicates the variable names assigned to each data field (i.e., "id" is the label for the questionnaire number, "tbq1" represents Taco Bell question 1, etc.). The numbers in the columns are the coded values that were entered. The dots indicate omitted responses. While the process is somewhat tedious, the analyst can view the actual entered data for accuracy and could tell exactly where any errors were located.

The final approach to error detection is to produce a data/column list procedure for the entered data. Once each error edit routine has been run, and any obvious errors corrected by viewing the actual data entry output, the analyst should request a data/column list table for each individual data field. A sample data/column list is shown in Exhibit 15.9. The rows of this output indicate the fields of the data record. The columns indicate the frequency of responses for each particular field. In data field 40, for example, 50 responses of 1 were entered, 20 responses of 2 were entered, and so on. A quick viewing of this data/column list procedure can indicate to the analyst whether inappropriate codes were entered into the data fields. The analyst can then find the corresponding questionnaire and correct the error as needed.

By initiating error edit routines, scanning actual raw data input, and producing a data/column list table, the researcher should be confident of error-free data entry. At this point the data should be ready for preliminary tabulation and data analysis. The In the Field box addresses additional issues of error detection.

Data Tabulation

Tabulation The simple process of counting the number of observations (cases) that are classified into certain categories.

One-way tabulation Categorization of single variables existing in a study.

Cross-tabulation Simultaneously treating two or more variables in the study; categorizing the number of respondents who have answered two or more questions, consecutively.

Tabulation is a simple process of counting the number of observations (cases) that are classified into certain categories. Two common forms of data tabulation are used in marketing research projects: one-way tabulations and cross-tabulations. A **one-way tabulation** is the categorization of single variables existing in the study. In most cases, a one-way tabulation shows the number of respondents who gave each possible answer to each question on the questionnaire. The actual number of one-way tabulations is directly related to the number of variables being measured in the study.

Cross-tabulation simultaneously treats two or more variables in the study. It categorizes the number of respondents who have responded to two or more consecutive questions. For example, a cross-tabulation could involve the number of respondents who spent more than $7.00 on fast food at McDonald's.

The use and purpose of tabulations range from further validation of the accuracy of the data to the communication of research results. Since each tabulation procedure serves its own unique purpose in the research study, each will be treated separately in our discussion.

One-Way Tabulation

One-way tabulations serve several purposes in the research project. First, they can be used to determine the degree of nonresponse to individual questions. Based on the coding scheme used for omitted responses, one-way tabulations will produce the actual number of respondents who omitted or failed to answer various questions on the questionnaire. Second, one-way tabulations can be used to locate simple blunders in data entry.

If a specific range of codes has been established for a given response to a question, say 1 through 5, a one-way tabulation can illustrate if an inaccurate code was entered, say a 7

EXHIBIT 15.8   Computer Output of Coded Values for 23 Observations

id	tbq1	harq1	kfcq1	wenq1	ralq1	popq1	kryq1	chrq1	mcdq1	bkq1	bybq1	arbq1	sonq1	otherq1	none
1	1						1					1	1		
2	1												1		
3	1	1	1	1			1		1	1					
4				1					1						
5	1	1		1					1						
6	1	1	1	1					1	1			1		
7	1								1	1					
8	1	1	1				1		1			1			
9		1								1		1			
10															
11		1		1											
12	1	1		1			1								
13									1	1					
14			1						1				1		
15	1			1			1		1		1				
16											1				
17	1	1					1								
18	1	1	1	1						1		1			
19	1								1	1					
20		1		1			1		1	1				1	
21	1								1						
22	1		1						1						
23	1	1		1			1		1	1		1			

A CLOSER LOOK AT RESEARCH   In the Field

Data Collection Should Not Be Manual Labor

With the computerization of survey design and dissemination, manual questionnaires have become a thing of the past. Computer-based surveys can accommodate vast and complex arrays of data, greatly increasing the capacity for data collection and substantially reducing confusion and errors by interviewers and respondents. Three of the major benefits are as follows:

1. **Encoding data without transcribing from paper.** The interviewer or respondent can enter encoded data directly into a computer database. Numerous hours of tedious effort can be eliminated by avoiding transcription from paper surveys.

2. **Minimizing errors in data.** Errors in data are less likely with computer data collection than with manual transcriptions of paper surveys. Researchers no longer have to decipher illegible interviewer or respondent handwriting.

3. **Speeding up data collection and coding.** Computer surveys can speed the process of gathering data at any or all of five points in the data collection process: (*a*) getting the questions to the respondent, (*b*) asking questions of the respondent, (*c*) recording the respondent's answers, (*d*) getting the answers back to the researcher, and (*e*) entering the answers into a computer database. Clearly, all of these add up to time savings, and potential cost savings.

EXHIBIT 15.9   Example of Data/Column List Procedure

Data Field	1	2	3	4	5	6	7
40	50	20	33	81	0	2	1
41	5	9	82	77	36	8	0
42	10	12	11	15	0	0	0
43	15	16	17	80	1	3	5
44	0	0	7	100	2	11	0
45	17	42	71	62	1	3	5
46	100	2	5	18	16	2	12
47	22	25	62	90	10	30	15
48	0	0	25	18	13	17	35
49	61	40	23	30	18	22	17
50	10	11	62	73	10	21	0
51	7	11	21	17	52	47	5
52	82	46	80	20	30	6	7

or 8, by providing a list of responses to the particular question. In addition, one-way tabulations are used to calculate summary statistics on various questions. Averages, standard deviations, and percentages are normally determined from the one-way tabulation. Finally, one-way tabulations are also used to communicate the results of the research project. One-way tabulations are used to profile sample respondents, establish characteristics that distinguish between groups (i.e., heavy users versus light users), and establish the percentage of respondents who respond differently to different situations (e.g., the percentage of people who purchase fast food from drive-thru windows, and those who use dine-in facilities).

The most basic way to illustrate a one-way tabulation is to construct a one-way frequency table. An example of this type of table is shown in Exhibit 15.10. A one-way frequency table illustrates the number of respondents who responded to questions given

EXHIBIT 15.10　　**Example of One-Way Frequency Distribution**

5. In the past TWO WEEKS, which fast-food restaurants in your area have you had food or beverage from?
(27) (DO NOT READ—MULTIPLE RESPONSE)

	Frequency	Percentage
1.　Andy's	3	.7
2.　Arby's	25	6.2
3.　Back Yard Burgers	26	6.4
4.　Burger King	48	11.9
5.　Church's Fried Chicken	3	.7
6.　Hardee's	22	5.4
7.　Kentucky Fried Chicken	39	9.7
8.　McDonald's	135	33.4
9.　Sonic	46	11.4
10.　Subway	14	3.5
11.　Taco Bell	67	16.6
12.　Wendy's	84	20.8
13.　Other	43	10.6
14.　Refused	1	.2
15.　Don't know	6	1.5
16.　None	52	12.9
17.　Pizza Hut	21	5.2
18.　Rally's	14	3.5
19.　Captain D's	9	2.2
Total qualified	404	100

the available alternatives. Exhibit 15.10 indicates that 48 customers (11.9 percent) ate at Burger King in the past two weeks, 135 (33.4 percent) ate at McDonald's, 84 (20.8 percent) ate at Wendy's, and so on. Normally, a computer printout will be produced with one-way frequency tables for each question on the survey. In addition to producing an absolute number of responses, one-way frequency tables also produce indications of missing data, valid percentages, and summary statistics.

1. **Indications of missing data.** One-way frequency tables indicate the absolute number of missing responses for each question. As illustrated in Exhibit 15.11, 17 respondents, or 3.8 percent of the sample, did not respond to how satisfied they were with the quality of food received during their last visit to a fast-food restaurant. It is important to recognize the actual number of missing responses when estimating percentages from a one-way frequency table. In order to establish valid percentages, missing responses must be removed from the calculation.

2. **Determining valid percentages.** The establishment of valid percentages is based on removing incomplete surveys or particular questions. For example, the one-way frequency table in Exhibit 15.11 actually constructs valid percentages (the fourth column). While the total number of responses for this particular question was 443, only 426 are used to develop the valid percentage of response across categories due to 17 missing responses.

3. **Summary statistics.** Finally, one-way frequency tables also can illustrate a variety of summary statistics relevant to the question being analyzed. Again in reference to Exhibit 15.11, the summary statistics for question 66, on quality of food, are mean, mode, median, and standard deviation. In the context of a one-way frequency table, these statistics allow the research analyst to get a better understanding concerning average responses. For example, with a mean of 4.681, most respondents were satisfied with the quality of food received during their last visit to a fast-food establishment. A full discussion of the significance and interpretation of summary statistics is given in Chapter 16.

Cross-Tabulation

Upon the construction of the one-way frequency table, the next logical step in preliminary data analysis is to perform cross-tabulation. Cross-tabulation is extremely useful when the analyst wishes to study relationships among and between variables. The purpose of the cross-tabulation is to determine whether certain variables differ when compared among various subgroups of the total sample. In fact, cross-tabulation is normally the main form of data analysis in most marketing research projects. Two key elements of cross-tabulation are how to develop the cross-tabulation and how to interpret the outcome.

Exhibit 15.12 shows a simple cross-tabulation between the number of visits and amount of money spent at fast-food establishments. The cross-tabulation shows frequencies and percentages, with percentages existing for both rows and columns. A simple way to interpret this table, for example, would be to isolate those individuals who visit fast-food establishments seven or more times per month. Generally speaking, they constitute 33.7 percent of the sample, with a majority of them spending $2 to $6 per visit (31.2 percent and 29.1 percent when viewed individually). While no relationship appears to exist between number of visits and dollars spent per visit, this cross-tabulation table still provides information about frequency of visits and how it may affect spending on fast food.

EXHIBIT 15.11   One-Way Frequency Table Illustrating Missing Data

Q65   CONVENIENTLY LOCATED

VALUE LABEL	VALUE	FREQUENCY	PERCENT	VALID PERCENT	CUM PERCENT
VERY DISSATISFIED	1	6	1.4	1.4	1.4
DISSATISFIED	2	5	1.4	1.4	2.8
SOMEWHAT DISSATISFIED	3	13	2.9	3.1	5.9
SOMEWHAT SATISFIED	4	57	12.9	13.4	19.2
SATISFIED	5	162	36.6	38.0	57.3
VERY SATISFIED	6	182	41.1	42.7	100.0
	*	17	3.8	MISSING	
		-----------	-----------	----------------	
	TOTAL	443	100.0	100.0	

MEAN	5.134	STD ERR	.049	MEDIAN	5.000
MODE	6.000	STD DEV	1.010	VARIANCE	1.020
KURTOSIS	3.398	S E KURT	.236	SKEWNESS	−1.607
S E SKEW	.118	RANGE	5.000	MINIMUM	1.000
MAXIMUM	6.000	SUM	2187.000		

VALID CASES   426   MISSING CASES   17

Q66   QUALITY OF FOOD

VALUE LABEL	VALUE	FREQUENCY	PERCENT	VALID PERCENT	CUM PERCENT
VERY DISSATISFIED	1	6	1.4	1.4	1.4
DISSATISFIED	2	11	2.5	2.6	4.0
SOMEWHAT DISSATISFIED	3	27	6.1	6.3	10.3
SOMEWHAT SATISFIED	4	126	28.4	29.6	39.9
SATISFIED	5	155	35.0	36.4	76.3
VERY SATISFIED	6	101	22.8	23.7	100.0
	*	17	3.8	MISSING	
		-----------	-----------	----------------	
	TOTAL	443	100.0	100.0	

MEAN	4.681	STD ERR	.052	MEDIAN	5.000
MODE	5.000	STD DEV	1.070	VARIANCE	1.145
KURTOSIS	1.019	S E KURT	.236	SKEWNESS	−.853
S E SKEW	.118	RANGE	5.000	MINIMUM	1.000
MAXIMUM	6.000	SUM	1994.000		

VALID CASES   426   MISSING CASES   17

EXHIBIT 15.12   Example of a Cross-Tabulation: Number of Visits × Money Spent

Q3 Count Row Pct Col Pct Tot Pct Q2		Under $2	$2.01 to $4	$4.01 to $6	$6.01 to $8	$8.01 to $10	$10.01 to $12	Over $12	Don't Remember	
	0	1	2	3	4	5	6	7	8	Total
0 None	1 100.0 100.0 .2									1 .2
1 One		1 2.0 14.3 .2	15 30.6 11.2 3.5	16 32.7 12.8 3.7	10 20.4 14.3 2.3	3 6.1 6.1 .7	1 2.0 5.0 .2	2 4.1 9.5 .5	1 2.0 33.3 .2	49 11.4
2 Two		1 1.7 14.3 .2	17 28.3 12.7 4.0	15 25.0 12.0 3.5	12 20.0 17.1 2.8	6 10.0 12.2 1.4	5 8.3 25.0 1.2	2 3.3 9.5 .5	2 3.3 66.7 .5	60 14.0
3 Three		1 2.3 14.3 .2	8 18.6 6.0 1.9	15 34.9 12.0 3.5	11 25.6 15.7 2.6	4 9.3 8.2 .9	2 4.7 10.0 .5	2 4.7 9.5 .5		43 10.0
4 Four			33 46.5 24.6 7.7	16 22.5 12.8 3.7	9 12.7 12.9 2.1	7 9.9 14.3 1.6	1 1.4 5.0 .2	5 7.0 23.8 1.2		71 16.5
5 Five			9 33.3 6.7 2.1	10 37.0 8.0 2.3	3 11.1 4.3 .7	3 11.1 6.1 .7	1 3.7 5.0 .2	1 3.7 4.8 .2		27 6.3
6 Six		1 2.9 14.3 .2	7 20.6 5.2 1.6	10 29.4 8.0 2.3	6 17.6 8.6 1.4	4 11.8 8.2 .9	2 5.9 10.0 .5	4 11.8 19.0 .9		34 7.9
7 Seven or more		3 2.1 42.9 .7	45 31.0 33.6 10.5	43 29.7 34.4 10.0	19 13.1 27.1 4.4	22 15.2 44.9 5.1	8 5.5 40.0 1.9	5 3.4 23.8 1.2		145 33.7
Column (Continued) Total	1 .2	7 1.6	134 31.2	125 29.1	70 16.3	49 11.4	20 4.7	21 4.9	3 .7	430 100.0

Regarding the development and interpretation of cross-tabulation tables, several issues need to be identified and examined.[5] Several different percentages are calculated within each cell of the cross-tabulation table. The top number within each cell represents the absolute frequency of responses for each variable or question (i.e., 33 respondents who visit fast-food establishments four times per month spend approximately $2 to $4 per visit). Below the absolute frequency is the row percentage per cell. For example, the 33 individuals who visit fast-food establishments four times per month and spend $2 to $4 per visit represent 46.5 percent of the total (which is 71) in that frequency category. The third number within each cell is the column percentage. In this example, of 134 respondents who spend $2 to $4 per visit, 24.6 percent of them average four visits per month. The last number within each cell represents the total percentage of respondents within cells based on the total sample. So, for example, with a total sample of 430, 7.7 percent of the sample visit fast-food restaurants four times per month and spend approximately $2 to $4 per visit.

When constructing the cross-tabulation table, the analyst must select the variable to use when examining relationships. As always, the selection of variables should be based on the objectives of the research project. Paired variable relationships should be selected on the basis of whether they answer the specific research questions put forth in the research project.

Best practices within the marketing research industry normally dictate the use of demographic variables or lifestyle/psychographic characteristics as the starting point in developing cross-tabulations. These variables normally constitute the column indicators of the cross-tabulation table, with purchase intention, usage, motivational factors, or actual sales variables constituting the rows. Cross-tabulation tables such as these calculate percentages on the basis of column variable totals. In turn, this allows the research analyst to make comparisons on the relationship between behaviors and intentions with predictor variables such as income, sex, and marital status. Preliminary analysis of this nature is especially useful if the researcher wants to establish subgroup differences in relation to certain actions. For example, Exhibit 15.13 illustrates the relationships between sex, marital status, and education in regard to number of visits to fast-food establishments.

As a preliminary technique, cross-tabulation provides the research analyst with a powerful tool for summarizing survey data. The technique is easy to understand and interpret, and can provide a valid description of both aggregate and subgroup data. Yet the simplicity of this technique can create certain problems. Certain survey approaches can lend themselves to the construction of an endless variety of cross-tabulation tables. In developing these tables, the analyst must always keep in mind both the project objectives and specific research questions the study will attempt to answer. The analyst should take care to construct cross-tabulations that accurately reflect information relevant to the objectives of the project. A variety of software and statistical packages can be used to generate cross-tabulation tables. Spreadsheets such as Lotus, Excel, Access, and Quattro Pro, along with statistical packages like SAS, SPSS, Querie, and Systat can all generate effective cross-tabulations. Chapter 16 will discuss various statistical techniques normally used in conjunction with cross-tabulation, as well as tests of association, significant differences, and measures of central tendency.

Graphical Illustration of Data

The next logical step following the construction of one-way frequency and cross-tabulation tables is to translate them into graphical illustrations. Graphical illustrations, as opposed to tables, can be very powerful for communicating key research results generated from preliminary data analysis to the client. Given the importance of this topic, an elaborate and detailed discussion will be provided in Chapters 16 through 19.

| EXHIBIT 15.13 | Example of a Cross-Tabulation: Demographic Variables × Behavior |

Q2 Visits per Month by Q1520 Gender

Q1520   Page 1 of 1

Count

Q2		Female 1	Male 2	Row Total
0	None	1	1	2 .5
1	One	27	23	50 11.8
2	Two	25	33	58 13.6
3	Three	16	25	41 9.6
4	Four	38	32	70 16.5
5	Five	12	14	26 6.1
6	Six	19	15	34 8.0
7	Seven or more	70	74	144 33.9
Column Total		208 48.9	217 51.1	425 100.0

Number of Missing Observations: 18

Q2 Visits per Month by Q1515 Marital status

Q1515   Page 1 of 1

Count

Q2		Married 1	Widowed 2	Separated 3	Divorced 4	Never Married 5	Row Total
0	None	2					2 .5
1	One	41	7		1	1	50 11.8
2	Two	46	4	1	3	4	58 13.7
3	Three	30	3		4	3	40 9.5
4	Four	53	6		6	5	70 16.6
5	Five	21	2			2	25 5.9
6	Six	31		1	1	1	34 8.1
7	Seven or more	116	6	1	12	8	143 33.9
Column Total		340 80.6	28 6.6	3 .7	27 6.4	24 5.7	422 100.0

Number of Missing Observations: 21

SUMMARY OF LEARNING OBJECTIVES

Illustrate the process of preparing data for preliminary analysis.

The value of marketing research is its ability to provide decision-making information to the user or client. To accomplish this, the raw data must be converted into usable information. After collecting data through the appropriate method, the task becomes one of ensuring that the data will provide meaning and value. Data preparation is the first part of the process of transforming raw data to usable information. This process takes into account five steps: (1) data validation, (2) editing and coding, (3) data entry, (4) error detection, and (5) data tabulation.

Demonstrate the procedure for assuring data validation.

Data validation attempts to determine whether surveys, interviews, or observations were conducted correctly and are free from fraud. In recontacting select respondents, the researcher asks whether the interview (1) was falsified, (2) was conducted with a qualified respondent, (3) took place in the proper procedural setting, (4) was completed correctly and accurately, and (5) was accomplished in a courteous manner.

Illustrate the process of editing and coding data obtained through survey methods.

The editing process involves the manual scanning of interviews or questionnaire responses to determine whether the proper questions were asked, proper answers recorded, and proper screening questions employed, as well as whether open-ended questions were recorded accurately. Once edited, all questionnaires are coded by assigning numerical value to all responses. Coding is the process of providing numeric labels to the data so they can be entered into a computer for subsequent statistical analysis.

Acquaint the user with data entry procedures.

There are four principal methods of entering coded data into a computer. First is the keyboard terminal or PC keyboard. Data may also be entered through terminals having touch-screen capabilities, or through the use of a handheld electronic pointer or light pen. Finally, data from certain questionnaires can be entered through a scanner using optical character recognition.

Illustrate the process of detecting errors in data entry.

Unfortunately, error detection normally occurs after the data have been entered into computer storage. Entry errors can be detected through the use of error edit routines, built or developed, into the data entry software. An additional approach is to visually scan the actual data after they have been entered. A data table is one approach for visually scanning entered data.

Discuss techniques used for data tabulation and data analysis.

Two common forms of data tabulations are used in marketing research. A one-way tabulation indicates the number of respondents who gave each possible answer to each question on a questionnaire. Cross-tabulation provides categorization of respondents by treating two or more variables simultaneously. Categorization is based on the number of respondents who have responded to two or more consecutive questions.

KEY TERMS AND CONCEPTS

Coding 482	**Data entry** 491	**One-way tabulation** 501
Cross-tabulation 501	**Data validation** 480	**Tabulation** 501
Curbstoning 480	**Editing** 481	

REVIEW QUESTIONS

1. Briefly describe the process of data validation. Specifically discuss the issues of fraud, screening, procedure, completeness, and courtesy.

2. What are the differences between data validation, data editing, and data coding?

3. Explain the differences between establishing codes for open-ended questions versus closed-ended questions.

4. Briefly describe the process of data entry. What changes in technology have simplified this procedure?

5. What are the three approaches to error detection? In your discussion be sure to describe the data/column list procedure.

6. What is the purpose of a simple one-way tabulation? How does this relate to a one-way frequency table?

DISCUSSION QUESTIONS

1. **EXPERIENCE THE INTERNET.** Go to the Web site for the Acxiom Corporation, at www.acxiom.com, and select the topic *Case in Point*. Once there select the topic *Newsletters* and select the newsletter for vol. 2, issue 1. Read the passage on cluster coding systems and comment on how they apply to preliminary data analysis.

2. **EXPERIENCE THE INTERNET.** At the Acxiom Web site select newsletter vol. 2, issue 3. Select the article on data warehousing and comment on how it relates to the coding of marketing data.

3. Obtain a copy of a marketing research questionnaire, and, based on your knowledge of developing codes, convert the questionnaire into a master code illustrating the appropriate values for each question and corresponding responses.

4. Look back at the quote at the beginning of this chapter. Based on what you now know about preparing data for analysis, explain what Robert W. Kneen meant by "garbage in, garbage out."

ENDNOTES

1. Barry DeVille, "The Data Assembly Challenge," *Marketing Research Magazine* (Fall/Winter 1995).

2. Ibid.

3. Paula Kephart, "The Spy in Aisle 3," *American Demographics* (May 1996).

4. Ibid.

5. Ken Gofton, "Pushing All the Right Buttons," *Marketing,* November 23, 1995.

MARKETING RESEARCH ILLUSTRATION

ASSESSING DATA COMPLETENESS OF A TRADITIONAL SHOPPER SURVEY

This illustration provides an example of how preliminary analysis is used to assess the completeness and accuracy of collected data. While at first glance the illustration may appear incomplete, the focus is on data validation and accuracy, not on making inferences from the data. This illustration also shows some common outcomes of open-ended questions.

Memphis Shopper Survey

Results of the shopper survey for Belz Factory Outlet World. Designations are: Mall = Responses from mall patrons ($n = 185$): Mail = Responses from mail survey ($n = 60$); Total = Total responses ($n = 245$).

Listed below are various shopping centers in the area. Which centers have you visited in the past two months? Check as many as apply. (Figures are percentage of responses.)

	Mall	Mail	Total
Mall of Memphis	18.9	26.7	20.85
Wolfchase Galleria	69.7	66.7	69.0
Belz Factory Outlet	51.4	20.0	43.7
Oak Court Mall	45.4	48.3	46.1
Hickory Ridge Mall	29.2	38.3	31.4
Raleigh Springs Mall	23.8	21.7	23.3
Southland Mall	4.9	5.0	4.9
Saddle Creek	19.5	20.0	19.6
Other	5.4	11.7	6.9

Listed below are a set of attributes (reasons) many people use when selecting a shopping center to visit. Regarding your most recent selection of a shopping center, please rank each attribute from 1 to 8, with "1" being the most important and "8" being the least important reason for visiting that center. (Figures are average responses.)

	Mall	Mail	Total
Variety of stores	2.5	3.0	2.6
Location	2.6	2.3	2.5
Safety	3.5	3.2	3.5
Entertainment	5.8	6.2	6.0
Restaurants	5.1	5.7	5.3
Specific store	3.1	3.0	3.1
Special events	6.8	6.9	6.8
Atmosphere	2.0	2.1	2.0

On your last visit to a shopping center which type of store(s) did you visit? Check as many as apply. (Figures are percentages of responses.)

	Mall	Mail	Total
Department store (Dillard's, Goldsmith's)	77.8	81.7	78.8
Discount store (Wal-Mart, Target)	48.6	55.0	50.2
Specialty store (The Gap, Circuit City)	52.4	50.0	51.8
Outlet store (stores in outlet malls)	48.6	16.7	40.8
Other			

Listed below are a variety of entertainment offerings available at most shopping centers. On your last visit to a shopping center, please indicate which entertainment offering you attended/visited? Check as many as apply. (Figures are percentage of responses.)

	Mall	Mail	Total
Movie theater	45.4	31.7	42.0
Video game arcade	11.4	3.3	9.4
Ice skating rink	5.4	3.3	4.9
Carousel	11.9	10.0	11.4
Food court	62.7	48.3	59.2
Special events such as car shows or craft shows	9.7	10.0	9.8
Other	2.2	0	1.6
None			

On your most recent visit to a shopping center, approximately how much time did you spend at the shopping center? (Figures are percentage of responses.)

	Mall	Mail	Total
Less than 1 hour	18.4	21.7	19.2
1 to 3 hours	70.3	76.7	71.8
4 to 6 hours	9.7	0	7.3
More than 6 hours	1.1	1.7	1.2

On your most recent visit to a shopping center, approximately how much did you spend on goods and services? (Figures are percentage of responses.)

	Mall	Mail	Total
Under $20	12.4	18.3	13.9
$21 to $40	10.9	20.0	18.0
$41 to $60	19.5	13.3	18.0
$61 to $80	17.3	15.0	16.7
$81 to $100	9.0	6.3	9.0
Over $100	29.7	25.0	28.6

On your last visit to a shopping center in the Memphis area, how far did you have to travel? (Figures are percentage of responses.)

	Mall	Mail	Total
Less than 5 miles	33.5	50.0	37.6
6 to 10 miles	33.0	38.3	34.3
11 to 15 miles	9.7	10.0	9.8
More than 15 miles	23.2	1.7	18.0

On your last visit to a shopping center which of the following products, from the categories below, did you purchase? Check as many as apply. (Responses are for total sample; figures are percentage of responses.)

Clothes	75.9	Shoes	34.3
Books/magazines	23.3	Household items	29.0
Furniture	6.1	Toys	11.0
Sporting goods	10.6	Appliances	2.4
Home electronics	12.2	Cosmetics	22.9
Hardware	11.0	Computer	3.7
Other	9.4		
None			

In the past month, have you heard or seen any advertisements for shopping centers in the Memphis area? (Figures are percentage of total sample.)

Yes	43.7
No	26.1
Don't remember	28.6

If yes, what shopping center? (See attached list.)

The following questions refer to your perceptions on the value and quality of Memphis area shopping centers. On a scale of 1 to 5, with "1" being strongly disagree and "5" being strongly agree, please rate the following statements. (Figures are average responses from total sample.)

In my opinion, all shopping centers are the same.	2.4
Shopping centers should include entertainment for the whole family.	3.5
I prefer to shop at smaller centers rather than large malls.	3.2
Shopping centers need to increase their security.	4.1
I generally go to a shopping center because of certain stores.	4.2
While I don't plan on it, I usually end up eating at a restaurant in the shopping center.	2.9
I consider shopping a social event.	2.4
I normally go to shopping centers that feature special events such as car shows or craft fairs.	1.9
Shopping centers need to offer customers entertainment such as movies, arcades, etc.	3.0
Type of stores located in the shopping center is the main reason why I go to the center.	4.3

Are you aware of a shopping center called the Belz Factory Outlet Mall? (Figures are percentage of responses.)

		Mall	Mail	Total
Yes ___	If yes, go to question 12.	91.4	91.7	91.4
No ___	If no, go to question 18.			

In the past six months how many times have you visited the Belz Factory Outlet Mall? (Figures are percentage of responses.)

	Mall	Mail	Total
None	27.6	60.0	92.9
1 to 3 times	14.6	0.00	6.1
4 to 6 times	47.0	30.0	42.9
More than six times	5.9	0.0	0.0

On a scale of 1 to 5 with "1" being very dissatisfied and "5" being very satisfied, how would you rate the Belz Factory Outlet Mall on the following factors. (Figures represent average responses.)

	Mall	Mail	Total
Type of stores available	2.7	2.8	2.7
Number of stores available	2.7	2.7	2.7
Variety of food offerings	2.1	2.3	2.1
Level of entertainment available	2.2	2.3	2.2
Quality of the food court	2.3	2.3	2.3

On your most recent visit to the Belz Factory Outlet Mall, which store(s) did you patronize?

See attached list.

In the past two months, do you recall seeing or hearing any advertising for the Belz Factory Outlet Mall? (Figures are percentage of total sample.)

No   53.4

Yes   38.4

If yes, where did you see or hear them?

Television	8.6	Radio	13.9
Newspaper	6.1	Billboard	20.4
Other			

On your last visit, what was your primary reason for visiting the Belz Factory Outlet Mall?

See Attached List.

If you could suggest an improvement to the Belz Factory Outlet Mall, what would that improvement be?

See Attached List.

On a scale of 0% to 100%, what percentage of your weekly television viewing time is devoted to cable TV networks such as ESPN, TBS, CNN, etc.?

Average response for total sample 38.1%

On a scale of 0% to 100%, what percentage of your weekly television viewing time is devoted to traditional TV networks such as ABC, CBS, NBC, etc.?

Average response for total sample 49.2%

Here is a list of different types of music. Would you please read down the list and check each type that you listen to fairly often? Check as many as apply. (Figures are percentages of total sample.)

Country/western	40.8	Soft rock	35.9
Country rock	21.6	New wave	14.7
Classic rock	38.4	Jazz	14.4
Hard rock	13.5	Gospel	20.4
Rhythm & blues	26.5	None of these	7.3

Which newspaper do you read most often? (Figures are percentages of total sample.)>

Name of newspaper:	See Attached List.
Don't read newspapers	12.7

Approximately what is your age? (Figures are percentages of total sample.)

Under 18	3.7
18 to 30	23.1
31 to 40	12.7
41 to 50	33.1
51 to 60	12.2
Over 60	9.8

Approximately, what is your total family household income? (Figures are percentages of total sample.)

Under $15,000	6.5
$15,001 to $20,000	2.0
$20,001 to $30,000	13.3
$30,001 to $40,000	13.1
$40,001 to $50,000	12.2
Over $50,000	38.6

Do you have any children? (Figures are percentages of total sample.)

Yes   54.7   No   39.2

If yes, how many children do you have living at home? (Figures are percentages of total sample.)

None   1.2   One   55.5   Two   11.0   Three   16.7   Four   6.9   Five or more   .8

What is your marital status? (Figures are percentages of total sample.)

Single   28.6   Married   53.5   Divorced/Separated   9.0   Widowed   3.0

Are you? Female   58.4   Male   35.1   **(Figures are percentages of total sample.)**

What is your occupation?

See Attached List.

What is your zip code?

See Attached List.

ADS FOR SHOPPING CENTERS SEEN OR HEARD

01	Wolf Chase
02	Dillards
03	Belz
04	Amber Chambre Fitch
05	Goldsmith
06	Outlet
07	Wal-Mart
08	Saddle Creek
09	Oak Court
10	Mall of Memphis
11	Target
12	Bill Board
13	Home Depot
14	Hickory Ridge Mall

STORES PATRONIZED ON MOST RECENT VISIT TO BELZ

01	Old Time Pottery	18	Stack Room
02	Corning	19	Foot Locker
03	Furniture	20	Lighthouse Factory
04	Hanes/Leggs	21	Book Store
05	Bass	22	Naturalizer
06	Van Heusen	23	Famous Footwear
07	Rack Room Shoes	24	Regal
08	Maiden Form	25	Silk Flowers
09	Bugle Boy	26	Carter's Outlet
10	Book Land	27	Craft
11	Casual Corner	28	Vitamin World
12	Capacity	29	Luggage Store
13	Toy Store	30	Optical Outlet
14	Saks	31	Claires
15	Saks-Off 5th	32	Musk Store
16	Music 4 Less	33	Danskin
17	Dress Barn	34	Ducks Unlimited

PRIMARY REASON FOR VISITING BELZ

01	Children's Clothes	14	Casual Corner
02	Rugs	15	Shoes
03	Pottery	16	Toy Store
04	Christmas Trees	17	Work
05	Underwear/Hose	18	Home Store
06	Clothes	19	Better Prices
07	Meet Friends	20	Christmas Shopping
08	Furniture	21	Car Show
09	Household Items	22	Ducks Unlimited
10	Dried Flowers	23	Vitamins
11	Bugle Boy	24	Glasses
12	Browsing	25	Craft
13	Check Sales	26	Books

SUGGESTED IMPROVEMENTS FOR BELZ MALL

01	Higher Quality Clothes
02	Upscale Outlets
03	Larger Food Selection
04	Known Name National Brands
05	Store Variety
06	Advertisement
07	Sales
08	More Store Selection
09	Entertainment
10	Men's Clothing (Only)
11	Better Prices
12	Handicap Accessories
13	Security
14	Merry-go-round
15	Kid's Stuff
16	Gift Stores
17	Theater
18	Woman's Clothing

NEWSPAPERS READ

01	Commercial Appeal	16	Fort Worth Telegram
02	USA Today	17	Indy Star & News
03	Wall Street Journal	18	New York Times
04	Memphis Flyer	19	Financial Times
05	Business Journal	20	Desoto Times Today
06	Germantown News	21	Dallas Morning News
07	Tennessean	22	Columbus (OH) Dispatch
08	Tribune	23	Jackson Sun
09	Daily Journal of Tupelo	24	Crockett Times
10	Don't Read Newspaper	25	Tri-State Defender
11	People	26	Star
12	Covington Leader	27	Bartlett Express
13	Jonesboro San	28	Chicago Sun Times
14	Dyersburg State Gazette	29	Shelby Sun Times
15	Paragould Daily Press		

OCCUPATION OF RESPONDENTS

01	Managerial
02	Professional
03	Sales
04	Clerical
05	Craftsman

MARKETING RESEARCH CASE EXERCISE

ENVIROSELL

This Case Exercise Pertains to the Video Case Envirosell

As you can see in the video, Envirosell is a marketing research firm that specializes in gathering data through observation. The video shows how consumers act and behave in certain store environments when initiating the purchase situation. Observation is becoming a widely used method of gathering data on consumers, yet, despite all the benefits associated with this method of data collection, it offers several challenges in the area of preparing data for analysis.

After viewing the video, what do you feel to be the major problems associated with preparing observation data for analysis? Specifically comment on the following issues:

1. How can a researcher validate observation data, especially with regard to fraud, screening, procedure, and completeness?

2. How should Envirosell categorize its collected data? Also, how should Envirosell handle verification of accuracy, error detection, and coding of responses?

Learning Objectives

After reading this chapter, you will be able to

1. Understand the mean, median, and mode as measures of central tendency.

2. Understand the range and standard deviation of a frequency distribution as measures of dispersion.

3. Understand how to graph measures of central tendency.

4. Understand the difference between independent and related samples.

5. Explain hypothesis testing.

6. Understand how to determine the error in hypothesis testing.

7. Understand univariate t- and z-tests for determining the significance for means and proportions.

8. Understand bivariate t- and z-tests for means and proportions.

9. Understand ANOVA and the various types of variance within it.

10. Understand how to determine the statistical significance of differences between means in ANOVA.

Data Analysis: Testing for Significant Differences

❝ The more I know, the more I know I don't know. ❞

ANONYMOUS

Statistical Software

Marketing research efforts often net significant amounts of data and information. However, many companies do not have or do not take the time to statistically analyze the information that they have obtained. Two software packages, SPSS and SAS, provide statistical processing capabilities for a variety of tasks. Each technique is briefly described below.

SPSS

The Statistical Product and Service Solutions (SPSS) software package is designed to be user-friendly, even for novice computer users. Released in the Microsoft Windows format and touted as "Real Stats. Real Easy," SPSS delivers easy data access and management, highly customizable output, complete just-in-time-training, and a revolutionary system for working with charts and graphs. The producers of SPSS proudly claim that "you don't have to be a statistician to use SPSS," an important characteristic for individuals who are somewhat afraid of computers and their power. Available in almost any format, SPSS provides immense statistical analysis capability while remaining one of the most user-friendly statistical packages available today. Information concerning SPSS is available online at www.spss.com.

SAS

The SAS (rhymes with *class*) system provides extensive statistical capabilities, including tools for both specialized and enterprisewide analytical needs. Research institutes, laboratories, marketing research firms, universities, pharmaceutical companies, government agencies, and banks all take advantage of the statistical capabilities of SAS. From traditional analysis of variance to exact methods of statistical visualization, the SAS system provides the tools required to analyze data and help organizations make the right statistical choices. Many heavy users of statistical software packages feel that SAS offers greater statistical analysis capability than SPSS. However, this increased statistical power is sometimes compromised by applications less user-friendly than those of SPSS. Information concerning SAS is available online at www.sas.com.

Value of Testing for Differences in Data

Once the data have been collected and prepared for analysis, there are some basic statistical analysis procedures the marketing researcher will want to perform. An obvious need for these statistics comes from the fact that almost all data sets are disaggregated; that is, it's hard to find out what the entire set of responses means because there are "too many numbers" to look at. Consequently, every set of data needs some summary information developed that describes the numbers it contains. Basic statistics and descriptive analysis were developed for this purpose.

Some of the statistics common to almost all marketing research projects are described in this chapter. The chapter also explains how to graphically display the data so decision makers can understand it. For example, if you conducted a study of people who buy Domino's pizza you would be able to most effectively show who the most frequent purchasers are compared to the least frequent purchasers, and perhaps why. The In the Field box describes how these statistics are used in the field.

First we describe measures of central tendency and dispersion. The advantages and pitfalls of each measure need to be understood so that the distribution of the information can be reasonably well described. Next, we discuss relationships of the sample data. The *t*-distribution and associated confidence interval estimation, the *z*-distribution, and sample proportions are all discussed in this second section. Third, we describe hypothesis testing, including tests for examining hypotheses related to differences between two sample

Birds of a Feather Flock Together

Marketers use geodemographic clusters to reach new customers, select business sites, target direct mail campaigns, and perform a multitude of other customer-centered tasks. Recently the major input data providers have incorporated the 1990 census data. The providers have revised their cluster systems in order to provide the best value to marketers seeking to identify and reach their best business prospects. Geodemographics is one of the most efficient segmentation systems available for capturing customers.

Geodemographics incorporates geographic segmentation with demographic information. The systems provide a methodical means of breaking down the nation's neighborhoods into similar groups, known as clusters. Cluster systems are predicated on the notion that birds of a feather tend to flock together. Susan Mitchell, a contributing editor of *American Demographics,* suggests that you look at your own neighborhood. The homes and cars are very likely to be similar in size and in value. The similarity within the cluster extends to what magazines are in the mailboxes and what breakfast cereals are on the table.

Popular cluster systems include Claritas's PRIZM; Strategic Mapping's Cluster Plus 2000; NDS/Equifax's Micro Vision; and CACI's ACORN. Each of these systems incorporates descriptive statistics from the 1990 decennial census to segment the nation into comparable clusters. Some of the clustering systems use catchy names, such as PRIZM's "Blue Blood Estates." Other systems use descriptive names such as "Urban New Families" in the Cluster Plus 2000 scheme.

Whatever the name, each system breaks the neighborhood into groups based on similarities in income, education, household type, attitudes, and product preferences. Each of the major segmentation systems is both dynamic and flexible. The 1990 census statistics provided an enormous amount of new data, which prompted two of the players to completely overhaul their systems and develop new sets of clusters organized in different ways.

Constructing a clustering system is no mean feat. It takes some fancy methods to tease out patterns that can be used to link millions of households. Marketers turned to biological science to find a way of matching census geography and postal service zip codes. Just as a species is a class of objects that have common attributes and is designated by a common name, a cluster is a class of households with common demographic and lifestyle characteristics.

Even deciding on the number of clusters is difficult. Clusters must be large enough to provide meaningful distinctions between groups, but small enough to be manageable. Imagine a clustering system that differentiates on every characteristic of Americans. Such a system would develop over 260 million clusters, each with a population of one individual. At the other extreme, a clustering system that incorporated only the characteristic of "living in the United States" would produce a single cluster with 260 million individuals. The challenge of clustering is to find a system that teases out homogeneous groups but provides sufficient diversity so that the clusters are not overly large.

One thing that is perfectly clear is that the segmentation scheme is only as good as the data that go into it. The marketing power of clustering lies in the ability to predict the consumers' behavior.

One marketing use of clustering is to find customers. Suppose a direct mail campaign gets a surprisingly strong response from a particular zip code. In effect, there are two ways to use segmentation systems to find customers. One way is for firms that already know who their customers are, and the other is for firms that need to find out who their customers are.

Clustering can reveal niches of potential customers in surprising locations. Perhaps even more important, clustering can show places that are poor prospects. Isuzu used clustering to determine that Chicago was an excellent place to sell convertible cars. Their models predicted sales would be strong, very much counterintuitively. However, the two top dealers in convertible sales were in Chicago.

Clustering can also be used for selecting business locations. Clustering allows the business to *(continued) (concluded)* skip the tedious process of driving through area after area to get a feel for the neighborhood. Clustering allows the firm to take a virtual tour of many areas very quickly while avoiding subjective bias from first impressions.

However, not every firm can make good use of a clustering system. Most experts think that 2,000 cus-tomers is the absolute minimum a firm should have to use a geodemographic clustering system. Many experts think that 5,000 to 10,000 customers is a more accurate minimum for best results.

Source: Susan Mitchell, "Birds of a Feather," *American Demographics,* February 1995, pp. 40+.

means, as well as appropriate terminology. Finally, the chapter closes with an introduction to analysis of variance, a powerful technique for detecting differences between three or more sample means.

Guidelines for Graphics

Graphics should be used whenever practical. They help the information user to quickly grasp the essence of the information developed in the research project. Charts also can be an effective visual aid to enhance the communication process and add clarity and impact. For example, the data in Exhibit 16.1 (from a study in which respondents were asked to rate the importance of having a compact disc player in a new automobile) are turned into a graph in Exhibit 16.2 to provide more expression to the data. The old saying "A picture is worth a thousand words" is still as true today as it ever has been.

Histograms and Bar Charts

A bar chart shows the data in the form of horizontal or vertical bars. Bar charts are excellent tools for depicting both absolute and relative magnitudes, differences, and change. A histogram is a form of a bar chart where each bar's height is the relative or cumulative frequency of a value of a specific variable (see Exhibits 16.2 and 16.3).

EXHIBIT 16.1 | **Frequency Distribution: Importance of a Compact Disc Player in a New Automobile**

Value Label	Value	Frequency (N)	Percent	Valid %	Cumulative %
Very important	1	25	6.3	6.6	6.6
Important	2	75	19.0	19.7	26.3
Somewhat important	3	100	25.3	26.3	52.6
Somewhat unimportant	4	89	22.5	23.4	76.1
Unimportant	5	65	16.5	17.1	93.2
Very unimportant	6	25	6.3	6.6	100.0
Missing	9	16	4.1	—	—
Totals		395	100.0		

EXHIBIT 16.2 **Importance of a Compact Disc Player in a New Automobile**

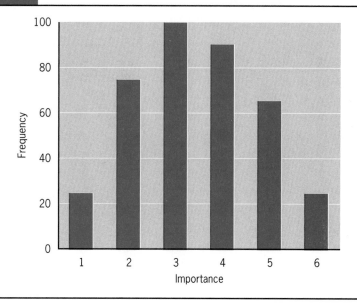

EXHIBIT 16.3 **Importance of a Compact Disc Player in a New Automobile Displayed as a Horizontal Bar Chart**

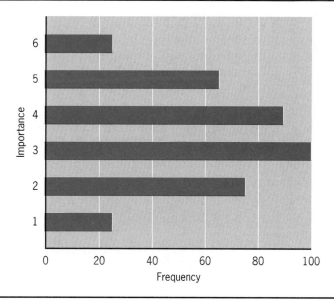

Line Charts

A line chart simply connects a series of data points with a continuous line. Line charts are frequently used to portray trends over several periods of time. In addition, several lines can be displayed on the same chart, allowing for multiple comparisons by the viewer. This can be very useful in explaining comparisons between variables. If multiple lines are used in the same chart, each line needs to have its own label and must be clearly different in form or color to avoid confusing the viewer. Exhibit 16.4 is a special form of a line chart, called

EXHIBIT 16.4	**Importance of a Compact Disc Player in a New Automobile Displayed as an Area Chart**

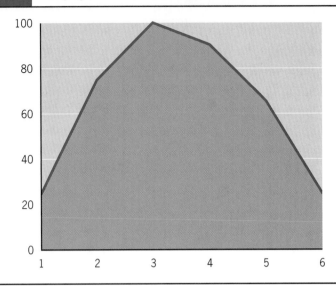

an area chart. In an area chart, the area below the line is filled in to dramatically display the information.

Pie or Round Charts

Pie charts are very good at displaying relative proportions. Each section of the pie is the relative proportion, as a percentage of the total area of the pie, associated with the value of a specific variable. The relative proportions of a set of data were used to create the chart in Exhibit 16.5. Pie charts are not useful for displaying comparative information between

EXHIBIT 16.5	**Importance of a Compact Disc Player in a New Automobile Displayed as a Pie Chart (Valid % of All Responses)**

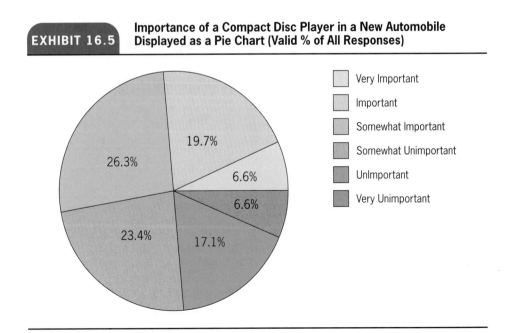

| **EXHIBIT 16.6** | **A *Good* Picture Is Worth a Thousand Words** |

Many people panic when confronted with mounds of statistics, but they are quick to rely on charts and graphs. The old saying "A picture is worth a thousand words" seems especially appropriate when applied to charts intended to simplify tables of numbers. The problem is, however, that the saying lacks one very important qualifier: a *good* picture is worth a thousand words. A *bad* picture is worth very little.

Unfortunately, we are all exposed to many charts that are bad pictures. A chart may be colorful, artistic, eye-catching, and even accurate but can still fail in its mission. Charts are supposed to dramatize the facts, but some—called "gee-whiz" charts—overstate the facts.

Gee-whiz chart is a term coined by Darrell Huff in his book *How to Lie with Statistics,* first published in 1954. No doubt Huff intended his book to help readers recognize misleading representations of data, though some readers may have misappropriated it as a primer for data muddling instead. Politicians, economists, marketing researchers, and many others with an ax to grind or a cause to promote have used gee-whiz charts to overdramatize their point.

It is simple to make a gee-whiz chart. Draw the chart correctly and cut off the bottom part. Insert a little jog in the vertical scale on the left to indicate that the scale is incomplete and you have created a chart that overdramatizes any trend, up or down, and makes it appear to be much more impressive.

Suppose annual sales of a brand of toothpaste dropped from 420 tons to 295 tons, a 30 percent decline. A good picture will show a 30 percent decline, but a gee-whiz chart would show something that looked like a 90 percent decline. While close examination of the numbers will reveal the actual decline to be 30 percent, the picture creates a stronger, and thus misleading, impression. The numbers tell, the picture shows—a sort of twisted version of a children's show-and-tell exercise.

Thomas Semon, a research consultant, bemoans the fact that he has seen many gee-whiz charts in research presentations. He notes that it is very unlikely that a marketing researcher would deliberately distort the actual results when expressed in numbers, yet some will distort the results visually in charts. A misleading chart is disinformation according to Semon. It is a deliberate attempt to create an erroneous impression or to make a trend appear more dramatic and noteworthy.

He suggests the following experiment. Look closely at every chart you see in the newspaper and magazines for the next week. Imagine what they would look like if they were correctly drawn. If many of the trends appear insignificant, it may be because the trend is insignificant. This is a useful thought to keep in mind when interpreting information.

As a final note, Semon says that while a lot of news is hype, research shouldn't be.

Sources: Based on Thomas T. Semon, "A Bad Picture Is Worth Very Few Words," *Marketing Research,* May 24, 1993, pp. 11+; and Edward R. Tufte, *The Visual Display of Quantitative Information* (Cheshire, CT: Graphics Press, 1983).

several variables or changes over time. Generally, seven sections are considered the practical maximum in a pie chart.

The researcher needs to exercise caution, however, when using charts and figures to explain the data. It is possible to misinterpret information in a chart and lead marketing research information users to inappropriate conclusions. (See Exhibit 16.6 for a discussion of this pitfall.)

Measures of Central Tendency

As described above, frequency distributions can be useful for examining the different values for a given variable. Frequency distribution tables are easy to read and provide a great deal of basic information. There are times, however, when the amount of detail is just too much. In such situations the researcher needs a way to summarize and condense all the information in order to get at the underlying meaning. Descriptive statistics are commonly used to accomplish this task. As we mentioned briefly in Chapter 12, the mean, median, and mode are measures of central tendency. These measures locate the center of the distribution. For this reason, the mean, median, and mode are sometimes also called measures of location.

Mean

Mean   The arithmetic average of the sample; all values of a distribution of responses are summed and divided by the number of valid responses.

The **mean** is the average value within the distribution, and is the most commonly used measure of central tendency. The mean tells us, for example, the average number of cups of coffee the typical student may drink during finals to stay awake. The mean can be calculated when the data scale is either interval or ratio. Generally, the data will show some degree of central tendency, with most of the responses distributed close to the mean.

The formula for the mean is

$$\text{Mean} = \frac{\sum^n X_i}{n}$$

where:

$$X_i = \text{All the values of the distribution of responses}$$

$$n = \text{Number of valid responses}$$

Generally the mean is a very robust measure of central tendency. It is fairly insensitive to data values being added or deleted. The mean can be subject to distortion, however, if extreme values are included in the distribution.

For the data in Exhibit 16.1, the mean is calculated as follows:

$$\text{Mean} = \frac{(25*1) + (75*2) + (100*3) + (89*4) + (65*5) + (25*6)}{379}$$

$$= 3.5$$

Mode

Mode   The most common value in the set of responses to a question; that is, the response most often given to a question.

The **mode** is the value that appears in the distribution most often. For example, the *average* number of cups of coffee students drink per day during finals may be 5 (the mean), while the number of cups of coffee that *most* students drink is only 3 (the mode). The mode is the value that represents the highest peak in the distribution's graph. The mode is especially useful as a measure for data that have been somehow grouped into categories. The mode in the data distribution presented in Exhibit 16.1 is 3.

Median

Median   The middle value of a rank-ordered distribution; exactly half of the responses are above and half are below the median value.

The **median** is the middle value of the distribution when the distribution is ordered in either an ascending or descending sequence. For example, if you interviewed a sample of students to determine their coffee-drinking patterns during finals, you might find that the median number of cups of coffee consumed is 4. The number of cups of coffee consumed above and below this number would be the same (the median number is the exact middle of the distribution). If the number of data observations is even, the median is generally considered to be the average of the two middle values. If there are an odd number of observations, the median is the middle value. The median is especially useful as a measure of central tendency for ordinal data. The median for the data in Exhibit 16.1 is 3, the same as the mode in this instance.

The three measures of central tendency can all be different within the same distribution, as described above in the coffee-drinking example. In the data presented in Exhibit 16.1, the median and the mode happen to be the same, but the mean is different from both.

Each measure of central tendency describes a distribution in its own manner, and each measure has its own strengths and weaknesses. For nominal data, the mode is the best measure. For ordinal data, the median is generally best. For interval or ratio data, the mean is generally used. If there are extreme values within the interval or ratio data, however, the mean can be distorted. In those cases, the median and the mode should be considered. SPSS and other statistical software packages are designed to perform such types of analysis.

Measures of Dispersion

Often measures of central tendency cannot tell the whole story about a distribution of responses. For example, if data have been collected about consumers' attitudes toward a new brand of a product, you could find out the mean, median, and mode of the distribution of answers, but you might also want to know if most of the respondents had similar opinions. One way to determine the answer to this question would be to examine the measures of dispersion associated with the distribution of responses to your questions.

Measures of dispersion (which we introduced briefly in Chapter 12) describe how close to the mean or other measure of central tendency the rest of the values in the distribution fall. Two measures of dispersion used to describe the variability in a distribution of numbers are the range and the standard deviation.

Range

Range The distance between the smallest and largest values in a set of responses.

The **range** defines the spread of the data. It is the distance between the smallest and largest values of the variable. Another way to think about it is that the range identifies the endpoints of the distribution of values. In Exhibit 16.1, the range is the difference between the response category 1 (smallest value) and response category 5 (largest value); that is, the range is 4. In this example, since we defined the response categories to begin with, the range doesn't tell us much. However, if we asked people questions, such as how often in a month they rent videotapes, or how much they would pay to buy a CD player that could also record songs, the range would be more informative. In this case, the respondents, not the researchers, would be defining the range by their answers. For this reason, the range is more often used to describe the variability of such open-ended questions as our videotape example.

The formula for the range is

$$\text{Range} = X_{\text{largest}} - X_{\text{smallest}}$$

For the data in Exhibit 16.1, the range is calculated as

$$\text{Range} = 5 - 1$$

$$= 4$$

Standard Deviation

Standard deviation The average distance of the distribution values from the mean.

The **standard deviation** describes the average distance of the distribution values from the mean. The difference between a particular response and the distribution mean is called a *deviation*. Since the mean of a distribution is a measure of central tendency, there should be about as many values above the mean as there are below it (particularly if the distribution is symmetrical). Consequently, if we subtracted each value in a distribution from the mean and added them up, the result would be close to zero (the positive and negative results would cancel each other out).

The solution to this difficulty is to square the individual deviations before we add them up (squaring a negative number produces a positive result). Once the sum of the squared deviations is determined, it is divided by the number of respondents minus 1. The number 1 is subtracted from the number of respondents to help produce an unbiased estimate of the standard deviation. The result of dividing the sum of the squared deviations is the average squared deviation. To get the result back to the same type of units of measure as the mean, we simply take the square root of the answer. This produces the standard deviation of the distribution. By the way, sometimes the average squared deviation is also used as a measure of dispersion for a distribution; it is called the **variance.** The variance is used in a number of statistical processes that analyze collected data.

Variance   The average squared deviation about the mean of a distribution of values.

Since the standard deviation is the square root of the average squared deviations, it represents the average distance of the values in a distribution from the mean. If the standard deviation is large, the responses in a distribution of numbers do not fall very close to the mean of the distribution. If the standard deviation is small, you know that the distribution values are close to the mean. For the data in Exhibit 16.1, the mean is 3.5, the variance is 1.72, and the standard deviation is 1.31. The formula for calculating the standard deviation of a distribution of numbers is

$$\text{Standard deviation} = \sqrt{\frac{\sum (x_i - \bar{x})}{n - 1}}$$

where:

$$x_i = \text{Value of the } i\text{th respondent in the sample}$$

$$n = \text{Sample size}$$

$$\bar{x} = \text{Mean}$$

Together with the measures of central tendency, these descriptive statistics can reveal a lot about the distribution of a set of numbers representing the answers to an item on a questionnaire. Often, however, marketing researchers are interested in more detailed questions that involve more than one variable at a time. The next section provides some ways to analyze those types of questions. The Using Technology box explains how technology helps us use these descriptive statistics.

Hypothesis Testing

Frequency distributions and measures of central tendency are very useful to marketing researchers. In most cases, however, the researcher will have some preconceived notion of the relationships the data should present. The preconception should be based on marketing theory or previous research. The preconception is called a **hypothesis.** An example of a hypothesis would be, "The average number of cups of coffee students consume during finals will be greater than the average they consume at other times." In this section of the chapter, we will introduce the concept of hypothesis testing, explain some related terms, and discuss some types of possible errors.

Hypothesis   An empirically testable though yet unproven statement developed in order to explain phenomena.

Independent samples Two or more groups of responses that are tested as though they may come from different populations.

Independent versus Related Samples

Often the marketing researcher will want to compare the means of two groups. There are two possible situations when comparing means. The first is when the means are from **independent samples,** and the second is when the samples are related. An example of indepen-

A CLOSER LOOK AT RESEARCH　　Using Technology

A Guide to Four Basic Statistical Tools in Lotus 1-2-3

Electronic spreadsheets such as Lotus's 1-2-3 product are outstanding at crunching large amounts of numbers. But what if you don't understand exactly what the numbers are telling you? The electronic spreadsheets are capable of producing a surprising array of statistics and are simple enough to produce that even novice statistics users can quickly reduce a very large amount of data to its meaningful essence. In an article in *PC World,* Michael Massagil described the commands necessary to produce four basic statistics in Lotus 1-2-3.

Assume the data come from a customer survey. You have data regarding four attributes of the firm rated on a five-point modified Likert scale anchored by "Excellent" (5) and "Very Poor" (1). Just for the sake of convenience, assume that there are 25 responses. Create the worksheet and enter the attribute labels in the range A1..E2. Enter the values in the range A3..E27.

One of the first measures of central tendency you will likely wish to calculate is the mean. The mean is a good indicator when the responses are separated by equal intervals, as is the case with Likert data.

To calculate the mean for each column in this hypothetical example, enter the formula @AVG(B3..B27) in cell B33. Copy that to the range C33..E33, which will calculate the mean for all the attributes.

A second statistic you will likely want to calculate is the variance. The variance helps put the mean into perspective. The variance describes the variability within the data set. A large variance indicates a great amount of dispersion within the data, while a small variance indicates closely clustered data. Essentially, the lower the variance, the more likely it is that a person's response is close to the mean. To calculate the variance with 1-2-3, you will use the @VARS function.

Enter the function @VAR(B3..B27) in cell B34. Copy that formula to the range C34..E34. Lotus will return the variance. The real power of the variance becomes apparent when you have a large amount of data and you can't get a good "feel" because you can't see all the data at one time.

A third basic statistic is the median, the middle response. As all values are taken into account when calculating the mean, extreme values can distort the average in the direction of the extremes. The median is simply the central value in an ordered array. It may be the better measure of central tendency if extreme values are distorting the mean.

To calculate the median in releases 4.x and higher, use the @Median(range) function. If the range you indicate has an odd number of values, Lotus 1-2-3 will return the middle value. If there is an even number of values, the spreadsheet will return the mean of the middle two values. Enter the formula @MEDIAN(B3..B27) in cell B35 and copy the formula to cells C35..E35.

In older releases of Lotus 1-2-3, it will be necessary to sort your data into ascending or descending sequence. Then you will have to visually scan the data set to determine the middle value. If there is an even number of values, find the middle two and take their average. If there is an odd number of values, find the middle one. Note that you have to sort each column separately so be sure to copy your data set so you don't destroy the integrity of your original.

The fourth basic statistic to describe the central tendency of the data is the mode. The mode is the most frequent response. Finding the mode is a good way to determine if the responses cluster in the upper or lower range of values. Unfortunately, Lotus 1-2-3 doesn't have an @MODE function in releases 5.x and below. However, you can use the Range/Analyze/Distribution command in releases 4.x and 5.0 for Windows or the Data/Distribution command in releases 2.x and 3.x for DOS. The Distribution command in the Lotus spreadsheet counts the number of occurrences of each response within a specified range (the range value) that fall within a specified numeric value (the bin range).

To find the mode first enter the labels in ranges A41..A65 and B38..C39 and fill range B41..B46 with the numbers 0 through 5, all possible responses in this example. Next, copy range B41..B46 tp cells B49, B57, and B65. In release 4.x and 5.0 for Windows, utilize the Range/Analyze/Distribution command. In the dialog box that pops up enter B3..B27 *(continued) (concluded)* in the Range of Values edit box, enter B41..B46 in the Bin Range box, and use the mouse to click "OK." The spreadsheet will return a count of each response in column C. In the older releases for DOS, use the Data/Distribution command. At the "Enter Values Range" prompt, enter B3..B27. At the "Enter Bin Range" prompt, enter B41..B46.

If you graph the results of your Distribution command, you can see the modal value.

Source: Based on Michael Massagil, "Statistics for Every User: Guide to Four Statistical Tools in all Versions of Lotus 1-2-3," *PC World* 13, no. 1 (January 1995), p. L16.

dent samples would be the results of interviews with male and female coffee drinkers. The researcher may want to compare the average number of cups of coffee consumed per day by male students to the average number of cups of coffee consumed by female students. An example of the second situation, **related samples,** is when the researcher compares the average number of cups of coffee consumed per day by male students to the average number of soft drinks consumed per day by the same sample of male students. Although the following paragraph presents an overview of related-sample testing, the remainder of this discussion assumes independent samples.

Related samples Two or more groups of responses that originated from the sample population.

In the related-sample situation, the marketing researcher must take special care in analyzing the information. Although the questions are independent, the respondents are the same. This is called a *paired sample.* When testing for differences in related samples the researcher must use what is called a *paired samples t-test.* The formula to compute the *t* value for paired samples is not presented here; the student is referred to more advanced texts for the actual calculation of the *t* value for related samples.

Developing Hypotheses

The first step in testing a hypothesis is, of course, to develop the hypothesis itself. As we have said in earlier chapters, hypotheses are developed not only prior to the collection of data but also as a part of the research plan. Hypotheses allow the researcher to make comparisons between two groups of respondents and to determine if there are important differences between the groups. For example, if the average number of cups of coffee consumed by female students per day during finals is 6.1, and the average number of cups of coffee consumed by males is 4.7, is this finding meaningful?

The groups compared in developing hypotheses may be from two different surveys or they may be different subsets of the total sample. In effect, the research is conducted under the assumption that the two groups potentially are from separate populations.

To illustrate, let's consider the fast-food industry. Suppose you have conducted research on fast-food restaurant patronage and find that of the 1,000 people surveyed this year, 18 percent say they visit fast-food establishments at least 15 times per month (in the United States this is a typical percentage for "heavy users" of fast food). But in a survey conducted last year, only 12 percent said they visited fast-food restaurants at least 15 times per month. In this example, the samples are independent. The question is whether or not the difference in the number of visits per month is meaningful. Stated another way, "Did the percentage of persons eating at fast-food restaurants 15 times per month increase from 12 percent last year to 18 percent this year?"

The answer appears to be straightforward, but as we have previously pointed out, some type of sampling error could have distorted the results enough so there may not be any real differences between this year's percentage of heavy users of fast-food restaurants and last year's. If the difference between the percentages is very large, one would be more confident that there is in fact a true difference between the groups. However, there would still be some uncertainty as to whether the difference is meaningful. In this instance we have intuitively factored in one of the most important components in determining whether important differences exist between two sample means: the magnitude of the difference between the means. But another important component to consider is the size of the sample used to calculate the means.

Null hypothesis A statement that asserts the status quo; that is, that any change from what has been thought to be true is due to random sampling error.

In hypothesis development, the **null hypothesis** states that there is no difference between the group means in the comparison. In this case, the null hypothesis states there is no difference between the 12 percent visiting fast-food restaurants an average of 15 times a month last year and the 18 percent found this year. The null hypothesis is the one that is always tested by statisticians and market researchers. Another hypothesis, called the **alternative hypothesis,** states that there is a true difference between the group means. If the null hypothesis is accepted, there is no change to the status quo. If the null hypothesis is rejected, we automatically accept the alternative hypothesis and conclude that there has been a change in opinions or actions.

Alternative hypothesis A statement that is the opposite of the null hypothesis, that is, that the difference exists in reality and is not simply due to random error.

A null hypothesis refers to a population parameter, not a sample statistic. The data will show that either there is a meaningful difference between the two groups (reject the null hypothesis) or there is not a large enough difference between the groups to conclude that groups are different (fail to reject the null hypothesis). In the latter case, the researcher would not be able to detect any significant differences between the groups. It is important to bear in mind that failure to reject the null hypothesis does not necessarily mean that the null hypothesis is true. This is because data from another sample from the same population could produce different results.

In marketing research the null hypothesis is developed in such a way that its rejection leads to an acceptance of the desired situation. In other words, the alternative hypothesis represents the condition desired. Using the visits at the fast-food establishments as an example, the null hypothesis is that there is no difference between the patronage levels this year and last year. The alternative hypothesis is that this year's fast-food patronage is different from last year's. Usually, the null hypothesis is notated as H_0 and the alternative hypothesis is notated as H_1. If the null hypothesis (H_0) is rejected, then the alternative hypothesis (H_1) is accepted. The alternative hypothesis always bears the burden of proof.

Small businesses need to test hypotheses just as large ones do. SPSS and SAS can help them do this, as shown in the Small Business Implications box.

Statistical Significance

Whenever the marketing researcher draws an inference regarding a population, there is a risk that the inference may be incorrect. That is, in marketing research, error can never be completely avoided. Thus, the test the marketing researcher performs in order to decide whether or not to reject the null hypothesis may produce incorrect results.

Type I error The error made by rejecting the null hypothesis when it is true; the probability of alpha.

There are two types of error associated with hypothesis testing that the marketing researcher needs to be aware of when forming conclusions based on the data analysis. The first type of error is termed Type I. **Type I error** is associated with rejecting the null hypothesis and accepting the alternative hypothesis in error. This type of error, frequently called alpha (α), occurs when the sample data lead to rejection of a null hypothesis that is in fact true. The probability of such an error is termed the **level of significance.** The level of significance is equivalent to the amount of risk regarding the accuracy of the test that the researcher is willing to accept. In other words, the level of significance is the probability that the rejection of the null hypothesis is in error. Usually, marketing researchers accept a level of significance of either .10, .05 or .01, depending on the research objectives. This

Level of significance The amount of risk regarding the accuracy of the test that the researcher is willing to accept.

A CLOSER LOOK AT RESEARCH   **Small Business Implications**

Small-business owners and managers can use information from the SPSS and SAS Web sites for a variety of marketing research purposes. The sites provide a wealth of information that can lead to idea generation for marketing research opportunities. (See the chapter opener for their addresses.)

In many small businesses, owners and managers possess limited statistical ability in terms of computer application. SPSS and SAS offer a variety of suggestions for how small-business owners can use

statistical analysis to benefit their business. Examples include uncovering trends in a particular niche market, identifying potential outliers (companies not following the standard path in that particular market), graphical representations of all market participants (which allows for easy visual comparison of competitors), and a host of additional techniques. With this technology, small-business owners can build sophisticated statistical networks within their organization one small step at a time.

means that the researcher is willing to accept some risk of incorrect rejection of the null hypothesis, but that level of risk is prespecified.

Type II error The error of failing to reject the null hypothesis when the alternative hypothesis is true; the probability of beta.

The second type of error, termed **Type II error,** is the error that occurs when the sample data produce results that fail to reject the null hypothesis when in fact the null hypothesis is false and should be rejected. Type II error is frequently called beta (β). Unlike α, which is specified by the researcher, β depends on the actual population parameter.

Sample size can help control Type I and Type II errors. Generally, the researcher will select an α and the sample size in order to increase the power of the test and β. However, in some research situations, the researcher may want to manage the type of risk (α or β) to help achieve the best results. For example, if a new drug is being tested with potentially serious side effects, the researcher would probably want to minimize the α error to minimize the possibility of concluding that the drug is effective (i.e., to reject the null hypothesis) when in fact the drug is not effective.

Analyzing Relationships of Sample Data

Once the researcher has formed the hypotheses and calculated the means of the groups, the next step is to actually analyze the relationships of the sample data. In this segment we will discuss the methods used to test hypotheses. We will introduce the t and z distributions and describe their function in testing hypotheses. This requires a review of some basic statistical terminology.

Sample Statistics and Population Parameters

The purpose of inferential statistics is to make a determination about a population on the basis of a sample from that population. As we explained in Chapter 11, a *sample* is a subset of all the elements within the population. For example, if we wanted to determine the average number of cups of coffee consumed per day during finals at your university, we would not interview all the students. This would be costly, take a long time, and might be impossible since we may not be able to find them all or some would decline to participate. Instead, if there are 16,000 students at your university, we may decide that a sample of 200 females and 200 males is sufficiently large to provide accurate information about the coffee-drinking habits of all 16,000 students.

Sample statistics are measures obtained directly from the sample or calculated from the data in the sample. A *population parameter* is a variable or some sort of measured characteristic of the entire population. Sample statistics are useful in making inferences regarding the population's parameters. Generally, the actual population parameters are unknown since the cost to perform a true census of almost any population is prohibitive.

A frequency distribution displaying the data obtained from the sample is commonly used to summarize the results of the data collection process. When a frequency distribution displays a variable in terms of percentages, then this distribution is representing proportions within a population. For example, a frequency distribution showing that 40 percent of the people patronize Burger King indicates the percentage of the population that meets the criterion (eating at Burger King). The proportion may be expressed as a percentage, a decimal value, or a fraction.

Univariate Tests of Significance

In many situations a marketing researcher will form hypotheses regarding population means based on sample data. This involves going beyond the simple tabulations incorporated in a frequency distribution and calculation of averages. In these instances, the researcher may conduct univariate tests of significance. Univariate tests of significance involve hypothesis testing using one variable at a time.

An Example of a Univariate Hypothesis Test

Suppose that a marketing researcher is interested in determining whether hospital patients are satisfied with the care they receive from the nursing staff. The researcher asks former patients to indicate how courteous the nursing staff seemed to be during the patient's stay in the hospital. The responses are recorded on a five-point modified Likert scale, on which 5 indicates "very courteous" and 1 indicates "very discourteous." The scale is assumed to be an interval scale, and previous research using this measure has shown that the distribution of responses is approximately normal.

Further, suppose the researcher hypothesizes that the hospital patients will feel that the nursing staff was neither courteous nor discourteous. The researcher has formed a hypothesis that the mean of the sample will be 3. More formally, the null hypothesis is $\bar{X} = 3$ and the alternative hypothesis is $\bar{X} \neq 3$.

A final step is to determine the area of rejection. In this instance, assume that the researcher wants to be 95 percent certain that the mean is not 3. That means that the researcher has decided to set the level of significance at .05. Setting the level of significance at .05 means that if the survey were conducted many times, the probability of incorrectly rejecting the null hypothesis when it is true would occur fewer than 5 times in 100 (.05).

Now the marketing researcher collects data. The researcher interviews 350 people and prepares a frequency distribution. The distribution shows a mean rating of nurses of 3.68 and a sample standard deviation of 1.5. If the population standard deviation is known, the researcher would use that information in testing the hypothesis, but the population parameter is seldom known. Therefore, the sample statistic will be used. A **z-test** is a hypothesis test that utilizes the *z* distribution and is used when the sample size is larger than 30 and the standard deviation is unknown.

z-test A hypothesis test that utilizes the *z* distribution; used when the sample size is larger than 30 and the standard deviation is unknown.

The values that lie on the boundary between accepting and rejecting the null hypothesis are called critical values. The upper-limit critical value is that value which the sample distribution mean cannot exceed without rejecting the null. Likewise, the lower-limit critical value is that value that the sample distribution cannot fall below without rejecting the null hypothesis. The critical values of *z* are +1.96 and –1.96 at a .05 significance level. Now, the marketing researcher must translate the *z* values to the sample data in order to test the hypothesis regarding the courtesy of the nursing staff.

The lower-limit critical value is $\mu - z\,S_{\bar{x}}$ or

$$\mu - z\left(\frac{S}{\sqrt{n}}\right) = 3.00 - 1.96\left(\frac{1.5}{\sqrt{350}}\right)$$

$$= 3.00 - 1.96(.08)$$

$$= 2.84$$

The upper-limit critical value is $\mu + z\,S_{\bar{x}}$ or

$$\mu + z\left(\frac{S}{\sqrt{n}}\right) = 3.00 + 1.96\left(\frac{1.5}{\sqrt{350}}\right)$$

$$= 3.00 + 1.96(.08)$$

$$= 3.16$$

Based on this survey data, the null hypothesis will be rejected. The survey data show a mean of 3.68, higher than the upper-limit critical value. In this instance, the researcher would say that the sample result is statistically significant beyond the .05 level.

Hospital management can interpret this result to mean that patients perceive the nursing staff to be courteous. It is very unlikely, below a 5 percent chance, that this result would have occurred due to simple random sampling error. The hospital may want to consider other aspects of service quality, but should not be so concerned with the courtesy of the nursing staff.

Univariate Hypothesis Testing Using the t Distribution

The process for univariate testing using the t distribution is very similar to using the z distribution. If the sample size is small and the standard deviation within the population is unknown, the researcher will use a ***t*-test.** The t distribution is a symmetrical, bell-shaped distribution with a mean of 0 and a standard deviation of 1. The t distribution is used when the sample size is small, less than 30, and when the population standard deviation is unknown. The following example will clarify univariate hypothesis testing using the t distribution.

t-test   One form of
hypothesis test that
utilizes the *t* distribution;
used when the sample
size is small (generally
less than 30) and the
standard deviation is
unknown.

Assume that a market researcher believes that, at a fast-food restaurant being studied, no more than 15 people per day are given refunds because their food is served cold. The restaurant's records indicate the number of refunds granted each day for the last four weeks. The researcher calculates the sample mean to be 17 and the sample standard deviation to be 2. The researcher's basic question is whether the sample mean is different enough from 15 people for him to revise his belief that no more than 15 people a day get refunds due to being served cold food.

The researcher states the null and alternative hypotheses to be as follows:

$$H_0: \mu \leq 15$$

$$H_1: \mu > 15$$

In the next step, the researcher calculates the standard error of the mean as follows:

$$S_{\bar{x}} = \frac{S}{\sqrt{n}}$$

$$= \frac{2}{\sqrt{28}}$$

$$= .38$$

The researcher specifies the level of statistical significance. In this example, we will assume a level of .05. Since the researcher is interested in whether the sample mean is significantly *higher* than 15, only an upper-limit critical value is needed. That is, we are only interested in one end (or tail) of the t distribution. To specify the upper value, the researcher needs a t value from the distribution to multiply with the standard error of the mean.

The t distribution table shows t values for a wide variety of sample sizes and α levels. For this example, we are interested in the t value associated with a .05 level of significance and 27 degrees of freedom ($n - 1$). For a two-tailed test, we would use $\alpha/2$ (.025). For this one-tailed test, the t value is 1.703. The formula for calculating the critical value is $\mu + t(S_{\bar{x}})$, or $\mu + t(2 / \sqrt{28}\,)$. For this example, the critical value is

$$\text{Upper limit} = 15 + 1.703 \left(\frac{2}{\sqrt{28}} \right)$$

$$= 15 + 1.703(.38)$$

$$= 15 + .65$$

$$= 15.65$$

Finally, the researcher makes the determination that the sample mean is not within the range for acceptance of the null hypothesis. The sample mean does not fall below 15.65. Therefore, the null hypothesis is rejected and the alternative hypothesis is accepted. In short, the number of refunds given per day for cold food is in fact higher than 15.

Hypothesis Test of a Sample Proportion

The population proportion can also be estimated from a sample, and this is often the case in marketing research. Conceptually, the hypothesis test of a proportion is similar to other univariate hypothesis testing, but the formula for the standard error of the proportion is different. The following example shows how a univariate proportion hypothesis test is done.

Customers entering and leaving a Walgreens drugstore.

Suppose that the Walgreens drugstore chain believes that 50 percent of its customers shop there once a week. Specifically stated, the null hypothesis is $\bar{X} = .5$ and the alternative hypothesis is $\bar{X} \neq .5$. Assume also that the researcher conducts a survey of 250 drugstore patrons and calculates $p = .6$; that is, 60 percent of the sample shop at Walgreens once a week. Although the population proportion is unknown, the large sample size allows for the z-test to be used. If the researcher sets the level of significance at .01 the critical z value is 2.58 for this hypothesis test. The formula for calculating the observed z value is

$$z_{obs} = \frac{(p - \rho)}{S_p}$$

where:

p = The sample proportion

ρ = Population proportion as hypothesized

S_p = Estimate of the standard error of the proportion

The standard error of the proportion is calculated as

$$S_p = \sqrt{\frac{(pq)}{n}} \quad \text{or} \quad \sqrt{\frac{p(1 - p)}{n}}$$

where:

S_p = Estimate of the standard error of the proportion

p = Proportion of success

$q = (1 - p)$ = Proportion of failure

In this example, the standard error estimate of the proportion is

$$S_p = \sqrt{\frac{(.5)(.5)}{250}}$$

$$= \sqrt{(.001)}$$

$$= .03$$

The Z_{obs} is now calculated as

$$z_{obs} = \frac{(p - \rho)}{S_p}$$

$$= \frac{(.6 - .5)}{.03}$$

$$= 3.33$$

In this example, the Z_{obs} is greater than the critical z value of 2.58, and the null hypothesis is rejected. That is, more than 50 percent of customers shop at Walgreens more than once a week, and in our sample we would conclude that the actual percentage is 60 percent (or at least closer to 60 percent than 50 percent).

Bivariate Hypotheses Tests

In many instances the marketing researcher will want to test hypotheses that compare the mean of one group to the mean of another group. For example, the marketing researcher may well be interested in determining whether there is any difference between older and younger new car purchasers in terms of the importance of a CD player. In situations where more than one group is involved, bivariate tests are needed. In the following section, we describe three bivariate hypothesis tests: the *t*-test to compare two means; a *z*-test to compare two proportions; and analysis of variance, which is a method to compare three or more group means.

In nearly all cases the null hypothesis is that there is no difference between the group means. This null hypothesis is specifically stated as follows:

$$\mu_1 = \mu_2 \text{ or that } \mu_1 - \mu_2 = 0$$

Using the t-*Test to Compare Two Means*

Just as with the univariate *t*-test, the bivariate *t*-test requires interval or ratio data. Also, the *t*-test is especially useful when the sample size is small ($n < 30$) and when the population standard deviation is unknown. Unlike the univariate test, however, we assume that the samples are drawn from populations with normal distributions and that the variances of the populations are equal.

Essentially, the *t*-test for differences between group means can be conceptualized as the difference between the means divided by the variability of random means. The *t* value is a ratio of the difference between the two sample means and the standard error. The *t*-test tries to provide a rational way of determining if the difference between the two sample means occurred by chance.

The formula for calculating the *t* value is

$$t = \frac{X_1 - X_2}{S_x}$$

where:

X_1 = Mean of group 1

X_2 = Mean of group 2

S_x = Pooled standard error of the difference between the means

The pooled standard error of the difference is calculated as follows:

$$S_x = \sqrt{\frac{(n_1 - 1)S_1 + (n_2 - 1)S_2}{n_1 + n_2 - 2}\left(\frac{1}{n_1} + \frac{1}{n_2}\right)}$$

where:

S_1 = Variance of group 1

S_2 = Variance of group 2

n_1 = Number in the sample of group 1

n_2 = Number in the sample of group 2

To illustrate the use of a *t*-test to test for the difference between two group means, suppose that older and younger customers' attitudes about having a CD player in their new car is measured on an interval scale. The customers are in two groups; one group is older customers (> 30) and the other group is younger customers (< 30). A high score indicates a favorable attitude toward the new product, while a low score indicates an unfavorable attitude. Exhibit 16.7 shows a comparison of the two groups.

EXHIBIT 16.7	Comparison of CD Survey Groups

Younger Customers	Older Customers
Mean = 15.3	Mean = 12.3
Variance = 2.3	Variance = 2.1
Sample size = 21	Sample size = 19

The calculation of S_x is

$$S_x = \sqrt{\frac{(n_1 - 1)S_1 + (n_2 - 1)S_2}{n_1 + n_2 - 2}\left(\frac{1}{n_1} + \frac{1}{n_2}\right)}$$

$$= \sqrt{\frac{(21 - 1)2.3 + (19 - 1)2.1}{21 + 19 - 2}\left(\frac{1}{21} + \frac{1}{19}\right)}$$

$$= .4702$$

The calculation of the t-statistic is

$$t = \frac{(15.3 - 12.3)}{S_x}$$

$$= \frac{3}{.4702}$$

$$= 6.38$$

The degrees of freedom (df) are calculated as

$$df = n - k$$

where:

$$n = \text{Combined sample size of both groups}$$

$$k = \text{Number of groups}$$

In this example, the degree of freedom is 38. If the significance level designed by the marketing researcher is .05, the critical t value is 2.01. Because the calculated t value exceeds the critical value of t, the researcher can say that there is a significant difference between the younger customers' perceptions of the value of a CD player and older customers' perceptions. In this example, the younger customers place a statistically significant higher value on having a CD player in their car.

If the population standard deviation is known or if the sample size is large enough, the z-test is the appropriate measure. The z-test is exactly the same as the t-test from a conceptual standpoint.

Comparing Two Proportions Using a z-Test

Suppose that Nike hires a marketing researcher to test the hypothesis that the percentage of wearers of Nike shoes is different in the northern region of the United States than in the southern region. The null hypothesis is that there is no difference between the proportions of Nike wearers in the North and the South, as defined by Nike and the researcher. Just as in the means test, the sample size is the criterion for selecting the z-test. The z-test of a proportion provides a rational method for determining whether an observed difference in proportion from a large sample is due to sampling error or is indicative of a true difference between the two groups (wearers of Nike shoes in the North and the South).

The formula for comparing the proportions of two groups is

$$z = \frac{(p_1 - p_2) - (\rho_1 - \rho_2)}{S_{p_1 - p_2}}$$

where:

p_1 = Proportion in sample group 1

p_2 = Proportion in sample group 2

$\rho_1 - \rho_2$ = Proportion hypothesized for group 1 minus the proportion hypothesized for group 2. Note that this difference is normally hypothesized to be 0 for the null hypothesis, so this term usually drops out of the calculation.

$S_{p_1 - p_2}$ = Pooled estimate of the standard error of the proportions

To calculate the pooled estimate of the standard error of the proportions, the following formula is used:

$$S_{p_1 - p_2} = \sqrt{pq\left(\frac{1}{n_1} + \frac{1}{n_2}\right)}$$

where:

p = Pooled estimate of proportion in the sample

$q = (1 - p)$, 1 minus the pooled estimate of the proportion

n_1 = Number in the sample of group 1

n_2 = Number in the sample of group 2

The pooled estimate of proportion is calculated as a weighted average of the sample proportions. This is usually necessary because under the null hypothesis, ρ is unknown. To calculate p, the following formula is employed:

$$p = \frac{n_1 p_1 + n_2 p_2}{n_1 + n_2}$$

Whether the researcher is comparing sample means or proportion, caution is needed in interpretation. Both the differences and the errors must always be assessed before drawing conclusions. Exhibit 16.8 provides an example of why such caution is needed.

Analysis of Variance (ANOVA)

Analysis of variance (ANOVA) A statistical technique that determines whether three or more means are statistically different from each other.

Analysis of variance (ANOVA) is used to determine the statistical difference between three or more means. For example, if a sample finds that the average number of cups of coffee consumed per day by freshman during finals is 3.7, while the average number of cups of coffee consumed per day by seniors and graduate students is 4.3 cups and 5.1 cups, respectively, are these observed differences statistically significant? The ability to make such comparisons can be quite useful for the marketing researcher.

While the name ANOVA can be disconcerting to many students, the technique is really quite straightforward. In this section we shall describe a one-way ANOVA. The

EXHIBIT 16.8	Focusing on Election Poll Point Spreads Instead of Percentages May Be Misleading!

Accurate reporting of research results is considered to be so important that it is specifically addressed in the American Marketing Association's *Marketing Research Code of Ethics*. However, the way preelection poll results are reported might be misleading and give rise to criticism of marketing survey research. At least one person, Thomas S. Gruca, an associate professor of marketing at the University of Iowa, thinks that one potential source of error in election polls is the focus on the point spread between the candidates. Professor Gruca's research supports the notion that the point spread between candidates is a dubious portrayal of survey research.

The problem with focusing on the point spread arises from the segment of voters who report themselves as undecided in the so-called trial-heat election polls. Research in the 1980s showed an interesting pattern in the disposition of undecided voters in incumbent reelections. In a study of 155 polls primarily from 1986 and 1988, it was shown that in most cases, most of the undecided vote appeared to go to the challenger. This finding, dubbed the "incumbent rule" has important implications for the analysis and interpretation of trial-heat election poll reporting.

Suppose an incumbent is facing a single challenger. The results of a trial-heat poll show that 48 percent of voters are for the incumbent and 40 percent for the challenger, with a margin of error of 2 percent. One could report the results of such a poll as an 8-point lead for the incumbent, or one could report the percentages. While the two reporting methods may seem equivalent, they are not.

Consider the following real election examples. In the 1993 New Jersey governor's race and the 1994 New York governor's race, the incumbents were leading in the preelection polls just a few days before the elections. The polls were conducted by prestigious organizations such as the Gallup Organization, *The New York Times*, Louis Harris and Associates, and others. Both incumbents lost.

In each case newspaper articles appeared trying to explain the surprising results in terms of late media blitzes, voter attitude swings, and other factors. Yet the real reason, according to Professor Gruca, was that the focus on the point spread missed the obvious. The polls may have been right, but assuming the point spread would hold through election day ignored the incumbency rule.

In effect, the focus on only point spread misleads readers in several ways. First, the actual election results will probably be closer than the poll suggests because the undecided vote will not be spread equally. Any lead by an incumbent is probably less than it appears. Focusing on only the point spread between candidates masks this phenomena.

Second, incumbents leading a single challenger but having less than a 50 percent share of the vote usually end up losing the election. This is a direct result of the opponent's receiving the majority of the undecided voters ballots in the actual election. It appears that the incumbent's chances of actually winning depend on how far under 50 percent he is and how close the race is.

Third, many polls that at first appear to be in error may actually be correct. The problem is the interpretation of the undecided vote. Given the name recognition and other advantages enjoyed by most incumbents, the fact that a voter is undecided close to election day is not necessarily good news.

Professor Gruca suggests that it is clear that caution must be used when reporting preelection poll results. The polls may be good at gauging an incumbent's support, but they are less good at projecting the final election results. Professor Gruca thinks that every polling story should incorporate a simple statement about the trend for undecided voters to swing to the challenger on election day.

Source: Based on Thomas S. Gruca, "Reporting Poll Results: Focusing on Point Spreads Instead of Percentages Can Be Misleading," *Marketing Research* (Winter 1996), pp. 29+.

term *one-way* is used since there is only one independent variable. ANOVA can be used in cases where multiple independent variables are considered, and allows the analyst to estimate both their individual and joint effects on the dependent variable.

Multiple dependent variables can be analyzed together using a related procedure called multivariate analysis of variance (MANOVA). The objective in MANOVA is identical to that in ANOVA—to examine group differences in means—only the comparisons are considered for a group of dependent variables. While a detailed discussion is beyond the scope of this text, a brief description of MANOVA is included at the end of this chapter.

An example of an ANOVA problem may be to compare light, medium, and heavy drinkers of Starbucks coffee on their attitude toward a particular Starbucks advertising campaign. In this instance there is one independent variable—consumption of Starbucks coffee—but it is divided into three different levels. Our earlier z and t statistics won't work here, since we have more than two groups to compare.

ANOVA requires that the dependent variable, in this case the attitude toward the Starbucks advertising campaign, be metric. That is, the dependent variable must be either interval or ratio scaled. A second data requirement is that the independent variable, in this case the coffee consumption variable, be categorical.

The null hypothesis for ANOVA always states that there is no difference between the ad campaign attitudes of the groups of Starbucks coffee drinkers. In specific terminology, the null hypothesis would be:

$$\mu_1 = \mu_2 = \mu_3$$

The ANOVA technique focuses on the behavior of the variance within a set of data. If you remember the earlier discussion of measures of dispersion, the variance of a variable is equal to the average squared deviation from the mean of the variable. The logic of the ANOVA technique says that if we calculate the variance *between* the groups and compare it to the variance *within* the groups, we can make a rational determination as to whether the means (attitudes toward the advertising campaign) are significantly different.[1]

Types of Variance in ANOVA

ANOVA is concerned with differences from the mean (variance); there are three specific types of variance that are possible: total variation (TV), variation between groups (VB), and variation within groups (VW). Each source of variation tells the marketing researcher about differences between means in the data set being analyzed.

Total variation (TV) deals with the variation of the individual observations about the grand mean. The grand mean is the average of the entire data set, that is, the overall attitude of all Starbucks coffee drinkers toward the advertising campaign. The sum of the squared differences between the individual observations and the grand mean makes up the TV. Remember, we mentioned earlier that squaring the differences is necessary to avoid the negative variation from canceling the positive variations, and vice versa, during the summing up process. The formula for TV is

$$\text{TV} = \sum_1^k \sum_1^{n_j} (X_{ij} - \overline{X})^2$$

where:

$$\overline{X} = \text{Grand mean}$$

$$k = \text{Number of groups included in the analysis}$$

$$n_j = \text{Number of observations of each group}$$

$$X_{ij} = \text{Value for observation } i \text{ in group } j$$

Variation between groups (VB) is the sum of the squared differences between the individual group means and the data set's grand mean. As before, the differences are squared to prevent positive and negative variations from washing each other out. The formula for VB is

$$\text{VB} = \sum_1^k n_j (\overline{X}_j - \overline{X})^2$$

where:

$$\overline{X} = \text{Grand mean}$$

$$k = \text{Number of groups included in the analysis}$$

$$n_j = \text{Number of observations of each group}$$

$$\overline{X}_j = \text{Mean of group } j$$

Variation within groups (VW) is the sum of the squared differences of each observation within the group as compared to the group mean. The formula for the VW is

$$\text{VW} = \sum_{1}^{k}\sum_{1}^{n_j}(X_{ij} - \overline{X}_j)^2$$

where:

$$\overline{X}_{ij} = \text{Group mean}$$

$$k = \text{Number of groups included in the analysis}$$

$$n_j = \text{Number of observations of each group}$$

$$X_{ij} = \text{Value for observation } i \text{ in group } j$$

Determining Statistical Significance in ANOVA

F-test   The test used to statistically evaluate the differences between the group means in ANOVA.

In ANOVA, the *F*-test is used to statistically evaluate the differences between the group means. For example, suppose the heavy users of Starbucks coffee rate the advertising campaign 4.4 on a five-point scale, with 5 = Very favorable. The medium users of Starbucks coffee rate the campaign 3.9, and the light users of Starbucks coffee rate the campaign 2.5. The *F*-test in ANOVA tells us if these observed differences are meaningful.

The total variance in a set of responses to a question can be separated into between-group and within-group variance. The *F* distribution is the ratio of these two components of total variance and can be calculated as follows:

$$F = \frac{\text{Variance between groups}}{\text{Variance within groups}}$$

The larger the difference in the variance between groups, the larger the *F* ratio. Since the total variance in a data set is divisible into between and within components, if there is more variance explained or accounted for by considering differences between groups than there is within groups, then the independent variable probably has a significant impact on the dependent variable. Larger *F* ratios imply significant differences between the groups. The larger the *F* ratio, the more likely it is that the null hypothesis will be rejected.

The second piece of information needed to examine statistical differences between groups in ANOVA is the degrees of freedom. Degrees of freedom are adjustments made to the different types of sums of squares in order to make them comparable. Degrees of freedom are calculated as the number of observations whose squared deviations are incorporated in the summing-up process minus the number of sample statistics calculated in the analysis.

Thus, to calculate the degrees of freedom for the grand mean, the formula is

$$\text{df}_{\text{total}} = (n - 1)$$

where:

$$n = \text{Number of observations}$$

To calculate the degrees of freedom for the within-group variation, the formula is

$$\text{df}_{\text{between}} = (k - 1)$$

where:

$$k = \text{Number of groups included in the analysis}$$

To calculate the degrees of freedom within groups, the formula is

$$\text{df}_{\text{within}} = (n - k)$$

where:

$$n = \text{Number of observations}$$

$$k = \text{Number of groups included in the analysis}$$

When the sum of squares between group variation and the sum of squares within group variation is divided by their respective degrees of freedom, the result is called a mean square. Thus, the F statistic formula can be restated as

$$F = \frac{\text{Mean square}_{\text{VB}}}{\text{Mean square}_{\text{VW}}}$$

If the mean squares between group is significantly larger than the mean squares within group, the F ratio will be large and the null hypothesis is not supported.

The test of statistical significance for the differences between group means is performed by looking up the value of F in the tables included in the back of this text. The tables show the critical values of F at various levels of significance. To find the appropriate F critical value, use the table associated with the level of significance desired (usually $\alpha =$ .05 or .01). Then, locate the value associated with $\text{df}_{\text{between}}$ and $\text{df}_{\text{within}}$ on the respective row and column. As you can see from the F value formula, Mean square$_{\text{VB}}$ / Mean square$_{\text{vw}}$, the first degree of freedom applies to the numerator (between-group df) and the second pertains to the denominator (within-group df).

If the F statistic calculated from the sample is not larger than the critical value F from the statistical table, the null hypothesis that there are no differences between the groups is not rejected. This means that we cannot conclude that the group means are different. However, if the calculated F statistic is larger than the critical F value, then the null hypothesis is rejected and the researcher can say, with whatever level of significance selected, that true differences exist between the means. In other words, rejecting the null implies that the observed differences between the groups are in fact true differences.

However, ANOVA is only able to tell the researcher that differences exist between the group means considered together. It cannot identify which pairs of means are significantly different from each other. In our example of Starbucks coffee drinkers' attitudes toward the advertising campaign, if we were able to conclude that differences in attitudes toward the advertising campaign exist between the three groups, we would not be able to point out just where the specific differences were. That is, we couldn't say whether the differences were between the heavy and medium drinkers, the medium and light drinkers, the heavy and light drinkers, or all groups. Thus, the marketing researcher is still saddled with the task of determining where the differences in means lie. Follow-up tests have been designed for just that purpose.

Follow-up test A test that flags the means that are statistically different from each other; follow-up tests are performed after an ANOVA determines there are differences between means.

There are several **follow-up tests** available in statistical software packages such as SPSS and SAS, including comparison tests by Tukey, Duncan, and Dunn. All of these methods involve multiple comparisons, or simultaneous assessment of confidence interval estimates of differences between the means. All means are compared two at a time. The differences between the techniques lie in their ability to control the error rate. We shall briefly describe the Scheffé procedure, although a complete discussion of these techniques is well beyond the scope of this book. Relative to the other follow-up tests mentioned, however, the Scheffé procedure is a more conservative method of detecting significant differences between group means.

The Scheffé follow-up test essentially establishes simultaneous confidence intervals, which holds the entire experiment's error rate to a specified α level. The test exposes differences between all pairs of means to a high and low confidence interval range. If the difference between each pair of means falls outside the range of the confidence interval, then we reject the null hypothesis and conclude that the pairs of means falling outside the range are statistically different. The Scheffé test might show that one, two, or all three pairs of means in our Starbucks example are different. The Scheffé test is equivalent to simultaneous two-tailed hypothesis tests, and the technique holds the specified analysis significance level. Because the technique holds the experimental error rate to α, the confidence intervals tend to be wider than in the other methods, but the researcher has more assurance that true mean differences exist.

n-Way ANOVA

The entire discussion of ANOVA to this point has been devoted to one-way ANOVA. In a one-way ANOVA there is only one independent variable. In the foregoing examples, the usage category (consumption of Starbucks coffee) was the independent variable. However, it is not at all uncommon for the researcher to be interested in several independent variables simultaneously. In that case an *n*-way ANOVA would be used.

Often, however, the market researcher may be interested in the region of the country where a product is sold as well as consumption patterns. Using multiple independent factors allows for an interaction effect, or the effects of the multiple independent factors acting in concert to affect group means. For example, heavy consumers of Starbucks coffee in the Northeast may have different attitudes about advertising campaigns than heavy consumers of Starbucks coffee in the West, and there may be still further differences between the various coffee-consumption-level groups, as shown earlier.

Another situation that may require *n*-way ANOVA is the use of experimental designs, where the researcher provides different groups in a sample with different information to see how their responses change. For example, a marketer may be interested in finding out whether consumers prefer a humorous ad to a serious one and whether that preference varies across gender. Each type of ad could be shown to different groups of customers (both male and female). Then, questions about their preferences for the ad and the product it advertises could be asked. The primary difference between the groups would be the difference in ad execution (humorous or nonhumorous) and customer gender. A *n*-way ANOVA could be used to find out whether the ad execution differences helped cause differences in ad and product preferences, as well as what effects might be attributable to customer gender.

From a conceptual standpoint, *n*-way ANOVA is very similar to one-way ANOVA, but the mathematics are more complex. However, statistical packages such as SPSS will conveniently allow the marketing researcher to perform *n*-way ANOVA.

Finally, a related technique, MANOVA, was mentioned earlier in this chapter. MANOVA is designed to examine multiple dependent variables across single or multiple independent variables. The technique considers the mean differences for a group of dependent measures. For example, a researcher might want to measure customers' use of several types of related products, such as golf balls, golf shoes, golf clubs, and golf clothing. Since use of one of these types of products is probably related to use of the others, MANOVA would be a good choice for examining the effect of independent variables like income or gender on use of the entire group of golf-related products. The statistical calculations for MANOVA are similar to *n*-way ANOVA and are typically included in the statistical software packages (such as SAS and SPSS) mentioned earlier.[2]

Statistical techniques are used globally as well as in the United States; the Global Insights box explains how.

GLOBAL INSIGHTS — BEST WESTERN

Best Western is the world's biggest hotel chain, with some 3,300 independently owned hotels. By using marketing research, Best Western has been able to identify its market segments. The hotel chain has discovered that business travelers tend to shy away from unknown, less expensive brands of hotels in favor of consistent quality brands, such as Best Western. The first table here shows the composition of the worldwide hotel market, and the second shows the source of business (domestic or foreign) by world region.

Composition of Business Traveler Market

Source of Business	Worldwide	Africa/Middle East	Asia/Australia	North America	Europe
Domestic	50.7%	24.6%	35.0%	84.6%	47.3%
Foreign	49.3	75.4	65.0	15.4	52.7
Total	100.0	100.0	100.0	100.0	100.0

Using marketing research to uncover facts about its market segments such as the ones above, Best Western has been able to focus its marketing strategy on business travelers. In addition, the hotel chain emphasizes domestic business in North America; focuses on both domestic and foreign business in Europe; and targets foreign business in Africa, Asia, Australia, and the Middle East.

Composition of the Worldwide Hotel Market

Market Segment Group	Percent of Total Market
Business travelers	36.0%
Individual travelers	24.5
Tour groups	13.5
Conference participants	12.7
Other groups	9.2
Government officials	4.1

Sources: "Hotel Chains Capitalize on International Travel Market," *Hotels and Restaurants International* (June 1989), pp. 81s–86s; and "Target Marketing Points to Worldwide Success," *Hotels and Restaurants International* (June 1989), p. 87s.

SUMMARY OF LEARNING OBJECTIVES

Understand the mean, median, and mode as measures of central tendency.

The mean is the most commonly used measure of central tendency and describes the arithmetic average of the values in a sample of data. The median represents the middle value of an ordered set of values. The mode is the most frequently occurring value in a distribution of values. All these measures describe the center of the distribution of a set of values.

Understand the range and standard deviation of a frequency distribution as measures of dispersion.

The range defines the spread of the data. It is the distance between the smallest and largest values of the distribution. The standard deviation describes the average distance of the distribution values from the mean. A large standard deviation indicates a distribution in which the individual values are spread out and are relatively farther away from the mean.

Understand how to graph measures of central tendency.

Distributions of numbers can be illustrated by several different types of graphs. Histograms and bar charts display data in either horizontal or vertical bars. Line charts are good choices for communicating trends in data, while pie charts are well suited for illustrating relative proportions.

Understand the difference between independent and related samples.

In independent samples the respondents come from different populations, so their answers to the survey questions do not affect each other. In related samples, the same respondent answers several questions, so comparing answers to these questions requires the use of a paired-samples *t*-test. Questions about mean differences in independent samples can be answered by using a student *t*-test statistic.

Explain hypothesis testing.

A hypothesis is an empirically testable though yet unproven statement about a set of data. Hypotheses allow the researcher to make comparisons between two groups of respondents and to determine whether there are important differences between the groups.

Understand how to determine the error in hypothesis testing.

Hypothesis tests have two types of error connected with their use. The first type of error (Type I error) is the risk of rejecting the null hypothesis on the basis of your sample data when it is, in fact, true for the population from which the sample data was selected. The second type of error (Type II error) is the risk of not detecting a false null hypothesis. The level of statistical significance (alpha) associated with a statistical test is the probability of making a Type I error.

Understand univariate *t*- and *z*-tests for determining the significance for means and proportions.

t statistics are tests of mean values that should be used when the sample size is small (less than 30) and the standard deviation of the population is unknown; *z*-tests are statistical tests of mean values best used when sample sizes are above 30 and the standard deviation of the population is known. Both tests involve the use of the sample mean, a *t* or *z* value selected from the respective distribution, and the standard deviation of either the sample or the population.

Understand bivariate *t*- and *z*-tests for means and proportions.

Tests of the differences between two groups require the use of *t*-tests for small samples (less than 30) and unknown population standard deviations. For larger samples and known population standard deviations, the *z*-test is used. The difference between the two means of interest is calculated and divided by the pooled standard error of the two groups. The resulting value is compared to a critical value (either *t* or *z* value) derived from the appropriate statistical distribution. If the calculated value is larger than the critical value, a statistically significant difference is indicated between the two means.

Understand ANOVA and the various types of variance within it.

ANOVA is used to determine the statistical significance of the difference between two or more means. The ANOVA technique calculates the variance of the values between groups of respondents and compares it to the variance of the responses within the groups. If the between-group variance is significantly greater than the within-group variance as indicated by the *F* ratio, the means are significantly different.

Understand how to determine the statistical significance of differences between means in ANOVA.

The statistical significance between means in ANOVA is detected through the use of a follow-up test. The Scheffé test is one type of follow-up test. The test examines the differences between all possible pairs of sample means against a high and low confidence range. If the difference between a pair of means falls outside the confidence interval, then the means can be considered statistically different.

KEY TERMS AND CONCEPTS

Alternative hypothesis 531

Analysis of variance (ANOVA) 539

***F*-test** 542

Follow-up test 543

Hypothesis 528

Independent samples 528

Level of significance 531

Mean 526

Median 526

Mode 526

Null hypothesis 531

Range 527

Related samples 530

Standard deviation 527

***t*-test** 534

Type I error 531

Type II error 532

Variance 528

***z*-test** 533

REVIEW QUESTIONS

1. Why are graphic approaches to reporting marketing research better than simply reporting numbers?

2. Explain the difference between the mean, the median, and the mode.

3. Why do we use hypothesis testing?

4. Why and how would you use t- and z-tests in hypothesis testing?

5. Why and when would you want to use ANOVA in marketing research?

6. What will ANOVA tests not tell you, and how can you overcome this problem?

DISCUSSION QUESTIONS

1. The measures of central tendency discussed in this chapter are designed to reveal information about the center of a distribution of values. Measures of dispersion provide information about the spread of all the values in a distribution around the center values. Assume you were conducting an opinion poll on voters' approval ratings of the job performance of the mayor of the city where you live. Do you think the mayor would be more interested in the central tendency or the dispersion measures associated with the responses to your poll? Why?

2. If you were interested in finding out whether or not young adults (21–34 years old) are more likely to buy products online than older adults (35 or more years old), how would you phrase your null hypothesis? What is the implicit alternative hypothesis accompanying your null hypothesis?

3. The level of significance (alpha) associated with testing a null hypothesis is also referred to as the probability of a Type I error. Alpha is the probability of rejecting the null hypothesis on the basis of your sample data when it is, in fact, true for the population you are interested in. Since alpha concerns the probability of making a mistake in your analysis, should you always try to set this value as small as possible? Why or why not?

4. Analysis of variance (ANOVA) allows you to test for the statistical difference between two or more means. Typically, there are more than two means tested. If the ANOVA results for a set of data reveal that the four means which were compared are significantly different from each other, how would you find out which individual means were statistically different from each other? What statistical techniques would you apply to answer this question?

5. **EXPERIENCE THE INTERNET.** Nike, Reebok, and Converse are strong competitors in the athletic shoe market. All three use different advertising and marketing strategies to appeal to their target markets. Use one of the search engines on the Internet to identify information on this market. Go to the Web sites for these three companies (www.Nike.com; www.Reebok.com; www.Converse.com). Gather background information on each, including its target market and market share. Design a questionnaire based on this information and survey a sample of students. Prepare a report on the different perceptions of each of these three companies, their shoes, and related aspects. Present the report in class and defend your findings.

6. **SPSS EXERCISE.** Form a team of three to four students in your class. Select one or two local franchises to conduct a survey on, such as Subway or McDonald's. Design a brief survey (10–12 questions) including questions like ratings on quality of food, speed of service, knowledge of employees, attitudes of employees, and price, as well as several demographic variables such as age, address, how often individuals eat there, and day of week and time of day. Obtain permission from the franchises to interview their customers at a convenient time, usually when they are leaving. Assure the franchiser you will not bother customers and that you will provide the franchise with a valuable report on your findings. Develop frequency charts, pie charts, and similar graphic displays of findings, where appropriate. Use statistics to test hypotheses, such as "Perceptions of speed of service differ by time of day or day of week." Prepare a report and present it to your class; particularly point out where statistically significant differences exist and why.

7. **SPSS EXERCISE.** Using SPSS and the fast-food database, provide frequencies, means, modes, and medians for all the relevant variable on the questionnaire. The actual questionnaire is presented in Chapter 15 as Exhibit 15.6. In addition, provide bar charts and pie charts for the data you analyzed.

ENDNOTES

1. For a more detailed discussion of analysis of variance, see Gudmund R. Iversen and Helmut Norpoth, *Analysis of Variance* (Newbury Park, CA: Sage, 1987); and John A. Ingram and Joseph G. Monks, *Statistics for Business and Economics* (San Diego, CA: Harcourt Brace Jovanovich, 1989).

2. For a more detailed conceptual discussion of multiple analysis of variance, see Joseph F. Hair, Jr., Rolph E. Anderson, Ronald L. Tatham, and William C. Black, *Multivariate Data Analysis,* 5th ed. (Englewood Cliffs, NJ: Prentice Hall, 1998); and James H. Bray and Scott E. Maxwell, *Multivariate Analysis of Variance* (Newbury Park, CA: Sage, 1985).

MARKETING RESEARCH ILLUSTRATION

USE OF CONSUMERS' ATTITUDINAL INFORMATION IN ASSESSING RESTAURANT IMAGE POSITIONS

This illustration focuses on the integrative impact of the following types of concepts: consumers' attitudinal data structures toward service quality and customer satisfaction; importance of restaurant choice features; importance-image performance (IIP) analysis; restaurant images; service/restaurant positioning strategies; diagnostic evaluations of marketing mix strategies; descriptive data analysis and testing for differences between mean values; and table construction.

Situation

About three years ago, Mr. John Smith, founder and corporate executive officer, opened Remington's Steak House, a retail theme restaurant located in a large southeastern metropolitan area. Prior to opening his restaurant, Smith wanted consumers to perceive his restaurant as being a unique, theme-oriented, conveniently located specialty restaurant with an excellent reputation for offering a wide assortment of high-quality yet competitively priced entrees and services and having very knowledgeable employees who listen and understand customers' needs and place heavy emphasis on satisfying the customer.

Smith used this image to guide the development and implementation of his restaurant's positioning and marketing strategies. Although Smith knows how to deliver dining experiences, he does not know much about developing, implementing, and assessing marketing strategies. The following statements highlight Smith's evaluation of his company's so-called strategies:

Service/product offerings	A wide variety of quality steak, chicken, and seafood entrees (e.g., steak, chicken, seafood specialties, appetizers, desserts, etc.) using only excellent-quality ingredients.
Pricing	Employs a traditional cost plus 50% contribution margin (with the margin percentage being based on cost structures, not selling price structures) for all items carried in the restaurant. Will run occasional food specials to meet the competition's specials.
Advertising	Relies heavily on positive word of mouth from past customers and limited direct mail to known past customers. Has an advertisement in the local Yellow Pages, and benefits from national advertisements on TV.
Service staff	All employees (managers and staff alike) attend continuous training seminars to advance their product, service, and store operation knowledge levels.
Location	Owns three 10,000-square-feet buildings located on heavy traffic arteries within the metropolitan area. There are several other specialty steak restaurants within a two-mile radius of each of the three Remington's restaurant locations.
Customer	Attracts customers who are price-conscious but under the impression that the higher the price, the greater the quality of the food and service offerings; they demand quality and expect any dining problems to be fixed right the first time.

Recently, Smith began asking himself some fundamental questions about his restaurant's operations and the future of his business. Smith expressed these questions to a hired marketing researcher and decided to do some research to better understand his customers' attitudes and feelings. More specifically, he wanted to gain some information and insights to the following set of questions:

1. Do the customers attach significantly different degrees of importance to the features that are the nucleus of Remington's Steak House's operations?

2. What image do customers have of Remington's?

3. Is Remington's providing quality and satisfaction to its customers?

4. Do any of Remington's current marketing strategies need to be modified? If so, in what ways?

To address Smith's questions, the marketing researcher conducted a comprehensive specialty restaurant image study via direct mail. A self-administered questionnaire, cover letter, and incentive were sent to 500 randomly selected individuals who were identified as known patrons of Remington's as well as users of similar restaurants (i.e., Remington's main competitors: Outback Steakhouse and Longhorn Steak House) within the market area. Three hundred usable surveys were returned within the prespecified time frame, for a 60 percent response rate. Respondents were asked their opinions about 14 selected restaurant features; see Exhibit 1 for a description.

To collect the needed importance data on the restaurant features, a six-point, ordinally-interval importance scale was used, where (6) = "Extremely Important to Me"; (5) = "Definitely Important to Me"; (4) = "Generally Important to Me"; (3) = "Somewhat Important to Me"; (2) = "Only Slightly Important to Me"; and (1) = "Not at All Important to Me." In turn, consumers' perceptions of the performance of those features were collected using an ordinally-interval semantic differential scale consisting of a set of seven-point, bipolar descriptors. Each bipolar scale ranged from (7), a "very positive (+) pole descriptor," to (1), a

EXHIBIT 1	Restaurant Food/Service Features and Descriptions

Feature	Description
1	**Quality of the restaurant's products and services.** The restaurant's services and products are dependable and consistent over many trials; service provider fixed the problem right the first time.
2	**Service providers' technical knowledge/competence.** Service providers thoroughly explain the technical aspects of each restaurant encounter and instill a sense of confidence in handling technical problems.
3	**Personnel's understanding of customers' needs.** Personnel understand the customers' needs.
4/5	**Credibility/reliability of restaurant's service providers.** Service providers keep promises, give customers information that can be trusted, do not make mistakes.
6	**Restaurant staff social skills in dealing with their customers.** The service providers are open, friendly, courteous, cheerful, warm, and helpful.
7	**Availability of quality restaurant food/service offerings.** A wide variety of food/services and delivery processes are offered.
8	**Restaurant's overall reputation.** Restaurant is seen as being the right place to go for an excellent dining experience and meal.
9	**Restaurant's concern of putting its customers "first."** Customer satisfaction is job number one.
10	**Flexibility in restaurant's operating hours.** Service staff are there when you need them; restaurant's hours fit customers' busy schedules.
11	**Restaurant's communication and listening skills.** Restaurant's employees explain the situation clearly so that customers understand and listen carefully so that mistakes are avoided or eliminated.
12	**Prices of the restaurant's products and services offerings.** Meals, appetizers, drinks, desserts, etc., are appropriately priced.
13	**Convenience of restaurant's location(s).** Restaurant is easy to drive to; provides prompt delivery of food/services.
14	**Appearance of the restaurant's facilities, equipment, personnel, etc.** Restaurant has modern, very comfortable facilities; uses up-to-date equipment in providing services; personnel look professional.

"very negative (−) pole descriptor." The critical importance and performance results are presented in Exhibit 2.

To determine whether consumers do attach different degrees of importance on restaurant features when selecting a restaurant to eat at, the researcher ran several multiple mean difference tests using z-testing procedures. These testing results are presented in Exhibit 3. To create the necessary information for addressing Mr. Smith's above-mentioned image and customer satisfaction/service quality questions, the researcher decided to perform an importance-image performance (IIP) analysis on the attitudinal and image performance data (see Exhibit 4).

Results

Differences in the Importance of Restaurant Features

Using z-testing procedures, the mean importance ratings of the 14 restaurant features displayed in Exhibit 2 were subjected to multiple mean difference tests. The test results sug-

EXHIBIT 2	**Importance and Image Performance Ratings for Remington's Steak House and Its Competitors**

Feature	Description	Mean* Importance Ratings	(Standard Error)	Mean Image Performance Ratings[†]		
				Outback	Remington's	Longhorn
1	Quality of product/service offerings (Truly Exceptional—7; Truly Terrible—1)	5.87	(.07)	5.92	**3.45**	2.49
2	Restaurant staff's competence/knowledge (Totally Awesome—7; Totally Incompetent—1)	5.82	(.06)	6.60	**3.51**	5.70
3	Understands customer's service needs (Really Understand—7; Definitely Clueless—1)	5.76	(.08)	4.50	**2.68**	5.22
4	Credibility of restaurant/promptness of service (Extremely Credible/Very Quick—7; Worthless/Unacceptably Slow—1)	5.45	(.08)	5.43	**3.52**	5.40
5	Reliability of restaurant/keeps promises (Extremely Reliable/Very Trustful—7; Totally Unreliable/Very Deceitful—1)	5.38	(.09)	5.60	**2.73**	4.28
6	Restaurant staff's personal social skills (Very Friendly—7; Very Rude—1)	5.27	(.10)	4.25	**5.34**	2.59
7	Restaurant food/service assortment (Truly Full Service—7; Only Basic Service—1)	5.18	(.12)	4.10	**5.78**	3.53
8	Restaurant's overall reputation (Truly Exceptional—7; Truly Terrible—1)	5.02	(.15)	5.10	**2.58**	4.34
9	Customer satisfaction (Truly Delighted—7; Totally Dissatisfied—1)	4.92	(.11)	5.15	**3.75**	5.63
10	Restaurant's operating hours (Extremely Flexible—7; Extremely Limited—1)	4.68	(.14)	6.12	**4.46**	2.90
11	Staff's communication & listening skills (Truly Exceptional—7; Truly Terrible—1)	4.45	(.14)	3.75	**4.11**	2.67
12	Prices of restaurant's food/services (Very Competitive Rates—7; Much Too High—1)	3.62	(.15)	4.53	**3.01**	4.53
13	Convenience of restaurant's locations (Very Easy to Get To—7; Too Difficult—1)	3.25	(.13)	4.80	**3.89**	2.42
14	Appearance of facilities, personnel, etc. (Very Professional—7; Very Unprofessional—1)	2.10	(.15)	3.20	**4.68**	3.92

*Importance scale scheme: A six-point scale was used with "Extremely Important to Me" (6); "Definitely Important to Me" (5); "Generally Important to Me" (4); "Somewhat Important to Me" (3); "Only Slightly Important to Me" (2); "Not at All Important to Me" (1).

[†]Performance scale scheme: A seven-point set of semantic differential scales was used with each bipolar scale ranging from "very positive (+) pole descriptor" (7) to "very negative (–) pole descriptor" (1).

gest that there are five significantly different degrees of importance that consumers can attach to restaurant features in their decision process. These five levels of importance and the features are reported in Exhibit 3. From a diagnostic perspective, consumers do attach different degrees of importance to restaurant features. There are three specific features that consumers feel are of "primary importance" in their decision of selecting a restaurant to eat at. Consumers assess the "quality of the restaurant's products and services" (feature 1); the "restaurant staff's competence/knowledge" (feature 2); and the "staff's ability to understand customers' service needs" (feature 3) as being equally and extremely important in nature. Without a restaurant having positive images of these three features, it is unlikely

EXHIBIT 3	Different Degrees of Importance of Restaurant Features

Extremely Important Primary Features

Feature 1: Quality of product/service offerings	(5.87)
Feature 2: Staff's competence/knowledge	(5.82)
Feature 3: Staff's understanding of customers' service needs	(5.76)

Very Important Secondary Features

Feature 4: Credibility of restaurant	(5.45)
Feature 5: Reliability of restaurant	(5.38)
Feature 6: Staff's personal social skills	(5.27)
Feature 7: Assortment of restaurant's food/service offerings	(5.18)
Feature 8: Restaurant's overall reputation	(5.02)

Important Features

Feature 9: Customer satisfaction	(4.92)
Feature 10: Restaurant's operating hours	(4.68)
Feature 11: Staff's communication & listening skills	(4.45)

Somewhat Important Features

Feature 12: Restaurant's prices	(3.62)
Feature 13: Convenience of restaurant's locations	(3.25)

Only Slightly Important Features

Feature 14: Appearance of facilities, equipment, personnel	(2.10)

Note: All five importance groupings are significantly different at $p > .05$.

that a potential customer would give that restaurant serious patronage consideration. In addition, consumers tend to establish five secondary restaurant features that also have a strong influence on their decision process—such as, the "credibility of the restaurant" (feature 4); the "reliability of the restaurant" (feature 5); the staff's social skills in dealing with customers" (feature 6); "assortment of quality food/service offerings" (feature 7); and the "restaurant's overall reputation" (feature 8). The features in these sets are viewed as being very important in restaurant patronage decisions. These results suggest that any restaurant that does not have positive images associated with these features will find it more difficult to attract regular customers.

Although the remaining six restaurant features have some degree of importance in the minds of consumers when selecting a restaurant to patronize, the degrees of importance attached to them, while significant, would not be considered key factors in the decision process.

Remington's Steak House's Current Performance Image

In investigating Smith's second question concerning Remington's current performance image, the researcher performed an importance-image performance (IIP) analysis by plotting Remington's importance and performance data from Exhibit 2 on the IIP grid displayed in Exhibit 4. To aid in understanding the IIP grid results, the grid forms several overall quadrants (A–D) that are narratively described as follows:

Quadrant A: Modifications are needed. The situation where customers or consumers feel that a particular feature was very important in selecting a steak-oriented restaurant but indicate low perceptual satisfaction with the restaurant feature's performance (high importance but low image performance).

Quadrant B: Good job—no need to modify. The situation where customers exhibit a high value toward a given feature and are pleased with that feature's perceived performance (high importance and high image performance).

EXHIBIT 4	Importance-Image Performance Grid for Remington's Steak House's Dining/Food/Service Feature Ratings

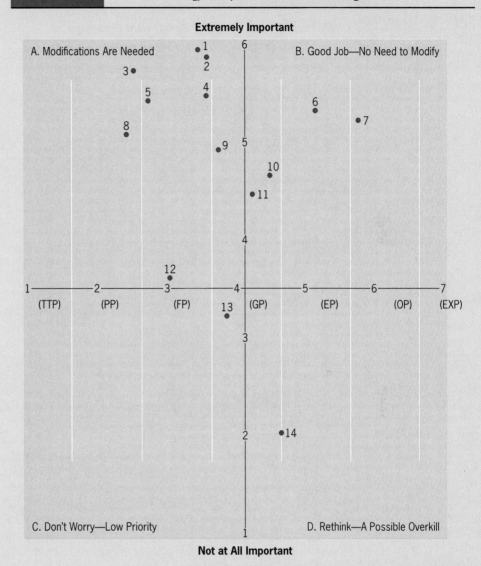

Quadrant C: Don't worry—low priority. Quadrant D: Rethink—A Possible Overkill

Quadrant C: Don't worry—low priority. The situation where a particular feature is perceived as being low in terms of performance, but consumers do not consider it as being very important (low importance and low image performance).

Quadrant D: Rethink—a possible overkill. The situation where a particular feature is judged as being good in terms of performance, but customers attach only slight importance to it (low importance and high image performance).

To add accuracy to the IIP grid and the diagnostic information, vertical performance ranges for each of the seven performance levels are added to the grid format. These performance ranges were statistically derived by calculating acceptance intervals similar to confidence intervals and are displayed in Exhibit 5. The performance of each restaurant

EXHIBIT 5	Image Performance Code Ranges	
Original Scale Code	**Performance Description**	**Statistical Mean Range***
7	Exceptional performance (EXP)	$6.70 \leq \overline{x} \leq 7.00$
6	Outstanding performance (OP)	$5.70 \leq \overline{x} \leq 6.69$
5	Excellent performance (EP)	$4.70 \leq \overline{x} \leq 5.69$
4	Good performance (GP)	$3.70 \leq \overline{x} \leq 4.69$
3	Fair performance (FP)	$2.70 \leq \overline{x} \leq 3.69$
2	Poor performance (PP)	$1.70 \leq \overline{x} \leq 2.69$
1	Truly terrible performance (TTP)	$.70 \leq \overline{x} \leq 1.69$

*Ranges are based on a 99% confidence level ($Z = 2.58$) and standard error of .30 for a sample size of 300 respondents.

feature was plotted on the IIP grid using each feature's corresponding "mean importance rating" and "mean image performance rating" from Exhibit 2.

The IIP grid results demonstrate that customers' perceptions of Remington's were much different from what Smith had desired when opening the restaurant. Out of the 14 features that customers could use to formulate their perceptual image of Remington's, the results indicate that the performances of eight features fall in Quadrant A (Modifications are needed). Among the top eight image-building restaurant features deemed extremely or very important to customers, only the restaurant staff's social skills (feature 6) and wide assortment of food and service offerings (feature 7) are viewed as having excellent or better performances. The three most important features—product/service quality (feature 1); staff's competence/knowledge (feature 2); and staff's understanding of customers' service needs (feature 3))—are viewed as performing at the poor to fair levels. In addition, customers felt that the restaurant's credibility (feature 4) and reliability (feature 5) are less than marginal and that its overall reputation of being the right place to go for an "excellent" dining experience and meal (feature 8) is poor.

While there are five features that are judged as good performers, customer satisfaction (feature 9) is at the lowest end of the good performance range and needs some modification. The staff's communication and listening skills (feature 11) are well below the desired "excellent" performance level. Although prices (feature 12) are only marginally important to customers, Remington's current prices are less than competitive.

Dining/Food/Service Quality and Customer Satisfaction

The data presented in Exhibit 2 and on the IIP grid strongly suggest that Remington's Steak House is falling short of providing the level of service quality and customer satisfaction demanded by its patrons. Customers feel that the quality of Remington's products and services (feature 1) and staff's competence (feature 2) are marginal, at best. The staff is almost clueless about patrons' service needs (feature 3). In addition, the restaurant's staff is having a difficult time putting the customer first, thus creating not only a low level of customer satisfaction (feature 9) but weak levels of credibility (feature 4) and reliability (feature 5); in turn, these negatively affect the restaurant's overall reputation (feature 8).

Need for Strategy Changes

IIP analysis by itself cannot offer specific strategy changes, but it does identify those image building features that are not performing as anticipated, and where Smith must focus attention in order to improve the restaurant's image. For example, to improve Remington's current image closer to the initial desired image, Smith must improve the restaurant's performance in the following areas: product and service quality; staff's competence and knowledge; staff's ability to understand the customer's needs; credibility and reliability of keeping promises and giving customers information that they can trust over time; making prices more competitive; and providing strong customer satisfaction to those patrons who frequent the restaurant. Finally, Smith must understand that many of the features that make up Remington's image are interactive. To achieve the desired "excellent" image of being a unique theme-oriented specialty dining restaurant, care must be given in assessing what impact changes in one strategy area have on the other strategy areas.

MARKETING RESEARCH CASE EXERCISE

HOW TO FLY ON THE INTERNET

Northern World Airlines is a national carrier contemplating a shift in its marketing strategy toward conducting more of its ticketing and customer service activities over the Internet. One of the alternatives Northern World is considering is the issuing of electronic airline tickets to its passengers. Customers booking their tickets through Northern World's Web site would be sent an e-mail confirmation as soon as the transaction was completed and registered in the company's database. The customer could then take the confirmation number to the airport terminal and check in at Northern World's ticket counter, where he or she would be issued a boarding pass and could check luggage if needed. This system would eliminate a substantial amount of paper processing for Northern World Airlines and would provide quicker service to the customer.

The managers at Northern World are unsure about whether ticket customers would expect lower prices for electronic tickets than for tickets issued in the traditional manner. To help answer this question, Northern World contracted with a marketing research firm to survey approximately 400 of its current customers. The research firm asked these customers three questions: (1) How likely would you be to book airline tickets through the Internet? (2) Would you expect to pay more, the same, or less for an electronic ticket? and (3) If tickets were $300, how much more or less would you be prepared to pay to buy your tickets online? The following table shows the average responses to the third question:

Responses to Northern World Airlines Customer Survey

Response Group	Average	Standard Deviation	Number of Respondents
Expect to pay more	$349	$30	216
Expect to pay less	$278	$22	184

The Northern World managers are interested in finding out whether customers were expecting to pay a substantial difference in prices for an electronic ticket. That is, were the customers expecting to pay more or less than the standard ticket price? If you consider the hypothetical ticket price of $300 used by the research firm in the survey, were the customers' answers significantly above or below that number?

Describe how you would analyze the data in the table above to answer this question. What analysis technique would you use? What would your null hypothesis be? How many statistical comparisons do you need to conduct? Based on your analysis, would you recommend that Northern World Airlines raise, lower, or keep its electronic ticket prices the same?

Learning Objectives

After reading this chapter, you will be able to

1. Understand the difference between testing for significant differences and testing for association.

2. Understand what a relationship is, as well as the various types of possible relationships.

3. Understand the concept of covariation and association.

4. Understand the various statistical tests and when they should be used.

5. Explain the concept of statistical significance versus practical significance.

6. Understand the difference between univariate, bivariate, and multivariate techniques.

7. Understand when and how to use regression analysis.

Data Analysis:
Testing for Association

❝ By far the most important things to a statistician are the quality of the data, the dimensionality of the data, and the completeness of the data. ❞

RANDY HLAVAC
President
Marketing Synergy, Inc.

Correlation and Regression

The Web site at www.med.umkc.edu provides a very basic introduction to correlation and regression. These statistical techniques are used in a variety of situations, including business applications, medical research, and government situations. This Web site provides, in sufficient detail, the history of correlation and regression, the appropriate application situations of both techniques, and step-by-step graphical and statistical examples that make the techniques easier to understand. Definitions of key terms are also provided.

For advanced statisticians, this Web site provides detailed discussions of correlation and regression applications. Exten-sive use of formulas and advanced statistical operations are included for individuals who desire greater depth in statistical presentations. Additional discussions center on the statistical significance of correlation and regression results and the predicted error of using correlation and regression.

Supplemental information on correlation and regression can be found on other Web sites. Using your Internet search engine and the search words *correlation* and *regression,* you will locate a variety of sites dedicated to the discussion of these specific statistical techniques.

Value of Testing for Association

Marketing managers are very often interested in detailed descriptions of the types of people who are most likely to buy their products. For example, consumers between the ages of 18 and 24 may be much more interested in buying the latest CD from a new alternative rock group than would consumers who are over 45 years old. Or people who often drink wine with their dinner may have higher income levels than those who drink beer at dinner.

Relationship   A consistent and systematic link between two or more variables.

Knowledge about these types of relationships between your customers' characteristics and their behavior can be very useful to marketers. A **relationship** is a consistent and systematic link between two variables. That is, knowledge about the behavior of one variable (e.g., age) gives you some information about the possible behavior of another variable (e.g., CD purchases). This does not mean that one variable causes another. The existence of a relationship simply means that the two items tend to change together.

There are three useful types of questions marketing researchers can ask about the connection between two variables. The most obvious one is whether two items or characteristics of an object are related at all. That is, does a relationship exist between these two elements? Does knowledge about the behavior of one variable allow us to make any sort of useful prediction about the behavior of another?

Linear relationship
A relationship between two variables whereby the strength and nature of the relationship remains the same over the range of both variables.

A second kind of beneficial question that can be asked is, "If variables Y and X are related, how strong is this relationship?" On the one hand, if the relationship between CD purchases (variable Y) and age (variable X) can be described as very weak, then changes in Y may only rarely be associated with changes in X. On the other hand, if the relationship between CD purchases (Y) and age (X) can be characterized as very strong, then nearly every time we see a change in CD purchases, we can also expect to see a change in age.

Curvilinear relationship
A relationship between two variables whereby the strength and/or direction of their relationship changes over the range of both variables.

Third, if two variables can be described as related, a very useful question to ask is, "What is the nature of the relationship?" How can the link between Y and X best be described? There are a number of different ways in which two variables can share a relationship. Variables Y and X can have a **linear relationship,** which means that the strength and nature of the relationship between them remains the same over the range of both variables, and can best be described using a straight line. Conversely, Y and X could have a **curvilinear relationship,** which would mean that the strength and/or direction of their relationship changes over the range of both variables (perhaps Y's relationship with X first gets stronger as X increases, but then gets weaker as the value of X continues to increase).

It may occur to you that a linear relationship would be much simpler to work with than a curvilinear relationship, and that is true. That is, if we know the value of variable X, then we can apply the formula for a straight line ($Y = a + bX$) to determine the value of Y. But when two variables have a curvilinear relationship, the formula that best describes that linkage will be more algebraically complex and possibly hard to determine. For these reasons, most marketing researchers tend to work with relationships that they believe are linear, or are close approximations. In fact, many of the statistics you learned about in preceding chapters are based on the assumption that a linear relationship is an efficient way to describe the link between two variables under investigation.

Using Covariation to Describe Variable Relationships

Covariation The amount of change in one variable that is consistently related to the change in another variable of interest.

Since we are interested in finding out whether two variables describing our customers are related, the concept of covariation is a very useful idea. **Covariation** is defined as the amount of change in one variable that is consistently related to a change in another variable of interest. For example, if we know that CD purchases are related to age, then we want to know the extent to which younger persons purchase more CDs, and ultimately which types of CDs. Another way of stating the concept of covariation is that it is the degree of association between two items (e.g., the change in the attitude toward Starbucks coffee advertising campaigns as it varies between light, medium, and heavy consumers of Starbucks coffee). If two variables are found to change together on a reliable or consistent basis, then we can use that information to make predictions as well as decisions on advertising and marketing strategies.

Scatter diagram A graphic plot of the relative position of two variables using a horizontal and vertical axis to represent the values of the respective variables.

One easy way of visually describing the covariation between two variables is with the use of a **scatter diagram.** A scatter diagram plots the relative position of two variables using a horizontal and vertical axis to represent the values of the respective variables. Exhibits 17.1 through 17.4 show some examples of possible relationships between two variables that might show up on a scatter diagram. In Exhibit 17.1, the best way to describe the visual impression left by the collection of dots representing the values of each variable is probably a circle. That is, there is no particular skewness or direction to the collection of

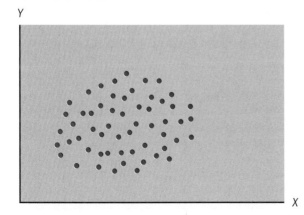

EXHIBIT 17.1 **No Relationship between *X* and *Y***

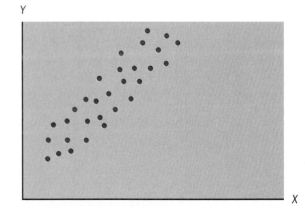

EXHIBIT 17.2 **Positive Relationship between *X* and *Y***

dots. Thus, if you take two or three sample values of variable *Y* from the scatter diagram and look at the values for *X*, there is no predictable pattern to the values for *X*. Knowing the values of *Y* or *X* would not tell you very much (maybe nothing at all) about the possible values of the other variable. Exhibit 17.1 suggests that there is no systematic relationship between *Y* and *X*, and that there is very little or no covariation shared by the two variables. If we measured the amount of covariation shared by these two variables (something you will learn how to do in the next section), it would be very close to zero.

In Exhibit 17.2, the two variables present a very different picture from that of Exhibit 17.1. There is a distinct pattern to the dots. As the values of *Y* increase, so do the values of *X*. This pattern could be very effectively described using the idea of a straight line or an ellipse (a circle that has been stretched out from both sides). We could also describe this relationship as positive, because increases in the value of *Y* are associated with increases in the value of *X*. That is, if we know the relationship between *Y* and *X* is a linear, positive relationship, we would know that the values of *Y* and *X* change in the same direction. As the values of *Y* increase, so do the values of *X*. Similarly, if the values of *Y* decrease, the values of *X* should decrease as well. If we try to measure the amount of covariation shown by the values of *Y* and *X*, it would be relatively high. Thus, changes in the value of *Y* are systematically related to changes in the value of *X*.

Exhibit 17.3 shows the same type of distinct pattern between the values of *Y* and *X*, but the direction of the relationship is opposite the one in Exhibit 17.2. There still seems to be the same linear pattern, but now increases in the value of *Y* are associated with decreases in the values of *X*. The values of *Y* and *X* change in the opposite direction. This type of relationship is known as a negative relationship. The amount of covariation shared between the two variables is still high, because *Y* and *X* still change together, though in a direction opposite from that shown in Exhibit 17.2. The concept of covariation refers to the amount of shared movement, not the direction of the relationship between two variables.

Finally, Exhibit 17.4 shows a more complicated type of relationship between the values of *Y* and *X*. This pattern of dots can be described as curvilinear. That is, the relationship between the values of *Y* and the values of *X* is different for different values of the variables. In the case of Exhibit 17.4, part of the relationship is positive (increases in the small values of *Y* are associated with increases in the small values of *X*), but then the relationship becomes negative (increases in the larger values of *Y* are now associated with decreases in the larger values of *X*).

| EXHIBIT 17.3 | **Negative Relationship**
 between *X* and *Y* | | EXHIBIT 17.4 | **Curvilinear Relationship**
 between *X* and *Y* |

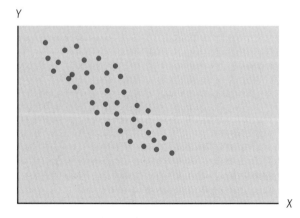

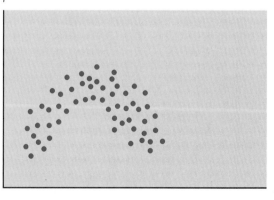

Situations often arise where many small-business owners and managers collect data from two relevant samples yet do not know how to statistically compare the two measures. When this occurs, the most frequently used statistical technique available to the small-business owner is correlation analysis.

Correlation analysis describes the degree of relationship between the two variables, often stated as an absolute value score between 0 and 1. The higher the correlation score, the stronger the relationship between the two variables. Through the use of correlation procedures, small-business owners can identify trends in their particular market.

A brief description of correlation analysis in action is described below. This example is only one of a variety of possible applications of correlation analysis.

A small-business owner might have information on the exact number of hours worked by salespeople in his company last year, and the amount of advertising sold by each sales representative that year. After ini-

tial graphical representation, the two measures would appear to be highly correlated. In other words, as the number of hours worked by salespeople increased, the amount of advertisements sold per individual would also increase.

While this brief example shows the possible inferences from correlation analysis, a common mistake in interpreting the correlation score for two variables is to assume that a high correlation score implies causation. No such conclusion is automatic. In the previous example, although the number of hours worked and sales productivity are highly correlated, other factors—such as territory or number of representatives in that area—play an important role in analyzing correlation. Assuming causation based solely on these two factors might ignore other important variables.

Therefore, small-business owners should use correlation analysis to analyze potential relationships but should be careful in attempting to determine causal relationships between two variables.

This pattern of dots could not easily be described as a linear relationship. An additional complication comes from the fact, noted earlier, that many of the statistics marketing researchers use to describe association assume the two variables have a linear relationship. These statistics don't perform very effectively when used to describe a curvilinear relationship. In Exhibit 17.4, we can still say the relationship is strong, or that the covariation exhibited by the two variables is strong. However, now we can't talk very easily about the direction (positive or negative) of the relationship, because the direction changes. To make matters more difficult, many statistical methods of describing relationships between variables cannot be effectively applied to situations where you suspect the relationship is curvilinear. The Small Business Implications box provides some insight on how correlations can be used in small businesses.

Treatment and Measures of Correlation Analysis

The use of a scatter diagram gives us a visual way to describe the relationship between two variables and a sense of the amount of covariation they share. For example, a scatter diagram can tell us that as age increases the average consumption of Starbucks coffee increases too. But even though a picture is worth a thousand words, it is often more convenient to use a quantitative measure of the covariation between two items.

Pearson correlation coefficient A statistical measure of the strength of a linear relationship between two metric variables.

The **Pearson correlation coefficient** measures the degree of linear association between two variables. It varies between –1.00 and +1.00, with 0 representing absolutely no association between two variables, and –1.00 or +1.00 representing a perfect link between two variables. The higher the correlation coefficient, the stronger the level of association. The

Is Starbucks coffee consumption related to levels of personal income?

correlation coefficient can be either positive or negative, depending on the direction of the relationship between two variables. As we explained earlier, if there is a negative correlation coefficient between Y and X, that means that increases in the value of Y are associated with decreases in the value of X, and vice versa.

The null hypothesis for the Pearson correlation states that there is no association between the two variables in the population and that the correlation coefficient is zero. For example, we may hypothesize that there is no relationship between Starbucks coffee consumption and income levels. If you take measures of two variables (coffee consumption and income) from a sample of the population and estimate the correlation coefficient for that sample, the basic question is, "What is the probability that I would get a correlation coefficient of this size in my sample, if the correlation coefficient in the population is actually zero?" That is, if you calculate a large correlation coefficient between the two variables in your sample, and your sample was properly selected from the population of interest, then the chances that the population correlation coefficient is really zero are relatively small. Therefore, if the correlation coefficient is statistically significant, the null hypothesis is rejected, and you can conclude with some confidence that the two variables you are examining do share some association in the population. In other words, Starbucks coffee consumption is related to income.

If you remember earlier in the chapter, we stated that the first question of interest was, "Does a relationship between Y and X exist?" This question is equivalent to asking whether a correlation coefficient is statistically significant. If this is the case, then you can move on to the second and third questions: "If there is a relationship between Y and X, how strong is that relationship?" and "What is the best way to describe that relationship?"

The size of the correlation coefficient can be used to quantitatively describe the strength of the association between two variables. Many authors have suggested some rules of thumb for characterizing the strength of the association between two variables based on the size of the correlation coefficient.

As Exhibit 17.5 suggests, correlation coefficients between +.81 and +1.00 are considered very strong. That is, covariance is shared between the two variables under study. At the other extreme, if the correlation coefficient is between +.00 and +.20, there is a good chance that the null hypothesis won't be rejected (unless you are using a large sample).

EXHIBIT 17.5	Rules of Thumb about the Strength of Correlation Coefficients

Range of Coefficient	Description of Strength
±.81 to ±1.00	Very strong
±.61 to ±.80	Strong
±.41 to ±.60	Moderate
±.21 to ±.40	Weak
±.00 to ±.20	None

You should realize that these numbers are only suggestions and that other ranges and descriptions of relationship strength are possible.

Pearson Correlation Coefficient Formula

The Pearson correlation coefficient formula makes several assumptions about the nature of the data to which it is applied. First of all, the two variables are assumed to have been measured using interval or ratio scale measures. If this is not the case, there are other types of correlation coefficients that can be computed that match the type of data on hand. We will devote more discussion to these coefficients after we have described the basic concepts.

A second implicit assumption made by the Pearson correlation coefficient (and most other correlation coefficient measures) is that the nature of the relationship that we are trying to measure is linear. That is, a straight line will do a reasonably good job of describing the relationship between the two variables of interest.

Use of the Pearson correlation coefficient also assumes that the variables you want to analyze come from a bivariate normally distributed population. That is, the population is such that all the observations with a given value of one variable have values of the second variable that are normally distributed. This assumption of normal distributions for the variables under study is a common requirement for many statistical techniques used by marketing researchers. Although a common assumption, finding out whether it holds for the sample data you are working with is sometimes hard to determine and often taken for granted.

The formula to calculate the Pearson correlation coefficient is shown below:

$$r_{xy} = \frac{(x_i - x)(y_i - y)}{n s_x s_y}$$

where:

x_i = Each x value

y_i = Each y value

x = Mean of the x values

y = Mean of the y values

n = Number of paired values

s_x = Standard deviation of x values

s_y = Standard deviation of y values

A hypothetical example may help to illustrate many of the basic ideas. In Exhibit 17.6, there are 14 observations; these describe the relationship between the sales revenue of 14

Canon copier distributors and each distributor's sales force. We are interested in finding out whether the two variables are related. That is, are sales revenues for each of the 14 distributors related to the size of their sales force?

The data in Exhibit 17.6 provide us with the information we need to calculate the correlation coefficient measuring the relationship between sales revenue and sales force size for the Canon copier distributors. The mean of $309.43 million for sales revenue (calculated across all 14 local distributors) is subtracted from each of the observations to develop an estimate of the variation present in the observations of sales revenue. The same calculation is conducted for the sales force size.

Notice that for one variable (sales) we are talking about millions of dollars, while in the other we are considering the number of individual salespersons. Unless we find a way to compare these two different quantities, any conclusions about the strength of the association between sales revenue and sales force size could be misleading. If you examine the numerator of the formula for the correlation coefficient above, the covariation of the two quantities is developed by multiplying the variation of each observation from its mean with the corresponding value from the other variable. Changing units of measure (say from millions to thousands of dollars) would affect the level of the covariation. For that reason, the numerator is divided by the product of the standard deviations of each variable and the number of observations. This step makes the covariation "unitless" (just like a percentage

EXHIBIT 17.6	Data on Sales Revenue and Sales Force Size (n = 14)				
Sales (Y) ($ million)	**Salespersons (X)**	**$(Y - \bar{Y})(Y - \bar{Y})$**	**$(X - \bar{X})$**	**$(Y - \bar{Y})(X - \bar{X})$**	
252	15	−57.43	−5.21	299.21	
263	15	−46.43	−5.21	241.90	
275	16	−34.43	−4.21	144.95	
225	15	−84.43	−5.21	439.88	
253	18	−56.43	−2.21	124.71	
279	19	−30.43	−1.21	36.82	
305	20	−4.43	−0.21	0.93	
310	14	0.57	−6.21	−3.54	
333	18	23.57	−2.21	−52.09	
345	25	35.57	4.79	170.38	
359	26	49.57	5.79	287.01	
399	31	89.57	10.79	966.46	
358	22	48.57	1.79	86.94	
376	29	66.57	8.79	585.15	
Average:	**Average:**				
309.43	20.21				
Standard deviation	**Standard deviation**				
53.34	5.56				

figure has no particular unit of measure). Now, the units in which each variable is measured don't have an impact on our calculations. This process is called standardizing the data to make it comparable in units.

If you take the information from Exhibit 17.6 and work through the formula, you see that the sum of the variation between the two variables is 3,328.71, and the product of the standard deviations and number of observations is 4,151.99. Dividing this into the numerator value produces a Pearson correlation coefficient of $r = .802$.

Statistical Significance

Although the size of the correlation coefficient for our sample of 14 observations is large, the statistical significance of the coefficient needs to be determined. We are interested in finding out whether the correlation is significantly different from zero. To do this, the correlation coefficient is converted into a t-test statistic. The formula for this conversion is shown below:

$$t = \frac{r(n - 2)}{1 - r^2}$$

The decision rule to follow is

> If the calculated value of t is less than the critical value of t, the null hypothesis cannot be rejected.

Using the t statistic formula above, $r = .802$, $n - 2 = 12$, and $1 - r^2 = .3568$. Consequently, the calculated t statistic is 4.65105. The critical value of t with 12 degrees of freedom in a table of t values at .05 probability (two-tailed test) is 3.0545. Using the decision rule above, we would reject the null hypothesis that the population correlation coefficient is zero and conclude that sales revenue of Canon copier distributors is related to the size of their sales force (both strongly and very strongly, according to our suggested guidelines for strength of association).

One note of caution should be emphasized here. Although it may seem logical that the number of people in a company's sales force would affect the level of sales revenue generated, we cannot make that causal statement. It is also conceivable that the company tends to reduce its sales force when its revenues drop, due to a shortage of cash. In that case, sales revenue might actually be what determines the size of the sales force. The point is that correlation coefficients can only show association; the causal implications must be developed from conceptual reasoning and good research design, not from the results of a statistical calculation. Statistics (even, as we will see, regression formulas) do not, in and of themselves, allow the researcher to make causal statements.

A final point to be made is that the Pearson correlation coefficient is intended to measure the degree of linear association between two variables. Sales revenue and sales force size for the Canon copier distributors could still be closely associated in a curvilinear fashion (remember the scatter diagram in Exhibit 17.4), and the Pearson correlation coefficient would be close to zero and statistically nonsignificant.

When the correlation coefficient is strong and significant, you can be confident that the two variables are associated in a linear fashion. In our example, we can be reasonably confident that the sales of the individual Canon copier distributors are in fact related to the size of their sales force. When the correlation coefficient is weak, then two possibilities must be considered: (1) there simply is no consistent, systematic relationship between the two items in the population you are interested in, or (2) the association exists, but it is not linear, and other types of relationships must be investigated further.

Substantive Significance of the Correlation Coefficient

In the formula for determining the statistical significance of the correlation coefficient discussed earlier, the denominator included a calculation formed by squaring the correlation coefficient and subtracting it from 1.00. It turns out that if you square the r correlation coefficient, you arrive at the **coefficient of determination, or r^2.** This number ranges from 0.0 to 1.0 and shows the proportion of variation explained or accounted for in one variable by another. In our example above, the correlation coefficient $r = .802$. The $r^2 = .643$, meaning that approximately 64 percent of the variation in sales revenue of the Canon copier distributors is associated with the size of the sales force. You could also state the reverse: 64 percent of the variation in the size of the sales force is associated with the level of sales revenue. The larger the size of the coefficient of determination, the stronger the linear relationship between the two variables under study. In our example, we have accounted for more than half of the variation in sales revenue by relating it to the size of sales force.

> **Coefficient of determination (r^2)** A number measuring the proportion of variation in one variable accounted for by another. The r^2 measure can be thought of as a percentage and varies from 0.0 to 1.00.

You need to remember that it is not sufficient to find only the statistical significance of a correlation coefficient; you also need to assess the substantive significance. That is, do the numbers you calculate mean anything useful? Since the statistical significance procedure for correlation coefficients includes information on the sample size, it is possible to find statistically significant correlation coefficients that are really too small to be of much practical use. For example, if we had compared the revenues and sales force sizes of 300 Canon copier distributors (a national survey instead of a regional survey) and the correlation coefficient was .40 (significant at .05 level), the coefficient of determination would be .16. Can we conclude that the results are meaningful? To say yes requires a little more thought. So you must always look at both types of significance (statistical and substantive) before you develop your conclusions. This is of particular importance when assessing information from global markets.

Influence of Measurement Scales on Correlation Analysis

A common occurrence in marketing research studies is that the answers to questions that marketing researchers are most interested in can be measured only with ordinal or even nominal scales. For example, if we are interested in learning more about Starbucks coffee consumption, we might consider consumption patterns of female versus male coffee drinkers. In these cases, applying the Pearson correlation coefficient to the data and assuming these measures of gender have interval or ratio scale properties (when they do not) will possibly produce misleading or overstated results.

> **Spearman rank order correlation coefficient** A statistical measure of the linear association between two variables where both have been measured using ordinal (rank order) scales.

What options are available to the researcher when ordinal scales are used to collect data, or when the data simply cannot be measured with an interval scale or better? The **Spearman rank order correlation coefficient** is the recommended statistic to use when two variables have been measured using ordinal scales. If either one of the variables is represented by rank order data, the best approach is to use the Spearman rank order correlation coefficient, rather than the Pearson product moment correlation coefficient. The Spearman rank order correlation coefficient tends to produce the lowest coefficient and is considered a more conservative measure.

In addition to the Spearman rank order correlation coefficient, there are other correlation coefficients that may be used to take into consideration the scale properties inherent in the data. For example, if you think that the gender of your customers makes a difference in the amount of your product they purchase, it would be possible to correlate customer gender (male/female) with product purchases (dollars) to answer your question. To do so, you would use a biserial correlation coefficient to make this calculation. Although the formula to calculate this value is somewhat more complicated than the ones we have already seen, the point is that you should try to use the appropriate statistic to match the characteristics of your data. There are formulas available to calculate almost any type of correlation coefficient to match the situation.

What Is Regression Analysis?

We have discussed correlation as a way of determining the existence of a relationship between two variables. The correlation coefficient also can be used to answer questions about the overall strength of the association and the direction of the relationship between the variables. There are instances, however, when these answers do not provide enough information to the marketing manager. We may still need to know how to describe the relationship between the variables we are examining in greater detail. One method for arriving at these more detailed answers is called regression analysis.

Often, a marketing manager may need to make predictions about future sales levels or how a potential price increase will affect the profits or market share of the company. There are a number of ways to make such predictions: (1) extrapolation from past behavior of the variable; (2) simple guesses; or (3) use of a regression equation that compares information about related variables to assist in the prediction. Extrapolation and guesses (educated or otherwise) usually assume that past conditions and behaviors will continue into the future. They do not examine the influences behind the behavior of interest. Consequently, when sales levels, profits, or other variables of interest to a manager differ from those in the past, extrapolation and guessing do not provide any means of explaining why.

Bivariate regression analysis is a statistical technique that uses information about the relationship between an independent or predictor variable and a dependent or criterion variable, and combines it with the algebraic formula for a straight line to make predictions. Particular values of the independent variable are selected and the behavior of the dependent variable is observed. This data is then applied to the formula for a straight line we discussed earlier. This formula is repeated here:

Bivariate regression analysis A statistical technique that analyzes the linear relationship between two variables by estimating coefficients for an equation for a straight line. One variable is designated as a dependent variable and the other is called an independent or predictor variable.

$$Y = a + bX + e$$

where:

Y = Dependent variable

X = Independent variable

a = Y intercept (where the line crosses the Y axis and $X = 0$)

b = Slope, or amount Y increases with each unit increase in X

e = Error – Difference between actual value and value predicted by regression line

For example, if you want to find the level of your company's current sales volume, you would apply the following straight-line formula:

Sales volume = $0 + (Price per unit) (Number of units sold)

You obviously would expect no sales revenue if nothing was sold. Price per unit dictates the amount that sales (or Y) increases with each unit sold (X). In this example, the relationship between sales volume and number of units sold is linear (i.e., it is consistent and positive over the values of both Y and X).

Once a regression equation has been developed to predict values of Y, we are interested in trying to find out how good that prediction is. An obvious place to begin would be the actual value we collected in our sample. By comparing this actual value Y_i with our predicted value Y_i, we can tell how far away our prediction is. In fact, this procedure of comparing actual values from a sample with predicted values from a regression equation is a commonly used method of determining the accuracy of a regression equation.

A couple of points should be made about the assumptions behind regression analysis. First, just like correlation analysis, regression analysis assumes that a linear relationship will provide a good description of the relationship between two variables. If the scatter diagram showing the positions of the values of both variables looks like the scatter plot in Exhibit 17.2 or Exhibit 17.3, this assumption would seem to be a good one. However, if the plot looks like Exhibit 17.1 or Exhibit 17.4, then regression analysis isn't a good choice.

Second, even though the common terminology of regression analysis uses the labels *dependent* and *independent* for the variables, those names don't mean that we can say one variable causes the behavior of the other. Regression analysis uses knowledge about the level and type of association between two variables to make predictions. Statements about the ability of one variable to cause changes in another must be based on conceptual logic or information other than just statistical techniques.

Finally, the use of a simple regression model assumes (1) the variables of interest are measured on interval or ratio scales (except in the case of dummy variables, which we will discuss later); (2) these variables come from a bivariate normal population (the same assumption made by correlation analysis); and (3) the error terms associated with making predictions are normally and independently distributed (we will also talk about this particular assumption and its validation later in this chapter).

In the case of bivariate regression analysis, we are looking at one independent variable and one dependent variable. Often, marketing managers will want to look at the joint influence of several independent variables on one dependent variable. For example, are CD purchases related only to age, or are they also related to income, ethnicity, gender, geographic location, education level, and so on? Multiple regression is the appropriate technique to measure these relationships and represents a straightforward extension of bivariate regression. We will go through the mechanics of conducting a bivariate or simple regression analysis before turning to a discussion of multiple regression analysis.

Developing and Estimating the Regression Coefficients

Remember that the regression equation examining the relationship between two variables is derived from the equation for a straight line. The slope coefficient b tells us how much we can expect Y to change, given a unit change in X. Once this equation is developed from sample data, we can use it to make predictions about Y, given different values of X.

At this point, you might be thinking, "Okay, so we use a straight line to describe the relationship between Y and X, but which one? Is it the best line, or the first line the computer program estimates?" It turns out there is a procedure called ordinary least squares (OLS), which guarantees that the line it estimates to describe the data is the best one. We said earlier that the best prediction would be one in which the difference between the actual value of Y and the predicted value of Y was the smallest. **Ordinary least squares** is a statistical procedure that results in equation parameters (a and b) that produce predictions with the *lowest* sum of squared differences between actual and predicted values.

The differences between actual and predicted values of Y are represented by e_i (the error term of the regression equation). If we square these errors for each observation (the difference between actual values of Y and predicted values of Y) and add them up, the total would represent an aggregate or overall measure of the accuracy of the regression equation. Regression equations calculated through the use of OLS procedures will always give the lowest squared error totals, and this is why both bivariate and multiple regression analysis are sometimes referred to as OLS regression.

Ordinary least squares
A statistical procedure that estimates regression equation coefficients which produce the lowest sum of squared differences between the actual and predicted values of the dependent variable.

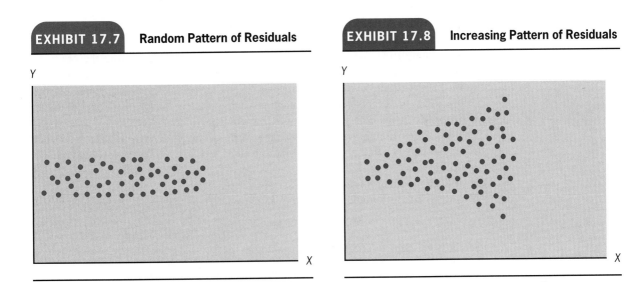

EXHIBIT 17.7 Random Pattern of Residuals

EXHIBIT 17.8 Increasing Pattern of Residuals

Besides allowing the researcher to evaluate the quality of the prediction produced by a regression equation, the error terms also can be used to diagnose potential problems caused by data observations that do not meet the assumptions described above. The pattern of errors produced by comparing actual Y values with predicted Y values can tell you whether the errors are normally distributed and/or have equal variances across the range of X values. Exhibits 17.7, 17.8, and 17.9 show several possible patterns of residuals (another term for the error between actual and predicted Y values).

In Exhibit 17.7, there is no discernible pattern to the error terms when you plot the predicted values against the residuals. In Exhibit 17.8, there is an apparent pattern; the predictions made for small values of Y are more precise than the predictions made for large values of Y. Obviously, our regression equation is more accurate for some values of the independent variable X than for others. There are transformation techniques that can be applied to the data to potentially help this problem.[1]

Exhibit 17.9 portrays a pattern to the error terms that suggests a nonlinear relationship between Y and X. In this case, the researcher's initial assumption that a straight line would

EXHIBIT 17.9 Nonlinear Pattern of Residuals

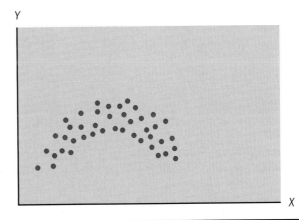

be the best way to describe the potential relationship may need to be changed. The best approach may be a nonlinear relationship-based technique.

Examination of the error terms and the pattern obtained by comparing the predicted values of Y against the residuals can tell us whether our initial assumptions about the appropriateness of using regression analysis to examine variable relationships are correct. In addition, this type of evidence can sometimes suggest the next type of analysis to undertake, given the characteristics of the data we have collected.

The use of an example will help illustrate the procedure for computing the regression equation parameters a and b. Once again, our Canon copier distributorship wants to know the impact of sales force size on revenues. Exhibit 17.10 shows the observations for sales force size (X) and sales volume (Y).

The regression formula to be used in this case is

$$y_i = a + bX_i + e_i$$

The slope coefficient, b, is computed according to the formula below:

$$b = \frac{nX_iY_i - (X_i)(Y_i)}{nX_i^2 - (X_i)^2}$$

The estimate of the intercept, a, can be found by using the following calculation:

$$a = \frac{1}{n(y_i - bX_i)}$$

EXHIBIT 17.10 Data for Sales Force Size and Sales Volume: Canon Copier Distributorship

Observation	X Size	Y – Sales ($000s)	XY	X²	Y	e²
1	0	10	0	0	10.15	.03
2	2	8	16	4	11.65	13.32
3	4	11	44	16	13.15	4.63
4	6	20	120	36	14.65	28.63
5	8	18	144	64	16.15	3.43
6	10	15	150	100	17.65	7.02
7	12	22	264	144	19.15	8.13
8	14	25	350	196	20.65	18.93
9	16	19	304	256	22.15	9.93
10	18	21	378	324	23.65	7.02
Sum	90	169	1,770	1,140		101.07
Mean	9.0	16.9				
Standard deviation	6.06	5.67				

Taking the data shown in Exhibit 17.10 and applying it to the formula for *b*, we get the following:

$$b = \frac{10(1,770) - (90)(169)}{10(1,140) - (90)^2}$$

$$b = \frac{17,700 - 15,210}{11,400 - 8,100} = \frac{2,490}{3,300}$$

$$b = .75$$

The intercept *a* calculation is

$$a = \frac{1}{10[169 - .75(90)]}$$

$$a = 10.15$$

Therefore, the regression equation that best explains the linear relationship between the size of the sales force and the sales revenue for Canon copier distributorship is

$$Y_i = 10.15 + .75 \, X_i + e_i$$

If *X* (sales force size) = 0, then sales for the copier distributorship are estimated to be $10,150 (recall that sales were measured in millions in Exhibit 17.6). The slope coefficient tells us that for every unit increase in *X*, *Y* will increase by .75 units. In the context of the example, for every salesperson we add to the sales force, copier sales revenue should increase by $75,000, on average.

Look at the last two columns on the right in Exhibit 17.10. The estimated values for *Y* (sales) are provided, along with the squared difference between the actual and predicted values. As you can see, our equation provides better predictions for some observations than for others. However, the ordinary least squares formulas we used mean that the values of *a* and *b* will produce the lowest squared error total.

Statistical Significance

Up to this point we have developed a regression coefficient for the slope and intercept for the data in our sample. The question we need to answer now is whether we would be likely to get these numbers if in fact the real values in the population from which our sample was taken were zero. This is the same type of null hypothesis we used when determining the statistical significance of the correlation coefficient. The statistical significance of the regression coefficient is calculated by the following formula:

$$t = \frac{b - 0}{S}$$

where:

b = Estimated regression coefficient in the sample

S = Standard error of estimate

For our data for copier distributorships, the standard error of the estimate = .196. The *t* statistic derived from the formula above is 3.83 [(.75 − .00)/.196]. The statistical significance of this *t* value is .05. Therefore, we can conclude that the chances of finding a regression coefficient of .75 when the actual population coefficient is 0 are .05 or less. From a practical standpoint, this means our regression coefficient is statistically significant and the size of the sales force and the sales volume for Canon copiers are related at .75.

The statistical significance of the intercept coefficient is calculated in the same manner. However, as a practical matter, the statistical significance of the intercept coefficient is not usually a matter of great interest to the marketing manager, since if the independent variable is 0, we may not be interested in the value of the dependent variable.

Substantive Significance

Once the statistical significance of the regression coefficients is determined, we have answered the first question about our relationship: "Is there a relationship between our dependent and independent variable?" In this case, the answer is yes. The second question we wanted to ask was: "How strong is that relationship?" The output of the regression analysis includes the coefficient of determination, or r^2. As we noted earlier, the coefficient of determination describes the amount of variation in the dependent variable associated with the variation in the independent variable. Another way of thinking about it is that the regression r^2 tells you what percentage of the total variation in your dependent variable you can explain by using the independent variable. The r^2 measure varies between .00 and 1.00, and is calculated by dividing the amount of variation you have been able to explain with your regression equation (found by summing the squared differences between your predicted value and the mean of the dependent variable) by the total variation in the dependent variable. In the Canon copier example, $r^2 = .643$. That means that approximately 64 percent of the variation in the sales volume is associated with the variation in the size of the sales force. Remember, we cannot say that sales force size causes changes in sales volume, only that changes in sales force size tend to be reliably associated with changes in copier sales volume.

When examining the substantive significance of a regression equation, you should look at the size of the r^2 obtained for the regression equation, and the strength of the regression coefficient, b_1. The regression coefficient may be statistically significant, but still be relatively small, meaning that your dependent measure won't change very much for a given unit change in the independent measure. In our case, the regression coefficient $b_1 = .75$, which is a relatively strong relationship. If the regression coefficient were significant, but only .15, then we would say a relationship is present in our population, but that it is very weak.

Multiple Regression Analysis

Multiple regression analysis A statistical technique which analyzes the linear relationship between a dependent variable and multiple independent variables by estimating coefficients for the equation for a straight line.

In most practical problems faced by marketing managers, there are several independent variables the manager wants to examine for their influence on a dependent variable of interest. **Multiple regression analysis** is the appropriate technique to use for these situations. The technique is a straightforward extension of the bivariate regression analysis we just discussed. Multiple independent variables are entered into the same type of regression equation, and for each variable a separate regression coefficient is calculated that describes its relationship with the dependent variable. These coefficients allow the marketing manager to examine the relative influence of each independent variable on the dependent variable.

The regression equation in multiple regression has the following form:

$$Y_i = a + b_1X_1 + b_2X_2 + b_3X_3 + \ldots + b_mX_m + e_i$$

where:

Y_i = Dependent variable for the ith observation

a = Intercept coefficient

b_1 = Slope coefficient for independent variable X_1

X_1 = Independent variable 1

b_2 = Slope coefficient for independent variable X_2

X_2 = Independent variable 2

b_3 = Slope coefficient for independent variable X_3

X_3 = Independent variable 3

b_m = Slope coefficient for independent variable X_m

X_m = Independent variable m

e_i = Error term for the regression equation for the ith observation

The type of relationship that exists between each independent variable and the dependent measure is still linear. However, now with the addition of multiple independent variables we have to think of multiple independent dimensions instead of just a straight-line description. The easiest way to analyze the relationships is to examine the regression coefficients for each independent variable. These coefficients still describe the average amount of change to be expected in Y given a unit change in the value of the particular independent variable you are examining. Moreover, each particular regression coefficient describes the relationship of that independent variable to the dependent variable.

With the addition of more than one independent variable, we have a couple of new issues to consider. One concern is the fact that each independent variable may be measured using a different scale. For example, if we want to try to predict the sales volume for our Canon copier distributorship using size of sales force (X_1), amount of advertising budget (X_2), and consumer attitudes toward the company's products (X_3), each of these independent variables would likely be measured in different units. The size of the sales force would be measured by the number of salespeople, the amount of the advertising budget would be in dollars, and the consumer attitude might be measured on a five-point scale from "Very Poor" to "Excellent."

Assume we had collected some data and performed a multiple regression analysis resulting in the following regression equation:

$$Y_i = 1053.45 + .75X_1 + 954.64X_2 + 1.23X_3 + e_i$$

where:

Y_i = Observed sales volume for the ith observation

X_1 = Size of the sales force

X_2 = Amount of the advertising budget

X_3 = Consumer attitude score towards brand

When multiple independent variables are measured with different scales, it is not possible to make relative comparisons between regression coefficients to see which independent

Beta coefficient An estimated regression coefficient that has been recalculated to have a mean of 0 and a standard deviation of 1. Such a change enables independent variables with different units of measurement to be directly compared on their association with the dependent variable.

variable has the most influence on the dependent variable. What we need is a way to make the regression coefficients comparable. The standardized regression coefficient, or **beta coefficient,** is calculated from the normal regression coefficient. The regression coefficient is recalculated to have a mean of 0 and a standard deviation of 1. Standardization removes the effects of different scales. We can make direct comparisons between independent variables using beta coefficients to determine which variables have the most influence on the dependent measure.

Statistical Significance

After the regression coefficients have been estimated, you still must examine the statistical significance of each coefficient. This is done in the same manner as the bivariate regression case. Each regression coefficient will be divided by its standard error to produce a *t* statistic, which is compared against the critical value to determine whether the null hypothesis can be rejected. The basic question we are trying to answer is still the same: "What is the probability that we would get a coefficient of this size in our sample if the real regression coefficient in the population were zero?" You should examine the *t*-test statistics for each regression coefficient. Many times not all the independent variables in a regression equation will be statistically significant. Practically speaking, if a regression coefficient is not statistically significant, that means the independent variable does not have a relationship with the dependent variable and the slope describing that relationship is relatively flat (i.e., the value of the dependent variable does not change at all as the value of the statistically insignificant independent variable changes).

When using multiple regression analysis, it is important to examine the overall statistical significance of the regression model. The amount of variation in the dependent variable that you have been able to explain with the independent measures is compared to the total variation in the dependent measure. This comparison results in a statistic called a **model *F* statistic.** This measure is compared against a critical value to determine whether or not to reject the null hypothesis. If the *F* statistic is statistically significant, it means that the chances of the regression model for your sample producing a large r^2 when the population r^2 is actually 0 are acceptably small.

Model *F* statistic A statistic that compares the amount of variation in the dependent measure "explained" or associated with the independent variables to the "unexplained" or error variance. A larger *F* statistic indicates that the regression model has more explained variance than error variance.

Substantive Significance

Once we have estimated the regression equation describing the relationships between our independent variables and the dependent variable, we need to assess the strength of the association that exists. From an overall perspective, the multiple r^2 or multiple coefficient of determination describes the strength of the relationship between all the independent variables in our equation and the dependent variable. If you recall our discussion of r^2 from the section on correlation analysis, the coefficient of determination is a measure of the amount of variation in the dependent variable associated with the variation in the independent variable. In the case of multiple regression analysis, the r^2 measure shows the amount of variation in the dependent variable associated with (or explained by) all of the independent variables considered together.

The larger the r^2 measure, the more of the behavior of the dependent measure is associated with the independent measures we are using to predict it. For example, if the multiple r^2 in our example above were .78, that would mean that we can account for, or explain, 78 percent of the variation in sales revenue by using the variation in sales force size, advertising budget, and customer attitudes toward our copier products. Higher values for r^2 mean stronger relationships between the group of independent variables and the dependent measure. As before, the measure of the strength of the relationship between an individual independent variable and the dependent measure of interest is shown by the regression coefficient or the beta coefficient for that variable.

Summarizing, the elements of a multiple regression model to examine in determining its significance include: the r^2; the model F statistic; the individual regression coefficients for each independent variable; their associated t statistics; and the individual beta coefficients. The appropriate procedure to follow in evaluating the results of a regression analysis is as follows: (1) assess the statistical significance of the overall regression model using the F statistic and its associated probability; (2) evaluate the obtained r^2 to see how large it is; (3) examine the individual regression coefficients and their t statistics to see which are statistically significant; and (4) look at the beta coefficients to assess relative influence. Taken together, these elements should give you a comprehensive picture of the answers to our basic three questions about the relationships between your dependent and independent variables.

The Use of Dummy Variables in Multiple Regression

Dummy variables Artificial variables introduced into a regression equation to represent the categories of a nominally scaled variable.

Sometimes the particular independent variables you may want to use to predict a dependent variable are not measured using interval or ratio scales (a basic assumption for the use of regression analysis). It is still possible to include such variables though the use of **dummy variables.** For example, if you wanted to include the gender of your customers to help explain their annual purchases of your product, it is obvious your measure would include only two possible values, male or female. Dummy variable coding involves choosing one category of the variable to serve as a reference category and then adding as many dummy variables as there are possible values of the variables, minus that reference category. The categories are coded as either 0 or 1. In the example above, if you choose the female category as the reference category, you would add one dummy variable for the male category. That dummy variable would be assigned the value of 1 for males and 0 for females. The regression equation would look like this:

$$Y_i = a + b_i D_1 + e_i$$

where:

Y_i = Annual purchases of your product for the ith observation

a = Intercept (represents the value of Y for females)

b_i = Regression coefficient (representing the difference in annual purchases between males and females)

D_1 = Dummy variable representing males (0 for females, 1 for males)

e_i = Error term for the equation

The dummy variable D_1 is given a value of 1 when the respondent is a male and 0 when the respondent is a female. Consequently, when the respondent is a female, the regression equation reduces to

$$Y_i = a + e_i$$

because $D_1 = 0$. When $D_1 = 1$, the regression coefficient, b_i, represents the difference in annual purchases for males compared to females. In other words, if the regression coefficient was, say, 2.57, we would say that compared to females, on average males purchase 2.57 more units of our product. This change in interpretation for the regression coefficient when using dummy variables is important to remember because it is entirely the researcher's choice about which response category to use as a reference category. In the example above, we could have just as easily used males as the reference category, and the regression coefficient would represent the difference in annual purchases for females compared to males.

It is also possible to use categorical independent variables with more than just two categories. Let's say you wanted to use consumers' purchase behavior of Starbucks coffee to help predict their purchase behavior for Maxwell House, and you had separated your sample into nonusers, light users, and heavy users. To use dummy variables in your regression model, you would pick one category as a reference group (nonusers) and add two dummy variables for the remaining categories. The variables would be coded as follows, using 0 and 1:

Category	D_1	D_2
Nonuser	0	0
Light user	1	0
Heavy user	0	1

As you can tell from the list above, when the respondent is a nonuser, D_1 and D_2 will be 0 and the intercept term will represent the average purchases of the dependent variable for nonusers. For light users, the regression coefficient for D_1 will represent the difference in annual purchases of the dependent variable, compared to nonusers. The regression coefficient associated with D_2 will represent the difference in annual purchases of the dependent variable for heavy users compared to nonusers.

The use of dummy variables in regression models allows different types of independent variables to be included in prediction efforts. The researcher must keep in mind the difference in the interpretation of the regression coefficient and the identity of the reference category that is represented by the intercept term.

Multicollinearity and Multiple Regression Analysis

Multicollinearity A situation in which several independent variables are highly correlated with each other. This characteristic can result in difficulty in estimating separate or independent regression coefficients for the correlated variables.

One common problem area for marketing researchers involves the situation in which the independent variables are highly correlated among themselves. This characteristic of the data presents a problem and is referred to as **multicollinearity.** The general definition of the regression coefficient that describes the relationship between one independent variable and the dependent variable of interest is that it signifies the average amount of change in the dependent variable associated with a unit change in the independent variable, *assuming all other independent variables in the equation remain the same.* If several independent variables are highly correlated (say, for example, the education level and annual income of a respondent), then clearly income level is not going to remain the same as the education level of a respondent changes.

The effect of high levels of multicollinearity is to make it difficult or impossible for the regression equation to separate out the independent contributions of the independent or predictor variables. The practical impact of multicollinearity relates to the statistical significance of the individual regression coefficients. Multicollinearity inflates the standard error of the coefficient and *lowers* the t statistic associated with it (recall that the regression coefficient is subtracted from the null hypothesis coefficient and divided by its standard error to calculate the t statistic). Therefore, it may be possible, if the multicollinearity is severe enough, for your regression model to have a significant F statistic, have a reasonably large

r^2, and still have no regression coefficients that are statistically significant from zero. Multicollinearity problems do not have an impact on the size of the r^2 or your ability to predict values of the dependent variable. The major impact is limited to the statistical significance of the individual regression coefficients.

SUMMARY OF LEARNING OBJECTIVES

Understand the difference between testing for significant differences and testing for association.

Examining variables to estimate whether they can be considered different from each other does not provide any information about the ability to predict one variable based on knowledge of another. To gain such information, the research analyst must investigate the existence and strength of a relationship between two variables. The techniques of correlation and regression are useful tools in such situations.

Understand what a relationship is as well as the various types of possible relationships.

Two variables may share a linear relationship, in which changes in one variable are accompanied by some change (not necessarily the same amount of change) in the other variable. As long as the amount of change stays constant over the range of both variables, the relationship is termed *linear*. Relationships between two variables that change in strength and/or direction as the values of the variables change are referred to as *curvilinear*.

Understand the concept of covariation and association.

The terms *covariation* and *association* refer to the attempt to quantify the strength of the relationship between two variables. Covariation is the amount of change in one variable of interest that is consistently related to change in another variable under study. The degree of association is a numerical measure of the strength of the relationship between two variables. Both these terms refer to linear relationships.

Understand the various statistical tests and when they should be used.

Pearson correlation coefficients are a measure of linear association between two variables of interest. The Pearson correlation coefficient is used when both variables are measured on an interval or ratio scale. When one or more variables of interest are measured on an ordinal

scale, the Spearman rank order correlation coefficient should be used.

Explain the concept of statistical significance versus practical significance.

Because some of the procedures involved in determining the statistical significance of a statistical test include consideration of the sample size, it is possible to have a very low degree of association between two variables show up as statistically significant (i.e., the population parameter is not equal to zero). However, by considering the absolute strength of the relationship in addition to its statistical significance, the research is better able to draw the appropriate conclusion about the data and the population from which they were selected.

Understand the difference between univariate, bivariate, and multivariate techniques.

Univariate techniques concern questions about a single variable and whether that variable is different from zero or different from some other hypothesized value. Bivariate techniques always involve questions about two variables and how they compare to each other, or how strongly they are associated with each other. Multivariate techniques are useful in dealing with questions about more than two independent variables and the relationship each shares with a specific dependent variable.

Understand when and how to use regression analysis.

Regression analysis is useful in answering questions about the strength of a linear relationship between a dependent variable and one or more independent variables. The results of a regression analysis indicate the amount of change in the dependent variable that is associated with a one unit change in the independent variables. In addition, the accuracy of the regression equation can be evaluated by comparing the predicted values of the dependent variable to the actual values of the dependent variable drawn from the sample.

KEY TERMS AND CONCEPTS

Beta coefficient 574

Bivariate regression analysis 567

Coefficient of determination (r^2) 566

Covariation 559

Curvilinear relationship 558

Dummy variables 575

Linear relationship 558

Model F statistic 574

Multicollinearity 576

Multiple regression analysis 572

Ordinary least squares 568

Pearson correlation coefficient 561

Relationship 558

Scatter diagram 559

Spearman rank order correlation coefficient 566

REVIEW QUESTIONS

1. Explain the difference between testing for significant differences and testing for association.

2. Explain the difference between association and causation.

3. What is covariation? How does it differ from correlation?

4. Which statistical tests should be used with nominal and ordinal data? Which can be used with interval and ratio data?

5. What are the differences between univariate, bivariate, and multivariate statistical techniques?

6. What is regression analysis? When would you use it? What is the difference between simple regression and multiple regression?

DISCUSSION QUESTIONS

1. Regression and correlation analysis both describe the strength of linear relationships between variables. Consider the concepts of education and income. Many people would say these two variables are related in a linear fashion. As education increases, income usually increases (although not necessarily at the same rate). Can you think of two variables that are related in such a way that their relationship changes over their range of possible values (i.e., in a curvilinear fashion)? How would you analyze the relationship between two such variables?

2. It is possible to conduct a regression analysis on two variables and obtain a significant regression equation (significant F ratio), but still have a low r^2. What does the r^2 statistic measure? How can you have a low r^2 yet still get a statistically significant F ratio for the overall regression equation?

3. The ordinary least squares (OLS) procedure commonly used in regression produces a line of "best fit" for the data to which it is applied. How would you define *best fit* in regression analysis? What is there about the procedure that guarantees a best fit to the data? What assumptions about the use of a regression technique are necessary to produce this result?

4. When using multiple independent variables to predict a dependent variable in multiple regression, multicollinearity among the independent variables is often a

concern. What is the main problem caused by high multicollinearity among the independent variables in a multiple regression equation? Can you still achieve a high r^2 for your regression equation if multicollinearity is present in your data?

5. **EXPERIENCE THE INTERNET.** A trend in marketing is to shop for products and services on the Internet. In the last decade or so, traditional retailers have begun selling through catalogs. More recently, they also are selling over the Internet. In fact, a new Web site is www.catalogsite.com. At this site, many retailers are listing this merchandise and hoping to sell it. Go to this site and review the catalogs. Compare the information on the Web site with traditional catalogs and retail stores. Prepare a questionnaire covering the common elements of these three approaches to selling. Select a retailer students are familiar with. Compile a sample of catalogs that offer similar merchandise. Then ask a sample of students to visit catalogs on the Web site, look at the catalogs you have brought to class, and then complete the questionnaire. Enter the data into a software package and assess your finding statistically. Prepare a report and be able to defend your conclusions.

6. **SPSS EXERCISE.** Choose one or two other students from your class and form a team. Identify the different retailers from your community where VCRs, CD players, and TVs are sold. Team members should divide up and visit all the different stores and describe the products and brands that are sold in each. Also observe the layout in the store, the store personnel, and the type of advertising the store uses. In other words, familiarize yourself with each retailer's marketing mix. Use your knowledge of the marketing mix to design a questionnaire. Interview approximately 100 people who are familiar with all the retailers you selected and collect their responses. Analyze the responses using a statistical software package such as SPSS. Prepare a report of your findings, including whether the perceptions of each of the stores are similar or different, and particularly whether the differences are statistically or substantively different. Present your findings in class and be prepared to defend your conclusions and your use of statistical techniques.

7. **SPSS EXERCISE.** Using the fast-food database provided in SPSS, run a regression analysis on 10 variables (you select the most appropriate variables) that appear to be the best predictors of who will visit a fast-food establishment.

ENDNOTE

1. For a more detailed conceptual discussion of transformations, see Joseph F. Hair, Jr., Rolph E. Anderson, Ronald L. Tatham, and William C. Black, *Multivariate Data Analysis,* 5th ed. (Englewood Cliffs, NJ: Prentice Hall, 1998).

MARKETING RESEARCH ILLUSTRATION

SPSS EXAMPLE: CUSTOMER SATISFACTION FACTORS IN A MANUFACTURING OPERATION

The plant manager of QualKote Manufacturing is interested in the impact his year-long effort to implement a total quality management (TQM) program is having on the satisfaction of his customers. The plant foremen, assembly-line workers, and engineering staff have closely examined their operation to determine which activities have the most impact on product quality and reliability. Together, the managers and employees have worked to better understand how each particular job affects the final delivered quality of the product as the customer perceives it.

To help answer his question about customer satisfaction, the plant manager has collected data from the plant workers and managers using a Likert scale to find out what they think about the new TQM system. The following are sample topics that were measured:

- The company's product quality program has improved the level of customer satisfaction. (Dependent measure A84.)

- Data from a variety of external sources (customers, competitors, suppliers, etc.) are used in the strategic product planning process. (Independent variable A14.)

- Customers are involved in the product quality planning process. (Independent variable A22.)

- Customer requirements and expectations of the company's products are used in developing strategic plans and goals. (Independent variable A24.)

- There is a systematic process to translate customer requirements into new/improved products. (Independent variable A35.)

- There is a systematic process to accurately determine customers' requirements and expectations. (Independent variable A50.)

A multiple regression was run using SPSS with 464 observations as input to the model. The output is shown in the following tables.

Descriptive Statistics

	Mean	Standard Deviation	N
A84	2.793E-02	.9972	464
A14	5.832E-02	.9518	464
A22	2.334E-02	.9876	464
A24	2.282E-02	.9852	464
A35	6.726E-02	.9607	464
A50	4.769E-02	.9805	464

Correlations

		A84	A14	A22	A24	A35	A50
Pearson correlation	A84	1.000	.467	.345	.491	.502	.432
	A14	.467	1.000	.428	.520	.512	.489
	A22	.345	.428	1.000	.569	.490	.509
	A24	.491	.520	.569	1.000	.568	.588
	A35	.502	.512	.490	.568	1.000	.580
	A50	.432	.489	.509	.588	.580	1.000

Correlations (concluded)

		A84	A14	A22	A24	A35	A50
Sig. (1-tailed)	A84	.	.000	.000	.000	.000	.000
	A14	.000	.	.000	.000	.000	.000
	A22	.000	.000	.	.000	.000	.000
	A24	.000	.000	.000	.	.000	.000
	A35	.000	.000	.000	.000	.	.000
	A50	.000	.000	.000	.000	.000	.
N	A84	464	464	464	464	464	464
	A14	464	464	464	464	464	464
	A22	464	464	464	464	464	464
	A24	464	464	464	464	464	464
	A35	464	464	464	464	464	464
	A50	464	464	464	464	464	464

Variables Entered/Removed*

Model	Variables Entered	Variables Removed	Method
1	A50, A14, A22, A35, A24[†]		Enter

*Dependent variable: A84.

[†]All requested variables entered.

Model Summary

Model	r	r Square	Adjusted r Square	Standard Error of the Estimate
1	.590*	.348	.341	.8098

*Predictors: (Constant), A50, A14, A22, A35, A24.

Model Summary

Model	Change Statistics				
	r Square Change	F Change	df1	df2	Sig. F Change
1	.348	48.811	5	458	.000

ANOVA*

Model		Sum of Squares	df	Mean Square	F	Sig.
1	Regression	160.040	5	32.006	48.811	.000[†]
	Residual	300.334	458	.656		
	Total	460.374	463			

*Dependent variable: A84.
[†]Predictors: (Constant), A50, A14, A22, A35, A24.

Coefficients*

Model		Unstandardized Coefficients		Standardized Coefficients		
		B	Standard Error	Beta	t	Sig.
1	(Constant)	−9.62E-03	.038		−.255	.799
	A14	.212	.050	202	4.277	.000
	A22	−2.28E-02	.049	−.023	−.467	.641
	A24	.217	.054	.214	3.984	.000
	A35	.252	.053	.243	4.737	.000
	A50	7.982E-02	.053	.078	1.517	.130

*Dependent variable: A84.

Coefficients*

Model		Correlations		
		Zero-order	Partial	Part
1	(Constant)			
	A14	.467	.196	.161
	A22	.345	−.022	−.018
	A24	.491	.183	.150
	A35	.502	.216	.179
	A50	.432	.071	.057

*Dependent variable: A84.

MARKETING RESEARCH CASE EXERCISE

QUANTUM SOFTWARE

Stuart Symington is busy studying a marketing research report that has just arrived on his desk from the research staff. Symington is the vice president for marketing of Quantum Software Company. Quantum Software produces computer games for the young-adult market. Stuart had given the research department the task of developing a regression model to predict the likelihood of computer game purchase by young adults. To make these predictions, Symington and several members of the marketing research staff had examined profiles of some 300 current customers and selected the following variables (measurement indicated in parentheses):

a. X_1 (number of years)

b. X_2 (female/male—dummy variables with female as the reference variable; i.e., female was coded as 0)

c. X_3 (number of years spent using personal computers)

d. X_4 (estimated annual household income)

e. X_5 (North/South–dummy variables with South as the reference variable; i.e., South was coded as 0)

The research department had developed a survey to collect this information and the report in front of Symington displayed the regression analysis results from a sample of approximately 500 respondents. The regression model resulting from this analysis was

$$\text{Likelihood of game purchase} = 3.46 + .67\, X_1 + .19\, X_2 + .54\, X_3 + .33\, X_4 + .40\, X_5 + \varepsilon_1$$

Based on this regression model, which independent variables have the most influence on young adults' likelihood of game purchase? How do you interpret the dummy variables of gender and geographic location? What does the number 3.46 represent in the regression model?

Data Analysis: Multivariate Techniques for the Research Process

❝ The unique yet ironic element associated with statistics is that they can be used to produce evidence to support any conclusions the researcher may make. ❞

HAROLD AUSTIN
President
Beta Dynamics, Inc.

NuvoMedia

Martin Eberhard, cofounder of NuvoMedia, recently launched the Rocket eBook. His book-shaped product weighs 22 oz., has a high-contrast, high-resolution, backlit black and white touchscreen, and stores 4,000 pages (upgradable up to 160,000 pages). Users can view an entire page on the screen, write notes in the margin with a stylus, and electronically download files of new books from online booksellers like barnesandnoble.com and powells.com. Eberhard's product has several competitors with similar products and prices (under $500). For more information on NuvoMedia, see www.nuvomedia.com.

The main task facing NuvoMedia at present is to discover and profile the characteristics of the people who will be most interested in buying this product. The situation seems ripe for the use of discriminant analysis. By surveying consumers about their likelihood of purchasing the new eBook and collecting additional descriptive information, NuvoMedia can uncover the descriptive characteristics that best separate the most interested from the least interested consumers. In addition, the results of the discriminant analysis should also reveal which types of descriptive data (e.g., income, age, occupation, etc.) are most important in predicting potential purchase by prospective customers.[1]

Value of Multivariate Techniques in Data Analysis

The majority of the questions posed to marketing researchers involve more than two variables. In the modern world, consumers and business decision makers tend to use a lot of information to make choices and decisions. Consequently, there are a lot of potential influences on consumer behavior and business reactions.

Multivariate techniques arose partially out of the need of businesses to address such complexity. The ability to determine the relative influence of different independent variables, as well as to assess the behavior of groups of dependent measures simultaneously, has become an important asset in the marketing researcher's toolbox. In addition, tremendous increases in computing power and portability have encouraged the adoption of multivariate analysis by individuals who were unable to realistically consider such approaches in earlier years.

Multivariate analysis

A group of statistical techniques used when there are two or more measurements on each element and the variables are analyzed simultaneously. Multivariate analysis is concerned with the simultaneous relationships among two or more phenomena.

What is multivariate analysis? **Multivariate analysis** refers to a group of statistical procedures that simultaneously analyze multiple measurements on each individual or object being investigated. The multivariate statistical procedures we will highlight in this chapter are extensions of the univariate and bivariate statistical procedures that were discussed in previous chapters. Many authorities consider any simultaneous statistical analysis of more than two variables to be multivariate analysis. The Small Business Implications box illustrates how these techniques can aid the small-business owner.

Multivariate analysis is extremely important in marketing research because most business problems are multidimensional. Corporations and their customers are seldom described on the basis of one dimension. An individual's decision to visit a fast-food restaurant is often dependent on such factors as the quality, variety, and price of the food; the restaurant's location; and the service. When corporations develop databases to better serve their customers, the database often includes a vast array of information—such as demographics, lifestyles, zip codes, purchasing behavior—on each customer. As marketing researchers become increasingly aware of the power of multivariate analysis, they will use multivariate techniques more and more in solving complex business problems. The In the Field box illustrates the value of using multivariate statistical techniques.

A CLOSER LOOK AT RESEARCH — Small Business Implications

Many small businesses can neither afford nor conform to large expensive statistical packages like SPSS or SAS. XLSTAT is an affordable and user-friendly statistical package designed for small businesses that utilize Microsoft Excel. XLSTAT is an add-on for Excel. It allows the small business user, working mainly in an Excel worksheet, to transfer stored data into the program for data analysis purposes.

XLSTAT can perform very simple techniques like Box Plots and Frequencies, or more complex multivariate techniques like discriminant analysis and regression. To see examples of data analyzed, and how XLSTAT performs discriminant analysis functions, consult the XSTAT Web page at www.xlstat.com.

A CLOSER LOOK AT RESEARCH — In the Field

Using Multivariate Data Analysis to Gain a Foothold in the Fast-Food Wars

Back Yard Burgers is a regional fast-food franchise specializing in hamburgers and chicken sandwiches. After a history of growth and expansion, the company found itself in a position of stagnant if not declining sales for several consecutive quarters. Top executives at Back Yard Burgers realized that after so many years of managing growth, they had never really listened to their customers. This omission may have been related to the stagnant sales they were currently experiencing in such a competitive industry.

Even though Back Yard Burgers was a relatively small regional franchise, it was competing with the likes of McDonald's, Wendy's, Burger King, and Kentucky Fried Chicken in every one of its markets. Competitors continually monitored customers via surveys.

Given the current market situation, executives at Back Yard Burgers decided that in order to remain competitive in this industry, they needed marketing research. When management met with a marketing research consultant, both parties agreed that they needed to gather information from their customers regarding their attitudes, perceptions, and behaviors toward Back Yard Burgers' competitors. Specifically, Back Yard Burgers was concerned with the following issues:

- What are the various market segments within the fast-food category? Can Back Yard Burgers appeal to all fast-food users, or are there certain segments that are more appropriate to target?

- What factors, demographic or other, can predict whether an individual who eats at fast-food restaurants more than twice a month will choose a hamburger or nonhamburger fast-food restaurant?

- What are consumers' perceptions of Back Yard Burgers? How do those perceptions compare with consumers' perceptions of the competition?

These kinds of questions involve analyzing intricate intervening variables. Multivariate procedures are powerful data analytical techniques used for addressing such issues.

Many statistical techniques can be considered multivariate data analysis procedures. In this chapter we will discuss the following five techniques: (1) cluster analysis, (2) factor analysis, (3) multidimensional scaling, (4) discriminant analysis, and (5) conjoint analysis. Another widely used multivariate technique—multiple regression analysis—was discussed separately in Chapter 17.

Classification and Application of Multivariate Techniques

Exhibit 18.1 presents a process for classifying selected multivariate procedures. This classification is based on three criteria concerning the nature and use of the data:

1. Are some of the variables dependent on others? For example, does a person's age, education, lifestyle, or marital status affect his or her frequency of visits to a fast-food restaurant?

2. How many variables are treated as being dependent on others?

3. How are the variables measured? Have the variables been measured on a nonmetric (categorical) or metric (continuous) scale?

EXHIBIT 18.1   **Classifying Multivariate Statistical Techniques**

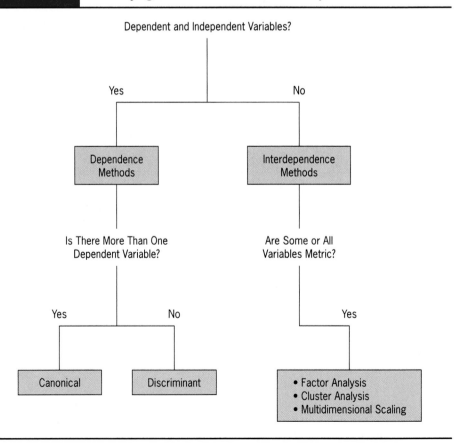

Criterion 1: Dependence or Interdependence Methods?

Dependence technique Multivariate technique appropriate when one or more of the variables can be identified as dependent variables and the remaining as independent variables.

When considering the classification and/or application of multivariate statistical techniques, the first question to be asked is, Can the data be divided into independent and dependent classifications? The answer to this question indicates whether a dependence or interdependence technique should be used. A **dependence technique** may be defined as one in which a variable or set of variables is identified as the dependent variable to be predicted or explained by other, independent variables. Dependence techniques include multiple regression analysis, discriminant analysis, and conjoint analysis. For example, many businesses today are very interested in predicting the dependent variable *customer loyalty,* or high-volume customers (e.g., heavy consumers of Starbucks coffee) versus light users, on the basis of numerous independent variables. Multiple discriminant analysis is a dependence technique that predicts customer loyalty based on several independent variables, such as how much is purchased and how often it is purchased.

Interdependence technique Multivariate statistical technique in which the whole set of interdependent relationships is examined.

In contrast, an **interdependence technique** is one in which no single variable or group of variables is defined as being independent or dependent. In this case, the multivariate procedure involves the analysis of all variables in the data set simultaneously. The goal of interdependence methods is to group things together. In this case, no one variable is to be predicted or explained by the others. Cluster analysis, factor analysis, and multidimensional scaling are the most commonly used interdependence techniques. For example, a marketing manager who wants to identify various market segments or clusters of fast-food customers (e.g., burgers, pizza, or chicken) might use these techniques.

Criterion 2: How Many Variables Are Dependent?

The next question in the classification or application of multivariate techniques is, How many dependent variables are there? Or stated another way, How many variables are you attempting to predict? This question must be answered to determine which dependence method to use. The dependence multivariate techniques such as multiple regression and multiple discriminant analysis involve the analysis of a single dependent variable. For example, to predict the single dependent variable of sales from multiple dependent variables such as advertising expenditures and number of salespeople the multivariate technique of multiple regression would be used. In contrast, if a company wants to predict a dependent variable of, say, group membership (e.g., heavy versus light users), multiple discriminant analysis could be used. If several dependent variables are included in the analysis, then a dependence method such as multivariate analysis of variance (MANOVA) is used. For example, if an advertising manager for Starbucks is interested in understanding the effectiveness of an advertising campaign using several dependent variables such as recall, recognition, and likability, and several independent variables, then all the variables can be analyzed simultaneously with a technique such as MANOVA.

Criterion 3: How Are the Variables Measured?

Measurement is very important in the classification or application of multivariate data. Nonmetric or categorical data are measured with nominal or ordinal scales. Metric or continuous data are measured with interval and ratio scales. As can be seen in Exhibit 18.1, the nature of measurement scales will determine which multivariate technique is appropriate for the data. The exhibit also illustrates that selection of a multivariate technique requires consideration of the types of measures used for both independent and dependent sets of variables. Regardless of the statistical technique selected, the outcome of the analysis is key. Review the Global Insights box to see how outcomes can change across markets.

GLOBAL INSIGHTS · *ANALYSIS FROM GLOBAL RESEARCH MAY YIELD INTERESTING FINDINGS*

Just Kids Inc., a marketing research firm specializing in the 2- to 12-year-old market, uncovered some interesting findings among youngsters in Great Britain. Kids in Great Britain seem to shed their childhood much earlier than their peers elsewhere. McDonald's and Coke are universally loved, but the same advertising that attracts a nine-year-old Yank does not appeal to the nine-year-old Brit. Asked to identify their favorite TV programs, kids in Great Britain named adult shows. Their responses also demonstrated more teen behavior than those of kids from other countries. For example, most of the nine-year-olds around the globe said they want to be like their mom and dad when they grow up. In Britain, nine-year-olds want to be rock stars and entertainers. The conclusion: If you're a marketer with a clown and a happy meal, you may have a problem in England.

Selecting the Appropriate Multivariate Technique

We will start our discussion of specific multivariate techniques with an analysis of interdependence methods. The purpose of techniques such as factor analysis, cluster analysis, and conjoint analysis is not to predict a variable from a set of independent variables, but to summarize and better understand a large number of variables or objects.

Factor Analysis

Factor analysis A class of procedures primarily used for data reduction and summarization.

Factor analysis is a multivariate statistical technique that is used to summarize the information contained in a large number of variables into a smaller number of subsets or factors. The purpose of factor analysis is to simplify the data. With factor analysis there is no distinction between dependent and independent variables; rather, all variables under investigation are analyzed together to identify underlying factors.

Many problems facing businesses today are often the result of a combination of several variables. For example, if the local McDonald's franchisor is interested in assessing customer satisfaction, many variables of interest must be measured. Variables such as freshness of the food, waiting time, taste, food temperature, cleanliness, and how friendly and courteous the personnel are would all be measured by means of a number of rating questions.

Let's look at an intuitive example of factor analysis. Data from five customers who each rated the fast-food restaurant on six characteristics are presented in Exhibit 18.2. Customers who gave lower ratings on waiting time also gave lower ratings on cleanliness and personnel. Another pattern is evident when one considers the customer ratings of food taste, food temperature, and freshness. In this case, the ratings were quite high on all three variables. Based on the patterns of data, these six measures can be combined into two summary measures, or factors, called *service quality* and *food quality* (see Exhibit 18.3).

As the above example illustrates, the general purpose of factor analysis is to summarize the information contained in a large number of variables into a smaller number of factors. The statistical purpose of factor analysis is to determine whether there are linear combinations of variables (e.g., waiting time, cleanliness, personnel) that will help the researcher summarize the data and identify underlying relationships.

Factor scores Composite scores estimated for each respondent on the derived factors.

The starting point in interpreting the statistics of factor analysis lies in the understanding of **factor scores.** A factor is a linear combination of variables or a weighted summary score of a set of related variables. Each measure in factor analysis is first weighted according to how much it contributes to the variation of each factor.

EXHIBIT 18.2 **Ratings of a Fast-Food Restaurant Assigned by Five Consumers**

Consumer	Waiting Time	Cleanliness	Personnel	Food Taste	Food Temperature	Freshness
Dino	2	2	1	6	5	5
Sammi	1	1	1	4	5	4
Frank	2	2	2	5	5	5
Debbie	2	1	2	4	6	5
Joey	1	3	1	6	5	5
Average	1.6	1.8	1.4	5.0	5.2	4.8

Let's develop factor scores based on our fast-food example. First, factor analysis calculates a factor score on each factor for each respondent in the data set. The following equation is used to determine factor scores:

$$F_i = W_i A_1 + W_i A_2 + W_i A_3 \ldots W_i A_k$$

where:

$$F_i = \text{Estimate of the } I\text{th factor}$$

$$W_i = \text{Weight of factor score coefficient}$$

$$k = \text{Variable number}$$

It is common to select weights or factor score coefficients so that the first factor explains the largest portion of the total variance. Then a second set of weights is often selected so that the second factor accounts for most of the residual variance. This process continues until all the variance is accounted for.

EXHIBIT 18.3 **Example of a Factor Analysis Application to a Fast-Food Restaurant**

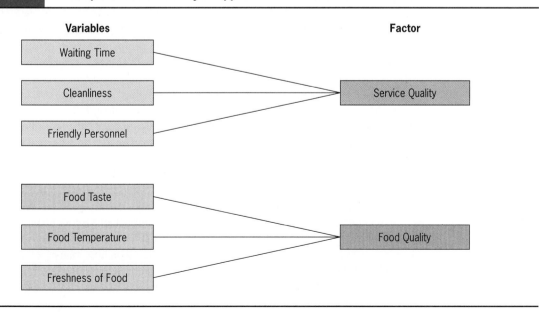

Therefore, continuing our fast-food example, the following equation would be used to determine factor scores for the two-factor model:

$$F_1 = .30A_1 + .25A_2 + .25A_3 + .05A_4 + .08A_5 + .02A_6$$

$$F_2 = .04A_1 + .06A_2 + .01A_3 + .40A_4 + .18A_5 + .22A_6$$

Using these formulas, factor scores could be calculated for each customer by substituting their ratings on the six variables into each equation. The weights or coefficients in the equations (e.g., .30, .25) are the factor scoring coefficients to be applied to each customer's ratings. For example, Dino's factor scores would be computed as follows:

$$F_1 = .30(2) + .25(2) + .25(1) + .05(6) + .08(5) + .02(5)$$

$$F_2 = .04(2) + .06(2) + .01(1) + .40(6) + .18(5) + .22(5)$$

In the first equation, the factor scoring coefficients for A_1, A_2, and A_3 (.30, .25, .25) are large, whereas the weights for A_4, A_5, and A_6 (.05, .08, .02) are small. The small weights on A_4, A_5, and A_6 indicate that these variables contribute only a small amount to the factor score variations on factor 1. Conversely, variables A_4, A_5, and A_6 make a large contribution to the factor score variations on factor 2. These two equations also show that variables A_1, A_2, and A_3 are relatively independent of A_4, A_5, and A_6 because each variable has larger weights in only one equation.

The size of the scoring coefficients is also important in understanding the mechanics of factor analysis. For example, variable A_4 (food taste), with a weight of .40, is a more important contributor to factor 2 variation than A_5 (food temperature), with a smaller weight of .18. The marketing manager of the fast-food chain may want to emphasize how good the food tastes in an advertising campaign.

Factor loading A simple correlation between the variables and the factors.

Once the researcher has an understanding of factor scores, the next concept of importance in factor analysis is factor loading. **Factor loading** refers to the correlation between each factor score and each of the original variables. Each factor loading is a measure of the importance of the variable in measuring each factor. Factor loadings, like correlations, can vary from +1.0 to –1.0. If variable A_4 (food taste) is closely associated with factor 2, the factor loading or correlation would be high. The statistical analysis associated with factor analysis would produce factor loadings between each factor score and each of the original variables. An illustration of the output of this statistical analysis is given in Exhibit 18.4. Variables A_1, A_2, and A_3 are highly correlated with scores on factor 1, and variables A_4, A_5, and A_6 are highly correlated with scores on factor 2. An analyst would say that variables A_1, A_2, and A_3 have "high loadings" on factor 1, which means that they help define that factor.

The next step in factor analysis is to name the resulting factors. The researcher examines the variables that have high loadings on each factor. There often will be a certain consistency among the variables that load high on a given factor. For example, the ratings on waiting time (A_1), cleanliness (A_2), and friendly personnel (A_3) all load on the same factor. We have chosen to name this factor *service quality* because the three variables deal with some aspect of a customer's service experience with the restaurant. Variables A_4, A_5, and A_6 all load highly on factor 2, which we named *food quality*. Naming factors is often a subjective process of combining intuition with an inspection of the variables that have high loadings on each factor.

A final aspect of factor analysis concerns the number of factors to retain. While our restaurant example dealt with two factors, many situations can involve anywhere from one factor to as many factors as there are variables. Deciding on how many factors to retain is a very complex process because there can be more than one possible solution to any factor analysis problem. A discussion of the technical aspects of this part of factor analysis is

EXHIBIT 18.4	Factor Loadings for the Two Factors

	Correlation with:	
Variable	Factor 1	Factor 2
A_1 (waiting time)	.79	.07
A_2 (cleanliness)	.72	.10
A_3 (friendly personnel)	.72	.05
A_4 (food taste)	.09	.85
A_5 (food temperature)	.11	.70
A_6 (freshness of food)	.04	.74

EXHIBIT 18.5	Percentage of Variation in Original Data Explained by Each Factor

Factor	Percentage of Variation Explained
1	50.3%
2	46.5
3	1.8
4	0.8
5	0.6

beyond the scope of this book, but we will provide an example of how an analyst can decide how many factors to retain.

An important measure to consider in deciding how many factors to retain is the percentage of the variation in the original data that is explained by each factor. A factor analysis computer program will produce a table of numbers that will give the percentage of variation explained by each factor. A simplified illustration of these numbers is presented in Exhibit 18.5. In this example, we would definitely keep the first two factors, because they explain a total of 96.8 percent of the variability in the five measures. Since the last three factors explain only 3.2 percent of the variation, they contribute little to our understanding of the data and would not be retained. Many marketing researchers often stop factoring when additional factors no longer make sense, because the variance they explain often contains a large amount of random variation.

Factor Analysis Applications in Marketing Research

While our fast-food example illustrated the power of factor analysis in simplifying customer perceptions toward a fast-food restaurant, the technique has many other important applications in marketing research:

- **Advertising.** Factor analysis can be used to better understand media habits of various customers.

- **Pricing.** Factor analysis can help identify the characteristics of price-sensitive and prestige-sensitive customers.

- **Product.** Factor analysis can be used to identify brand attributes that influence consumer choice.

- **Distribution.** Factor analysis can be employed to better understand channel selection criteria among distribution channel members.

Cluster Analysis

Cluster analysis A multivariate interdependence technique whose primary objective is to classify objects into relatively homogeneous groups based on the set of variables considered.

Cluster analysis is another interdependence multivariate method. As the name implies, the basic purpose of cluster analysis is to classify or segment objects (e.g., customers, products, market areas) into groups so that objects within each group are similar to one another on a variety of variables. Cluster analysis seeks to classify segments or objects such that there will be as much likeness within segments and as much difference between segments as possible. Thus, this method strives to identify natural groupings or segments among many variables without designating any of the variables as a dependent variable.

We will start our discussion of cluster analysis with this intuitive example. Our fast-food restaurant wants to open an eat-in restaurant in a new, growing suburb of a major metropolitan area. Marketing researchers surveyed a large sample of households in this suburb and collected data on characteristics such as demographics, lifestyles, and expenditures on eating out. The fast-food chain wants to identify one or more household segments that are likely to visit its new restaurant. Once this segment is identified, the firm's advertising and services would be tailored to them.

A target segment can be identified for the company by conducting a cluster analysis of the data it has gathered. The results of the cluster analysis will identify segments, each of which contains households that have similar characteristics and differs considerably from the other segments. Exhibit 18.6 identifies four potential clusters or segments for our fast-food chain. As our intuitive example illustrates, this growing suburb contains households that seldom visit restaurants at all (cluster 1), households that tend to frequent dine-in

EXHIBIT 18.6 **Cluster Analysis Based on Two Characteristics**

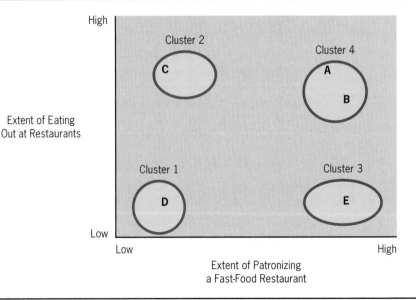

restaurants exclusively (cluster 2), households that tend to frequent fast-food restaurants exclusively (cluster 3), and households that frequent both dine-in and fast-food restaurants (cluster 4). By examining the characteristics associated with each of the clusters, management can decide which clusters to target and how best to reach them through marketing communications.

Statistical Procedures for Cluster Analysis

Several cluster analysis procedures are available, each based on a somewhat different set of complex computer programs. However, the general approach in each procedure is the same and involves measuring the similarity between objects on the basis of their ratings on the various characteristics. The degree of similarity between objects is often determined through a distance measure. This process is best illustrated with our earlier example involving two variables:

$$V_1 = \text{Extent of eating out at fancy restaurants}$$

$$V_2 = \text{Extent of eating out at fast-food restaurants}$$

Data on V_1 and V_2 are plotted on the two-dimensional graph shown in Exhibit 18.6. Each dot represents the position of one consumer with regard to the two variables V_1 and V_2. The distance between any pair of points is positively related to how similar the corresponding individuals are when the two variables are considered together. Thus, individual A is more like B than either C, D or E. As can be seen, there are four distinct clusters identified in the exhibit.

This analysis can inform marketing management of the proposed new fast-food restaurant that customers are to be found among those who tend to eat at both fancy and fast-food restaurants (cluster 4). To develop a marketing strategy to reach this cluster of households, management would like to identify demographic, psychographic, and behavioral profiles of the individuals in cluster 4.

Clusters are often developed from scatter plots, as we have done with our fast-food restaurant example. This is a very complex trial-and-error process. Fortunately, computer algorithms are available, and must be used if the clustering is to be done in an efficient, systematic fashion. While the mathematics are beyond the scope of this chapter, the algorithms are all based on the idea of starting with some arbitrary cluster boundaries and modifying the boundaries until a point is reached where the average interpoint distances within clusters are as small as possible relative to the average distances between clusters.

Cluster Analysis Applications in Marketing Research

While our fast-food example illustrated how cluster analysis segmented groups of households, it has many other important applications in marketing research:

- **New-product research.** Clustering brands can help a firm examine its product offerings relative to competition. Brands in the same cluster often compete more fiercely with each other than with brands in other clusters.

- **Test marketing.** Cluster analysis groups test cities into homogeneous clusters for test marketing purposes.

- **Buyer behavior.** Cluster analysis can be employed to identify similar groups of buyers who have similar choice criteria.

- **Market segmentation.** Cluster analysis can develop distinct market segments on the basis of geographic, demographic, psychographic, and behavioristic variables.

Multidimensional Scaling

Multidimensional scaling
A class of procedures for representing perceptions and preferences of respondents spatially by means of a visual display.

Multidimensional scaling is the last interdependence multivariate method to be discussed in this chapter. This method provides the market researcher with a procedure for measuring objects in multidimensional space on the basis of respondents' perceptions of similarity (or preferences) among a set of objects. Like factor and cluster analysis, multidimensional scaling does not include a predictor or dependent variable. The technique is intended to identify the underlying dimensions from a series of similarity and/or preference judgments provided by customers about objects (e.g., companies, brands, products). Perceived similarity or preferences can be in the form of ranking data (i.e., nonmetric) or in the form of customer ratings (i.e., metric).

To illustrate multidimensional scaling, we'll use an example involving analysis of similarities based on ranking of fast-food restaurants. A customer is given a list of six fast-food restaurants and asked to express how he or she perceives the similarity of each restaurant to the others. The customer is asked to compare pairs of restaurants and rank the pairs from most similar to least similar. Since this analysis involves six restaurants, 15 separate pairs are possible. The ranks, based on the customers' perceptions, are presented in Exhibit 18.7.

Multidimensional scaling is a complex, iterative process that can be carried out by using one of several computer programs. A computer program using the data in Exhibit 18.7 would attempt to generate a geometric configuration of the restaurants such that distances between pairs of stores are as consistent as possible with the customers' similarity ranks. In other words, the pair of restaurants ranked number 1 (Back Yard Burgers and Wendy's) would be closest together, and the pair ranked number 15 (Back Yard Burgers and McDonald's) would be farthest apart.

Perceptual map   A graphic representation of respondents' beliefs about the relationship between objects with respect to two or more dimensions (usually attributes or features of the objects).

Multidimensional scaling can also provide the researcher with a perceptual map of the data. A **perceptual map** is a visual representation of customer perceptions of the data (e.g., rankings of brands or restaurants). Again, with the aid of a complex computer program, the rankings, or **similarity judgments,** are statistically transformed into distances by placing the fast-food restaurants into a specified multidimensional space. The distance between similar objects on the perceptual map is small for similar objects and large for dissimilar objects.

Similarity judgments
A direct approach to gathering perceptual data for multidimensional scaling, where the respondents use a Likert scale to rate all possible pairs of brands in terms of their similarity.

Exhibit 18.8 illustrates a perceptual map of the six restaurants in two-dimensional space. This map is based on customers' perceptions of each restaurant on two dimensions—freshness of food and food temperature. Inspection of the map illustrates that Wendy's and Back Yard Burgers were perceived as quite similar to each other. Arby's and Hardee's were also

---

EXHIBIT 18.7   **Similarity Rankings of Six Fast-Food Restaurants**

	McDonald's	Burger King	Wendy's	Back Yard Burgers	Arby's	Hardee's
McDonald's		3	14	15	13	9
Burger King			7	8	12	4
Wendy's				1	10	11
Back Yard Burgers					6	5
Arby's						2
Hardee's						

**Customers ordering food at a Wendy's fast-food
restaurant chain.**

EXHIBIT 18.8 A Perceptual Map of Six Fast-Food Restaurants

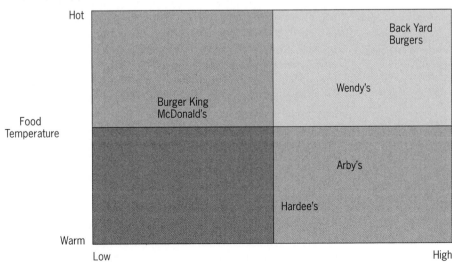

perceived as somewhat similar. However, Back Yard Burgers and McDonald's were perceived as dissimilar.

Multidimensional Scaling Applications in Marketing Research

While our fast-food example illustrated how multidimensional scaling grouped pairs of restaurants together based on similarity rankings, it has many other important applications in marketing research:

- **New-product development.** Multidimensional scaling can be used to search for gaps in perceptual maps in an attempt to position new products.

- **Image measurement.** Multidimensional scaling can help analysts to develop perceptual maps of a company relative to competition in an attempt to identify the image of the company.

- **Advertising.** Multidimensional scaling and perceptual mapping can be used to assess advertising effectiveness in positioning the brand.

- **Distribution.** Multidimensional scaling could be used to assess similarities of brands and channel outlets.

Analysis of Dependence

We now focus our discussion on the multivariate techniques that deal with analysis of dependence. The purpose of techniques such as discriminant analysis and conjoint analysis is to predict a variable from a set of independent variables.

Discriminant Analysis

Discriminant analysis

A technique for analyzing marketing research data when the criterion or dependent variable is categorical and the predictor or independent variables are intervals.

Discriminant analysis is a multivariate technique used for predicting group membership on the basis of two or more independent variables. There are many situations where the marketing researcher's purpose is to classify objects or groups by a set of independent variables. Thus, the dependent variable in discriminant analysis is nonmetric or categorical. In marketing, consumers are often categorized on the basis of heavy versus light users of a product, or viewers versus nonviewers of a media vehicle such as a television commercial. Conversely, the independent variables in discriminant analysis are metric and often include characteristics such as demographics and psychographics. Additional insights into discriminant analysis can be found in the Using Technology box.

Let's begin our discussion of discriminant analysis with an intuitive example. Our fast-food company wants to see whether a lifestyle variable such as eating a nutritious meal (X_1) and a demographic variable such as household income (X_2) are useful in distinguishing households visiting their restaurant from those visiting other fast-food restaurants. Marketing researchers have gathered data on X_1 and X_2 for two random samples of households. Discriminant analysis procedures would plot these data on a two-dimensional graph, as shown in Exhibit 18.9.

The scatter plot in Exhibit 18.9 yields two groups, one containing primarily Back Yard Burgers' customers and the other containing primarily households that patronize other fast-food restaurants. From this example, it appears that X_1 and X_2 are critical discriminators of fast-food restaurant patronage. Although the two areas overlap, the extent of the overlap does not seem to be substantial. This minimal overlap between groups, as in Exhibit 18.9, is an important requirement for a successful discriminant analysis.

A CLOSER LOOK AT RESEARCH   Using Technology

Discriminant analysis is used primarily to classify individuals or experimental units into two or more uniquely defined populations. An example of the use of discriminant analysis could include a credit card company that would like to classify credit card applicants into two groups: (1) individuals who are considered good credit risks, and (2) individuals who are considered poor credit risks.

Based on this classification, individuals considered good credit risks would be offered credit cards, while individuals considered poor credit risks would not be offered credit cards. Different factors that could help the credit card company in determining which of the two groups applicants would fall into include salary, past credit history, level of education, and number of dependents. The statistical software package SPSS could be used to determine where the line should be drawn between these two groups.

To learn more about the use of discriminant analysis in SPSS, go to the SPSS Web site at
www.spss.com.

Discriminant function

The linear combination of independent variables developed by discriminant analysis which will best discriminate between the categories of the dependent variable.

Let us now turn to the fundamental statistics of discriminant analysis. Remember, the prediction of a categorical variable is the purpose of discriminant analysis. From a statistical perspective, this involves studying the direction of group differences based on finding a linear combination of independent variables—the **discriminant function**—that shows large differences in group means. Thus, discriminant analysis is a statistical tool for determining linear combinations of those independent variables.

A linear function can be developed with our fast-food example. We will use a two-group discriminant analysis example in which the dependent variable, Y, is measured on a nominal scale (i.e., patrons of Back Yard Burgers versus other fast-food restaurants).

EXHIBIT 18.9 **Discriminant Analysis Scatter Plot of Lifestyle and Income Data for Fast-Food Restaurant Patronage**

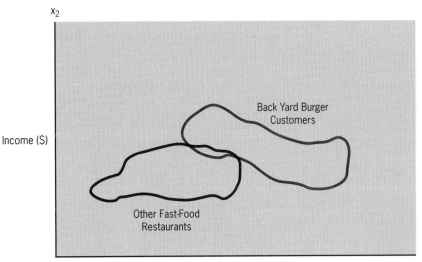

x_2

Income ($)

Back Yard Burger Customers

Other Fast-Food Restaurants

x_1

Lifestyle—Eating Nutritious Meals

Again, the marketing manager believes it is possible to predict whether a customer will patronize a fast-food restaurant on the basis of lifestyle (X_1) and income (X_2). Now the researcher must find a linear function of the independent variables that shows large differences in group means.

Discriminant score   In discriminant analysis, the score of each respondent on the discriminant function.

The **discriminant score,** or the Z score, is the basis for predicting to which group the particular individual belongs and is determined by a linear function. This Z score will be derived for each individual by means of the following equation:

$$Z_i = b_1X_{1i} + b_2X_{2i} + \ldots + b_nX_{ni}$$

where

$$Z_i = i\text{th individual's discriminant score}$$

$$b_n = \text{Discriminant coefficient for the } n\text{th variable}$$

$$X_{ni} = \text{Individual's value on the } n\text{th independent variable}$$

Discriminant function coefficients   The multipliers of variables in the discriminant function when the variables are in the original units of measurement.

Discriminant weights (b_n), or **discriminant function coefficients,** are estimates of the discriminatory power of a particular independent variable. These coefficients are computed by means of the discriminant analysis computer program. The size of the coefficients associated with a particular independent variable is determined by the variance structure of the variables in the equation. Independent variables with large discriminatory power will have large weights, and those with little discriminatory power will have small weights.

Returning to our fast-food example, suppose the marketing manager finds the standardized weights or coefficients in the equation to be

$$Z = b_1X_1 + B_2X_2$$

$$= .32X_1 + .37X_2$$

These results show that income (X_2) is the more important variable in discriminating between those patronizing Back Yard Burgers and those who patronize other fast-food restaurants. The lifestyle variable (X_1) with a coefficient of .32 also represents a variable with good discriminatory power.

Another important goal of discriminant analysis is classification of objects or individuals into groups. In our example, the goal was to correctly classify consumers into Back Yard Burger user and nonuser groups. To determine whether the estimated discriminant function is a good predictor, the **confusion (or prediction) matrix** is used. The confusion matrix in Exhibit 18.10 shows that the discriminant function correctly classified 84.5 percent of the actual users as users and incorrectly classified 15.5 percent of the actual users as nonusers. Regarding nonusers, the discriminant function correctly classified 77.9 percent as nonusers and incorrectly classified 22.1 percent as users. Our classification matrix in Exhibit 18.10 shows that the number of correctly classified consumers (93 users and 95 nonusers) out of a total of 232 equals 81 percent correctly classified. This resulting percentage is much higher than would be expected by chance. Statistical tests can be performed to determine whether the percentage of correct classification is statistically significant.

Confusion (or prediction) matrix   The classification matrix in discriminant analysis that contains the number of correctly classified and misclassified cases.

Discriminant Analysis Applications in Marketing Research

While our example illustrated how discriminant analysis helped classify users and nonusers of the restaurant based on independent variables, other applications include the following:

- **Product research.** Discriminant analysis can help to distinguish between heavy, medium, and light users of a product in terms of their consumption habits and lifestyles.

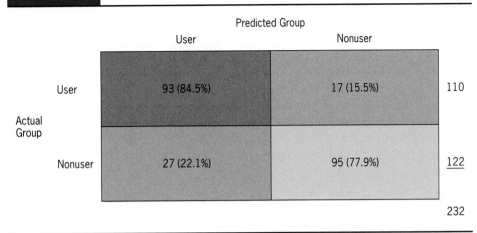

EXHIBIT 18.10   **Confusion Matrix**

	Predicted Group		
	User	Nonuser	
User	93 (84.5%)	17 (15.5%)	110
Nonuser	27 (22.1%)	95 (77.9%)	122
			232

- **Image research.** Discriminant analysis can discriminate between customers who exhibit favorable perceptions of a store or company and those who do not.

- **Advertising research.** Discriminant analysis can assist in distinguishing how market segments differ in media consumption habits.

- **Direct marketing.** Discriminant analysis can help in distinguishing characteristics of consumers who respond to direct marketing solicitations and those who don't.

Conjoint Analysis

Conjoint analysis A multivariate technique that estimates the utility of the levels of various attributes or features of an object, as well as the relative importance of the attributes themselves.

Conjoint analysis is a multivariate technique which estimates the relative importance consumers place on the different attributes of a product or service, as well as the utilities or value they attach to the various levels of each attribute. This dependence method assumes that consumers choose or form preferences for products by evaluating the overall utility or value of the product. This value is composed of the individual utilities of each product feature or attribute. Conjoint analysis tries to estimate the product attribute importance weights that would best match the consumer's indicated product choice or preference.

For example, assume that our fast-food company wants to determine the best combination of restaurant features to attract customers. A marketing researcher could develop a number of descriptions or restaurant profiles, each containing different combinations of features. Exhibit 18.11 shows two examples of what these profiles might look like. Consumers

EXHIBIT 18.11   **Sample Conjoint Survey Profiles**

Attribute	Restaurant Profile A	Restaurant Profile B
Price level	Inexpensive ($3 – $6)	Moderate ($7–$10)
Atmosphere	Family style	Upscale
Menu type	Sandwiches	Salad, entrée, dessert
Service level	Self-service	Table service

would then be surveyed, shown the different profiles, and asked to rank the descriptions in order of their likelihood of patronizing the restaurant. Note that with the conjoint analysis technique, the researcher has to do a lot more work than the survey respondent. The researcher must choose the attributes that are likely to affect consumer choice or preference, and must also pick the levels of each attribute to include in the survey. All that is required of the consumer is to rank order the profiles.

If each of the four attributes shown in Exhibit 18.11 had two levels or values (e.g., price level: inexpensive versus moderate), there would be 16 possible combinations for consumers to rank. Once those data were collected, applying conjoint analysis to the responses would produce a **part-worth estimate** for each level of each attribute.

Part-worth estimate

An estimate of the utility that survey respondents place on each individual level of a particular attribute or feature.

The statistical process underlying conjoint analysis uses the customer ranking of the profiles as a target. The process then assigns a part-worth estimate for each level of each attribute. The overall utility is estimated using the following formula:

$$U(\chi) = \alpha_{11} + \alpha_{12} + \alpha_{21} + \alpha_{22} + \ldots + \alpha_{mn}$$

where:

$U(\chi)$ = Total worth for product

α_{11} = Part-worth estimate for level 1 of attribute 1

α_{12} = Part-worth estimate for level 2 of attribute 1

α_{21} = Part-worth estimate for level 1 of attribute 2

α_{22} = Part-worth estimate for level 2 of attribute 2

α_{mn} = Part-worth estimate for level n of attribute m

Once the total worths of the product profiles have been estimated, the process compares it to the consumer's actual choice ranking. If the predictions are not accurate, then the individual part-worth estimates are changed and the total worths recalculated. This process continues until the predictions are as close to the consumer's actual rankings as possible. The ability of the estimated part-worth coefficients to accurately predict the consumer rankings can be determined through inspection of the model statistics, such as r^2. Just as in regression, a high r^2 indicates a good fit to the data (i.e., the model predictions closely match the consumer rankings).

Returning to our fast-food example above, Exhibit 18.12 shows graphs of the part-worth estimates for the various levels of the four attributes. The importance of each attribute across its different levels is indicated by the range of the part-worth estimates

EXHIBIT 18.12   Conjoint Part-Worth Estimates for Restaurant Survey

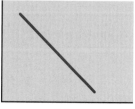

Price

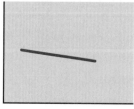

Atmosphere

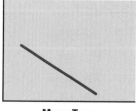

Menu Type

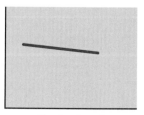

Service Level

Attribute importance estimate The importance of an attribute of an object as estimated by conjoint analysis; calculated by subtracting the minimum part-worth estimate from the maximum part-worth estimate.

for that attribute; that is, by subtracting the minimum part-worth for the attribute from the maximum part-worth. Once the **attribute importance estimate** has been determined, the relative importance of each attribute can be calculated as a percentage of the total importance scores of all the attributes in the model. The formula for the attribute importance is

$$I_i = \{\text{Max}(\alpha_{ij}) - \text{Min}(\alpha_{ij})\} \text{ for each attribute } i$$

And the formula for the relative attribute importance is

$$R_i = \frac{I_i}{\Sigma I_i}$$

If we take the part-worth estimates shown in Exhibit 18.12 and calculate the importance of each attribute and its relative importance, we get the results shown in Exhibit 18.13.

As you can see, the price level of the potential restaurant is the most important attribute to consumers in choosing a place to eat, followed by menu type.

Once the importance weights of the attributes have been estimated, it is relatively easy to make predictions about the overall preference for particular combinations of product features. Comparisons of alternative products can then be made to determine the most feasible alternative to consider bringing to market.

The main advantages of conjoint analysis techniques are (1) the low demands placed on the consumer to provide data; (2) the ability to provide utility estimates for individual levels of each product attribute; and (3) the ability to estimate nonlinear relationships among attribute levels. The limitations placed on the researcher by conjoint analysis are (1) that the researcher is responsible for choosing the appropriate attributes and attribute levels that will realistically influence consumer preferences or choice, and (2) that consumers may have difficulty making choices or indicating preferences among large numbers of profiles, so the number of attributes and levels used cannot be too large.

Conjoint Analysis Applications in Marketing Research

The fast-food example used in this discussion illustrates one possible use of conjoint analysis to identify the important attributes that influence consumer restaurant choice.

EXHIBIT 18.13 **Importance Calculations for Restaurant Data**

Attribute	Description	Part-worth	Attribute Importance	Relative Importance
Price level 1	Inexpensive ($3–$6)	1.762		
Price level 2	Moderate ($7–$10)	−1.762	3.524	0.600
Atmosphere 1	Family style	0.244		
Atmosphere 2	Upscale	−0.244	0.488	0.083
Menu type 1	Sandwiches	0.598		
Menu type 2	Salad, entrée, dessert	−0.598	1.196	0.203
Service 1	Self-service	0.337		
Service 2	Table service	−0.337	0.674	0.115

There are other important applications of this technique in marketing research, such as the following:

- **Market share potential.** Products with different combinations of features can be compared to determine the most popular design.

- **Product image analysis.** The relative contribution of each product attribute can be determined for use in marketing and advertising decisions.

- **Segmentation analysis.** Groups of potential customers who place different levels of importance on the product features can be identified for use as high and low potential market segments.

SUMMARY OF LEARNING OBJECTIVES

Define multivariate analysis.

Multivariate analysis refers to a group of statistical procedures used to simultaneously analyze three or more variables. Factor analysis, cluster analysis, multidimensional scaling, discriminant analysis, and conjoint analysis are commonly used multivariate statistical techniques.

Understand how to use multivariate analysis in marketing research.

Multivariate analysis is extremely important in marketing research because most business problems are multidimensional. Marketing managers are often concerned with various aspects of the consumer (e.g., demographics, lifestyles); consumers' purchasing process (e.g., motives, perceptions); and competition. Thus, techniques such as factor analysis, cluster analysis, and discriminant analysis assist marketing managers in simultaneously assessing a set or sets of important variables.

Distinguish between the two basic methods in multivariate analysis: dependence methods and interdependence methods.

Multivariate data analysis techniques can be classified into dependence and interdependence methods. A dependence method is one in which a variable or set of variables is identified as the dependent variable to be predicted or explained by other, independent variables. Dependence techniques include multiple regression analysis, discriminant analysis, and conjoint analysis. An interdependence method is one in which no single variable or group of variables is defined as being independent or dependent. The goal of interdependence methods is data reduction, or grouping things together. Cluster analysis, factor analysis, and multidimensional scaling are the most commonly used interdependence methods.

Define and understand factor analysis and cluster analysis.

Factor analysis and cluster analysis are both interdependence methods. Factor analysis is used to summarize the information contained in a large number of variables into a smaller number of factors. Cluster analysis classifies observations into a small number of mutually exclusive and exhaustive groups. In cluster analysis, these groups should have as much similarity within each group and as much difference between groups as possible.

Understand multidimensional scaling and perceptual mapping.

Another interdependence multivariate method is multidimensional scaling. This method measures objects in multidimensional space based on consumers' similarity judgments. In perceptual mapping, graphic representations can be produced from multidimensional scaling programs. The maps provide a visual representation of how companies, products, brands, or other objects are perceived relative to each other on key attributes such as quality of service, food taste, and food preparation.

Define and use discriminant analysis and conjoint analysis.

Multiple discriminant analysis and conjoint analysis are dependence methods. The purpose of techniques such as discriminant and conjoint analysis is to predict a variable from a set of independent variables. Discriminant analysis uses independent variables to classify observations into mutually exclusive categories. Discriminant analysis can also be used to determine whether statistically significant differences exist between the average discriminant score profiles of two or more groups. Conjoint analysis is a technique that uses consumer ranking or preference ratings of a group of product profile descriptions to estimate attribute importance coefficients through the use of part-worth estimates. Each level of each attribute in the product description is given a weight and the weights are added together to form a product utility. Conjoint can be used to compare consumer preferences for different product attribute combinations.

KEY TERMS AND CONCEPTS

Attribute importance estimate 603

Cluster analysis 594

Confusion (or prediction) matrix 600

Conjoint analysis 601

Dependence technique 589

Discriminant analysis 598

Discriminant function 599

Discriminant function coefficients 600

Discriminant score 600

Factor analysis 590

Factor loading 592

Factor scores 590

Interdependence technique 589

Multidimensional scaling 596

Multivariate analysis 586

Part-worth estimate 602

Perceptual map 596

Similarity judgments 596

REVIEW QUESTIONS

1. Why are multivariate statistical analysis methods so important to managers today? How do multivariate methods differ from univariate methods?

2. What is the difference between dependence and interdependence multivariate methods?

3. What is the goal of factor analysis? Give an example of a marketing situation that would call for factor analysis.

4. How does cluster analysis differ from factor analysis? Give an example of how cluster analysis is used in marketing research.

5. What is the purpose of multidimensional scaling? How is perceptual mapping related to multidimensional scaling?

6. What is the purpose of discriminant analysis? How might it be used to solve a marketing problem or identify a marketing opportunity?

DISCUSSION QUESTIONS

1. Cluster analysis is a commonly used multivariate analysis technique in segmentation studies. Its primary objective is to classify objects into relatively homogeneous groups based on a set of variables. Once those groups are identified by a cluster analysis, what is the next logical analysis step a marketer might want to take? Will the results of a cluster analysis also reveal the characteristics of the members in each group? Why not?

2. Describe how you would use the results of a multidimensional scaling analysis which produced a perceptual map of customers' opinions of the quality and value of several brands of watches. What importance would you attach to the location of a

consumer's ideal watch compared to other available watch brands? What role would the distance between the brands on the perceptual map play in your conclusions?

3. Discriminant analysis is a frequently used multivariate technique when the objective is to identify important variables in identifying group membership of some type. What is the role of the discriminant function coefficients in identifying these important variables? In the chapter on regression, multicollinearity among the independent variables in a regression equation was highlighted as a potential problem for interpretation of the results. Do you think multicollinearity would also pose a problem for interpreting discriminant analysis results? Why or why not?

4. Conjoint analysis is used to determine the important perceptions of respondents regarding the features of a product or service. Respondents are typically asked to rank-order product or service descriptions containing different combinations of the attributes or features of interest. What is the role of the part-worth utility coefficient produced by a conjoint analysis? How should the researcher go about deciding which features to include in the product descriptions? How do you think the quality of the conjoint analysis results are affected if a potentially important feature is left out of the descriptions respondents are asked to rank-order?

5. **EXPERIENCE THE INTERNET.** Access the Internet and select a particular search engine. Use various key words and identify five major market research providers listed on the Web. Compare and contrast their Web sites and suggest the strength and weaknesses of each. Which would you choose to conduct a marketing research project for you? Why? Prepare a report for class so you can share your findings with other students.

6. **SPSS EXERCISE.** Using the fast-food data set and the questionnaire found in Exhibit 15.6 (Chapter 15), conduct the following tasks:

   a. Use questions 2 and 3, and with SPSS, create a new variable from these questions called *Usage*. With this new variable create the following categories:

   Light users = Those individuals who responded "1" and "2" to question 2, and "under $2" and "$2.01 to $ 4.00" in question 3.

   Medium users = Those individuals who responded "3," "4," and "5" to question 2, and "$4.01 to $6.00," "$6.01 to $8.00," and "$8.01 to $10.00" on question 3.

   Heavy users = Those individuals who responded "6" and "7 or more" to question 2, and "$10.01 to $12.00" and "more than $12" on question 3.

   b. Using these new categories and the statements from question 7, perform a three-group discriminant analysis on the data.

7. **SPSS EXERCISE.** With the same data set and questionnaire used in question 6 above, perform a factor analysis on the lifestyle statements contained in question 9.

ENDNOTE

1. Carol Vinzant, "Electronic Books Are Coming at Last," *Fortune,* July 6, 1998, pp. 119–24.

COMPUTER COMPANIES STRIVE TO UNDERSTAND DIFFERENCES IN MARKET SEGMENTS

This illustration is designed to show how marketing practitioners and researchers can use a multivariate analysis technique like discriminant analysis to gain insights into the important factors used in market segmentation activities.

As America enters the 21st century, there is little doubt that computer technology will remain a pervasive force in our society that has many beneficial consequences. The fast-growing advancements of technology, high-cost structures of new-product innovations, and the increasing pressures for successful product introductions have many of today's high-tech firms turning to consumer market segments for opportunities of market expansion and profitablility. Two of the most challenging tasks facing today's marketers are (1) the successful introduction of new technology-based product innovations into consumer markets, and (2) stimulating the diffusion of those innovations to acceptable penetration levels. To meet these challenges, researchers must be able to gain clearer insights of the key factors people might use in deciding whether or not to adopt computer technology innovations.

Recently, a study was conducted to investigate the use of postpurchase behavioral factors among adopters of personal computers (PCs) for in-home use. The study concentrated on determining whether or not differences do exist between *innovator* and *late adopter* market segments with respect to usage, satisfaction, and product integration patterns. The main question that the computer company was trying to address was, "Are there significant post-adoption PC opinions and behavioral profile differences between consumers who are considered members of the innovator versus late adopter market segments for in-home PCs?"

The research procedure used to collect the necessary data was a direct mail survey, characterized as descriptive and exploratory. A specifically designed cover letter was attached to the questionnaire to enhance the participation of the selected personal computer owners as well as to ensure the legitimacy of the study. The population frame was defined as adult personal computer owners who had purchased either an IBM or Apple PC for primarily in-home use and not for business or commercial use. A probabilistic simple random sampling technique was employed to draw a representative sample of 1,200 IBM and Apple PC owners. A final total of 356 usable questionnaires (47 percent Apple owners, 53 percent IBM owners) was returned by the specified deadline date, for a response rate of about 30 percent. The five-page questionnaire contained questions for measuring PC users' adoptive innovativeness, PC activity, use innovativeness, PC integration, and a standard set of demographic characteristics. Other than some of the demographic variables, all the scale measurements of the key factors were designed as having either ordinal, interval, or ratio scaling properties. Exhibit 1 summarizes the demographic variables, electronic product ownership/experience, and key factors used in the investigation as well as the reliability estimates of those factors.

To investigate the main question, it was necessary to classify the respondents as either an innovator or late adopter of the in-home PC. The identification process was enhanced with the aid of a known and widely accepted stepwise discriminant analysis procedure in which the variable that maximizes the F ratio and minimizes Wilks's lambda (a measure of group discrimination) is used to investigate differences between the innovator and late-adopter test groups' centroids. For clarity, the resulting group profile relationships were further investigated for distinguishable opinions, usage patterns, and behavioral integration habit differences through the use of standard z-tests and chi-square statistical testing procedures. Exhibit 2 presents the stepwise discriminant analysis results.

EXHIBIT 1   Summary of Demographic Variables, Dependent Variable, and Independent Variables

Demographic Variables	Factors	Number of Items in Factor	Cronbach's Alpha	Electronic Product Ownership/Experience
Marital Status*	Use Innovativeness[†]			Videodisc player
Family size*	Multiple use subscale	7	0.84	Videocassette player
Occupation*	Creativity/curiosity subscale	9	0.56	Cordless phone
Length of PC ownership[†]	PC Integration[†]			
Primary PC user*	Current use	5	0.73	Microwave oven
Primary PC purchaser*	Usage pattern	4	0.26	Videotape camera
Degree of prior computer experience[†]	Expected future use	2	0.74	ATM bank card
	PC satisfaction	3	0.68	Telephone answering machine
	PC Accessory Purchase Behavior*			
	Number of additional PC hardware	10	0.82	
	Number of additional PC software	10	0.76	Mobile telephone

*Data collected using nominal scaling designs.
[†]Data collected using ordinally-interval scale designs.

EXHIBIT 2   Standard Discriminant Function and Classification Function Coefficients

Variables	Discriminant Function Coefficients*	Classification Function Coefficients[†]	
		Innovators	Late Adopters
Degree of prior computer experience	−0.22	0.31	0.46
Use innovativeness—multiple use subscale	−0.41	0.65	0.79
Use innovativeness—creativity curiosity subscale	0.27	1.92	1.83
Extent of electronic product ownership	−0.18	2.33	2.48
PC integration—expected future use	0.47	3.36	2.88
PC integration—current PC usage behavior	0.32	1.69	1.59
PC integration—postadoption PC satisfaction	−0.58	1.41	1.80
Postadoption—additive hardware purchases	0.45	1.22	0.90
Constant		−60.14	−59.12

*The standardized discriminant function significantly discriminated between the two groups ($X^2 = 48.72$, df = 8, $p < 0.0005$).

[†]Overall, the percentage correctly classified (hit ratio) = (100) (73 = 184/356) = 72.19%; with the percentage correctly classified in analysis = (100) (38 = 76/148) = 77.03%; and in classification = (100) (35 + 108/208) = 68.75%

Results

Postadoption Attitude-Behavior Profile Differences

To determine whether profile differences do exist, a wide array of postadoption PC opinion and use behavior factors were submitted to a varimax rotated stepwise discriminant analysis procedure. The total sample was divided into an *analysis subgroup* of 148 respondents and a *holdout subgroup* of 208 respondents. Using the chi-square testing procedure, the standardized canonical discriminant function discriminated significantly between the two groups of respondents ($X^2 = 48.72$, df = 8, $p < 0.005$). The reported discriminant function correctly classified 77.3 percent of the analysis subgroup and 68.75 percent of the holdout subgroup. Furthermore, the function's overall "hit ratio" was compared to the "proportional chance criterion" (C prop) model. Overall, the study's standardized canonical discriminant function correctly classified approximately 72 percent of the 356 respondents, which was significantly greater than C prop (54%) at the 0.001 level and minimum 25 percent increase standard.

The discriminant analysis results suggest there are distinguishable traits relating to postadoption PC use innovativeness and PC integration habits, which could be used by marketing management to identify those PC adopters who might be considered innovators of in-home PCs and those characterized as being late adopters. It seems that PC owners' opinions toward their multiple use habits serve as dominant postadoption and use innovativeness monitoring factors. From a PC integration perspective, the subjects' attitudes toward their expected future PC use habit and postadoption PC satisfaction serve as the salient product-integration-related traits. Furthermore, the results suggest that such monitoring traits as degree of prior ownership, PC adopters' creativity/curiosity traits, electronic product ownership as well as current usage behavior were significant, but demonstrate lower discriminatory capabilities. The findings suggest that PC use innovativeness, PC integration patterns, degree of prior experience with computers, and electronic product ownership traits can serve as meaningful postadoption traits that PC marketers could use to monitor the diffusion of PCs within the in-home consumer market segment.

Using *z*-tests to establish the detailed profile differences between innovators and late adopters of in-home PCs, the major differences in the profiles can be summarized as follows:

- Innovators are more likely to be more curious about how the product works and more willing to develop additional uses for the PC. To accomplish this, they purchase additional items of hardware and software. They like multipurpose innovations.

- Innovators use their PCs quite frequently and expect to continue to use their PCs heavily in the future.

- As a result of their level of involvement with the PC, innovators are very satisfied with their purchase and become a positive force in influencing their friends to purchase one.

- Innovators own a lot of electronic products in their homes, and lack of prior experience with computers does not deter them from purchasing one.

Overall, the use of discriminant analysis can help today's PC marketers gain better understanding of their potential market segments. This study demonstrated that in-home PCs have left the innovation stage of the diffusion process. PC manufacturers and retail marketers alike must now focus on developing strategies that can attract the large number of potential late adopters (i.e., nonadopters who have yet to purchase a PC for in-home use).

MARKETING RESEARCH CASE EXERCISE

EXAMINING LIFESTYLE DATA

The marketing director of a large consumer products firm that sells toys and recreational equipment has commissioned a lifestyle study of the firm's customers. The director wants to better understand the activities, interests, and opinions of the people who buy products from the firm. The lifestyle survey contains approximately 250 questions concerning respondents' preferences for: (1) various types of activities (e.g., snow skiing, hiking, playing chess); (2) interests (e.g., watching sports shows, collecting stamps); and (3) opinions (e.g., political attitudes, opinions about fashion). Respondents' answers to these questions have been collected, and now a large stack of tables containing the mean scores to each question and the distribution of the answers to each question sits in front of the marketing director.

The director wonders if there is a better way to summarize the patterns of answers provided by the respondents. Perhaps the questions could be grouped together in some fashion and the scores summarized by groups. What multivariate analysis techniques would you recommend to the director to help him understand the knowledge contained in the stack of tables sitting in front of him? Could more than one approach be used? Remember, the director's objective is to find out more about the lifestyle patterns of his customers so he can decide how best to market his firm's products to them.

CHAPTER 19

Preparing the Marketing Research Report and Presentation

Learning Objectives

After reading this chapter, you will be able to

1. Understand the primary objectives of a research report.

2. Explain how a marketing research report is organized.

3. List problems that one may encounter when preparing the report.

4. Understand the importance of presentations in marketing research.

5. Identify different software options available for developing presentations.

6. Understand the advantages and disadvantages of different software options available for developing presentations.

" Many times what you say may not be as important as how you say it. "

ANONYMOUS

Back Yard Burger Focus Group Summary: Presenting Focus Group Results

To: All Executive Officers, Department Heads, Franchisees
Topic: Results and Dialogue Pertaining to July 20 Focus Group
Date: July 29, 1999

EXECUTIVE SUMMARY

While we at Back Yard Burger (BYB) have just scratched the surface of the information needed to correct the climate in Little Rock, many interesting comments were realized in the July focus group session. Based on this discussion it appears quite obvious that immediate attention must be given to operations and marketing in the Little Rock market. Overall, we lack consistency. More important, we need to enhance our commitment to solving the issues that need correction. These issues center on customer service, facility curb appeal, and general customer awareness. From this perspective, the following recommendations are set forth.

All stores in Little Rock need to be cleaned up. Exterior repairs, landscaping improvements, and enhancement of reader boards need to be systematically addressed. In-store employees need to improve their physical appearance and dress. This is particularly important for all window personnel. Cleanliness is a major issue with the Little Rock consumer. This is complicated by the fact that double-drive-thru formats are evaluated on cleanliness based on their exterior appearance.

Regarding internal operations, we have three problems that need immediate attention: bland, mundane attitudes at point of sale; employee confusion in kitchen areas; and a habit of getting customer orders wrong. The surest way to alienate a Little Rock customer is to get his or her order wrong. Another big turnoff is charging the customer for additional condiments. In my opinion, there is no excuse for this, since by saving five cents we run the risk of losing long-term loyalty and revenue. Many of these problems can be dissipated with the QSR program. We need to implement this program in all Little Rock locations. Little Rock customers do not perceive value at a QSR; they view all QSRs in terms of price. The only differentiated feature among QSRs is the level of service quality perceived by our customers.

From a marketing perspective, we have great burgers, but beyond that customers don't know what we offer— they lack awareness of our menu variety. Given the fact that healthier food is desired by our patrons, we need to increase our emphasis on our chicken product line specifically and our full menu variety in general. Little Rock customers want to be treated with respect. They appreciate community involvement on the part of local businesses. They like to know who owns and operates those businesses. Given this attitude, BYB needs to implement a two-pronged approach to communication strategy. First, we need to project an overall image of how good we are regarding food and service. With a credible spokesperson, we need to tell the people of Little Rock that BYB is a great place to visit. Second, we need a tactical communication focused on our extensive menu variety, with an emphasis on our chicken line.

Coupons may not be an effective price incentive for Little Rock. Free samples, in-store point-of-sale price discounts, and employee/manager interaction at community events may prove more effective than coupons in generating first-time purchases.

With the high level of expectations for service quality among Little Rock customers, it is important that marketing be accountable for customer satisfaction. Therefore, marketing needs direct input into the QSR program and mystery shopper function. These programs are critical at developing lasting customer relationships and enhancement of our overall image. Given the severe ramifications that can result from these programs, and the emphasis needed on curb appeal and customer contact personnel, marketing needs to accept responsibility for these programs.

Attached are the findings from the July 20 focus group held in Little Rock. The report is in a question-and-answer format. We strongly urge all parties to read this report. It will provide insights into what customers believe to be occurring in the QSR industry, and BYB operations. Also attached is a fax from one of the focus group participants regarding her most recent visit to BYB. Let's see if we can't prevent this from happening.

Value of Preparing the Marketing Research Report

The opening section is an excerpt from an executive summary of a marketing research report. What is being communicated in this excerpt are recommendations that should be implemented based on information obtained from a focus group study. While this is not a complete executive summary, it does illustrate some issues surrounding the role and purpose of the marketing research report.

Best practices within the marketing research industry suggest that no matter how perfectly the research project was designed and implemented, if the results cannot be effectively communicated to the client, the research project cannot be considered a success. Effectively designing and developing the marketing research report is one way to ensure that the time, effort, and money that went into the research project will be completely realized. The purpose of this chapter is to introduce the style and format of the marketing research report. We will identify how the marketing research report is established and designed, and explain the specific objectives of each section of the report. We will then discuss industry best practices regarding effective presentation of the research report, focusing on the use of computer technology to build credibility. A complete marketing research report from a focus group interview is included in the Marketing Research Illustration at the end of this chapter.

The Written Marketing Research Report

The professional marketing research report must achieve four primary objectives: (1) to effectively communicate the findings of the marketing research project, (2) to provide interpretations of those findings in the form of sound and logical recommendations, (3) to illustrate the credibility of the research project, and (4) to serve as a future reference document for strategic or tactical decisions.

The first and foremost objective of the research report is to effectively communicate the findings of the marketing research project. Since the primary purpose of the research project was to obtain information that will answer specific questions in relation to a specific business problem, the report must explain both how the information was obtained and what relevance it has to the research questions. Best practices suggest that a detailed description of the following factors be communicated to the client:

1. The specific research objectives.

2. The specific research questions the study was to answer.

3. Specific procedural information relevant to the collection of secondary data (if necessary).

4. A description of the research methods employed.

5. Findings displayed in tables, graphs, or charts.

6. An accurate interpretation and summation of the findings.

7. Conclusions based on data analysis.

8. Recommendations and suggestions for their implementation.

Far too often, the researcher is so concerned about communicating results that he or she forgets to provide a clear, logical interpretation of those results. The researcher must always be aware that his or her level of understanding regarding sampling methods and statistics, for example, may not be the same as that of the user. Therefore, the researcher must always attempt to take technical or complex information and present it in a manner that is understandable to all parties concerned. Most researchers are often fully armed with statistics, computer output, questionnaires, and other project-related material. In presenting such information to the client, the researcher should always rely on the original research objectives. The task is to focus on each objective and communicate how each part of the project is related to the accomplishment of that objective.

For example, Exhibit 19.1 was prepared to illustrate a research objective defining the significant predictors of heavy versus moderate users of fast-food restaurants. While a volume of numerical data was necessary to fulfill this objective, the use of appropriate terminology provides a clear and understandable interpretation of the data. One can easily see from Exhibit 19.1 that, compared to moderate users, heavy users are more loyal to national brands, have a low orientation to fashion, are not as concerned about food prices, and have a low preference for combination meals.

EXHIBIT 19.1   **Simple Interpretation of Data**

Significant Predictors of User Class: Fast-Food Eating Segments

Predictor	Moderate User Class	Heavy User Class
Opinions		
Nutritious meals	High	Low
Information	Leaders	Seekers
Eating	Skip lunch	Routine
Children	Less child oriented	High child oriented
Brand orientation	More loyal to national brands	Less loyal to national brands
Eating	Avoid fat and cholesterol	Lower tendency
Packaging	No preference	Prefer single-serving items
Novelty	Like to buy new and different things	Less likely
Dress	High fashion orientation	Low fashion orientation
Leadership	Leaders	Followers
Eating	Avoid salt	No preference
TV ads	Zappers	Less likely
Fast-Food Attitudes		
Store visits	Convenience	Convenience
Food prices	Important	Not important
Perception of outlets	All the same	Some differences
Price/quality	Quality	Quality
Food types	Salad bars	Salad bars
Breakfast	Low visits	High visits
Combo meals	Prefer	Low preference
Advertising impact	Low	Moderate

Credibility The quality of a report that is related to its accuracy, believability, and professional organization.

A critical dimension of the research report is to establish **credibility** of the research methods, findings, and conclusions. This can be accomplished only if the report is accurate, believable, and professionally organized. These three dimensions cannot be treated separately, for they collectively operate to build credibility into the research document. For the report to be accurate, all of the input must be accurate. No degree of carelessness in handling data, reporting statistics, or phasing outcomes must be tolerated. Errors in mathematical calculations, grammatical errors, and incorrect terminology are just a few types of inaccuracies that can serve to diminish the credibility of the entire report.

Believability The quality of a report that is based on clear and logical thinking, precise expression, and accurate presentation.

Clear and logical thinking, precise expression, and accurate presentation constitute **believability**. When the underlying logic is fuzzy or the presentation imprecise, readers may have difficulty understanding what they read. In most instances, if readers don't understand what they read, they may not believe what they read. For example, a client may have a notion that half of all respondents find the company's store locations very convenient. If the actual results deviate from this expectation, the client may not feel comfortable with the research results. In such cases, the researcher needs to explain the results clearly, especially if they result from some type of error. Improper question wording, sampling bias, or nonresponse error may all be at work to create the discrepancy between the client's expectations and the findings.

Finally, the credibility of the research report can be affected by the quality and organization of the document itself. It is critical that the report is clearly developed and professionally organized. This means the researcher must know exactly what he or she wants to say. It also means that the researcher must make every effort to organize the document around the preferences and technical sophistication of the reader.

The following advice is helpful in developing the report: Make an outline of all major points, with supporting details in their proper position and sequence. Always keep the reader informed of where the topical development of the report is going. Use short, concise sentences and paragraphs. Always say exactly what you intend to say; don't leave the reader "hanging" or "grasping" for more information. Always select wording that is consistent with the background and knowledge level of the reader. Rewrite the report several times; this will force you to remove clutter and critically evaluate the document for errors. Professional organization of the research report will also be discussed in the next section on report format.

The fourth and final objective of the research report is to maintain reference status. Once it is fully completed, the research report will have a life of its own as a reference source. Most marketing research studies cover a variety of different objectives and seek to answer a multitude of research questions. This is normally accomplished with large volumes of information in both statistical and narrative formats. To retain all of this information at any one time is virtually impossible for the client. Consequently, the research report normally becomes a reference document that is cited over an extended period.

In addition, many marketing research reports become just one element of a larger project conducted in various stages over time. It is not uncommon for one marketing research report to serve as a baseline or benchmark for additional studies. Also, many reports are used for comparison purposes. Companies use them to measure promotional changes, image building tactics, or even strengths and weaknesses of the firm.

Format of the Marketing Research Report

Every marketing research report is unique in some way—due to client needs, research purpose, study objectives, and so on—yet all reports contain some common elements. Although the terminology may differ among industry practices, the basic format discussed in this section will help researchers plan and prepare reports for various clients. The parts common to all marketing research reports are as follows:

1. Title page

2. Table of contents

3. Executive summary
   a. Research objectives
   b. Concise statement of method
   c. Summary of findings
   d. Conclusion and recommendations

4. Introduction

5. Research method and procedures

6. Data analysis and findings

7. Conclusions and recommendations

8. Limitations

9. Appendixes

Title Page

The title page indicates the subject of the report and the name of the recipient, along with his or her position and organization. Any necessary numbers or phrases to designate a particular department or division should also be included. Most important, the title page must contain the name, position, employing organization, address, and telephone (and fax) number of the person or persons submitting the report, as well as the date the report is submitted.

Table of Contents

The table of contents lists the specific topics of the report in sequential order. Normally, the contents page will highlight each topical area, the subdivisions within each area, and corresponding page numbers. It is also common to include tables and figures and the pages where they may be found.

Executive Summary

Executive summary
The part of a marketing research report that presents the major points; it must be complete enough to provide a true representation of the document but in summary form.

The **executive summary** is the most important part of the report. Many consider it the soul of the report, insofar as many executives will only read the report summary. The executive summary must present the major points of the report; it must be complete enough to provide a true representation of the entire document but in summary form.

The executive summary must be written to fulfill several purposes: (1) it must convey how and why the research was undertaken, (2) what the findings were, (3) what the findings mean for the reader, and (4) what future action must be taken. In other words, the executive summary must contain the research objectives, a concise statement of method, a summary of the findings, and specific conclusions and recommendations.

The research objectives should be as precise as possible, and confined to approximately one page. The research purpose, along with the questions or hypotheses that guided the project, should also be stated in this section. Next, a brief description of the sampling method, the research design, and any procedural aspects should be addressed in one or two paragraphs. Following this should come a statement of findings. The findings presented in the summary must, of course, agree with those found in the findings section of the full report. Best practices suggest including only key findings that specifically relate to the research objectives. Again, this part of the executive summary should be no more than two or three paragraphs. Finally, the summary must contain a brief statement of conclusions and recommendations derived from the research. Conclusions are given as opinions based on the findings. They are merely statements of what the research generated and what meaning can be attached to the findings. Recommendations, in contrast, are statements for appropriate future actions. Recommendations are generated by the process of logical deduction and focus on specific marketing tactics or strategies the client should use to gain a competitive advantage. Normally, conclusions and recommendations can be stated in one to two paragraphs of the executive summary.

Introduction

The introduction contains background information necessary for a complete understanding of the report. A definition of terms, relevant background, specific circumstances surrounding the study, and the study's scope and emphasis are communicated in the introduction.

This section should also list specific research objectives and questions the study was designed to achieve. Specific hypotheses, length and duration of the study, and any research-related problems would also be contained in the introduction. Upon reading the introduction, the client should know exactly what the report is about, why the research was conducted, and what relationships exist between the current study and past research endeavors.

Research Method and Procedures

The objective of the method-and-procedures section is to communicate to the user specifically how the research was conducted. Issues addressed in this section must include the following:

1. What research design was used: exploratory, descriptive, causal.

2. What types of secondary data were used in the study.

3. If primary data were collected, what procedure was employed (observation, questionnaire), and what administration procedures were employed (personal, mail, telephone).

4. What sample and sampling process were used. Within this description the following questions must be addressed:
   a. How was the sample population defined and profiled?
   b. What sampling units were used (businesses, households, individuals, etc.)?
   c. How was the sampling list generated?
   d. How was the sample size determined?
   e. Was a probability or nonprobability sampling plan employed?

Many times when generating the method-and-procedures section, the writer gets bogged down in presenting too much detail on the study. If upon completion of this section, the reader can say what was done, how it was done, and why it was done, the objective of the writer has been fulfilled. The Marketing Research Illustration at the end of the chapter exemplifies many of these principles.

Data Analysis and Findings

Because each project is so specific with regard to data analysis, little can be said in reference to the analysis technique per se. Nonetheless, if the researcher is reporting the output of a chi-square, for example, best practices suggest that he or she define the concept of statistical significance of the test, give the general rationale for performing the test, and list the various assumptions associated with the procedure.

For more sophisticated analysis techniques, such as multiple regression analysis or ANOVA, it is always good practice to provide a brief interpretation of the technique specifically, along with why it is being used and what outcomes can occur.

The actual results of the study—the findings—will constitute the majority of this section of the report. Findings should always consist of a detailed presentation, with supporting tables, figures, and graphs. All results must be detailed and logically arranged so as to correspond to each research objective or research question indicated earlier in the report. Best practices suggest that tables, figures, and graphs be used accordingly when presenting any results. These illustrations should represent a simple summation of the data in a clear, concise, and nontechnical manner. For example, Exhibit 19.2 contains a table illustrating the results for the research question "To which fast-service hamburger restaurant were consumers most favorably predisposed?" This table illustrates the data output in a simple and concise manner, allowing the reader to easily view the most preferred/least preferred restaurant.

More sophisticated or technical graphs should be reserved for the appendixes of the report. Unlike Exhibit 19.2, the chart contained in Exhibit 19.3 is highly complex and to

---

EXHIBIT 19.2   **Findings Illustrating Simple Readable Results**

To which fast-service hamburger restaurant were consumers most favorably predisposed?

√ **Memphis**

	Predisposition			
	Total Favorable			
	Most Preferred	Would Consider	Neutral	Unfavorable
Wendy's	37%	54%	8%	1%
Back Yard Burgers	28	57	14	1
Burger King	17	61	12	10
McDonald's	9	60	8	23
Rally's	4	60	31	5

√ **Little Rock**

	Predisposition			
	Total Favorable			
	Most Preferred	Would Consider	Neutral	Unfavorable
Back Yard Burgers	41%	49%	7%	3%
Wendy's	28	58	8	6
Rally's	11	66	16	7
Burger King	9	61	15	15
McDonald's	8	60	13	19

EXHIBIT 19.3 **Findings Illustrating Complex, Technical Results**

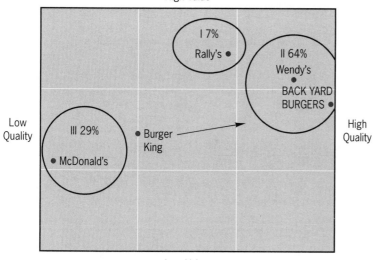

QUALITY/VALUE POSITIONING™
Back Yard Burgers

High Value

I 7% Rally's •

II 64% Wendy's • BACK YARD BURGERS •

Low Quality

III 29% • Burger King • McDonald's

High Quality

Low Value

++	= Major Strength
+	= Above Average
o	= Average
−	= Below Average
− −	= Major Weakness

* While BACK YARD BURGERS naturally fits in Position II, its image is shown in Positions I and III to indicate how good a fit it has in Positions I and III.

→ Burger King's current Position (II) is indicated by the arrow. Burger King is not shown in Position II because it does not provide the expected level of Quality and Value associated with Position II.

	Image of:	
Position I Influences:	Rally's	(BACK YARD BURGERS)*
1. Speed of service	++	(−)
2. Prices of food items	++	(−)
3. Gets orders correct	++	(++)
4. Friendly employees	++	(+)

	Image of:	
Position III Influences:	McDondald's	(BACK YARD BURGERS)*
1. Specials and promotions	++	(− −)
2. Attention getting signs	++	(− −)
3. Offers children's menu	++	(− −)
4. Convenient location	++	(− −)
5. Fun place to go	++	(−)
6. Selection of desserts	++	(+)

		Image of:	
			BACK
	Burger		YARD
Position II Influences:	King	Wendy's	BURGERS
1. Unique menu items	−	++	++
2. Variety of food	−	++	− −
3. Large hamburger	++	+	++
4. Method of cooking hamburgers	++	−	++
5. Good tasting food	+	++	++
6. Prepares food to customer's special request	++	++	+
7. Each order prepared fresh	−	++	++
8. Quality of ingredients	−	++	++
9. Consistent quality every visit	−	++	+
10. Portion size	+	++	++
11. Selection of types of french fries	−	− −	++
12. Food well prepared	−	+	++
13. Gets orders correct	−	+	++
14. Uses extra lean ground beef	−	+	++
15. Healthy food	−	++	+

some extent difficult to interpret. While this chart is directly related to the research objectives concerning image of restaurants, it needs detailed explanation to simplify the intent for the reader. A chart such as this is better suited for the appendix section of the report.

Conclusions and Recommendations

Conclusions and recommendations are derived specifically from the findings. Conclusions can be considered broad generalizations that focus on answering questions related to the research objectives. They are condensed pieces of information derived from the findings

EXHIBIT 19.4	Illustration of Conclusions within a Marketing Research Report

Conclusions

Awareness

- Building unaided awareness is directly related to consistent efforts in advertising, promotions, and signage.

- Among its competitors, Back Yard Burgers has the lowest levels of advertising recall, awareness of specials and promotions, and attention-getting signage.

- On the other hand, BYB has a very high reputation among qualified consumers—those who most prefer or are favorable to the restaurant. This is an indication that BYB is satisfying consumers with its products and service.

Patronage

- Among restaurants that serve large hamburgers and grilled chicken sandwiches, Wendy's is the pacesetter.

Strengths

- BYB scores the strongest of all competitors on three of the top five consumer attributes. BYB is delivering what consumers want most!

that communicate the results of the study to the reader. As illustrated in Exhibit 19.4, conclusions take the form of descriptive statements generalizing the results, not necessarily the numbers generated by any statistical analysis. Each conclusion is made in direct reference to the research objectives.

Recommendations are generated by critical thinking. The task is one where the researcher must critically evaluate each conclusion and develop specific areas of applications for strategic or tactical actions. Recommendations must focus on how the client can solve the problem at hand through the creation of a competitive advantage.

Exhibit 19.5 outlines the recommendations that correspond to the conclusions displayed in Exhibit 19.4. You will notice that each recommendation, unlike the conclusions, is in the form of a clear action statement.

Limitations

Limitations Extraneous events that place certain restrictions on the report and are normally mentioned when communicating results.

While all attempts are made to develop and implement a flawless study for the client, certain extraneous events are always present to place **limitations** on the project. All researchers must be aware of the limitations surrounding a project, and inform the client of such events. Common limitations associated with marketing research include sampling bias, financial limitations, time pressures, measurement error, and demand artifacts, to name a few.

Every study has limitations, and it is the responsibility of the researcher to make the client aware of them. The researcher must not be embarrassed by limitations but rather must admit openly that they exist. Treatment of limitations in the research report normally involves a discussion of results and accuracy. For example, researchers should inform the client about the generalizability of the results beyond the sample used in the study. Weaknesses of specific scales should be addressed, along with potential sources of nonsampling error. If limitations are not stated and later discovered by the client, mistrust and skepticism toward the entire report may result. Limitations rarely diminish the credibility of the

---

EXHIBIT 19.5	Illustration of Recommendations within a Marketing Research Report

Recommendations

Back Yard Burgers has a strong story to tell, but it must raise its voice in order to be heard.

As much as consumers may enjoy your products, they need reminding. Meals are an occasion, and very often an impulse.

Specifically:

1.
   a. Consider your major strengths on the top 20 attributes, where you have clear superiority.
   b. Recall your present positioning—``Fresh Gourmet Fast" and the symbolism of *Back Yard Burger.*
   c. Develop a marketing and advertising program based on your strengths—those qualities that make you unique.

2. Address your own brand of specials and promotions.

3. Conduct some focus group research on new signage concepts.

4. Consider menu display options that will dramatize the variety of your offerings.

5. Consider branding some of your menu items—the object is to raise awareness and differentiate your products.

6. Explore marketing options for increasing dinner or evening visits.

---

report but rather serve to improve the perceptions clients may hold toward the quality of the document.

Appendixes

Appendix A section following the main body of the report; used to house complex, detailed, or technical information.

An **appendix,** many times referred to as a "technical appendix," is developed to house complex, detailed, or technical information not necessary for the formal report. Common items contained in appendixes include questionnaires, interviewer forms, statistical calculations, detailed sampling maps, and even highly detailed tables such as the one in Exhibit 19.6. A researcher must recognize that the appendix is rarely read in the same context as the report itself. In fact, most appendixes are treated as points of reference in the report. That is to say that information in the appendix may be cited in the report to guide the reader to further technical or statistical detail.

Common Problems Encountered When Preparing the Marketing Research Report

Many times we get so involved with the mere writing of a research report that we fail to keep in mind key issues that later may present themselves as problems. Such simple things as language may even go overlooked in some cases. Industry best practices suggest to always keep in mind five problem areas that may arise when writing a marketing research report:

1. **Lack of data interpretation.** In some instances, we get so involved in constructing tables of results that we fail to provide proper interpretation of the data within the tables. It is always the responsibility of the researcher to provide unbiased interpretations of any findings.

EXHIBIT 19.6   **Example of Detailed Results Table Suitable for Appendix Section**

SUMMARY TABLE

		Total Motivational Profile	Image Profiles				
			Back Yard Burgers	Wendy's	Rally's	Burger King	McDonald's
1	Unique menu items	132	169+	184+	55–	114	82–
2	Variety of food	131	92–	201+	18–	104	109
3	Large hamburger	130	225+	142	103	189+	43–
4.5	Method of cooking hamburgers	124	253+	110	85–	223+	31–
4.5	Good-tasting food	124	222+	155+	109	143	33–
6	Specials and promotions	121	31–	139	91–	92	166+
7	Speed of service	118	114	110	236+	75–	126
8	Prepares food to customer's special request	113	139	149+	103	153+	36–
9	Each order prepared fresh	112	179+	170+	139	82	23–
10	Quality of ingredients	110	206+	150+	97	102	27–
11	Consistent quality every visit	106	132	143+	103	85	63–
12	Portion size	105	160+	139+	109	124	27–
13	Prices of food items	104	77	82	267+	95	110
14	Selection of types of french fries	103	256+	62–	200+	73	76
15	Attention-getting signs	102	43–	96	109	63–	157+
16	Food well prepared	99	176+	130	109	87	33–
17.5	Gets orders correct	94	154+	96	151+	85	54–
17.5	Food hot when served	94	145+	124	115	80	37–
19.5	Offers children's menu	90	25–	70	36–	63	173+
19.5	Convenient location	90	34–	91	115	65	123+
21.5	Uses extra lean ground beef	88	166+	99	67	78	49–
21.5	Fun place to go	88	65	76	30–	92	123+
23	Healthy food	87	114	144+	36–	63	34–
24	Cleanliness	82	65	108	48–	51	84
25	Friendly employees	77	92	90	127+	48	62
26	Selection of desserts	72	95	58	6–	46	109+
27	Easy to understand menu	65	80	53	170+	53	54
28	Drink prices	62	34	58	170+	58	56
29	Employees can answer questions and solve problems	61	89	68	61	44	52
	Average image profile		126	115	110	91	74

+ = Major strength; – = Major weakness

A CLOSER LOOK AT RESEARCH | **In the Field**

What is marketing research? It's certainly not a profession and it's certainly not academia. Apart from focus groups, marketing research consists mainly of sampling consumers, asking questions, adding up the answers, and supplying the results to clients. And the main change to date resulting from the convergence of computers and telephones is the speed of getting answers. The slowest change has been in the presentation of results, and it is there that change is most needed. Speed of data collection has leapt ahead; but often the results are printed out on paper in too much detail and clients are bombarded with information.

Progress in results presentation is essential. Nowadays most clients have PCs on their desks. The voice of the consumer should be made available to them in an interactive format that allows for immediate action.

This is some way away from conventional table analysis. It means quickly identifying what matters in the data, comparing it with past data for changes, and giving the client what is needed. In this way data can be used to make swift decisions and match the almost daily changes in the marketplace. To provide useful research, suppliers must know their clients' business. They can no longer be providers of tables only, but of data specifically tailored to the needs of their clients.

The future will see more specialization by research companies: data collection and data presentation will separate. There will be research companies collecting data, and research companies using the data to inform clients. And most of the new developments will be in the area of presenting data in a form that clients can use interactively. That's a long way from the old-style presentation of data in large bound volumes of tables.

2. **Unnecessary use of multivariate statistics.** In order to impress the client, many researchers will unnecessarily subject data to sophisticated multivariate statistical techniques. In 75 percent of all research reports, the most sophisticated statistical technique required will be a chi-square test. Try to avoid using statistical methods unless they are essential in deriving meaning from the data.

3. **Emphasis on packaging instead of quality.** With the abundance of computer software packages available today, many researchers go out of their way to make the report look classy or flamboyant with sophisticated computer-generated graphics. While graphic representation of the results is essential in the report, never lose sight of the primary purpose—to provide valid and credible information to the client.

4. **Lack of relevance.** Reporting data, statistics, and information that are not consistent with the study's objectives is a major problem with writing the report. Always develop the report with the research objectives clearly in focus. Avoid adding unnecessary information just to make the report bigger. Always remain in the realm of practicality; suggest ideas that are relevant, doable, and consistent with the results of the study. A further discussion of relevance appears in the In the Field box.

5. **Placing too much emphasis on a few statistics.** Never base all conclusions or recommendations on one or a few statistically significant questions or results. Always attempt to find various supporting evidence for any recommendation or conclusion.

Always remember, the final research document is the end product of the researcher. Individual credibility can be enhanced or damaged by the report, and credibility is what helps a researcher gain repeat business and referrals from clients. The quality, dedication, and honesty one places into the report have the potential to generate future business, promotions, and salary raises.

The Critical Nature of Presentations

The *presentation* of marketing research results can be as important, if not more so, than the results of the research itself. This is true for several reasons. First, any research, no matter how well done or how important, cannot be properly acted upon if the results are not effectively communicated to those who are seeking to use the information in making decisions. Managers need accurate information if they are going to make good decisions, and if they do not understand the marketing research findings, they may well make poor decisions that lead to difficulty and hardship not only for the organization but also for those individuals in the organizations that are affected by those decisions. Second, the report or presentation is often the only part of the marketing research project that will be seen by those commissioning the report. Senior managers often do not have the time to review all aspects of a research project, so they rely on the researcher to carry out the research properly and then present the findings clearly and concisely. Third, the content and the presentation form of the research are closely intertwined. Poorly organized presentations presented in an unclear, lengthy, difficult-to-access format often lead audiences to discount the content. Presentations that use high-technology applications and methods are often perceived as having more merit than presentations that use older, low-tech methods. Thus, the method of presentation can influence the perception of the value or merit of the information presented.

Presenting Marketing Research Results

Traditional presentation methods include chalkboards, whiteboards (dry-erase boards), and overhead projectors with handmade transparencies. These tried-and-true methods may be preferable in situations where simple concepts and ideas are to be communicated to relatively small audiences. More frequently, however, they are being seen as being too limited for communicating more complex ideas. The desire to create cleaner, more professional-looking presentations of marketing research results has led to the development of a wide variety of computer-based presentation applications, from computer-generated overhead transparencies to full-blown multimedia presentations, complete with text, graphics, sound, and video or animation.

These marketing researchers prepare to make a presentation using video conferencing.

Using Computer Software for Developing Presentations

Currently, there are many different computer presentation software packages, and more are being introduced every day. Recognizing that there is no way to discuss all of the various options, we shall focus on two major formats useful in presenting market research findings: computer screen projection and World Wide Web pages. Projecting the computer screen has several advantages. Researchers often find it easy to develop the presentation on a computer and import information from the research project computer files as needed. The computer helps the researcher stay organized during presentations, with little chance of lost or out-of-order transparencies. It also allows for greater use of color and other graphics, giving presenters flexibility in developing the look of their presentations. It also allows presenters to reduce costs, since they no longer need to pay for costly color transparencies.

PowerPoint A software package used to develop slides for electronic presentation of research results.

One of the most widely used presentation software packages is Microsoft's **PowerPoint.** PowerPoint can be used to develop transparencies, 35-mm slides, and on-screen electronic presentations; it can also be used to develop notes, audience handouts, and outlines, all from the same information. Thus, the presenter has to type or import information only once to develop the research presentation. Presentation software such as PowerPoint can be used to develop eye-catching, organized presentations that convey research findings clearly, concisely, and smoothly. A detailed discussion on developing a PowerPoint presentation is given in the appendix to this chapter.

Hypertext markup language (HTML) Computer language used to create Web pages for communicating results on the Internet.

Another emerging format for presentations is the use of **hypertext markup language (HTML)** to create Web pages. This is the format for communications over the World Wide Web. By using the Web, researchers are able to communicate market information to their audiences around the world, without the restrictions of time or geography. No longer do all members of the audience need to be in the same location at a given time to receive information during a presentation. Marketing research results can be posted on Web pages and viewed at leisure. Furthermore, not only the presentation itself but also the supporting materials—including text, sound, graphics, and animation or movie files—can be available for viewers to download and inspect, and articles on similar topics can be linked together for easy reference. Also, developing technology is leading to the possibility of real-time video conferencing, where participants at different geographical locations take part in meetings, seeing and hearing each other through their computers over the World Wide Web.

In developing Web page–based presentations, researchers have several options. They can put their information on a World Wide Web server (a computer permanently linked to the World Wide Web, designated for maintaining Web pages and other Internet-accessible files) for the world to view, and let those interested in the information know where to access it so they can receive the information independently, at their convenience. Or, if the researcher wishes to present the information at a given time and location, he or she can either place the information on a World Wide Web server or on his or her own computer, and then personally lead the presentation of the information to the audience, adding input and guiding the presentation along. In this section, we will focus on the creation and development of Web page–based presentations that will be placed on a server for geographically dispersed audiences to view independently, but keep in mind that the presenter can just as easily use this format in actual presentations of research outcomes to a local audience. The flexibility and power of the Web page–based presentation makes it an attractive format for use where time or distance is a problem in disseminating information.

Claris Home Page Software used to create Web pages that can integrate text and graphics with other types of computer files.

Again, there are many different software packages for developing Web pages. One easy-to-use software package is **Claris Home Page,** which is used to create Web pages and can integrate text, graphics, and other types of computer files. While there are several different software packages available for Web page development, they are similar enough in operation that an understanding of Claris Home Page should provide a sound foundation for using any of the other packages.

Advantages and Disadvantages of Computer Formats

Computer screen projection and Web page presentation formats each have their own advantages and disadvantages. Both formats allow presenters to easily import text outlines into the presentation software. Both formats also allow the integration of text and graphics to create eye-catching presentations, and the use of coloring, background shading, and textures to highlight certain topics or major points. However, both formats also require at least the use of computers and their basic power requirements—it would be difficult to give a computer-based presentation to a group of farmers in a Kansas wheatfield, without a nearby source of electricity. Both formats also require the presenter, or both the presenter and the audience, to have some basic level of computer competence.

The use of software such as Microsoft PowerPoint in computer screen projection allows presenters to have control over their presentation, in terms of timing, highlighting key points, and making transitions between topics. A disadvantage, however, is that it requires the audience to be physically present at a given location at a given time. Also, the amount of information presented is usually limited to the main points, with supporting documentation usually distributed in printed form, requiring added printing expense. Finally, animations and other high-tech graphics are not easily integrated into this presentation format.

Web page–based presentations of marketing research have the primary advantage of not requiring the audience to be physically present at any given time or location. Members of the audience can access the information at any time, from many different locations. (One example of this is a student at the University of Memphis who accessed his marketing class's Web page and downloaded the reading materials while traveling from Nashville to Memphis, using a laptop computer, a modem, and his cellular phone.) Further, additional information with supporting documentation, graphics, animation, or sounds can be readily available through the computer if requested. Also, similar information on other Web pages can be linked so that the audience can easily and quickly access a wealth of relevant information. Finally, the World Wide Web itself can be used by the audience to conduct further investigations. Computer searches can be conducted to find out what other information is available, or possibly where it may be found. Using the World Wide Web has its drawbacks, however. The main drawback is that the presenter loses some control over the presentation, so the information must be presented in a more self-explanatory fashion. This requires presenters to spend more time in developing their presentations, with greater organization and an eye toward heading off possible misunderstandings. Another consideration is that the speed at which files are transmitted over the Internet can be a problem, particularly if large graphics files must be transmitted. Finally, creating Web page–based presentations requires presenters to have the relevant computer skills, since, for example, graphics files must often be converted and saved in particular file formats for use in Web pages.

SUMMARY OF LEARNING OBJECTIVES

Understand the primary objectives of a research report.

The key objective of a marketing research report is to provide the client with a clear, concise interpretation of the research project. The research report is a culmination of the entire study and therefore must communicate the systematic manner in which the study was designed and implemented. Secondary objectives of the report are to provide accurate, credible, easy-to-understand information to the client. The end result of the report is its ability to act as a reference document to guide future research and serve as an information source.

Explain how a marketing research report is organized.

The research report generally includes the following: a title page; a table of contents; and an executive summary, which includes a statement of the research objectives, a detailed statement of the research method and procedures, a brief statement of findings, and conclusions and recommendations. Following the executive summary is the introduction of the report, a description of the methodology employed, and a discussion of data analysis techniques and findings. The final elements are a conclusion, a set of recommendations, and a description of limitations. An appendix may include technical explanations or illustrations.

List problems that one may encounter when preparing the report.

Problem areas that may arise in the preparation of the research report are (1) lack of data interpretation, (2) unnecessary use of multivariate statistics, (3) emphasis on packaging rather than quality, (4) lack of relevance, and (5) placing too much emphasis on a few statistical outcomes.

Understand the importance of presentations in marketing research.

Presentations are important because research results must be effectively communicated to those who are seeking to use the information in making decisions. The report or presentation may be the only part of the research project that will be seen by those commissioning the report. The content of the research and the presentation form of the research are closely intertwined.

Identify different software options available for developing presentations.

Computers can be used to create overhead transparencies, on-screen presentations based on slides or Web pages, and actual Web pages. The two major formats for presenting information are (1) computer screen projection, in which computer slides are projected to a live audience, and (2) Web page–based presentation to a live audience or to a general Internet audience.

Understand the advantages and disadvantages of different software options available for developing presentations.

Computer screen projection requires the audience to be physically present at a given time and location but allows the presenter to control the presentation, receive immediate feedback from the audience, and answer any questions. Web pages allow audiences to access the information anytime from anywhere they have computer access.

KEY TERMS AND CONCEPTS

Appendix 621	**Credibility** 615	**Limitations** 620
Believability 615	**Executive summary** 616	**PowerPoint** 625
Claris Home Page 625	**Hypertext markup language (HTML)** 625	

REVIEW QUESTIONS

1. What are the four primary objectives of the marketing research report? Briefly discuss each objective and why they are so important.

2. In the context of the marketing research report, what is the primary goal of the executive summary?

3. What is the primary purpose of the research method and procedures section of a marketing research report?

4. Why are conclusions and recommendations included in a marketing research report?

5. What are the five common problems associated with the marketing research report?

6. Why is Microsoft PowerPoint such a valuable tool for preparing marketing research presentations?

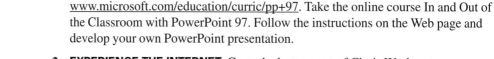

DISCUSSION QUESTIONS

1. **EXPERIENCE THE INTERNET.** Go to the home page of Microsoft PowerPoint, at www.microsoft.com/education/curric/pp+97. Take the online course In and Out of the Classroom with PowerPoint 97. Follow the instructions on the Web page and develop your own PowerPoint presentation.

2. **EXPERIENCE THE INTERNET.** Go to the home page of Claris Works, at www.claris.com/smallbiz. Explore the availability of product offerings and experience how Claris Works operates.

3. Using the information in the appendix to this chapter, develop a PowerPoint presentation on a topic of your choice.

4. How can a World Wide Web page be used for communication of marketing research results?

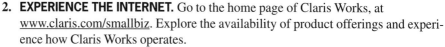

APPENDIX: USING MICROSOFT POWERPOINT 7.0

Getting Started

Microsoft PowerPoint 7.0 has some built-in features called *wizards* that greatly simplify presentation development, but in this appendix we will walk through the development process without relying on the wizards in an effort to better explain what to do. Also, previous versions of PowerPoint may not have these wizards. Another thing to keep in mind is that in PowerPoint each page is referred to as a slide, whether it is to be printed out as an actual slide or not. Finally, there are often several different methods you can use to perform any given task on a computer. Feel free to experiment, using the Help files, until you find the methods you prefer.

Step 1: Saving the Outline

In your word processing software package, save your complete presentation outline in what is called rich text format (RTF). This allows the outline structure to be preserved for the importing process. Other word processing software will be slightly different, but the basics are the same.

Step 2: Opening the Outline in PowerPoint

With PowerPoint up and running, go up to the File menu and select Open. This will bring up a dialog box from which you can select the RTF file Outline.RTF that you just saved. You may need to change the file type at the bottom of the dialog box so that PowerPoint will show All readable outlines.

Step 3: Different Views in PowerPoint

You will see your outline open up within PowerPoint. At this point, you may want to save the file as a PowerPoint presentation file. You may call it Outline.PWP, meaning Outline in PowerPoint format.

Step 4: Editing in PowerPoint

Now would be a good time to edit your presentation outline, checking your spacing, alignment, and so on. Editing is done in much the same way as in a word processor—you select the text you want to edit and either cut-and-paste, delete, or make other changes. You can add information to individual slides, delete information, or make other changes as you see fit. You may need to switch to single slide view to make some editing changes. Note that these changes affect only that one slide. To make editing changes that will affect all of your slides, you need to view the Slide Master.

Step 5: Changing the Slide Master

Go up to the menu bar, and under the View menu, you will select the option View/ Master/Slide Master. This will bring up your Slide Master, which is the basic template determining the way all of your slides look. To make changes, simply select text and change the alignment, the spacing, the location on the page, and so on. When you are satisfied with the way your slides look, exit the Slide Master by simply clicking on one of the View buttons at the bottom left corner of the window.

Step 6: Additional Slides

There are several ways to add slides to your presentation. You can click on the New Slide button at the lower right of your screen, you can position the cursor at the end of an existing slide (while in Outline View) and press the Return key, or you can click on the New Slide button at the top center of your screen.

Step 7: Adding the Content of the Additional Slide

Once you have added a new slide, in Outline View you can simply type in the heading of the slide. Press Return, and you have added another slide to your presentation. Select the slide below the one you are working on, and click on the Demote arrows at the left of your screen, and the last slide created will change into the body of the slide you are working on. The Demote and Promote arrows are used to keep elements of your outline organized, with each major topic of your outline having a slide. Of course, you may want to have several slides covering one major topic. Simply copy-and-paste the slide heading onto each slide, and use the Demote and Promote keys to keep everything organized according to your original outline.

Step 8: Adding Charts or Graphs

You may well want to add a chart or other illustration to your presentation. To demonstrate, we will add a pie chart illustrating the various faculty ranks represented in a hypothetical sample of respondents. In our study, we surveyed 148 faculty, 58 of whom were assistant professors, with 24 associate professors and 66 full professors. This information we have entered into a new slide in the middle of our presentation. To create a graph within Power-Point, begin in the Slide View mode, click the Insert Chart button at the top of your screen, and then enter your data in the window that appears. When you have entered the data, click outside the graph, and you will see your graph inserted into your slide. You can move it around, resize it, or make other changes to it.

Step 9: Picking a Template for a Consistent Look

To give your presentation slides a more colorful look, go up to the Main Menu bar, and select the Pick a Look Wizard from the Format menu. This helper will lead you through the steps necessary for adding one of several predrawn background templates to your slides.

Step 10: Adding Clip Art

To add a small picture (often called clip art, because you can clip-and-paste these pictures into files) to your presentations, simply open up the clip-art file in whatever software package is available, select the clip art you want, and copy it to the computer's clipboard. Switch back into PowerPoint, go to the slide where you want the clip art to be, and paste it into the slide. You can then move and resize the clip art to suit your needs.

Once you have your slides organized and looking just right, it is time to prepare your presentation of the slides. Click on the small button at the bottom of the window that has four small slides on it; this takes you to the Slide Sorter View. Once in Slide Sorter View, you will see miniatures of all of your slides, in the order that they will be presented. (Note: If you wish to re-order your slides, this is the easiest place to do it.) In the next step, we will demonstrate how to change the manner in which PowerPoint transitions from one slide to another. When you click on the Slide Show dialog button beside the other view buttons at the bottom of the window, you will view your presentation, one slide at a time. PowerPoint is set up so that clicking the mouse button (even though you cannot see the cursor) advances from slide to slide. The default transition from slide to slide is to simply change slides quickly. You can change this, and have PowerPoint roll slides off one side of the screen as the next slide rolls onto the screen or perhaps have it "checkerboard" from slide to slide. This is done using the Transitions menu. Further, you can direct PowerPoint to build your slides on the screen, one item per mouse click. This feature is similar to the Transition function, but it affects each item on a slide, whereas the Transition function affects the change from slide to slide.

Step 11: Selecting Transition and Build Modes

Transition and Build are both done in the same manner. The easiest way is to select all of the slides, using the Command+A keys if using an Apple computer, and the Control+A keys if using a DOS-based machine. (Or use the Edit menu to Select All.) Once you have selected all of your slides, click on the Transitions pop-up menu at the top of the window, and scroll down to select the effect of your choice. Build effects are changed in the same way. Experiment and see which effects give your presentation the most visual impact. If you wish one slide to have a different Transition or Build effect, simply select only that slide, and then modify it accordingly.

You have now created a presentation, beginning with just the outline you had from your research report. To present your information, you can either print out your slides or transparencies and use the traditional overhead projector, or you can use a Computer Screen Projection device to show your presentation to your audience. Note that Power-Point has many more features than we discussed here. You can use PowerPoint to time your presentations as you practice them, so that you know how long you spend on each topic. You can configure PowerPoint to automatically change from slide to slide, so that you do not have to be near the computer to click the mouse and transition from slide to slide. There are many other features and benefits of PowerPoint, and other presentation software packages; do not be hesitant to try them out in your efforts to develop more effective presentations.

The illustration contained in the next section uses a focus group report to illustrate many of the concepts addressed in this chapter.

Introduction

This focus group report is prepared for the area known as the Jackson community, located in the north central section of Memphis, Tennessee. The focus of this report is to communicate findings that were revealed in a focus group interview performed on July 18, 1998. Elements of discussion centered on the trends and market dynamics of the business environment within the Jackson community.

Research Purpose

Issues pertaining to the business climate of the Jackson community will be explored. The purpose of this study is twofold. First, to explore the business trends, market dynamics, and growth potential of the Jackson community for the purpose of providing insights into future business development in the area. Second, to obtain data on market characteristics to be used in a subsequent survey method for determining residents' buying power and spending habits within the community. In order to address these issues, the following research objectives were developed.

Research Objectives

In order to obtain usable and reliable data pertaining to future business development in the Jackson area, the following research objectives were set forth:

1. To determine the current level of saturation and oversaturation of business activities in the Jackson community.

2. To assess opportunities for new and emerging businesses regarding trends and potential of the Jackson market.

3. To discover potential barriers to entry and growth in such areas as capital, markets, banking, and suppliers.

4. To explore related business issues such as racial variables, supplier/vendor relations, receivables, financial variables, leasing, and location, along with selling strategies.

5. To assess positive city-delivered services to the Jackson community.

6. To explore business and neighborhood relations.

7. To discuss what can be done to improve the Jackson community business environment.

8. To learn how businesses in the Jackson community market themselves.

9. To address the future of the economy and business climate regarding customer segments, spending behavior, and consumer decision making.

Sample Characteristics

Based on a random sample of the university business community, eight business owners/managers were used in the focus group procedure:

Mr. Harry Grayden	Johnson Supply
Mr. Warren Bowling	Plastic Fabrication
Ms. Emma Roberson	Temporary Employment
Ms. Anna Hogan	Sheet Metal Services, Inc.
Mr. Tom Brockway	Target Medical, Inc.
Mr. Sam Jorce	Retail Glass Co.
Mr. Andy Hammond	Retail Auto Parts
Mr. Hilliard Johnson	Carpet Cleaning

Research Findings

To best illustrate the findings of this focus group interview, results will be categorized in narrative form as they pertain to each research objective, following a general overview of the Jackson community.

General Overview of the Jackson Community

MAJOR POSITIVE ASPECTS. Jackson community is a very centralized location, with easy access to all areas of the city and surrounding communities. Good area to conduct manufacturing or wholesaling businesses. Very stable, yet very dependent on the economy—first area to lose jobs when the economy softens. Major competitive advantage is the central location.

MAJOR NEGATIVE ASPECTS. Major problems in the area are drugs and prostitution centering around two motels located off of Summer Ave., and the Paris adult bookstore. Crime is very high—**all participants in the study were victims of break-ins during the past two years.** In addition, the uncertainty of the Sam Cooper Expressway extension has created a lot of anxiety among businesses.

1. Saturation and Oversaturation of Business Activities

Not unlike other areas of the city, the Jackson community is oversaturated in low-entry-barrier businesses. These include:

Pawn shops	Title companies
Used-car lots	Small, home-based businesses
Credit agencies	Medium-sized distribution businesses

A major concern of the participants was the increased appearance of small mom-and-pop-type businesses. The Jackson area offers very low rental space that makes it attractive for many small, novice businesses to operate with a severe level of undercapitalization. The Broad/Tillman area is an example of undercapitalized businesses that fail in the first year, leading to distressed commercial property.

2. Opportunity Assessment and Market Trends

Growth in the Jackson area is very uncertain, given the extension of Sam Cooper Expressway. High level of business turnover leads to both distressed commercial and residential property.

Several participants labeled the area as a good "incubation" area for small businesses, given its central location and low rent for commercial property.

BUSINESS TRENDS AND MARKET POTENTIAL. The Jackson community has an excellent opportunity for growth due to the high level of business turnover and low cost of rental property. Certain businesses can take advantage of a low barrier to entry but need to understand how to operate a business successfully without intensifying the level of saturation.

Businesses that were identified by the participants include:

Hardware stores	Large manufacturing plants
Grocery stores	Warehousing and logistical businesses
Movie theaters	Fast-food restaurants
Entertainment businesses	Discount stores

All participants were in agreement that the Jackson area is a great magnet area due to the high level of employment that brings working people into the area.

3. Potential Barriers to Entry and Growth

Area is good for business growth if certain conditions exist. A very neglected area that needs to be cleaned up, especially distressed property resulting from evicted tenants; there appears to be no code enforcement in the area. Prostitution and drugs are keeping many businesses out.

4. Related Business Issues

- **Racial variables.** No real racial barriers or biases; no real minority problems regarding day-to-day business activities.

- **Supplier/vendor relations.** No problems with supplier because of the high volume of warehousing, distribution, and manufacturing in the community.

- **Controlling receivables.** Heavy inflow of dollars into the community from all parts of the statistical metropolitan area. Most accounts are large, high volume. Receivables are normally paid within 30 days; usual business cycles.

- **Financial variables.** Most financial institutions have moved out of the area due to crime. The level of financial support is still good in the community, but more so for service businesses and not as supportive for retail.

- **Leasing and location.** Low rent, convenient access, and central location are the major positives of the area. Yet many facilities are in the process of relocating because large spaces are not available in the area. Office space is high priced relative to other areas, retail space is normal, and warehousing and distribution space is very cheap in the community.

- **Selling strategies.** The community is excellent for business-to-business activity; not so good, given current conditions, for retail trade. Appeal to drive up business, not a conducive area for pedestrian traffic. No real community support for retail business.

5. Positive Aspects of City Services

Businesses in the community are very disgruntled with city officials; aside from electric and water they feel that the community is ignored by the city. Especially a lack of concern from the department of public works. Lack of city services distracts from the community, making it unappealing for consumers to shop in the area. The city has done nothing to promote the area in general, and nothing to promote business growth. The infrastructure of the community is deteriorating; high level of break-ins in the community.

6. Business and Neighborhood Relationships

Community commitment is low among both residential and business entities. Community has no sense of identity. Low community support for retail businesses.

Heavy migration to East Memphis for shopping/specialty goods due to a lack of discount stores in the area and unpleasant shopping centers. The lack of adequate retailers is forcing people to other communities, specifically, east.

Curb appeal of many businesses is low; unsightful area needs to be cleaned up, with emphasis on the distressed property, both commercial and residential.

7. How to Improve the Business Environment in the Jackson Community

- Clean up distressed property from evicted housing; enforce city codes on property.

- Resolve the problems with the rail tracks.

- Provide some certainty as to the Sam Cooper Expressway extension.

- Add more foliage; make the streets look more attractive.

- Start enforcing housing codes for both residential and commercial property.

8. How Do Businesses Market Themselves?

- Focus on the business-to-business market, not on retail.

- Have good labor supply; provide security for the employees.

- Provide a safe, appealing, and convenient environment for your customers and employees.

- Train employees.

- Take advantage of any form of low-cost advertising and promotions.

- Provide quality service; don't promise what you can't deliver.

9. Future Direction of the Economy and Business Community in the Jackson Area

- It's a very static area—will probably go unchanged for the immediate future. Possibly a slow decline in the area due to many larger businesses relocating to other areas of the city.

- Perception of the area needs to change if businesses are to remain there.

- Major opportunity for the community is to position it as a warehousing/distribution park.

- Not a good area for retail—too many distressed neighborhoods, too many home-based businesses.

- Sam Cooper Expressway extension will determine the future of the community; need better leadership by the city to correct crime problems.

- Area is ideally suited for small manufacturing businesses or transportation businesses; not really conducive for retail—bad pedestrian traffic area.

- Provide the area with a focus of what it should be—industrial, residential, etc.; develop much of the vacant land with businesses that reinforce that focus.

MARKETING RESEARCH CASE EXERCISE

V-8, MAIDENFORM, AND AT&T

This Case Corresponds to the Video Case The Advertising Research Foundation: Goodbye Guesswork

After viewing the video *Goodbye Guesswork*, use one of the three examples presented—V-8, Maidenform, or AT&T—to develop and write a marketing research report. Pay careful attention to the video and note how the research process is implemented in each example. Then construct your report using the headings described in the section "Format of the Marketing Research Report" at the beginning of this chapter.

TABLE 1   Cumulative Standard Unit Normal Distribution

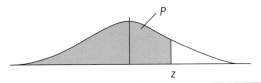

Values of P corresponding to Z for the normal curve. Z is the standard normal variable. The value of P for $-Z$ equals one minus the value of P for $+Z$, (e.g., the P for -1.62 equals $1 - .9474 = .0526$).

Z	.00	.01	.02	.03	.04	.05	.06	.07	.08	.09
.0	.5000	.5040	.5080	.5120	.5160	.5199	.5239	.5279	.5319	.5359
.1	.5398	.5438	.5478	.5517	.5557	.5596	.5636	.5675	.5714	.5753
.2	.5793	.5832	.5871	.5910	.5948	.5987	.6026	.6064	.6103	.6141
.3	.6179	.6217	.6255	.6293	.6331	.6368	.6406	.6443	.6480	.6517
.4	.6554	.6591	.6628	.6664	.6700	.6736	.6772	.6808	.6844	.6879
.5	.6915	.6950	.6985	.7019	.7054	.7088	.7123	.7157	.7190	.7224
.6	.7257	.7291	.7324	.7357	.7389	.7422	.7454	.7486	.7517	.7549
.7	.7580	.7611	.7642	.7673	.7704	.7734	.7764	.7794	.7823	.7852
.8	.7881	.7910	.7939	.7967	.7995	.8023	.8051	.8078	.8106	.8133
.9	.8159	.8186	.8212	.8238	.8264	.8289	.8315	.8340	.8365	.8389
1.0	.8413	.8438	.8461	.8485	.8508	.8531	.8554	.8577	.8599	.8621
1.1	.8643	.8665	.8686	.8708	.8729	.8749	.8770	.8790	.8810	.8830
1.2	.8849	.8869	.8888	.8907	.8925	.8944	.8962	.8980	.8997	.9015
1.3	.9032	.9049	.9066	.9082	.9099	.9115	.9131	.9147	.9162	.9177
1.4	.9192	.9207	.9222	.9236	.9251	.9265	.9279	.9292	.9306	.9319
1.5	.9332	.9345	.9357	.9370	.9382	.9394	.9406	.9418	.9429	.9441
1.6	.9452	.9463	.9474	.9484	.9495	.9505	.9515	.9525	.9535	.9545
1.7	.9554	.9564	.9573	.9582	.9591	.9599	.9608	.9616	.9625	.9633
1.8	.9641	.9649	.9656	.9664	.9671	.9678	.9686	.9693	.9699	.9706
1.9	.9713	.9719	.9726	.9732	.9738	.9744	.9750	.9756	.9761	.9767
2.0	.9772	.9778	.9783	.9788	.9793	.9798	.9803	.9808	.9812	.9817
2.1	.9821	.9826	.9830	.9834	.9838	.9842	.9846	.9850	.9854	.9857
2.2	.9861	.9864	.9868	.9871	.9875	.9878	.9881	.9884	.9887	.9890
2.3	.9893	.9896	.9898	.9901	.9904	.9906	.9909	.9911	.9913	.9916
2.4	.9918	.9920	.9922	.9925	.9927	.9929	.9931	.9932	.9934	.9936
2.5	.9938	.9940	.9941	.9943	.9945	.9946	.9948	.9949	.9951	.9952
2.6	.9953	.9955	.9956	.9957	.9959	.9960	.9961	.9962	.9963	.9964
2.7	.9965	.9966	.9967	.9968	.9969	.9970	.9971	.9972	.9973	.9974
2.8	.9974	.9975	.9976	.9977	.9977	.9978	.9979	.9979	.9980	.9981
2.9	.9981	.9982	.9982	.9983	.9984	.9984	.9985	.9985	.9986	.9986
3.0	.9987	.9987	.9987	.9988	.9988	.9989	.9989	.9989	.9990	.9990
3.1	.9990	.9991	.9991	.9991	.9992	.9992	.9992	.9992	.9993	.9993
3.2	.9993	.9993	.9994	.9994	.9994	.9994	.9994	.9995	.9995	.9995
3.3	.9995	.9995	.9995	.9996	.9996	.9996	.9996	.9996	.9996	.9997
3.4	.9997	.9997	.9997	.9997	.9997	.9997	.9997	.9997	.9997	.9998

Source: Paul E. Green, *Analyzing Multivariate Data* (Chicago: Dryden Press, 1978).

TABLE 2 — Selected Percentiles of the χ^2 Distribution

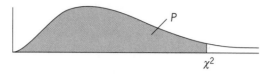

Values of χ^2 corresponding to P

v	$\chi^2_{.005}$	$\chi^2_{.01}$	$\chi^2_{.025}$	$\chi^2_{.05}$	$\chi^2_{.10}$	$\chi^2_{.90}$	$\chi^2_{.95}$	$\chi^2_{.975}$	$\chi^2_{.99}$	$\chi^2_{.995}$
1	.000039	.00016	.00098	.0039	.0158	2.71	3.84	5.02	6.63	7.88
2	.0100	.0201	.0506	.1026	.2107	4.61	5.99	7.38	9.21	10.60
3	.0717	.115	.216	.352	.584	6.25	7.81	9.35	11.34	12.84
4	.207	.297	.484	.711	1.064	7.78	9.49	11.14	13.28	14.86
5	.412	.554	.831	1.15	1.61	9.24	11.07	12.83	15.09	16.75
6	.676	.872	1.24	1.64	2.20	10.64	12.59	14.45	16.81	18.55
7	.989	1.24	1.69	2.17	2.83	12.02	14.07	16.01	18.48	20.28
8	1.34	1.65	2.18	2.73	3.49	13.36	15.51	17.53	20.09	21.96
9	1.73	2.09	2.70	3.33	4.17	14.68	16.92	19.02	21.67	23.59
10	2.16	2.56	3.25	3.94	4.87	15.99	18.31	20.48	23.21	25.19
11	2.60	3.05	3.82	4.57	5.58	17.28	19.68	21.92	24.73	26.76
12	3.07	3.57	4.40	5.23	6.30	18.55	21.03	23.34	26.22	28.30
13	3.57	4.11	5.01	5.89	7.04	19.81	22.36	24.74	27.69	29.82
14	4.07	4.66	5.63	6.57	7.79	21.06	23.68	26.12	29.14	31.32
15	4.60	5.23	6.26	7.26	8.55	22.31	25.00	27.49	30.58	32.80
16	5.14	5.81	6.91	7.96	9.31	23.54	26.30	28.85	32.00	34.27
18	6.26	7.01	8.23	9.39	10.86	25.99	28.87	31.53	34.81	37.16
20	7.43	8.26	9.59	10.85	12.44	28.41	31.41	34.17	37.57	40.00
24	9.89	10.86	12.40	13.85	15.66	33.20	36.42	39.36	42.98	45.56
30	13.79	14.95	16.79	18.49	20.60	40.26	43.77	46.98	50.89	53.67
40	20.71	22.16	24.43	26.51	29.05	51.81	55.76	59.34	63.69	66.77
60	35.53	37.48	40.48	43.19	46.46	74.40	79.08	83.30	88.38	91.95
120	83.85	86.92	91.58	95.70	100.62	140.23	146.57	152.21	158.95	163.64

Source: Adapted with permission from *Introduction to Statistical Analysis* (2nd ed.) by W. J. Dixon and F. J. Massey, Jr., © 1957 McGraw-Hill.

| TABLE 3 | | Upper Percentiles of the *t* Distribution | | | | | |

v \ $1-\alpha$	.75	.90	.95	.975	.99	.995	.9995
1	1.000	3.078	6.314	12.706	31.821	63.657	636.619
2	.816	1.886	2.920	4.303	6.965	9.925	31.598
3	.765	1.638	2.353	3.182	4.541	5.841	12.941
4	.741	1.533	2.132	2.776	3.747	4.604	8.610
5	.727	1.476	2.015	2.571	3.365	4.032	6.859
6	.718	1.440	1.943	2.447	3.143	3.707	5.959
7	.711	1.415	1.895	2.365	2.998	3.499	5.405
8	.706	1.397	1.860	2.306	2.896	3.355	5.041
9	.703	1.383	1.833	2.262	2.821	3.250	4.781
10	.700	1.372	1.812	2.228	2.764	3.169	4.587
11	.697	1.363	1.796	2.201	2.718	3.106	4.437
12	.695	1.356	1.782	2.179	2.681	3.055	4.318
13	.694	1.350	1.771	2.160	2.650	3.012	4.221
14	.692	1.345	1.761	2.145	2.624	2.977	4.140
15	.691	1.341	1.753	2.131	2.602	2.947	4.073
16	.690	1.337	1.746	2.120	2.583	2.921	4.015
17	.689	1.333	1.740	2.110	2.567	2.898	3.965
18	.688	1.330	1.734	2.101	2.552	2.878	3.922
19	.688	1.328	1.729	2.093	2.339	2.861	3.883
20	.687	1.325	1.725	2.086	2.528	2.845	3.850
21	.686	1.323	1.721	2.080	2.518	2.831	3.819
22	.686	1.321	1.717	2.074	2.508	2.819	3.792
23	.685	1.319	1.714	2.069	2.500	2.807	3.767
24	.685	1.318	1.711	2.064	2.492	2.797	3.745
25	.684	1.316	1.708	2.060	2.485	2.787	3.725
26	.684	1.315	1.706	2.056	2.479	2.779	3.707
27	.684	1.314	1.703	2.052	2.473	2.771	3.690
28	.683	1.313	1.701	2.048	2.467	2.763	3.674
29	.683	1.311	1.699	2.045	2.462	2.756	3.659
30	.683	1.310	1.697	2.042	2.457	2.750	3.646
40	.681	1.303	1.684	2.021	2.423	2.704	3.551
60	.679	1.296	1.671	2.000	2.390	2.660	3.460
120	.677	1.289	1.658	1.980	2.358	2.617	3.373
∞	.674	1.282	1.645	1.960	2.326	2.576	3.291

v = degrees of freedom

Source: Taken from Table III of R. A. Fisher and F. Yates: *Statistical Tables for Biological, Agricultural, and Medical Research*, published by Longman Group UK Ltd., London (previously published by Oliver & Boyd Ltd., Edinburgh, 1963), and used by permission of the authors and publishers.

TABLE 4 Selected Percentiles of the *F* Distribution

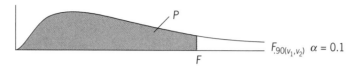

$F_{.90(v_1, v_2)}$ $\alpha = 0.1$

v_1 = degrees of freedom for numerator

v_2 \ v_1	1	2	3	4	5	6	7	8	9	10
1	39.86	49.50	53.59	55.83	57.24	58.20	58.91	59.44	59.86	60.19
2	8.53	9.00	9.16	9.24	9.29	9.33	9.35	9.37	9.38	9.39
3	5.54	5.46	5.39	5.34	5.31	5.28	5.27	5.25	5.24	5.23
4	4.54	4.32	4.19	4.11	4.05	4.01	3.98	3.95	3.94	3.92
5	4.06	3.78	3.62	3.52	3.45	3.40	3.37	3.34	3.32	3.30
6	3.78	3.46	3.29	3.18	3.11	3.05	3.01	2.98	2.96	2.94
7	3.59	3.26	3.07	2.96	2.88	2.83	2.78	2.75	2.72	2.70
8	3.46	3.11	2.92	2.81	2.73	2.67	2.62	2.59	2.56	2.50
9	3.36	3.01	2.81	2.69	2.61	2.55	2.51	2.47	2.44	2.42
10	3.29	2.92	2.73	2.61	2.52	2.46	2.41	2.38	2.35	2.32
11	3.23	2.86	2.66	2.54	2.45	2.39	2.34	2.30	2.27	2.25
12	3.18	2.81	2.61	2.48	2.39	2.33	2.28	2.24	2.21	2.19
13	3.14	2.76	2.56	2.43	2.35	2.28	2.23	2.20	2.16	2.14
14	3.10	2.73	2.52	2.39	2.31	2.24	2.19	2.15	2.12	2.10
15	3.07	2.70	2.49	2.36	2.27	2.21	2.16	2.12	2.09	2.06
16	3.05	2.67	2.46	2.33	2.24	2.18	2.13	2.09	2.06	2.03
17	3.03	2.64	2.44	2.31	2.22	2.15	2.10	2.06	2.03	2.00
18	3.01	2.62	2.42	2.29	2.20	2.13	2.08	2.04	2.00	1.98
19	2.99	2.61	2.40	2.27	2.18	2.11	2.06	2.02	1.98	1.96
20	2.97	2.59	2.38	2.25	2.16	2.09	2.04	2.00	1.96	1.94
21	2.96	2.57	2.36	2.23	2.14	2.08	2.02	1.98	1.95	1.92
22	2.95	2.56	2.35	2.22	2.13	2.06	2.01	1.97	1.93	1.90
23	2.94	2.55	2.34	2.21	2.11	2.05	1.99	1.95	1.92	1.89
24	2.93	2.54	2.33	2.19	2.10	2.04	1.98	1.94	1.91	1.88
25	2.92	2.53	2.32	2.18	2.09	2.02	1.97	1.93	1.89	1.87
26	2.91	2.52	2.31	2.17	2.08	2.01	1.96	1.92	1.88	1.86
27	2.90	2.51	2.30	2.17	2.07	2.00	1.95	1.91	1.87	1.85
28	2.89	2.50	2.29	2.16	2.06	2.00	1.94	1.90	1.87	1.84
29	2.89	2.50	2.28	2.15	2.06	1.99	1.93	1.89	1.86	1.83
30	2.88	2.49	2.28	2.14	2.05	1.98	1.93	1.88	1.85	1.82
40	2.84	2.44	2.23	2.09	2.00	1.93	1.87	1.83	1.79	1.76
60	2.79	2.39	2.18	2.04	1.95	1.87	1.82	1.77	1.74	1.71
120	2.75	2.35	2.13	1.99	1.90	1.82	1.77	1.72	1.68	1.65
∞	2.71	2.30	2.08	1.94	1.85	1.77	1.72	1.67	1.63	1.60

v_2 = degrees of freedom for denominator

Source: Adapted with permission from *Biometrika Tables for Statisticians*, Vol. 1 (2nd ed.), edited by E. S. Pearson and H. O. Hartley, Cambridge University Press, 1958.

12	15	20	24	30	40	60	120	∞
60.71	61.22	61.74	62.00	62.26	62.53	62.79	63.06	63.33
9.41	9.42	9.44	9.45	9.46	9.47	9.47	9.48	9.49
5.22	5.20	5.18	5.18	5.17	5.16	5.15	5.14	5.13
3.90	3.87	3.84	3.83	3.82	3.80	3.79	3.78	3.76
3.27	3.24	3.21	3.19	3.17	3.16	3.14	3.12	3.10
2.90	2.87	2.84	2.82	2.80	2.78	2.76	2.74	2.72
2.67	2.63	2.59	2.58	2.56	2.54	2.51	2.49	2.47
2.50	2.46	2.42	2.40	2.38	2.36	2.34	2.32	2.29
2.38	2.34	2.30	2.28	2.25	2.23	2.21	2.18	2.16
2.28	2.24	2.20	2.18	2.16	2.13	2.11	2.08	2.06
2.21	2.17	2.12	2.10	2.08	2.05	2.03	2.00	1.97
2.15	2.10	2.06	2.04	2.01	1.99	1.96	1.93	1.90
2.10	2.05	2.01	1.98	1.96	1.93	1.90	1.88	1.85
2.05	2.01	1.96	1.94	1.91	1.89	1.86	1.83	1.80
2.02	1.97	1.92	1.90	1.87	1.85	1.82	1.79	1.76
1.99	1.94	1.89	1.87	1.84	1.81	1.78	1.75	1.72
1.96	1.91	1.86	1.84	1.81	1.78	1.75	1.72	1.69
1.93	1.89	1.84	1.81	1.78	1.75	1.72	1.69	1.66
1.91	1.86	1.81	1.79	1.76	1.73	1.70	1.67	1.63
1.89	1.84	1.79	1.77	1.74	1.71	1.68	1.64	1.61
1.87	1.83	1.78	1.75	1.72	1.69	1.66	1.62	1.59
1.86	1.81	1.76	1.73	1.70	1.67	1.64	1.60	1.57
1.84	1.80	1.74	1.72	1.69	1.66	1.62	1.59	1.55
1.83	1.78	1.73	1.70	1.67	1.64	1.61	1.57	1.53
1.82	1.77	1.72	1.69	1.66	1.63	1.59	1.56	1.52
1.81	1.76	1.71	1.68	1.65	1.61	1.58	1.54	1.50
1.80	1.75	1.70	1.67	1.64	1.60	1.57	1.53	1.49
1.79	1.74	1.69	1.66	1.63	1.59	1.56	1.52	1.48
1.78	1.73	1.68	1.65	1.62	1.58	1.55	1.51	1.47
1.77	1.72	1.67	1.64	1.61	1.57	1.54	1.50	1.46
1.71	1.66	1.61	1.57	1.54	1.51	1.47	1.42	1.38
1.66	1.60	1.54	1.51	1.48	1.44	1.40	1.35	1.29
1.60	1.55	1.48	1.45	1.41	1.37	1.32	1.26	1.19
1.55	1.49	1.42	1.38	1.34	1.30	1.24	1.17	1.00

TABLE 4   *(Continued)*

$$F_{.95}(v_1, v_2) \qquad \alpha = 0.05$$

v_1 = degrees of freedom for numerator

v_2 \ v_1	1	2	3	4	5	6	7	8	9	10
1	161.4	199.5	215.7	224.6	230.2	234.0	236.8	238.9	240.5	241.9
2	18.51	19.00	19.16	19.25	19.30	19.33	19.35	19.37	19.38	19.40
3	10.13	9.55	9.28	9.12	9.01	8.94	8.89	8.85	8.81	8.79
4	7.71	6.94	6.59	6.39	6.26	6.16	6.09	6.04	6.00	5.96
5	6.61	5.79	5.41	5.19	5.05	4.95	4.88	4.82	4.77	4.74
6	5.99	5.14	4.76	4.53	4.39	4.28	4.21	4.15	4.10	4.06
7	5.59	4.74	4.35	4.12	3.97	3.87	3.79	3.73	3.68	3.64
8	5.32	4.46	4.07	3.84	3.69	3.58	3.50	3.44	3.39	3.35
9	5.12	4.26	3.86	3.63	3.48	3.37	3.29	3.23	3.18	3.14
10	4.96	4.10	3.71	3.48	3.33	3.22	3.14	3.07	3.02	2.98
11	4.84	3.98	3.59	3.36	3.20	3.09	3.01	2.95	2.90	2.85
12	4.75	3.89	3.49	3.26	3.11	3.00	2.91	2.85	2.80	2.75
13	4.67	3.81	3.41	3.18	3.03	2.92	2.83	2.77	2.71	2.67
14	4.60	3.74	3.34	3.11	2.96	2.85	2.76	2.70	2.65	2.60
15	4.54	3.68	3.29	3.06	2.90	2.79	2.71	2.64	2.59	2.54
16	4.49	3.63	3.24	3.01	2.85	2.74	2.66	2.59	2.54	2.49
17	4.45	3.59	3.20	2.96	2.81	2.70	2.61	2.55	2.49	2.45
18	4.41	3.55	3.16	2.93	2.77	2.66	2.58	2.51	2.46	2.41
19	4.38	3.52	3.13	2.90	2.74	2.63	2.54	2.48	2.42	2.38
20	4.35	3.49	3.10	2.87	2.71	2.60	2.51	2.45	2.39	2.35
21	4.32	3.47	3.07	2.84	2.68	2.57	2.49	2.42	2.37	2.32
22	4.30	3.44	3.05	2.82	2.66	2.55	2.46	2.40	2.34	2.30
23	4.28	3.42	3.03	2.80	2.64	2.53	2.44	2.37	2.32	2.27
24	4.26	3.40	3.01	2.78	2.62	2.51	2.42	2.36	2.30	2.25
25	4.24	3.39	2.99	2.76	2.60	2.49	2.40	2.34	2.28	2.24
26	4.23	3.37	2.98	2.74	2.59	2.47	2.39	2.32	2.27	2.22
27	4.21	3.35	2.96	2.73	2.57	2.46	2.37	2.31	2.25	2.20
28	4.20	3.34	2.95	2.71	2.56	2.45	2.36	2.29	2.24	2.19
29	4.18	3.33	2.93	2.70	2.55	2.43	2.35	2.28	2.22	2.18
30	4.17	3.32	2.92	2.69	2.53	2.42	2.33	2.27	2.21	2.16
40	4.08	3.23	2.84	2.61	2.45	2.34	2.25	2.18	2.12	2.08
60	4.00	3.15	2.76	2.53	2.37	2.25	2.17	2.10	2.04	1.99
120	3.92	3.07	2.68	2.45	2.29	2.17	2.09	2.02	1.96	1.91
∞	3.84	3.00	2.60	2.37	2.21	2.10	2.01	1.94	1.88	1.83

v_2 = degrees of freedom for denominator

12	15	20	24	30	40	60	120	∞
243.9	245.9	248.0	249.1	250.1	251.1	252.2	253.3	254.3
19.41	19.43	19.45	19.45	19.46	19.47	19.48	19.49	19.50
8.74	8.70	8.66	8.64	8.62	8.59	8.57	8.55	8.53
5.91	5.86	5.80	5.77	5.75	5.72	5.69	5.66	5.63
4.68	4.62	4.56	4.53	4.50	4.46	4.43	4.40	4.36
4.00	3.94	3.87	3.84	3.81	3.77	3.74	3.70	3.67
3.57	3.51	3.44	3.41	3.38	3.34	3.30	3.27	3.23
3.28	3.22	3.15	3.12	3.08	3.04	3.01	2.97	2.93
3.07	3.01	2.94	2.90	2.86	2.83	2.79	2.75	2.71
2.91	2.85	2.77	2.74	2.70	2.66	2.62	2.58	2.54
2.79	2.72	2.65	2.61	2.57	2.53	2.49	2.45	2.40
2.69	2.62	2.54	2.51	2.47	2.43	2.38	2.34	2.30
2.60	2.53	2.46	2.42	2.38	2.34	2.30	2.25	2.21
2.53	2.46	2.39	2.35	2.31	2.27	2.22	2.18	2.13
2.48	2.40	2.33	2.29	2.25	2.20	2.16	2.11	2.07
2.42	2.35	2.28	2.24	2.19	2.15	2.11	2.06	2.01
2.38	2.31	2.23	2.19	2.15	2.10	2.06	2.01	1.96
2.34	2.27	2.19	2.15	2.11	2.06	2.02	1.97	1.92
2.31	2.23	2.16	2.11	2.07	2.03	1.98	1.93	1.88
2.28	2.20	2.12	2.08	2.04	1.99	1.95	1.90	1.84
2.25	2.18	2.10	2.05	2.01	1.96	1.92	1.87	1.81
2.23	2.15	2.07	2.03	1.98	1.94	1.89	1.84	1.78
2.20	2.13	2.05	2.01	1.96	1.91	1.86	1.81	1.76
2.18	2.11	2.03	1.98	1.94	1.89	1.84	1.79	1.73
2.16	2.09	2.01	1.96	1.92	1.87	1.82	1.77	1.71
2.15	2.07	1.99	1.95	1.90	1.85	1.80	1.75	1.69
2.13	2.06	1.97	1.93	1.88	1.84	1.79	1.73	1.67
2.12	2.04	1.96	1.91	1.87	1.82	1.77	1.71	1.65
2.10	2.03	1.94	1.90	1.85	1.81	1.75	1.70	1.64
2.09	2.01	1.93	1.89	1.84	1.79	1.74	1.68	1.62
2.00	1.92	1.84	1.79	1.74	1.69	1.64	1.58	1.51
1.92	1.84	1.75	1.70	1.65	1.59	1.53	1.47	1.39
1.83	1.75	1.66	1.61	1.55	1.50	1.43	1.35	1.25
1.75	1.67	1.57	1.52	1.46	1.39	1.32	1.22	1.00

TABLE 4   *(Continued)*

$$F_{.975}(v_1, v_2) \qquad \alpha = 0.025$$

v_1 = degrees of freedom for numerator

v_2 \ v_1	1	2	3	4	5	6	7	8	9	10
1	647.8	799.5	864.2	899.6	921.8	937.1	948.2	956.7	963.3	968.6
2	38.51	39.00	39.17	39.25	39.30	39.33	39.36	39.37	39.39	39.40
3	17.44	16.04	15.44	15.10	14.88	14.73	14.62	14.54	14.47	14.42
4	12.22	10.65	9.98	9.60	9.36	9.20	9.07	8.98	8.90	8.84
5	10.01	8.43	7.76	7.39	7.15	6.98	6.85	6.76	6.68	6.62
6	8.81	7.26	6.60	6.23	5.99	5.82	5.70	5.60	5.52	5.46
7	8.07	6.54	5.89	5.52	5.29	5.12	4.99	4.90	4.82	4.76
8	7.57	6.06	5.42	5.05	4.82	4.65	4.53	4.43	4.36	4.30
9	7.21	5.71	5.08	4.72	4.48	4.32	4.20	4.10	4.03	3.96
10	6.94	5.46	4.83	4.47	4.24	4.07	3.95	3.85	3.78	3.72
11	6.72	5.26	4.63	4.28	4.04	3.88	3.76	3.66	3.59	3.53
12	6.55	5.10	4.47	4.12	3.89	3.73	3.61	3.51	3.44	3.37
13	6.41	4.97	4.35	4.00	3.77	3.60	3.48	3.39	3.31	3.25
14	6.30	4.86	4.24	3.89	3.66	3.50	3.38	3.29	3.21	3.15
15	6.20	4.77	4.15	3.80	3.58	3.41	3.29	3.20	3.12	3.06
16	6.12	4.69	4.08	3.73	3.50	3.34	3.22	3.12	3.05	2.99
17	6.04	4.62	4.01	3.66	3.44	3.28	3.16	3.06	2.98	2.92
18	5.98	4.56	3.95	3.61	3.38	3.22	3.10	3.01	2.93	2.87
19	5.92	4.51	3.90	3.56	3.33	3.17	3.05	2.96	2.88	2.82
20	5.87	4.46	3.86	3.51	3.29	3.13	3.01	2.91	2.84	2.77
21	5.83	4.42	3.82	3.48	3.25	3.09	2.97	2.87	2.80	2.73
22	5.79	4.38	3.78	3.44	3.22	3.05	2.93	2.84	2.76	2.70
23	5.75	4.35	3.75	3.41	3.18	3.02	2.90	2.81	2.73	2.67
24	5.72	4.32	3.72	3.38	3.15	2.99	2.87	2.78	2.70	2.64
25	5.69	4.29	3.69	3.35	3.13	2.97	2.85	2.75	2.68	2.61
26	5.66	4.27	3.67	3.33	3.10	3.94	2.82	2.73	2.65	2.59
27	5.63	4.24	3.65	3.31	3.08	2.92	2.80	2.71	2.63	2.57
28	5.61	4.22	3.63	3.29	3.06	2.90	2.78	2.69	2.61	2.55
29	5.59	4.20	3.61	3.27	3.04	2.88	2.76	2.67	2.59	2.53
30	5.57	4.18	3.59	3.25	3.03	2.87	2.75	2.65	2.57	2.51
40	5.42	4.05	3.46	3.13	2.90	2.74	2.62	2.53	2.45	2.39
60	5.29	3.93	3.34	3.01	2.79	2.63	2.51	2.41	2.33	2.27
120	5.15	3.80	3.23	2.89	2.67	2.52	2.39	2.30	2.22	2.16
∞	5.02	3.69	3.12	2.79	2.57	2.41	2.29	2.19	2.11	2.05

v_2 = degrees of freedom for denominator

12	15	20	24	30	40	60	120	∞
976.7	984.9	993.1	997.2	1001	1006	1010	1014	1018
39.41	39.43	39.45	39.46	39.46	39.47	39.48	39.49	39.50
14.34	14.25	14.17	14.12	14.08	14.04	13.99	13.95	13.90
8.75	8.66	8.56	8.51	8.46	8.41	8.36	8.31	8.26
6.52	6.43	6.33	6.28	6.23	6.18	6.12	6.07	6.02
5.37	5.27	5.17	5.12	5.07	5.01	4.96	4.90	4.85
4.67	4.57	4.47	4.42	4.36	4.31	4.25	4.20	4.14
4.20	4.10	4.00	3.95	3.89	3.84	3.78	3.73	3.67
3.87	3.77	3.67	3.61	3.56	3.51	3.45	3.39	3.33
3.62	3.52	3.42	3.37	3.31	3.26	3.20	3.14	3.08
3.43	3.33	3.23	3.17	3.12	3.06	3.00	2.94	2.88
3.28	3.18	3.07	3.02	2.96	2.91	2.85	2.79	2.72
3.15	3.05	2.95	2.89	2.84	2.78	2.72	2.66	2.60
3.05	2.95	2.84	2.79	2.73	2.67	2.61	2.55	2.49
2.96	2.86	2.76	2.70	2.64	2.59	2.52	2.46	2.40
2.89	2.79	2.68	2.63	2.57	2.51	2.45	2.38	2.32
2.82	2.72	2.62	2.56	2.50	2.44	2.38	2.32	2.25
2.77	2.67	2.56	2.50	2.44	2.38	2.32	2.26	2.19
2.72	2.62	2.51	2.45	2.39	2.33	2.27	2.20	2.13
2.68	2.57	2.46	2.41	2.25	2.29	2.22	2.16	2.09
2.64	2.53	2.42	2.37	2.31	2.25	2.18	2.11	2.04
2.60	2.50	2.39	2.33	2.27	2.21	2.14	2.08	2.00
2.57	2.47	2.36	2.30	2.24	2.18	2.11	2.04	1.97
2.54	2.44	2.33	2.27	2.21	2.15	2.08	2.01	1.94
2.51	2.41	2.30	2.24	2.18	2.12	2.05	1.98	1.91
2.49	2.39	2.28	2.22	2.16	2.09	2.03	1.95	1.88
2.47	2.36	2.25	2.19	2.13	2.07	2.00	1.93	1.85
2.45	2.34	2.23	2.17	2.11	2.05	1.98	1.91	1.83
2.43	2.32	2.21	2.15	2.09	2.03	1.96	1.89	1.81
2.41	2.31	2.20	2.14	2.07	2.01	1.94	1.87	1.79
2.29	2.18	2.07	2.01	1.94	1.88	1.80	1.72	1.64
2.17	2.06	1.94	1.88	1.82	1.74	1.67	1.58	1.48
2.05	1.94	1.82	1.76	1.69	1.61	1.53	1.43	1.31
1.94	1.83	1.71	1.64	1.57	1.48	1.39	1.27	1.00

TABLE 4   *(Concluded)*

$$F_{.99}(v_1, v_2) \qquad \alpha = 0.01$$

v_1 = degrees of freedom for numerator

v_2 \\ v_1	1	2	3	4	5	6	7	8	9	10
1	4052	4999.5	5403	5625	5764	5859	5928	5982	6022	6056
2	98.50	99.00	99.17	99.25	99.30	99.33	99.36	99.37	99.39	99.40
3	34.12	30.82	29.46	28.71	28.24	27.91	27.67	27.49	27.35	27.23
4	21.20	18.00	16.69	15.98	15.52	15.21	14.98	14.80	14.66	14.55
5	16.26	13.27	12.06	11.39	10.97	10.67	10.46	10.29	10.16	10.05
6	13.75	10.92	9.78	9.15	8.75	8.47	8.26	8.10	7.98	7.87
7	12.25	9.55	8.45	7.85	7.46	7.19	6.99	6.84	6.72	6.62
8	11.26	8.65	7.59	7.01	6.63	6.37	6.18	6.03	5.91	5.81
9	10.56	8.02	6.99	6.42	6.06	5.80	5.61	5.47	5.35	5.26
10	10.04	7.56	6.55	5.99	5.64	5.39	5.20	5.06	4.94	4.85
11	9.65	7.21	6.22	5.67	5.32	5.07	4.89	4.74	4.63	4.54
12	9.33	6.93	5.95	5.41	5.06	4.82	4.64	4.50	4.39	4.30
13	9.07	6.70	5.74	5.21	4.86	4.62	4.44	4.30	4.19	4.10
14	8.86	6.51	5.56	5.04	4.69	4.46	4.28	4.14	4.03	3.94
15	8.68	6.36	5.42	4.89	4.56	4.32	4.14	4.00	3.89	3.80
16	8.53	6.23	5.29	4.77	4.44	4.20	4.03	3.89	3.78	3.69
17	8.40	6.11	5.18	4.67	4.34	4.10	3.93	3.79	3.68	3.59
18	8.29	6.01	5.09	4.58	4.25	4.01	3.84	3.71	3.60	3.51
19	8.18	5.93	5.01	4.50	4.17	3.94	3.77	3.63	3.52	3.43
20	8.10	5.85	4.94	4.43	4.10	3.87	3.70	3.56	3.46	3.37
21	8.02	5.78	4.87	4.37	4.04	3.81	3.64	3.51	3.40	3.31
22	7.95	5.72	4.82	4.31	3.99	3.76	3.59	3.45	3.35	3.26
23	7.88	5.66	4.76	4.26	3.94	3.71	3.54	3.41	3.30	3.21
24	7.82	5.61	4.72	4.22	3.90	3.67	3.50	3.36	3.26	3.17
25	7.77	5.57	4.68	4.18	3.85	3.63	3.46	3.32	3.22	3.13
26	7.72	5.53	4.64	4.14	3.82	3.59	3.42	3.29	3.18	3.09
27	7.68	5.49	4.60	4.11	3.78	3.56	3.39	3.26	3.15	3.06
28	7.64	5.45	4.57	4.07	3.75	3.53	3.36	3.23	3.12	3.03
29	7.60	5.42	4.54	4.04	3.73	3.50	3.33	3.20	3.09	3.00
30	7.56	5.39	4.51	4.02	3.70	3.47	3.30	3.17	3.07	2.98
40	7.31	5.18	4.31	3.83	3.51	3.29	3.12	2.99	2.89	2.80
60	7.08	4.98	4.13	3.65	3.34	3.12	2.95	2.82	2.72	2.63
120	6.85	4.79	3.95	3.48	3.17	2.96	2.79	2.66	2.56	2.47
∞	6.63	4.61	3.78	3.32	3.02	2.80	2.64	2.51	2.41	2.32

v_2 = degrees of freedom for denominator

12	15	20	24	30	40	60	120	∞
6106	6157	6209	6235	6261	6287	6313	6339	6366
99.42	99.43	99.45	99.46	99.47	99.47	99.48	99.49	99.50
27.05	26.87	26.69	26.60	26.50	26.41	26.32	26.22	26.13
14.37	14.20	14.02	13.93	13.84	13.75	13.65	13.56	13.46
9.89	9.72	9.55	9.47	9.38	9.29	9.20	9.11	9.02
7.72	7.56	7.40	7.31	7.23	7.14	7.06	6.97	6.88
6.47	6.31	6.16	6.07	5.99	5.91	5.82	5.74	5.65
5.67	5.52	5.36	5.28	5.20	5.12	5.03	4.95	4.86
5.11	4.96	4.81	4.73	4.65	4.57	4.48	4.40	4.31
4.71	4.56	4.41	4.33	4.25	4.17	4.08	4.00	3.91
4.40	4.25	4.10	4.02	3.94	3.86	3.78	3.69	3.60
4.16	4.01	3.86	3.78	3.70	3.62	3.54	3.45	3.36
3.96	3.82	3.66	3.59	3.51	3.43	3.34	3.25	3.17
3.80	3.66	3.51	3.43	3.35	3.27	3.18	3.09	3.00
3.67	3.52	3.37	3.29	3.21	3.13	3.05	2.96	2.87
3.55	3.41	3.26	3.18	3.10	3.02	2.93	2.84	2.75
3.46	3.31	3.16	3.08	3.00	2.92	2.83	2.75	2.65
3.37	3.23	3.08	3.00	2.92	2.84	2.75	2.66	2.57
3.30	3.15	3.00	2.92	2.84	2.76	2.67	2.58	2.49
3.23	3.09	2.94	2.86	2.78	2.69	2.61	2.52	2.42
3.17	3.03	2.88	2.80	2.72	2.64	2.55	2.46	2.36
3.12	2.98	2.83	2.75	2.67	2.58	2.50	2.40	2.31
3.07	2.93	2.78	2.70	2.62	2.54	2.45	2.35	2.26
3.03	2.89	2.74	2.66	2.58	2.49	2.40	2.31	2.21
2.99	2.85	2.70	2.62	2.54	2.45	2.36	2.27	2.17
2.96	2.81	2.66	2.58	2.50	2.42	2.33	2.23	2.13
2.93	2.78	2.63	2.55	2.47	2.38	2.29	2.20	2.10
2.90	2.75	2.60	2.52	2.44	2.35	2.26	2.17	2.06
2.87	2.73	2.57	2.49	2.41	2.33	2.23	2.14	2.03
2.84	2.70	2.55	2.47	2.39	2.30	2.21	2.11	2.01
2.66	2.52	2.37	2.29	2.20	2.11	2.02	1.92	1.80
2.50	2.35	2.20	2.12	2.03	1.94	1.84	1.73	1.60
2.34	2.19	2.03	1.95	1.86	1.76	1.66	1.53	1.38
2.18	2.04	1.88	1.79	1.70	1.59	1.47	1.32	1.00

ability to participate   The availability of both the interviewer and the respondent to get together in a question-and-answer interchange.

acquiescence error   A specific type of response bias that can occur when the respondent perceives what answer would be the most desirable to the sponsor.

administrative error   Bias that can stem from either data processing mistakes, interviewer distortion of the respondents' answers, or systemic inaccuracies created by using a faulty sampling design.

affect global approach   The theoretical approach of viewing the structure of a person's attitude as nothing more than the overall (global) expression of his or her favorable or unfavorable feeling toward a given object or behavior.

affective component   That part of an attitude which represents the person's feelings toward the given object, idea, or set of information.

alpha factor   The desired or acceptable amount of difference between the expected and actual population parameter values; also referred to as the *tolerance level of error (α)*.

alternative hypothesis   A statement that is the opposite of the null hypothesis, where the difference in reality is not simply due to random error.

ambiguity   Contamination of internal validity measures due to unclear determination of cause–effect relationships between investigated constructs.

analysis of variance (ANOVA)   A statistical technique that determines whether two or more means are statistically different from each other.

anonymity   The assurance that the prospective respondent's name or any identifiable designation will not be associated with his or her responses.

appendix   A section at the end of the final research report used to house complex, detailed, or technical information.

archives   Secondary sources of recorded past behaviors and trends.

area sampling   A form of cluster sampling where clusters are formed by geographic designations such as cities, subdivisions, and blocks. Any geographic unit with boundaries can be used, with one-step or two-step approaches.

assignment   The scaling property that allows the researcher to employ any type of descriptor to identify each object (or response) within a set; this property is also known as *description* or *category*.

attitude   A learned predisposition to react in some consistent positive or negative way to a given object, idea, or set of information.

attitude-toward-behavior   A multiplicative-additive model approach that attempts to capture a person's attitude toward a behavior rather than their attitude to the object itself; where the attitude is a separate, indirectly derived composite measure of a person's combined thoughts and feelings for or against carrying out a specific action or behavior.

attitude-toward-object   A multiplicative-additive model approach that attempts to capture a person's attitude about a specific object; where the attitude is a separate indirectly derived composite measure of a person's combined thoughts and feelings for or against a given object.

attribute-importance estimate   The importance of an attribute of an object as estimated by conjoint analysis. It is calculated by subtracting the minimum part-worth estimate from the maximum part-worth estimate.

auspices error   A type of response bias that occurs when the response is dictated by the image or opinion of the sponsor rather than the actual question.

automatic replenishment system   A continuous, automated inventory control system designed to analyze inventory levels, merchandise order lead times, and forecasted sales.

availability of information   The degree to which the information has already been collected and assembled in some type of recognizable format.

bad question setup   Any question or directive that obscures, prevents, or distorts the fundamental communications between respondent and researcher.

balancing positive/negative scale descriptors   The researcher's decision to maintain objectivity in a scale that is designed to capture both positive and negative state-of-mind raw data from respondents; the same number of relative magnitudes of positive and negative scale descriptors are used to make up the set of scale points.

bar code   A pattern of varied-width electronic-sensitive bars and spaces that represents a unique code of numbers and letters.

behavioral intention scale   A special type of rating scale designed to capture the likelihood that people will demonstrate some type of predictable behavior toward purchasing an object or service.

believability   The quality achieved by building a final report that is based on clear, logical thinking, precise expression, and accurate presentation.

benefit and lifestyle descriptive studies   Studies conducted to examine similarities and differences in needs; used to identify two or more segments within a market for the purpose of identifying customers for the product category of interest to a particular company.

beta coefficient   An estimated regression coefficient that has been recalculated to have a mean of 0 and a standard deviation of 1. This statistic enables the independent variables with different units of measurement to be directly compared on their association with the dependent variable.

bias   A particular tendency or inclination that skews results, thereby preventing accurate consideration of a research question.

bivariate regression analysis   A statistical technique that analyzes the linear relationship between two variables by estimating coefficients for an equation for a straight line. One variable is designated as a dependent variable, and the other as an independent (or predictor) variable.

Boolean operators   Key words that form a logic string to sort through huge numbers of sites on the World Wide Web.

brand awareness   The percentage of respondents having heard of a designated brand; brand awareness can be either unaided or aided.

business ethics   The moral principles and standards that guide behavior in the world of business.

buying power index (BPI)   A statistical indicator that provides weighted-average population, retail sales, and effective buying income data on different geographic areas of the United States.

call record sheet   A recording document that gathers basic summary information about an interviewer's performance efficiency (e.g., number of contact attempts, number of completed interviews, length of time of interview, etc.).

cardinal numbers   Any set of consecutive whole integers.

causal research   Research that focuses on collecting data structures and information that will allow the decision maker or researcher to model cause–effect relationships between two or more variables under investigation.

census   A study that includes data about or from every member of a target population. Sampling is often used because it is impossible or unreasonable to conduct a census.

central limit theorem (CLT)   The theoretical backbone of sampling theory. It states that the sampling distribution of the sample mean ($\bar{x}$) or the sample proportion ($\bar{p}$) value derived from a simple random sample drawn from the target population will be approximately normally dis-

tributed provided that the associated sample size is sufficiently large (e.g., when n is greater than or equal to 30). In turn, the sample mean value ($\bar{x}$) of that random sample with an estimated sampling error ($SE_{\bar{x}}$) (e.g., estimated standard error) fluctuates around the true population mean value (μ) with a standard error of σ/n and has a sampling distribution that is approximately a standardized normal distribution, regardless of the shape of the probability frequency distribution curve of the overall target population.

cheating   The deliberate falsification of respondents' answers on a survey instrument.

Claris Home Page   A specific software program that can be used to create Web pages that can integrate both text and graphics with other types of computer files.

cluster analysis   A multivariate interdependence technique whose primary objective is to classify objects into relatively homogeneous groups based on the set of variables considered.

clusters   The mutually exclusive and collectively exhaustive subpopulation groupings that are then randomly sampled.

cluster sampling   A method of probability sampling where the sampling units are selected in groups (or clusters) rather than individually. Once the cluster has been identified, the elements to be sampled are drawn by simple random sampling or all of the units may be included in the sample.

code of ethics   A set of guidelines that states the standards and operating procedures for ethical decisions and practices by researchers.

coding   The activities of grouping and assigning values to various responses from a survey instrument.

coefficient alpha   See Cronbach's alpha.

coefficient of determination (r^2)   A statistical value (or number) that measures the proportion of variation in one variable accounted for by

another variable; the r^2 measure can be thought of as a percentage and varies from .00 to 1.00.

cognitive component   That part of an attitude which represents the person's beliefs, perceptions, preferences, experiences, and knowledge about a given object, idea, or set of information.

commercial/syndicated data   Data that have been compiled and displayed according to some standardized procedure.

company ethics program   The framework through which a firm establishes internal codes of ethical behavior to serve as guidelines for doing business.

competitive intelligence analysis   Specific procedures for collecting daily operational information pertaining to the competitive companies and markets they serve.

completeness   The depth and breadth of the data.

completion deadline date   Part of the information included in a cover letter that directly communicates to a prospective respondent the date by which his or her completed questionnaire must be returned to the researcher.

complexity of the information   One of the two fundamental dimensions used to determine the level of information being supplied by the information research process; it relates to the degree to which the information is easily understood and applied to the problem or opportunity under investigation.

computer-administered survey   A survey design that incorporates the use of a computer to ask questions and record responses.

computer-assisted personal interviewing   An interview in which the interviewer reads respondents the questions from a computer screen and directly keys in the response.

computer-assisted self-interviewing   An interview in which respondents are directed to a computer where they read questions from the computer screen and directly enter their responses.

computer-assisted telephone interview (CATI) The computer controls and expedites the interviewing process.

computer-assisted telephone survey A survey that uses a fully automated system in which the respondent listens to an electronic voice and responds by pushing keys on a Touch-Tone telephone keypad.

computer disks by mail A survey procedure in which computer disks are mailed to respondents; the respondents complete the survey on their own computer and return the disk to the researcher via the mail.

computer-generated fax survey A survey procedure in which a computer is used to send a survey to potential respondents via fax; the respondent completes the survey and returns it via fax or mail.

computerized secondary data sources Data sources designed by specific companies that integrate both internal and external data with online information sources.

conative component That part of an attitude which refers to the person's behavioral response or specific action/reaction toward the given object, idea, or set of information; it tends to be the observable outcome driven by the interaction of a person's cognitive and affective components toward the object or behavior.

confidence interval A statistical range of values within which the true value of the target population parameter of interest is expected to fall based on a specified confidence level.

confidence levels Theoretical levels of aassurance at which the probability that a particular confidence interval will accurately include or measure the true population parameter value. In information research, the three most widely used levels are 90 percent, 95 percent, and 99 percent.

confidentiality to client The agreement between a researcher and the client that all activities performed in the process of conducting marketing research will remain private and the property of the client, unless otherwise specified by both parties.

confidentiality to respondent The expressed assurance to the prospective respondent that his or her name, while known to the researcher, will not be divulged to a third party, especially the sponsoring client.

confirmation/invitation letter A specific follow-up document sent to prospective focus group participants to encourage and reinforce their willingness and commitment to participate in the group session.

conformance to standards The researcher's ability to be accurate, timely, mistake free, and void of unanticipated delays.

confusion or predictor matrix The classification matrix in discriminant analysis that contains the number of correctly classified and misclassified cases.

conjoint analysis A multivariate technique that estimates the utility of the levels of various attributes or features of an object, as well as the relative importance of the attributes themselves.

connect time The length of time, frequently measured in minutes and seconds, that a user is logged on to an electronic service or database. The amount of connect time is generally used to bill the user for services.

connectors Logic phrases and symbols that allow search terms to be linked together in a Boolean logic format.

consent forms Formal signed statements of agreement by the participants approving the taping or recording of the information provided in group discussions and releasing that data to the moderator, researcher, or sponsoring client.

constant sums rating scale A scale format that requires the respondents to allocate a given number of points, usually 100, among several attributes or features based on their importance to the individual; this format requires a person to value each separate feature relative to all the other listed features.

construct development An integrative process of activities undertaken by researchers to enhance understanding of what specific data should be collected for solving defined research problems.

construct development error A type of nonsampling (systematic) error that is created when the researcher is not careful in fully identifying the concepts and constructs to be included in the study.

constructs Hypothetical variables comprised of a set of component responses or behaviors that are thought to be related.

construct validity The degree to which researchers measure what they intended to measure, and to which the proper identification of the independent and dependent variables were included in the investigation.

consumer panels Large samples of households that provide certain types of data for an extended period of time.

content analysis The technique used to study written or taped materials by breaking the data into meaningful aggregate units or categories using a predetermined set of rules.

content validity That property of a test which indicates that the entire domain of the subject or construct of interest was properly sampled. That is, the identified factors are truly components of the construct of interest.

control group That portion of the sample which is not subjected to the treatment.

controlled test markets Test markets performed by an outside research firm that guarantees distribution of the test product through prespecified outlets in selected cities.

control variables Extraneous variables that the researcher is able to account for according to their systematic variation (or impact) on the functional relationship between the independent and dependent variables included in the experiment.

convenience sampling   A method of nonprobability sampling where the samples are drawn based on the convenience of the researcher or interviewer; also referred to as *accidental sampling*. Convenience sampling is often used in the early stages of research because it allows a large number of respondents to be interviewed in a short period of time.

convergent validity   The degree to which different measures of the same construct are highly correlated.

cost analysis   An analysis of alternative logistic system designs that a firm can use for achieving its performance objective at the lowest total cost.

covariation   The amount of change in one variable that is consistently related to the change in another variable of interest.

cover letter   A separate letter that either accompanies a self-administered questionnaire or is mailed prior to an initial interviewer contact call and whose main purpose is to secure a respondent's willingness to participate in the research project; sometimes referred to as a letter of introduction.

cover letter guidelines   A specific set of factors that should be included in a cover letter for the purpose of increasing a prospective respondent's willingness to participate in the study.

credibility   The quality that comes about by developing a final report that is accurate, believable, and professionally organized.

critical questions   Questions used by a moderator to direct the group to the critical issues underlying the topics of interest.

critical tolerance level   The observed difference between a sample statistic value and the corresponding true or hypothesized population parameter.

critical z value   The book z value and the amount of acceptable variability between the observed sample data

results and the prescribed hypothesized true population values measured in standardized degrees of standard errors for given confidence levels.

Cronbach's alpha   A widely used measurement of the internal consistency of a multi-item scale in which the average of all possible split-half coefficients is taken.

cross-tabulation   The process of simultaneously treating (or counting) two or more variables in the study. This process categorizes the number of respondents who have responded to two or more questions consecutively.

curbstoning   Cheating or falsification of data during the collection process that occurs when interviewers fill in all or part of a survey themselves.

curvilinear relationship   An association between two variables whereby the strength and/or direction of their relationship changes over the range of both variables.

customer satisfaction studies   Studies designed to assess both the strengths and weaknesses customers perceive in a firm's marketing mix.

cycle time   The time that elapses between taking a product or service from initial consumer contact to final delivery.

data   Facts relating to any issue or subject.

data analysis error   A "family" of nonsampling errors that are created when the researcher subjects the raw data to inappropriate analysis procedures.

database   A collection of secondary information indicating what customers are purchasing, how often they purchase, and how much they purchase.

database technology   The means by which data are transformed into information.

data coding errors   The incorrect assignment of computer codes to the raw responses.

data enhancement   The process of weaving data into current internal data structures for the purpose of

gaining a more valuable categorization of customers relative to their true value to the company.

data editing errors   Inaccuracies due to careless verifying procedures of raw data to computer data files.

data entry   The direct inputting of the coded data into some specified software package that will ultimately allow the research analyst to manipulate and transform the raw data into data structures.

data entry errors   The incorrect assignment of computer codes to their predesignated location on the computer data file.

data field   A basic characteristic about a customer that is filled in on a database.

data interaction matrix   A procedure used to itemize the type and amount of data required by each functional area of the company regardless of the cost of data collection.

data processing error   A specific type of nonsampling error that can occur when researchers are not accurate or complete in transferring raw data from respondents to computer files.

data structures   The output analysis results of combining a group of reported raw data using some type of quantitative or qualitative analysis procedure.

data validation   A specific control process that the researcher undertakes to ensure that his or her representatives collected the data as required. The process is normally one of recontacting about 20 percent of the selected respondent group to determine that they did participate in the study.

debriefing analysis   The technique of comparing notes, thoughts, and feelings about a focus group discussion between the moderator, researcher, and sponsoring client immediately following the group interview.

decision opportunity   The presence of a situation in which market performance can be significantly improved by undertaking new activities.

decision problem A situation in which management has established a specific objective to accomplish and there are several courses of action that could be taken, each with its own risks and potential benefits.

defined target population A specified group of people or objects for which questions can be asked or observations made to develop the required data structures and information; also referred to as the *working population*. A precise definition of the target population is essential when undertaking a research project.

degree of manipulation The extent to which data structures and results have been interpreted and applied to a specific situation.

deliberate falsification When either the respondent and/or interviewer intentionally gives wrong answers or deliberately cheats on a survey.

demand analysis The estimating of the level of customer demand for a given product as well as the underlying reasons for that demand.

demand characteristics Contamination to construct validity measures created by test subjects trying to guess the true purpose behind the experiment and therefore give socially acceptable responses or behaviors.

demographic characteristics Physical and factual attributes of people, organizations, or objects.

deontologists Individuals who emphasize good intentions and the rights of the people involved in an action; they are much less concerned with the results from any ethical decision.

dependence techniques Appropriate multivariate procedures when one or more of the variables can be identified as dependent variables and the remaining as independent variables.

dependent variable A singular observable attribute that is the measured outcome derived from manipulating the independent variable(s).

depth of data The overall number of key data fields or variables that will comprise the data records.

descriptive questionnaire design A questionnaire design that allows the researcher to collect raw data that can be turned into facts about a person or object. The questions and scales primarily involve the collecting of state-of-being and state-of-behavior data.

descriptive research Research that uses a set of scientific methods and procedures to collect data structures that are used to identify, determine, and describe the existing characteristics of a target population or market structure.

diffusion of treatment Contamination to construct validity measures due to test subjects discussing the treatment and measurement activities to individuals yet to receive the treatment.

direct cognitive structural analysis A data analysis procedure in which respondents are simply asked to determine the extent to which an attribute is part of the construct's structural makeup and its importance to construct.

direct (positive) directional hypothesis A statement about the perceived relationship between two questions, dimensions, or subgroups of attributes that suggests that as one factor moves in one direction, the other factor moves in the same direction.

direct mail survey A questionnaire distributed to and returned from respondents via the postal service.

direct observation The process of observing actual behaviors or events and recording them as they occur.

direct self-administered questionnaire A survey instrument designed to have the respondent serve as both an interviewer and a respondent during the question-and-answer encounter.

directness of observation The degree to which the researcher or trained observer actually observes the behavior/event as it occurs; also termed *direct observation*.

discretion of primary descriptors The carefulness that a researcher must use in selecting the actual words used to distinguish the

relative magnitudes associated with each of the primary descriptors in a scale design.

discriminant analysis A multivariate technique for analyzing marketing research data when the dependent variable is categorical and the independent variables are interval.

discriminant function The linear combination of independent variables developed by discriminant analysis which will best discriminate between the categories of the dependent variable.

discriminant function coefficient The multipliers of variables in the discriminant function when the variables are in the original units of measurement.

discriminant score In discriminant analysis, this represents the score of each respondent on the discriminant function.

discriminant validity The degree to which measures of different constructs are uncorrelated.

discriminatory power of the scale The scale's ability to significantly differentiate between the categorical scale responses (or points).

disguised observation An observation technique in which the test subjects are completely unaware that they are being observed and recorded.

disguised sponsorship When the true identify of the person or company for which the research is being conducted is not divulged to the prospective respondent.

disproportionate stratified sampling A form of stratified sampling in which the size of the sample drawn from each stratum is independent of the stratum's proportion of the total population.

distance The scaling property that when activated allows the researcher and respondent to identify, understand, and accurately express in a unit measurement scheme the exact (or absolute) difference between each of the descriptors, scale points, or raw responses.

diversity of respondents The degree to which the respondents in the study share some similarities.

domain of observables   The set of observable manifestations of an variable that is not itself directly observable. A domain represents an identifiable set of components that indirectly make up the construct of interest.

drop-off survey   A questionnaire that is left with the respondent to be completed at a later time. The questionnaire may be picked up by the researcher or returned via some other mode.

dummy variables   Artificial variables introduced into a regression equation to represent the categories of a nominally scaled variable (such as sex or marital status). There will be one dummy variable for each of the nominal categories of the independent variable and the values will typically be 0 and 1, depending on whether the variable value is present or absent for a particular respondent (e.g., male or female).

editing   The process in which the interviews or survey instruments are checked for mistakes that may have occurred by either the interviewer or the respondent during data collection activities.

effective buying income (EBI)   The measure of personal income less federal, state, and local taxes.

electronic database   A high-speed, computer-assisted information source or library.

electronic data interchange   A specific system designed to speed the flow of information as well as products from producer to distributor to retailer.

electronic test markets   Test procedures that integrate the use of selected panels of consumers who use a special identification card in recording their product purchasing data.

element   The name given to the object about which information is sought. Elements must be unique, countable, and, when added together, comprise the whole of the target population.

e-mail survey   A survey in which electronic mail is used to deliver a questionnaire to respondents and receive their responses.

empirical testing   The actual collection of data in the real world using research instruments and then subjecting that data to rigorous analysis to either support or refute a hypothesis.

ending questions   Questions used by a focus group moderator to bring closure to a particular topic discussion; encourages summary-type comments.

environmental forecasting   The projection of environmental occurrences that can affect the long-term strategy of a firm.

environmental information   Secondary information pertaining to a firm's suppliers and/or distributors.

equivalent form reliability   A method of assessing the reliability associated with a scale measurement; the researcher creates two basically similar yet different scale measurements for the given construct and administers both forms to either the same sample of respondents or two samples of respondents from the same target population.

error   The difference between the true score on a research instrument and the actual observed score.

estimated sample standard deviation   A quantitative index of the dispersion of the distribution of drawn sampling units' actual data around the sample's arithmetic average measure of central tendency; this sample statistical value specifies the degree of variation in the raw data responses in such a way that allows the researcher to translate the variations into normal curve interpretations.

estimated sample variance   The square of the estimated sample standard deviation.

estimated standard error of the sample statistic   A statistical measurement of the sampling error that can be expected to exist between the drawn sample's statistical values and the actual values of all the sampling units' distributions of those concerned statistics. These indexes are referred to as *general precision*.

estimates   Sample data facts that are transformed through interpretation procedures to represent inferences about the larger target population.

ethical dilemmas   Specific situations in which the researcher, decision maker, or respondent must choose between appropriate and inappropriate behavior.

ethics   The field of study that tries to determine what behaviors are considered to be appropriate under certain circumstances by established codes of behavior set forth by society.

evaluation apprehension   Contamination to construct validity measures caused by test subjects being fearful that their actions or responses will become known to others.

executive interview   A person-administrated interview of a business executive. Frequently, these interviews will take place in the executive's office.

executive summary   The part of the final research report that illustrates the major points of the report in a manner complete enough to provide a true representation of the entire document.

expected completion rate (ECR)   The percentage of prospective respondents who are expected to participate and complete the survey; also referred to as the *anticipated response rate*.

experimental design reliability   The degree to which the research design and its procedures can be replicated and achieve similar conclusions about hypothesized relationships.

expert systems   Advanced computer-based systems that function in the same manner as a human expert, advising the analyst on how to solve a problem.

exploratory research   Research designed to collect and interpret either secondary or primary data in an unstructured format using sometimes an informal set of procedures.

external secondary data   Data collected by outside agencies such as the federal, state, or local government; trade associations; or periodicals.

external validity   The extent to which the measured data results of a study based on a sample can be expected to hold in the entire defined target population. In addition, it is the extent that a causal relationship found in a study can be expected to be true for the entire defined target population.

extraneous variables   All variables other than the independent variables that affect the responses of the test subjects. If left uncontrolled, these variables can have a confounding impact on the dependent variable measures that could weaken or invalidate the results of an experiment.

extremity error   A type of response bias when the clarity of extreme scale points and ambiguity of midrange options encourage extreme responses.

facilitating agencies   Businesses that perform a marketing research function as a supplement to a broader marketing research project.

factor analysis   A class of statistical procedures primarily used for data reduction and summarization.

factor loadings   Simple correlations between the variables and the factors.

factor scores   Composite scores estimated for each respondent on the derived factors.

facts   Pieces of information that are observable and verifiable through a number of external sources.

faulty recall   The inability of a person to accurately remember the specifics about the behavior under investigation.

fax survey   A questionnaire distributed to the sample via fax machines.

field experiments   Causal research designs that manipulate the independent variables in order to measure the dependent variable in a natural test setting.

finite correction factor (fcf)   An adjustment factor to the sample size

that is made in those situations where the drawn sample is expected to equal 5 percent or more of the defined target population. The fcf is equal to the overall square root of $N - n/N - 1$.

flowerpot approach   A specific, unique framework or blueprint for integrating different sets of questions and scale measurements into an instrument that is capable of collecting the raw data needed to achieve each of the established information objectives.

focus group   A formalized process of bringing a small, select group of people together for an interactive and spontaneous discussion of one particular topic or concept.

focus group facility   A professional facility that offers a set of specially designed rooms for conducting focus group interviews; each room contains a large table and comfortable chairs for up to 13 people, with a relaxed atmosphere, built-in audio equipment, and normally a one-way mirror for disguised observing by the sponsoring client or researcher.

focus group incentives   Specified investment programs to compensate focus group participants for their expenses associated with demonstrating a willingness to be a group member.

focus group moderator   A special person who is well-trained in interpersonal communications; listening, observation, and interpretive skills; and professional mannerisms and personality. His or her role in a session is to draw from the participants the best and most innovative ideas about an assigned topic or question.

follow-up test   A statistical test that flags the means that are statistically different from each other; follow-up tests are performed after an ANOVA determines there are differences between means.

forced-choice scale measurements Symmetrical scale measurement designs that do not have a logical "neutral" scale descriptor to divide the positive and negative domains of response descriptors.

formal rating procedures   The use of structured survey instruments or questionnaires to gather information on environmental occurrences.

***F*-ratio**   The statistical ratio of between-group mean squared variance to within-group mean squared variance; the *F* value is used as an indicator of the statistical difference between group means in an ANOVA.

free-choice scale measurements Symmetrical scale measurement designs that are divided into positive and negative domains of scale-point descriptors by a logical center "neutral" response.

frequency distributions   A summary of how many times each possible raw response to a scale question/setup was recorded by the total group of respondents.

full-text   Option of having the entire document, news story, article, or numerical information available for downloading.

fully automated self-interviewing   A procedure in which respondents independently approach a central computer station or kiosk, read the questions, and respond—all without researcher intervention.

fully automated telephone interviewing   A data collection procedure in which the computer calls respondents and asks questions; the respondent records his or her answers by using the keypad of a Touch-Tone telephone.

fully automatic devices   High-tech devices that interact with respondents without the presence of a trained interviewer during the question/response encounter.

functional relationship   An observable and measurable systematic change in one variable as another variable changes.

garbage in, garbage out   A standard phrase used in marketing research to represent situations where the process of collecting, analyzing, and interpreting data into information contains errors or biases, creating less than accurate information.

generalizability   The extent to which the data are an accurate portrait of the defined target population; the representativeness of information obtained from a small subgroup of members to that of the entire target population from which the subgroup was selected.

generalizability of data structures   The degree to which sample data results and structures can be used to draw accurate inferences about the defined target population, that is, the extent to which the research can extrapolate results from a sample to the defined target population.

general precision   The amount of general sampling error associated with the given sample of raw data that was generated through some type of data collection activity; no specific concern for any level of confidence.

graphic rating scale   A scale point format that presents respondents with some type of graphic continuum as the set of possible raw responses to a given question.

group dynamics   The degree of spontaneous interaction among group members during a discussion of a topic.

hits   The number of documents or other items that meet the search terms in an online search.

human observation   Data collection by a researcher or trained observer who records text subjects' actions and behaviors.

hypertext markup language (HTML)   The language used to create Web pages for communicating the research results as well as other information on the Internet.

hypothesis   A yet-unproven proposition or possible solution to a decision problem that can be empirically tested using data that are collected through the research process; it is developed in order to explain phenomena or a relationship between two or more constructs or variables.

hypothesis guessing   Contamination to construct validity measures due to test subjects believing they know the desired functional relationship prior to the manipulation treatment.

iceberg principle   The general notion indicating that the dangerous part of many marketing decision problems is neither visible nor well understood by marketing managers.

importance-performance analysis   A research and data analysis procedure used to evaluate a firm's and its competitors' strengths and weaknesses, as well as future actions that seek to identify key attributes that drive purchase behavior within a given industry.

inadequate preoperationalization of variables   Contamination to construct validity measures due to inadequate understanding of the complete makeup of the independent and dependent variables included in the experimental design.

inappropriate analysis bias   A type of data analysis error that creates the wrong data structure results and can lead to misinterpretation errors.

incidence rate   The percentage of the general population that is the subject of the marketing research.

independent samples   Two or more groups of responses that are tested as though they may come from different populations.

independent variable   An attribute of an object whose measurement values are directly manipulated by the researcher, also referred to as a *predictor* or *treatment variable*. This type of variable is assumed to be a causal factor in a functional relationship with a dependent variable.

in-depth interview   A formalized, structured process of asking a subject a set of semistructured, probing questions by a well-trained interviewer usually in a face-to-face setting.

indirect observation   A research technique in which researchers or trained observers rely on artifacts that, at best, represent specific reported behavioral outcomes from some earlier time.

information   The set of facts derived from data structures when someone—either the researcher or decision maker—interprets and attaches narrative meaning to the data structures.

information objectives   The clearly stated reasons why raw data must be collected; they serve as the guidelines for determining the raw data requirements.

information requirements   The identified factors, dimensions, and attributes within a stated information objective for which raw data must be collected.

information research process   The 10 systematic task steps involved in the four phases of gathering, analyzing, interpreting, and transforming data structures and results into information for use by decision makers.

information research questions   Specific statements that address the problem areas the research study will attempt to investigate.

in-home interview   A person-administrated interview that takes place in the respondent's home.

instrumentation   Contamination to internal validity measures from changes in measurement processes, observation techniques, and/or measuring instruments.

intelligibility of the questions   The degree to which questions can be understood by the respondents making up the defined target population to whom the scale will be administered to.

intention to purchase   A person's planned future action to buy a product or service.

interdependence techniques   Multivariate statistical procedures in which the whole set of interdependent relationships is examined.

internal consistency reliability   The extent to which the items of a scale represent the same domain of content and are highly correlated both with each other and summated scale scores. It represents the degree to which the components are related to the same overall construct domain.

internal quality movement   One of the underlying factors for which many organizations are restructuring away from old traditional functional control/power systems of operating to new cross-functional structures where team building, decision teams, and sharing of information and responsibility are the important factors, not control and power.

internal secondary data   Facts that have been collected by the individual company for accounting and marketing activity purposes.

internal validity   The certainty with which a researcher can state that the observed effect was caused by a specific treatment; exists when the research design accurately identifies causal relationships.

Internet   A network of computers and technology linking computers into an information superhighway.

Internet survey   The method of using the Internet to ask survey questions and record responses of respondents.

interpersonal communication skills   The interviewer's abilities to articulate the questions in a direct and clear manner so that the subject understands what she or he is responding to.

interpretive bias   Error that occurs when the wrong inference about the real world or defined target population is made by the researcher or decision maker due to some type of extraneous factor.

interpretive skills   The interviewer's capabilities of accurately understanding and recording the subject's responses to questions.

interval scales   Any question/scale format that activates not only the assignment and order scaling properties but also the distance property; all scale responses have a recognized absolute difference between each of the other scale points (responses).

interviewer error   A type of nonsampling error that is created in situations where the interviewer distorts information, in a systematic way, from respondents during or after the interviewer/respondent encounter.

interviewer/mechanical devices   The combination of highly skilled people who are aided by high-technology devices during the questioning/responding encounters with respondents.

interviewer's instructions   The vehicle for training the interviewer on how to select prospective respondents, screen them for eligibility, and conduct the actual interview.

introductory questions   Questions used by a focus group moderator to introduce the general topic of discussion and opportunities of reflecting their past experiences.

inverse (negative or indirect) directional hypothesis   A statement about the perceived relationship between two questions, dimensions, or subgroupings of attributes that suggests that as one factor moves in one direction, the other factor moves in an opposite fashion.

judgment sampling   A nonprobability sampling design that selects participants for a sample based on an experienced individual's belief that the participants will meet the requirements of the research study.

junk mail   A categorical descriptor that prospective respondents attach to surveys that are administered through the direct mail delivery system or an unwanted telephone interview that is viewed as being nothing more than a telemarketing gimmick to sell them something they do not want or need.

knowledge level of respondent   The degree to which the selected respondents feel they have experience (or knowledge) with the topics that are the focus of the survey's questioning.

lead country test markets   Field test markets that are conducted in specific foreign countries.

leading questions   A question that tends to purposely elicit a particular answer.

library   A large group of related information.

lifetime value models   Procedures developed using historical data, as well as actual purchase behavior, not probability estimates, to predict consumer behavior.

Likert scale   A special rating scale format that asks respondents to indicate the extent to which they agree or disagree with a series of mental belief or behavioral belief statements about a given object; it is a cognitive-based scale measurement.

limitations   A section of the final research report in which all extraneous events that place certain restrictions on the report are fully communicated.

linear relationship   An association between two variables whereby the strength and nature of the relationship remains the same over the range of both variables.

listening skills   The interviewer's capabilities of understanding what the respondent is communicating.

lottery incentive approach   A unique incentive system that pools together either individual small cash incentives into a significantly larger dollar amount or a substantial nonmonetary gift and then holds a drawing to determine the winner or small set of winners. The drawing procedure is designed so that all respondents who complete and return their survey have an equal chance of receiving the larger reward.

mail panel   A representative sample of individual respondents who have agreed in advance to participate in a mail survey.

mall-intercept   An interview technique in which mall patrons are stopped and asked for feedback. The interview may take place in the mall's common areas or in the research firm's offices at the mall.

managerial function software system   A computer-based procedure that includes forecasting, brand management, and promotional budget capabilities.

marketing decision support system (MDSS)   A computer-based system intended for use by particular marketing personnel at any functional level for the purpose of solving information and/or semistructured problems. Within this system databases are developed and used to analyze the firm's performance as well as control its marketing activities.

marketing knowledge   A characteristic that complements a researcher's technical competency.

marketing research   The function that links an organization to its market through the gathering of information. The information allows for the identification and definition of market-driven opportunities and problems. The information allows for the generation, refinement, and evaluation of marketing actions.

market performance symptoms   Conditions that signal the presence of a decision problem and/or opportunity.

maturation   Contamination to internal validity measures due to changes in the dependent variable based on the natural function of time and not attributed to any specific event.

mean   The arithmetic average of all the raw responses; all values of a distribution of responses are summed and divided by the number of valid responses.

measurement   Rules for assigning numbers to objects so that these numbers represent quantities of attributes.

measurement/design error   A "family" of nonsampling errors that result from inappropriate designs in the constructs, scale measurements, or survey measurements used to execute the asking and recording of people's responses to a study's questions.

measures of central tendency   The basic sample statistics that could be generated through analyzing the collected raw data; they are the mode, the median, and the mean.

measures of dispersion   The sample statistics that describe how all the raw data are actually dispersed around a given measure of central tendency; they are the frequency distribution, the range, and the estimated sample standard deviation.

mechanical devices   High-technology instruments that can artificially observe and record either current behavioral actions or physical phenomena as they occur.

media panels   Selected households that are primarily used in measuring media viewing habits as opposed to product/brand consumption patterns.

median   The sample statistic that splits the raw data into a hierarchical pattern where half the raw data is above the median statistic value and half is below.

method bias   The error source that results from selecting an inappropriate method to investigate the research question.

misinterpretation error   An inaccurate transformation of data structures and analysis results into usable bits of information for the decision maker.

mode   The most frequently mentioned (or occurring) raw response in the set of responses to a given question/setup.

model *F*-statistic   A statistic which compares the amount of variation in the dependent measure "explained" or associated with the independent variables to the "unexplained" or error variance. A larger *F*-statistic value indicates that the regression model has more explained variance than error variance.

moderator's guide   A detailed document that outlines the topics, questions, and subquestions that serve as the basis for generating the spontaneous interactive dialogue among the focus group participants.

modified Likert scale   Any version of the agreement/disagreement-based scale measurement that is not the original five-point "strongly agree" to "strongly disagree" scale.

monetary compensation   An individual cash incentive used by the

researcher to increase the likelihood of a prospective respondent's willingness to participate in the survey.

monomethod bias   A particular type of error source that is created when only a single method is used to collect data about the research question.

moral philosophy   A person's basic orientation toward problem solving. Within the ethical decision making process, philosophical thinking will come from teleology, deontology, and/or relativity orientations.

mortality   Contamination to internal validity measures due to changing the composition of the test subjects in the experiment.

multiattribute trilogy approach   The theoretical approach of viewing a person's attitude toward an object as consisting of three distinct components: cognitive, affective, and conative.

multicollinearity   A situation in which several independent variables are highly correlated with each other. This characteristic can result in difficulty in estimating separate or independent regression coefficients for the correlated variables.

multiple regression analysis   A statistical technique which analyzes the linear relationships between a dependent variable and multiple independent variables by estimating coefficients for the equation for a straight line.

multivariate techniques   Statistical procedures used when there are two or more measurements on each element and the variables are analyzed simultaneously. Multivariate techniques are concerned with the simultaneous relationships among two or more phenomena.

mystery shopper studies   Studies in which trained, professional shoppers visit stores, financial institutions, or companies and "shop" for various products and assess service quality factors or levels.

nominal scales   Question/scale structures that ask the respondent to provide only a descriptor as the raw response; the response does not contain any level of intensity.

nomological validity The extent to which one particular construct theoretically networks with other established constructs which are related, yet different.

nonapplicable response descriptor The alternative response attached to even-point (or forced-choice) scale designs that allows respondents not to directly respond to a given scale dimension or attribute if they feel uncomfortable about expressing thoughts or feelings about a given object because they lack knowledge or experience.

nondirectional hypothesis A statement regarding the existing relationship between either two questions, dimensions, or subgroupings of attributes as being significantly different but lacking an expression of direction.

nonequivalent control group A quasi-experimental design that combines the static group comparison and one-group, pretest-posttest pre-experimental designs.

nonmonetary compensation Any type of individual incentive excluding direct cash (e.g., a free T-shirt) used by the researcher to encourage a prospective respondent's participation.

nonprobability sampling Sampling designs in which the probability of selection of each sampling unit is not known. The selection of sampling units is based on the judgment or knowledge of the researcher and may or may not be representative of the target population.

nonresponse error An error that occurs when the portion of the defined target population not represented or underrepresented in the response pool is systematically and significantly different from those that did respond.

nonsampling error A type of bias that occurs in a research study regardless of whether a sample or census is used.

not at home A specific type of nonresponse bias that occurs when a rea-

sonable attempt to initially reach a prospective respondent fails to produce an interviewer/respondent encounter.

null hypothesis A statement of the perceived existing relationship between either two questions, dimensions, or subgroupings of attributes as being not significantly different; it asserts the status quo condition, and any change from what has been thought to be true is due to random sampling error.

objectivity The degree to which a researcher uses scientific procedures to collect, analyze, and create nonbiased information.

observation The systematic process of witnessing and recording the behavioral patterns of objects, people, and occurrences without directly questioning or communicating with them.

observing mechanism How the behaviors or events will be observed; *human observation* is when the observer is either a person hired and trained by the researcher or the researcher, himself; *mechanical observation* refers to the use of a technology-based device to do the observing rather than a human observer.

odd or even number of scale points When collecting either state-of-mind or state-of-intention data, the researcher must decide whether the positive and negative scale points need to be separated by a neutral scale descriptor; even-point scales (known as forced-choice scales) do not require a neutral response, but odd-point scales (known as free-choice scales) must offer a neutral scale response.

one-group, pretest-posttest A pre-experimental design where first a pretreatment measure of the dependent variable is taken (O_1), then the test subjects are exposed to the independent treatment (X), then a post-treatment measure of the dependent variable is taken (O_2).

one-shot study A single group of test subjects exposed to the independent

variable treatment (X), and then a single measurement on the dependent variable is taken (O_1).

one-way tabulation The categorization of single variables existing in the study.

online services Providers of access to electronic databases and other services in real time.

opening questions Questions used by a focus group moderator to break the ice among focus group participants; identify common group member traits; and create a comfort zone for establishing group dynamics and interactive discussions.

operationalization The process of precisely delineating how a construct is to be measured. The variables are specified in such a manner as to be potentially observable or manipulable.

opportunity assessment The collection of information on product-markets for the purpose of forecasting how they will change in the future. This type of assessment focuses on gathering information relevant to macroenvironments.

optical scanner An electronic device that optically reads bar codes; this scanner captures and translates unique bar code numbers into product information.

order The scaling property that activates the existence of relative magnitudes between the descriptors used as scale points (or raw responses); it allows the researcher to establish either a higher-to-lower or lower-to-higher rank order among the raw responses.

ordinally-interval scales Ordinal questions or scale formats that the researcher artificially redefines as being interval by activating an assumed distance scaling property into the design structure; this hybrid-type scale format incorporates both primary ordinal scale descriptors and a secondary set of cardinal numbers used to redefine the original primary descriptors.

ordinal scales A question/scale format that activates both the assignment and order scaling properties; the respondent is asked to express relative magnitudes between the raw responses to a question.

ordinary least squares A statistical procedure that estimates regression equation coefficients which produce the lowest sum of squared differences between the actual and predicted values of the dependent variable.

origin The scaling property that activates a unique starting (or beginning) point in a set of scale points that is designated as being a "true zero" or true state of nothing.

overall incidence rate (OIR) The percentage of the defined target population elements who actually qualify for inclusion into the survey.

overall reputation The primary dimension of perceived quality outcomes. Quality of the end product can be gauged in direct proportion to the level of expertise, trust, believability, and contribution the research brings to the client.

overregistration When a sampling frame contains all of the eligible sampling units of the defined target population plus additional ones.

paired comparison rating scale A scale format in which preselected groups of product characteristics or features are paired against one another and the respondents are asked to select which feature in each pairing is more important to them.

part-worth estimates Estimates of the utility survey that respondents place on each individual level of a particular attribute or feature.

Pearson correlation coefficient A statistical measure of the strength and direction of a linear relationship between two metric variables.

perceptual map A graphic representation of respondents' beliefs about the relationship between objects with respect to two or more dimensions (usually attributes or features of the objects).

performance rating scale A scale that uses an evaluative scale point format that allows the respondents

to express some type of postdecision evaluative judgment about an object.

person-administered survey A survey in which an individual interviewer asks questions and records responses.

phantom respondents A type of data falsification that occurs when the researcher takes an actual respondent's data and duplicates it to represent a second (nonexisting) set of responses.

physical audits (or traces) Tangible evidence (or artifacts) of some past event or recorded behavior.

plus-one dialing The method of generating telephone numbers to be called by choosing numbers randomly from a telephone directory and adding one digit.

population The identifiable total set of elements of interest being investigated by a researcher.

population mean value The actual calculated arithmetic average parameter value based on interval or ratio data of the defined target population elements (or sampling units).

population proportion value The actual calculated percentage parameter value of the characteristic of concern held by the target population elements (or sampling units).

population size The determined total number of elements that represent the target population.

population specification error An incorrect definition of the true target population to the research question.

population standard deviation A quantitative index of the dispersion of the distribution of population elements' actual data around the arithmetic average measure of central tendency.

population variance The square of the population standard deviation.

positioning The desired perception that a company wants to be associated with its target markets relative to its products or brand offerings.

posttest-only, control group A true experimental design where the test subjects are randomly assigned to either the experimental or control

group; the experimental group is then exposed to the independent treatment after which both groups receive a posttreatment measure of the dependent variable.

Powerpoint A specific software package used to develop slides for electronic presentation of the research results.

precise precision The amount of measured sampling error associated with the sample's raw data at a specified level of confidence.

precision The degree of exactness of the raw data in relation to some other possible response of the target population.

predictions population estimates that are carried into a future time frame; they are derived from either facts or sample data estimates.

predictive bias A specific type of data analysis error that occurs when the wrong statistical facts and estimates invalidate the researcher's ability to predict and test relationships between important factors.

predictive questionnaire design A design that allows the researcher to collect raw data that can be used in predicting changes in attitudes and behaviors as well as testing hypothesized relationships. The question/scales primarily involve the collecting of state-of-mind and state-of-intention data.

predictive validity The extent to which a scale can accurately predict some event external to the scale itself.

pre-experimental designs A family of designs (one-shot study, one-group pretest-posttest, static group comparison) that are crude experiments that are characterized by the absence of randomization of test subjects; they tend not to meet internal validity criteria due to a lack of equivalent group comparisons.

pretesting The conducting of a simulated administering of a designed survey (or questionnaire) to a small, representative group of respondents.

pretest-posttest, control group A true experimental design where the test subjects are randomly assigned to either the experimental or control group and each group receives a pretreatment measure of the dependent variable. Then the independent treatment is exposed to the experimental group after which both groups receive a posttreatment measure of the dependent variable.

primary data   Data structures of variables that have been specifically collected and assembled for the curent research problem or opportunity situation; they represent "firsthand" structures.

primary information   Firsthand facts or estimates that are derived through a formalized research process for a specific current problem situation.

probability distribution of the population   The relative frequencies of a population's parameter characteristic emulating a normal bell-shaped pattern.

probability sampling   Sampling designs in which each sampling unit in the sampling frame (operational population) has a known, nonzero probability of being selected for the sample.

probing questions   The outcome of an interviewer taking the subject's initial response to a question and using that response as the framework for asking the next question.

problem definition   A statement that seeks to determine precisely what problem management wishes to solve and the type of information necessary to solve it.

product analysis   Methods that identify the relative importance of product selection criteria to buyers and rate brands against these criteria.

project costs   The price requirements of doing marketing research.

proportionate stratified sampling   A form of stratified sampling in which the sample size from each stratum is dependent on that stratum's size relative to the total population.

purchase intercept   An interview similar to a mall intercept except that the respondent is stopped at the point of purchase and asked a set of predetermined questions.

qualitative research   Selective types of research methods used in exploratory research designs where the main objective is to gain a variety of preliminary insights to discover and identify decision problems and opportunities.

quality of the information   One of the two fundamental dimensions that is used to determine the level of information being provided by the research process; it refers to the degree to which the information can be depended on as being accurate and reliable.

quantitative research   Data collection methods that emphasize using formalized, standard, structured questioning practices where the response options have been predetermined by the researcher and administered to significantly large numbers of respondents.

quasi-experimental designs   Designs in which the researcher can control some variables in the study but cannot establish equal experimental and control groups based on randomization of the test subjects.

query   Part of an MDSS that enables the user to retrieve information from the system without having to have special software requirements.

questionnaire   A set of questions and scales designed to generate enough raw data for accomplishing the information requirements that underlie the research objectives.

questionnaire development process   A specific yet integrative series of logical activities that are undertaken to design a systematic survey instrument for the purpose of collecting primary raw data from sets of people (respondents).

questionnaire format/layout   The integrative combination of sets of question/scale measurements into a systematic structured instrument.

question/setup element   The question and/or directive that is asked to the respondent for which the respondent is to supply a raw response; it is one of the three elements that make up any scale measurement.

quota sampling   The selection of participants based on specific quotas regarding characteristics such as age, race, gender, income, or specific behaviors. Quotas are usually determined based on specific research objectives.

quota sheets   A simple tracking form that enhances the interviewer's ability to collect raw data from the right type of respondents; the form helps ensure that representation standards are met.

random error   An error that occurs as the result of chance events affecting the observed score.

random-digit dialing   A random selection of area code, exchange, and suffix numbers.

randomization   The procedure whereby many subjects are assigned to different experimental treatment conditions, resulting in each group averaging out any systematic effect on the investigated functional relationship between the independent and dependent variables.

random sampling error   The statistically measured difference between the actual sampled results and the estimated true population results.

ranges   Statistics that represent the grouping of raw data responses into mutually exclusive subgroups with each having distinct identifiable lower and upper boundary designation values in a set of responses.

rank-order rating scale   A scale point format that allows respondents to compare their responses to each other by indicating their first preference, then their second preference, then their third preference, etc., until all the desired responses are placed in some type of rank order, either highest to lowest or lowest to highest.

rating cards   Cards used in personal interviews that represent a reproduction of the set of actual scale points and descriptions used to respond to a specific question/setup in the survey. These cards serve as a tool to help the interviewer and respondent speed up the data collection process.

ratio scales   Question/scale formats that simultaneously activate all four scaling properties; they are the most sophisticated scale in the sense that absolute differences can be identified not only between each scale point but also between individuals' raw responses. Ratio scales request that respondents give a specific singular numerical value as their response to the question.

raw data   The actual firsthand responses that are obtained about the investigated object by either asking questions or observing the subject's actions.

reachable rate (RR)   The percentage of active addresses on a mailing list or other defined population frame.

reader sorter   An electronic mechanism located at the point-of-purchase (POP) that resembles a miniature automated bank teller machine. This device enables consumers to pay for transactions with either credit cards, ATM cards, or debit cards.

refusal   A particular type of nonresponse bias that is caused when a prospective respondent declines the role of a respondent, or simply is unwilling to participate in the question/answer exchange.

related samples   Two or more groups of responses that originated from the sample population.

relational database   A database in table format of rows and columns, with tables (not data fields) being linked together depending on the output requirements.

relationships   The degree (relative magnitude) and direction of a consistent and systematic linkage (dependence) between two or more variables; this type of information can be derived from either facts or sample data estimates; in special cases, the researcher can determine the existence of cause–effect associations between two or more variables.

relativists   Individuals who let present practice set the standard for ethical behavior.

reliability   The extent to which the measurements taken with a particular instrument are repeatable.

reliability of data   Data structures that are consistent across observations or interviews.

reliability of the scale   The extent to which the designed scale can reproduce the same measurement results in repeated trials.

reliability of service   The researcher's ability to be consistent and responsive to the needs of the client.

reputation of the firm   The culmination of a research firm's ability to meet standards, reliability of service, marketing knowledge, and technical competency for purposes of providing quality outcomes.

research instrument   A microscope, radiation meter, ruler, questionnaire, scale, or other device designed for a specific measurement purpose.

research objectives   Statements that the research project will attempt to achieve. They provide the guidelines for establishing a research agenda of activities necessary to implement the research process.

research proposal   A specific document that serves as a written contract between the decision maker and researcher.

respondent characteristics   The attributes that make up the respondents being included in the survey; three important characteristics are diversity, incidence, and participation.

respondent error   The type of nonsampling errors that can occur when selected prospective respondents either cannot be initially reached to participate in the survey process, do not cooperate, or demonstrate an unwillingness to participate in the survey.

respondent participation   The overall degree to which the selected people have the ability and the willingness to participate as well as the knowledge of the topics being researched.

response error   The tendency to answer a question in a particular and unique systematic way. Respondents may consciously or unconsciously distort their answers and true thoughts.

response rate   The percentage of usable responses out of the total number of responses.

sample   A randomly selected group of people or objects from the overall membership pool of a target population.

sample design error   A family of nonsampling errors that occur when sampling plans are not appropriately developed and/or the sampling process is improperly executed by the researcher.

sample mean value   The actual calculated arithmetic average value based on interval or ratio data of the drawn sampling units.

sample percentage value   The actual calculated percentage value of the characteristic of concern held by the drawn sampling units.

sample selection error   A specific type of sample design bias that occurs when an inappropriate sample is drawn from the defined target population because of incomplete or faulty sampling procedures or by not following the correct procedures.

sample size   The determined total number of sampling units needed to be representative of the defined target population; that is, the number of elements (people or objects) that have to be included in a drawn sample to ensure appropriate representation of the defined target population.

sampling   The process of selecting a relatively small number of elements from a larger defined group of elements so that the information gathered from the smaller group allows one to make judgments about that larger group of elements.

sampling distribution   The frequency distribution of a specific sample statistic value that would be found by taking repeated random samples of the same size.

sampling error   Any type of bias in a survey study that is attributable to mistakes made in either the selection process of prospective sampling units or determining the size of a sample required to ensure its representativeness of the larger defined target population.

sampling frame   A list of all eligible sampling units for a given study.

sampling frame error   An error that occurs when a sample is drawn from an incomplete list of potential or prospective respondents.

sampling gap   The representation difference between the population elements and sampling units in the sample frame.

sampling plan   The blueprint or framework used to ensure that the raw data collected is, in fact, representative of a larger defined target population structure.

sampling units   Those elements that are available for selection during the sampling process.

satisfaction of experience   A person's evaluative judgment about his or her postpurchase consumption experience of a specified object.

scale dimensions and attributes element   The components of the object, construct, or concept that is being measured; it identifies what should be measured and is one of the three elements of a scale measurement.

scale measurement   The process of assigning a set of descriptors to represent the range of possible responses that an individual gives in answering a question about a particular object, construct, or factor under investigation.

scale point descriptor element   The set of assigned descriptors that designate the degrees of intensity to the responses concerning the investigated characteristics of an object, construct, or factor; it is one of the three elements that make up scale measurements.

scale reliability   The extent to which a scale can produce the same measurement results in repeated trials.

scatter diagram   A graphic plot of the relative position of two variables

using a horizontal and vertical axis to represent the values of the respective variables.

scientific method   The systematic and objective process used to develop reliable and valid firsthand information by using the information research process.

scoring models   Procedures that attempt to rank customer segments based on their potential profitability to the company.

screening forms   A set of preliminary questions that are used to determine the eligibility of a prospective respondent for inclusion in the survey.

screening question/scales   Specific questions or scales that are used to qualify prospective respondents for a survey or eliminate unqualified respondents from answering question/scales in a study.

search   A computer-assisted scan of the electronic databases.

search engine   An electronic procedure that allows the researcher to enter "key" words as search criteria for locating and gathering secondary information off the Internet.

search words   The terms that the computer looks for in electronic databases.

secondary data   Historical data structures of variables that have been previously collected and assembled for some research problem or opportunity situation other than the current situation.

secondary information   Information (facts or estimates) that has already been collected, assembled, and interpreted at least once for some other specific situation.

selection bias   Contamination of internal validity measures created by inappropriate selection and/or assignment processes of test subjects to experimental treatment groups.

selective perception bias   A type of error that occurs in situations where the researcher or decision maker uses only a selected portion of the survey results to paint a tainted picture of reality.

self-administered survey   A survey in which the respondent reads the survey questions and records their responses without the assistance of an interviewer.

semantic differential scale   A special type of symmetrical rating scale that uses sets of bipolar adjectives and/or adverbs to describe some type of positive and negative poles of an assumed continuum; it is used to capture respondents' cognitive and affective components of specified factors and create perceptual image profiles relating to a given object or behavior.

semistructured question   A question that directs the respondent toward a specified topic area, but the responses to the question are unbounded; the interviewer is not looking for any preconceived right answer.

separate sample, pretest-posttest   A quasi-experimental design where two different groups of test subjects are drawn for which neither group is directly exposed to the independent treatment variable. One group receives the pretest measure of the dependent variable; then after the insignificant independent treatment occurs, the second group of test subjects receive a posttest measure of the dependent variable.

sequential system   A sorting procedure that displays data in a very simple pattern, usually where the data is organized by a simple path, linkage, or network.

service quality studies   Studies designed to measure the degree to which an organization conforms to the quality level expected by customers; they concentrate on attributes determined to be most important to customers.

service sensitivity analysis   A procedure that helps an organization in designing a basic customer service program by evaluating cost-to-service trade-offs.

similarity judgments   A direct approach to gathering perceptual data for multidimensional scaling; where the respondents use a Likert scale to rate all possible pairs of brands in terms of their similarity.

simple random sampling (SRS) A method of probability sampling in which every sampling unit has an equal, nonzero chance of being selected. Results generated by using simple random sampling can be projected to the target population with a prespecified margin of error.

simulated test markets Quasi-test market experiments where the test subjects are preselected, then interviewed and observed on their purchases and attitudes toward the test products; also referred to as *laboratory tests* or *test market simulations*.

situation analysis An informal process of analyzing the past, present, and future situations facing an organization in order to identify decision problems and opportunities.

situational characteristics Factors of reality such as budgets, time, and data quality that affect the researcher's ability to collect accurate primary data in a timely fashion.

skip interval A selection tool used to identify the position of the sampling units to be drawn into a systematic random sample design. The interval is determined by dividing the number of potential sampling units in the defined target population by the number of units desired in the sample.

skip questions/scales Questions designed to set the conditions which a respondent must meet in order to be able to respond to additional questions on a survey; also referred to as *conditional* or *branching questions*.

snowball sampling A nonprobability sampling method that involves the practice of identifying a set of initial prospective respondents who can, in turn, help in identifying additional people to be included in the study.

social desirability A type of response bias that occurs when the respondent assumes what answer is socially acceptable or respectable.

Solomon Four Group A true experimental design that combines the Pretest-Posttest, Control Group, and Posttest Only, Control Group designs and provides both "direct" and "reactive" effects of testing.

Spearman rank order correlation coefficient A statistical measure of the linear association between two variables where both have been measured using ordinal (rank-order) scale instruments.

split-half test A technique used to evaluate the internal consistency reliability of scale measurements that have multiple attribute components.

standard deviation The measure of the average dispersion of the values in a set of responses about their mean.

standard error of the population parameter A statistical measure used in probability sampling that gives an indication of how far the sample result lies from the actual population measure we are trying to estimate.

standard industrial classification (SIC) codes The numerical scheme of industrial listings designed to promote uniformity in data reporting procedures for the U.S. government.

staple scales Considered a modified version of the semantic differential scale; they symmetrically center the scale point domain within a set of plus (+) and minus (−) descriptors.

state-of-being data Raw responses that are pertinent to the physical and/or demographic or socioeconomic characteristics of individuals, objects, or organizations.

state-of-behavior data Raw responses that represent an individual's or organization's current observable actions or reactions or recorded past actions/reactions.

state-of-intention data Raw responses that represent an individual's or organization's expressed plans of future actions/reactions.

state-of-mind data Raw responses that represent the mental attributes of individuals which are not directly observable nor available through some type of external source.

static group comparisons A pre-experimental design of two groups of test subjects; one is the experimental group (EG) and is exposed to the independent treatment; the second group is the control group (CG) and is not given the treatment; the dependent variable is measured in both groups after the treatment.

statistical conclusion validity The ability of the researcher to make reasonable statements about covariation between constructs of interest and the strength of that covariation.

statistical regression Contamination to internal validity measures created when experimental groups are selected on the basis of their extreme responses or scores.

statistical software system A computer-based system that has capabilities of analyzing large volumes of data and computing basic types of statistical procedures, such as means, standard deviations, frequency distributions, and percentages.

store audits Formal examinations and verifications of how much of a particular product or brand has been sold at the retail level.

strata The subgroupings that are derived through stratified random sampling procedures.

stratified random sampling (STRS) A method of probability sampling in which the population is divided into different subgroups (called strata) and samples are selected from each stratum.

structured questions Questions that require the respondent to make a choice among a limited number of prelisted responses or scale points; they require less thought and effort on the part of the respondent; also referred to as closed-ended questions.

structuredness of observation The degree to which the behaviors or events are specifically known to the researcher prior to doing the observations.

subjective information Information that is based on the decision maker's or researcher's past experiences, assumptions, feelings, or interpretations without any systematic assembly of facts or estimates.

subject's awareness The degree to which subjects consciously know their behavior is being observed; *disguised observation* is when the subject is completely unaware that he or she is being observed, and *undisguised observation* is when the person is aware that he or she is being observed.

supervisor's instructions A form that serves as a blueprint for training people on how to execute the interviewing process in a standardized fashion; it outlines the process by which to conduct a study that uses personal and telephone interviewers.

survey instrument design error A "family" of design or format errors that produce a questionnaire that does not accurately collect the appropriate raw data; these nonsampling errors severely limit the generalizability, reliability, and validity of the collected data.

survey instrument error A type of error that occurs when the survey instrument induces some type of systematic bias in the response.

survey research methods Research design procedures for collecting large amounts of raw data using interviews or questionnaires.

symptoms Conditions that signal the presence of a decision problem or opportunity; they tend to be observable and measurable results of problems or opportunities.

systematic error The type of error that results from poor instrument design and/or instrument construction causing scores or readings on an instrument to be biased in a consistent manner; creates some form of systematic variation in the raw data that is not a natural occurrence or fluctuation on the part of the surveyed respondents.

systematic random-digit dialing The technique of randomly dialing telephone numbers, but only numbers that meet specific criteria.

systematic random sampling (SYMRS) A method of probability sampling that is similar to simple random sampling but requires that the defined target population be naturally ordered in some way.

table of random numbers A table of numbers that have been randomly generated.

tabulation The simple procedure of counting the number of observations, or data items, that are classified into certain categories.

task characteristics The requirements placed on the respondents in their process of providing answers to questions asked.

task difficulty How hard the respondent needs to work to respond, and the level of preparation required to create an environment for the respondent.

technical competency The degree to which the researcher possesses the necessary functional requirements to conduct the research project.

teleologists Individuals who follow a philosophy that considers activities to be ethical if they produce desired results.

telephone-administered survey A survey in which individuals working out of their homes or from a central location use the telephone medium to ask participants questions and record the responses.

telephone interview A question-and-answer exchange that is conducted via telephone technology.

test marketing A controlled field experiment conducted for gaining information on specified market performance indicators or factors.

test-retest approach A procedure used to assess the reliability of a scale measurement; it involves repeating the administration of the scale measurement to either the sample set of sampled respondents at two different times or two different samples of respondents from the same defined target population under as nearly the same conditions as possible.

test-retest reliability The method of accumulating evidence of reliability by using multiple administrations of an instrument to the same sample. If those administrations are consistent, then evidence of test-retest reliability exists.

topic sensitivity The degree to which a specific question or investigated issue leads the respondent to give a socially acceptable response.

topographically integrated geographic encoding and referencing (TIGER) system The U.S. government's new system that provides the researcher with the ability to prepare detailed maps of a variety of areas within the United States.

traditional test markets Test markets that use experimental design procedures to test a product and/or a product's marketing mix variables through existing distribution channels; also referred to as *standard test markets*.

trained interviewers Highly trained people, with excellent communication and listening skills, who ask research participants specific questions and accurately record their responses.

trained observers Highly skilled people who use their various sensory devices to observe and record either a person's current behaviors or physical phenomena as they take place.

transactional data Secondary information derived from transactions by consumers at the retail level.

transition questions Questions used by a moderator to direct a focus group's discussion toward the main topic of interest.

true experimental designs Designs that ensure equivalence between the experimental and control groups of subjects by random assignment of subjects to the groups ("pretest-posttest, with control group," "posttest-only, with control group," Solomon Four Group).

***t*-statistic** A hypothesis test procedure that uses the *t*-distribution: *t*-tests are used when the sample size of subjects is small (generally less than

30) and the standard deviation is unknown.

Type I error The error made by rejecting the null hypothesis when it is true; represents the probability of alpha error.

Type II error The error of failing to reject the null hypothesis when the alternative hypothesis is true; represents the probability of beta error.

underregistration When eligible sampling units are left out of the sampling frame.

undisguised sponsorship When the true identity of the person or company for which the research is being conducted is directly revealed to the prospective respondent.

unstructured questions Question/scale formats that require respondents to reply in their own words; this format requires more thinking and effort on the part of respondents in order to express their answers; also called open-ended questions.

validity The degree to which a research instrument serves the purpose for which is was constructed; it also relates to the extent to which the conclusions drawn from an experiment are true.

validity of data The degree to which data structures actually do represent what was to be measured.

variability A measure of how data are dispersed; the greater the dissimilarity or "spread" in data, the larger the variability.

variable Any observable, measurable element (or attribute) of an event.

variance The average squared deviations about a mean of a distribution of values.

virtual test markets Completely computerized systems that allow the test subjects to observe and interact with the product as though they were actually in the test store's environment.

Web home page The guide to a Web site; generally the home page is the first Web page accessed at the Web site.

Web page A source of secondary information that is likely to be linked to other complementary pages; includes text, graphics, and even audio.

Web site An electronic location on the World Wide Web.

width of data The total number of records contained in the database.

willingness to participate The respondent's inclination or disposition to share his or her thoughts and feelings.

World Wide Web (WWW) A graphical interface system that allows for text linkage between different locations on the Internet.

wrong mailing address A type of nonresponse bias that can occur when the prospective respondent's mailing address is outdated or no longer active.

wrong telephone number A type of nonresponse bias that can occur when the prospective respondent's telephone number either is no longer in service or is incorrect on the sample list.

z **statistic** A hypothesis test procedure that uses the z distribution; z-tests are used when the sample size is larger than 30 subjects and the standard deviation is unknown.

Chapter 1 3, ©Robert Brenner/PhotoEdit. 10, ©Bonnie Kamin/PhotoEdit.

Chapter 2 27, ©Jose Luis Pelaez Inc./Stock Market. 33, ©Spencer Grant/Liaison Agency.

Chapter 3 53, ©Fabricius & Taylor/Liaison Agency. 65, ©Chuck Nacke/Woodfin Camp & Associates.

Chapter 4 89, ©Chuck Savage/Stock Market. 95, ©Paul Conklin/PhotoEdit.

Chapter 5 119, ©Telegraph Colour Library/FPG International. 128, Courtesy of AltaVista/Feldman & Associates.

Chapter 6 147, ©David Young Wolff/PhotoEdit. 150, ©Bill Aron/PhotoEdit.

Chapter 7 181, ©Charles Gupton/Stock Market. 188, ©David Young Wolff/Tony Stone Images.

Chapter 8 213, ©Spencer Grant/PhotoEdit. 220, ©Spencer Grant/PhotoEdit.

Chapter 9 251, ©Ron Chapple/FPG International. 264, ©John Turner/Tony Stone Images.

Chapter 10 285, ©David Young Wolff/Tony Stone Images. 289, ©David Young Wolff/PhotoEdit.

Chapter 11 325, ©Tony Freeman/PhotoEdit. 332, ©Billy E. Barnes/PhotoEdit.

Chapter 12 369, ©Doug Handel/Stock Market. 377, ©Amy Etra/PhotoEdit.

Chapter 13 405, ©David Young Wolff/PhotoEdit. 409, ©Michael Newman/PhotoEdit.

Chapter 14 437, ©Rhoda Sidney/PhotoEdit. 451, ©James Wilson/Woodfin Camp & Associates.

Chapter 15 479, ©Robert E. Daemmrich/Tony Stone Images. 499, ©Paul R. Kennedy/Liaison Agency.

Chapter 16 519, ©Michael Newman/PhotoEdit. 535, ©Bonnie Kamin/PhotoEdit.

Chapter 17 557, ©David Young Wolff/PhotoEdit. 562, ©Cathyln Melloan/Tony Stone Images.

Chapter 18 585, Courtesy of NuvoMedia, Inc. 597, ©Spencer Grant/PhotoEdit.

Chapter 19 611, ©Telegraph Colour Library/FPG International. 624, ©Bruce Ayers/Tony Stone Images.